T0180335

Lecture Notes in Computer Science 13158

Founding Editors

Gerhard Goos
Karlsruhe Institute of Technology, Karlsruhe, Germany

Juris Hartmanis
Cornell University, Ithaca, NY, USA

Editorial Board Members

Elisa Bertino
Purdue University, West Lafayette, IN, USA

Wen Gao
Peking University, Beijing, China

Bernhard Steffen
TU Dortmund University, Dortmund, Germany

Gerhard Woeginger
RWTH Aachen, Aachen, Germany

Moti Yung
Columbia University, New York, NY, USA

More information about this subseries at https://link.springer.com/bookseries/7411

Yevgeni Koucheryavy · Sergey Balandin ·
Sergey Andreev (Eds.)

Internet of Things, Smart Spaces, and Next Generation Networks and Systems

21st International Conference, NEW2AN 2021
and 14th Conference, ruSMART 2021
St. Petersburg, Russia, August 26–27, 2021
Proceedings

 Springer

Editors
Yevgeni Koucheryavy ⓘD
Tampere University
Tampere, Finland

Sergey Balandin ⓘD
FRUCT Oy
Helsinki, Finland

Sergey Andreev ⓘD
Tampere University
Tampere, Finland

ISSN 0302-9743   ISSN 1611-3349 (electronic)
Lecture Notes in Computer Science
ISBN 978-3-030-97776-4   ISBN 978-3-030-97777-1 (eBook)
https://doi.org/10.1007/978-3-030-97777-1

LNCS Sublibrary: SL5 – Computer Communication Networks and Telecommunications

© Springer Nature Switzerland AG 2022, corrected publication 2022
This work is subject to copyright. All rights are reserved by the Publisher, whether the whole or part of the material is concerned, specifically the rights of translation, reprinting, reuse of illustrations, recitation, broadcasting, reproduction on microfilms or in any other physical way, and transmission or information storage and retrieval, electronic adaptation, computer software, or by similar or dissimilar methodology now known or hereafter developed.
The use of general descriptive names, registered names, trademarks, service marks, etc. in this publication does not imply, even in the absence of a specific statement, that such names are exempt from the relevant protective laws and regulations and therefore free for general use.
The publisher, the authors and the editors are safe to assume that the advice and information in this book are believed to be true and accurate at the date of publication. Neither the publisher nor the authors or the editors give a warranty, expressed or implied, with respect to the material contained herein or for any errors or omissions that may have been made. The publisher remains neutral with regard to jurisdictional claims in published maps and institutional affiliations.

This Springer imprint is published by the registered company Springer Nature Switzerland AG
The registered company address is: Gewerbestrasse 11, 6330 Cham, Switzerland

Preface

We welcome you to the joint proceedings of the 21st International Conference on Next Generation Teletraffic and Wired/Wireless Advanced Networks and Systems (NEW2AN 2021) and the 14th Conference on the Internet of Things and Smart Spaces (ruSMART 2021) held in St. Petersburg, Russia, during August 30–31, 2021.

Originally, the NEW2AN conference was launched by the International Teletraffic Congress (ITC) in St. Petersburg in June 1993 as an ITC-sponsored Regional International Teletraffic Seminar. The first edition was entitled "Traffic Management and Routing in SDH Networks" and held at the R&D Institute (LONIIS). In 2002, the event received its current name, NEW2AN. In 2008, NEW2AN acquired a new companion in the Conference on Smart Spaces, ruSMART, hence boosting interaction between researchers, practitioners, and engineers across different areas of ICT. From 2012, the scope of the ruSMART conferences has been extended to cover the Internet of the Things and related aspects.

NEW2AN and ruSMART are well-established conferences with a unique cross-disciplinary mixture of telecommunications-related research and science, featuring outstanding keynotes from speakers at universities and companies across Europe, the USA, and Russia.

The NEW2AN 2021 technical program addressed various aspects of next-generation data networks, while special attention was given to advanced wireless networking and applications. In particular, the authors demonstrated novel and innovative approaches to performance and efficiency analysis of 5G and beyond systems, game-theoretical formulations, advanced queuing theory, and machine learning. It is also worth mentioning the rich coverage of the Internet of Things, optics, and signal processing, as well as business aspects.

RuSMART 2021 provided a forum for academic and industrial researchers to discuss new ideas and trends in the emerging areas of the Internet of Things and smart spaces that create new opportunities for fully-customized applications and services. The conference brought together leading experts from top institutions around the world. This year, we saw participation from representatives of various players in the field, including academic teams and industrial companies, particularly representatives of Russian R&D centers, which have a solid reputation for high-quality research and business in innovative service creation and development of applications. The conference was held virtually due to the COVID-19 pandemic.

We would like to thank the Technical Program Committee members of the two conferences, as well as the invited reviewers, for their hard work and important contributions to the conference. This year, the conference program met the highest quality criteria with an acceptance ratio of around 35%. The number of submissions sent for peer review 118, while the number of full papers accepted is 41. A single-blind peer-review process was employed.

This year's conferences were organized in cooperation with the IEEE Communications Society Russia Northwest Chapter, YL-Verkot Oy, the Open Innovations Association FRUCT, Tampere University, the Peter the Great St. Petersburg Polytechnic University, the Peoples' Friendship University of Russia (RUDN University), the National Research University Higher School of Economics (HSE), the St. Petersburg State University of Telecommunications, and the Popov Society. The conference was held within the framework of the "RUDN University Program 5–100."

We believe that the NEW2AN 2021 and ruSMART 2021 conferences delivered an informative, high-quality, and up-to-date scientific program. We also hope that participants enjoyed both technical and social conference components, the Russian ways of hospitality, and the beautiful city of St. Petersburg.

August 2021   Yevgeni Koucheryavy
                                                      Sergey Balandin
                                                      Sergey Andreev

Organization

Conference Chair

Yevgeni Koucheryavy — Tampere University, Finland

Techncial Program Co-chairs

Sergey Balandin — FRUCT, Finland
Sergey Andreev — Tampere University of Technology, Finland

Technical Program Committee

Torsten Braun — University of Bern, Switzerland
Paulo Carvalho — Universidade do Minho, Portugal
Chrysostomos Chrysostomou — Frederick University, Cyprus
Roman Dunaytsev — Saint Petersburg State University of Telecommunications, Russia
Dieter Fiems — Ghent University, Belgium
Alexey Frolov — Skolkovo Institute of Science and Technology, Russia
Ivan Ganchev — University of Limerick, Ireland
Jiri Hosek — Brno University of Technology, Czech Republic
Alexey Kashevnik — SPIIRAS, Russia
Joaquim Macedo — Universidade do Minho, Portugal
Ninoslav Marina — UIST, Macedonia
Aleksandr Ometov — Tampere University, Finland
Pavel Masek — Brno University of Technology, Czech Republic
Edison Pignaton de Freitas — Federal University of Rio Grande do Sul, Brazil

Publicity Chair

Nikita Tafintsev — Tampere University, Finland

Contents

New Generation of Smart Services

Fast Data Processing by IoT Devices 3
  Alexander Anufrienko

On Smart Greenhouse Issues 9
  Manfred Schneps-Schneppe and Gunars Lacis

Smart Contract Enabled Decentralized Reputation System for E-Commerce
Reviews 22
  Carl Kugblenu, Petri Vuorimaa, and Barbara Keller

Estimation of Quality of Service in Tactile Internet, Augmented Reality
and Internet of Things 35
  Abbas Alzaghir, Alexander Paramonov, and Andrey Koucheryavy

The Challenges with Internet of Things Security for Business 46
  Ievgeniia Kuzminykh, Bogdan Ghita, and Jose M. Such

Information and Communications Technology in the Development
of Territories Based on Designing "Smart Cities" 59
  Viktoria Bondarenko, Natalia Guzenko, Tatiana Romanishina,
  Valery Leventsov, and Vladimir Gluhov

Next Generation Wired/Wireless Advanced Networks and Systems

Developing Smart Cities: The Risks of Using Information
and Communications Technology 71
  Viktoria Bondarenko, Tatiana Romanishina, Natalia Guzenko,
  Natalya Mukhanova, and Sergey Salkutsan

Influence of Digital Technology and Telecommunications
on the Customer-Oriented Development of Electronic Commerce 81
  Olga Chkalova, Yury Trifonov, Pavel Shalabaev, Ekaterina Abushova,
  and Elena Kasianenko

Utilization of Organizational-Economic Mechanism for Selection
and Management of Spectrum Sharing Scenarios to Increase Economic
Efficiency of 5G Operators 95
  Valery Tikhvinskiy, Roman Umanskiy, Arseny Plossky,
  and Vladimir Makarov

Sustainable Development of Small and Medium Business in View
of the Rapid Growth of Telecommunications and Digital Economy
in the Russian Federation 108
   Marina Efremova, Maxim Tcvetkov, Nikolay Shimin, Oksana Evseeva,
   and Efimov Alexey

Info-Communications-Based Interaction of Companies and Consumers
on the Grocery Retail Market 122
   Olga Chkalova, Inna Bolshakova, Natalia Kopasovskaya,
   Tatyana Nekrasova, and Sergey Salkutsan

Transforming the Strategic Benchmarks of Russian Telecommunications
Companies in the Sustainable Development Paradigm 147
   Irina Krasyuk, Oksana Evseeva, Maria Kolgan, and Yulia Medvedeva

Study of Relationship Between the Corporate Governance Factors
and ESG Ratings of ICT Companies from the Developed Markets 158
   Sergei Grishunin, Svetlana Suloeva, Tatyana Nekrasova,
   and Alexandra Erorova

Improving Project Management for the Development of New Internet
Applications 170
   Tatyana Nekrasova and Natalia Alekseeva

Specifics of Forming an Innovation Sector When Developing Industry 4.0
Technology 179
   Valery Leventsov, Vladimir Gluhov, Anna Kamyshova,
   and Denis Skripnichenko

Increasing the Competitiveness of Info-Telecommunications Enterprises
Through Building a Mobile Eco-system 191
   Irina Krasyuk, Valery Leventsov, Olga Kartavenko, Maria Kolgan,
   and Yulia Medvedeva

Structural Shifts on Derivatives Markets at the Time of Increasing
Digitalization and Post-pandemic Transformation of the Market 201
   Vladimir Gluhov, Olga Kartavenko, Anna Kamyshova,
   Ekaterina Popova, and Nikita Kapustin

Coarse Estimation of the Distance to the Harmonic Sound Source by DAS
for the Determination of Optical Cable Location 212
   Vladimir A. Burdin, Olga Yu. Gubareva, and Vladimir O. Gureev

Fiber Optic System for Monitoring Coolant Parameters in Nuclear Power
Plants 221
    Roman Davydov, Semen Logunov, Denis Nikolaev, Vadim Davydov,
    and Valentin Dudkin

Fiber-Optic Sensor for Monitoring Radiation Level 230
    Diana S. Dmitrieva, Valeria M. Pilipova, Valentin I. Dudkin,
    Roman V. Davydov, and Vadim V. Davydov

Experimental Study of Temperature Impact on Fiber Optic Current Sensor
Elements 240
    Valentina Temkina, Andrei Medvedev, Alexey Mayzel,
    Eduard Sivolenko, Ekaterina Poletaeva, and Iuliia Dudnik

Fiber-Optic Recirculating Memory Loop for Wideband Microwave Signal 254
    Sergei I. Ivanov, Alexander P. Lavrov, Dmitrii V. Kondakov,
    and Yurij A. Matveev

Simulation and Experimental Study of Multi-source Application Layer
ARQ for FANET 268
    Irina Kaisina, Albert Abilov, Danil Vasiliev, Mohammed Amin Lamri,
    and Anatoli Nistyuk

Deep Learning Approach for Predicting Energy Consumption of Drones
Based on MEC 284
    Ali R. Abdellah, Abbas Alzaghir, and Andrey Koucheryavy

Predicting Energy Consumption for UAV-Enabled MEC Using Machine
Learning Algorithm 297
    Abbas Alzaghir, Ali R. Abdellah, and Andrey Koucheryavy

Investigation Methods of Dehydrated Protein Films for Biomolecular
Electronics 310
    Maksim Baranov and Elena Velichko

Applying Deep Learning Techniques to Extract Diagnostic Information
from ECG Images 321
    Georgy M. Kostin, Vitalii A. Pavlov, Sergey V. Zavjalov,
    and Tatiana M. Pervunina

Application of Wavelet Transform for ECG Processing 329
    Veronika Malysheva, Diana Zaynullina, Alena Stosh,
    and Gregory Cherepennikov

Analysis of Nonlinear Distortions of FTN Signals Transmitted Through
TWT Amplifier 339
   Ekaterina Smirnova and Sergey Makarov

Selecting a Receiver for Wideband Spectrum Sensing in Cognitive Radio
Systems Based on an Assessment of the Signal Environment Complexity 352
   *Alexey S. Podstrigaev, Andrey V. Smolyakov, Vladimir P. Likhachev,
   Sergei E. Efimov, and Vadim V. Davydov*

Instantaneous Interference Evaluation Model for Smart Antennas in 5G
Ultra-Dense Networks 365
   Vadim Davydov, Grigoriy Fokin, Angelina Moroz, and Vitaly Lazarev

The Effect of Error Burst When Using a Decision Feedback Algorithm
for Receiving Non-orthogonal Multi-frequency Signals 377
   *Sergey B. Makarov, Dac Cu Nguyen, Sergey V. Zavjalov,
   Anna S. Ovsyannikova, and Canh Minh Nguyen*

Software Implementation of the Algorithm for Optimal Joint Estimation
and Detection of an Arbitrary Waveform 390
   Nikita Ilchenko and Eugenii Popov

Application of Neural Network to Demodulate SEFDM Signals 405
   Anastasiia I. Semenova and Sergey V. Zavjalov

Electromagnetic Waves Propagation in Low-Profile SIW Structures 413
   Ekaterina Kiseleva, Artem Galushko, and Alexander Sochava

Observation Interval Analysis for Faster-Than-Nyquist Signals Coherent
Detection with Decision Feedback 427
   Ilya Lavrenyuk, Sergey Makarov, and Wei Xue

Heuristic Design Algorithm for Scheduling of URLLC and eMBB Traffics
in 5G Cellular Networks 438
   Jerzy Martyna

Geometrical Approach to the Plane Tessellation in the IEEE 802.11
Networks Channel Planning 449
   Anton Vikulov, Alexander Paramonov, and Tatiana Tatarnikova

Advancement of Fingerprint Polarimetric Scheme for Purposes
of Authentication 470
   Trubin Pavel, Murashov Aleksandr, Suntsov Dmitriy, and Velichko Elena

Network Slice Degradation Probability as a Metric for Defining Slice
Performance Isolation 481
*Nikita Polyakov, Natalia Yarkina, Konstantin Samouylov,
and Yevgeni Koucheryavy*

Using a Machine Learning Model for Malicious URL Type Detection 493
*Suet Ping Tung, Ka Yan Wong, Ievgeniia Kuzminykh, Taimur Bakhshi,
and Bogdan Ghita*

Correction to: Internet of Things, Smart Spaces, and Next Generation
Networks and Systems C1
Yevgeni Koucheryavy, Sergey Balandin, and Sergey Andreev

Author Index 507

New Generation of Smart Services

Fast Data Processing by IoT Devices

Alexander Anufrienko[✉]

Department of Electronic Engineering, Higher School of Economics, 20 Myasnitskaya Ulitsa,
Moscow 101000, Russia
alexanuf@gmail.com

Abstract. In this paper presented model of Internet-of-Things system with propagation delays of the main devices and limitations of communication channels
between devices. Were proposed an expression that defines the balance between
the frequency of characters, the order of the filter, and the bandwidth of the communication channel between the modem and the gate. Were researched the utilization for hardware resources (FPGA-based implementation) and maximum performance at different bit width of the input data stream. The system is based on a
method of matched filtering adapted for IoT devices, with a truncated order N,
which allows solving the problem of detecting various signals when implemented
on discrete end devices.

Keywords: Internet-of-Things · Industrial IoT · Cross-correlation · Matched
filter · Storage · Platform · Streaming

1 Introduction

The modern Internet-of-Things systems operate with huge data generated from IoT
devices. The amount of data generated by sensors, devices, social networks, medical
applications, temperature sensors, and various other software applications and digital
devices that continuously generate large amounts of structured, unstructured, or semi-
structured data. IoT applications will represent more than 50 Percent of global devices
and connections by 2021 [1]. As a result, there are problems associated with the transmission, processing and storage of data. There are various scientific and practical approaches
to solving these problems.

From the point of view of computational approaches and IoT architectures, systems
are divided into two polarities-Cloud computing and Edge/Fog computing [2–9]. But
key issues related to data processing on the first point of sensor network -end IoT devices
are still relevant and unresolved.

In paper [10] was presented method for reducing the amount of data transmitted and
stored in IoT systems. Instead of expensive and complex network devices, developers
can use cheap and proven low-speed solutions (ZigBee, NB IoT, BLE). Correlation
processes were described in detail, and the architecture of endpoints for the processing
method was proposed. The presented model of the system is based on correlators, which
store a copy of the signal with the full and reduced length of the correlation sequence.

© Springer Nature Switzerland AG 2022
Y. Koucheryavy et al. (Eds.): NEW2AN 2021/ruSMART 2021, LNCS 13158, pp. 3–8, 2022.
https://doi.org/10.1007/978-3-030-97777-1_1

Consider the model of the Internet of Things system from the point of view of the basic devices that transmit, receive and process data, as well as key characteristics. It is assumed that all data processing is carried out in digital, not analog form, that is, even when transmitting data from sensors to the processor, we operate with samples of a fixed bit depth.

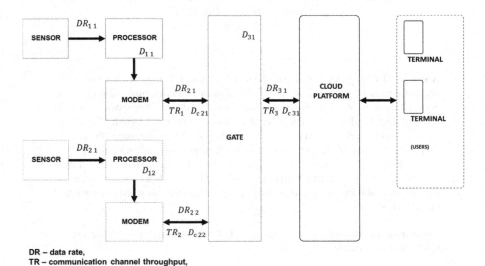

DR – data rate,
TR – communication channel throughput,
D – delay

Fig. 1. IoT system model with processing devices

The sensor, processor, and modem form the end device (module. Let's define the key parameters related to data transmission (Table 1).

Table 1. Key parameters

DR	Data rate, bit/s (Symbols/s)
TR	Throughput of communication channel, bit/s (Symbols/s)
D	Data processing delay (Number of clocks or ms)

For the first module (processor, sensor and modem):

DR_{11} – data rate between the sensor and the processor.
D_{11} – data processing delay.
DR_{21} – data rate between the Modem and the Gate.
TR_1 – throughput of communication channel between the Modem and the Gate.

Same parameters (DR_{31}; TR_3; D_3) are applied to the "Gate-Cloud" communication channel.

Generally:

$$TR_1 \leq TR_3;$$
$$TR_1 \geq M * DR_{21},$$

(1)

where $M < 1$ [11].

This model of the Internet of Things system that considers devices, the bandwidth of communication channels, and the processing delays on the devices from sensors to the Cloud. Next, we will consider approaches to correlation signal processing in order to further analyze the digital processing approach on the end device of the Internet of Things operating as part of an IoT-system. Data processing by end devices is particularly effective for Industrial applications (Industrial IoT).

Let's move on to the analysis of existing approaches to correlation signal processing in order to further consider the integrated approach of processing on the end device as part of an IoT system.

Table 2. Comparison of data volumes for transmission and storage for three methods

Interval, min	0	10	20	30	40	50	60
Bypass method, GB	0	12	23	34	45	56	68
Simple threshold method, GB	0	5,1	10,1	15,1	20,1	25,1	30,1
Correlation method, B	0	120	240	360	480	600	720

As we can see from the Table 2, the direct method is the most expensive in terms of the data required for transmission and storage (up to 68 GB @ 60 min). A simple threshold method, with obvious simplicity of implementation, also requires significant amounts for data transfer and storage (up to 30.1 GB @ 60 min). Choosing a threshold level in real-world conditions is difficult. However, the value of the information received is limited. Additional analysis is required on the receiving side (in the Cloud).

Let's analyze the effect of the bit width of the input data stream and the length of the filter (pulse response) on the required hardware resources. The Cyclone IV E [12] (Intel/Altera) FPGA family was used as the basis for prototyping the system. This is one of the most popular families in the line, optimized for energy-efficient applications. The models were implemented using MATLAB. For implementation on the FPGA, the Verilog HDL was used.

The expression for the cross-correlation function [13, 14], taking into account normalization, has the form:

$$\rho_{12}(j) = \frac{r_{12}(j)}{\frac{1}{N}\sqrt{[\sum_{n=0}^{N-1} x_1^2(n) * \sum_{n=0}^{N-1} x_2^2(n)]}}$$

(2)

Square root and division operations are some of the most resource intensive operations for digital devices. It is more efficient to replace the denominator calculation with a truncation operation. Design and results will be presented in the next chapter.

2 Design and Results

In the experiment, a triangular signal was used, for number of taps N = 4, 8, 12, 16, 20, 24, 28 and 32. The bit width = 14-bits; 10-bits and 8-bits. Thus, 24 matched filters were implemented on the FPGA, in accordance with the models made in MATLAB (Table 3).

Table 3. Utilization of resources depending on N, with different bit depth

N of taps	4	8	12	16	20	24	28	32
Number of LE (14-bit)	199	647	795	1304	1588	1802	2158	2846
Number of LE (10-bit)	113	454	556	900	1081	1210	1430	1856
Number of LE (8- bit)	75	339	419	677	819	917	1092	1410

Similar results were obtained for the required FPGA hardware resources for 10-bit and 8-bit input sequence widths. In particular, for 10-bits: when increasing the filter order N by 2 times (from N = 4 to N = 8), the amount of required resources increases by 4 times. With an increase in N by 8 times (from N = 4 to N = 32), the amount of required resources increases by 16.4 times.

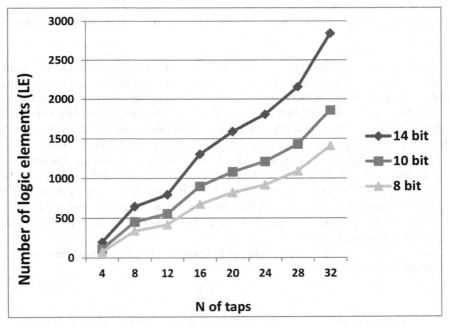

Fig. 2. Number of required hardware resources (LE) depending on the filter order.

For 8-bits: when increasing the filter order N by 2 times (from N = 4 to N = 8), the number of required resources increases by 4.5 times. With an increase in N by 8 times (from N = 4 to N = 32), the amount of required resources increases by 18.8 times (Fig. 2).

3 Processing

The processing delay for proposed method in accordance with the algorithm will be:

$$D_{11} = N + 3 \, [\text{time units}] \tag{3}$$

which corresponds to 7 clocks at N = 4, and 11 clocks at N = 8. So The the delay corresponds to the filter order.

In a time domain, the delay is equivalent to:

$$D_{11} = \frac{(N + 3)}{SR} [\text{sec}] \tag{4}$$

that at a sampling frequency of SR = 10 MSamples/s of the input sequence corresponds to the delay duration of 7 us at N = 4, and 11 us at N = 8, from the input data to the input values to the interface converter.

$$\frac{SR}{N} \leq M * DR \tag{5}$$

This expression defines an important relationship between the frequency of characters at the processor input and the bandwidth of the modem-gate communication channel (according to model Fig. 1), which is true for the number of samples per unit of time.

4 Conclusion

The main results presented here are summarizing methods for reducing the amount of data transmitted and stored in Internet-of-Things systems. Total processing delay corresponds to N (filter order). Another important tool for improving the efficiency of the proposed correlation method of processing on the end device as part of the Internet of Things system is the use of proprietary IoT protocols to further reduce the volume due to the service information in the transmitted packet.

With an increase in the order of the filter N, there is a non-linear increase in the required resources; the steepness of the characteristic of the required resources for the 14-bit bit rate is higher than for the 8-bit rate. Up to the order of N = 20, the growth of is linear, and then there is a nonlinear growth of the required hardware resources, which automatically has a negative impact on the maximum performance.

The maximum operation frequency F_{max} (system performance) is achieved by minimizing the bit depth of the system and minimizing the order of the filter N. Moreover, this fact may not always mean a decrease in the dynamic range (input data range), but a purposeful narrowing of the operating range around the average value x of the input data sequence.

Were proposed expressions that define the balance between the frequency of characters, the order of the filter, and the bandwidth of the communication channel between the modem and Gates.

References

1. Cisco Visual Networking Index Predicts Global Annual IP Traffic to Exceed Three Zettabytes by 2021 (2017)
2. Weyrich, M., Ebert, C.: Reference architectures for the internet of things. IEEE Softw. **33**(1), 112–116 (2016)
3. Bonomi, F., Milito, R., Natarajan, P., Zhu, J.: Fog computing: a platform for internet of things and analytics. In: Bessis, N., Dobre, C. (eds.) Big Data and Internet of Things: A Roadmap for Smart Environments. SCI, vol. 546, pp. 169–186. Springer, Cham (2014). https://doi.org/10.1007/978-3-319-05029-4_7
4. Marjani, M., et al.: Big IoT data analytics: architecture, opportunities, and open research challenges. IEEE Access **5**, 5247–5261 (2017)
5. Engines in the Data Cloud, 10 April 2018
6. Bhuiyan, M.Z.A., Jie, W., Wang, G., Wang, T., Hassan, M.M.: e-sampling: event-sensitive autonomous adaptive sensing and low-cost monitoring in networked sensing systems. ACM Trans. Auton. Adapt. Syst. **12**(1), 1–29 (2017)
7. Harb, H., Makhoul, A.: Energy-efficient sensor data collection approach for industrial process monitoring. IEEE Trans. Ind. Informat. **14**(2), 661–672 (2018)
8. Tayeh, G.B., Makhoul, A., Laiymani, D., Demerjian, J.: A distributed real-time data prediction and adaptive sensing approach for wireless sensor networks. Pervasive Mob. Comput. **49**, 62–75 (2018)
9. Tayeh, G.B., Makhoul, A., Demerjian, J., Laiymani, D.: A new autonomous data transmission reduction method for wireless sensors networks. In: Proceedings of IEEE Middle East North Africa Communications Conference (MENACOMM), pp. 1–6, April 2018
10. Anufrienko, A.: Methods for reducing the amount of data transmitted and stored in IoT systems. In: Galinina, O., Andreev, S., Balandin, S., Koucheryavy, Y. (eds.) Internet of Things, Smart Spaces, and Next Generation Networks and Systems. LNCS, vol. 12525, pp. 21–31. Springer, Cham (2020). https://doi.org/10.1007/978-3-030-65726-0_3
11. Kurose, J.F., Ross, K.W.: Computer Networking: A Top-Down Approach, 7th edn. Pearson Education Limited (2017). 6th edn, pp. 264–266
12. Cyclone IV Device Handbook, 490 p, March 2016. https://www.intel.com/content/dam/www/programmable/us/en/pdfs/literature/hb/cyclone-iv/cyclone4-handbook.pdf
13. Ifeachor, E., Jervis, B.: Digital Signal Processing: A Practical Approach. Hardcover, 2nd edn, pp. 184–245. Prentice Hall, USA (2001)
14. Oppenheim, A.V., Schafer, R.W., Buck, J.R.: Discrete-Time Signal Processing. Hardcover, 2nd edn, pp. 746–753. Prentice Hall, USA (1998)

On Smart Greenhouse Issues

Manfred Schneps-Schneppe[1]([✉]) [iD] and Gunars Lacis[2] [iD]

[1] Ventspils International Radio-Astronomy Centre, Ventspils University of Applied Sciences,
Ventspils 3601, Latvia
manfreds.sneps@gmail.com
[2] Institute of Horticulture, Latvia University of Life Sciences and Technologies,
Dobele 3701, Latvia
gunars.lacis@llu.lv

Abstract. Rapid climate change, the explosion of the population and the reduction of arable land call for new approaches to ensure sustainable agriculture and food supply in the future. Emerging Internet of Things (IoT) technologies, which include smart sensors, devices, network topologies, big data analysis and smart decision making, are considered to be the solution to the key challenges facing greenhouse farming. Under the IoT greenhouse environment, numerous sensors and actuators can be utilized for connection throughout the greenhouse, capable of monitoring and detecting the change in the environment. The readings from these sensors can be used in analytics and providing to supervision applications. The paper shows an architecture of mesh network for greenhouse IoT system. A Biene Electronics platform embedded with GSM 2.5G receiver and microcontroller units serves as a local host in the network. Smart greenhouse basics are explained and some emergency issues pointed out. Exampled by plant disease detection, the question: what a method is more efficient - discriminant functions or neural networks, is discussed. In conclusion, some future works are mentioned, mainly relating IoT software.

Keywords: Internet of Things · Smart greenhouse · Neural network · Discriminant function

1 Introduction

Rapid climate change, the explosion of the population and the reduction of arable land call for new approaches to ensure sustainable agriculture and food supply in the future. Greenhouse farming is seen as a viable alternative and a sustainable solution that can combat the future food crisis by controlling the local environment throughout the year and growing crops even in harsh outdoor conditions. However, greenhouse farms still face many challenges to efficient operation and management.

Emerging Internet of Things (IoT) technologies, which include smart sensors, devices, network topologies, big data analysis and smart decision making, are considered to be the solution to the key challenges facing greenhouse farming. IoT allows individuals and objects to connect, communicate and coordinate with each other, share

© Springer Nature Switzerland AG 2022
Y. Koucheryavy et al. (Eds.): NEW2AN 2021/ruSMART 2021, LNCS 13158, pp. 9–21, 2022.
https://doi.org/10.1007/978-3-030-97777-1_2

information and coordinate decisions. IoT transforms traditional objects into intelligent smart objects using enabling technologies such as communication technologies, Internet protocols, applications and sensor networks. The global smart agriculture market is expected to reach $ 18.0 billion by the end of 2024, compared to $ 5 billion in 2016 [1].

Smart agriculture will become an important area of IoT use in agricultural-based exporting countries. There are challenges in developing a green IoT-based farming solution, including hardware, data analysis, maintenance, mobility and infrastructure. Hardware issues relate to sensor selection and distance to IoT devices. The challenge of data analysis concerns the use of predictive algorithms and machine learning (such as deep learning approaches and others) in IoT data to obtain a productive solution for smart farming. One of the challenges of the widespread use of smart farming is the cost of both initial implementation and maintenance, as well as the need for a highly qualified support and advisory system.

The maintenance problem applies to the sensory performance of all IoT devices, as they can be easily damaged in agriculture. The mobility challenge concerns the type of wireless communication (eg 2G, 4G, WiFi, 6LowPan, LoRa) that can connect sensors distributed over a large field in agriculture. The design and implementation of various sensor, data transmission and analysis systems must consider the environmental conditions at the place of operation. Mostly they are unfriendly to electronic devices. Infrastructure problems concern the installation and development of IoT network architecture using new technologies such as fog computing, edge computing, cloud computing, network virtualization, and so on.

Fig. 1. IoT-enabled greenhouse.

Under the IoT greenhouse environment, numerous sensors and actuators can be utilized for connection throughout the greenhouse, capable of monitoring and detecting the change in the environment. The readings from these sensors can be used in analytics and providing to supervision applications. Figure 1 shows an architecture of mesh network for greenhouse IoT system (discussed in more detail in Sect. 4). A platform embedded with RF receiver and microcontroller units serves as a local host in the network. Sections 2 and 3 explains smart greenhouse basics and point out some emergency issues. Section 5 is about the highly hot issue - plant disease detection: what a method is more efficient - discriminant functions or neural networks? In conclusion, some future works are mentioned, mainly relating software.

2 Smart Greenhouse Basics

Let us start with a small greenhouse. Given a space about $10\,m^2$, an automated hydroponic greenhouse could be set up (see Fig. 2). At the top of a tank is a floating sheet. It can help containers to float above water. At the bottom of the container are the water pump and oxygenator. We need to control the environment for the greenhouse. There will be 7 factors to control: humidity, temperature, CO_2, light, electrical conductivity (EC), pH, and dissolved oxygen. Those factors have corresponding sensors and actuators. Sensors will help IoT system to collect these data, and actuators will receive data from cloud to react to corresponding changes on these 7 factors. After data is being collected, they will be sent to a local server (data logger) through the sensor network. And the local server will send data to the cloud server (Decision Support System, DSS) by using 2.5G mobile network protocol. After computing, the data will send to the local server. Local server will send data to actuators (Fig. 3).

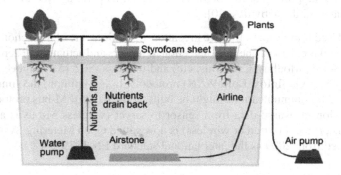

Fig. 2. Bubbleponics [3].

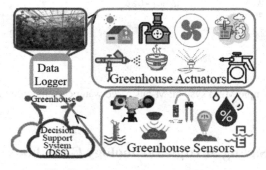

Fig. 3. Smart greenhouse basics [2].

The five types of sensors are employed in the greenhouse sensor network:

(1) humidity and temperature sensors,
(2) light sensors (light exposure creates a profound influence on crop growth in the natural environment),
(3) CO2 sensors (the content of CO2 in the air could control the photosynthesis rate of plants),
(4) electrical conductivity (EC) and pH sensors (EC and pH are two important conditions for hydroponics),
(5) dissolved oxygen sensors are in the water (ensuring the root could breathe normally, the water needs enough oxygen).

There are five actuators that adjust circumstance in order to achieve:

(1) The ideal atmosphere environment. For atmosphere, there are three actuators: CO2 generator, dehumidifier, and air-conditioner (used at High Technology Greenhouse Farms, due to energy saving).
(2) Water condition (a pump system will adjust the water condition),
(3) Light (LED light bar is used to enhance light).

A Decision Support System (DSS) acts as the central operating system which governs and coordinates all the activities [20].

Resume 1. Used for the cost-effective greenhouse solution, one of hard choice is – what kind of protocol is cheapest one for connection to sensors and actuators? There is a plenty of wired (RS-485, Modbus, CAN Bus, etc) and wireless (802.15.4, Zigbee, 868 MHz, 900 MHz, WiFi, 4G, Sigfox, LoRaWAN) protocols. In our opinion, the simplest wired version of M2M communications might be built on the basis of M-bus protocol (Fig. 4) for transmission measured data from sensor to server (wireless M-bus is available as well). M-Bus protocol (wired or wireless) is now called Open Metering System (OMS) and distributed from 2009 as the international standard EN 13757.

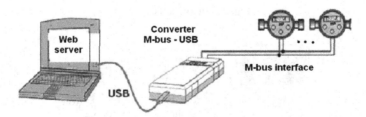

Fig. 4. A simple M2M system: M-bus based water consumption measuring.

3   On Energy Saving at High Technology Greenhouse Farms

The maintenance of the greenhouse farms is quite strenuous as it needs more resources than the traditional farms [7]. HTG farms have all the advanced climate control technologies, making it suitable for any climatic conditions [8]. It can control the heating by sensing the internal climatic conditions and provide forced cooling and ventilation. Also, it can control the humidity, luminous level and CO_2 levels inside the greenhouse (Figs. 5, 6, 7 and 8). As an exiting case, one can recall the Egypt's new national project to establish 100,000 greenhouses [9].

Fig. 5. High technology greenhouse farm.

An industrial dehumidifier (Fig. 6) will be used to dehumidification by condensation (cooling the air the water vapor phase to a liquid) and reheat the air.

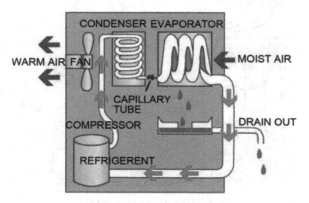

Fig. 6. Dehumidifier [3].

Temperature is under control by DSS and absorption refrigerator. DSS burn the fuel to heat. And the absorption refrigerator (Fig. 7) will cool the air.

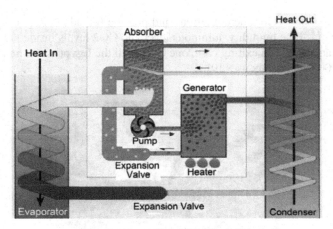

Fig. 7. Absorption refrigerator [3].

A pump system contains water pump and air pump. A water pump system, such an auto-dosing system (Fig. 8), can control water condition by pumping the different liquid. For example, adding consistent pH down or pH up can adjust pH, and pumping water or nutrient solution can control EC.

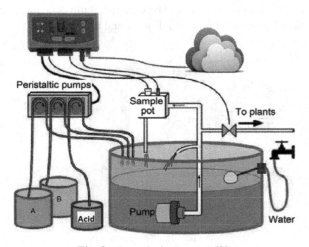

Fig. 8. Auto-dosing system [3].

Resume 2. Used for the cost-effective High Technology Greenhouse, the key problem is – to develop Decision Support System, especially from a view-point of energy saving. At the same time, the greenhouse system must ensure optimal growing conditions for obtaining the maximum possible yield.

4   Smart Greenhouse Case (Biene Electronics)

A connected farm based on IoT systems for a smart farming system was recently proposed by Beene Electronics, Latvia (http://www.bieneelectronics.com/). The proposed connected farm system has four main components such as connected IoT devices (sensors and actuators), Data logger, IoT gateway, and IoT service platform (Cloud). Many physical sensors and controls will provide the means for monitoring and controlling of the environmental conditions of the farm. These sensors and data loggers (controllers) are connected to an IoT gateway. By smartphone application (GSM 2.5G phone), the end user can monitor and control in the farming system remotely (Fig. 9).

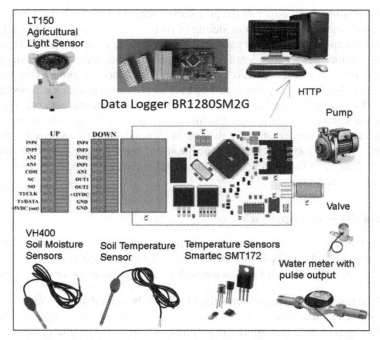

Fig. 9. GPRS Data Logger BR1280SM2G for data remote monitoring and SMS remote alarming and control applications (http://www.bieneelectronics.com/).

Biene Electronics offers two GPRS Data Logger versions BR1280SM2G and BR1280SM3G. The first one works in 2G Quad-band GSM/GPRS/EDGE 850/900/1800/1900MHz networks. The second - in 2G Dual-band GSM/GPRS/EDGE 900/1800MHz and 3G Dual-band WCDMA/HSPA 900/2100MHz networks.
Features:

- 12/11/10/9/8 digital input ports
- 8 analogue inputs (0-10V/0-5V/0-20/4-40mA)
- 8 digital open drain outputs (optionally – 4 solid-state relay outputs)

- 1/2/3 Smartec SMT172 or SMT160-30 temperature sensor inputs
- 2 Pulse inputs (optional)
- On-board power supply monitoring
- Easy to programming via RS232 interface (software included) and via SMS.
- Error notification using SMS messaging via cell phone
- Data Logging using GPRS
- Configuration from any cell phone or PC

5 On Plant Disease Detection: By Discriminant Functions or Neural Networks?

There are many unsolved issues in the greenhouse area. One of the hottest issues is the timely plant disease detection and modeling of further actions to control it. Early identification of disease symptoms has particular importance, and can often only be ensured by technical solutions (sensor-identifiable changes in plants, hyperspectral imagining) [21]. The neural network approach is the most popular method for pattern recognition in nowadays [22–24]. Some 50 years ago, the linear discriminant analysis was widely used [10, 11]. What is a difference between these methods? To use neural network, one needs high computational power. In case of discriminant analysis, enough to have smartphone but a rather complex mathematical knowledge is required. Both the approaches are popular till now. As per Google Scholar on the question "plant disease detection" and only from 2020, there are 17800 references to the neural network use and 8380 references to the discriminant analysis.

5.1 Neural Networks Approach

A range of plant diseases infect the vegetative parts, especially leaves of the plant which effect the growth and quality of agriculture crop. To avoid these economic loss, early detection and identification of leaf disease will be a better solution for this problem.

Case 1. The research [12] implements the idea of early plant disease detection. It concerns the early identification of leaf disease symptoms on the plant by acquiring leaf images from greenhouse and apply image processing techniques and computer vision algorithm on it. The VGA camera is comprised of 20 pins ports connected with Arduino Uno microcontroller. The pixel size of camera comprises of 3.6 μm $\times$ 3.6 μm. The VGA camera is getting leaf images (Fig. 10).

The identification of disease symptoms on plant leaf is applied by implementing Convolutional Neural Network (CNN) with AlexNet algorithm. The AlexNet performance optimized algorithm contains eight layers for learning including five convolutional and three fully connected layers. The primary convolutional layer filters the $224 \times 224 \times 3$ input image with 96 kernels of size $11 \times 11 \times 3$ with a length of 4 pixels. Fully connected layers comprise of 4096 neurons in each. Similarly, the AlexNet neural specification has 60 million parameters.

The leaf disease detection was implemented with MATLAB simulation software. For the experiment purposes, two fruit crops were selected including apple and grape

Fig. 10. Leaf images [9].

along with three vegetables including corn (maize), potato and tomato with overall 25 categories of diseases including i.e. apple scab, septoria spot, early blight etc. with 375 infected and healthy leaf image datasets. After the training process completed, the infected and healthy test images can be applied to test whether the leaf is infected with disease or healthy.

Case 2. In [13], convolutional neural network (CNN) models were developed to perform plant disease detection and diagnosis using simple leaves images of healthy and diseased plants, through deep learning methodologies. The training of the models was performed using an openly available database of 87,848 photographs, taken in both laboratory conditions and real conditions in cultivation fields. The data comprises 25 plant species in 58 distinct classes of plant/disease combinations, including some healthy plants. The most successful model architecture, a VGG convolutional neural network, achieved a success rate of 99.53% in the classification of 17,548 previously unseen by the model plant leaves images (testing set). Based on that high level of performance, it becomes evident that convolutional neural networks are highly suitable for the automated detection and diagnosis of plant diseases through the analysis of simple leaves images.

Total training time for that model was about 5.5 days (!). Training algorithms were implemented on the GPU of an NVIDIA GTX1080 card, using the CUDA parallel programming platform, in Linux environment (Ubuntu 16.04 LTS operating system). Classification of an image takes on average about 2 ms on the same GPU that was used for training.

5.2 The Usage of Linear Discriminant Functions

Some 50 years ago, the linear discriminant analysis was popular, particularly, for medical diagnosis [11, 14]. The linear discriminant function (LDF) is the following:

$$F = \omega_1 x_1 + \omega_2 x_2 + \ldots + \omega_m x_m$$

In this record, $x_1, x_2, \ldots x_m$ denote the symptoms (signs) that in each particular case (patient) have certain numerical values; $\omega_1, \omega_2, \ldots, \omega_m$ - coefficients that include the diagnostic value of symptoms; m- number of symptoms (usually equal to tens or even hundreds). Qualitative symptoms that may correspond to "white" or "black" should be coded with numbers such as "white" $= 0$, "black" $= 1$.

Such a geometric interpretation can be given to the discriminant function and to the decision-making process itself. Let's start with two symptoms, because then everything can be represented graphically. So, when measuring the symptoms x_1 and x_2, one of the two decisions D_1 or D_2 must be made. To do this, you need to know the numerical value of the discriminant function

$$F = \omega_1 x_1 + \omega_2 x_2$$

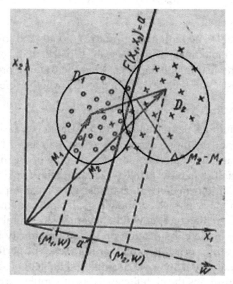

Fig. 11. Construction of LDF in case of two symptoms and two diagnoses (two domains D_1 and D_2).

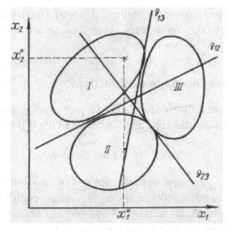

Fig. 12. In the case of three diagnoses (three domains), one needs for differential diagnosis three LDFs: g_{12}, g_{13}, g_{23}

i.e. to know the coefficients ω_1 un ω_2 as well as the limit number a. The numerical values of ω_1, ω_2 and a are obtained by processing medical histories, which show not only the values of the symptoms, but also the diagnosis that has been reliably determined, for example, after surgery. Thus, N_1 medical histories with a diagnosis of D_1 and N_2 medical histories with a diagnosis of D_2 should be taken. Each of the histories for two symptoms can be represented by a dot in the plane.

In the Fig. 11, each case of diagnosis D_1 is shown with a circle, the case of diagnosis D_2 - with a cross. If patient groups are represented geometrically, they are usually grouped according to diagnosis. The discriminant function F, which in the case of two symptoms is a straight line $\omega_1 x_1 + \omega_2 x_2 = a$, divides the plane into two parts. The straight-line equation should be chosen to best distinguish patient groups from each other. Geometrically, any line $F_1 = \omega x_1 + \omega_2 x_2$ is perpendicular to the vector ω. From all these lines, choose the one that best divides the sets. It also determines the cut-off number a. The three diagnoses case is more complicated (Fig. 12).

Breast Cancer [14]. 180 medical histories with a diagnosis of "cancer" and 115 histories in cases where there were no pathological changes in the breast were processed. The number of symptoms was 39. They all related to the patient survey. The computer selected the 22 most informative features and based on them designed the LDF, which makes the decision "cancer" or "non-cancer" with 77% accuracy. To verify the decision rule, 600 women were surveyed in a Moscow factory. The nurse collected the questionnaire data (answers to 22 questions) and entered it into the calculator. Thus, 170 women who had to undergo a further health examination were presented. As a result, three cases of cancer were detected and operations were performed in the early stages of cancer.

Lung Cancer [14]. In another similar case, 1,100 verified medical histories (from P. Hertsen Moscow Oncology Research Institute data base) were treated (550 cancers and 550 non-cancers). These were only conclusions on fluorograms: the presence of darkening in the lungs, their contours, contrast, etc. The nurse reviewed each fluorogram and entered into the card 33 signs characterizing the fluorogram. Of the 33 signs, the computer selected the most informative 11 signs. These 11 signs yielded 90% correct diagnoses on testing histories. This is the level of correct diagnoses that a highly qualified doctor achieves, and what is important - on condition of unhurried work. As a rule, the doctor has to view fluorograms in a hurry and therefore he makes mistakes more often. The main conclusion is that a nurse using a computer can achieve the accuracy of diagnoses of a highly qualified unhurry doctor.

Resume 3. Returning to the subject, namely, disease detection in plant, there is reason to carry on a study described just now. The greenhouse worker notices the damaged leaf, enters the signs of the disease into a standardized questionnaire on the smartphone and instantly receives a diagnosis with the precision of a highly qualified agronomist. It's tempting! Of course, a smartphone has camera and the defected leaf image could be transmitted to computer and processed by CNN software in 2 ms. Therefore, in our opinion, the choice between discriminant functions or neural networks is still open.

6   Conclusion

Rapid climate change, the explosion of the population and the reduction of arable land call for new approaches to ensure sustainable agriculture and food supply in the future. Greenhouse farming is seen as a viable alternative. However, greenhouse farms still face many challenges to efficient operation and management.

Some emergency issues in greenhouse industry are pointed out above, namely, (1) what kind of protocol is cheapest one for the cost-effective greenhouse solution; in our opinion, the preferable is M-bus protocol now called Open Metering System (OMS) and distributed from 2009 as the international standard EN 13757; (2) used for the cost-effective High Technology Greenhouse, the key problem is – to develop Decision Support System, especially from a view-point of energy saving; (3) is reason to carry on a study to confere the efficiency of discriminant functions versus neural networks in the field of pattern recognition.

High Technology Greenhouse industry needs a sophisticated Decision Support System. In great extent, it concerns software [15–18] and relates to the future work. To continue the above discussed disease detection in plant, one needs to produce the biostimulants in a form of extracts from medical plants [19].

Honesty speaking, all of the above greenhouse issues are only a few.

References

1. Lipper, L., et al.: Climate-smart agriculture for food security. Nat. Clim. Change **4**, 1068–1072 (2014)
2. Tripathy, P.K., et al.: MyGreen: an IoT-enabled smart greenhouse for sustainable agriculture. IEEE Consum. Electron. Mag. **10**(4), 57–62 (2021). https://doi.org/10.1109/MCE.2021.305 5930
3. Li, N., et al.: Smart agriculture with an automated IoT-based greenhouse system for local communities. Adv. Internet Things **9**, 15–31 (2019). https://doi.org/10.4236/ait.2019.92002
4. Schneps-Schneppe, M.A.: M2M communications based on the M-bus protocol. Autom. Control. Comput. Sci. **46**(2), 83–89 (2012)
5. Sneps-Sneppe, M., Namiot, D.: About M2M standards and their possible extensions. In: 2012 2nd Baltic Congress on Future Internet Communications, BCFIC 2012, pp. 187–193, 6218001 (2012)
6. Schneps-Schneppe, M., et al.: Wired smart home: energy metering, security, and emergency issues. In: International Congress on Ultra Modern Telecommunications and Control Systems and Workshops, pp. 405–410, 6459700 (2012)
7. Rayhana, R., Xiao, G., Liu, Z.: Internet of things empowered smart greenhouse farming. IEEE J. Radio Freq. Identif. **4**(3), 195–211 (2020)
8. Kipp, J.: Optimal climate regions in Mexico for greenhouse crop production, Wageningen UR Greenhouse Horticulture, Bleiswijk, The Netherlands, Report GTB-1024 (2010)
9. Egypt's new national project to establish 100,000 greenhouses. https://scoopempire.com/egy pts-new-national-project-to-establish-100000-greenhouses/
10. Smirnov, I.P., Shneps-Shneppe, M.A.: Medical system engineering. Proc. IEEE **57**(11), 1869–1879 (1969). https://doi.org/10.1109/PROC.1969.7432
11. Smirnov, I.P., Shneps-Shneppe, M.A.: Medical Systems Engineering, Moscow (1972). (in Russian)

12. Khan, F.A., et al.: Environmental monitoring and disease detection of plants in smart greenhouse using internet of things. J. Phys. Commun. **4**(5), 055008 (2020). https://doi.org/10.1088/2399-6528/ab90c1
13. Ferentinos, K.P.: Deep learning models for plant disease detection and diagnosis. Comput. Electron. Agric. **145**, 311–318 (2018)
14. Shneps-Shneppe, M.A.: Mathematics and Health Care, Moscow (1982). (in Russian)
15. Sneps-Sneppe, M., Namiot, D.: M2M applications and open API: what could be next? In: Andreev, S., Balandin, S., Koucheryavy, Y. (eds.) NEW2AN/ruSMART -2012. LNCS, vol. 7469, pp. 429–439. Springer, Heidelberg (2012). https://doi.org/10.1007/978-3-642-32686-8_40
16. Namiot, D., Sneps-Sneppe, M.: On software standards for smart cities: API or DPI. In: Proceedings of the 2014 ITU Kaleidoscope Academic Conference: Living in a Converged World - Impossible Without Standards? K 2014, pp. 169–174, 6858494 (2014)
17. Namiot, D., Sneps-Sneppe, M.: On internet of things programming models. In: Vishnevskiy, V., Samouylov, K., Kozyrev, D. (eds.) Communications in Computer and Information Science, vol. 678, pp. 13–24. Springer, Cham (2016). https://doi.org/10.1007/978-3-319-51917-3_2
18. Namiot, D., Sneps-Sneppe, M., Pauliks, R.: On data stream processing in IoT applications. In: Galinina, O., Andreev, S., Balandin, S., Koucheryavy, Y. (eds.) NEW2AN/ruSMART -2018. LNCS, vol. 11118, pp. 41–51. Springer, Cham (2018). https://doi.org/10.1007/978-3-030-01168-0_5
19. Sneps-Sneppe, M., Kalis, H.: On diffusion processes and medical plants processing. Современные информационные технологии и ИТ-образование**16**(1), 132–138 (2020). http://sitito.cs.msu.ru. ISSN 2411-1473
20. Zhai, Z., Martínez, J.F., Beltran, V., Martínez, N.L.: Decision support systems for agriculture 4.0: Survey and challenges. Comput. Electron. Agric. **170**, 105256 (2020). https://doi.org/10.1016/j.compag.2020.105256
21. Basnet, B., Bang, J.: The state-of-the-art of knowledge-intensive agriculture: a review on applied sensing systems and data analytics. J. Sens. **2018**, Article ID 3528296 (2018). https://doi.org/10.1155/2018/3528296
22. Nagaraju, M., Chawla, P.: Systematic review of deep learning techniques in plant disease detection. Int. J. Syst. Assur. Eng. Manag. **11**(3), 547–560 (2020). https://doi.org/10.1007/s13198-020-00972-1
23. Kodors, S., Lacis, G., Zhukov, V., Bartulsons, T.: Pear and apple recognition using deep learning and mobile. Eng. Rural Dev. (2020). https://doi.org/10.22616/ERDev.2020.19.TF476
24. Kodors, S., Lacis, G., Sokolova, O., Zhukovs, V., Apeinans, I., Bartulsons, T.: Apple scab detection using CNN and Transfer Learning. Agron. Res. **19**(2), 507–519 (2021). https://doi.org/10.15159/AR.21.045

Smart Contract Enabled Decentralized Reputation System for E-Commerce Reviews

Carl Kugblenu$^{(\boxtimes)}$ (ID), Petri Vuorimaa, and Barbara Keller

Department of Computer Science, Aalto University, Espoo, Finland
{carl.kugblenu,petri.vuorimaa,barbara.keller}@aalto.fi

Abstract. E-commerce has seen a surge in growth in the wake of the ongoing pandemic and is gaining ground worldwide. Inherently, product reviews by customers have fueled purchasing decisions. Blockchain is a decentralized ledger technology where a history of transactions are managed in an immutable manner. This technology is gaining traction as a result of general distrust and fragmentation in centralized systems. This paper proposes a smart contract enabled decentralized reputation system on a permissioned blockchain for E-commerce reviews. We present an overview of the limitations of current reputation system. We show how our approach addresses the fragmentation and credibility issues of product reviews in current reputation systems.

Keywords: Blockchain · Reputation system · Smart contracts · Hyperledger fabric · E-commerce

1 Introduction

Global e-commerce was showing an unprecedented growth and has seen a surge in adoption due to the COVID pandemic. According to NASDAQ, it has been estimated that by 2040, over 95% of purchases will be by e-commerce services [8]. Customers are continually seeking verifiable and genuine reviews and over 60% read reviews in some form before making a purchasing decision [9].

There has been a proliferation of fraudulent reviews on the major online retailers like Amazon, Walmart and Alibaba and they are facing challenges in mitigating them despite their best efforts [14]. Additionally, the centralized nature of the existing review systems by the retailers leaves some level of mistrust in the reviews. Retailers occasionally employ techniques to label products as top rated without elaborating on the metrics used. As a result, healthy competition becomes a challenge as the methods of boosting certain products are opaque and thereby limiting the ability of the customer to make well informed purchasing decisions [13].

Blockchain is a technology that involves an immutable distributed ledger with committed transactions stored in a chain of blocks. It has garnered interest

© Springer Nature Switzerland AG 2022
Y. Koucheryavy et al. (Eds.): NEW2AN 2021/ruSMART 2021, LNCS 13158, pp. 22–34, 2022.
https://doi.org/10.1007/978-3-030-97777-1_3

in industry and academia with some of its key features including transparency, decentralization and auditability [12]. A subsequent feature, smart contract support, has given it a broader appeal for more generalized use cases [4].

Research efforts on blockchain and reputation systems are gaining momentum in order to reduce the reliance on centralized reputation systems. These efforts have not been without their setbacks as decentralization also poses unique challenges including attack vectors such as Sybil based attacks [11]. Trade-offs in performance for transparency are necessitated especially for the use case of a decentralized reputation system.

In this paper, we present a smart contract enabled decentralized reputation system on a permissioned blockchain. Our proposed system combines review information of products purchased on recognized retailer platforms and aggregates them. There are multiple attacks that are possible on the e-commerce sites due to the centralized nature of the review systems being utilized. Due to the transparent nature of our approach, malicious activity [7] will be difficult to obscure. An example is review bombing where multiple identities are created and used to give high or low reviews after purchase. This becomes challenging in a centralized approach as they must mitigate all forms of malicious activity.

By utilizing smart contracts, we ensure similar capabilities of centralized reputations systems with the added element of transparency. Customers are guaranteed a high level of privacy by utilizing multiple pseudonymous identities, since reviews are connected to a verified proof of purchase. Reviews can be flagged by parties specialized in detecting fake reviews. A smart contract based state machine is designed to achieve this functionality. Customers now have the choice of the third party to trust for flagging anomalous reviews.

Our contributions are:

1. Design of a decentralized reputation system with local verification of proof of purchase
2. Smart Contract design and state transitions that leverages protocols over platforms
3. Implementation of a prototype using Hyperledger Fabric.

The remainder of the paper is structured as follows. In Sect. 2, we present the related work. In Sect. 3, we give an overview of our proposed architecture and design goals. In Sect. 4, we detail the smart contract design and state transitions. The product review process flow is discussed in this section. Section 5 details the implementation with Hyperledger Fabric blockchain. In Sect. 6, we discuss some limitations of our approach and possible solutions before finally concluding with main takeaways in Sect. 7.

2   Related Work

Dennis et al. [5] first proposed a novel generalized reputation system built atop the Bitcoin blockchain showing the benefits in comparison to centralized reputation systems. The paper highlights the issues of centralized reputation and the negative impacts of a single entity controlling the reputation information and making changes to how reputation is computed in an obscure manner. However, the system has limitations in transaction speed, block size and the choice of the Proof of Work [6] consensus algorithm.

Carboni [3] presents a blockchain reputation system based on an incentive model. The paper highlights key requirements a decentralized feedback management system needs and expands on how the Bitcoin blockchain helps in this regard. The decentralized approach highlights a key benefit of an architecture without a single point of failure. The possibility of a motivated malicious actor to set up multiple identities to boost reputation is mentioned. However, the incentive mechanism presented mitigates malicious activity only to an extent and other methods of highlighting abuse and fraud need to exist in a reputation system. The use of a public blockchain like Bitcoin does not take into consideration the stakeholders of a feedback reputation system.

Liu et al. [10] propose a blockchain based reputation system with a focus on preserving customer identities. The approach taken ensures that the high level reputation of the retailers is transparent while ensuring the privacy of the customers. Smart contracts are heavily utilized for retailer review aggregation unlike in [3]. The emphasis is placed on the importance of transparency, privacy and how blockchain enabled technologies achieve this within a reputation system. However, it does not take into consideration anomalous reviews that bypass the verified proof of purchase mechanism and the ability to flag such reviews in a decentralized fashion.

Wang et al. [15] present a decentralized review system that utilizes two Ethereum blockchains for on-chain and off-chain validation of reviews. The benefits of smart contracts to model centralized review systems are highlighted. The dependence of validation from a supply chain could pose a bottleneck to the system.

The existing research has shown the benefits of utilizing smart contracts and blockchains for designing reputation systems, but research is lacking in how fraudulent reviews are mitigated adequately. The system we propose presents a solution to this by providing a transparent mechanism for flagging reviews and supporting interested parties that have competencies in participating in the blockchain network.

3   Proposed Architecture

Our approach is a smart contract enabled reputation system that aggregates product ratings from multiple retailer platforms and mitigates attacks common on centralized reputation. The system will center around a permissioned blockchain, Hyperledger Fabric, as the stakeholders or participants of the system are known. The participants are online retailers, customers, sellers and interested parties.

1. Customer. A customer represents an individual capable of creating multiple pseudonymous identities to leave reviews of products, view reviews and update past reviews.
2. Retailer. A retailer represents the e-commerce platforms that hosts sellers for the purchase and delivery of products. The retailer is capable of validating reviews via proof of purchase and will flag reviews if there is evidence of malicious reviews.
3. Seller. A seller represents an individual or group that has listed products on multiple online retailers.
4. Interested Party. An interested party represents an individual or group that wishes to participate in the blockchain network to get access to the product review data in exchange for running a node. An example is a company that has competencies in detecting fake reviews using machine learning techniques.

As a result of the known entities participating in the blockchain network as shown in Fig. 1, identity management and access control is managed via certificate authorities [2]. A root Certificate Authority (CA) issues Intermediate CAs to retailers and interested parties due to their specific access control. The retailers issue certificates to sellers as proof for being a seller on their specific platforms. Intermediate CAs issue certificates to customers as end users.

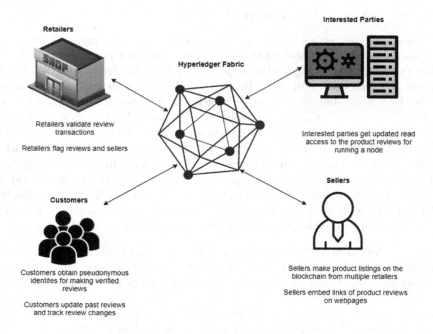

Fig. 1. Decentralized reputation architecture

The important elements of the design as follows:

- Multiple Identities. A customer has the ability to choose an identity from multiple pseudonymous identities to leave a review.
- Local Storage. All personal information of the customer is stored locally and only used to verify the purchase within the client application.
- Review Portability. The reviews of a product that exists on multiple recognized retailers are aggregated to give a full impression of customer satisfaction.
- Embedded Reviews. A customer has the ability to view and make reviews of purchased products on web-pages with embedded tags that have integrated the review system. These embedded tags on specific pages can give aggregated reviews about a product without visiting the ecommerce website.
- Review Chaining. A customer has the ability to update a past review and track past updates of a review to see the evolution of impressions made about the product.
- Flagged Reviews. A customer's review can be flagged if malicious intent or monitored threat models are detected. This is due to reputation systems being the target of malicious actors and coordinated attacks. It is with this functionality that customers can then choose to trust reviews based on the external reputation of the Interested Party.

3.1   Description of Our Approach

The main goals of our proposed system are two folds - to aggregate customer impressions of a product that exists on recognized retailer platforms in a decentralized fashion and to mitigate the majority of attacks leveled against reputation systems in a transparent manner. Retailers and product owners will play a key role in the system and serve as stakeholders. Due to the transparency considerations, assigned permissions and roles can be revoked if malicious activity is observed. We follow the major online retailers review data model; the numeric score and supporting review text. When a customer who has the web extension installed makes a purchase on a recognized retailer platform, the order information is associated with a selected pseudonymous identity. The customer can in the future leave a review with the selected identity, which will then be validated and submitted as a transaction on the blockchain. A permissioned blockchain is an ideal fit for our solution and the reasons are as follows:

1. Stakeholders contributing in a trust-less environment lends itself to a permissioned blockchain solution. The ability to use appropriate consensus algorithms like Proof of Stake and Proof of Authority instead of Proof of Work [6].
2. It has been observed that a permissioned blockchain delivers better performance than public blockchains since the stakeholders are known and their roles defined.

Retailers have the ability to flag questionable reviews in a transparent manner. It will be made possible by standardized smart contracts that are enforced specific to the retailer role. The reviews of a product that is available from multiple retailers are aggregated. Reviews are accessible on platforms that contribute a node to the blockchain with more of a read-only access control. Customers can update their review and track past reviews. Product owners and sellers can use embedded links to make their product reviews accessible in a decentralized fashion.

4   Smart Contract

This section details the process flows in the proposed system that are enabled by smart contracts [2]. The review life-cycle is presented followed by process flow of the customer and seller.

4.1   Review Life-Cycle

Hyperledger Fabric models specific users as Participants who can interact with entities as Assets. An example of an asset pertaining to reviews is shown in Fig. 2. These Assets are modifiable and transferable by Participants. In our proposed system, the Customer, Retailer, Seller and Interested Party are all Participants and have specific access controls and operations enforced by smart contracts.

```
{
    "reviewerID": "A2SUAM1J3GNN3B",
    "listingID": "ADHFEDSSWWF3B",
    "reviewText": "Works as expected",
    "overall": 5.0,
    "summary": "Positive",
    "reviewTimestamp": 1252800000,
    "status": "validated"
}
```

Fig. 2. Example of a review asset

Figure 3 presents the full process of a product review made by a customer. Firstly, a review asset is submitted by a customer. Then, the review is validated by a retailer using a smart contract leveraging a proof of purchase. A customer can later make an update to the review using the same pseudonymous identity. A review can be flagged as fraudulent by a retailer and reason stated in a transparent manner. The flagged review can be revoked back to an updated state by a specific Interested Party.

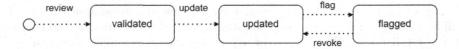

Fig. 3. Smart contract state diagram

4.2   Customer Process Flow

From the point of view of a customer, the customer goes through the process as shown in Fig. 4. The customer has access to multiple pseudonymous identities to tie a review to. These identities are in a wallet application either running in a web extension or as an application on a phone. The customer can only make a review after a verified proof of purchase. In the proposed design, this occurs locally via a web extension retrieving the order information from an active session on the retailer's web page. The submitted review is checked and enforced by a smart contract before storage on the blockchain. The customer is then notified of a successful validation of their submitted review.

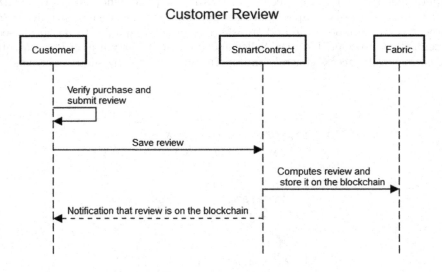

Fig. 4. Customer flow

The blocks and transitions described in Fig. 3 are described at a high level to show the transactions and the smart contract logic that is executed.

4.3   Seller Process Flow

From the point of view of a seller, the seller goes through the process as shown in Fig. 5. The seller can only make a listing after a verified proof of ownership. In

---

Algorithm 1: SubmitReview Transaction

Input: Review Asset
Result: Transaction Status
initialization with proof of purchase parameters;
if *Proof of Purchase* **then**
    Initialize connection to blockchain;
    set reviewState to Invalid;
    submit review asset to blockchain;
end

Algorithm 2: ValidateReview Transaction

Input: Review Asset
Result: Transaction Status
Verify proof of purchase;
set reviewState to Valid;

Algorithm 3: UpdateReview Transaction

Input: Review Asset
Result: Transaction Status
if *Past Review exists* **then**
    Initialize connection to blockchain;
    update review asset;
    set updatedState to True;
    submit updated asset to blockchain;
end

Algorithm 4: FlagReview Transaction

Input: Review Asset
Result: Transaction Status
Initialize connection to blockchain;
update review asset;
set flaggedState to True;
submit asset to blockchain;

---

the proposed design, this occurs if a supported retailer issues a CA to the seller. With these access rights, the seller can make a listing of products being sold on multiple retail platforms to be able to aggregate the reviews. When a seller submits a listing, a smart contract verifies ownership and checks for duplicates on the blockchain. The seller is then notified of a successful validation of their submitted review.

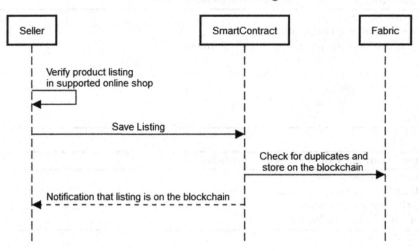

Fig. 5. Seller process flow

5 Implementation

The proposed design is implemented with the Hyperledger Fabric v1.4 and the smart contracts written as chaincode in golang. The system is evaluated based on the smart contract enabled review lifecycle testing the state transitions and Participant interactions. The blockchain test network was set up in Docker Engine 19.03 deployed on Google Cloud virtual instance e2-medium machine with 4GB of RAM. Each component runs as a container on the virtual machine and using one peer node for testing.

5.1 Experimental Setup

We leveraged Hyperledger Caliper, a performance testing tool used to run workloads on blockchain platforms including Hyperledger Fabric. A key advantage of this tool is that it abstracts away the complexity of the communication by the client and the blockchain to focus more on the test scenarios.

5.2 Measurements

We measure the latency and throughput of executing the smart contract and querying a review to compare the results. The workload specifies a fixed send rate, specified in transactions per second (tps) each round and gradually increase the rate to observe the performance at each step show in Table 1. The test scenario are executed for the "SubmitReview" chaincode and retrieving a review. Caliper collects the results for each fixed send rate.

Table 1. Metrics for performance evaluation.

Metrics	Send rate (tps)	Number of transactions
Latency	50, 100, 200, 300, 400 tps	1000
Throughput	50, 100, 200, 300, 400 tps	1000

6   Results and Discussion

Figure 6 shows the average latency in seconds of the transaction types at different transaction send rates. The "SubmitReview" transaction has a higher latency in comparison with "GetReview" transaction due to the overhead of validation checks and writing to the Hyperledger Fabric blockchain. The latency is also constrained by the test environment shown by the increasing latency in "SubmitReview".

Figure 7 shows the throughput in transactions per second (tps) at different transaction send rates. It can be observed from the results that the "SubmitReview" transactions had a throughput limit of 66 tps before leveling off. When the send rate is increased to 100 tps and beyond, the latency of continues to increase while the throughput remains the same or decreases slightly. This shows the limitations of the specific test environment ability to handle 66 tps of the "SubmitReview" transaction without impacting network latency significantly.

However, the "GetReview" transactions handled 173 tps with a delay of up to 0.03 s from Fig. 6. The low latency results are as a result of the relatively low overhead in querying the blockchain.

The key takeaway from the results are as follows:

- Performance of the blockchain network is impacted by the type of transactions and complexity of the smart contract.
- Throughput levels out when it exceeds the maximum transaction send rate and is limited by the test environment.

7   Limitations

A key limitation is the incentive model of the stakeholders participating in the decentralized reputation system. A case could be made for sellers being incentivized to make available the reviews of their products across multiple avenues. However, a clear incentive for retailers is a challenge as they are more incentivized to continue to improve their centralized platforms and be gatekeepers for the data.

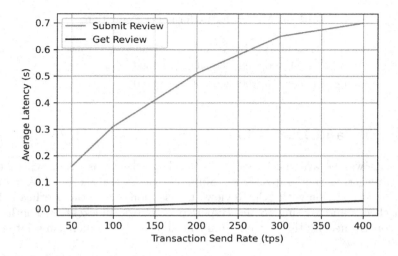

Fig. 6. Latency results

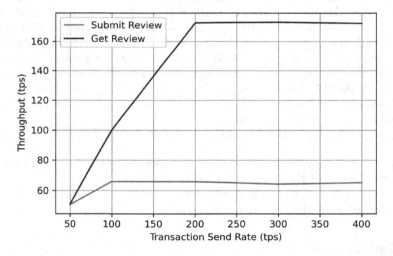

Fig. 7. Throughput results

Another challenge is the limited storage capabilities of the blockchain. Current centralized review systems include images and video. The decentralized reputation system in its current form cannot handle multimedia content and would need a backing store. The InterPlanetary File System (IPFS) [1] has shown potential as a possible decentralized storage, but more research is needed to ascertain the feasibility in a production environment.

A limitation of our system is that although it is effectively guards against objective attacks like bad-mouthing attacks and Sybil attacks on reputation systems [11], subjective or opinion based attacks are a major issue. However, the benefits of transparency on the permissioned blockchain will highlight coordinated review manipulation for it to be adequately flagged if enough evidence is present.

8   Conclusion

In this paper, we presented a smart contract enabled decentralized reputation system to solve the challenges of product reviews on centralized retailer platforms. The proposed approach details a decentralized solution that addresses the fragmentation of product reviews and how malicious attacks like bad-mouthing attacks, are mitigated as a result of utilizing a permissioned blockchain. We also present the architecture and smart contract state transitions. The system was implemented and tested with Hyperledger Fabric. The results showed that customers can submit verified reviews in a decentralized manner with pseudonymous identities. The throughput and latency results of the transaction types showed the impact of the system configuration of the test environment. We discussed some limitations and presented possible solutions to address these issues.

A possible future research direction is to conduct similar tests with multiple permissioned blockchains to evaluate their performance, robustness and scalability. Other approaches of identity management on a permissioned blockchain could be explored to test effectiveness and ease of use. Also, a standard for the smart contracts could be proposed to address the disparity in the ecosystem as it changes quickly and technologies get deprecated.

References

1. Benet, J.: IPFS-content addressed, versioned, P2P file system. arXiv preprint arXiv:1407.3561 (2014)
2. Cachin, C.: Architecture of the Hyperledger blockchain fabric. In: Workshop on Distributed Cryptocurrencies and Consensus Ledgers (DCCL 2016) (2016). https://www.zurich.ibm.com/dccl/papers/cachin_dccl, http://bytacoin.io/main/Hyperledger.pdf
3. Carboni, D.: Feedback based Reputation on top of the Bitcoin Blockchain (2015). http://arxiv.org/abs/1502.01504
4. Cong, L.W., He, Z.: Blockchain disruption and smart contracts. Rev. Finan. Stud. **32**(5), 1754–1797 (2019)
5. Dennis, R., Owen, G.: Rep on the block: a next generation reputation system based on the blockchain. In: 2015 10th International Conference for Internet Technology and Secured Transactions, ICITST 2015, pp. 131–138 (2016). https://doi.org/10.1109/ICITST.2015.7412073
6. Ferdous, M.S., Chowdhury, M.J.M., Hoque, M.A., Colman, A.: Blockchain consensuses algorithms: a survey. arXiv preprint arXiv:2001.07091 (2020)
7. Hoffman, K., Zage, D., Nita-Rotaru, C.: A Survey of attacks on Reputation Systems, pp. 7–13 (2007). http://docs.lib.purdue.edu/cgi/viewcontent.cgi?article=2676&context=cstech

8. Kitonyi, N.: UK Online Shopping and E-Commerce Statistics for 2017—Nasdaq. https://www.nasdaq.com/articles/uk-online-shopping-and-e-commerce-statistics-2017-2017-03-14. Accessed 2 Feb 2021

9. Lipsman, A.: Global Ecommerce 2019 - eMarketer Trends, Forecasts and Statistics. https://www.emarketer.com/content/global-ecommerce-2019. Accessed 2 Feb 2021

10. Liu, D., Alahmadi, A., Ni, J., Lin, X., Shen, X.: Anonymous reputation system for IIoT-enabled retail marketing atop PoS blockchain. IEEE Trans. Ind. Inf. **15**(6), 3527–3537 (2019). https://doi.org/10.1109/TII.2019.2898900

11. Mohaisen, A.: The sybil attacks and defenses: a survey. Smart Comput. Rev. **3**(6) (2013). https://doi.org/10.6029/smartcr.2013.06.009

12. Nakamoto, S.: Bitcoin: A Peer-to-Peer Electronic Cash System (2008)

13. Palmer, A.: Amazon Choice badge recommends unsafe, fake products. https://www.cnbc.com/2019/12/23/amazon-choice-badge-recommends-unsafe-fake-products.html. Accessed 2 Feb 2021

14. Schoolov, K.: Amazon Reviews: Thousands are fake, here's how to spot them. https://www.cnbc.com/2020/09/06/amazon-reviews-thousands-are-fake-heres-how-to-spot-them.html. Accessed 2 Feb 2021

15. Wang, K., Zhang, Z., Kim, H.S.: ReviewChain: smart contract based review system with multi-blockchain gateway. In: Proceedings - IEEE 2018 International Congress on Cybermatics: 2018 IEEE Conferences on Internet of Things, Green Computing and Communications, Cyber, Physical and Social Computing, Smart Data, Blockchain, Computer and Information Technology, iThings/GreenCom/CPSCom, pp. 1521–1526 (2018). https://doi.org/10.1109/Cybermatics_2018.2018.00256

Estimation of Quality of Service in Tactile Internet, Augmented Reality and Internet of Things

Abbas Alzaghir[(✉)], Alexander Paramonov, and Andrey Koucheryavy

The Bonch-Bruevich Saint-Petersburg State University of Telecommunications, St. Petersburg 193232, Russia
abbasaltamimi89@gmail.com

Abstract. In this paper the researchers provide a model to analyse the traffic streams of Tactile Internet and Augmented Reality with the concept Internet of Things. In addition, the directions in traffic served by communication networks, construct a real time interactive system between human and machine and present a novel evolution in human to machine communication. The key requirement in the implementation of augmented reality and Tactile Internet is how to achieve a low latency transmission. In this work the effect of Internet of Things, augmented reality and tactile internet traffic, is investigated, formed by surveillance and dispatching control systems, when the properties of this traffic are qualified by regular data stream properties. The researchers evaluate the effect of such traffic stream on key QoS indicators that represent the probability of packet loss and time delivery delay. The queuing system (QS) is used with a combined service discipline as a constructed model of a communication network. The simulation results of the analytical model turned satisfying.

Keywords: Tactile Internet · Augmented reality · Internet of Things · Traffic · Queuing system · Quality of service

1 Introduction

Continuing technical development led to changes in the info-communication systems. These developments will lead to a big increase of mobile and wireless traffic volume. It is also predicted that today's dominating scenarios of human-centric communication will be complemented by a huge increase in the numbers of communicating machines. The coexistence of human-centric and machine-type applications will lead to a large diversity of communication characteristics [1]. Furthermore, 5G technology will support demanding services like massive Machine-Type Communications, enhanced Mobile Broadband, Ultra-Reliable and Low Latency Communications, which require high data rates, low latency of few milliseconds as well as connecting millions of devices per square kilometer [2]. This will require high quality of service such as QoS in Internet of Things (IoT) that will play an important role in 5G technology. The IoT is a machine-to-machine

---

The original version of this chapter was revised: an orthographic error in an author's name was corrected. The correction to this chapter is available at
https://doi.org/10.1007/978-3-030-97777-1_42

© Springer Nature Switzerland AG 2022, corrected publication 2022
Y. Koucheryavy et al. (Eds.): NEW2AN 2021/ruSMART 2021, LNCS 13158, pp. 35–45, 2022.
https://doi.org/10.1007/978-3-030-97777-1_4

(M2M) communication which requires a low latency communication and promising to interconnect billions of sensors, and augment multiple levels of cognition to accelerate and perfect sensory acquisition from heterogeneous circumstances. The development of IoT is an extremely important step, as it affects almost all areas of human activity. The diffusion of the Internet of Things will pay to the accessibility of more and more information, the evolution of its analysis capabilities, the establishment of decisions and activities based on its outcomes. Another technology which requires ultra-low latency, high quality of service QoS is the Tactile Internet (TI). The Tactile Internet (TI) is construction on the idea of remote action in supposed real-time [3]. The TI will utilize the traditional wired internet, the mobile internet, and the IoT as the infrastructure of transportation from an end-to-end perspective. Furthermore, it is predictable that TI provides a novel perspective for human-machine communications with its low latency in constructing real-time cooperative systems [4]. The third important technology that has developed in 5G network is the Augmented Reality (AR) that also requires low latency communication and is used in many applications such as: control of robots, unmanned aerial vehicles (UAVs), medicine, maintenance and repair of the complex equipment, gaming and entertainment industry; military as well as management and monitoring of telecommunication networks [5–7]. The data delivery requirement between large numbers of devices, which potentially can significantly exceed the number of subscribers of existing communication networks, sets the task of ensuring the availability, QoS, reliability and stability of the operation of communication networks in such conditions. The traffic produced by the Internet of Things devices can be served and collected with other traffic of communication services, such as, wireless access point, base stations, etc. In fact, the nature of Internet of Thing traffic in general is different from the traffic of other services; it makes intelligence to measure its characteristics and influence on QoS [6]. The study [9] presented an investigation of Machine to Machine (M2M) traffic models and introduced the definition of flow types in case of mass event detection. "Traffic flow types for testing quality of service parameters on model networks" modification. Additionally, the paper [11] introduced a service model and traffic pattern for augmented reality joint with the concept of the Internet of Things, and established a method for Quality of Experience estimation. Furthermore, the paper [12] proposed a queuing system (QS) as communication model to estimate the Quality-of-Service QoS for Tactile Internet technology sharing with Internet of Things concept.

In this paper the researchers provide an analytical model for traffic streams of Tactile Internet (IT), Augmented Reality (AR) and Internet of Things (IoT) to estimate the Quality of Service represented as probability of packet loss and time delivery delay.

The reminder of the article is organized as follows: Section 2 describes the system model and problem statement. Section 3 provides an analytical model of our work, and Sect. 4 presents the simulation model that proposed in this paper, Sect. 5 shows the achieved results and finally, Sect. 6 concludes the article.

2 System Model and Problem Statement

The system model of our work consists of three traffic generators which are: tactile internet traffic generator designated as (H2H + TI, H2H - Human to Human, TI - tactile Internet), augmented reality traffic generator (AR) and internet of things traffic generator (IoT) that simulates as one or more of IoT devices in addition, all these traffic generators are aggregated to one communication node and entering to queuing system (QS) with Combined Service Discipline which include delay and losses as shown in the Fig. 1.

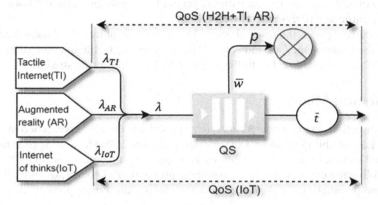

Fig. 1. System model

The traffic that Internet of Thing devices generate are categorized into three characteristic kinds [8, 9]:

1) Deterministic: These are produced by devices operating on a fixed schedule
2) Deterministic technological – These are they types that are essential to maintain the system functioning.
3) Mediated: These are a generation which are a reaction to some external events.

The traffic that the Internet of Things devices generate may be together served.

with the traffic of other services of communication, for instance, wireless access points, base stations and other network nodes. Because the nature of Internet of Thing traffic generally differs from other services traffic, it is possible to assess its characteristics as well as impact on QoS [12].

As seen from Fig. 1, the first source denoted by λ_{TI} is the intensity of the tactile internet traffic (H2H + TI), the second source is λ_{AR} which is the intensity of the augmented reality traffic and the third source is the intensity of internet of things traffic represented by λ_{IoT}, all these sources are aggregated into one stream in the output and denoted by $\lambda = \lambda_{TI} + \lambda_{AR} + \lambda_{IoT}$. At the input of a system in which all positions in the queue are occupied, the packet arrives with a certain probability p of failure, leading to some losses. Because the system has aggregated three different sources of traffic, each has its own properties, so the system will have a mixed properties of traffic stream of all aggregated traffic streams differ from traditional traffic.

The services that generate the traffic in different communication networks have a quality of service according to their requirements. In this work, the quality-of-service QoS of the system will be determined by the probability of failure packets (packet loss) and time delay of packets, where the delay occurs because of waiting time $\overline{w}$ in queue system and service time where the average service time of packets represented by $\overline{t}$ as shown in the Fig. 1.

At the system input, the characteristics of the mixed stream are decided by the properties of both streams. Hence, it differs generally from the properties of both Internet of Things traffic and traditional traffic.

In the current paper, the researchers will present the joint impact of measured traffic stream and evaluation the QoS indicators separately for the tactile internet traffic stream (H2H + TI), augmented reality traffic stream (AR) and IoT traffic stream.

3   Analytical Model

In this subsection, the considered analytical model for the aforementioned system to evaluate the probability of losses and time delay of packets due to waiting time in queue system and service time, where the represented queue system model is G/G/1/k system.

The following expression is to estimate the probability of packet losses with known distribution parameters that describe the traffic and packet service process [8, 12]

$$p = \frac{1-\rho}{1 - \rho^{\frac{2}{C_a^2 + C_s^2} n_b + 1}} \rho^{\frac{2}{C_a^2 + C_s^2} n_b} \tag{1}$$

Where, ρ is the load of system, n_b buffer size, C_a^2 and C_s^2 are the quadratic coefficients of variation of the distribution of incoming stream and service time.

Additionally, the expression to estimate the time delivery of packets by using the following equation [8, 12]:

$$T = \frac{\rho \overline{t}}{2(1-\rho)} \left(\frac{\sigma_a^2 + \sigma_s^2}{\overline{t}^2} \right) \left(\frac{\overline{t}^2 + \sigma_s^2}{\overline{a}^2 + \sigma_s^2} \right) + \overline{t} \tag{2}$$

Where, σ_a^2 and σ_s^2 are the values of the variance of the time interval between packets and the service time, $\overline{a}$ – is the average value of the interval between packets, $\overline{t}$ – average service time.

Because of the system it is characterized by having a QoS separately for each traffic (tactile internet, augmented reality, and IoT traffic), it enables to complete the applicability of the above approximations to estimate the QoS of the aggregated traffic stream. Due to a large percentage of traffic in modern communication networks is video transmission, so the traffic stream of tactile internet and augmented reality has a self-similar flow property. On other hand, the IoT (Machine-to-Machine) traffic has a deterministic flow property [9, 10], defined as a periodic process of sending monitoring system data. The assumption is based on the fact that in many cases machine-machine traffic is produced by monitoring and dispatch control systems [12].

4   Simulation Model

The simulation environment of our model was implemented by using Anylogic simulator system. As mentioned above, the first two traffics (TI and AR) have a self-similar flow properties and require generating a sequence of independent events and time intervals between them to be changed randomly. They have a Pareto and Poisson distributions [5, 7], respectively. The probability density function of Pareto distribution is:

$$f(x) = \begin{cases} \frac{\alpha x_m^\alpha}{\alpha^{k+1}} & x \geq x_m \\ 0 & x < x_m \end{cases} \tag{3}$$

Where x_m and α are distribution parameters.

The expected value and variance value are calculated from the expressions bellow:

$$E(x) = \frac{\alpha x_m}{\alpha - 1} \tag{4}$$

$$V(x) = \frac{\alpha x_m^2}{(\alpha - 1)^2 (\alpha - 2)} \tag{5}$$

Additionally, for Poisson distribution:

$$f(x) = \frac{(\lambda_r)^x e^{-\lambda_r}}{x!} \tag{6}$$

Where $\lambda_r > 0$ is the expected rate of events, and x is the number of events ($x = 0,1, 2,...$). The expected value and variance value are equally to λ:

$$E(x) = V(x) = \lambda_r \tag{7}$$

The example of implementation of simplest stream with hurst coefficient H = 0.88, and self-similar stream with H = 0.5 are shown in the Fig. 2.

Meanwhile, the implementation of aggregated traffic streams for (tactile internet, augmented reality and IoT) with hurst coefficient H = 0.6 is shown in the Fig. 3.

Furthermore, the hurst coefficients are valued by evaluating the variance change, where the diagrams of the dependence of the variance for inputting and outputting streams with intervals of aggregated streams are shown in Fig. 4. As shown in the figure, the hurst coefficient depends on the intensity of the load, where its decrease with increasing intensity of load and vice versa.

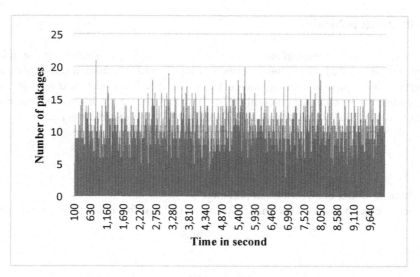

Fig. 2. The simplest and self-similar traffic stream

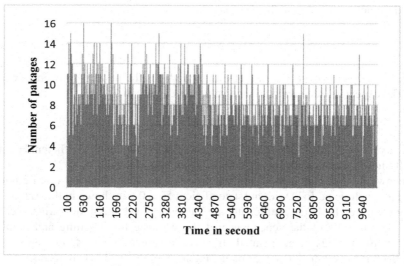

Fig. 3. The aggregated traffic streams

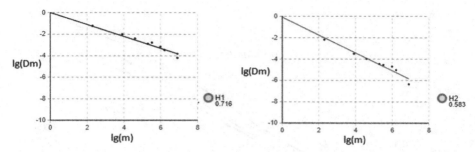

Fig. 4. The hurst coefficients for input (H = 0.716) and output (H = 0.583) streams

5 Simulation Results

In this section the researchers present the estimation results of the current work using anylogic analytic program as well as the mathematical model presented in Eq. (1) and (2).

Figures 5 and 6 show the estimation of probability of losses versus intensity of load ρ with different buffer sizes n equal to 2 and 10. As mentioned above, the results were obtained by using formula (1) in terms of losses as well as the anylogic simulator where the dashed curves represent the results obtained by using formula (1), whereas the solid curves represent the outcomes from anylogic simulator. For deterministic flow, the probability of packet loss on intensity of load was obtained differentially representing the Internet of things traffic, since the red dashed and solid curves show in both Figs. 5 and 6 buffer sizes 2 and 10. As illustrated, the simulation results obtained by using formula (1) give a slightly overvalued loss factor in both cases of buffer size.

Additionally, for self-similar flow the probability of packet loss on intensity of load for the tactile internet traffic (light blue curve) and augmented reality traffic (dark blue curve), since the blue dashed obtained by using formula (1) and solid curves show in both Figs. 5 and 6 the buffer sizes 2 and 10. Also, the simulation results obtained by using formula (1) give a slightly high loss factor in case of buffer size $n = 2$. While, in case of buffer size $n = 10$ the simulation results give a slightly low loss factor when using formula (1). Moreover, the results show that the probability of loss in terms of augmented reality is a slightly higher than the probability of loss of tactile internet and IoT traffic.

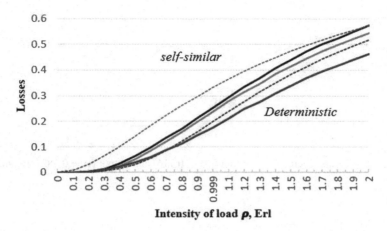

Fig. 5. The probability of losses vs intensity of load, buffer size ($n = 2$) (Color figure online)

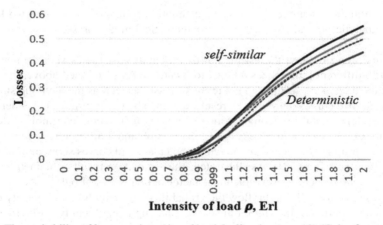

Fig. 6. The probability of losses vs intensity of load, buffer size ($n = 10$) (Color figure online)

The Figs. 7 and 8 shows the packet delivery delay versus intensity of load ρ for self-similar (blue and orange curves) and deterministic flow (red curve) as well as for aggregated model (gray curve) formula (2) with different buffer sizes n equal to 2 and 10.

The results were achieved by using the formula (2) in terms of time delivery delay, as well as using the anylogic simulator for comparison between them where the gray curve represented the results obtained by using formula (2), whereas the blue, orange, and red curves represented the results gained from anylogic simulator. For deterministic flow which represent the internet of things traffic the time delivery delay on intensity of load is less than the time delay for self-similar flow of tactile internet and augmented reality for both cases of buffer size. Also, we see that the time delay for augmented reality traffic (blue curve) in case buffer size is equal 2 a little higher than the time delay of tactile internet traffic (orange curve). Whereas, in case buffer size is equal 10, the time delay of augmented reality traffic is less than the time delay of tactile internet traffic. In comparison the results of formula (2) for aggregated traffic streams (gray curve) with a result of anylogic simulator we see that the packet loss is close to zero when the intensity of load is (0–0.5 Erl) in case buffer size $n = 2$, whereas in case buffer size $n = 10$ the packet loss is close to zero when the intensity of load is (0–0.9 Erl).

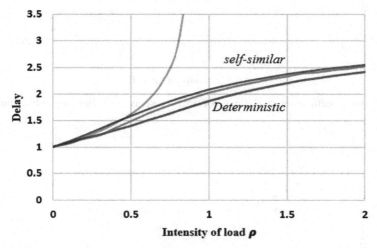

Fig. 7. The packet delivery delay versus intensity of load with buffer size ($n = 2$) (Color figure online)

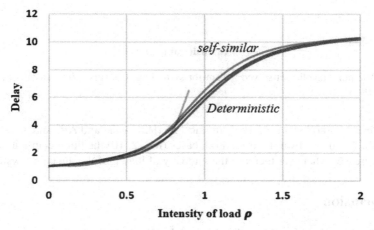

Fig. 8. The packet delivery delay versus intensity of load with buffer size ($n = 10$) (Color figure online)

The hurst coefficients for output of system versus intensity of load are shown in the Figs. 9 and 10 with different buffer sizes. Where the analytical results for aggregated

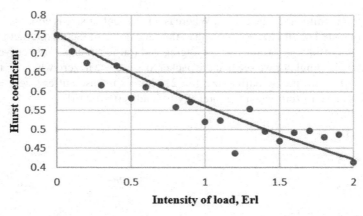

Fig. 9. The hurst coefficient served stream for system outputs versus intensity of load, buffer size *n = 2*

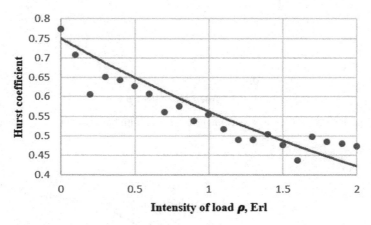

Fig. 10. The hurst coefficient served stream for system outputs versus intensity of load, buffer size *n = 10*

traffic streams by collection the self-similar flow (H2H + TI and AR) and deterministic flow (IoT). As shown from figure in both cases (n = 2, 10) the hurst coefficients at the output decreases whenever increase the intensity of load ρ of the queueing system.

6 Conclusion

In this paper, we provided the analytical model to estimate the Quality-of-Service QoS which include the probability of packet losses and time delivery delay for Tactile Internet, Augmented Reality and Internet of Things traffic streams. The proposed model of Internet of Things traffic takes into account the obtained component of dispatching and monitoring services. The model for traffic of tactile internet and augmented reality has a self-similar stream property was proposed. While a model for Internet of Things traffic is a regular stream property. The simulation results that achieved displayed that the Quality-of-Service parameters of the Internet of Things traffic and background traffic are notably different when servicing an aggregate stream. An investigation of the simulation results of the process of aggregated stream service indicated that the random stream (H2H + TI and AR) is more than loss probability for regular stream packets. In addition, this difference becomes more significant when the intensity of the incoming load increases.

Acknowledgements. This research is based on the Applied Scientific Research under the SPbSUT state assignment 2021.

References

1. Marchetti, N.: Towards the 5th generation of wireless communication systems. arXiv preprint arXiv:1702.00370 (2017)
2. Navarro-Ortiz, J., et al.: A survey on 5G usage scenarios and traffic models. IEEE Commun. Surv. Tutor. **22**(2), 905–929 (2020)
3. Oteafy, S.M., Hassanein, H.S.: Leveraging tactile Internet cognizance and operation via IoT and edge technologies. Proc. IEEE **107**(2), 364–375 (2018)
4. Yahiya, T.I., Kirci, P.: Issues and challenges facing low latency in tactile internet. UKH J. Sci. Eng. **3**(1), 47–58 (2019)
5. Makolkina, M., Koucheryavy, A., Paramonov, A.: Investigation of traffic pattern for the augmented reality applications. In: Koucheryavy, Y., Mamatas, L., Matta, I., Ometov, A., Papadimitriou, P. (eds.) WWIC 2017. LNCS, vol. 10372, pp. 233–246. Springer, Cham (2017). https://doi.org/10.1007/978-3-319-61382-6_19
6. Makolkina, M., et al.: The use of UAVs, SDN, and augmented reality for VANET applications. DEStech Trans. Comput. Sci. Eng. Aiie **134**, 153–157 (2017)
7. Iversen, V.B.: Teletraffic Engineering Handbook. COM Center Technical University of Denmark Building 343, DK-2800 Lyngby Tlf.: 4525 3648. www.tele.dtu.dk/teletra
8. Muthanna, A., Khakimov, A., Ateya, A.A., Paramonov, A., Koucheryavy, A.: Enabling M2M communication through MEC and SDN. In: Vishnevskiy, V.M., Kozyrev, D.V. (eds.) DCCN 2018. CCIS, vol. 919, pp. 95–105. Springer, Cham (2018). https://doi.org/10.1007/978-3-319-99447-5_9
9. Paramonov, A., Koucheryavy, A.: M2M traffic models and flow types in case of mass event detection. In: Balandin, S., Andreev, S., Koucheryavy, Y. (eds.) NEW2AN 2014. LNCS, vol. 8638, pp. 294–300. Springer, Cham (2014). https://doi.org/10.1007/978-3-319-10353-2_25
10. Chornaya, D., Paramonov, A., Koucheryavy, A.: Investigation of machine-to machine traffic generated by mobile terminals. In: 2014 6th International Congress on Ultra Modern Telecommunications and Control Systems and Workshops, ICUMT 2014, pp. 210–213 (2015)
11. Koucheryavy, A., Makolkina, M., Paramonov, A.: Applications of augmented reality traffic and quality requirements study and modeling. In: Vishnevskiy, V.M., Samouylov, K.E., Kozyrev, D.V. (eds.) DCCN 2016. CCIS, vol. 678, pp. 241–252. Springer, Cham (2016). https://doi.org/10.1007/978-3-319-51917-3_22
12. Mahmood, O.A., Khakimov, A., Muthanna, A., Paramonov, A.: Effect of heterogeneous traffic on quality of service in 5G network. In: Vishnevskiy, V.M., Samouylov, K.E., Kozyrev, D.V. (eds.) DCCN 2019. LNCS, vol. 11965, pp. 469–478. Springer, Cham (2019). https://doi.org/10.1007/978-3-030-36614-8_36

The Challenges with Internet of Things Security for Business

Ievgeniia Kuzminykh[1]([⊠]) [iD], Bogdan Ghita[2] [iD], and Jose M. Such[1]

[1] King's College London, Strand, London WC2R 2LS, UK
`ievgeniia.kuzminykh@kcl.ac.uk`
[2] University of Plymouth, Drake Circus, Plymouth PL4 8AA, UK
`bogdan.ghita@plymouth.ac.uk`

Abstract. Many companies consider IoT as a core element for increasing competitiveness. Despite the growing number of cyberattacks on IoT devices and the importance of IoT security, no study has yet primarily focused on the relationship between the potential impact of IoT security measures and the security challenges when implementing them. This paper presents a review of the current state of the art in IoT security for companies that produce IoT products and started transitioning towards the digitalization of their products and processes. The analysis of challenges in IoT security was conducted while mapping the relevant solutions for strengthening security to the already existing challenges. Based on the analysis, we conclude that almost all companies have an understanding of basic security measures such as encryption, but do not understand threat surface and not aware of advanced methods of protecting data and devices. The analysis shows that most companies do not have internal experts in IoT security and prefer to outsource operations to security providers.

Keywords: Business strategy · IoT certification · IoT security · Regulations

1 Introduction

The global market and society are currently undergoing the process of digitalization of the objects. Internet of things, digital twins, big data, blockchain are all evidence of a global trend of moving valuables and activities from the physical world to the digital world that drive growth of the business and raise the competitiveness. IoT came to simplify and optimize business processes, improve society lives, allow people to control connected products, save money and time, while maintaining our security and privacy. Are companies ready for the secure transmission, processing, and storage of IoT services data which are increasingly becoming part of their products and processes?

According to the Cisco Annual Internet report, we will have 29.3 billion networked devices by 2023 including smart TV, smartphones and M2M applications, such as smart meters, healthcare monitoring, transportation, and package or asset tracking [1].

The report Worldwide Global Data Sphere IoT Device and Data Forecast, 2019–2023, provides a forecast of 41.6 billion connected IoT devices, or "things", generating 79.4 zettabytes (ZB) of data in 2025 [2].

© Springer Nature Switzerland AG 2022
Y. Koucheryavy et al. (Eds.): NEW2AN 2021/ruSMART 2021, LNCS 13158, pp. 46–58, 2022.
https://doi.org/10.1007/978-3-030-97777-1_5

But the level of security of new online technologies, including IoT, remains quite low. According to Gartner report in 2018 [3] most of the companies considered IoT security IoT security not as part of the business strategy but as line-of-business unit. Therefore, the poor "security by design", and little control over the technology within connected devices were the consequences of the strategy and led to the growing number of cyberattacks on the IoT. In the period from 2015 to 2018 about 20% of the organizations were exposed to the attacks on IoT system, as reported by Gartner survey.

The number of cyberattacks on IoT devices is growing rapidly, as more and more customers, companies, municipal services start to use "smart" devices, such as routers, DVR cameras, smart traffic lights, asset trackers, smart meters, connecting to the Internet but not everyone is concerned about security [4]. By themselves, these devices may not be of interest to the cybercriminals. However, hackers crack them to use as robots to create botnets - networks of infected smart devices to conduct DDoS attacks - or as a proxy server for other types of malicious actions. Hackers simply need to discover the place where devices are connected not properly to be able to get into the system. And often, nine times out of ten they are successful. Most owners of hacked devices do not even suspect how their IoT devices are used. Cybercriminals see more and more financial opportunities to use such devices.

Regardless the number of attacks on IoT the Gartner report predicted that even in 2020 the security of the Internet of things would not be a priority for business [3]. In addition, the implementation of best security practices and tools in IoT planning would be ignored. Due to these two constraints, the companies can lose their reputation.

In this paper, we will take a look on the current state of the IoT security of the companies by analyzing the resources and available documentation on security in IoT. The purpose of the study is to identify and make analysis of the challenges that enterprises are faced when they plan and deploy IoT security at their products and processes. Moreover, several solutions to reduce risks related to IoT security have been analyzed as well and been mapped against identified issues.

Despite the growing importance of IoT, no study has yet primarily focused on the impact of IoT security on the business strategy or business models. For example, Z. Bi et al. in [5] investigated the impact of IoT on manufacturing and enterprises, K. Wnuk and B.Teja in [6] analyzed the impact of IoT on software business and requirements engineering, H. C. Y. Chan in [7] made analysis of value chain elements and stakeholders for IoT business model and validated proposed business models through the case studies of some companies. But none of these works had considered IoT security factor when developing or analyzing the impact of IoT on the business strategy or business model of enterprise. Our study is intended to fill this gap.

The organization of the paper is as follows: Sect. 2 presents most important challenges raised with IoT security for businesses. In Sect. 3, the possible solutions to strengthen the IoT security are described, and analyzed in Sect. 4. Finally, Sect. 5 presents the conclusions.

2 Challenges in IoT Security

The following list outlines the challenges that enterprises are faced during planning and deploying IoT security. Totally, the discovered challenges can be divided in two categories: internal and external. Each category has number of challenges related to certain source that summarised on the Fig. 1. Regardless the end user concerns about security of IoT services and products are high, the SMEs do not consider it as a challenge for business.

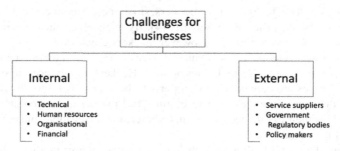

Fig. 1. The sources of challenges with IoT security for businesses.

Non-Trusted Third Parties. According to the report of Gemalto report about state of IoT security [8] most companies see the challenges with trying to secure their IoT products and services in ensuring data privacy and amount of data being collected. This user data can be shared between or even sold to various companies, violating the rights for privacy and security. Since data have a long way from its producer to the end consumer, including cloud, communication, and IoT service providers, most of the companies consider third-party risk as a serious threat to sensitive and confidential information. This stated in the report of Ponemon about State of Cybersecurity in Small and Medium Sized Businesses [9] with numbers of 57% who consider that third parties expose their companies to risk regarding a data privacy, and 58% who are not confident that their primary third party would notify them if it had a data breach.

Lack of Awareness. Regardless the fact that more than half (54%) of consumers own an IoT device (on average, two devices per person), only 14% consider themselves knowledgeable about the security of these devices [8]. This knowledge includes awareness about security measures, and principal understanding of what measure mitigate or eliminates what risk. Such statistics show that both consumers and enterprises need additional education in this area.

Unknown Threat Surface. The biggest mistake of the businesses that data from IoT system is often not considered critical until it is used for billing and accounting. In their opinion, the device sending sensor measurement periodically does not carry critical information and is not of interest to hackers. The report [10] showed that number of companies that have no confidence in identifying assets for threat model [11–13], as well as in understanding and assessing cyber risks, raised from 9% in 2018 to 18% in 2019 which is caused by the emergence of new technologies like IoT, blockchain, big data, etc., that brought the complexity of an organization's technology footprint, including threat and cyber risk assessment.

Lack of Support from Top Management. Regarding the level of investment in security, the survey [10] showed that IoT device manufacturers and service providers spend only 11% of their total IoT budget on securing IoT devices. Regardless the 92% of companies have seen an increase in sales or use of the product following the implementation of IoT security measures, the company leaders are not encouraged by the widespread use of IoT security, they are more interested in getting their products to market quickly, rather than taking the necessary steps to build security.

Top managers pay attention to security in cases when IoT system is dealing with personal sensitive information, as customers' medical, financial, or tax records, otherwise the security is out of priority of management. Security financial investment, especially advanced, is painful for top management, therefore, the level of security measures remains low in IoT and leads to so many successful attacks.

Lack of In-House Expertise. Since IoT services is a new technology, for most of the companies is unknown territory that requires additional competence, and a finding an expert that skilled enough in IoT solutions can be challenging. For example, security professionals need practical knowledge of embedded devices, sensors, and computer-computer data communications, they should have experience in integrating heterogeneous protocols for data transfer, communications and network design both within the local Internet of things infrastructure and in cloud environments.

According to IoT Signals report from Microsoft [14] about half of the companies (47%) do not have enough workers skilled in IoT, and 44% are not having enough finances to invest in IoT security training for employees. Lack of external regulation on how to secure IoT devices and services, lack of internal knowledge of how to provide security measures were pointed as challenging in dealing with IoT. Moreover, inside organizations it is not clear who is responsible for IoT security and who does what: responsibilities and competencies are fragmented within the companies that causes uncertainty among companies and customers.

Undefined Metrics for IoT Security. The studies showed that companies really recognize the importance of protecting the IoT devices and data that they generate or transmit, and 50% of companies provide security based on a design approach. Two-thirds (67%) of organizations report using encryption as the main method of protecting IoT assets with 62% data encryption immediately upon reaching the IoT device, and 59% upon exiting the device [8]. But at the same time the organizations state that it is hard to define the right level of security, determine when that's fine enough. Basic encryption is good, but this is an artifact measure inherent to IT security in general, however, more specific measures to ensure the security of IoT are not popular due to lack of understanding of IoT system features, as limited memory and computational resources of IoT devices [15], special communication and information exchange protocols, supply chain complexity and increased connectivity of IoT ecosystems, as well as not understanding the essence of these measures.

Lack of Standards. The security of the Internet of things suffers from a lack of generally accepted standards. All businesses revealed the lack of standards, guidelines and/or checklists on how to ensure the security of IoT [8–10]. Adding new devices or their components to the IoT ecosystem given that there are no standards, increase the risk of penetrating into critical systems (e.g. industrial, municipal, energy, etc.) by intruders with the subsequent termination of operations.

Although, there are many best practices and recommendations for IoT security from the security-focused organizations, there is no single coherent structure. Large vendors, world leader companies have their own specific standards, while each IoT domain has its own incompatible standards from industry leaders in certain domain. The variety of these standards makes it difficult not only to protect systems, but also to ensure interoperability between them.

3   Measures to Strengthen IoT Security

The following list outlines the measures for the companies that reduce risks related to IoT security.

Investment. Increasing investment into IoT security carries almost unlimited potential benefits in rise of protection, operational efficiency and in creating trustful relationships with customers. As survey [16] showed that the performing of better investment in the security allows for the business to stop more attacks, find and fix breaches faster and have less breach impact.

IoT Security as Part of Cybersecurity Business Strategy. The changing of business strategy forward new technologies trends related to digital transformation allows to achieve greater efficiency while also better protecting the business. However, in the process of including IoT development to the business strategy the organizations should not forget about the risks associated with IoT. Internet of things security, as part of cybersecurity policy, must be woven into corporate strategy, product design, budgets, and permeated with everyday business activities. Companies are required to change the approach to information security and the nature of their IT budgets, move their security mindset from technology-based defenses to new models for the implementation of information security, to proactive steps that include technology, process, and education.

IoT Security as Part of Cybersecurity Business Strategy. Most of the companies (99%) feel insufficient expertise to ensure the security of their products and processes, so they attract external consultants [17]. Using external suppliers and consultants in security operations can significantly increase the level of service and products without investment in technology or expert hiring.

An outsourcing continues to be popular solution in providing security measures for the companies: they prefer to outsource the security operations related to IoT, even if they have expertise, to do some operations as risk assessment, monitoring the traffic for malicious activities, incident response service. The outsourcing is more common trend among small and medium businesses, that was observed in previous years [18].

Allocating Responsibility within IoT Ecosystem. Nowadays, all businesses are not standalone production but complicated enterprise ecosystem with set of hardware, software and services. The potential breaches occurred in the company will affect not only company itself but hardware/software manufactures and all level of society. Cybersecurity could be one of these managed services that helps the company to tackle the IoT security risks. Third-party supplier can play a responsible role on helping the companies to protect against cyberattacks and providing security training for employees. Therefore, it is important to map the responsibility within all interacting elements in company's IoT ecosystem to specify and divide duties and responsibilities.

Allocating Responsibility within Company. Having cybersecurity team inside company with allocated task related to IoT security can improve cyber resilience, provide faster incident detection, shorter response time and in-time recovery process. Well organized, supported and managed by company leaders IoT security will help to deal with the pervasive risks of the IoT technology for business.

Implementing IoT Security Measures. After series of the attack and misusing of IoT devices the companies are forced to add security measures to their products or include into already running processes. The implementing of best practices and security measures as stated by ENISA in [19] can help ensure overall security of IoT system and devices, prevent or properly respond to potential cyberattacks. There two approaches of implementing security measures to the product: at the design stage for new customers, and after the product is on the market. The first approach is the most effective and secure.

Both approaches can be accompanied by a systematic implementation or driven by customer requirements. During systematic implementation of IoT security the process is starting with threat modelling, risk assessment, and required security measures towards components of product and ending with mitigation, planning, and the optimal solution for each customer. But many companies admit that selection of IoT security measures is primary driven by customer requirements, and that some customers are not security-driven at all, they just need to have their data collected by IoT.

Standardization and Legacy Regulation. The legal standards and regulatory frameworks aimed at IoT service providers and manufacturers, with large fines and working instructions, can raise responsibilities of the business for IoT security, as well as, both non-trusted third parties and not defined IoT security metrics challenges can be resolved with it. The set of dedicated compliance and standards how to handle and store sensitive IoT data can help with ensuring protection of user data and lead to more trust towards third parties who have access to the data.

Standardization and legacy regulation will be a driving factor in the development of cybersecurity hygiene and culture, raising awareness and responsibility. Mandatory set of measures and requirements for the security level in different IoT domains will increase customer confidence towards manufacturers of IoT products and services. Moreover, companies will no longer be unaware of what a sufficient level of security is, and there will be no need in search of an individual solution for each client that will allow save time and resources. The certification procedure for IoT devices should not be bureaucratic and provide the buyer with a guarantee that it has a certain degree of protection against hacker attacks.

Raising awareness about security of companies is one of the measures to improve IoT product security standards. Many authors and reports [9, 20] emphasize higher general awareness among customers and business can drive a market growth, increase the understanding of cybersecurity and data privacy. A high level of competences will create a more skilled workforce that can serve as a differentiator by itself.

4   Analysis of IoT Security Measures

In this section the result of the analysis of measures for strengthening IoT security and risks associated with their implementation will be presented.

Investment. A number of security reports from Ponemon, Accenture, Deloitte, Hiscox, PwC [9, 16, 17, 21, 22] have already noticed that in the past 5 years the companies have begun to pay more attention to security, have larger percentage of investments in security. The reports of 2018 and 2020 [21, 23] showed that companies spend 10–12.5% of budget on cybersecurity programs.

Although 83% of organisations agree that new technologies are necessary and crucial, investment is lagging. Only two out of five companies invest in new technologies, including IoT. However, companies are ready in the near future to increase investment in security of Internet of things: about half of the companies expressed a desire to do this, of which the most interested in investing were areas such as the automotive industry, industrial goods and technology [22].

IoT Security as Part of Cybersecurity Business Strategy can help strengthen the security of IoT products and processes, but first, organizations need to change their approach to security because existing security strategies in the form of security appliance (FW, anti-virus solutions, intrusion detection systems) are becoming not enough. All organisations, including large businesses, continue to struggle with insufficient, outdated security strategies and plans that do not consider fully all risks and threats.

There is no research that can show business strategy of the companies towards the IoT security, but mindset regarding common security strategy in the company shows that there is three way of focus [24]:

- security operations operate under stealth and secrecy (60%)
- security efforts prioritize external threats (55%)
- security efforts mainly focus on prevention (55%)

In total, 42% of companies have no governance policies associated with IoT risks included to the business continuity plan [16].

The most *common reason* why these enterprises do not consider it necessary to include security into the business plan is because they consider themselves too small or insignificant to justify such measures. The opinion that prevails in this category of respondents is that their IoT system will not be affected by cyberattacks.

The *second popular reason* for business is that cybersecurity is not considered enough in priority. Companies prefer to place functionality of the products and processes related to IoT on the higher level than security.

Outsourcing Security Operations to Third-Party. The organizations believe that outsourcing is a cost-effective way to attract additional expert knowledge since it is quite difficult to convince management of in-house investments in such a narrow sector as IoT security.

The types of security services requested by companies from security suppliers can be divided into two types:

1) outsourcing that oriented on providing certain service, and
2) outsourcing that focused on the whole product.

Some companies purchase just additional pentesting of the product in addition to the pentesting conducted inside company, and some purchase all spectre of services during transmission, hosting and processing of data, including server security, authentication and authorization of users for granting access to data collected by IoT devices.

From the analysis of the reports we can conclude that the reasons for outsourcing are not only the lack of expertise in IoT security, but also the lack of time or human resources, therefore majority (93%) of companies indicated that they turn to suppliers in providing more than 10% of security operations, vulnerability management and incident monitoring. Only 8% of companies are highly confident in external suppliers and 55% stated that they are fairly confident [8]. Therefore, with such a low level of trust, it is better to have internal expert in-house with basic level of understanding the security measures, and proper evaluate what can be outsourced.

Generally, the involvement of professional service providers or security consultants should be considered as positive aspect that gives confidence in ensuring cyber and IoT security.

Allocating Responsibility Within IoT Ecosystem. The allocating IoT security operations to the external supplier demonstrates the trust relations inside value chain, and in many cases, relieves liability from the company itself. Another approach of managing security in company is to do it with its own efforts and do not delegate security operation to outsourcing parties. The allocating IoT security to the department or person in the company demonstrates a willingness to move towards including IoT security into the business strategy. In this case, all responsibility in providing protection and recovering measures lays on the company itself.

The Gemalto report [8] shows that there is no clear understanding who is responsible for what operation in IoT system deployed in the company. If with responsibility for stored in the cloud IoT data all is clear, and cloud service provider is responsible for security, then the responsibility for other stages of operation of the IoT system are split between manufacturers of IoT products, IoT service providers, API developers and third-party security suppliers and specialists.

Allocating Responsibility Within Company. For a long time, cybersecurity has been the responsibility of IT departments. The most common misconception among business leaders is that they believe that Information Security is part of IT. But security is a separate area that requires time.

In many cases the task of dealing with IOT security is done by the person who just interested in this field. This person has *no expertise* in security or has little, but spend his/her time on getting knowledge and implementing security measures. This approach is more appropriate to medium and small companies mostly due to lack of the resources.

Regardless the high concern about cybersecurity of IoT (80% think that a security incident related to unsecured IoT product could be catastrophic [9]), the top management rarely participates in cybersecurity discussions regarding, for example, building security into product designs. Earlier research showed that only 22% of companies have business leaders are accountable for cybersecurity [16], and only 21% monitor the risk of their IoT products [9]. But even these numbers need to be shifted more towards responsibility of top management because nowadays the cybersecurity is becoming a common task for all company employees.

Implementing of IoT Security Measures. Regardless the most companies (80%) are interested in IoT security [9], they are not in a rush with implementing security measures. According to [8] almost one-quarter of companies is aware of cybersecurity risks, but some companies do not have IoT security measures in place at all. This is because with the adopting of new technologies (IoT, AI, block chain, cloud computing), the main preference for half of companies (50%) was the pushing ahead a digital transformation, despite the potential security risks associated with them [8].

After series of the attacks against IoT devices, companies are forced to add security measures into their marketed products. Some companies have hung with a basic security measures as encryption and passwords and do not progress more due to the lack of awareness and guidance of how to do it. But it is required to keep balance between cryptography algorithm and level of security. Some of the algorithms are high energy consuming that can reduce the lifetime of IoT devices that powered by battery [25].

Half of the companies implements their security measures based on the current cybersecurity needs and customer demands, and do not consider future pervasive risks and needs [16]. The more aware customers about security risks and threats, the bigger the demand for IoT security measures. Therefore, it is very important to help consumers really understand what is happening with their data and teach them how it is possible to protect it.

Some companies have more than basic level with a systematic approach based on one of the cyber security frameworks, e.g. ISO 27001 [26], IoT Security Foundation [27], NIS directives [28], NIST SP 800-53 [29], IEC 62443 [30] UL 2900 series [31], and Cyber Essentials in UK [32].

The most important security measures in IoT should be focused on authentication, secure communication, handling, storage, which are aimed to protecting data in transit, protecting data in process, and protecting data at rest [33]. All companies should strive for providing all set of the data-centric security measures. This is not only correct, but also important if organizations have serious intension towards protecting their assets and the data of customers [11, 12, 19].

Standardization and Legacy Regulation. While certification promises a solution to many problems for business and for consumers of IoT services, a unified standard still does not exist. However, the large amount of IoT vulnerabilities forced the organizations focused on providing guides for security to make a number of recommendations on protecting IoT devices and IoT infrastructures.

Among bodies involved in the producing of recommendation for security of IoT devices, such as OWASP, ENISA, IoT Security Foundation, NCSC. The recommendations partially duplicate each other, are *advisory in nature*, therefore, cannot be considered as legacy regulations, and most companies simply ignore them.

Due to the fact that passwords are the most common weakness, the principal recommendation in all guidelines relates to the strengthening and control of the use and procedure of generating passwords. All passwords of user IoT devices should be unique and without the ability to reset them to factory settings.

Another measure of enhancing of IoT security stated in many guidelines is the ability to provide product updates, either remotely or in place. Usage of old versions of software are identified as high security risk in many regulations on ensuring IoT security.

Given the heterogeneity of applications by end-user (private person, company, state) and application domain (health, automotive, HVAC), the system of standards will be multi-level, varying in degree of coverage and detail [34].

While mitigating the risk associated with the low trust to suppliers the appearing of new standards and regulation can pose another challenge related to compliance with various standards, legal and regulatory structures.

Raising Awareness. The IoT security training for employees, customers and business leaders is required to build effective cybersecurity culture. It could be done through the educational institutions, roundtables, workshops, security consultancy firms, etc. [35].

IoT security training has not yet been widely disseminated in most organizations. The percentage of organizations that conduct educational training for employees and third parties about the risks in IoT remains small - only 24% of companies currently provide such information and education [9]. However, it is promising that three out of ten business leaders plan to invest more in IoT security training in the future [23].

Finally, the effectiveness of each security measure and its impact towards the identified challenge is presented in Table 1.

Table 1. Impact of the measures on the issues with IoT security.

	Third parties	Lack of awareness	Threat surface	No support from management	No in-house expertise	Undefined metrics	Missing standard
Investment	Medium	High		Medium	High	Low	
IoT security strategy		Medium	High	High		Medium	Low
Outsourcing			Medium				
Ecosystem leadership	High			High	Low		
Company leadership	Medium			High	Medium		
IoT security measures			High			Low	Medium
Standardization						High	High
Raising awareness		High	High		High		Medium

Regardless its popularity the outsourcing is not effective strategy of the company in solving the issues related to IoT security. This measure leaves the company blind in relation to the threat surface, possible security solutions, does not increase knowledge within the company. The most effective method for solving a series of the most cutting-edge problems is an investment but not all companies are willing to spend more on security and on staff education.

Raising awareness is one more effective way to solve the set of the issues related to personal expertise inside company. During training the employees can expand their knowledge about IoT technology, attack surface, protection security measures, and, also, help the client to select IoT solution.

Using this matrix, the companies will be able to navigate in the selection of security measures and choose the most effective way to solve their specific issues.

5   Conclusions

The paper was aimed at identifying challenges with IoT security for business and finding possible measures to overcome these challenges. The proposed mapping of the impact of each of the security measure will help companies change their mindset towards IoT security, increase the protection of devices, processes and customers data, and thus, business competitiveness.

Our findings continue to highlight the importance of implementing the IoT security as part of the business strategy. Among the reasons why companies have difficulties with creating a stronger IoT security posture are 1) lack of in-house expertise, 2) not understanding how to protect against IoT cyberattacks, 3) not a priority issue, 4) lack of collaboration with other functions, 5) management does not see cyberattacks on IoT products as a significant risk. First two are primary reasons for not implementing the IoT security, others are main reasons for companies to consider IoT security as afterwards because operational processes considered as more important.

Only two of ten companies monitor the risk of their IoT products and processes. This is catastrophic because these products go to the market, start operate in the customer houses or monitor engines without any cyber security check. Another challenge is related to implementing security measures, they are either basic in form of encryption and secure data transmission or have necessary for customer level.

Standardization and regulatory control of IoT security will make security of IoT tangible and understandable for business and, therefore, uses IoT security as a driving force for growth.

Finally, while more organizations are concerned about IoT security, the analysis showed that implementation of IoT security is not a priority task. Increasing understanding of IoT security risks and threats among top management and business leaders may facilitate the change of strategy towards inclusion of IoT security in the company's priority tasks. The companies must update the way they plan and execute IoT security.

References

1. Cisco Public: Cisco Annual Internet Report (2018)
2. MacGillivsry, C., Reinsel, D.: Worldwide Global DataSphere IoT Device and Data Forecast, 2019–2023. 13 (2019)
3. Contu, R., Middleton, P., Alaybeyi, S., Pace, B.: Forecast: IoT Security, Worldwide, 2018. 26 (2018)
4. Kuzminvkh, I.: Development of traffic light control algorithm in smart municipal network. In: Proceedings of 13th International Conference on Modern Problems of Radio Engineering, Telecommunications and Computer Science, TCSET 2016, pp. 896–898 (2016). https://doi.org/10.1109/TCSET.2016.7452218
5. Chengen, W., Da Li, X., Zhuming, B.: Internet of things for enterprise systems of modern manufacturing. IEEE Trans. Ind. Inform. 10(2), 1537–1546 (2014)
6. Wnuk, K., Murari, B.T.: The impact of internet of things on software business models. In: Maglyas, A., Lamprecht, A.-L. (eds.) Software Business. LNBIP, vol. 240, pp. 94–108. Springer, Cham (2016). https://doi.org/10.1007/978-3-319-40515-5_7
7. Chan, H.C.Y.: Internet of things business models. In: Internet of Things and Data Analytics Handbook, pp. 735–757 (2017). https://doi.org/10.1002/9781119173601.ch45
8. Gemalto: The State of IoT Security (2018)
9. Ponemon Instsitute: Exclusive Research Report 2019 Global State of Cybersecurity in Small and Medium-Sized Businesses (2019)
10. Marsh: 2019 Global Cyber Risk Perception Survey. Microsoft Insights, pp. 1–36 (2019)
11. Kuzminykh, I.: Avatar conception for thing representation in internet of things. In: Proceedings of 14th Swedish National Computer Networking Workshop (2018)
12. Kuzminykh, I., Carlsson, A.: Analysis of assets for threat risk model in avatar-oriented IoT architecture. In: Galinina, O., Andreev, S., Balandin, S., Koucheryavy, Y. (eds.) NEW2AN/ruSMART -2018. LNCS, vol. 11118, pp. 52–63. Springer, Cham (2018). https://doi.org/10.1007/978-3-030-01168-0_6
13. Bakhshi, T., Ghita, B., Kuzminykh, I.: Securing IoT firmware - technologies and research challenges. Unpublished manuscript

14. Microsoft: IoT SIGNALS. 80 (2019)
15. Kuzminykh, I., Carlsson, A., Yevdokymenko, M., Sokolov, V.: Investigation of the IoT device lifetime with secure data transmission. In: Galinina, O., Andreev, S., Balandin, S., Koucheryavy, Y. (eds.) NEW2AN/ruSMART -2019. LNCS, vol. 11660, pp. 16–27. Springer, Cham (2019). https://doi.org/10.1007/978-3-030-30859-9_2
16. Accenture: Building Pervasive Cyber Resilience Now. Securing the Future Enterprise Today – 2018. https://www.accenture.com/_acnmedia/pdf-81/accenture-build-pervasive-cyber-resilience-now-landscape.pdf
17. Deloitte: 2019 Future of cyber survey I Deloitte I Risk (2019)
18. Cyber Security Breaches Survey 2020. Comput. Fraud Secur. **2020**, 4 (2020). https://doi.org/10.1016/s1361-3723(20)30037-3
19. ENISA: Good Practices for Security of Internet of Things in the context of Smart Manufacturing. Eur. Union Agency Netw. Inf. Secur. 1–118 (2018)
20. Furnell, S., Gennatou, M., Dowland, P.S.: Promoting security awareness and training within small organisations. In: Proceedings of 1st Australian Information Security Management Workshop (2000)
21. Wharton, G.: The Hiscox Cyber Readiness Report 2019 I Hiscox UK. R (2019)
22. Randeria, Z., Horne, R.: Global State of Information Security® Survey. PwC UK (2018)
23. Accenture: State of Cybersecurity Report 2020 (2020)
24. Accenture: The Cyber Security Leap: From Laggard to Leader (2015)
25. Kuzminykh, I., Yevdokymenko, M., Sokolov, V.: Encryption algorithms in IoT: security vs lifetime. Lect. Notes Data Eng. Commun. Technol. (2021)
26. International Standard Organization: IEC/ISO 27001:2013 Information technology — Security techniques — Information security management systems (2013)
27. IoT SF: IoT Security Compliance Framework Release 2.1 (2020)
28. Markopoulou, D., Papakonstantinou, V., De Hert, P.: The new EU cybersecurity framework: the NIS directive, ENISA's role and the general data protection regulation. SSRN Electron. J. (2021). https://doi.org/10.2139/ssrn.3493561
29. National Institute of Standards and Technology: NIST Special Publication 800-53: Security and Privacy Controls for Federal Information Systems and Organizations (2013)
30. IEC: Industrial communication networks – Network and system security - IEC 62443
31. UL Standards: ANSI/CAN/UL Standard for Software Cybersecurity for Network-Connectable Products, Part1: General Requirements - UL2900-1 (2017)
32. Such, J.M., Ciholas, P., Rashid, A., Vidler, J., Seabrook, T.: Basic cyber hygiene: does it work? Computer (Long. Beach. Calif.) **52**, 21–31 (2019). https://doi.org/10.1109/MC.2018.2888766
33. Inside Secure: IOT SECURITY SOLUTIONS White paper
34. Huawei: Iot_Security_White_Paper_2018_V2_En.Pdf (2018)
35. Kuzminykh, I., Yevdokymenko, M., Yeremenko, O., Lemeshko, O.: Increasing Teacher Competence in Cybersecurity using the EU Security Frameworks. Manuscr. Submitt. Publ. (2021)

Information and Communications Technology in the Development of Territories Based on Designing "Smart Cities"

Viktoria Bondarenko[1], Natalia Guzenko[1], Tatiana Romanishina[1],
Valery Leventsov[2](✉), and Vladimir Gluhov[2]

[1] Rostov State University of Economics (RINH), Rostov-on-Don, Russia
[2] Peter the Great St. Petersburg Polytechnic University, Saint-Petersburg, Russia
{vleventsov,vicerector.me}@spbstu.ru

Abstract. This paper analyzes the leading role of information and communications technology in developing territories based on the smart city concept. It is noted that the main significance of this concept is the ability to quickly process large amounts of information, to join together the interests of managers, businesses and the population, and to calculate the current and future demands of an area and its consumer groups within the selected positive growth scenario. An example of such solutions is the "living urban technology labs", where the situation in a specific area is assessed using artificial intelligence and ICT development, and this assessment is then used to design urban landscapes with affordable housing, healthcare services, including telehealth, as well as traffic control and other sectors. Researching the role of information and communications technology in the development of a territory based on designing "smart cities" suggests a need to: 1) assess the role of the smart city concept in transforming territories based on adopting information and communications technology; 2) validate the possibilities of Russian regions where megapolises are the driving force in the positive transformation of the socio-economic system of a territory on a digital basis to provide an information and communications infrastructure. In Russia, the driving forces in the development of the smart city concept are modern large cities, in the majority of which initiatives on positively transforming the planning and management strategy for a smart urban environment are being carried out. With their developed ICT, they help generate the growth of their local region, contributing to its transformation into a smart territory. Foreign experience concerning both local examples of renovating industrial regions of urban areas as well as scaling the smart city concept within the framework of interregional projects similar to the experience of China can be demanded and tested in Russia, above all, in regions with the most developed ICT today.

Keywords: Information and communications technology · Development drivers · Megapolises · Concept scaling · Smart cities · Smart territories

© Springer Nature Switzerland AG 2022
Y. Koucheryavy et al. (Eds.): NEW2AN 2021/ruSMART 2021, LNCS 13158, pp. 59–68, 2022.
https://doi.org/10.1007/978-3-030-97777-1_6

1 Introduction

Information and communications technology (ICT) currently allows for the development of a set of actions [1] that make it possible to develop territories using completely new principles that mediate initially calculated solutions* to the needs of the local communities (residents), locally active businesses and management, in charge of strategic planning and tactical steps for positive transformations in the long run [2].

The originality of these adopted principles is above all the ability to quickly process a large amount of information, join together the interests of managers, businesses and the population, to calculate the current and future demands of an area and its consumer groups within the selected positive growth scenario. An example of such decisions is the "living urban technology labs", where the situation in a specific area is assessed using artificial intelligence and ICT development, and this assessment is then used to design urban landscapes with affordable housing, healthcare services, including telehealth, as well as traffic control and other sectors [3].

ICT-based projects for transforming city landscapes are being carried out, for example, in Copenhagen with the renovation of the old industrial port and creation of a "smart space" there for the citizens to work and live in [4]. Similar solutions for redeveloping and using industrial regions are being implemented in Helsinki, where renovations of industrial zones are being based on digital BIM technology (Building Information Model), giving the opportunity to create digital prototypes and understand all possible complications and necessary resources [4].

Information and communications technology also makes it possible to scale successful solutions of a megapolis that acts as a flagship in the development of a specific area for the whole region, as well as to include the region itself in ongoing large-scale projects that allow it to succeed and be competitive, including at an international level. One of the most well-known projects being carried out for the digital information and communications infrastructure is the Eurasian Land Bridge (OBOR concept (One Belt One Road), which is based on the construction of smart cities [5]. This project involves cities in China as well as smart territories in Germany, Malaysia and Kenya, where companies such as ZTE and Huawei are actively working [6].

In relation to the situation in Russia, it is noted that the development of an information and communications infrastructure also plays a key role. However, according to currently existing assessments that are based on large-scale research of the provision of a telecommunications infrastructure, 41 regions of the country have not achieved the industry-average indicator corresponding to the subindex [7]. To calculate this subindex, the provision of broadband internet, fixed-line and mobile communication to the people in a region was evaluated. The number of organizations equipped with broadband internet was also evaluated. The leading regions in this regard (according to the corresponding subindex value calculated) are given in Fig. 1.

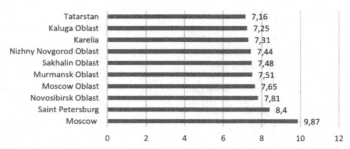

Fig. 1. Leading Russian regions in indicator of telecommunications infrastructure development (based on the obtained subindex) in 2020 [7]

Naturally, Moscow and Saint Petersburg are included in the leading regions for this indicator. A defined increase is noticed in all federal subjects of the country. At the same time, there are territories in which this indicator is minimal in comparison to the other subjects (Fig. 2).

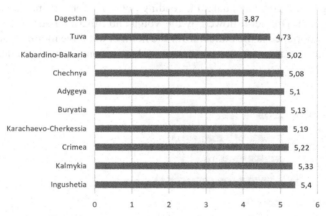

Fig. 2. Russian republics lagging in indicator of telecommunications infrastructure development (based on the obtained subindex) in 2020 [7]

The development of this emerging infrastructure has in large part a defining role in the possibilities of constructing "smart territories", since the insufficient amount of modern telecommunications technology provided to the population, businesses and organizations acts as a negative precursor to deepening the disparity in territorial development growing in the digital realm [8].

To understand the development of the presented segment in the context of Russian federal districts (since the state of the telecommunications infrastructure is one of determining significance in carrying out the national project "Digital Economy of the Russian Federation" [9]), information about the number of active fixed-line broadband internet access subscribers (both individuals and legal entities) is presented (Fig. 3).

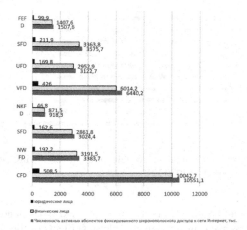

Fig. 3. Data on the number of active fixed-line broadband internet subscribers in Russia for 2019 in the context of the federal districts (thous.) [10]

According to the presented data, the leading positions for this indicator are held by the Central Federal District followed by the Volga and Siberian Federal Districts.

Of equal importance is the indicator for the number of active mobile communication subscribers that use internet access services (also in context of the federal districts) (Fig. 4).

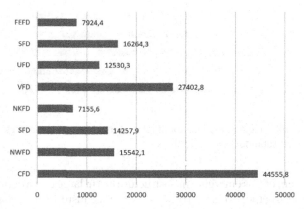

Fig. 4. Number of active mobile communication subscribers that use internet access services in the context of Russian federal districts in 2019 (thous.) [10]

It is shown that the same federal districts lead in this indicator as well. In light of the existing trends to develop smart cities as well as the wide-scale regional and interregional projects being carried out based on adopting single information and communications technology established in foreign practice, there is considered to be a justified need to assess the possibilities of developing smart cities in Russia based on introducing such a practice in regions where megapolises act as flagships in the evolution of the area.

It is believed that the given circumstances suggest a refined role for information and communications technology in establishing smart cities and understanding the idea of the concept for transforming territories. They also suggest identifying the established positions for providing an information and communications infrastructure in the regions of Russia where megapolises are the driving forces in the positive transformation of the area's socio-economic system on a digital basis.

2   Research Method

Researching the role of information and communications technology in developing a territory based on designing smart cities suggests a need to:

- assess the role of the smart city concept in transforming territories based on adopting information and communications technology.
- validate the possibilities of Russian regions where megapolises are the driving forces in the positive transformation of the socio-economic system of a territory on a digital basis to provide an information and communications infrastructure.

2.1   Assessing the Role of the Smart City Concept in Transforming Territories Based on Adopting Information and Communications Technology

According to the opinions presented in scientific literature on the successful and competitive operation of territories at a modern level, it is necessary to create conditions in which highly educated individuals, who form their intellectual capital and are capable of positively transforming the place where they live and pursue their professional endeavors, can develop [11, 12, 13]. Such conditions are created by actively using information and communications technology in designing smart cities [14].

In terms of Russia, where three fourths of the country's population lives in cities, managing the urban economy and making strategic decisions based on digital solutions is the priority [15].

In order to understand the idea behind the smart city concept, it is advised to look at the main terms related to it and the interpretations of various authors associated with this concept (Table 1).

It is noted that all of the interpretations listed include information and communications technology that, on the one hand, act as an infrastructure element or platforms for smart cities to operate on. On the other hand, along with providing an infrastructure, this technology is the main idea (essence) behind joining the interests of target audiences in relation to the future development of a megapolis and the strategic solutions for its transformation. Accordingly, ICT plays a defining role in both the material support and conceptual embodiment of a smart city.

Table 1. Interpretations associated with the smart city concept [11, 12, 16, 17]

Interpretation	General concept
Wired city	Urban environment that operates based on laying fiberoptic cables to connect infrastructure elements and exchange data
E-globalization city	Information technology is fully implemented and applied in all sectors and areas of activity
Intellectual city	Digital technology and a comfortable urban environment help attract highly intellectual individuals synthesizing knowledge and driving innovation
Information city	An active exchange of information between businesses, government and the local community carried out on an ICT platform
Digital city	Management and communications subsystems functioning on an IT basis
Smart community	Widespread use of ICT in communication, education, business activities and in the interaction between government, businesses and the population. Interested people working together with the goal of developing the territory
City of knowledge	A highly developed ICT sector and a telecommunications infrastructure that allows there to be a constant growth in the knowledge required for communities involved in developing the territory
Learning city	A smart city in which education plays a permanent role for individuals and organizations. Constant education and improvement based on ICT use is an organic component to the urban society life
Sustainable city	Focused on social and environmental effects as well as economical ones. Forecasts, data exchange and monitoring of activities are carried out on a digital platform
"Green" city	Digital solutions are adopted with the goal of sustainable development to reduce the environmental stress on the land and to increase the quality of life for citizens, as well as to ensure acceptable living conditions for future generations

2.2 Validating the Possibilities of Russian Regions Where Megapolises are the Driving Force in the Positive Transformation of the Socio-Economic System of a Territory on a Digital Basis to Provide an Information and Communications Infrastructure

It is advised to conduct a comparative analysis of the provided information and communications infrastructure of Russian regions in which cities with a population of over one million act as the flagship of growth. This position appears to be justified, since cities of such size are an attraction point for investments and human capital and are an element that shapes the development path and vector for the whole region, scaling its own economic model to it. They are the basis for creating smart territories based on the smart city concept.

The regions for comparison according to the research method given include Moscow, Saint Petersburg, Moscow Oblast and Leningrad Oblast (despite the fact that these are individual subjects, Moscow and Saint Petersburg have a significant impact on their growth), Novosibirsk Oblast, Sverdlovsk Oblast, Rostov Oblast, Nizhny Novgorod Oblast, Tatarstan, Chelyabinsk Oblast, Omsk Oblast, Samara Oblast, Bashkiria, Krasnoyarsk Krai, Perm Oblast, Voronezh Oblast, Volgograd Oblast, Krasnodar Krai. Thus, 18 regions of Russia are included in the spectrum for comparison.

In relation to the information and communications infrastructure, the parameter given for comparison was the number of devices with mobile communications plans per 1,000 people (Fig. 5).

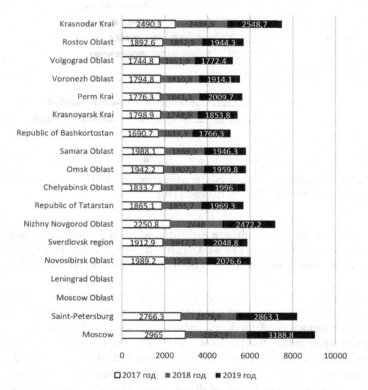

Fig. 5. Changes in number of devices with mobile communications plans per 1,000 people in the analyzed regions of Russia for 2017–2019 (units) [10]

Data on the specified parameters is not given for the Moscow and Leningrad Oblasts. For all regions except Sverdlovsk Oblast, an increase in the analyzed indicator can be observed. The top indicators are found in Moscow, Saint Petersburg, Krasnodar Krai, Nizhny Novgorod Oblast and Novosibirsk Oblast.

The next parameter to be analyzed is the number of active mobile broadband internet subscribers per 100 people (Fig. 6).

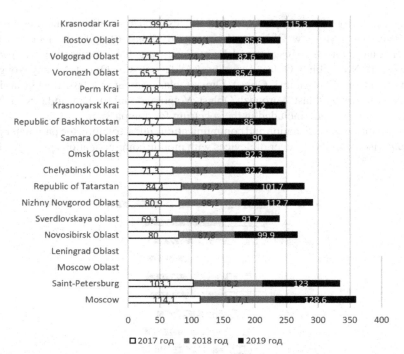

Fig. 6. Changes in number of active mobile broadband internet subscribers per 100 people in the analyzed regions of Russia for 2017–2019 (units) [10]

The leaders for the given indicator are Moscow, Saint Petersburg, Krasnodar Krai, Tatarstan and Nizhny Novgorod Oblast. Data for the Moscow and Leningrad Oblasts is not given. An increase in this indicator is a common positive trend for all of the subjects analyzed.

In regions such as Moscow, Saint Petersburg and Tatarstan, there is already significant initiative to create a smart city and involve in this process managers, businesses and active representatives of the local community, whose efforts are joined through information and communications technology [17, 18]. The infrastructural component of developing smart cities makes it possible to create comfortable and accessible conditions for the population. Therefore, great attention is given to the effective operation of the trade environment under conditions of digitalization [19, 20]. These territories can be considered to have promising potential to develop a smart urban environment.

It is believed that these subjects specifically are expected to significantly increase the development of the regional economy thanks to introducing in practice the smart city concept and scaling it for the region, thereby transforming it into a "smart territory". Looking forward, the noted practice will spread to other regions of Russia, contributing to the positive evolution of their socio-economic systems, which will in large part take place on the basis of digital solutions.

3 Conclusion

1. The development of smart cities and scaling this concept for smart territories is a practically certain scenario in terms of the possibilities for the positive evolution of territories.
2. Smart cities are becoming attraction points for intellectual capital in the form of highly educated individuals involved in the issues of ensuring a future for territories based on adopting targeted applications of the concept of sustainable development and who carry out their communication possibilities using ICT.
3. All theoretical positions connected to the smart city concept are based on the use of information and communications technology as an infrastructure platform and idealogical construct bringing together administrative messages, business solutions and intentions of the local community.
4. In Russia, the driving forces in the development of smart cities should be considered the megapolises, the majority of which are already carrying out initiatives on the positive transformation of the strategy for planning and managing an urban environment. These megapolises have well-developed ICT and act as generators for the development of their local region, contributing to its transformation into a smart territory.
5. The current foreign experience concerning both local examples of renovating industrial regions of urban areas as well as scaling the smart city concept within interregional projects similar to the experience of China can be demanded and tested in Russia, above all, in regions with the most developed ICT today.

Acknowledgments. The reported study was funded by RFBR, project number 20-010-00942 A.

References

1. Kurcheeva, G.I., Klochkov, G.A.: Developing a smart city process-based model [Rasrabotka protsessnoy modeli "Umnyy gorod"]. Eur. Sci. J. **5**(42) (2017). https://cyberleninka.ru/art icle/n/razrabotka-protsessnoy-modeli-umnyy-gorod. Accessed 27 Apr 2021
2. Gavrikova, K.V., Grigorieva, M.S.: Integrating the smart city concept into the Russian system of strategic management of an urban area [Integratsiya kontseptsii "umnogo goroda" v rossiyskuyu sistemu strategicheskogo upravleniya gorodskim prostranstvom]. Soc.: Politics Econ. Law **5** (2018). https://cyberleninka.ru/article/n/integratsiya-kontseptsii-umnogo-goroda-v-rossiyskuyu-sistemu-strategicheskogo-upravleniya-gorodskim-prostranstvom. Accessed 27 Apr 2021
3. Kupriyanovsky, V.P., et al.: Smart monotowns as zones for the economic development of a digital economy [Umnye monogoroda kak zony ekonomicheskogo ravitiya tsifrovoy ekonomiki]. Int. J. Open Inf. Technol. **1** (2018). https://cyberleninka.ru/article/n/umnye-monogoroda-kak-zony-ekonomicheskogo-razvitiya-tsifrovoy-ekonomiki. Accessed 27 Apr 2021
4. Belyaeva, N.B., Mingaleeva, E.D.: Smart city concept and its implementation in Northern Europe and Russia [Kontseptsiya umnogo goroda i eyo realizatsiya v Severnoy Evrope I Rossii]. UNECON News **5–1**(119), 95–98 (2019)

5. Tsvetkova, N.N.: Regional integration projects and new technology: the digital Silk Road [Proekty regional'noy integratsii i novye tekhnologii: tsifrovoy Shelkovyy put']. Eastern Anal. **1** (2019). https://cyberleninka.ru/article/n/proekty-regionalnoy-integratsii-i-novye-teh nologii-tsifrovoy-shelkovyy-put. Accessed 27 Apr 2021

6. Beijing's Silk Road Goes Digital [Electronic resource]. https://www.cfr.org/blog/beijings-silk-road-goes-digital. Accessed 27 Apr 04 2021

7. Analytical overview InfraOne Research "Infrastructure of Russia: development index of 2020". https://infraone.ru/sites/default/files/analitika/2020/index_razvitiia_infrastruktury_rossii_2020_infraone_research.pdf. Accessed 09 Mar 2021

8. Sharif'yanov, T.F.: Smart cities: a new turn in the digital inequality of territories [Smart-siti - novyy vitok territorial'nogo tsifrovogo neravenstva]. Reg. Econ. Theory Pract. **2**(449) (2018). https://cyberleninka.ru/article/n/smart-siti-novyy-vitok-territorialnogo-tsifro vogo-neravenstva. Accessed 27 Apr 2021

9. Published document of the national program "Digital Economy of the Russian Federation". http://government.ru/info/35568/. Accessed 02 Mar 2021

10. Russian regions. Socio-economic indicators. 2020: Statistical bulletin/Federal State Statistics Service. M. 1242, pp. 1006–1007 (2020)

11. Veselova, A.O., Khatskelevich, A.N., Ezhova, L.S.: Possibilities for creating smart cities in Russia: systemizing problems and directions for their solution [Perspektivy sozdaniya "um-nykh gorodov" v Rossii: sistematizatiya problem I napravleniy ikh resheniya. Perm University Herald. Economy **13**(1), 75–89 (2018)

12. Florida, R.: The Rise of the Creative Class: and How It's Transforming Work, Leisure, Community and Everyday Life, p. 432. Basic Books, New York (2007)

13. Bakici, T., Almirall, E., Wareham, J.: A smart city initiative: the case of Barcelona. J. Knowl. Econ. **4**(2), 135–148 (2013)

14. Inyutsyn, A.Y.: Smart technology is becoming more accessible to cities [Umnye tekhnologii stanovyatsya dostupnee dlya gorodov]. Municipal Gov. Pract. **2**, 46–55 (2017)

15. Pierce, P., Andersson, B.: Challenges with smart cities initiatives – a municipal decision makers' perspective. In: Proceedings of the 50th Hawaii International Conference on System Sciences, pp. 2804–2813 (2017). http://aisel.aisnet.org/hicss-50/eg/smart_cities_smart_gov ernment/3/. Accessed 25 Apr 2021

16. Arkin, P., Abushova, E., Bondarenko, V., Przdetskaya, N.: The concept of "smart cities": prospects for the telecommunications business and the current trend in the development of modern society. In: Galinina, O., Andreev, S., Balandin, S., Koucheryavy, Y. (eds.) Internet of Things, Smart Spaces, and Next Generation Networks and Systems, pp. 308–317. Springer, Cham (2020). https://doi.org/10.1007/978-3-030-65729-1_26

17. Vidyasova, L.A., Tensina, Y.D., Vidyasov, E.Y.: Perception of the smart city concept by active citizens in St. Petersburg [Vospriyatie kontseptsii "umnogo goroda" aktivnymy gorozhanami v Peterburge]. Vestnik of St. Petersburg University. Sociology **11**(4), 404–419 (2018)

18. Maksimov, S.N.: "Smart city": on the issue of the term and concept ["Umnyy gorod": k voprosu o ponyatii i kontseptsii]. Probl. Mod. Econ. **1**(61), 117–120 (2017)

19. Krasyuk, I., Medvedeva, Y.: Resource support in business analytics of innovative development of trade and technological systems. In: 2019 Proceedings of the 33rd International Business Information Management Association Conference, IBIMA 2019: Education Excellence and Innovation Management through Vision, pp. 8807–8817 (2020)

20. Krasyuk, I.A., Medvedeva, Y.Y.: Drivers and obstacles for the development of marketing in Russian retailing. In: 2019 Proceedings of the 33rd International Business Information Management Association Conference, IBIMA 2019: Education Excellence and Innovation Management through Vision 2020, pp. 4838–4844 (2020)

Next Generation Wired/Wireless Advanced Networks and Systems

Developing Smart Cities: The Risks of Using Information and Communications Technology

Viktoria Bondarenko[1], Tatiana Romanishina[1], Natalia Guzenko[1],
Natalya Mukhanova[2]([✉]), and Sergey Salkutsan[2]

[1] Rostov State University of Economics (RINH), Rostov-on-Don, Russia
[2] Peter the Great St. Petersburg Polytechnic University, Saint-Petersburg, Russia
{nmukhanova,salkutsan}@spbstu.ru

Abstract. This paper analyzes the role of the smart city concept, which has been positively proven in foreign practice and is actively being introduced in Russia, making it possible to form within its territories a concentrated area for investments, innovation and intellectual human resources, thereby establishing sustainable development on a digital platform of modern information and communications technology. It was determined that the regions generating positive transformations in Russia are those with a concentrated amount of megapolises that are the most active in attracting investments and intellectual resources and adequately equipped with an information and communications infrastructure. The conceptual model they introduce can and should be further scaled for other regions of the country. Likewise, this paper identifies the main risks of introducing this concept based on modern ICT and the possible ways to mitigate their impact. Research of the advantages of introducing the smart city concept, along with the possible difficulties of actively using information and communications technology, suggests the need to: 1) determine the positive results for strategically managing territories, as well as the positive effects for businesses and society; 2) evaluate, identify and characterize the risks and complications associated with using information and communications technology. Introducing the smart city concept based on the ubiquitous use of ICT leads to positive results for everyone involved in this process. The local community has an opportunity to quickly solve issues they are concerned with, while the government can synchronize existing requests, assess the needs of businesses and the population and integrate relevant management technology into a single system that is efficient and versatile. Meanwhile, businesses can operate in a comfortable urban environment favorable for business. It is advised to differentiate the risks and complications related to using information and communications technology into systemic ones, appearing everywhere and associated with the technical and cultural component and the safe use of ICT, and ones that are characteristic for the conditions in Russia, consisting of a difficulty in attracting financing and organizing processes and administrative barriers. These specific risks and difficulties can be controlled by the timely planning and synchronizing of organizational and management processes "on the ground", while systemic difficulties cannot be completely and totally eliminated. However, it is possible to localize them and take a timely accounting of them while mitigating their impact on how well a smart city system operates when there are initially

© Springer Nature Switzerland AG 2022
Y. Koucheryavy et al. (Eds.): NEW2AN 2021/ruSMART 2021, LNCS 13158, pp. 71–80, 2022.
https://doi.org/10.1007/978-3-030-97777-1_7

high demands for the safety and reliability of the information and communications infrastructure and for the training of workers, education and involvement of youth and development of ICT in all regions of the country.

Keywords: Information and communications technology · Information and communications infrastructure · Megapolises · Positive effects · Smart cities · Risks and difficulties

1 Introduction

In the current situation, the phenomenon of developing megapolises and attracting businesses, investments and creative individuals involved in improving the landscape of cities is a practically unavoidable scenario for territories that plan on being competitive and attractive for internal and external target audiences. In Russia, the scenario of improving the well-being of the population, the success of businesses and finding optimal options for management is also connected to megapolises that are developing their business activities in the way of "smart cities" [1].

Smart cities produce their own opportunities based on information and communications technology, acting as an infrastructural basis and connecting element of communication and exchange of necessary information between the interacting sides. Such intellectual education in a territory forms a point of attraction for work resources by creating promising job positions, forming ties between management and innovation-oriented businesses, as well as by organizing the necessary exchange of information between those interested and those involved in the process of developing the territory [2, 3].

In smart cities, information and communications technology is involved in building relationships with a territory's local communities. Such intellectual urban areas are focused on following valuable guidelines of the sustainable development concept, which take into account not only economical and environmental benchmarks but socials ones as well.

Smart cities based on digital solutions offer visible advantages for their residences, local businesses, as well as the management division with its ability to rely on modern tools of analyzing and developing strategies and tactics, including the use of artificial intelligence, to take practical steps towards improving the urban landscape and creating an urban environment that is comfortable for businesses and the population [4, 5].

A smart digital environment based on the ubiquitous introduction of information and communications technology is popular in Russian regions and has already been found in administrative work when planning a strategy for transforming a megapolis such as Moscow [6].

According to the distribution of this concept, its popularity in a number of other regions in Russia can also be judged by the media (Fig. 1).

The development of the smart city concept in Russia today uses the active involvement of such companies as Rostelecom, Rosatom, MegaFon and others. Based on the introduction of information and communications technology, electronic services are being developed, and AI technology is being used for housing construction, processing

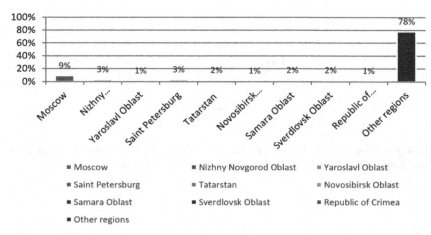

Fig. 1. Distinguishing mentions of the smart city concept in the media by Russian regions [7]

requests for traffic organization, lighting and camera systems and for managing housing and communal services as a whole [8–11].

Accordingly, given the key trends in the context of developing an information and communications infrastructure at a global and federal level, if there can be noted a focus on the information security of its smooth operation, the global nature of covering the fields of activity, and a need to train workers and attract investments in its development, then at a regional level, there can be seen a fostering of solutions carried out by practically implementing the smart city concept.

In the authors' opinion, the regions with the highest and prioritized chances for effectively introducing this concept are those with a concentration of megapolises that are the most active in attracting investments and intellectual workers and that are sufficiently equipped with an information and communications infrastructure.

Based on the calculations given, which reflect the positions of a number of regions, including cities with over a million people, the regions holding the top five leading places were determined. In the context of providing a telecommunications infrastructure, the leading regions for the indicator of number of devices with a mobile service subscription per 1,000 people are: Moscow, Saint Petersburg, Krasnodar Krai, Nizhny Novgorod Oblast and Novosibirsk Oblast (Fig. 2).

According to the indicator for the number of active mobile broadband internet subscribers per 100 people, the leading regions were Moscow, Saint Petersburg, Krasnodar Krai, Tatarstan and Nizhny Novgorod Oblast (Fig. 3).

Along with the Russian regions given above, leading in their information and communications infrastructure, other territories can also count on certain benefits from introducing the smart city concept into their management strategies and direct business practices.

However, any phenomenon demonstrating positive effects and new opportunities can, at the same time, produce previously hidden risks. This is true of the issues of digitally supporting an urban infrastructure and introducing the smart city concept based on

Fig. 2. Regions leading in the indicator for number of devices with a mobile service subscription per 1,000 people (calculated by the authors based on source data [12])

Fig. 3. Regions leading in the indicator for number of active mobile broadband internet subscribers per 100 people (calculated by the authors based on source data [12])

information and communications technology. For this reason, by recognizing that there is no alternative to the selected development path in the direction of smart cities, it can be considered relevant to clarify the advantages that this economic option gives to the territories where it is introduced and to identifying and characterizing the risks and difficulties associated with using information and communications technology.

2   Research Method

Along with the possible difficulties of actively using information and communications technology, researching the advantages of introducing the smart city concept suggests the need to:

- determine the positive results for the strategic management of territories as well as the positive effects for businesses and society.
- assess, identify and characterize the risks and difficulties associated with using information and communications technology.

2.1   Determining the Positive Results for the Strategic Management of Territories as well as the Positive Effects for Businesses and Society

Some of the visible, tangible effects capturing attention when designing smart cities is the comfort and human factors for the residents and businesses, as well as the promotion of efficient products aimed at local communities and engaged audiences. Certain advantages can be found, for example, among investors, who can assess potential complications and required resources using digital technology, including with the help of BIM technology when designing urban areas [5].

In the context of the strategic management of territories, it can be noted that the smart city concept makes it possible to carry out outlined plans and tactical solutions in initially designated and prioritized guidelines for the sustainable development of Russian regions.

Experts and practice show that the smart city concept in terms of realized effects relies on the 3Cs model, which includes the issues of gathering information resources, communications technology and analytical data processing [13].

In relation to the tasks of strategically managing cities, an important criterion is the possibility of eliminating the negative effects of extraordinary events with a fast reaction provided by focusing on the information and communications platform. A key priority for citizens is management's focus on following their request in terms of designing the urban landscape [14]. The smart city infrastructure (city, transport, society, engineering, innovation, information, etc.), operating on a single digital platform, simultaneously ensures the conservation and recycling of resources, as well as the quality of life and comfortable conditions for business operations [15].

Researchers also noted, for example, that the most tangible results for citizens of megapolises can be access to necessary data on a smart city basis and the involvement of local community representatives in creating client-oriented products and services [16].

In terms of the readiness of citizens in megapolises for using predominantly electronic services when contacting government representatives, for instance, research results demonstrating the population's preference when solving possible problems can be given [17]. Regarding citizens' preferred method of contacting government departments, the use of information and communications technology is clearly prevalent (Fig. 4).

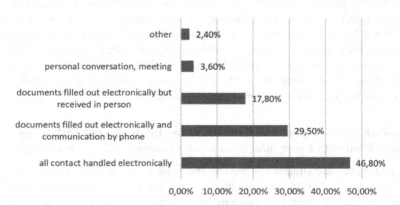

Fig. 4. Preferences of citizens when contacting government representatives, % [15]

According to the data give, around 48%* prefer a purely electronic form of communication and around another 47% expressed that a mixed format was acceptable for them at this stage.

Likewise, within the given research, the citizens rated how efficient it currently was to solve a number of tasks using electronic forms of communication. The maximum score was five. The scores of the local community representatives surveyed were modest, but the authors believe that this is related not to the quality of using information and communications technology but, overall, to their understanding of the quality of the problems being solved (Fig. 5).

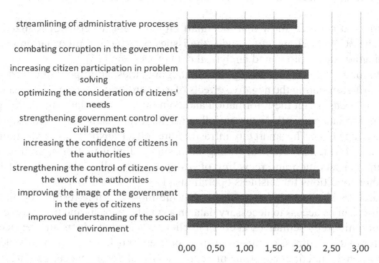

Fig. 5. Assessment from citizens about the efficiency of using electronic forms of communication in solving a number of tasks, score [15]

Despite the modest scores given, the involvement of the local community in the smart city project and the growing amount of people preferring electronic interaction is clearly broad. Likewise, government-solved issues related to construction, development of territories, improvement of services, and business, which are carried out in the context of the smart city concept, have visible advantages for the management system itself, through efficiency and versatility, and for the society, including the business spheres, which makes this a desirable vector of development.

2.2 Assessing, Identifying and Characterizing the Risks and Difficulties Associated with Using Information and Communications Technology

By characterizing the situation related to the appearance of risks accompanying the operation of smart cities, it can be highlighted that a number of these risks are systemic in nature, existing in virtually all megapolises, forming a concept of management and efficient transformations based on information and communications technology.

Most of these types of problems identified can be defined in the following way: risks of losing control over information/data leaks (appearing in the form of cyber espionage, identity and financial theft using electronic communication); risks of technical malfunctions (failures in software and communication channels leading to the distortion and/or misrepresentation of information); risks of catastrophic incidents (when cyberattacks create digital chaos, which impacts the accepted world order, causing concern among the citizens, mass panic, overload of requests though ICT, and eliminating the possibility of digital services working).

It is noted that similar failures, in particular, those associated with the risk of losing personal data and technical malfunctions, raise concerns both for those in charge and for citizens, who understand that a divide between their "digital identity" and their real one can occur in this case, and it would be difficult for them to prove their right to anything or to restore access, return their valuable assets or even get the necessary help in a timely fashion [18]. These risks highlight the need for the initial development of ways to keep the information and communications infrastructure used safe and secure.

Furthermore, risks appearing in modern society, the catalysts for which include smart cities, are ones such as: risks of cultural development (displacement of the usual cultural format by digital alternatives and a general reduction in the cultural level among the younger generations, who prefer to spend their free time on gadgets, used on the time killer principle); the risk of complete technology dependence (appearing in isolation from nature and real living environment, a "dying" of abilities and skills, since all necessary everyday life operations are handled by specialized gadgets controlled by artificial intelligence); the risk of a lower level of education (a phenomenon noted by psychologists and doctors, which is related to the formation of "clip mentality" among both children and teenagers, who are unable to concentrate for long periods of time and are prone to depression and general despondency) [19]. The difficulties mentioned suggest a need to introduce an adapted education system, instilling the required universal skills for individuals and the desire to expand one's own world view, possibly in a gamification format.

Other researchers rightfully determine risks associated with the possibilities of territorial development, particularly, in terms of Russian regions [20]. In this context, it is advised to note that it is necessary to increase the information and communications infrastructure provided in different regions of the country to ensure for their residents equal access to smart city technology, including in remote territories. Besides the active introduction of an information and communications infrastructure in various regions of the country, it is also necessary to develop a system of motivating the involvement of businesses, the population and management in the use of digital technology, as well as to instill media culture and media literacy in the population as a whole.

Along with the risks characterized above, associated with creating smart cities, it is also possible to identify those that currently create specific difficulties for the full implementation of this concept in Russia. Based on the results of empirical research, specialists include among them difficulties with attracting investments in new business models, existing administrative barriers, when, despite the digital platform, decisions are made over several months, communication difficulties between all members of an interaction within a smart city project, problems integrating this concept into current development plans for a territory, urbanization plans, insufficient number of trained workers that can develop ICT projects, difficulties forming a system of planning and reporting indicators, as well as insufficient popularization of this project among target audiences and the whole local community in a region [21].

The noted difficulties appearing within the formation of smart cities in Russia can be conditionally divided into a number of areas (Fig. 6).

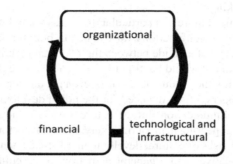

Fig. 6. Distinction of problems of a smart city characteristic for Russian conditions based on conditional groups [19]

It is believed that these difficulties, characteristic for the national circumstances, can be resolved when planning and formulating the smart city concept, introducing technology solutions in parallel to the launch of the concept, as well as when preparing appropriate human resources and synchronizing plans for the strategic development of a territory and "smart" solutions initially embedded in this format, understanding the pursued goals in the development of a territory, which based on the interests of the people and businesses (internal and external investors) [20, 21]. Realizing these goals will make it possible to integrate in a planned and congruent manner the smart city concept into the management paradigm of positively transforming the regions of Russia.

3   Conclusion

1. The smart city concept has been positively proven in foreign practice, is actively being introduced in Russia and makes it possible to create a concentrated area in territories for investments, innovation, intellectual human resources, establishing sustainable development on a digital platform of modern ICT.
2. In Russia, the regions generating positive transformations are those with a concentrated amount of megapolises that are the most active in attracting investments and intellectual resources and adequately equipped with an information and communications infrastructure. The conceptual model they introduce can and should further be scaled for other regions of the country.
3. Introducing the smart city concept based on the ubiquitous use of information and communications technology leads to positive results for everyone involved in this process. Citizens have an opportunity to quickly solve issues they are concerned with, while the government can synchronize existing requests, assess the needs of businesses and the population and integrate relevant management technology into a single system that is efficient and versatile. Meanwhile, businesses can operate in a comfortable urban environment favorable for business.

4. Since any positive phenomenon has negative effects as well, it was necessary to clarify the list of risks and difficulties associated with using information and communications technology, which, in the authors' opinion, is worth distinguishing into systemic ones, appearing everywhere and associated with the technical and cultural component and the safe use of ICT, and ones that are characteristic for conditions in Russia, consisting of a difficulty in attracting financing and organizing processes and administrative barriers.

5. It appears that these specific risks and difficulties can be controlled by the timely planning and synchronizing of organizational and management processes "on the ground", while systemic difficulties cannot be completely and totally eliminated. However, it is possible to localize them and take a timely accounting of them while mitigating their impact on the quality of a smart city system's operation when there are initially high demands for the safety and reliability of the information and communications infrastructure and for the training of workers, the education and involvement of youth and the development of ICT in all regions of the country.

References

1. Arkin, P., Abushova, E., Bondarenko, V., Przdetskaya, N.: The concept of "smart cities." In: Prospects for the Telecommunications Business and the Current Trend in the Development of Modern Society. LNCS, pp. 308–317. Springer, Cham (2020). https://doi.org/10.1007/978-3-030-65729-1_26

2. Florida, R.: The Rise of the Creative Class: And How it's Transforming Work, Leisure, Community and Everyday Life, 432 p. Basic Books, New York (2007)

3. Bakici, T., Almirall, E., Wareham, J.: A smart city initiative: the case of Barcelona. J. Knowl. Econ. 4(2), 135–148 (2013)

4. Veselova, A.O., Khatskelevich, A.N., Yezhova, L.S.: Future of creating smart cities in Russia: systemizing problems and directions for their solution [Perpesktivy sozdaniya "umnykh gorodov" v Rossii: systematizatsiya problem i napravleniy ikh resheniya]. Perm University Herald. Economy. 13(1), 75–89 (2018). Belyaeva, N.B., Mingaleeva, E.D.: Concept of a smart city and its realization in Northern Europe and Russia [Kontseptsiya umnogo goroda i eyo realizatsiya v Severnoy Evrope i Rossii]. UNECON News. 5–1(119), 95–98 (2019)

5. Gavrikova, K.V., Grigor'eva, M.S.: Integrating the smart city concept into the Russian system of strategically managing an urban area [Integratsiya kontseptsiya "umnogo goroda" v rossiyskuyu sistemu strategicheskogo upravleniya gorodskim prostranstvom]. Soc. Polit. Econ. Law №. 5 (2018). https://cyberleninka.ru/article/n/integratsiya-kontseptsii-umnogo-goroda-v-rossiyskuyu-sistemu-strategicheskogo-upravleniya-gorodskim-prostranstvom. Accessed 27 Apr 2021

6. Kupriyanovsky, V.P., et al.: Smart monotowns as zones for the economic development of a digital economy [Umnye monogoroda kak zony ekonomicheskogo ravitiya tsifrovoy ekonomiki]. Int. J. Open Inf. Technol. №. 1 (2018). https://cyberleninka.ru/article/n/umnye-monogoroda-kak-zony-ekonomicheskogo-razvitiya-tsifrovoy-ekonomiki Accessed 27 Apr 2021. Information Center of the Moscow Government [Electronic Resource]. https://icmos.ru/news/58083-sobyaninporuchil-razrabotat-programmu-umnyy-gorod/. Accessed 16 Apr 2020

7. Inyutsyn, A.Y.: Smart technology is becoming more accessible to cities [Umnye tekhnologii stanovyatsya dostupnee dlya gorodov]. Municip. Govern. Pract. 2, 46–55 (2017)

8. Russian Regions. Socio-economic indicators. In: 2020: Statistical Bulletin/Federal State Statistics Service. M., vol. 1242, pp. 1006–1007 (2020)
9. Smart Cities Readiness Guide. The planning manual for building tomorrow's cities today. In: Smart Cities Council (2015). readinessguide.smartcitiescouncil.com/. Accessed 04 July 2017
10. Nekrasova, T., Leventsov, V., Gluhov, V.: Development of infocommunications services in Russia. In: Galinina, O., Andreev, S., Balandin, S., Koucheryavy, Y. (eds.) NEW2AN/ruSMART -2019. LNCS, vol. 11660, pp. 505–514. Springer, Cham (2019). https://doi.org/10.1007/978-3-030-30859-9_43
11. Konnikov, E., Konnikova, O., Leventsov, V.: IT Services market as a driver for the development of the artificial intelligence market. IOP Conf. Ser. Mater. Sci. Eng. **497**(1), 012043 (2019). https://doi.org/10.1088/1757-899X/497/1/012043
12. Mamaeva, T.: Outrage against traffic in Moscow [Vozmuscheniye protiv dorozhnogo dvizheniya v Moskve] [Electronic Resource]. Ibid. http://strelka.com/ru/research/project/mos cow-traffic-outrage. Accessed 06 May 2021
13. Kurcheeva, G.I., Klochkov, G.A.: Developing a smart city process-based model [Rasrabotka protsessnoy modeli "Umnyy gorod"]. Eur. Sci. J. 5(42) (2017). https://cyberleninka.ru/art icle/n/razrabotka-protsessnoy-modeli-umnyy-gorod. Accessed 27 Apr 2021
14. Abella, A., Ortiz-de-Urbina-Criado, M., De-Pablos-Heredero, C.: A model for the analysis of data-driven innovation and value generation in smart cities' ecosystems. Cities **64**, 47–53 (2017)
15. Vidyasova, L.A., Tensina, Y.D., Vidyasov, E.Y.: Perception of the smart city concept by active citizens in St. Petersburg [Vospriyatie kontseptsii "umnogo goroda" aktivnymy gorozhanami v Peterburge]. Vestnik of St. Petersburg University. Sociology 11(4), 404–419 (2018)
16. Stefanova, N.A., Grankin, O.V.: Smart cities ["UMNYE" GORODA]. Curr. Iss. Mod. Econ. **3**, 94 (2017)
17. Stefanova, N.A., Khirsavova, Y.S.: Risks of smart cities [Riski "umnykh" gorodov]. Karelian Sci. J. **72**(23), 125–126 (2018)
18. Sharif'yanov, T.F.: Smart cities: a new turn in the digital inequality of territories [Smartsiti - novyy vitok territorial'nogo tsifrovogo neravenstva]. Region. Econ. Theory Pract. **2**(449) (2018). https://cyberleninka.ru/article/n/smart-siti-novyy-vitok-territorialnogo-tsifro vogo-neravenstva. Accessed 27 Apr 2021
19. Veselova, A.O., Khatskelevich, A.N., Yezhova, L.S.: Future of creating smart cities in Russia: systemizing problems and directions for their solution [Perpesktivy sozdaniya "umnykh gorodov" v Rossii: systematizatsiya problem i napravleniy ikh resheniya]. Perm University Herald. Economy. **13**(1), 75–89 (2018)
20. Krasyuk, I., Medvedeva, Y.: Resource support in business analytics of innovative development of trade and technological systems. In: Proceedings of the 33rd International Business Information Management Association Conference, IBIMA 2019: Education Excellence and Innovation Management through Vision 2020, pp. 8807–8817 (2019)
21. Krasyuk, I.A., Medvedeva, Y.Y.: Drives and obstacle for the development of marketing in Russian retailing. In: Proceedings of the 33rd International Business Information Management Association Conference, IBIMA 2019: Education Excellence and Innovation Management through Vision 2020, pp. 4838–4844 (2019)

Influence of Digital Technology and Telecommunications on the Customer-Oriented Development of Electronic Commerce

Olga Chkalova[1], Yury Trifonov[1], Pavel Shalabaev[1], Ekaterina Abushova[2], and Elena Kasianenko[2(✉)]

[1] Lobachevsky State University of Nizhny Novgorod, Nizhny Novgorod, Russian Federation
ochkalova@iee.unn.ru
[2] Peter the Great St. Petersburg Polytechnic University, Saint-Petersburg, Russia
{abushova_ee,kasyanenko_eo}@spbstu.ru

Abstract. It is shown that under conditions of a pandemic and telecommunications, one emerging global economic trend is the development of electronic commerce. The rapid growth of e-commerce intensifies the search for competitive strategies. It is established that a customer-oriented strategy is an effective development strategy. The factors forming use value in e-commerce are studied. Under e-commerce conditions, the customer-oriented approach is focused on creating use value and is connected with consumer behavior. It is shown that consumer actions in e-commerce conditions are becoming more and more irrational.

The goal of this paper is to identify the patterns in consumer behavior changes in e-commerce by identifying factors that impact consumer behavior, expressed as the percentage of internet visitors wanting to sell/buy products and services based on the latest methods of data analysis.

The research methods include the use of content analysis of the current base of published studies for the studied subject and the newest analysis tools based on neural networks. For the analysis, the Deductor neural network was used along with a multilayer perceptron for the forecasting method. The modeling was carried out using two layers of neural networks with five neurons in the first layer and three neurons in the second. Data from surveys by region and consumer characteristics, conducted by the Federal State Statistical Service from 2013 to 2019, were processed. A data forecast of the percentage of internet visitors wanting to sell/buy products and services depending on the values of factors influencing value showed that the neural network was trained and chosen correctly.

The data obtained can be used in the activities of various organizations and businesses operating on the internet. This allows for an adjustment to be made to the forecast sales taking into account the peculiarities of consumer behavior and their value benchmarks.

Keywords: Electronic commerce · Internet of Things · Use value · Consumer behavior · Neural network

© Springer Nature Switzerland AG 2022
Y. Koucheryavy et al. (Eds.): NEW2AN 2021/ruSMART 2021, LNCS 13158, pp. 81–94, 2022.
https://doi.org/10.1007/978-3-030-97777-1_8

1   Introduction

A global trend in the development of retailers over the past years has been the shift in the vector of their development in the online space. From 2011 to 2019, online sales in Russia grew by almost seven times. These processes accelerated noticeably after the start of the pandemic. In 2020, e-commerce grew 78% in comparison to 2019. 883 million shipments were delivered in 2020, which is 35% more than in 2019. The main growth factor for e-commerce is currently the growth in the number of orders based on repeat and new purchases that overlap the growth by the average order total. The selection of e-commerce products is fairly broad, but the largest growth is observed in the FMCG category at 145%. The fastest growing internet platforms are: Ozon, AliExpress, Wildberries, Lamoda, Bonprix [1].

A similar situation with the growth of e-commerce is seen across the whole world. According to an estimate by Digital Commerce 360, sales volumes in the USA reached $861.12 B in 2020, which is 44.0% more than in 2019. This is the highest annual growth of e-commerce in the USA and is three times higher than the 2019 growth relative to 2018, which came to 15.1%.

In conditions of global competition, e-business needs strategies that ensure a competitive position in the long run in order to grow. Assortment and pricing strategies are becoming no longer relevant, since products can easily be copied and reproduced by competitors. Under the new competition conditions, strategic success is based less on superior products and more on strategies focused on customer relations.

The term "relationship marketing" was introduced into scientific parlance in 1983 by the American scientist L.L. Berry and involves winning over customers and maintaining and strengthening relationships with them [2].

The theoretical basis of relationship marketing (client-oriented, customer-focused, customer-driven, customer centricity, customer–centric approach) in world science started developing in the mid-1950s and had grown significantly by the start of the 2000s [3–6].

In 1993, D. Peppers and M. Rogers (USA) proposed a system for managing customer relationships. Since that time, the customer-focused approach has come to be known by the abbreviation CRM (Customer Relationship Management) [7].

The uniqueness of the customer-oriented strategy was confirmed by scientific research. Professor at University of Michigan C. Fornell found a dependence between the growth of the customer satisfaction indicator (CSI) and the growth of a large company's capitalization: a 1% CSI growth leads to a 3% growth in a company's capitalization; the average cumulative effect of profitability growth (11.5% in five years) starts at 1% of the annual CSI growth) [8].

Nowadays, the topic of the customer-oriented approach is at the center of attention of researchers worldwide. Current studies are devoted to the customer centricity of personnel [9–11], the development of customer-oriented business processes [12], carrying out customer-oriented suggestions based on the order information model [13], and the effectiveness of customer-oriented strategies [14, 15].

The need to rethink approaches to developing e-commerce based on a customer-oriented strategy forms the basis for this research. Customer-oriented development of e-commerce involves studying and creating value for consumers. The modern concept of value comes from the position about what advantages and benefits consumers get. Thus, according to data from the Forrester Research, almost 70% of internet users appreciate that e-commerce helps save time; 63% find that the balance of supply and demand is better online, and 60% value the integrated electronic products offered [16]. Other researchers emphasize the comfort, freedom and convenience of making purchases over the internet, the familiar environment when shopping, for example, at home, the lack of physical lines at the store and other factors given in Fig. 1 [17].

Fig. 1. Factors influencing the value of shopping in e-commerce [18]

Along with the factors mentioned above, which form the value proposition, there is the communications aspect, which takes on a new character and transforms into a completely new channel of interaction in e-commerce [19, 20]. Potential customers have the opportunity to select information that is provided by search engines by special inquiries and to read reviews from other customers on websites of retailers or on third-party forums, not controlled by the sellers/manufacturers. Initial interest in a product can often occur as a result of seeing a message on a social network. Thus, in the digital environment, customers can follow a fundamentally new decision making path. Nowadays, consumers that actively use online services can conveniently learn about the consumer features of products from other customers instead of learning about highly technical features. To this end, internet users exchange information in online communities and come together to shop. In the presented research, it is pointed out that reviews are used when deciding to make a purchase in 9 out of 10 online orders: customers read reviews, look at photos and videos and ask questions to other customers. In 2 out of 10 online orders, reviews play no crucial role [21] (Fig. 2).

The biggest number of respondents (31.5%) noted that they preferred to shop online, since they read product reviews before buying. Slightly less than 30% of respondents compared similar products and their prices in different stores.

What shoppers did before buying

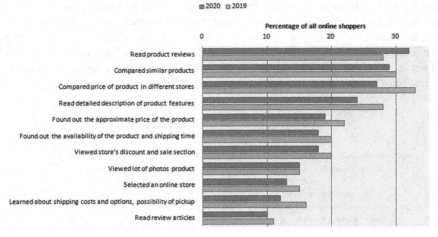

Fig. 2. Reasons affecting purchases in the electronic environment [22]

In scientific literature, a great number of other effects are described, which transform consumer behavior in the electronic environment: reactions to a purchase, forming an impression after purchasing [23–26].

E-commerce consumers traditionally try to be more rational, getting access to a large amount of information online and studying the experience of other consumers. However, as a number of researchers point out, consumer behavior, specifically in e-commerce, is becoming more and more irrational [27]. This is in many ways explained by the specifics of the human mind, which is certainly a limited resource. Our minds cannot possibly capture all the information or alternatives, calculate all possible scenarios, constantly take into account all already known facts when making decision and so on. The capability of the human mind to determine tasks and solve difficult problems is incomparable at the level of problems whose solution is necessary for objective rational behavior overall. Human behavior is only rational in terms of the potential desire to act rationally. In reality, people are only capable of this to a limited degree. From the perspective of the traditional economic theory, it is not possible to obtain and analyze all the information about the whole market before making a decision [28, 29]. In a digital economy, it is not information that is lacking but instead time, trust and attention.

In literature, a number of different effects are described, which illustrate the irrationality of consumer behavior. An important aspect causing irrational behavior among digital consumers is their completely different perception of electronic money, which is spent much more easily and significantly faster than in traditional commerce. The real value of electronic money is not felt, and it can be parted with easily without the consumer experiencing feelings of guilt over the money spent. Evidence for this is seen in the data of public monitoring of delivery service quality conducted by Roskachestvo and NAFI (Table 1).

Table 1. Question: "In your estimation, did you spend on average more, less or the same amount of money on groceries during self-isolation when you ordered online?", % of those who order home delivery of groceries online.

Respondent answers	% of those who order home delivery of groceries online
Spent more on groceries	46
Spent the same	35
Spent less on groceries	15
Not sure	3

According to experts, sales online will continue to grow. In order to manage sales more effectively, it is necessary to know from a marketing standpoint how consumer behavior is related to value and influences sales.

From the traditional point of view, the buying process is influenced by the two-factor demand model, in which price and volume are the main factors. However, research shows that this model cannot be used to describe or predict consumer behavior in the electronic environment due to the effects of the irrationality of consumer behavior [30]. Under these conditions, fundamentally different research methods are needed, which allow for working with large data sets [31, 32]. Literature analysis shows this technology to be neural networks and artificial intelligence. This technology is already being used to determine optimal markets and model the correlation between product quality and customer loyalty [33–37].

Neural network technology is also starting to be used in e-commerce, for example, for customer segmentation [33].

The goal of this research is to predict consumer behavior in the electronic environment to create use value based on the concept of relationship marketing.

2 Research Method

Within this research, a neural network was used when predicting consumer behavior.

Research objectives:

To predict the indicator for the percentage of the population that uses the internet for specific goals (finding information to make decisions about purchases, downloading files, etc.) by relying on factors related to describing consumer characteristics and to the peculiarities of their behavior and the use value created.

The object for analysis is the reason for which a consumer turns to the internet. The analysis result (output parameter) is the predicted indicator of the percentage of people that use the internet to achieve a set goal.

The following factors, which influence this indicator, were determined:

- Current portion of population using the internet for a specific purpose;
- Average consumer income;
- Device used to access the internet;

- Share of urban and rural population in the population structure in Russia;
- Portion of consumers with different educational backgrounds in the population structure;
- Portion of men and women in the population structure.

It is assumed that based on this data, the neural network will predict the portion of the population that uses the internet for a specific purpose, adjusting this indicator with consideration of the input factors. The neural network software tool Deductor is used for analysis. The method of prediction is the multilayer perceptron.

The Deductor software is designed for visually planning the logic of decision making. All actions are configured using only four masters: import, export, processing and visualization. It allows the analyst to automate routine operations for data processing, to concentrate on intellectual work and formalize the rules of decision making.

The principle for how the software works is presented in Fig. 3.

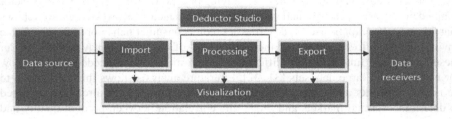

Fig. 3. Logic of how software works

Combining all of the mechanisms described above provides a fundamentally new quality of analysis: quick processing and adaptation of solutions, integration into the existing infrastructure, evolutionary development from simple reporting to deeper analytics.

To cluster the structure of the population that uses the internet. Unlike the general classification where the number of object groups is fixed and predetermined by a set of ideals, here, neither the groups nor their quantity are determined in advance and are formed in the process of the system's operation based on a certain measure of proximity of the objects. The input parameters in this case are:

- share of men and women.
- income of population.
- urbanization factor.
- purposes of internet visitors.

It is planned to study the neural network and determine the structure of the goals of a specific type of consumer for the future period using the forecast feature. Furthermore, it is possible to identify a consumer based on the parameters by using the neural network to determine which group they belong to.

3 Results

Questions about researching consumer behavior based on the collected statistics on various indicators are examined.

A neural network is used to describe consumer behavior. To do this, the software Deductor is used. The input and output data is presented in Table 2.

Table 2. Description of input and output data for the neural network

Factor	Description
X	Goal code
X1	Portion of population using the internet for a specific purpose, period N-1
X2	Portion of population using the internet for a specific purpose, period N-2
X3	Portion of population using the internet for a specific purpose, men, period N
X4	Portion of population using the internet for a specific purpose, woman, period N
X5	Portion of population using the internet for a specific purpose, city, period N
X6	Portion of population using the internet for a specific purpose, rural area, period N
X7	Nominal average wage of workers for a full range of organizations for the Russian economy as a whole, period N, thous. rubles
Y	Portion of population using the internet for a specific purpose, period N

The system of goals that internet visitors wish to achieve are presented in Table 3.

Table 3. Description of formulating goals for visiting the internet

Goal code	Goal formulation
1	Activity in social networks
2	Phone calls or videos calls via the internet (using Skype, for example)
3	Communicating using instant messaging systems (chats, ICQ, QIP and others)
4	Searching for information about products and services
5	Financial transactions
6	Downloading films, images, music; watching videos; listening to music or the radio
7	Sending or receiving emails
8	Obtaining knowledge and references on any topic using Wikipedia, online encyclopedias, etc.
9	Searching for information related to health or services in the healthcare field

(continued)

Table 3. (*continued*)

Goal code	Goal formulation
10	Uploading personal files (books/articles/journals, photos, music, videos, programs, etc.) onto websites, social networks, cloud storage for public access
11	Selling/buying products and services (including using auction websites)
12	Playing video and computer games/games for mobile phone or for download
13	Reading and downloading online newspapers, magazines or e-books
14	Searching for information about cultural heritage sites and cultural events; taking virtual tours of museums, galleries, etc.
15	Searching for information about education, courses, training and so on
16	Searching for jobs
17	Downloading software (other than computer games)
18	Participating in online voting or consultations about social and political issues
19	Distance learning
20	Posting opinions about social and political issues through websites or participation in forums
21	Participating in professional websites (for example, LinkedIn, Xing, E-xecutive.ru and so on)

The neural network makes it possible to:

- predict the portion of the population that uses the internet for a specific purpose, taking into account consumer characteristics.
- present the characteristics of consumers that use the internet for their own needs.
- highlight the peculiarities of consumer behavior when making purchases.
- form the elements of use value within the concept of the customer-oriented approach.

For this research, data from annual surveys conducted by the Federal State Statistics Service by region and consumer characteristics were used. The main data for constructing the neural network is presented in Table 4 (a fragment of it is presented).

Table 4. Initial data for training the neural network

X	X1	X2	X3	X4	X5	X6	X7	Y
1	77.8	78.1	74.2	79	77.3	74.6	47419.83	76.7
1	78.1	76	75.3	80.1	78	77.3	43431.31	77.8
1	76	74.6	74.9	81	77.9	78.6	39147.75	78.1

(*continued*)

Table 4. (*continued*)

X	X1	X2	X3	X4	X5	X6	X7	Y
2	52.6	48.8	70.7	71.3	73.3	63	47419.83	71
2	48.8	43.6	51.8	53.3	54.7	45.3	43431.31	52.6
2	43.6	41.3	48.4	49.1	50.9	41.3	39147.75	48.8
3	20.6	20.3	60.2	60.1	62.6	51.5	47419.83	60.1
3	20.3	14.6	21	20.3	22.7	13.4	43431.31	20.6
3	14.6	12.6	21.1	19.5	21.9	14.3	39147.75	20.3
4	54.1	51.7	52.6	59.9	60.2	43.7	47419.83	56.5
4	51.7	43.8	49.9	57.9	57.2	43.5	43431.31	54.1
4	43.8	39.6	46.7	56.2	55.2	38.9	39147.75	51.7
5	39	30.9	49.6	53.4	54.9	40.4	47419.83	51.6
5	30.9	22.5	36.8	41.1	42.6	26.6	43431.31	39
5	22.5	16.9	28.9	32.7	33.5	21.5	39147.75	30.9
6	49.2	53.3	53.8	42.1	49.3	41.5	47419.83	47.6
6	53.3	51.4	55.2	43.9	51.5	41.4	43431.31	49.2
6	51.4	49.6	59.9	47.4	55.2	46.2	39147.75	53.3

Two layers were used during the training of the neural network. There were five neurons in the first layer and three neurons in the second.

Working with Deductor resulted in a scatter plot. This is presented in Fig. 4.

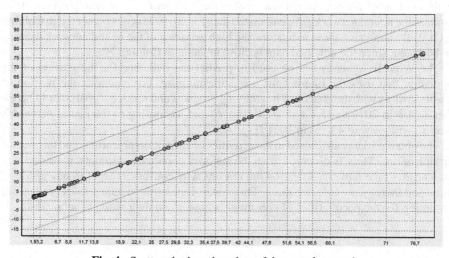

Fig. 4. Scatter plot based on data of the neural network.

It shows that the neural network built a quality model with data closest to the input values.

As a result, the program gives the following predicted indicators. Figure 5 reflects part of the output data obtained.

X	X1	X2	X3	X4	X5	X6	X7	Y	Y_OUT	Y_ERR
1	77,8	78,1	74,2	79	77,3	74,6	47419,83333	76,7	76,8024881724794	1,80899578712028E-6
1	78,1	76	75,3	80,1	78	77,3	43431,30505	77,8	77,388375456713	2,91804900483256E-5
1	76	74,6	74,9	81	77,9	78,6	39147,74931	78,1	77,4775109341666	6,67349765229894E-5
2	52,6	48,8	70,7	71,3	73,3	63	47419,83333	71	70,9909176330318	1,42065344248528E-8
2	48,8	43,6	51,8	53,3	54,7	45,3	43431,30505	52,6	52,6278467935309	1,33548940478925E-7
2	43,6	41,3	48,4	49,1	50,9	41,3	39147,74931	48,8	48,7518832537508	3,98733349454593E-7
3	20,6	20,3	60,2	60,1	62,6	51,5	47419,83333	60,1	60,110344040443	1,84276721513956E-8
3	20,3	14,6	21	20,3	22,7	13,4	43431,30505	20,6	20,5628957955973	2,3723041458164E-7
3	14,6	12,6	21,1	19,5	21,9	14,3	39147,74931	20,3	20,0780754137877	8,48205130260763E-6
4	54,1	51,7	52,6	59,9	60,2	43,7	47419,83333	56,5	56,5598705338439	6,173284874651E-7
4	51,7	43,8	49,9	57,3	57,2	43,5	43431,30505	54,1	54,0816614344797	5,79189633135673E-8
4	43,8	39,6	46,7	56,2	55,2	38,9	39147,74931	51,7	51,7306913105327	1,62226173388887E-7
5	39	30,9	49,6	53,4	54,9	40,4	47419,83333	51,6	51,556883117084	3,20173047924981E-7
5	30,9	22,5	36,8	41,1	42,6	26,6	43431,30505	39	39,0360309407025	2,23584276751966E-7
5	22,5	16,9	28,9	32,7	33,5	21,5	39147,74931	30,9	30,946152024261	3,6683567614408E-7
6	49,2	53,3	53,8	42,1	49,3	41,5	47419,83333	47,6	47,6003978104398	2,72547629867906E-11
6	53,3	51,4	55,2	43,9	51,5	41,4	43431,30505	49,2	49,0935923457199	1,95000531985233E-6
6	51,4	49,6	59,9	47,4	55,2	46,2	39147,74931	53,3	53,2836990375375	4,57632176004794E-8
7	42	44,1	41,2	44,8	48	26,2	47419,83333	43,1	43,0559225502687	3,34597718191035E-7
7	44,1	41,6	40,2	43,7	46,6	26,1	43431,30505	42	41,9921105171754	1,07198109752115E-8
7	41,6	41,7	42,9	45,2	47,9	30,2	39147,74931	44,1	44,0969418554407	1,6106681796933E-9
8	39,7	44,6	36,5	41,4	42,5	27,3	47419,83333	39,1	39,0961933797506	2,49556659898822E-9
8	44,6	40,6	37,2	42	43,5	26,5	43431,30505	39,7	39,7291341876238	1,461826676064E-7
8	40,6	36,9	42,5	46,6	47,9	32,7	39147,74931	44,6	44,5784342099975	8,00978393701566E-8
9	35,5	33,9	24,8	48,8	40,3	27,9	47419,83333	37,5	37,3901751395262	2,07726248408325E-6
9	33,9	27,2	23	46,7	37,9	27,2	43431,30505	35,5	35,5204809333444	7,2241964208132E-8
9	27,2	23,6	20,6	45,7	36,1	25,9	39147,74931	33,9	33,8943728183282	5,45345746581731E-9

Fig. 5. Predicted indicators obtained using the work of the trained neural network

Results of neural network. The figure shows Column Y, which shows the value for the portion of the population that visited the internet for a specific purpose. After learning, the neural network gave calculated data for 2019, which is presented in Column Y_OUT. By analyzing these indicators, the high accuracy of the neural network training can be noted, since the obtained data is close in value to Column Y.

The What-If Analysis can be used to predict the indicator for the portion of the population that uses the internet for a specific purpose. For example, the portion of website visitors with the goal of selling/buying products and services (goal code 11) grew from 33.4% in 2019 to 35.7% in 2020 (Fig. 6) and, according to the neural network's forecast, will grow to 43.1% in 2021 (Fig. 7).

The obtained data can be used in the activities of various organizations and businesses working online. Thus, in order to attract the majority of online consumers, it is necessary that websites take into consideration the reasons why consumers want to buy products online and thereby provide use value. This makes it possible to adjust sales predictions accounting for the peculiarities of consumer behavior and their value benchmarks.

Field	Value
⊟ Input	
12 X	11
9.0 X1	33,4
9.0 X2	27,5
9.0 X3	31,18
9.0 X4	36,1
9.0 X5	37,12
9.0 X6	24,8
9.0 X7	51016
⊟ Output	
9.0 Y	35,6812820738874

Fig. 6. Adjusted portion of consumers for 2020

Field	Value
⊟ Input	
12 X	11
9.0 X1	35,7
9.0 X2	33,4
9.0 X3	35,56
9.0 X4	37,4
9.0 X5	39,45
9.0 X6	28,4
9.0 X7	53027
⊟ Output	
9.0 Y	43,0979158557104

Fig. 7. Predicted portion of consumers for 2021 with the goal of selling/buying products and services

4   Conclusions

Consumer behavior in conditions of growing economic digitalization is undergoing significant changes, while the presence of initial preconditions for the growth of its rationality in terms of information supply is canceled by cognitive and time limitations. When researching consumer behavior in conditions of a rapidly changing decision-making environment, an important role is played by modern methods, particularly neural networks, which allow for the use of diverse data sets in studies and for constructing a forecast of the changes in the studied variables based on its training.

At the same time, an important aspect for consumers when making decisions and when following the customer-oriented approach is the growth of use value generated in the process of e-commerce. The conducted research shows that under current conditions, the e-commerce turnover is growing significantly, which makes it possible to provide consumers with a high use value in terms of making a more reasonable choice, saving time, etc.

The analysis method used in the research, which is based on neural networks using the Deductor software, allowed the neural network to be trained to predict the indicator for the portion of the population that uses the internet for a specific purpose. At the same time, the growth of the latter indicates the growth of value propositions in e-commerce and its generation of use value.

During the research, the authors chose the following factors/input parameters for training the neural network: portion of the population that uses the internet for a specific purpose, period N-1; portion of the population that uses the internet for a specific purpose, period N-2; portion of the population that uses the internet for a specific purpose, men, period N; portion of the population that uses the internet for a specific purpose, women, period N; portion of the population that uses the internet for a specific purpose, city, period N; portion of the population that uses the internet for a specific purpose, rural area, period N; nominal average wage of workers for a full range of organizations for the Russian economy as a whole, period N, thous. rubles. The output parameter of the model in the research was the portion of the population that uses the internet for a specific purpose, period N. In order to train the neural network, the authors used microdata from population surveys about the issues of using information technology conducted by the Federal State Statistics Service since 2013. The use of the Deductor software and the data set allowed for the successful training of the neural network to predict the output indicator.

These methods can be developed by broadening the range of input parameters, which include, for example, quality data from surveys of the population about the factors of forming use value and consumer satisfaction. Specialized surveys and information from social networks can serve as the information sources for the factors. Furthermore, an important aspect influencing the value is the level of the transaction costs of exchange, which include the costs of the opportunistic behavior of the subjects, which, as studies show, can also grow during the digitalization process due to the uneven distribution of information (information asymmetry) between the different sides.

References

1. E-Commerce in Russia 2020. Research by Data Insight (2020). https://datainsight.ru/sites/default/files/DI_eCommerce2020.pdf. Accessed 19 Apr 2021
2. Berry, L.L.: Relationship marketing. In: Leonard, L., Berry, G., Shostack, L., Upah, G.D. (eds.) Emerging Perspectives on Service Marketing, pp. 25–48. American Marketing Association, Chicago (1983). https://doi.org/10.1300/J366v01n01_05
3. Coltman, T., Devinney, T.M., Midgley, D.F.: Customer relationship management and firm performance. J. Inf. Technol. **26**(3), 205–219 (2010). https://doi.org/10.1057/jit.2010.39
4. Fader, P.: Customer Centricity: Focus on the Right Customers for Strategic Advantage (Wharton Executive Essentials), p. 128. Wharton Digital Press (2012)

5. Gebauer, H., Kowalkovski, C.: Customer-focused and service focused orientation in organizational structures. J. Bus. Indust. Market. **27**(7), 527–537 (2012). https://doi.org/10.1108/08858621211257293

6. Rebyazina, V.A., Smirnova, M.M.: Klientoorientirovannost' rossijskikh kompanij: rezul'taty ehmpiricheskogo issledovaniya. In: XIV Mezhdunarodnaya nauchnaya konferentsiya po problemam razvitiya ekonomiki i obshhestva. M.: NIU VSHE, pp. 265–270 (2013)

7. Peppers, D., Rogers, M.: Managing Customer Relationships: A Strategic Framework. Wiley, New York (2004)

8. Fornell, C., Rust, R., Dekimpe, M.: The effect of customer satisfaction on consumer spending growth. J. Mark. Res. **47**(1), 28–35 (2010). https://doi.org/10.1509/jmkr.47.1.28

9. Hughes, D.E., Richards, K.A., Calantone, R., Baldus, B., Spreng, R.A.: Driving in-role and extra-role brand performance among retail frontline salespeople: antecedents and the moderating role of customer orientation. J. Retail. **95**(2), 130–143 (2019). https://doi.org/10.1016/j.jretai.2019.03.003

10. Yanga, S.-Y., Tsai, K.-H.: Lifting the veil on the link between absorptive capacity and innovation: the roles of cross-functional integration and customer orientation. Indust. Market. Manag. **82**, 117–130 (2019)

11. Liu, Y., Chen, D.Q., Gao, W.: How does customer orientation (in) congruence affect B2B electronic commerce platform firms' performance? Ind. Market. Manage. **87**, 18–30 (2020). https://doi.org/10.1016/j.indmarman.2020.02.027

12. Kreuzer, T., Röglinger, M., Rupprecht, L.: Customer-centric prioritization of process improvement projects. Dec. Supp. Syst. **133**, 113286 (2020). https://doi.org/10.1016/j.dss.2020.113286

13. Giannikas, V., McFarlane, D., Strachan, J.: Towards the deployment of customer orientation: a case study in third-party logistics. Comput. Ind. **104**, 75–87 (2019). https://doi.org/10.1016/j.compind.2018.10.005

14. Frambach, R.T., Fiss, P.C., Ingenbleek, P.T.: How important is customer orientation for firm performance? A fuzzy set analysis of orientations, strategies, and environments. J. Bus. Res. **69**, 1428–1436 (2016). https://doi.org/10.1016/j.jbusres.2015.10.120

15. Smirnova, M.M., Rebiazina, V.A., Fröséna, J.: Customer orientation as a multidimensional construct: evidence from the Russian markets. J. Bus. Res. **86**, 457–467 (2018). https://doi.org/10.1016/j.jbusres.2017.10.040

16. Jitender, M.: Forrester Research World Online Population Forecast. 2012 To 2017 (Global) (2015). http://www.forrester.com

17. Pankina, T.V., Nikishin, A.F., Boykova, A.V.: Attracting and retaining customers in e-commerce [Privlecheniye i uderzhaniye pokupateley v elektronnoy torgovle]. Russ. Entrepr. **3** (2018). https://doi.org/10.18334/rp.19.3.38826

18. Digital 2020. Research by "Yandex.Market" and GfK Rus. https://e-pepper.ru/news/bolee-poloviny-rossiyan-pokupayut-tovary-v-internete.html. Accessed 14 Apr 2021

19. Christodoulides, G., Michaelidou, N.: Shopping motives as antecedents of e-satisfaction and e-loyalty. J. Mark. Manage. **27**(1–2), 181–197 (2010). https://doi.org/10.1080/0267257X.2010.489815

20. Butkovskaya, T.V., Statkus, A.V.: Digital marketing: consumer behavior [Tsifrovoy marketing: povedeniye potrebiteley]. University Herald **5**, 5–11 (2019)

21. Reviews and Recommendations in E-Commerce. Research by AliExpress Russia and Data Insight. https://datainsight.ru/DI_AliExpress_GuidedBuying

22. Digital 2020. Research by We Are Social and Hootsuite. https://e-pepper.ru/news/bolee-poloviny-rossiyan-pokupayut-tovary-v-internete.html

23. Musatova, Z.B., Skorobogatykh, I.I., Avvakumova, I.V., Musatov, B.V.: Influence of information technology on the transformation of the consumer experience [Vliyaniye informatsionnykh tekhnologiy na transformatsiyu potrebitel'skogo opyta]. Plekhanov Russ. Univ. Econ. **3–4**, 55–59 (2018)

24. Deputatova, Y.Y., Uryaseva, T.I., Cheglov, V.P., Leonova, J.G., Baskakov, V.A.: Methodical approach to identifying buying motives within various sales channels based on behavioral segmentation. J. Adv. Res. Law Econ. **10**(2(40)), 515–527 (2019)

25. Chkalova, O., Bolshakova, I., Kopasovskaya, N., Mukhanova, N., Gluhov, V.: Transformation of online consumer behavior under the influence of the pandemic and the development of telecommunications. In: Galinina, O., Andreev, S., Balandin, S., Koucheryavy, Y. (eds) Internet of Things, Smart Spaces, and Next Generation Networks and Systems. NEW2AN 2020, ruSMART 2020, vol. 12526, pp. 338–347. Lecture Notes in Computer Science. Springer, Cham (2020). https://doi.org/10.1007/978-3-030-65729-1_29

26. Pupentsova, S., Leventsov, V., Livintsova, M., Alexeeva, N., Vodianova, S.: Assessment of the Internet of Things projects on the real estate market. IOP Conf. Ser. Mater. Sci. Eng. **618**(1), 012041 (2019). https://doi.org/10.1088/1757-899X/618/1/012041

27. Menzeleev, I.A.: Changes in model of rational economic behavior caused by e-commerce [Peremeny v modeli ratsional'nogo ekonomicheskogo povedeniya, vyzvannye razvitiyem internet-torgovli]. J. Inst. Stud. **8**(1), 132–146 (2016). https://doi.org/10.17835/2076-6297.2016.8.1.132-146

28. Balakrishnan, K., Vashishtha, R., Verrecchia, R.: Foreign competition for shares and the pricing of information asymmetry: evidence from equity market liberalization. J. Acc. Econ. **67**(1), 80–97 (2019). https://doi.org/10.1016/j.jacceco.2018.08.015

29. Khalil, S., Mansi, S., Mazboudi, M., Zhang, A.J.: Information asymmetry and the wealth appropriation effect in the bond market: evidence from late disclosures. J. Bus. Res. **95**, 49–61 (2019). https://doi.org/10.1016/j.jbusres.2018.09.022

30. Greene, M.N., Morgan, P.H., Foxall, G.R.: Neural networks and consumer behavior: neural models, logistic regression, and the behavioral perspective model. Behav. Anal. **40**(2), 393–418 (2017). https://doi.org/10.1007/s40614-017-0105-x

31. Kliegr, T., Bahník, Š, Fürnkranz, J.: Advances in machine learning for the behavioral sciences. Am. Behav. Sci. **64**(2), 145–175 (2020). https://doi.org/10.1177/0002764219859639

32. Lukiyanchuk, I.N., Panasenko, S.V., Kazantseva, S.Y., Lebedev, K.A., Lebedeva, O.E.: Development of online retailing logistics flows in a globalized digital economy. Rev. Inclusion. **7**(S2–1), 407–416 (2020)

33. Hamed, F.: A DSS-based dynamic programming for finding optimal markets using neural networks and pricing. Iranian J. Manag. Stud. **14**(1), 87–106 (2021)

34. Yosini, D., Adiyatma, R.I.: Understanding consumer loyalty using neural network. Pol. J. Manag. Stud. **16**(2), 51–61 (2017)

35. Xiao, G., Zhou, M.: WITHDRAWN: analysis of electric vehicle purchase behavior based on FPGA system and neural network. Microprocess. Microsyst **2020**, 103361 (2020). https://doi.org/10.1016/j.micpro.2020.103361

36. Krasyuk, I., Medvedeva, Y.: Resource support in business analytics of innovative development of trade and technological systems. In: Proceedings of the 33rd International Business Information Management Association Conference, IBIMA 2019: Education Excellence and Innovation Management through Vision 2020, pp. 8807–8817 (2019)

37. Krasyuk, I.A., Medvedeva, Y.Y.: Drives and obstacle for the development of marketing in Russian retailing. In: Proceedings of the 33rd International Business Information Management Association Conference, IBIMA 2019: Education Excellence and Innovation Management through Vision 2020, pp. 4838–4844 (2019)

Utilization of Organizational-Economic Mechanism for Selection and Management of Spectrum Sharing Scenarios to Increase Economic Efficiency of 5G Operators

Valery Tikhvinskiy[1,3], Roman Umanskiy[2], Arseny Plossky[3(✉)], and Vladimir Makarov[4]

[1] Bauman Moscow State Technical University (BMSTU), Moscow, Russia
[2] Moscow Technical University of Communication and Informatics (MTUCI), Moscow, Russia
[3] FSUE Radio Research & Development Institute (NIIR), Moscow, Russia
[4] The Bonch-Bruevich Saint-Petersburg State University of Telecommunications, St. Petersburg, Russia

Abstract. The main topic of the article is the development of organizational-economic mechanism (OEM) for selecting and managing various scenarios to increase the economic efficiency of 5G network operators based on the influence of external market and internal technological factors. As the main scenarios for spectrum sharing in 5G networks, the authors proposed the following: licensed vertical shared access (primary/secondary access - LVSA); licensed shared access (access for licensed users - LSA); dynamic spectrum sharing (DSS); unlicensed horizontal sharing access ("first come, first use" for unlicensed spectrum - uLHSA).

Keywords: 5G network operator · Radio-frequency spectrum · Organizational-economic mechanism · Economic efficiency · Spectrum sharing scenario

1 Introduction

One of the development directions of modern economic science is the economy of sharing of productive resources of modern enterprises [1]. Some examples of the production resources sharing are the modern robotic production park with maximum utilization 24 × 7 × 365, car-sharing scenarios for the car-renting companies and time-share scenarios for the travel/hotel companies. The radio frequency spectrum has a dual nature at the same time being both a natural and a productive resource [2], which is increasingly being used by telecom operators for various types of mobile communications, satellite communications, television and radio broadcasting and the scarcity of spectrum resource is most acutely for mobile communications operators. The increase of spectrum demand and market entry of 5G operators lead to the high relevance of studies on spectrum sharing to increase the economic efficiency of mobile operators [3–6]. At the same time, existing studies on economic aspects of spectrum sharing [7] do not provide a

© Springer Nature Switzerland AG 2022
Y. Koucheryavy et al. (Eds.): NEW2AN 2021/ruSMART 2021, LNCS 13158, pp. 95–107, 2022.
https://doi.org/10.1007/978-3-030-97777-1_9

solution to operators on the feasibility and cost-effectiveness of using one or another type of spectrum sharing. To develop a scientific approach to the selection of a spectrum sharing scenario in order to increase the economic efficiency of the productive activities of 5G operators, authors considered these scenarios and justified the need to develop an organizational-economic mechanism for their selection and management.

2   Spectrum Sharing Scenarios

Spectrum sharing scenarios used by mobile operators at their production activities will be determined by the type of spectrum access which is set by the national regulatory authority (NRA) in the field of spectrum management. Currently, the Radio Regulations (RR) [8] identifies 2 such types:

– Individual authorized access (licensed access (LA));
– General authorized access (license exempt (LE)).

For the first type, RR and national telecommunication legislations distinguish primary and secondary use of spectrum and/or allotment of the spectrum that determines the priority for spectrum access. However, in order to increase the efficiency of the use of spectrum, especially for the introduction of new technologies, including 5G, a scenario is proposed based on the spectrum sharing utilization at the activities of mobile operators. By this scenario there are a different levels of a spectrum shared access (SA) and spectrum sharing models within the LA type.

Licensed Shared Access (LSA) is a regulatory approach, developed by EU countries, aiming to facilitate the introduction of radio communication systems operated by a limited number of licensees under an individual licensing regime in a frequency band already assigned or expected to be assigned to one or more incumbent users [9]. Under the LSA approach, the additional users are authorized to use the spectrum (or part of the spectrum) in accordance with sharing rules included in their rights of use of the spectrum, thereby allowing all the authorized users, including incumbents, to provide a certain quality of service. Accordingly, by this scenario, incumbent operator will provide access to licensed spectrum in certain frequency band upon the commercial agreements for the one or more other telecom operators under the conditions set by NRA [10].

Another spectrum sharing scenario, named Dynamic Spectrum Sharing (DSS), is used as a solution for intrasystem compatibility for mobile networks [11], which simultaneously used different radio technologies in a certain frequency range within the LA type. Utilization of the DSS scenario allows the shared use of certain frequency ranges allocated for 4G and 5G services within the combined network.

Unlicensed Horizontal Spectrum Access (uLHSA) scenario intended for cases of need to set the priority of spectrum access upon the commercial agreement between the operators who shared the certain frequency range of licensed spectrum.

Finally, Unlicensed Horizontal Spectrum Access (uLHSA) is used by the principle "first come – first serve" for unlicensed spectrum, for example in 2,4 GHz and 5 GHz bands.

The proposed classification of spectrum sharing scenarios for 5G operators is shown in Fig. 1.

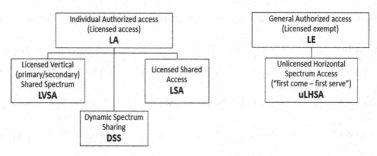

Fig. 1. Classification of spectrum sharing scenarios.

The analysis of the proposed classification shows four scenarios for spectrum sharing for 5G operators, three of them are used within individual authorized access and one – within the general authorized access.

The implementation of each of the proposed spectrum sharing scenarios has its own cost (CAPEX and OPEX) and efficiency, both technological and economic. This conclusion expects the development of an organizational-economic mechanism (OEM) for selecting and managing various scenarios of spectrum sharing to ensure the maximum economic efficiency of 5G operators in the provision of telecommunication services.

The relevance of the development of this OEM is confirmed by the fact that mobile operators have already begun investments in individual technical solutions for the implementation of certain spectrum sharing scenarios. So, at the beginning of 2021, 36 mobile operators around the world are investing in horizontal sharing (9 with deployed or commercial networks) and 12 operators – in vertical sharing (3 with deployed or commercial networks).

3 Estimation of Operators' Costs for Spectrum Sharing

Operators' costs for spectrum sharing are determined according to the formulas given in Table 1 and include the total CAPEX and OPEX and the costs of providing various spectrum sharing scenarios, respectively.

The main CAPEX for the construction of a 5G network are the costs of the radio access network, the modernization of the transport network, the core network, as well as the spectrum resource. The main OPEX during the operation of the 5G network are the costs of renting sites, power supply, maintaining the operability of the transport and backbone networks, as well as spectrum fees.

According to the data of mobile operators, the approximate spectrum fees are from 1 to 1,4 billion rubles per year, while the cost of organizational-technical measures (OTM) is about 100 million rubles (7–10% from spectrum fees).

The costs of the LVSA scenario implementation will include the costs of OTM on release the spectrum and ensure intersystem electromagnetic compatibility (EMC) with radio-electronic means [12] operating in the area where spectrum is allocated to the operator on a primary basis.

The costs of the LSA scenario implementation will include the cost of the equipment of the spectral "manager" of the 5G network [13], the geolocation database, containing

Table 1. Estimating the total costs of a 5G operator and its spectrum sharing costs.

Spectrum sharing scenarios	Total costs	Total spectrum sharing costs
Scenario 1 - LVSA	$S_{CAPEX} + S_{OPEX} + \Delta S_{LVSA}$	$\Delta S_{LVSA} = Sss^{LVSA}{}_{CAPEX} + Sss^{LVSA}{}_{OPEX}$
Scenario 2 - LSA	$S_{CAPEX} + S_{OPEX} + \Delta S_{LSA}$	$\Delta S_{LSA} = Sss^{LSA}{}_{CAPEX} + Sss^{LSVA}{}_{OPEX}$
Scenario 3 - DSS	$S_{CAPEX} + S_{OPEX} + \Delta S_{DSS}$	$\Delta S_{DSS} = Sss^{DSS}{}_{CAPEX} + Sss^{LVSA}{}_{OPEX}$
Scenario 4 – uLHSA	$S_{CAPEX} + S_{OPEX} + \Delta S_{uLHSA}$	$\Delta S_{uLHSA} = Sss^{uLHSA}{}_{CAPEX} + Sss^{uLHSA}{}_{OPEX}$

Notes: $S_{CAPEX} + S_{OPEX}$ - total capital and operating expenditures of a mobile operator without sharing costs for the nth 5G scenario

the date on the spectrum load in the area where spectrum is allocated to other operators on a primary basis [14–16], as well as the spectral server that manages the LSA algorithms [13].

The costs of the DSS scenario implementation will include the cost of the core network and the radio access network of the operator of the co-located 4G/5G network, implementing a multicast broadcast single frequency network (MBSFN) and evolved Multimedia Broadcast/Multicast Service (eMBMS).

The costs of the uLHSA [18] scenario implementation will include the cost of the equipment with Listen-Before-Talk (LBT) and Listen-Before-Receive (LBR) technologies [19].

4 Organizational-Economic Mechanism for Choosing a Spectrum Sharing Scenario by a 5G Operator

One of the methods for solving the problem of increasing the economic efficiency of the use of the radio frequency spectrum by the 5G operator in the provision of mobile communications and the Internet of Things (IoT) services is the development and implementation of OEM for choosing spectrum sharing by the operator.

OEM of efficiency management of spectrum used by 5G operator can be viewed in a broad and narrow sense. In a broad sense, the OEM for choosing spectrum sharing scenarios determines the form of organization of interaction between the operator of the 5G mobile services market, the network infrastructure and subscribers of the telecom operator, internal business processes, as well as economic methods and mechanisms for ensuring spectrum sharing as a valuable productive and natural resource.

The basic OEM for choosing a spectrum sharing scenario by a 5G operator is a mechanism for ensuring the operation of the main management functions, which is a combination of methods, rules, management, and decision-making procedures, and could significantly affect the economic efficiency of using the radio frequency spectrum in the provision of mobile communications and IoT services.

By the OEM for choosing a spectrum sharing scenario of a 5G operator, authors will assume a set of organizational and economic means influencing of the managing subject on a 5G mobile operator in order to maximize revenue from mobile and the IoT services by developing management decisions that ensure the choice of the optimal set of spectrum sharing scenarios.

The elements of the OEM for managing the choice of the spectrum sharing scenario are principles, methods, means and forms of its implementation. The set of principles, methods, and forms of implementation of OEM management, organizational and economic means of influence (which are elements of the forms of implementation of OEM management) can determine the structure of the formation of OEM management by a 5G operator in terms of efficient use of the spectrum.

A methodological approach to the formation of a control scheme for choosing a spectrum sharing scenario by a 5G operator in the provision of mobile communications and IoT services, implemented using OEM, is shown in Fig. 2.

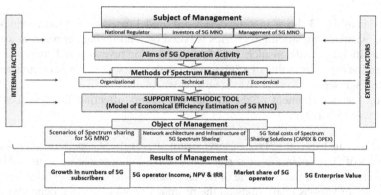

Fig. 2. An approach to the formation of an organizational-economic mechanism for managing spectrum sharing scenarios of a 5G operator.

To preserve the approaches to managing spectrum sharing scenarios by the 5G operator, the OEM is based on the selection mechanism existing in the operator companies, which has been transformed into the current OEM. The developed OEM, in contrast to the subjective mechanism of random selection or copying of the available a posteriori spectrum sharing by mobile operators, uses a model for assessing the economic efficiency of choosing a spectrum sharing scenario [20, 21].

The use of such a model in the OEM of choosing a spectrum sharing scenario by a 5G operator allows, on the basis of modeling the economic efficiency indicators of a 5G operator, taking into account the spectrum sharing scenario for specified external and internal environmental factors in the implementation of its operating activities, to assess the economic efficiency of a 5G operator for each of the spectrum sharing scenarios [13–20] and to make the optimal choice of the scenario or set of scenarios and volume of investments, CAPEX and OPEX, target segments of the 5G services market.

The proposed model for assessing the economic efficiency of operating activities of 5G company is shown in Fig. 3.

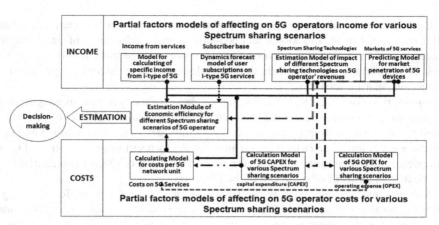

Fig. 3. Model for assessing the economic efficiency spectrum sharing scenarios of 5G operators.

Analysis of Fig. 3 shows that the developed model for assessing the economic efficiency of 5G spectrum sharing scenarios is based on a profitable approach to assessing economic efficiency and considers both factors affecting revenues and costs and factors that determine the future value of a 5G operator in the market of mobile communications and the IoT services.

During the development of the model, the factors affecting the revenues of 5G operators were attributed:

- specific income from the ith type of service provided by the 5G operator, per subscriber;
- dynamics of changes in the subscriber base of the 5G operator by years, taking into account the stage of the life cycle of development of services in the 5G network;
- the impact of various restrictions on the revenues of 5G operators, depending on the chosen network development and spectrum sharing scenarios;
- state of demand and capacity of regional and vertical markets by years of operator development, including the dynamics of penetration of 5G devices into the market.

Factors affecting the costs of 5G operators were attributed:

- unit cost for construction and maintenance of the ith type of 5G network element;
- used technologies of 5G radio access and spectrum sharing;
- the impact of various restrictions on the costs of 5G operators, depending on the chosen network development and spectrum sharing scenarios.

One of the important tasks of introducing an OEM for choosing a spectrum sharing scenario is to find and develop tools for its implementation in the course of managing the production activities of a 5G operator. The tools for implementing the OEM for choosing a spectrum sharing scenario of a 5G operator, depending on the current stage of the operator's life cycle, can be:

- Development strategy of the 5G operator;

- System project of a network of a mobile operator;
- Expert mechanism of the NRA for making a decision on the issuance of licenses for the provision of mobile services to a 5G operator;
- Reengineering plan for 5G operator to implement spectrum sharing.

At the stages of the 5G operator's life cycle, various tools for the implementation of the developing OEM can be used in its activities. So at the stage of creating a mobile operator (greenfield), the first three of the proposed tools can become the main tools for implementing the organizational and economic mechanism, and at the stage of maturity (brownfield) - the redevelopment plan of a mobile operator.

In the scenario of the reference operator, based on an assessment of the dynamics of penetration of 5G devices in the Russian Federation up to 2030, a forecast was made on the number of users of enhanced mobile broadband (eMBB) services in 5G networks, as well as IoT services. Further, based on the ARPU forecast for each type of services provided, calculated as the average monthly income from the sale of services per subscriber, the level of annual revenue was calculated for the reference operator providing services on the 5G network, which is the reference operator of the 5G network is going to achieve within 10 years of its activity under the given parameters.

5 Modeling the Economic Efficiency of a 5G Operator

Modeling the economic efficiency of a 5G operator was simulated for various spectrum sharing scenarios. The scenario in which the 5G operator received a ready-to-use radio frequency spectrum on a primary basis, incurred capital and operating costs for the development and implementation of the 5G project, connected subscribers and received revenues for 10 years was adopted as a reference scenario.

At the same time, the key task of the calculation was not to calculate the exact business plan and financial result to assess the payback of the 5G project for the reference operator, since not all the factors/costs that the operators will bear in the functioning of the constructed 5G network were taken into account in the model, but to calculate the incremental effect that will be achieved by the operator when choosing and implementing various spectrum sharing scenarios in comparison with the reference scenario in the framework of a single approach to taking into account the list and assessment of services and costs.

First, to calculate the economic efficiency of the incremental effect, it was assumed that the reference operator plans to work on creating a 5G network in all 15 cities of the Russian Federation with a population of more than 1 million people.

In the scenario of the reference operator, based on an assessment of the dynamics of penetration of 5G devices in the Russian Federation up to 2030, a forecast was made on the number of users of enhanced mobile broadband (eMBB) services in 5G networks, as well as IoT services. Further, based on the ARPU forecast for each type of services, calculated as the average monthly income from the sale of services per subscriber, the level of annual revenue was calculated for the reference operator providing services on the 5G network, which is the reference 5G operator is going to achieve within 10 years of its activity under the given parameters.

Further, based on the required technical characteristics and the specified parameters of the 5G network functioning, the construction and the annual maintenance costs of the 5G network were calculated for 10 years.

Based on obtained results, taking into account the expert estimations, a model was built for calculating the incremental effect of changes in income and costs on the implementation of various spectrum sharing scenarios, shown in Table 2.

Table 2. Model for calculating the incremental effect of changes in income and costs on the implementation of various spectrum sharing scenarios

Spectrum sharing scenarios	Description	Incremental income	Incremental cost				
			Spectrum release fee	Spectrum fee	Change of OPEX[a]	Spectrum sharing fee	Change of CAPEX[a]
LVSA	Utilizing the released spectrum for 5G on a secondary Basis	Increase in the number of subscribers due to the introduction of new services at new frequencies/Growth of traffic volume	+	+	+	+	+
LSA	Using the spectrum of another licensed operator using a dedicated frequency management server	Growth of traffic volume	−	+	+	+	+
DSS	Using special DSS equipment	Increase in the number of subscribers due to the introduction of new services at new frequencies/Growth of traffic volume	−	−	+	−	+
uLHSA	Utilization of regulation-free frequencies based on equipment Listen before talk	Growth of traffic volume for indoor solutions	−	+	+	−	+

[a]Not all cost elements that are included in the OPEX and CAPEX structure are changed when calculating the incremental effect. A part of the costs in comparison with the reference option may remain unchanged depending on the considered spectrum sharing scenario

To calculate the main indicators of the payback of the construction of a 5G network project, an assumption of a discount rate of 7.5% was used, and an analysis of the calculations of the discounted cash flow over a planning horizon of 10 years showed that the payback of the reference scenario occurs in the 9th year after the start of work, at the same time the annual free cash flow becomes positive for the 6th year of the project. The

NPV indicator is 33.9 million rubles, and the IRR is 16.1%, which indicates the effectiveness of the project implementation. It should be emphasized that the effectiveness of the project directly depends on the dynamics of penetration of 5G devices, as well as on the speed of subscriber base advancements.

The calculation results of the 5G operator using the developed economic-mathematical model for assessing the incremental effect of the selected spectrum sharing scenario in comparison with the 5G reference operator in the 10-year forecast period are presented in Table 3.

Table 3. Estimates of the incremental effect of the selected spectrum sharing scenarios

Indicators	LVSA	LSA	DSS	uHLSA
Incremental net present value (in comparison with the reference scenario), million rubles	−340	15 506	−15 913	−14 406
Incremental discounted payback period (in comparison with the reference scenario), years	0,4	−0,3	0,4	0,6
Incremental effect of calculating the internal rate of return (in comparison with the reference scenario),%	−3,0%	2,3%	−3,4%	−4,4%

At first glance, the only advantageous sharing spectrum option for the operator is to use the LSA scenario, since it has a higher NPV for the period under review in comparison with the baseline scenario, as well as a more advantageous payback period and IRR. Moreover, this scenario is not only more effective in comparison with the reference scenario, but also in comparison with other scenarios of RFS sharing (Fig. 4).

To confirm the obtained conclusions about the advisability of using a sharing scenario, an incremental calculation of the change in the cost of a 5G operator's project should be made for various spectrum sharing scenarios. The results of modeling the indicators of the value of the enterprise value (EV) and the terminal value (TV) when assessing the value of the 5G operator using various scenarios of spectrum sharing are shown in Table 4.

When calculating the cost of a 5G operator's project using spectrum sharing, discounted cash flows of 10 years (forecast period) do not have a significant effect on its formation, and the terminal value (TV) indicator of the 5G operator, which forms the value estimate, considering its functioning in the post-forecast period. To estimate the TV, the Gordon Growth Model was used [22], in which the WACC indicator (weighted average cost of capital) of 7.5% was used as assumptions, as well as the 3.5% indicator as a constant steady rate of growth of free cash flow in the post-forecast period.

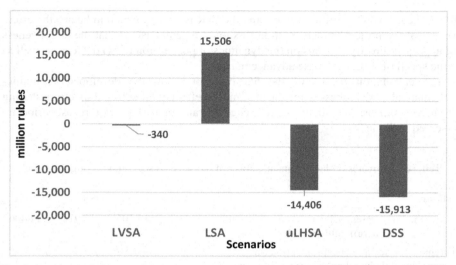

Fig. 4. Incremental change of NVP depending on the selected spectrum sharing scenario, million rubles

Table 4. EV and TV indicators for different spectrum sharing scenarios

Indicators	LVSA	LSA	DSS	uHLSA
Incremental discounted terminal value (TV), million rubles	361 945	171 959	−171 191	58 897
Incremental effect of calculating Incremental enterprise value (EV), million rubles	**361 605**	**187 465**	**−187 104**	**44 492**

Analysis of Fig. 5 shows that calculating the incremental cost of an operator's project leads to the state where vertical sharing of the spectrum becomes a more attractive scenario. This is due to the specific nature of calculating TV, which in the last year of the forecast period is higher for vertical sharing due to the presence of a more prospective frequency resource.

To summarize the results obtained, it can be concluded that, given the uncertainty of the development of the 5G services market and low growth rates of subscribers and revenue, the LSA scenario due to lower implementation costs is more economically preferable. However, in the case of active growth of subscribers and revenues, this scenario becomes less attractive in comparison with the scenario of introducing LVSA. At the same time, the calculation of the enterprise value did not consider the effect of the influence of the cost of an additional dedicated asset (additional spectrum resource for vertical sharing).

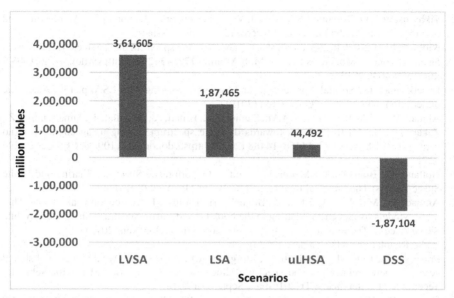

Fig. 5. Incremental change in the 5G operator's enterprise value (EV) depending on the spectrum sharing scenario, million rubles

6 Conclusion

Studies on the development of an organizational-economic mechanism for selecting spectrum sharing scenarios for 5G operators in order to increase the economic efficiency of their activities is an urgent area for the modern 5G services market.

Implementation of such a mechanism for choosing a spectrum sharing scenario which considering such factors as the business model used for building networks of a 5G operator, the life cycle stage and maturity of the operator, the amount of investment in the creation and development of a 5G operator, radio access technologies of a 5G operator that implements the selected spectrum sharing scenario, and other parameters will allow obtaining scientifically based recommendations for mobile operators entering the 5G service market, maximizing the economic efficiency of their activities and the future value of the company.

In addition to developing practical recommendations for 5G operators on choosing a spectrum sharing scenario, detailed development of tools for implementing the organizational-economic mechanism of this choice at the operator and industry levels of management and the improvement of the regulatory framework for both operator activities and spectrum management at the national level will be required.

References

1. Becker, T., Stern, H.: Impact of resource sharing in manufacturing on logistical key figures. Proc. CIRP **41**, 579–584 (2016)

2. Tikhvinskiy, V.O., Terentiev, S.V., Koval, V.A.: 5G Networks: Technologies, Architecture and Services, 376 p. Media Publisher, Moscow (2019). (in Russian)
3. Nidhi, A.M., Prasad, R.: Spectrum sharing and dynamic spectrum management techniques in 5g and beyond networks: a survey. J. Mob. Multim. **17**, 1–3 (2021). https://doi.org/10.13052/jmm1550-4646.17133
4. Lähetkangas, K.: Special Applications and Spectrum Sharing with LSA, p. 130. Academic dissertation, University of Oulu, Oulu (2019)
5. Ahmad, W.S.H.M.W., Radzi, N.A.M., Samidi, F.S., Ismail, A., Abdullah, F., Jamaludin, M.Z., Zakaria, M.N.: 5G technology: towards dynamic spectrum sharing using cognitive radio networks. IEEE Access **8**, 14460–14488 (2020). https://doi.org/10.1109/ACCESS.2020.2966271
6. Holland, O., Bogucka, H., Medeisis, A. (eds.): Opportunistic Spectrum Sharing and White Space Access: The Practical Reality, p. 736. Wiley, Hoboken (2015)
7. Ahmadi, H., Macaluso, I., Khan, Z., Bogucka, H., DaSilva, L.A.: Economic and Game Theoretic Models for Spectrum Sharing in the book Opportunistic Spectrum Sharing and White Space Access: The Practical Reality, pp. 393–406. Wiley, Hoboken (2015)
8. Radio Regulations. ITU, Geneva (2020)
9. Frascolla, V., Butt, M., Marchetti, N., Morgado, A.J., Gomes, A.: Dynamic licensed shared access: a new architecture and spectrum allocation techniques. In: IEEE 84th Vehicular Technology Conference: VTC2016-Fall, September 2016
10. Omana, R.: Using spectrum sharing to deploy 4G/5G capable wireless networks. In: Conference SCTE ISBE and NCTA, New Orleans, 30 September–3 October 2019
11. 5G NR and 4G LTE Coexistence. White Paper: A Comprehensive Deployment Guide to Dynamic Spectrum Sharing, p. 30. MediaTek (2020)
12. Koval, V.A., Tikhvinskiy, V.O.: Economical efficiency assessment model of spectrum conversion for new mobile wireless technologies. In: Proceedings of the 2014 ITU Kaleidoscope Academic Conference: Living in a Converged World - Impossible Without Standards, pp. 229–232 (2014)
13. 5G PPP, Deliverable D3.1. 5G spectrum scenarios, requirements and technical aspects for bands above 6 GHz, Version: v1.0 (2016)
14. ETSI TR 103 113 (V1.1.1,07/2013). System Reference Document for LSA. Mobile broadband services in the 2 300 MHz–2 400 MHz frequency band under Licensed Shared Access regime (2013)
15. ETSI TS 103 154 (V0.0.9, Draft 01/2014). System Requirements for LSA. System requirements for operation of Mobile Broadband Systems in the 2300 MHz–2400 MHz band under Licensed Shared Access (2014)
16. ETSI TS 103 235 (V0.0.1, Draft 01/2014) – System Architecture for LSA. System Architecture and High Level Procedures for Operation of Licensed Shared Access (LSA) in the 2300 MHz–2400 MHz band (2014)
17. Tikhvinskiy, V.O., Deviatkin, E.E., Aitmagambetov, A., Kulakaeva, A.: Provision of IoT Services for Co-Located 4G/5G Networks Utilization with Dynamic Frequency Sharing. In: Conference: 2020 International Conference on Engineering Management of Communication and Technology (EMCTECH), October 2020
18. 3GPP R1-1804313, 3GPP TSG RAN WG1 92bis Meeting. Channel access and co-existence for NR-U operation, April 2018
19. Optimized spectrum use with LSA/ASA. White paper. Version 3.0, GTI TDD (2014)
20. Report ITU-R SM.2404-0. Regulatory Tools to Support Enhanced Shared Use of the Spectrum. ITU, Geneva (2017)

21. Report ITU-R SM. 2012 Economic Aspects of Spectrum Management. ITU, Geneva (2018)
22. Gass, Y.M., Tikhvinskiy, V.O., Umanskiy, R.Y.: Economic efficiency operation activity modelling of mobile virtual network operator based on income and cost structure estimation. Druke. Vest. (3), 64–78 (2020)

Sustainable Development of Small and Medium Business in View of the Rapid Growth of Telecommunications and Digital Economy in the Russian Federation

Marina Efremova[1](✉), Maxim Tcvetkov[1], Nikolay Shimin[1], Oksana Evseeva[2], and Efimov Alexey[2]

[1] National Research Lobachevsky State University of Nizhny Novgorod, Nizhniy Novgorod, Russia
{efremovamv,shimin}@iee.unn.ru
[2] Peter the Great St. Petersburg Polytechnic University, St. Petersburg, Russia
evseeva@spbstu.ru, efimov@kafedrapik.ru

Abstract. The paper discusses the studied results of the use of telecommunications and digital technologies by small and medium enterprises in Russia, the readiness of enterprises to develop in the context of global digitalization and challenges of the new COVID-19 pandemic. In order to meet the research objective, we combined a number of methods and techniques, namely desk research, statistical analysis, and analysis of empirical data obtained by means of a survey. Digital technologies and telecommunications are more and more actively penetrating the realm of small and medium business while the digital maturity of enterprises and their capability of using telecommunications is going to become a major survival factor in the post-pandemic world. Enterprises that apply digital technologies and telecommunications are more adapted to the new market requirements and have better chances to survive.

Keywords: Telecommunications · Digitalization · Digital technologies · Small and medium business · Small and medium enterprises · Entrepreneurship · COVID-19 pandemic · Russia

1 Introduction

In well-developed countries, small and medium enterprises (SME) are a driving force of the economy. They form about half of GDP and up to 70% of jobs [14, 15]. In China this figure is even higher and amounts to 60% [27].

Small and medium business accounts for 50% of all tax payments into China's budget, 62% of all investments into fixed assets (excluding farmsteads), 90% of internal trade, 48% of exports, over 70% of innovative products, inventions and technical innovations [27].

© Springer Nature Switzerland AG 2022
Y. Koucheryavy et al. (Eds.): NEW2AN 2021/ruSMART 2021, LNCS 13158, pp. 108–121, 2022.
https://doi.org/10.1007/978-3-030-97777-1_10

In this respect, Russia is falling behind the world figures. Small and medium enterprises form just one fifth of GDP and provide about a quarter of the population with jobs [24]. As of March 10, 2021, the number of small and medium business agents reduced in comparison with the same period of the previous year by 228.8 thousand units [23]. The main destabilizing factor was the new COVID-19 pandemic.

Most researchers agree that the COVID-19 pandemic has caused irreversible damage to all sectors of the economy, but small and medium enterprises turned out to be the most vulnerable [6, 10, 11]. These types of enterprises play a crucial role in the economy as they form the biggest share of gross domestic product, stimulate economic growth, create employment, satisfy the needs of the public in products and services. Thus, encouraging the effective growth of small and medium business is a major goal of the Russian and world economy.

Today further effective development of small and medium business neither in Russia, nor abroad is possible without telecommunications and digital technologies. Obviously, digital maturity is the main factor determining survival on the market [22].

During the new COVID-19 pandemic, small and medium enterprises have become even more dependent on telecommunications. Representatives of small and medium business understand that digitalization is not the matter of choice, but rather the matter of life and death. According to Cisco [22], on a four-stage scale, only a quarter of small and medium enterprises reached the final fourth stage while 4% are still at the first stage. Remarkably, the most mature small and medium enterprises, which reached the 3rd and 4th stages of digital maturity, demonstrate the highest recovery results after the COVID-19 pandemic. They are capable of reacting promptly to external changes and grow their incomes at quicker rates.

Despite the enormous damage that the COVID-19 pandemic did to the entire world economy, it has considerably accelerated the processes of telecommunications development. Over 70% of the respondent small and medium enterprises all over the world have sped up the introduction of digital technologies as a result of the pandemic [21]. Researchers believe that the pandemic has given great momentum to business digitalization and telecommunications development. The lockdown stimulated entrepreneurs to transfer to remote working and quickly develop channels and services to build online business. The economic situation formed a new experience and increased the penetration of digitalization in users' life [21]. Telecommunications present unique opportunities for working remotely.

In this respect, it seems interesting to study the results of analysis of the behavior of small and medium enterprises in the time of digitalization and widespread introduction of telecommunications. In order to note the key changes in the behavior of market players, the current state of small and medium business in Russia has to be investigated, the problems faced by small and medium enterprises on their way to digitalization and use of telecommunications must be identified, the opinions of the companies about new growth options in the pandemic and post-pandemic time have to be collected.

The paper is aimed at presenting the results of the research undertaken to study how digital technologies and telecommunications are used by small and medium enterprises in Russia, their ability to develop in the time of global digitalization, to face the challenges of the COVID-19 pandemic, to react effectively and fast to the changes that take place and to make informed management decisions.

The structure of the paper includes an introduction; a literature review, describing the problems of behavior of small and medium enterprises in the time when digitalization and telecommunications are rapidly developing and the companies' reactions to the challenges of the COVID-19 pandemic; a methodology section, which describes the context, the processes of data acquisition and analysis; discussion of the situation at small and medium enterprises in the Russian Federation and digital literacy of the public; conclusions and areas of further research, which finalize the paper.

2 Literature Review

The growing spread of digitalization and telecommunications in all spheres of entrepreneurship allows the researchers, who study the processes of digital transformation of business and use of different types of innovative technologies in small and medium enterprises, to conclude about Revolution 4.0 or Industry 4.0, which is grounded on digitalization of all aspects of life [2, 18]. Fast progress of Industry 4.0 will enable small and medium enterprises to overcome difficulties caused by production of technically advanced products and development of logistic chains [18, 25, 28, 29].

Pointing out the significant contribution of small and medium enterprises in the production of the world GDP and highlighting their leading role in providing economic stability [13, 19], experts observe 5 major digital trends in the activities of small and medium enterprises [19]: transferring more operations into an online format, wide use of chat-bots, introduction of cloud technologies, use of social media, adapting business to the needs of millennial clients. Telecommunications provide unprecedented opportunities for doing all the above. The major spheres where telecommunications are used include the internet, mobile communications, data transmission networks, satellite communications systems, digital and analog TV, telephone communications and e-banking. Fast digitalization of business introduces changes to the business processes and infrastructure of small and medium enterprises, their organizational culture, sales structure and communication with customers [7].

Nationally and regionally, researchers identify the following problems related to digital transformation of small and medium enterprises [1, 17, 18]: lack of patterns for digital standardization and consistent support of small and medium business on the part of the state, insufficient funding of digital technologies introduction on the part of company owners, difficulties with teaching employees to use various elements of digitalization on every day basis.

The new COVID-19 pandemic and its effects proved to be the most serious destabilizing factor for small and medium business. Researchers point out that the spread of the disease led to logical inconsistences, reduced volumes of production, critically low demand in such service sectors as catering, tourism and hospitality [6]. At the same time, some authors highlight that the worsening economic situation, caused by the rapid spread of COVID-19 and the lockdown, have pushed small and medium enterprises towards more decisive actions in order to speed up the processes aimed at digital transformation and obtaining new knowledge in management and technology [10].

Thus, despite objective difficulties, the adaptation of digital technologies and telecommunications by small and medium business together with the subsequent digital transformation of business processes and processes of communication with customers is not only a way to respond to the challenges of the present, but also an attempt to form the scenarios of the future.

3 Method of Research

In order to achieve its goal, the research relies on the statistical analysis and analysis of the empirical data obtained by Sberbank RF thanks to the study of payment systems, and the data of the NAFI Analytical Center, acquired from surveying some representatives of small and medium enterprises.

The general state of small and medium business and the level of digital literacy in Russia were evaluated based on some open sources of information: official data of Rosstat by forms for statistical reporting; Sberbank of Russia's monitoring of cash flow by sectors; indices of consumer activity of the population and activity of small and medium enterprises, data from the register of small and medium enterprises of the Federal Tax Service.

4 Results

4.1 The State of Small and Medium Business in the Russian Federation

The damaging effect of the COVID-19 pandemic was felt especially strongly by small and medium enterprises [6, 12]. As a result of the first wave of the pandemic, the number of small and medium business entities in Russia reduced considerably from 6.052 million in June 2020 to 5.602 million in September 2020 [23]. By the end of 2020, there was a slight growth of small and medium enterprises – up to 5.702 million. As of March 10, 2021, this figure grew again and amounted to 5.732 million. The number of employees at these enterprises rose from 15.270 million people in June 2020 to 15.515 million in March 2021, which can be explained by a growth in the number of self-employed people during the quarantine (Fig. 1).

The most objective picture of the state of small and medium enterprises during the pandemic can be obtained from the analysis of dynamics of consumer expenses and the Consumer Activity Index weekly published by Sberbank [26]. Experts of Sberbank use the information collected from payment systems and open sources to present quantitative characteristics of socio-economic processes that take place in the country at the macro- and micro-economic levels. Only aggregated impersonal data are used in the analysis.

The Consumer Activity Index shows how many various goods and services are paid by consumers and helps to understand the changing pattern of buying habits at the time of the COVID-19 pandemic. The expenses of consumers on December 30th (the most active day in a year) are taken as the value of Index 100. The index falls in case the number of online and offline outlets where consumers make purchases during the day reduces. The results of the analysis give evidence that the most difficult month for business was April 2020. In this period consumer spending on products and services

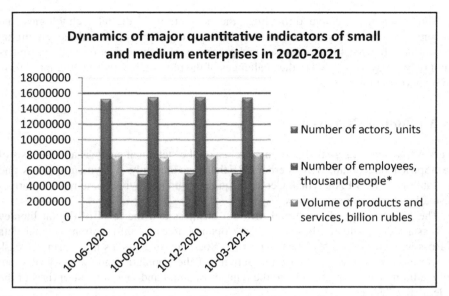

Fig. 1. Dynamics of major quantitative indicators of small and medium enterprises in the RF in 2020–2021

reduced by 26.2% in comparison with the same period in 2019 [26]. The Consumer Activity Index amounted to 50.2 points, which implies that consumers' buying activity halved against the comparable period in 2019.

Due to the dramatic fall in demand, a lot of small and medium enterprises had to close down [8]. Most of them were service enterprises [9]. In April 2020 the decline in consumer spending on services was unprecedented: it decreased by 57.7% in comparison with the same period of the previous year [26].

Tourism, sports and entertainment sectors suffered most of all [3, 5]. In summer 2020 due to the lockdown, the number of tourists going abroad reduced by 83.2% in comparison with the same period of the previous year while in winter 2021 this figure fell by 81.3%, respectively. From April to August 2020, sixty tourist operators were excluded from the All-Russian Register [16]. As the borders were closed, some tourists re-orientated on travel inside Russia. Thanks to this, the demand for domestic tourist slightly increased in summer 2020 (by 10.8%). However, in winter 2020–2021, the demand went down by 15% again, which partially may be explained by the limited capacities of Russia's winter resources whose infrastructure is not advanced enough, as well as by the wish of prospective tourists to stay home in the time of the second wave of the COVID-19 pandemic (Fig. 2).

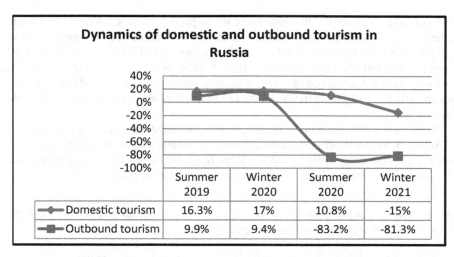

Fig. 2. Dynamics of domestic and outbound tourism in Russia

By 2021 the situation of small and medium enterprises had been improving. Thus, as of January 2021, the reduction of spending on services reduced down to 16% against 57.7% in April 2020 [26]. However, in the tourism and entertainment sector, the period of stagnation did not come to an end: the sales of air tickets in January 2021 fell by 78.1% in comparison to the same period in 2020, the demands for services of tourist agencies reduced by 50%, the sales of entertainment services decreased by 41.6%, the demand for the services of hotels went down by 29.3%, those of cafés and restaurants – by 23% (Fig. 3).

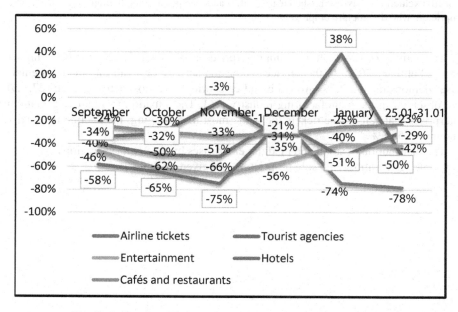

Fig. 3. Dynamics of consumer spending on services in 2020/2019.

As of June 2020, for the first time since the beginning of the COVID-19 pandemic, the level of activity of small and medium business was documented in comparison with year 2019 [26]. As of the end of June 2020, the turnover of SME increased by 1.5% in comparison with the same period of 2019. A fall over 50% against the levels of the previous year is still observed only in two sectors: tourism and sports and entertainment industry (86.1% and 50.6% respectively in comparison with the same period of the previous year).

Despite a slight increase in the number of small and medium enterprises, as of March 10, 2021 their total number is lower than the figures of the same period in 2020 (by 3.2%). Micro- and small enterprises turned out to be the most vulnerable: the reduction was 3.9% and 3.2% respectively in comparison with the previous year (Table 1).

Table 1. Dynamics of performance indicators of small and medium business in 2020–2021 (The Unified Register of Small and Medium Enterprises, 2021)

Categories of SME agents	Number of agents, units		Number of employees, people[a]		Volume of products and services, trillion rubles	
	10.03.21	10.03.20	10.03.21	10.03.20	10.03.21	10.03.20
Micro-enterprises	5,498,069	5,720,459	7,490,237	7,390,457	6 879	5138
Small enterprises	215,802	222,899	6,133,453	6,180,175	1 235	1134
Medium enterprises	17,699	16,998	1,834,864	1,706,016	238	245
Total	5,731,570	5,960,356	15,458,554	15,276,648	8352	6517

[a]Note. The average number of staff employed by small and medium enterprises (legal entities and sole proprietors which hired employees in the year preceding the year in which the Register was formed) excluding newly-established legal entities and sole proprietors, without reference to sole proprietors who did not hire employees.

The activity of small and medium enterprises as of March 15, 2021 is 6.5% higher than in February 2020. In the service sector, the activity of small and medium enterprises demonstrated a 9.6% growth by all categories. The most active growth (27.1%) was observed in the manufacturing industry [26]. The situation in small and medium enterprises that sell airline tickets looks the most discouraging: the decline in activity amounts to 55.2%.

The distribution of small and medium enterprises by the country's regions is broken down into legal entities and sole proprietors and given in Table 2.

Table 2. The number of legal entities and sole proprietors as of March 10, 2021 [26]

Region	Total	Legal entities				Sole proprietors			
		Total	Including		Medium enterprise	Total	Including		Medium enterprise
			Micro-enterprise	Small enterprise			Micro-enterprise	Small enterprise	
RF	5,731,570	2 387,972	2 181,026	189,554	17,392	3 343 598	3 317 043	26 248	307
CFD	1788 387	819 899	745 827	67 332	6 740	968 488	962 301	6 098	89
NWFD	665 657	316 516	289 658	24 697	2 161	349 141	346 725	2 391	25
SFD	666 950	187 202	170 842	14 980	1 380	479 748	476 240	3 478	30
NCFD	194 003	49 324	45 028	3 842	454	144 679	143 869	799	11
PFD	1016 916	426 306	388 168	35 074	3 064	590 610	584 645	5 908	57
UFD	489 658	207 087	190 208	15 507	1 372	282 571	279 978	2 561	32
SbFD	605 104	259 679	238 731	19 352	1 596	345 425	342 283	3 102	40
FEFD	304 895	121 959	112 564	8 770	625	182 936	181 002	1 911	23

The quantitative indicators characterizing the status of small and medium business vary significantly in the regions of the country. In absolute terms, the majority of small and medium enterprises are in the Central Federal District and the Volga (Privolzhsky) Federal District, while the Far-Eastern Federal District shows the lowest figure (Table 3).

Table 3. Number of small and medium enterprises per 10,000 people as of March 10, 2021[a]

Region	Population, people	Number of small and medium enterprises, units	Number of small and medium enterprises per 10,000 people, units
Russian Federation	146,171,015	5,731,570	392.1
Central FD	39,250,960	1 788 387	455.6
Northwestern FD	13,941,959	665 657	477.5
Southern FD	16,482,488	666 950	404.7
North Caucasus FD	9,967,301	194 003	194.6
Privolzhsky FD	29,070,827	1 016 916	349.8
Urals FD	12,329,500	489 658	397.1
Siberian FD	17,003,927	605 104	355.9
Far Eastern FD	8,124,053	304 895	375.3

[a]Compiled by the authors

When the number of small and medium enterprises is calculated per 10 thousand people, the situation changes dramatically: the leader is the Northwestern Federal District (477.5), the runner-up is the Central Federal District (455.6), while the third place is taken by the South Federal District (404.7). The last in the ranking is the Far Eastern Federal District (375.3). On average, in Russia there are 392 small and medium enterprises per 10,000 people.

4.2 Digital Competence and Telecommunications in Russia: Survey Results

Since 2018 the NAFI Analytical Center has been doing research on digital literacy in Russia [21]. The 2018 and 2019 studies measured five key indicators: information literacy, computer literacy, communicative literacy, media literacy and attitude to technological innovations (G20 methodology [4]). In 2020 the researchers used DigComp (Digital Competence Framework for Citizens), designed by the European Commission. According to the methodology, digital competences were assessed using 5 major parameters: information and data literacy, communication and collaboration, digital content creation, digital safety and problem-solving in digital environment.

As a result of a survey, which was conducted in January 2020 and included 1300 respondents aged 18 and above in 70 regions of Russia, it is revealed that about a quarter of Russians developed a high level of digital literacy. The Digital Literacy Index of

Russians in the first quarter of 2020 was 58 points (DigComp methodology, scale from 0 to 100), information literacy was 59 points, communication and collaboration was 62 points, digital content creation was 53 points, safety was 60 points and problem-solving in digital environment was 58 points.

The study shows that, due to the lack of knowledge and skills in the field of digital technologies, many respondents find it difficult to work remotely in the time of self-isolation and lockdown. The need to master digital technologies is recognized by most of the respondents: 65% of respondents find it probable that if digital technologies are introduced in the company they work for, it can be the reason for staff reduction. Every fourth employee thinks that they can lose their job if they lack the necessary skills. Notably, the activity in the matters of additional digital learning is demonstrated by those respondents whose level of skills in this field is already high.

More than a half of the interviewed (53%) reckon that the knowledge of information technology is a mandatory condition for successful work. A quarter of the respondents (26%) think that they can lose their job if they do not learn how to use digital technologies. The respondents admitted having insufficient digital competences in the following areas: critical evaluation of information in the digital environment, use of state digital services, internet communication skills, readiness for self-development in the field of digital technologies.

The level of digital literacy is higher than the national average in Russian capitals (62 against 58 points) and lower than the national average in smaller towns and villages (55 points). Those living the Northwestern Federal District demonstrated higher indicators of digital literacy in comparison with the national average figures. The Southern and North Caucasus Federal Districts had the lowest indicators of digital literacy.

Gender, age and professional activity are noted among socio-demographic factors affecting digital literacy. No significant difference in learning digital skills is observed between males and females (60 points for men and 57 for women). Women are weaker in digital environment (56 points against 59 points for males). Those aged 44 and younger demonstrate the highest indicators of digital literacy (59–61 points). The lowest figures are documented for Russians aged over 55. Employed students demonstrated the highest values of the Digital Literacy Index (64 points). Retired senior citizens are the weakest in digital environment. Their level of digital literacy amounted to 51 points.

Another report by the "NAFI" [20] contains the results of interviews with the key experts in the field of digital technologies. The survey was conducted in 2020. One of the key experts is Yves Punie, Deputy Head of Unit at the European Commission. He disposes the opinion that the younger generation born in the digitalization era have advanced digital competences by default. He believes that the problem of insufficient digital literacy is acute even for the countries that have well-developed digital economy. Thus, in the EU countries 35% of employable population do not have enough digital skills and this is the reason why almost half of them (42%) cannot find a job. Consequently, picking up digital skills is an urgent problem of today's society both in Russia and abroad.

4.3 Development of Digital Technologies and Telecommunications in Small and Medium Enterprises

Bank Otkritie and *the Moscow School of Management SKOLKOVO* published the results of a study about the readiness of small and medium business to digital economy [21]. The Business Digitalization Index (BDI) is suggested as an indicator of the readiness of small and medium enterprises to digital transformation. It combines five indices: data storage and transmission channels (use of cloud services, corporate e-mail, messengers, automation systems, etc.), integration of digital technologies (level of introduction of digital technologies such as artificial intelligence, the Internet of Things, 3D-printing, online document, electronic document management systems, etc.), internet use (digital tools for promotion and development of companies), information security (introducing the culture of protecting digital information, using specialized anti-virus programs), human capital (involvement of management in self-development and staff development in the sphere of digital technologies).

A representative all-Russian survey of 598 representatives of small and medium business carried out in 8 federal districts of Russia (year 2020) showed that the level of digitalization of small and medium enterprises rose from 45 points (year 2019) to 50 points (year 2020) on the scale from 1 to 100 [21]. In spite of the growth, the figures imply that in 2929 only a half of enterprises demonstrate digital literacy.

The number of websites of small and medium enterprises increased to 75% in 2020 against 54% in 2019. The share of entrepreneurs who believe that digitalization enhances the comfort of doing business grew from 34% in 2019 to 57% in 2020; those who think digitalization increases the speed of work went up from 33% in 2019 to 53% in 2020; those who believe digitalization improves client service grew from 15% in 2019 to 22% in 2020. 11% of enterprises have a high level of digitalization (70 points and above). This share reaches 20% among medium enterprises, 10% among sole proprietors and 12–15% among micro- and small enterprises.

A growing number of small and medium enterprises use such telecommunications as corporate e-mail (48% in 2019, 56% in 2020), cloud solutions (46% and 52%, respectively) and automated client contact systems (23% and 33%, respectively).

The demand for digital technologies and telecommunications is forever increasing: 2020 saw a growing number of small and medium enterprises using the technology of the Internet of Things, AI-based technologies and 3D-printing. The internet coverage of companies for doing business reached 94% (against 92% in 2019). Small and medium enterprises use electronic document management systems more and more willingly with 81% of them having rejected paper document management either partially or completely.

Small and medium enterprises widely use telecommunications when dealing with customers and partners. The share of managers who choose only face-to-face communication with clients reduced from 38% to 30%. Social media and messengers are actively used to communicate with customers: every second representative of small and medium business in Russia (47%) has a page on social media, and 80% of them use messengers.

Small and medium enterprises increasingly often use telecommunications channels and means for the purposes of promotion (44% in 2020 against 34% in 2019). In Moscow, entrepreneurs prefer to use *Instagram* and *Facebook* for promotion, while *Vkontakte* seems to be the most popular social media in the regions.

According to entrepreneurs, the main obstacle on the way to the digitalization of business is the lack of money, budget constraints (24%). This was mentioned especially often by entrepreneurs from the regions. Another problem highlighted by the respondents was the lack of interest to digitalization on the part of the heads of companies (14%), their low level of knowledge and skills in digital environment (9%).

5 Discussion and Conclusions

From the conducted studies it follows that the development level of small and medium business in the Russian Federation is much lower than the world level. The problems of Russian small and medium business are aggravated by the unstable economic situation caused by the COVID-19 pandemic. April 2020 was the most difficult month for business. The consumer spending on products and services reduced by 26.2% in comparison with the same period in 2019. Service enterprises proved to be the most vulnerable, especially enterprises operating in the tourism, sports and entertainment sectors. By and large, consumer spending on services fell by 57.7% in comparison with the same period of the previous year. Despite the general insignificant recovery of small and medium business, the number of small and medium enterprises reduced by 3.2% against the previous period.

Under these conditions, the digital maturity and the development level of telecommunications are becoming the major survival factor for small and medium enterprises. A high level of digital literacy was confirmed only by a quarter of respondents. 65% of respondents find it probable that if digital technologies are introduced in the company they work for, it can be the reason for staff reduction. Every fourth employee thinks that they can lose their job if they lack the necessary skills. The level of digital literacy is higher than the national average in Russian capitals (62 against 58 points). The population of the Southern and North Caucasus Federal Districts demonstrate the lowest indicators of digital literacy.

In 2020 the level of digitalization of small and medium enterprises grew up to 50 points against 45 points in 2019. The share of entrepreneurs who have the following beliefs went up: digitalization enhances the comfort of doing business (from 34% to 57%); increases the speed of work (from 33% to 53%); improves client service (from 15% to 22%). 11% of enterprises have a high level of digitalization (70 points and above).

Small and medium enterprises widely use telecommunications when dealing with customers and partners. Social media and messengers are actively used to communicate with customers: every second representative of small and medium business in Russia (47%) has a page on social media, and 80% of them use messengers.

2020 saw a growing number of small and medium enterprises using the technology of the Internet of Things, AI-based technologies and 3D-printing. The internet coverage of companies for doing business reached 94%. Small and medium enterprises are more and more committed to electronic document management and actively use social media and messengers to communicate with clients.

Small and medium enterprises force the use of telecommunications and digital technologies for the purposes of promotion. In 2020 promotion base on digitalization was confirmed by 44% respondents against 34% in 2019. In the capital of the country, entrepreneurs prefer to use *Instagram* and *Facebook* to promote their business, while in the regions *Vkontakte* seems to be the most popular media for promotion. Entrepreneurs believe that the main barriers preventing the use of telecommunications and digitalization in business are the lack of money, budget constraints, insufficient interest in digitalization on the part of the heads of companies, their low level of digital knowledge and skills.

References

1. Alraja, M.N., Hussein, M.A., Ahmed, H.M.S.: What affects digitalization process in developing economies? An evidence from SMEs sector in Oman. Bull. Electr. Eng. Inf. **10**(1), 441–448 (2021). https://doi.org/10.11591/eei.v10i1.2033
2. Andriani, D.P., Aini, A.P.N., Anwar, A.A., Adnandy, R.: Risks analysis on digital platforms adoption to elevate SME businesses in developing country. J. Phys. Conf. Ser. **1569**, 022096 (2020). https://doi.org/10.1088/1742-6596/1569/2/022096
3. Atar, S., Atar, I.: An invited commentary on «The socio-economic implications of the coronavirus and COVID-19 pandemic: a review». Int. J. Surg. **78**, 122 (2020). https://doi.org/10.1016/j.ijsu.2020.04.054
4. Chetty, K., Qigui, L., Gcora, N., Josie, J., Wenwei, L., Fang, C.: Bridging the digital divide: measuring digital literacy. Econimics **12**, 23 (2018). https://doi.org/10.5018/economics-ejournal.ja.2018-23
5. Gössling, S., Scott, D., Michael Hall, C.: Pandemics, tourism and global change: a rapid assessment of COVID-19. J. Sustain. Tour. **29**(1), 1–20 (2020). https://doi.org/10.1080/09669582.2020.1758708
6. Guo, H., Yang, Z., Huang, R., Guo, A.: The digitalization and public crisis responses of small and medium enterprises: implications from a COVID-19 survey. Front. Bus. Res. China **14**, 19 (2020). https://doi.org/10.1186/s11782-020-00087-1
7. Hervé, A., Schmitt, C., Baldegger, R.: Digitalization, entrepreneurial orientation and internationalization of micro-, small- and medium-sized enterprises. Technol. Innov. Manag. Rev. **10**(4), 5–17 (2020). https://doi.org/10.22215/timreview/1343
8. Holtemöller, O., Muradoglu, Y.G.: Corona shutdown and bankruptcy risk. IWH Online, 3/2020, Halle (Saale) (2020). http://hdl.handle.net/10419/219390
9. Jones, P., Comfort, D.: A commentary on the COVID-19 crisis, sustainability and the service industries. J. Publ. Affairs **2020**, e2164 (2020). https://doi.org/10.1002/pa.2164
10. Klein, V.B., Todesco, J.L.: COVID-19 crisis and SMEs responses: the role of digital transformation. Knowl. Process. Manag. **2021**, 1–17 (2021). https://doi.org/10.1002/kpm.1660
11. Kottika, E., et al.: We survived this! What managers could learn from SMEs who successfully navigated the Greek economic crisis. Ind. Mark. Manage. **88**(2020), 352–365 (2020). https://doi.org/10.1016/j.indmarman.2020.05.021
12. Milzam, M., Mahardika, A., Amalia, R.: Corona virus pandemic impact on sales revenue of micro small and medium enterprises (MSMEs) in Pekalongan City. J. Vocat. Stud. Appl. Res. **2**(1), 7–10 (2020). https://doi.org/10.14710/jvsar.2.1.2020.7-10
13. Naushad, M., Sulphey, M.M.: Prioritizing technology adoption dynamics among SMEs. TEM J. **9**(3), 983–991 (2020). https://doi.org/10.18421/TEM93-21
14. Ribeiro-Soriano, D.: Small business and entrepreneurship: their role in economic and social development. J. Entrepr. Reg. Dev. **29**(1–2), 1–3 (2017). https://doi.org/10.1080/08985626.2016.1255438

15. Sharma, N.: COVID-19: challenges and opportunities for small and medium enterprises (SMEs). SSRN Electron. J. (2020). https://doi.org/10.2139/ssrn.3650473
16. Sheresheva, M., Efremova, M., Valitova, L., Polukhina, A., Laptev, G.: Russian tourism enterprises' marketing innovations to meet the COVID-19 challenges. Sustainability **13**(7), 3756 (2021). https://doi.org/10.3390/su13073756
17. Strouhal, J., Horák, J., Bokšová, J.: Corporate perceptions on digitalization of public services: from the perspective of Czech SMEs. WSEAS Trans. Bus. Econ. **18**, 231–236 (2021). https://doi.org/10.37394/23207.2021.18.24
18. Türkes, M.C., Oncioiu, I., Aslam, H.D., Marin-Pantelescu, A., Topor, D.I., Capusneanu, S.: Drivers and barriers in using Industry 4.0: a perspective of SMEs in Romania. Processes **7**(3), 153 (2019). https://doi.org/10.3390/pr7030153
19. Viswanathan, R., Telukdarie, A.: A systems dynamics approach to SME digitalization. Proc. Comput. Sci. **180**(2021), 816–824 (2021). https://doi.org/10.1016/j.procs.2021.01.331
20. The NAFI Analytical Center. The project "Digital economy and Russian companies: level of use and readiness to transfer to digital technologies" [Electronic resource] – Access mode (2020). https://nafi.ru/projects/predprinimatelstvo/tsifrovaya-ekonomika-i-rossiyskie-kompanii/. Accessed 15 Apr 2021
21. The NAFI Analytical Center. The project "Pandemic and transfer of companies to "telecommuting". The digitalization index of small and medium business" [Electronic resource] – Access mode (2020). https://nafi.ru/analytics/pandemiya-i-perekhod-kompaniy-na-udalenku-indeks-tsifrovizatsii-malogo-i-srednego-biznesa/. Accessed 10 Apr 2021
22. Bakhur, V.: Study of Cisco: by 2024 small enterprises will be able to increase global GDP by $2.3 trillion. [Electronic resource] – Access mode (2020). https://www.cnews.ru/news/line/2020-09-15_issledovanie_cisco_k_2024_gmalye. Accessed 10 Apr 2021
23. Unified Register of Small and Medium Enterprises. [Electronic resource] – Access mode (2021). https://rmsp.nalog.ru. Accessed 05 Apr 2021
24. Efremova, M.V., Chkalova, O.V.: Effective development of small and medium enterprises as a factor of economic security of the country. On Guard Econ. **1**(16), 39–47 (2021)
25. Nevmyvaiko, V.P.: Digital tools of Industry 4.0 as a platform for providing dynamic stability of small and medium business. Probl. Mark. Econ. **4**, 137–150 (2020). https://doi.org/10.33051/2500-2325-2020-4-137-150
26. Sberbank, R.F.: Project "SberIndex" [Electronic resource] – Access mode (2021). https://sberindex.ru/ru. Accessed 08 Apr 2021
27. Chuvankova, V.V.: Developing small and medium business in China over 40 years of economic reforms: outcomes and prospects. In: Proceedings of the Conference "40 Years of Economic Reforms in the People's Republic of China", Moscow, 1–2 April 2019, pp. 222–237 (2019)
28. Krasyuk, I., Medvedeva, Y.: Resource support in business analytics of innovative development of trade and technological systems. In: Proceedings of the 33rd International Business Information Management Association Conference, IBIMA 2019: Education Excellence and Innovation Management through Vision 2020, pp. 8807–8817 (2019)
29. Krasyuk, I.A., Medvedeva, Y.Y.: Drivers and obstacles for the development of marketing in Russian retailing. In: Proceedings of the 33rd International Business Information Management Association Conference, IBIMA 2019: Education Excellence and Innovation Management through Vision 2020, pp. 4838–4844 (2019)

Info-Communications-Based Interaction of Companies and Consumers on the Grocery Retail Market

Olga Chkalova[1]($\boxtimes$), Inna Bolshakova[1], Natalia Kopasovskaya[1], Tatyana Nekrasova[2], and Sergey Salkutsan[2]

[1] Lobachevsky State University of Nizhni Novgorod, Nizhni Novgorod, Russian Federation
ochkalova@iee.unn.ru
[2] Peter the Great St. Petersburg Polytechnic University, Saint Petersburg, Russia

Abstract. The paper studies today's conditions for the operation of grocery delivery services on the intensively developing info-communication market. The object of the research is a regional market (Volga Federal District) of grocery e-commerce and delivery. Based on the analysis of some open data on the internet and the results of sociological research, the authors evaluated the competitive situation on the market of grocery delivery services in the region. This study characterizes the development and expansion of services that function based on modern internet communications, including, among other things, the influence of the pandemic. It also reveals the trends for market segmentation. A survey was conducted to determine the degree to which consumers are involved in using innovative services, their readiness to use the latter in future, and the specifics of taking a decision about buying groceries online as a whole or use individual services in particular. The features of an "ideal" grocery delivery service have been identified from the customer's perspective. Such a service should be able to use modern information technology so as to provide the customer with the widest possible range of food products and offer quick and punctual delivery at a minimal delivery price. It is proven that the highest level of penetration has been achieved by universal food product intermediaries who cooperate with offline hypermarkets and express delivery and discount services. The study was carried out independently for consumers who already have experience in buying groceries online and for prospects who do not have this experience yet. The diffusion of innovation theory developed by E. Rogers and the methodology for mapping *brand strength* and building the NPS index were used in the course of the analysis.

Keywords: Info-communications in retail business · Grocery delivery online service · Express delivery · Online grocery retailing · Regional market · Innovation diffusion · Customer attraction and retention · Delivery quality

1   Introduction

The matters of online grocery shopping have been actively researched by various authors starting from about 2009. The studies can be grouped by several categories.

© Springer Nature Switzerland AG 2022
Y. Koucheryavy et al. (Eds.): NEW2AN 2021/ruSMART 2021, LNCS 13158, pp. 122–146, 2022.
https://doi.org/10.1007/978-3-030-97777-1_11

First of all, attention is paid to the first purchase of groceries via internet communications. Thus, the work by Degeratu et al. [1] highlights the benefits customers get if they buy groceries online. Hand et al. [2] determine the factors that influence the decision of customers to buy food products online for the first time. Studies [3] consider the general problems related to the transformation of retailing caused by the digitalization of all trade and technology processes.

Apart from the advantages, researchers study the relative transaction costs incurred by households when they choose between online and offline channels of the same supermarket chain [4] and by the entire society in the course of development of this business segment [5]. According to [6], one of the major obstacles to the development of this business is the inability to use all sensory organs when groceries are chosen via info-communications.

With the growth in grocery e-commerce, it has been more and more important to study the factors that influence the satisfaction of customers with the buying process and their readiness for visiting the websites again [7], the frequency of repeat purchases [8] of both the entire range of groceries and their specific groups such as fresh vegetables and fruit [9]. In particular, [10] points out that online customers find the convenience of placing an order and obtaining the purchase essential. Consequently, the issues [11] arise concerning the development of logistics in the segment of online grocery retailing. That is why logistics is considered to be one of the factors that forms customer loyalty [12].

It should be noted that the authors do not come to a single opinion about how the revealed factors must be ranked, but instead focus on studying how each of these factors affects the purchase process. Studies are carried out both about all food products as a whole [13] and about individual specific groups [14]. The specifics of e-commerce development of individual groups of groceries were also investigated by [15, 16] and [17].

Over the last years, the focus of studies is shifting towards more global matters. These matters include, for example, development of a model of the modern "responsible, digital and smart consumer". The main features of buying behavior are defined in this model [18]. Chinese experts Wang and Somogyi [19] evaluate the ratio of early adopters and conservative buyers of online groceries in large Chinese cities. The work by Wang et al. [20] proves that online and offline markets refer to different business models, require different approaches on the part of entrepreneurs – brand owners and call for a new differentiated product on the internet. The attempts to build a conceptual marketing model of online grocery retailing, which reflects consumers' behavioral patterns in this segment, can be considered the outcome of many studies, carried out by authors, for example, such as: Khandpur et al. [21]. In parallel with the research of online grocery retailing, studies are conducted to learn about the ready meal delivery market [22] and express deliveries of ready meals [23].

The events of year 2020 connected with the COVID-19 pandemic activated the growth of the retail market based on modern info-communications as a whole and grocery retail market, in particular. Now, studying about what stimulates consumers to turn to online purchases is often substituted with investigating the reasons why some consumers still reject the opportunity [24]. However, new internet communications appear on the grocery online retail market all the time (express delivery, marketplaces etc. entering the market), capturing new and new territories. In the process of their development, regional patterns become quite obvious.

The study presented below is aimed at researching the dynamics and trends of the grocery retail market based on modern info-communications in the provincial regions of Russia (in particular, Volga Federal District). It also investigates the factors that influence the behavior of the consumers of such services and the behavior of those who still refuse to use them.

It should be noted that in this paper the term "delivery service" is used to refer to the: a) logistic divisions of offline retail chains which deliver groceries; b) subsidiaries of offline food retail chains, which were set up to do deliveries and are separated organizationally from their parent company; c) retail chains that have no offline outlets and only do deliveries from a warehouse (dark store); d) logistic intermediaries that deliver orders from shops of some retail chains.

The authors began to study the regional online grocery retail market for the first time in the early 2019. At that moment, most of the more or less significant services of this kind were concentrated in Moscow, St. Petersburg, Moscow and Leningrad Oblasts. These services were presented to a minor extent in VFD, including Nizhny Novgorod and Tatarstan: the regional chain SPAR in Nizhny Novgorod and igooods, a company from St. Petersburg, which was expanding its activities in Kazan.

Other deliveries of orders were most often carried out by diverse local companies, whose common distinction was a really small turnover and unclear development prospects. Up to the first half of 2020, it made sense only to speak about the percentage of provincial customers who were aware, in principle, of the possibility of buying groceries online. Only few federal delivery services, which were gradually penetrating the regions, could somehow affect the market. The first signs of this process could be observed at the end of 2019. However, the pandemic spurred the process dramatically in 2020.

In the time of the pandemic, the development of the grocery delivery market has become explosive not only in terms of the number of orders, new customers and turnovers, but also in terms of the variety of delivery channels. This paper considers only the delivery of the range of products that is similar to the assortment of a usual super- or hypermarket. The research does not take into account the delivery of non-food products such as, for instance: clothes, footwear, furniture and ready meals.

However, despite these limitations, we can observe a large variety of business models used by services, which are developing now not just in the capital cities, but also in provincial regions. Today customers in these regions can be quite rightly asked if they know about these diverse possibilities, whether they use one service all the time or change them depending on the situation, what are the reasons for their behaving in one way or another as they select a delivery service.

The aim of the research is to identify and analyze the specifics of consumers' behavior in provincial regions when it comes to buying groceries using modern internet-communications of delivery services, and to evaluate the depth of penetration of these services and the patterns their work.

The object of the research is a regional (Volga Federal District, Russia – VRD) market of e-commerce and delivery of food products, including customers living in the cities and towns of the region who buy or can buy groceries online and the services (delivery services) that sell and deliver food products.

The objectives of the research include giving the characteristics of the online grocery retail market in VFD, identifying the 2020 major trends and competitors on the regional market; finding out about the attitudes consumers have towards the possibility of buying groceries online as a whole and to the delivery services available in the region, in particular; defining the difference in the attitude to buying food products online among two main groups of consumers (those who have and those who do not have experience in making such purchases).

2   Research Methodology

The study uses the data about consumers living in Volga Federal District of Russia and the delivery services operating in this region. Volga Federal District was chosen to study the issues of market development outside the capital regions (Moscow, St. Petersburg, Moscow and Leningrad Regions), where we can observe a higher level of innovation spread, larger concentrations of population, including urban population and bigger incomes per capita. Although it is not a capital region, VFD is located relatively close to the capitals and accounts for 29 million inhabitants with almost three quarters of them living in cities and towns. The region has 5 cities whose population exceeds one million and 8 cities with more than 500,000 inhabitants. The natural conditions and the development of the transportation system make it possible to quickly deliver goods to smaller settlements as well.

In order to investigate the market, the presence of delivery services in VFD regions was analyzed focusing on the time when these services appeared on this territory. For this purpose, the authors monitored the websites of the delivery services, their mobile applications and advertising materials in the local press that contained data on the regions of operation. For the goals of the research all delivery services were divided into "new" ones, which came to the market since the end of 2019, and the "old" ones, operating on the VFD market in the early 2019.

In order to study the specific attitudes of the region's consumers to buying groceries online, a survey was conducted.

The survey was carried out in February–March 2021. Given the events of year 2020, it can be stated that by the time of the survey all the respondents had already faced the need to buy groceries in unusual conditions, since tight quarantine regulations were enforced in all big cities of VFD for quite a while. Food could be bought online in all the cities included in the survey because grocery delivery services appeared there before early 2020 and actively grew afterwards. The information about the work of delivery services was increasingly available as in 2020 many of them ran promotion campaigns and were the objects of news reports.

Thus, in any case, by early 2021 the respondents had to have some attitude towards buying food online using modern internet communications: thanks to their own experience, their friends' experience or the influence of mass media. Respondents from two largest cities in the region (Nizhny Novgorod and Kazan) and cities with population around 500,000 (Penza and Kirov) took part in the survey. 284 people were interviewed. All the respondents were divided into two groups and received different variants of questionnaires, one for those who had experience in buying groceries online and one for those who did not.

In order to evaluate the penetration of the innovative form of commerce into the region, the model developed by E. Rogers was used. The model suggests customer segmentation into groups of Innovators, Early Adopters, Early Majority, Late Majority, and Laggards. The conclusion about the quantity of consumers involved in the market was made based on the analysis of the following question from the questionnaire: "Have you ever used a grocery delivery service? for the entire VFD and for its individual regions. Apart from the direct analysis of the questionnaire results, several standardized techniques were used to evaluate the brand strength, awareness and loyalty of delivery services: brand strength mapping and NPS index.

3   Discussion

3.1   Competitive Situation on the Market

Stronger competition on the grocery delivery market becomes obvious after some data were generalized about the appearance of new services in the regions in late 2019–2020 (Table 1). Over this period VFD saw 6 new delivery services, which altogether opened 36 regional branches.

It is obvious that the penetration of Sbermarket to the region had been planned and started in the late fall of 2019, when about 10 cities around Russia, including Kazan, Nizhny Novgorod, Samara and Ufa, were chosen for the first stage of expansion of the service. Today, Sbermarket is presented in all 14 regions of VFD. Its further growth since spring 2020 is due to smaller cities and towns of the region (Togliatti, Orsk, Sterlitamak, Engels, Dzerzhinsk, Kstovo). Except for Togliatti, whose population amounts to 700,000 people, all the other cities and towns have population fewer than 250,000 people. Every other service, independently on their ideas of promotion in the regions actually started the process only in April 2020 with the advent of lockdown. Now, in the early 2021, the process is going on. In particular, igooods service is getting ready to be launched in Nizhny Novgorod.

In most cases the above six services were launched on the market of VFD not in a uniform way. As can be seen from Table 2, the biggest coverage of the regions at the end of 2020 was demonstrated by Sbermarket and Lentochka, while Samokat and Yandex.Lavka went outside the limits of the capital regions only in the third quarter of 2020 and have just 3 representative offices altogether in VFD. The regions where the competition between large delivery services is the strongest are Nizhny Novgorod Region and Tatarstan. At the same time, one should not forget that apart from the six new services, some other services (igooods, SPAR) have been operating here since 2017–2018.

In Moscow, Sbermarket offers its customers delivery from over 10 companies, which include not just supermarkets. In the province, the region is usually switched to 2–4 chains, like METRO, Lenta, Auchan, O'Key. In some rare cases, there can be other profile

Table 1. Spread of grocery delivery services in the regions of VFD in late 2019–2020[a]

Period	Delivery service	Growth in the number of regions where the service is active, units
4 Quarter 2019	Sbermarket	4
1 Quarter 2020	Sbermarket	5
2 Quarter 2020	Sbermarket	5
	Pyaterochka.Dostavka	1
3 Quarter 2020	Perekrestok.Vprok	1
	Samokat	1
	Yandex.Lavka	1
	Pyaterochka.Dostavka	1
	Lentochka	12
4 Quarter 2020	Perekrestok.Vprok	2
	Samokat	1
	Pyaterochka.Dostavka	2
Total	6 Services	36

[a]Compiled by the authors using data from open publications

Table 2. Number of new delivery services in the VFD regions (late 2019–early 2021)[a]

Region	Sbermarket	Pyaterochka	Perekrestok	Lentochka	Samokat	Yandex.Lavka	Total
Bashkiria	+	+		+			3
Kirov Oblast	+						1
Mary-El	+			+			2
Mordovia	+			+			2
Nizhny Novgorod Oblast	+	+	+	+	+	+	6
Orenburg Oblast	+			+			2
Penza Oblast	+			+			2
Perm Krai	+						1
Samara Oblast	+	+		+			3
Saratov Oblast	+			+			2
Tatarstan	+	+	+	+	+		5
Udmurtia	+			+			2
Ulyanovsk Oblast	+			+			2
Chuvashia	+		+	+			3
Total	14	4	3	12	2	1	36

shops: children's shop Dochki-Sinochki in Nizhny Novgorod, pet shop "Beethoven" in Togliatti. Infrequently, some local chains of grocery stores become the partners of Sbermarket: "Semia" (Perm Krai), Bakhetle (Tatarstan).

Having strengthened its positions in the regional centers, Sbermarket has been spreading its services on other cities in the regions since as early as April–May 2020. Other delivery services, which are not yet present in all the regions, are also following this path. At the moment, delivery is usually spread, with an exception of regional centers, either on territories closest to the main city in the region or on the largest cities in the region. Thus, in Nizhny Novgorod, which has just one really large center, delivery services (Sbermarket, Perekrestok, Samokat) embrace, to a certain degree, its satellite cities (Dzerzhinsk, Bor, Kstovo) or can move from them along the main routes (Bogorodsk, Gorokhovets, Gorodets). In Samara Region, differently from Nizhny Novgorod Region, delivery services actively operate in Samara, Novokuibyshevsk (located close to Samara), Togliatti (located relatively far from Samara but has a comparable population).

In the nearest time we are likely to witness further movement of online grocery retailing inside the regions and the issue of selecting and switching between grocery delivery services is going to become important for those who live in small provincial towns too.

The grocery delivery services can be categorized according to the following characteristics: ownership of the channel (retailer's own channel, intermediary's channel); number of channels (one or many); delivery time in the channel (usual delivery, express delivery), delivery transport (automobile or foot (bicycle) delivery); assembly place of delivery (dark stores, shops).

The biggest role for choosing one or another service by the consumer is played by the ownership of the channel and delivery time. Delivery transport is closely connected with time and determines the radius of delivery coverage. The assembly place has an indirect impact on the consumer's choice.

Ownership and number of channels. Using one's own channel implies that there is a clearly defined point of interaction between the customer and the shop. Most frequently this is a branded mobile application which can be combined with a website. Applications like this are used by X5 Retail Group (Perekrestok.Vprok, Pyaterochka.Dostavka), Lenta (Lentochka), VkusVill, SPAR (Moi SPAR), Auchan. The applications and websites can be easily found by the name of the store where a purchase is desired. X5 Retail Group and SPAR only use their own delivery service and receive orders via their own websites and applications. But at least two more options are possible.

First of all, Samokat and Yandex.Lavka services use their own delivery service and mobile applications, but an order can be placed through aggregators: Delivery Club for Samokat and Yandex.Eda for Yandex.Lavka. Here aggregators act rather as information intermediaries.

Secondly, many chains combine their own service and services of intermediaries. Thus, VkusVill started by developing its own service, but during the pandemic has been actively using the help of diverse intermediaries. On the contrary, Lenta has been working with intermediaries for a long time and began forming its own delivery service called Lentochka only since April 2020.

When intermediaries (usually several ones) are involved, the number of points of interaction with the consumer in the process of an order gets quite big. For example, in Nizhny Novgorod you can order goods from the Auchan hypermarket chain not only via the company's website and application, but also via the websites or applications of Sbermarket or Delivery Club. In Kazan, products from Auchan can also be bought through igooods. In this case the consumer does not have to download the applications of various stores. Using the application or the website of an intermediary you can easily click links to move from Auchan to Lenta or O'Key. Thus, the delivery services functioning in this sector have not worked out any clear and beneficial operating schemes for themselves. Just having started their way the companies are forever experimenting, looking for new projects, because it is still too difficult to evaluate the efficiency of such solutions.

Delivery time and transport. The delivery time in a channel is a sign according to which the market can be divided into two segments: regular and express delivery. Committing to one of the kinds determines not only the time interval of delivery but also the radius of delivery, the size of an order and average check. At the end of the day, it is about two types of living situations in which the consumer can make different decisions about the delivery service he or she chooses.

Regular delivery implies a time interval of about 2 h. Delivery is carried out using automobile transport. If the company has a threshold of free delivery, it is rather big. Such services can be provided either through the company's own shops or through intermediaries. An order in this case is an alternative to going to a large supermarket, which does not happen too often. This scheme is used by Perekrestok.Vprok, Sbermarket, igooods, etc.

Express delivery is well known in selling ready meals. But express delivery of groceries from a shop is a far more recent phenomenon. The best known services operating on the territory of VFD are Yandex.Lavka and Samokat. The delivery time interval in this case reduces down to 30 min. If the location is convenient, delivery time can be even less (about 15 min). Delivery is carried out by couriers going on foot or riding a bicycle. At the time of peak loads during lockdown, in some cities companies could cooperate with car-sharing firms or use drivers from Yandex.Taxi (Yandex.Lavka).

A foot-mobile courier cannot be used to deliver a very large order. In this case the volume of delivery is limited to approximately 10 kilos. Such services are more like visiting a shop next door. The demand for such orders is felt by many sellers. Thus, Perekrestok, in addition to the Perekrestok.Vprok service, is trying to develop Perekrestok.Bystro (rus. Perekrestok.Prompt), although foot-mobile couriers are not necessarily going to be involved in this project.

It can be assumed that the services that do not specialize in express delivery are going to try to fill this niche working towards reducing the delivery time. For example, in Kazan and Nizhny Novgorod Pyaterochka.Dostavka, Lentochka and Sbermarket are striving for minimizing the delivery time, noting on their websites that in case of low workload of the transportation system and smaller number of orders, delivery is possible within one hour. Trying to be as transparent as possible for its online customer, Pyaterochka.Dostavka shows on its website the exact time when the order is placed and will be delivered, down to minutes.

The assembly place of an order is not obvious and often unknown by the consumer. No clear dependence is observed between the classification of a service by first four characteristics and the assembly place. Thus, Perekrestok.Vprok assembles orders at dark stores, while SPAR, which has put the stake on its own delivery service, collects orders from its own shop. If customers visit aggregator websites, they simultaneously see Samokat, which works from dark stores, and Lenta, which assembles groceries directly in its shop. Perekrestok delivers goods in a 2 h's interval while Samokat, which also uses dark stores, does it in time less than 30 min.

3.2 Customer Attraction to the Online Grocery Delivery Market

In spite of the active introduction of online grocery delivery services, by the moment of the survey only 44.7% of urban population in VFD noted that they had used such services. Diffusion or spread of the innovative form of servicing on the market under consideration is far from being over. The groups of Innovators (2.5%), Early Adopters (13.5%) and Early Majority must amount to the total of 50% of prospective consumers. Thus, it can be said that Innovators, Early Adopters and a considerable part of Early Majority have already been attracted to the online grocery delivery market (Fig. 1). The Innovators were placing online orders for groceries as early as in 2018–2019, the Early Majority was stimulated to do so by the pandemic and quarantine.

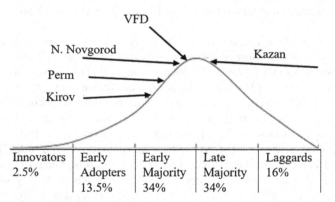

Fig. 1. Diffusion of innovations on the online grocery delivery market (VFD)

The respondents who in early 2021 had not yet placed online orders for groceries refer to the Late Majority and Laggards. It could be expected that older people will prevail in this consumer category as they are less used to applying modern technologies and more conservative. In reality, no clear divide by age is observed. For example, 53,1% of the respondents aged 18–30 have never bought groceries online, while this figure is almost the same for those who are aged 46–55 (57.1%). In all age groups the proportion of consumers that have no experience in placing online orders for groceries is over 50%.

Nevertheless, there is differentiation by cities. The smallest number of respondents who have no experience in buying groceries on the internet is in Nizhny Novgorod

(52.67%) and Kazan (43.75%). As can be seen from Table 2, it is Nizhny Novgorod and the Republic of Tatarstan where the biggest number of delivery services operate. Thus, 47.33% and 56.25% of prospective consumers, respectively, are attracted to the market in these cities, including some proportion of Late Majority in Kazan. In Perm 61.54% of people have not bought groceries online, while in Kirov this figure is 71.14%. In these regions the activity of delivery services is lower, so 38.46% and 28.86% of consumers, i.e. not even all Early Majority have been attracted to the market yet (Fig. 1).

3.3 Analyzing Consumers Who Have no Experience in Buying Groceries Online

Awareness. Even the Late Majority and Laggards could not but hear of grocery delivery services or at least see their advertisement once. High spontaneous brand recognition is a major competitive advantage in the life cycle of any enterprise. Strong brand awareness can be demonstrated both by those customers who have experience in using this brand and by those who do not. Customers who have no experience in buying the product, but who show strong brand awareness are extremely important. According to the brand recognition theory, a high indicator (over 50%) by this criterion says in favor of the fact that customers perceive the brand as one of the leaders in the industry. These customers are likely to use the goods of this brand in the long term. The evaluation of spontaneous recognition demonstrated by the respondents who have no experience in online buying has shown as follows.

Only 11.18% of the respondents could not choose any name from the list suggested. The older the respondent, the more chances that he or she finds it hard to do this task. Among the respondents aged 18–30, this answer was given by just 6.32%, those aged 31–45 – 12.00%, aged 46–65 – 29.41%, aged over 65 – 60.00%.

Those who could choose the services they know from the list gave 5–6 names on average. Virtually nobody used the possibility of supplementing the list. Table 3 illustrates the distribution of answers regarding the services that proved most popular among the respondents.

Table 3. Awareness about grocery delivery services among customers who have no experience in buying food products online[a]

City	Sbermarket	Pyaterochka	MySPAR	Vkus-Vill	Express Delivery	
					Samokat	Yandex Lavka
N.Novgorod	65.22	44.93	30.43	30.43	75.36	66.67
Penza	65.63	37.50	25.00	43.75	*6.25*	*37.50*
Kazan	57.14	57.14	21.43	21.43	35.71	*28.57*

[a]Each respondent could choose more than 1 answer. The delivery services that did not operate in the relevant cities at the time of the survey are italicized.

The respondents who have never bought groceries online most frequently mention Sbermarket (57–65%), which was actively entering the regions in 2020 and accompanied this process with a massive promotion campaign. It is worth mentioning the fact that express delivery services are known not only in the cities where they operate. Thus, Samokat is absent from Penza, but some respondents (6.25%) still know about this company. Yandex.Lavka does not work in Kazan and Penza and is less known there than in Nizhny Novgorod. But due to the support of an internet giant such as Yandex, it is much more recognizable than Samokat in these cities.

Market places such as Ozon, Wildberries and AliExpress should be highlighted separately. These services used to offer groceries with long life shelf. However, on the wave of increased demand for fresh food products, they took an attempt to enter the quickly-growing market. Ozon set up the OzonExpress division, which delivers fresh food products in Moscow and Moscow Region. AliExpress launched the AliExpressEst! application, integrated with the main application of the company. Wildberries only at the end of 2020 announced the possibility of delivering fresh groceries in Moscow and Moscow Region.

Nevertheless, the brands of market places are well-recognized and the respondents point them together with the services specializing in delivering groceries. Out of 16 names of delivery services, Ozon and Wildberries end up with equal results at places 4–5, AliExpress at place 7. Moreover, 7.9% of respondents pointed out only these three market places (one or several) as grocery delivery services they are familiar with.

On the one hand, it means that consumers are ready to accept the reality in which the well-known market places also deliver groceries. It is quite possible that customers will find it convenient to place complex orders including food and non-food products in the service they know very well.

On the other hand, if a brand is well-know, it can also lead to a stable negative experience. The most common answer (leaving far behind every other name) to the question "Which delivery service would you never buy groceries from?" was "AliExpress" (26.97%). The reasons for such an attitude are the lack of trust, negative reviews, lack of associations with the delivery of groceries, supposedly long delivery time. In more than a half of cases (57%), the reason is the lack of offline shops of the company where customers could get acquainted with the products.

Such claims are not made against Ozon and Wildberries, which do not have any offline shops too. It is obvious that customers expect to find here food products of the brands that they know very well. AliExpress is, to a larger extent, associated with lesser-known shops, many of which are outside Russia. In order to attract consumers, the market place will have to fight these associations. Thus, now AliExpress emphasizes in its advertising that with the opening of the Russian branch of AliExpress, the delivery time is going to reduce considerably. The respondents were asked to point out one service where they are most likely to place an online order for groceries (Table 4).

Table 4. Readiness for placing a grocery order online in a specific delivery service as % of the number of the respondents

Name	Nizhny Novgorod	Penza	Kazan	Total
Sbermarket	14.04	18.75	21.43	15.13
Yandex.Lavka	26.32	6.25	7.14	13.82
MySPAR	15.79	9.38	7.14	10.53
Samokat	15.79	3.13	0.00	8.55
Pyaterochka.Dostavka	5.26	15.63	14.29	6.58
Auchan	7.02	3.13	0.00	5.92
Have difficulty in answering	21.05	15.63	28.57	20.39

The outcomes of the answer to the question about which services the respondents know are given above (Table 3). However, in the first case the respondents named several services independently on their level of trust in them. Here, when choosing the most probable place for the first online purchase, only one name had to be given. Nevertheless, it is obvious that the selection of the most mentioned services in both cases is approximately the same: Sbermarket, Yandex.Lavka, MySpar, Samokat, Pyaterochka.Dostavka. I.e. the consumers who have no experience in buying groceries online draw a clear parallel between the awareness of the delivery service and their readiness to make their first purchase in it. Thus, a comparatively higher indicator of brand awareness is a major competitive advantage from the perspective of sales market expansion by the owner of this brand.

From the regional perspective, it is seen that in Nizhny Novgorod, which has virtually become a pilot region for express delivery services, trust in Yandex.Lavka and Samokat is much bigger. MySPAR, which was the first company to operate in the region, long before the advent of large federal services, is also popular. In Kazan and Penza consumers prefer Sbermarket and Pyaterochka. Perhaps, this picture will change after express services become more active in these regions.

Choosing the service. What can encourage consumers to try to buy groceries online? Among the respondents, 7.9% (Table 5) claim that they will never buy food products on the internet. The age of the respondents does not affect this answer significantly. Each age group contains about 7–12% of people of this kind.

The youngest of the prospective consumers point out that their interest in buying food products online is going to grow if they are sure that they can save money (60% of the respondents aged under 18% and 22.1% of the respondent aged 18–30). For the older respondents, the quality of goods comes to the first place (36.0% of the respondents aged 31–45 and 41.2% of the respondents aged 46–65). Those older than that found it hard to answer this question.

In terms of groceries, most of the consumers (61.84%) prefer door-to-door delivery. Another 14% are ready to use various means of receiving an order depending on the situation. Ways of delivery that are common for the non-food sector such as drop boxes and postamats are rarely mentioned when it comes to the delivery of groceries.

Table 5. Factors increasing consumer interest in delivery services, % of the respondents[a]

Factor	Share of respondents	Age group, years old				
		Under 18	18–30	31–45	46–65	Over 65
Precision of order fulfilment	6.6	0.0	6.3	16.0	0.0	0.0
Quality	25.7	**20.0**	**21.1**	*36.0*	*41.2*	**20.0**
Economy	23.7	*60.0*	*22.1*	20.0	17.6	**20.0**
Wide range of products	9.2	0.0	14.7	0.0	0.0	0.0
Help with first order	2.0	0.0	3.2	0.0	0.0	0.0
Big size/weight of order	11.2	0.0	13.7	8.0	11.8	0.0
Have difficulty in answering	13.8	10.0	11.6	12.0	**17.6**	*60.0*
Never	7.9	10.0	7.4	8.0	11.8	0.0
Total	100.0	100.0	100.0	100.0	100.0	100.0

[a]Positions in the first place in this age group are marked in bold-italicized, positions in the second place in this age group are marked in bold.

Under today's conditions, the respondents who have never bought groceries online (for any reason), independently on their intentions, may end up in a situation when online purchase is going to be the best solution (quarantine, illness, inability to leave a small child or an elderly person at home, intensive remote work, etc.). In this situation the customer will have to take specific decisions and clearly choose an algorithm of actions.

Answering the question "Your actions in case you need to buy groceries online", the majority of consumers (34.87%) choose an option to use the delivery service of the offline shop they know well (Table 6). This result correlates with the data from Table 5, where trust in the quality and ability of saving money take the first positions among the factors that increase interest in buying groceries online. Buying from the delivery service of a well-known shop, the consumer is familiar with the quality of most of the assortment and with the most advantageous items, which is why they feel more sure when placing an order.

Selecting options 2, 4, 5, the consumer gives preference to external information and somebody else's experience rather than their own one. Consumers are more inclined to trust their friends in this respect (27.63%), rather than advertising (8.55%) or information on the internet (4.61%). Thus, those who have never placed online orders for groceries manifest themselves as quite conservative, distrustful and suspicious. They know about the presence of delivery services (Table 3), including the services operating in the settlement where they live and express their readiness to place an order in one of the services in case of need (Table 4), predominantly pointing out those services that

Table 6. Actions of consumers in case they need to buy groceries online

Order will be placed in the:	Share of respondents, %
1. Delivery service of the shop where I usually buy offline	34.87
2. Service recommended by friends	27.63
3. Service with a high level of the most important parameter (range of products, price, delivery time, etc.)	13.82
4. Service advertised most actively	8.55
5. Service having the best reviews on the internet	4.61
6. Only available service in my region	3.95
7. Service in the first link to the enquiry "buying groceries online in the city of …"	2.63
8. Service having offline food stores	2.63
9. Via the mobile application of the offline shop chain installed earlier and having the feature of online order placing	0.66
10. Have difficulty in answering	0.66
Total	100

sound familiar to the majority of consumers. But in reality, they will place an order either based on their offline experience, or following their friends' recommendations.

3.4 Analyzing Consumers Who Have Experience in Buying Groceries Online

Brand awareness or popularity in the consumer environment does not always shape customers' actions in terms of their choice of place for a purchase. For example, 63% of the interviewed online customers in Kazan and 70% of the interviewed online customers in Nizhny Novgorod pointed out that they know Sbermarket brand, but only 25% in Kazan and 20% in Nizhny Novgorod have bought from it (Table 7).

The brand awareness of Pyaterochka.Dostavka is not so general. About 56% of the respondents from Kazan pointed out that they know this brand, but purchases were made there by virtually everybody who said that they know this brand, i.e. every second respondent from Kazan. Citizens of Nizhny Novgorod do not know MySPAR, Pyaterochka.Dostavka, Perekrestok.Vprok (56%, 49% and 37%, respectively) as well as, for example, Sbermarket. However, it does not prevent them from actively buying from these services. Sbermarket is known by 70% of the respondents, but only 20% of them used its serveces. For MySPAR these figures are 56% and 34%, respectively.

In order to evaluate the attractiveness of the grocery delivery services for customers, a Brand Strength Map was drawn for the VFD market (this method can be also called Conversion-Retention Map, Attraction Index Vs Retention Index). Brand Strength shows how well customers know a trademark. With all the subjectivity of this concept, it can still be measured and evaluated through the degree of "advancement" of the brand on a certain market. For this purpose, the degree of brand awareness and the degree of

Table 7. Comparative analysis of the degree of brand awareness and customer attraction to various delivery sectors in Kazan and Nizhny Novgorod, %

Name	Kazan			Nizhny Novgorod		
	Know	Placed orders	Placed orders most frequently	Know	Placed orders	Placed orders most frequently
Auchan	44	–	–	44	9	3
VkusVill	38	6	–	34	9	3
Lentochka	19	–	–	25	5	–
MySPAR	38	6	–	56	34	14
Perekrestok Vprok	19	–	–	37	22	5
Pyaterochka. Dostavka	56	50	31	49	25	12
Sbermarket	63	25	6	70	20	7
Samokat	81	44	31	76	44	26

involvement in buying this brand are measured among the customers on the market. As a rule, customer attraction is understood as the share of those who buy the brand among those who are familiar with it, while customer retention is believed to be the proportion of those who choose the brand more frequently among those who have ever bought it. This model can be used by companies to work out the strategy for expanding the sales market, focusing either on increasing brand awareness or on intensifying sales.

The matrix was built using the following data: number of the respondents who know the brand (X); number of the respondents from the set X who have bought groceries from this brand (Y), number of the respondents from the set Y who have bought from this brand more frequently (Z). Then the customer attraction coefficient is defined as Y/X ratio and the customer retention coefficient as Z/Y ratio.

According to the results of estimation, the Brand Strength Map was drawn to demonstrate the position of each brand from the perspective of attraction and retention (Fig. 2). The red line in the figure shows the average value of the indicator given the totality of the indicator values obtained in this research. For brand "attraction", the average indicator is 16%, while for brand "retention", it is 45%. It should be noted that the figure 16% means that the average share of those who made purchases among the consumers knowing about the online grocery services we consider is just 16%. Thus, despite the pandemic and growing demand for online purchases, selling groceries via the internet is still a relatively narrow market for many brands, which attracts a limited number of customers in VFD cities.

The estimates above show that brands such as Samokat and Pyaterochka.Dostavka have the highest Customer Attraction and Retention indicators and so they are the

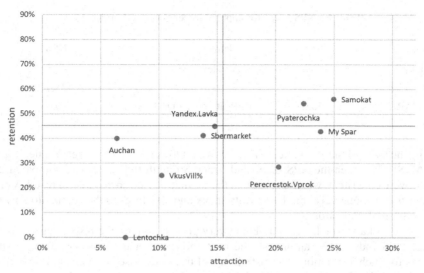

Fig. 2. Brand Strength Map of the delivery service market in VFD

strongest. Samokat has both the highest Brand Attraction indicator (the share of customers among those who are familiar with the brand is 25%) and Brand Retention indicator (the share of customers who most frequently buy from these brand is 56%).

Yandex.Lavka takes a marginal position, which makes it a niche service in the matrix. Indeed, this brand operates in few VFD regions and insignificantly increased the number of its representations over the period considered. So far it is relatively less attractive for customers (the share of those who buy from it is 15% in the total number of those who know the brand), but its Customer Retention Indicator is higher than that of many other brands (45%). MySPAR is close to the leader group. It has a very good Customer Attraction Indicator (24%), but its retention strength is weaker than that of the leaders. Probably, more efforts to stimulate sales should be taken.

Sbermarket service is also close to a marginal position. It can be suggested that Sbermarket just taking a little effort might quickly join the group of leaders. Perekrestok.Vprok, the same as MySPAR is an "attracting" brand. This company is able to persuade a relatively large number of consumers to order groceries from its delivery service, but it finds it hard, in comparison with the leaders, to retain loyalty. The services that fall behind by the Retention and Attraction Indicators are Auchan, VkusVill, Lentochka and, to a smaller degree, Sbermarket.

NPS Index was selected as another method to measure brand attraction (Table 8). This indicator was calculated by estimating the share of "Promoters" (choosing 9–10 points) and the share of "Critics" (choosing 0–6 points) in the answer to the question "To what extent are you ready to recommend this service to your friends and family on a scale from 1 to 10?". The difference between the share of Promoters and the share of Critics is the value of the index.

When the NPS Index is used to measure the degree of customer loyalty for the most popular grocery delivery services, it can be found out that Samokat has the highest index

Table 8. NPS Index for popular grocery delivery services, %

Name	NPS	Name	NPS
Samokat	66.6	Yandex.Lavka	44.5
Sbermarket	57.1	Perekrestok.Vprok	25.0
MySPAR	50.0	Pyaterochka.Dostavka	0.0

among the users of these services. The NPS is a bit lower for Sbermarket, Yandex.Lavka and MySPAR. When the NPS Index and Brand Strength Indicator were compared, the results were consistent, which proves that the estimations are correct. Perekrestok.Vprok demonstrates a relatively smaller Loyalty Index and also loses to the competitors by the Brand Strength Indicator.

Pyaterochka.Dostavka, despite being very popular among the respondents, has the lowest NPS Index (0%) among all the other brands. Let us consider some possible reasons for such a situation. The NPS Index of this enterprise is relatively low both on the online and offline markets. It has been pointed out many times by the press that the NPS Index is considerably lower for discounters than other chain retailers operating in Russia [24, 25]. Thus, it can be concluded that the customers' opinion has been affected by the stable image of a discounter enterprise in offline sales.

As mentioned above, Pyaterochka.Dostavka does not operate in Penza Region. However, the respondents pointed out that they make purchases there. The analysis of the market showed that some services delivering groceries from Pyaterochka and having a similar name work in Penza (v-5 ka.ru, dostavka-produktov-dom.ru/pyaterochka etc.). Inexperienced in the field of grocery deliveries, the respondents pointed out that they bought groceries online in Pyaterochka.Dostavka, whereas in reality they placed orders on the websites of Pyaterochka's local partners. As a rule, such delivery services operate quite independently on the local market and the main brand (like Pyaterochka) cannot be directly responsible for the quality of such services. This may worsen the brand reputation on the online market and reduce its competitiveness.

The awareness of a seller's brand and its image can play both a positive and a negative role when a decision about buying or not buying is taken. The less controllable the grocery delivery process is on the part on a brand, the higher the risk of forming a negative attitude on the customer's mind. So when they work with partnership delivery services, brand owners must meticulously monitor the quality of work provided by these delivery services.

When the attraction of various brands is analyzed from the perspective of customer age (Table 9), it is seen that the share of respondents aged over 30 most frequently choosing Samokat as a grocery delivery service is almost equal to the share of the youth choosing the same service in its age group (35.3% aged over 30 and 38.5% aged not older than 30).

Samokat is an express service for delivering groceries and has specific characteristics by the size of an order and the range of products. The popularity of Samokat, independently on the age characteristics means that the respondents in different age groups are

Table 9. Distribution of respondents' answers to the question "Where exactly have you placed an order for groceries most frequently? (age groups), %

Name	Age group		Name	Age group	
	Under 30	Over 30		Under 30	Over 30
Samokat	38.5	35.3	Perekrestok.Vprok	5.1	11.8
Pyaterochka.Dostavka	25.6	17.7	Auchan	5.1	0.0
Yandex.Lavka	20.5	0.0	VkusVill	2.6	5.9
My SPAR	12.8	17.6	Other	0.0	11.8
Sbermarket	18.0	0.0	Total	100.0	100.0

more likely to buy online in a situation when they need groceries as fast as possible. At the same time, a big food basket is not demanded by them, as might be expected.

The respondents over 30 years old pointed out Pyaterochka.Dostavka and MySPAR as the delivery services where they tend to buy groceries. This trend is getting even more noticeable when the respondents aged over 46 are interviewed. 55% and 32% of the respondents aged over 30 know about Sbermarket and Yandex.Lavka, respectively. This means that the older generation is more inclined to trust in the well-known brands that have offline chains of shops.

The youth aged 30 or under use delivery services such as Yandex.Lavka, Sbermarket and Auchan to buy groceries more often than other services. Consequently, younger customers, differently from the older generation, are more likely to trust new online grocery retail companies. It can be even assumed that such customers have less experience in filling their food basket and rely on their offline buying experience to a lesser extent.

Thus, the study proves that brand awareness has a decisive significance when the first purchase of groceries is made online. When choosing a service, prospective customers rely on the knowledge they have about the market of grocery sellers and on their knowledge of the offline market. However, as customers gain experience in buying online and become more conscious of some factors such as delivery time, range of products, delivery quality, price, etc., they may change their preferences towards brands that may be less known but capable of meeting their specific online requirements.

In order to study the enquiries of consumers on delivery services, the respondents were asked a question about what they mean by saying "the best grocery delivery service". It turned out that, first of all, the customers would like the service to have free delivery and keep the average level of food prices (53% of all answers), as well as to offer the widest range of groceries possible (47%). "The best service" should have the best quality of delivery, i.e. deliver groceries promptly and on time (50% of all answers). The reasons that can make the customer reject their regular delivery service or the service they have used at least once were also studied. The answers of the respondents well fit the model of today's (very spoilt) customer, who is not ready to put up with the errors in the work of a service (inconsistency with the quality of products, the quality of delivery and return policy).

Facing the question "Which delivery service would you never use to buy groceries?" 68% of the older age group (over 30 years old) and 49% of the youth (not older than 30 years old) had difficulty in answering (Table 10). It means that, in principle, most of the respondents are not biased against any concrete delivery services and can choose any available service that meets their requirements.

Table 10. Distribution of respondents' answers to the question "Which delivery service would you never buy groceries from?", %

Answer	Share	Answer	Share
Have difficulty in answering	54.0	MySPAR»	2.9
AliExpress	8.8	VkusVill	2.9
iGooods	5.9	Wildberries	2.9
Produktoff	5.9	Lentochka	0.0
Cdek.market	3.9	Other	6.9
Sbermarket	3.9	Total	100.0
Pyaterochka.Dostavka	2.9		

AliExpress is the leader among the services the respondents would not order groceries from (8.8% of all respondents). Non-specialized market places (AliExpress, Wildberries) were included in the survey, because in 2020 they took some active, even though not very noticeable attempts to enter the rapidly growing market. The second place is taken by "iGooods" (5.9%) and "Produktoff" (5.9%). Thus, the first positions were taken by the services well-known by our respondents, but not associated with food products or, vice versa, by lesser-known services that are weakly positioned on the markets of the VFD cities.

If this question is studied in the regional perspective, it can be noted that people living in cities with population below 1 million (60% of the respondents in this group), who are not spoiled by the competition of the federal chains, found it especially hard to name the service where they would not order groceries. More "picky" citizens of Kazan and Nizhny Novgorod had less difficulty in answering (50.0% and 42.6%, respectively).

By and large 43% of the interviewed users of delivery services cannot formulate the reasons why they could reject to buy from some concrete service. The second most common answer (34%) was "I will not buy if I know nothing about the service". Other reasons why customers do not or will not buy groceries online in some concrete service are mostly related to their negative experience or a deeply-rooted image of the service ("have negative experience in making an online purchase", "very expensive", "very long delivery", "modest range of products" and "unfriendly website"), the figure being 18%. That means that the majority of the respondents are not really biased, which gives a chance to the companies to expand their audience, including through better customer awareness.

The fact that consumers do not firmly reject to buy groceries online at all or from some concrete service does not mean that they are fully satisfied with all the elements of the selling process (Table 11). Contemplating about an ideal service, customers expect promptness and punctuality whereas the real services obtain rather low scores for promptness and, especially, punctuality.

Table 11. Ranking delivery quality of some services, points (1 is very bad, 5 is excellent).

Name	Average score of all respondents					Average score of the service by all characteristics
	Promptness	Punctuality	Politeness	Helpfulness	Cleanliness	
Samokat	3.9	3.7	3.8	3.3	3.7	3.68
Pyaterochka.Dostavka	3.0	2.8	3.2	3.1	3.2	3.06
Yandex.Lavka	3.8	3.7	4.0	4.0	3.5	3.80
MySPAR	3.3	3.3	3.4	3.4	3.4	3.36
Sbermarket	3.7	3.7	4.1	3.9	4.0	3.88
Average score by characteristic for all services	3.54	3.44	3.70	3.54	3.56	3.56

In total, the enterprises included in the study were not able to gain more than 3.56 points. That means that the respondents were really critical when evaluating the quality of delivery services. Sbermarket and Yandex.Lavka have the highest and very close values of the average score (3.88 and 3.8, respectively). Thus, even though Sbermarket and Yandex.Lavka as a brand demonstrate a relative weakness of their competitive position in terms of customer attraction and retention, they are evaluated quite high by their customers in terms of the service quality. Furthermore, the consumers learned about these brands only recently, and Yandex.Lavka only operates in few regions. With the good score given by users about their quality, these services have excellent development prospects.

The highest score for some important delivery characteristics such as promptness and punctuality were given to Samokat (3.9 and 3.8, respectively) and Yandex.Lavka (3.8 and 3.7, respectively). It is consistent with the strategy adopted by these services (delivery within 15–30 min). However, the respondents evaluated what was the actual delivery time against the time claimed by the services, which led to lower scores. The lowest score for punctuality was given to Pyaterochka.Dostavka (2.8).

The analysis of reviews about the general level of prices in those delivery services where the respondents prefer to order groceries did not let us conclude about the impression the customers have about prices of competitors, because the dispersion of opinions turned out to be very big. About a quarter of all the respondents failed to evaluate the level of prices of the service they use and chose the answer "I do not know". It can be assumed that each customer and each purchase they make is unique, in a sense. That is why customers can characterize the level of prices in the same online or offline shop depending on the composition of their food basket, the ability to compare the prices of goods they buy at a time with the prices of competitors, previous experience in making offline and online purchases and, finally, the established price image of the company.

The consequence of the above circumstances is that online customers are not aware of what is a clear price position of a brand in online sales. It seems that they will need more time and more buying experience to be able to clearly differentiate the delivery services by their price levels. On the other hand, online grocery retailers are now at the starting point in their competitive struggle for customers. A well-thought brand promotion policy and clear positioning of the brand in the customers' eyes are the major objectives for extending influence on the market. Those offline sellers who position themselves as discounters and strive for maintaining this position in e-commerce have to rigorously monitor the price policy of their competitors.

The fact that the established brand image affects the evaluation of the online price level is proved by the data of the questionnaire on Pyaterochka.Dostavka. The majority of the customers who prefer to buy groceries through Pyaterochka.Dostavka (71%) answered that the food products of this service are, on average, cheaper or much cheaper than those of the competitors. Another example is retail chain SPAR. A half of all the respondents who prefer to buy groceries from MySPAR evaluated the price level of this service as equivalent to that of the competitors, which corresponds to the offline image of this retail chain positioning itself as a brand with the main focus on the quality of its services, rather than prices [27–29].

Table 12. Actions of consumers (who have experience in buying groceries online) in case they need to buy food products online

Order will be made via the:	Share of respondents, %
1. Delivery service of the shop where I usually buy offline	32.8
2. Service with a high level of the most important parameter (assortment, price, delivery time, etc.)	16.4
3. Service recommended by friends	15.6
4. Service that has awarded bonuses for the previous purchase	9.4
5. The mobile application of the offline chain of shops that has been established before and has an online order feature	7.8
6. Service that is most actively advertised	7.0
7. Service that has the best reviews on the internet	6.3
8. Service that has offline food shops	2.9
9. Only available service in my region	1.0
10. Service in the first link to the enquiry "buying groceries online in the city of …"	1.0
11. Have difficulty in answering	1.0
Total	100.0

The experience of offline interaction with the brand is of paramount importance (Table 12) when a delivery service is selected in a concrete situation (32.8% of respondents). None of the following diverse marketing techniques even altogether give this effect: bonuses (9.4%), advertising (7%), reviews on the internet (6.3%), an installed mobile application (7.8%). Apart from offline experience, the consumers are ready to be guided, to a considerable degree, by their friends' opinions (15.6%) and correspondence to the parameter that is most important for the customer in a particular situation.

The results obtained demonstrate that the customer choice of various channels of communications is influenced significantly. Once again they highlight a low level of loyalty towards some brands on the part of customers and the great facilities that the main players have for affecting this process.

4 Conclusions

1. The competition on the regional market of grocery delivery services grew considerably in 2020. Large federal services are capturing bigger and bigger territory and gradually pushing out small local companies, applying a variety of cutting-edge info-communication methods.
2. The spread of delivery services is not uniform. This process is most actively developing in the areas with the largest share of urban population and highest incomes per capita (Nizhny Novgorod and Samara Regions, Tatarstan). Competition is strongest in regional, republican and district centers. However, delivery services are gradually penetrating smaller cities and towns.
3. The expansion of the delivery service market leads to the appearance of market niches: regular (an alternative to a hypermarket) and express delivery (an alternative to a next-door shop). Express delivery looks like a second stage of development. A separate segment combines the services for which groceries are not part of the main range of products (market places).
4. The grocery delivery market of VFD is far from saturation. The degree of penetration of innovations is about 50% and can be less in some regions. The main work should be done with the consumers who refer to the Early Majority and, in perspective, with the consumers from the Late Majority group.
5. Most of the consumers who have no experience in buying groceries online are well aware of the presence and diversity of such services, even when it comes to the services that do not operate in the city of the respondent. Express delivery services actively attract the attention of inexperienced consumers. Non-core services (market places with a wide range of products) are well-known, but their ability of delivering groceries causes some doubts due to the existing stereotypes.
6. Most of the consumers who have no experience in buying groceries online (about 92%), independently of their age do not exclude the probability of using such services in future. The youth's (up to 30) main focus is the ability to save money, the middle-aged people (up to 65) prefer the quality of products, and those older than 65 are somewhat confused and have difficulty in answering this question.
7. When choosing a service, consumers who have no experience in buying groceries online tend to trust their own offline buying experience and their friends' experience.

This fact must be considered in promotion to attract new customers. The existing offline chains can actively offer their customers modern info-communications in the form of an online delivery service and do that directly in shops. Referral marketing actions are also possible.

8. By and large, the general attraction of the delivery services in the VFD cities we considered is relatively low. The average indicator of a grocery purchase among those who know about the possibility of making such a purchase in the 9 services we considered is only 16%, but there are brands that attract 24–25% of the customers who are aware of these brands.

9. The leaders of the market in terms of customer attraction and retention are services such as Samokat and Pyaterochka.Dostavka, while Lentochka, VkusVill and Auchan are falling behind. Brand attraction can vary depending on the region or age. Firstly, it depends on the degree of coverage of the territory by a brand, and, secondly, on older consumers' traditional preferences, which they acquired on the offline food market.

10. The model of an ideal delivery service from the position of an "experienced" customer is a prompt and punctual service with the best price and minimal delivery cost, as well as the widest range of groceries. For this reason, non-core services (market places), which started experimenting with grocery delivery during the pandemic, has not been very successful so far.

11. The customers do not value high the existing delivery services, with the average score of the service quality being 3.56 out of 5 points. The customers are especially picky about the punctuality of delivery. This is the circumstance that brings express delivery services to the leaders of the ranking.

12. The evaluation of the service quality and loyalty index (NPS Index) can be affected by factors not directly related to the company or controlled by it (for example, operation of many small intermediary firms, which deliver goods from the shops of the well-known brands).

13. The customers who has online buying experience is still not loyal for one specific service. Their concept of prices in various services is largely dependent on the image of the same offline brand. When they have to choose a delivery service in a concrete life situation, they are ready to rely on their own offline experience. To a lesser degree this is true for the customers aged under 30, who are quite ready to experiment and switch to the services that have no offline shops.

14. In general, the regional, provincial grocery delivery market in Russia is in the early stage of its growth. Individual market niches are appearing and specialized info-communications start being applied. Market players have great facilities for influencing customer loyalty, including through offline buying experience and references from friends.

References

1. Degeratu, A.M., Rangaswamy, A., Wu, J.: Consumer choice behavior in online and traditional supermarkets: the effects of brand name, price, and other search attributes. Int. J. Res. Mark. **17**(1), 55–78 (2000). https://doi.org/10.1016/s0167-8116(00)00005-7

2. Hand, C., Riley, F.D., Harris, P., Singh, J., Rettie, R.: Online grocery shopping: the influence of situational factors. Eur. J. Mark. **43**(9), 1205–1219 (2009). https://doi.org/10.1108/030905 60910976447
3. Ramazanov, I.A., Panasenko, S.V., Cheglov, V.P., Krasilnikova, E.A., Nikishin, A.F.: Retail transformation under the influence of digitalisation and technology development in the context of globalisation. J. Open Innov. Technol. Mark. Complex. **7**(1), 49 (2021). https://doi.org/10.3390/joitmc7010049
4. Chintagunta, P.K., Chu, J., Cebollada, J.: Quantifying transaction costs in online/off-line grocery channel choice. Mark. Sci. **31**(1), 96–114 (2012). https://doi.org/10.1287/mksc.1110.0678
5. Liu, D., Deng, Z., Zhang, W., Wang, Y., Kaisar, E.I.: Design of sustainable urban electronic grocery distribution network. Alex. Eng. J. **60**(1), 145–157 (2021). https://doi.org/10.1016/j.aej.2020.06.051
6. Munson, J., Tiropanis, T., Lowe, M.: Online grocery shopping: identifying change in consumption practices (2017). https://doi.org/10.1007/978-3-319-70284-1_16. www.scopus.com
7. Sreeram, A., Kesharwani, A., Desai, S.: Factors affecting satisfaction and loyalty in online grocery shopping: an integrated model. J. Indian Bus. Res. **9**(2), 107–132 (2017). https://doi.org/10.1108/JIBR-01-2016-0001
8. Mortimer, G., Fazal e Hasan, S., Andrews, L., Martin, J.: Online grocery shopping: the impact of shopping frequency on perceived risk. Int. Rev. Retail Distrib. Consum. Res. **26**(2), 202–223 (2016). https://doi.org/10.1080/09593969.2015.1130737
9. Jin, S., Li, H., Li, Y.: Preferences of Chinese consumers for the attributes of fresh produce portfolios in an e-commerce environment. Br. Food J. **119**(4), 817–829 (2017). https://doi.org/10.1108/BFJ-09-2016-0424
10. Bragin, L.A., Panasenko, S.V., Nikishin, A.F., Pankina, T.V., Aleksina, S.B.: Supply chain management in delivery of goods to increase customer loyalty in electronic commerce. Int. J. Supply Chain Manag. **9**(4), 740–745 (2020). www.scopus.com
11. Gatta, V., Marcucci, E., Maltese, I., Iannaccone, G., Fan, J.: E-groceries: a channel choice analysis in Shanghai. Sustainability **13**(7), 3625 (2021). https://doi.org/10.3390/su13073625
12. Bragin, L.A., Panasenko, S.V., Nikishin, A.F., Pankina, T.V., Aleksina, S.B.: Supply chain management in delivery of goods to increase customer loyalty in electronic commerce. Int. J. Supply Chain Manag. **9**(4), 740–745 (2020)
13. Ukolov, V.F., Solomatin, A.V., Solomatin, Y.V., Chernikov, S.U., Ukolov, A.V.: Food-sharing economy pattern comparison in UK and Russian markets. Int. Bus. Manag. **10**(18), 4268–4282. www.scopus.com
14. Wang, O., Somogyi, S.: Motives for luxury seafood consumption in first-tier cities in China. Food Qual. Preference **79**. https://doi.org/10.1016/j.foodqual.2019.103780
15. Galati, A., Crescimanno, M., Tinervia, S., Siggia, D.: Website quality and internal business factors: an empirical investigation in the Italian wine industry. Int. J. Wine Bus. Res. **28**(4), 308–326 (2016). https://doi.org/10.1108/IJWBR-08-2015-0026
16. Krasnostavskaia, N., Pletneva, N., Kupriyanova, M., Golovkina, S.: The level of involvement and the nature of the stimulus as factors in the decision-making process on the purchase of handmade goods on the internet. IOP Conf. Ser. Mater. Sci. Eng. **940**(1), 012069 (2020). https://doi.org/10.1088/1757-899X/940/1/012069. www.scopus.com
17. Konnikov, E., Konnikova, O., Leventsov, V.: IT services market as a driver for the development of the artificial intelligence market. IOP Conf. Ser. Mater. Sci. Eng. **497**(1), 012043 (2019). https://doi.org/10.1088/1757-899X/497/1/012043
18. Aleshnikova, V., Beregovskaya, T., van der Voort, E.: A smart consumer is a challenge for business. (2021). https://doi.org/10.1007/978-3-030-59126-7_191. www.scopus.com

19. Wang, O., Somogyi, S.: Consumer adoption of online food shopping in China. Br. Food J. **120**(12), 2868–2884 (2018). https://doi.org/10.1108/BFJ-03-2018-0139

20. Wang, H.H., Hao, N., Zhou, Q., Wetzstein, M.E., Wang, Y.: Is fresh food shopping sticky to retail channels and online platforms? Evidence and implications in the digital era. Agribusiness **35**(1), 6–19 (2019). https://doi.org/10.1002/agr.21589

21. Khandpur, N., et al.: Supermarkets in cyberspace: a conceptual framework to capture the influence of online food retail environments on consumer behavior. Int. J. Environ. Res. Public Health **17**(22), 1–15 (2020). https://doi.org/10.3390/ijerph1722863

22. Brar, K., Minaker, L.M.: Geographic reach and nutritional quality of foods available from mobile online food delivery service applications: novel opportunities for retail food environment surveillance. BMC Publ. Health, **21**(1) (2021). https://doi.org/10.1186/s12889-021-104 89-2

23. Tian, D., Tang, J., Ren, Y.: Improving operation resilience of instant delivery service in online to offline business model. Xitong Gongcheng Lilun Yu Shijian/Syst. Eng. Theory Pract. **41**(2), 310–318 (2021). https://doi.org/10.12011/SETP2020-1622

24. Klepek, M., Bauerová, R.: Why do retail customers hesitate for shopping grocery online? Technol. Econ. Dev. Econ. **26**(6), 1444–1462 (2020). https://doi.org/10.3846/tede.2020. 13970

25. Klyzhenko, L.: *Pyaterochka* and *Magnit* – do customers see the difference? 3 Nov 2017. https://www.retail.ru/news/pyaterochka-i-magnit-vidyat-li-pokupateli-raznitsu/. Accessed 30 Apr 2021

26. Ivanov Index: a record number of respondents saving on groceries. 10–04–2019. https://1pr ime.ru/experts/20190410/829881439.html. Accessed 30 Apr 2021. 2019 Annual Report of SPAR International

27. https://spar-international.com/wp-content/uploads/2020/08/Russian-SPAR-Annual-Report-2019.pdf/. Accessed 30 Apr 2021

28. Krasyuk, I., Medvedeva, Y.: Resource support in business analytics of innovative development of trade and technological systems. In: Proceedings of the 33rd International Business Information Management Association Conference, IBIMA 2019: Education Excellence and Innovation Management through Vision 2020, pp. 8807–8817 (2019)

29. Krasyuk, I.A., Medvedeva, Y.Y.: Drives and obstacle for the development of marketing in Russian retailing. In: Proceedings of the 33rd International Business Information Management Association Conference, IBIMA 2019: Education Excellence and Innovation Management through Vision 2020, pp. 4838–4840 (2019)

Transforming the Strategic Benchmarks of Russian Telecommunications Companies in the Sustainable Development Paradigm

Irina Krasyuk[1], Oksana Evseeva[1]([✉]), Maria Kolgan[2], and Yulia Medvedeva[2]

[1] Peter the Great St. Petersburg Polytechnic University, Saint Petersburg, Russia
evseeva@spbstu.ru
[2] Don State Technical University, Rostov-on-don, Russia
{mkolgan,ymedvedeva}@donstu.ru

Abstract. The need to adapt enterprises to the volatile market environment and reconstruct managerial and financial activities in response to the challenges of the market makes top managers face difficulties as they choose strategic development alternatives and make strategic decisions. Economic thought offers enterprises new development concepts, one of which is the concept of sustainable development. Firms operating in the same sector can choose various strategic benchmarks to achieve sustainability and competitive advantage. Telecommunications companies encourage and speed up social, economic and ecological sustainable growth and development for everyone. The paper discusses the conditions and strategic directions for sustainable development of Russian information and communication companies (MTS, MegaFon, Beeline, Tele 2) based on the content analysis of annual reports and sustainable development reports. Based on the results obtained, it can be concluded that all the companies take part in offering incentives, education and good working conditions to their employees, provide support to the local community, organize charity activities. However, in practice not all the companies implement strategic management based on sustainable development. The companies MTS and Beeline demonstrate more focus on sustainable development in their strategic goals and business strategies. In addition to the declared orientation in its report, Beeline presents concrete results on achieving the goals of sustainable development.

Keywords: Info-communications · Sustainable development · Strategy · Mobile operators

1 Introduction

Strategic management lays a foundation for all major management decisions, such as decisions about the line of business, products and markets, production capacities, investments and organizational structure. In a successful company strategic planning is used to find and seize business opportunities. At the same time, it is a mechanism of corporate protection as it helps the firm to avoid expensive mistakes when choosing a product on the market or investing [1].

© Springer Nature Switzerland AG 2022
Y. Koucheryavy et al. (Eds.): NEW2AN 2021/ruSMART 2021, LNCS 13158, pp. 147–157, 2022.
https://doi.org/10.1007/978-3-030-97777-1_12

Another reason why strategic management is important is that it gives the members of the organization the sense of direction and help them understand what their efforts should be aimed at [2]. Without a strategic plan managers of the organization can focus on everyday activities only to find that their competitor has attained a more advantageous position having a more comprehensive, long-term perspective of strategic areas.

We believe that one of the most consistent definitions of enterprise strategy was given by P. Drucker. According to him, enterprise strategy is the implementation of the theory of business in practical activity [3]. Drucker emphasizes that having a strategy allows the enterprise to find opportunities for achieving the desired results in a non-controlled environment, since the company focuses on consciously looking for and using any suitable circumstances to its favor.

Strategic management of telecommunications companies is grounded on the need to create conditions for buy and sell process and providing some additional services. Thus, it forms premises for choosing the best development strategy.

In their turn, telecommunications companies contribute to achieving the UN Sustainable Development Goals (SDGs) [4], as they provide access to educational tools and platforms that improve the quality of life, form infrastructure for building smart cities, and help fight climate change.

2   Method of Research

Annual reports, press releases, and sustainable development reports of Russia's leading telecommunications companies, such as MTS, MegaFon, Beeline, and Tele 2 were studied using content analysis of the mission, strategies and business models presented in the reports.

2.1   Prospects of Sustainable Development of the Information and Communications Industry

An intention of an organization to move towards sustainable development is an attempt of management to integrate cognitive, learning and improving elements of every enterprise with a prevailing model of competitive advantages [5]. In this context, the primary need is to clarify the definition of company sustainability in precise terms. The concept of sustainable development is based on the concept "sustainability", which is multi-aspect.

Sustainability is an integrated approach to managing enterprises aimed at creating and maximizing long-term economic, social and ecological value [6]. Sustainability is the responsibility for the impact an organization makes on the environment in business, ecological and social terms. Conscious managing of the impact results in reduced costs, improved external relations and better risk management [7, 8].

Sustainability is the understanding of the fact that each agent is surrounded by stakeholders [9]. Building and developing a good rapport with stakeholders through cooperation and dialog is crucial, because not only does it affect the ability of managing risks but also fosters development and gives the organization a competitive advantage. Transforming business by managing sustainability leads to the following gains: the areas that create the long-term value of the organization are defined; business is stable as it is based on good relationships with key stakeholders; operating costs reduce due to the more effective management of resources through the entire supply chain; loyalty and trust of customers due to dialog and interaction; effective management of economic, social and environmental risks. The basis for the competitiveness of the telecommunications business is the openness and readiness of a company to communicate with society so as to find effective digital solutions that can influence the social problems in a consistent way [10].

The Covid-19 pandemic has demonstrated the need to develop and ensure reliable functioning of digital economy, which is dependent on a convenient and high-quality access to the internet and a whole set of digital services both for individuals and companies.

An example of social significance of developing telecommunications technologies may be the creation of new opportunities in the health care sector. According to the study by V.A. Bondarenko et al., introducing telecommunications technologies in the health care sector leads to a positive social effect due to the provision of quality medical services to the population in remote regions of the country, the transfer of medical experience to personnel, and increased economic efficiency of medical service systems [11]. In Russia there are initiatives on the digitalization of the health care system and use of modern telecommunications technologies.

The main idea of including sustainability in business management is based on the postulate that delivery and acceptance must support a successful company in the long run [12]. Since any company is integrated into a complex system of interdependences inside and outside the firm, this supporting character must be implemented thanks to the commitment of the company to protect the environment or reduce its carbon footprint, as well as thanks to the general acceptance of its corporate behavior by society inside and outside the firm. In their research Daniela Ebner and Dr. Rupert J. Baumgartner coin the term "corporate social responsibility" (CSR) as a social component of the concept "sustainable development" (SD), which is basically built on rational approach of stakeholders [13].

CSR focuses, first of all, on corporate interaction implementing its responsibilities as a member of society and living up to the expectations of all stakeholders. Sustainable development is considered to be an aesthetic concept, which suggests ideas regarding sustainable orientation on the macro-level [14]. The concept of sustainable development on the corporate level is formulated as corporate sustainability, which is based on three pillars of economic, ecological and social problems, so the social dimension is called CSR. Corporate orientation on sustainability is especially susceptible to the influence of external factors, which are preconditioned by specific orientation on sustainability on the macro-level:

- legal/institutional factors: laws, human rights, etc.
- technological factors: new technologies
- market: suppliers, competitors, customers, trends
- social: NGOs, society
- culture: attitude, behavior
- environment: nature, availability of resources [15].

According to the concept by Prahalad and Krishnan, business is moving towards shifting focus on every consumer and this trend is bound to lead us to the world with coordinates N = 1 и R = G. N = 1 implies the orientation of a trade enterprise on the needs of every individual customer [16]. The principle R = G allows us to find out about the nature of the resource base of large firms and understand how to get access to high-quality resources at low costs using platform business models. Companies are not capable of maintaining and controlling most of the resources they need, but they can provide easy and convenient access to resources bases if they form global supply chains and have many suppliers that they communicate with. In our opinion, this concept is consistent with today's transformations of telecommunications services market that is drifting to sustainable development as it has no more capacity to grow intensively any longer.

2.2 Drivers and Obstacles for Sustainable Development of Telecommunications Companies in Russia

The ITU data (ITU - International Telecommunication Union) show that in 2019 over 50% of people on the planet used the internet (51.4% around the world by the end of 2019), 75% of the entire population of the world had an active subscription to mobile broadband communication, while the subscription to fixed broadband communication increased to slightly over than 15% [17]. Today more than 57 households have access to the internet at home. Moreover, the demand for data is growing due to increasingly intensive services. The international capacity was on average 36% in the period from 2017 to 2020, while the average capacity per one internet user in the period from 2017 to 2019 was 26%.

The typical features of the modern market where telecommunications companies (TCs) operate is commoditization and consumer consolidation. The bargaining power is shifting from providers to consumers while margins are getting diluted. All of these bring forward the need to focus on consumer value [18]. Growing commoditization is preconditioned by a rising consumption of know-how and intensifying competition with the initially unique products and services losing their distinction and value. So telecommunications companies are consolidated, which leads to monopolistic competitiveness and oligopoly. The Russian market of mobile communications is presented by four major operators: MegaFon, MTS, Beeline (VEON) and Tele2. The direct consequence of the trend is the general shift of the bargaining power from sellers to consumers. The combined effect of commoditization on client concentration and bargaining power, which goes from the providers' hands to those of customers, is negative for business profitability.

The above changes of the market and the increasingly fierce competition caused by the global economic crisis exert pressure on companies. Most companies face the challenge of adapting their market strategy and tactics to the target markets in order to reduce the negative influence of today's recession. So as to solve the problem, the attitude towards the organization of strategic management of telecommunications companies must be changed. The competitiveness of telecommunications business is grounded on the openness and readiness of a company to interact with society and find effective digital solutions that could have a consistent effect on social problems.

In the field of ICT regulation, there is a new paradigm of cooperation between regulating bodies and directive bodies, aimed at faster digital transformation for everybody. This new paradigm is manifested in joint regulation, which must involve a wide range of stakeholders in informed law- and decision-making process that is based on actual data and considers social and economic consequences. While the arguments for cooperation are strong, progress can be hampered due to the race for power, lack of resources and poor vision of stakeholders' aims [17]. Joint regulation is regulation favoring people. It is aimed at sustainability and long-term benefits, rather than profit maximization of the sector and exceptional economic growth.

Telecommunications companies of Russia are developing in the time of fierce competition and their sustainable development reports reveal their economic, ecological and social responsibility [19]. It is done to show the transparency of all their activities related to economic, ecological and social aspects, which must be presented to various stakeholders.

According to the UN sustainable development goals, maximizing access to and use of ICT is one of the areas of sustainable development. It should be noted that the largest Russian cellular providers are still gaining big profits from mobile communications, but no serious growth of companies' profits is observed. Revenues from mobile communications services amounts to over 80% of the total revenues of each company, while the net profit of the companies from this line of business is low. In 2019 MTS had the highest and MegaFon the lowest net profit (127.2 million rubles and 5.2 million rubles, respectively). This is due to high business and administrative expenses and high costs of rendered services. At the same time the leaders of the Russian market have a stable subscriber base and their revenues are growing mostly due to the increasing sales of digital products and services of the company's ecosystem. The dynamics of the number of subscribers of the four largest telecommunications companies in Russia is presented in Fig. 1.

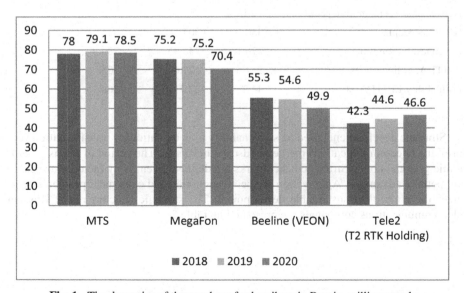

Fig. 1. The dynamics of the number of subscribers in Russia, million people

At an estimate by the GSMA Intelligence the level of penetration by the number of subscribers in Russia in 2019 amounted to 89 and, according to the forecast for 2025, this figure is not going to change [20].

The change of the strategic benchmarks of the telecommunications companies in the paradigm of sustainable development is caused by the fact that, in the time of stagnation of the subscriber base, the companies develop new business models and new associated markets using technological advances. For example, digital financial services (DFS) are going to allow the operators to diversify their activities outside communications, compensate the stagnation of major revenues and expand their presence in the digital eco-system.

2.3 Strategic Benchmarks of the Largest Telecommunications Companies in Russia

The main performance indicators of telecommunications companies in Russia are shown in Table 1. The Russian market of mobile communications is presented by four main operators: MegaFon, MTS, Beeline and Tele2.

It does not seem possible to present comparable data on Tele2 due to the restructuring processes in the company. Traditional mobile services are still the biggest share of the telecommunications market (57% in 2019). However, an increasingly important role is played by digital services (Internet of Things, mobile TV, M2M, e-commerce, big data), which are provided by all market players.

Table 1. Performance indicators of the largest telecommunications companies in Russia, year 2019 [19–23]

Indicator	MTS	MegaFon	Beeline (VEON)
Active subscribers, million people	79.1	75.2	54.6
ARPU, $/people	350	307	335
Revenues, billion rubles	476.1	348.96	289.9
EBITDA, billion rubles	214.6	127.6	105
Profitability EBITDA, %	44.2	37.2	36.2

Strategic development based on sustainability is an evolutionary transformation vector of the telecommunications market landscape in Russia. The period of intensive economic growth is over. Strategic benchmarks are defined given many factors intrinsic to competitive advantage. Aggravation of social, economic and ecological problems actualizes the concept of sustainable development. The strategic benchmarks of Russian telecommunications companies are presented in Table 2.

Table 2. Characteristics of strategic benchmarks (according to the companies reports) [19–23]

Company	Mission	Business strategy
MTS	Creating an extensive eco-system of new digital products based on the acquired expertise and leadership achievements in telecommunications business. The social mission is to create high-quality products and services to meet customers' needs in various spheres of life and maximize value for customers and the company	Customer Lifetime Value2.0 (aimed at building full-scale digital business on stable telecommunications base.)
MegaFon	We take part in building a digital world, whose facilities will improve the life of every client. The social mission is to create opportunities in the field of communications, socializing, family care, employment, and education. We inspire people to find and grasp all opportunities to the maximum extent	"Developing a digital world". The company keeps on focusing on digital clients and increasing their LTV (Lifetime Value) for sustainable growth
Beeline (VEON)	Using the business expertise, brand strength and technology resources to improve people's life and achieve progress in the society, economy and environment. The social strategy has three components: developing an inclusive society, technologies for the social sector, stable business-processes	Market growth, efficiency, cooperation. To become more than a telecom and grow faster than the market. In the interests of our clients. In the interests of our stakeholders and partners. In the interests of the society
T2 RTK Holding	The social mission: We create an alternative to market practices. We bring new quality of life to mobile services consumers: honest, transparent, favorable offers, high-quality partnership programs and services	Lifestyle enabler. Tele2 creates simple, beneficial and convenient mobile services for its subscribers in very different spheres of human life and, in this way, increases the value created by the company for the society, having adopted the company strategy as a strategy of sustainable development

MegaFon is in the process of developing a digital eco-system. The priorities of sustainable development are the happiest client (focus on clients' need also contributes to sustainable achievement of business goals; digitalization of the state and industries as a way of finding new sources of growth and bringing added value to other players of the Russian market; staff education, professional development and support, charity and volunteering support, care for the environment [21]. The company pays special attention to the digitalization of Russia's economy (for example, participation in creating an ecological monitoring platform, online platforms for automated transport logistics, water online monitoring).

Even though the principles of sustainable development have been introduced, the business strategy of MegaFon is declarative in terms of its orientation on the goals of sustainable development. The company does not submit a sustainable development report but presents the data on sustainable development in the annual report.

Sustainable development reports are presented to the public by MTS, Tele2 and Beeline. The reports of the above companies meet the Global Reporting Initiative Standards (GRI Standards) in the field of sustainable development.

In 2019 MTS, the largest operator of mobile communications, announced about rebranding and approval of a new development strategy called "Customer Lifetime Value2.0", which is an appropriate response to digitalization and growing demands of business for new technology [22, 23]. At the moment the company positions itself as an ecosystem of digital services. The range of these services includes traditional communications services, financial services, cloud and digital solutions, media. Since 2008 MTS Group annually publishes Sustainable Development Reports. The reports demonstrate the contribution of MTS to the development of digital economy, point out the presence regions, highlight the company's strategy and range of activity, corporate management system, results of responsible business practice, key projects in terms of cooperation with the state and local communities. MTS has the following priorities of sustainable development. Customer: ensuring for equal opportunity of access to the company services, increasing loyalty; safety and responsibility for services provided, creating an innovative environment for solving social problems; ecological responsibility of business. MTS. Lifetime: focus on maintaining loyalty and emotional attachment, including through taking socially and environmentally responsible actions; developing services that increase environmental sustainability; carrying out projects on environmental protection and rational use of resources. Value: enhancing the image of a socially responsible company (Sustainable Development Report, ESG, JAC and CDP); creating transparency for stockholders, investors, suppliers and partners; building up the corporate spirit and reputation of MTS.

In its sustainable development report, Beeline (VEON) claims a business strategy that reflects the principles and goals of sustainable development set by the company. The business strategy of the company consists of three elements: market growth, efficiency and cooperation. Each of the elements opens up in the strategy through the prism of sustainable development. Market growth relies on technological improvement and inclusiveness; efficiency is considered in terms of rational use of resources; cooperation is seen as an opportunity to react promptly to the needs of clients and partners. In 2019 Beeline PJSC VimpelCom (VEON) became the first Russian company that joined

The Valuable 500 movement (500 companies implementing the program of available environment and popularizing sustainable development among their key partners) [24].

In its sustainable development report, Tele2 highlights the target benchmarks grouped by two categories: those aimed at achieving the social and ecological effect from the core activities of the company and those aimed at social investing [25]. Virtually all the UN sustainable development goals are mentioned by the company as top priority. However, no description of real opportunities to achieve them and no measurable results are given. The report reflects the interests of stakeholder groups and the company's activities within these interests. However, no strategy formed on the basis of sustainable development is revealed at the level of business strategy.

3 Conclusion

The research led to the following main results:

1. Telecommunications companies form the infrastructure of sustainable economic, social and ecological development. The landscape on which such companies operate is transforming: the mobile communications market is being saturated and the subscriber base stops growing. The competition between companies is substituted for the competition between eco-systems based on platform business models.
2. New strategic development benchmarks of telecommunications companies in Russia lie in the sphere of sustainable development. On the one hand, this is determined by the changing market conditions, commoditization, shifting bargaining power from providers to consumers. On the other hand, the regulating effect is determined by the new global paradigm of joint regulation.
3. Mobile communications operators are becoming service companies working on the basis of the eco-system of a progressive platform business model. The strategic benchmarks of the telecommunications companies in Russia are not transforming due to consistent regulation or a general industry-specific trend. However, MTS (the leader of the sector and the only large Russian operator which has been submitting a separate report on sustainable development for 15 years) has already readjusted its strategic priorities. Beeline, which is not the leader of the market, does not limit itself to the declarative approach to sustainable development. The report presents the real results of strategic management based on the concept of sustainable development.
4. Further research may be dedicated to the comparative evaluation of the sustainable development priorities for telecommunications companies in the context of stakeholders' priorities. This evaluation would help understand which groups of stakeholders have interests that are top priority for every company and why. Finding and determining the degree of substantiation of such a focus would make it possible to adjust sustainable development business strategies of telecommunications companies.

References

1. Webster Jr., F.E.: Marketing IS management: the wisdom of Peter Drucker. J. Acad. Market. Sci. **37**(1), 20–27 (2009)
2. Porter, M.E.: What is strategy? Harv. Bus. Rev. **74**(6), 61–78 (1996)
3. Drucker, P.F.: Economic realities and enterprise strategy. In: Vogel, E.F. (ed.) Modern Japanese Organization and Decision-Making, pp. 228–248. University of California Press, Berkeley (2020). https://doi.org/10.1525/9780520311589-014
4. Organisation for Economic Cooperation and Development. Sustainable Manufacturing and Eco-Innovation: Framework, Practices and Measurement. OECD (2009)
5. Chkalova, O., Efremova, M., Lezhnin, V., Polukhina, A., Sheresheva, M.: Entrepreneurship and sustainability issues innovative mechanism for local tourism system management: a case study *. Entrep. Sustain. Issues (2019)
6. White, K., Habib, R., Hardisty, D.J.: How to SHIFT consumer behaviors to be more sustainable: a literature review and guiding framework. J. Mark. (2019). https://doi.org/10.1177/002 2242919825649
7. Sheth, J., Parvatiyar, A.: Sustainable marketing: market-driving, not market-driven. J. Macromark. **41**, 027614672096183 (2020). https://doi.org/10.1177/0276146720961836
8. Nekrasova, T., Leventsov, V., Axionova, E.: Forecasting of investments into wireless telecommunication systems. In: Balandin, S., Andreev, S., Koucheryavy, Y. (eds.) NEW2AN 2014. LNCS, vol. 8638, pp. 519–525. Springer, Cham (2014). https://doi.org/10.1007/978-3-319-10353-2_47
9. Bespalko, V.A., Voronov, A.A., Martynenko, O.V.: Marketing and operational aspects of the strategy of industrial import substitution. Int. J. Econ. Bus. Adm. (2019). https://doi.org/10.35808/ijeba/285
10. Pupentsova, S., Leventsov, V., Livintsova, M., Alexeeva, N., Vodianova, S.: Assessment of the internet of things projects on the real estate market. IOP Conf. Ser. Mater. Sci. Eng. **618**(1), 012041 (2019). https://doi.org/10.1088/1757-899X/618/1/012041
11. Bondarenko, V., Kostoglodov, D., Nekrasova, T.: Telecommunications techniques in the healthcare development: foreign experience and Russian realities. In: Galinina, O., Andreev, S., Balandin, S., Koucheryavy, Y. (eds) Internet of Things, Smart Spaces, and Next Generation Networks and Systems. NEW2AN 2020, ruSMART 2020. LNCS, vol. 12526, pp. 318–327. Springer, Cham (2020). https://doi.org/10.1007/978-3-030-65729-1_27
12. Salvioni, D., Bosetti, L.: Sustainable development and corporate communication in global markets. SYMPHONYA Emerg. Issues Manag. **1**, 1–19 (2014). https://doi.org/10.4468/2014. 1.03salvioni.bosetti
13. Ebner, D., Rupert, D., Baumgartner, R.: The relationship between sustainable development and corporate social responsibility. In: Corporate Responsibility Research Conference (CRRC) (2006)
14. Nekrasova, T., Leventsov, V., Gluhov, V.: Development of infocommunications services in Russia. In: Galinina, O., Andreev, S., Balandin, S., Koucheryavy, Y. (eds.) NEW2AN/ruSMART -2019. LNCS, vol. 11660, pp. 505–514. Springer, Cham (2019). https://doi.org/10.1007/978-3-030-30859-9_43
15. Klochkov, Y., Gazizulina, A., Muralidharan, K.: Lean six sigma for sustainable business practices: a case study and standardization. Int. J. Qual. Res. **13**(1), 47–74 (2019)
16. Prahalad, K.K., Krishnan, M.S.: The new age of innovation (2012)
17. Digital Trends in the Commonwealth of Independent States Region 2021. https://www.itu.int/en/myitu/Publications/2021/04/19/15/12/Digital-trends-in-the-Commonwealth-of-Independent-States-region-2021

18. Kashani, K.: Why is Not Traditional Marketing Valid? (in Czech). Computer Press, Brno (2007)
19. Nekrasova, T., Mukhanova, N., Kretsy, S., Polyjanova, N.: Modern digital technologies and telecommunications mechanisms in the implementation of socio-economic policy at the local and regional level. In: Galinina, O., Andreev, S., Balandin, S., Koucheryavy, Y. (eds) Internet of Things, Smart Spaces, and Next Generation Networks and Systems. NEW2AN 2020, ruSMART 2020. LNCS, vol. 12526, pp. 297–307. Springer, Cham (2020). https://doi.org/10. 1007/978-3-030-65729-1_25
20. Mobile Economy: Russia and the CIS 2020. https://www.gsma.com/mobileeconomy/wp-con tent/uploads/2020/12/GSMA_MobileEconomy2020_RussiaCIS_Rus.pdf
21. The Annual Report of MegaFon (2019). https://ar2019.megafon.ru/ru. Accessed 30 Apr 2021
22. Yearly Financial Report of MTS (2019). https://moskva.mts.ru/about/investoram-i-akcion eram/korporativnoe-upravlenie/raskritie-informacii/godovaya-otchetnost. Accessed 28 Apr 2021
23. The Sustainable Development Report of MTS Group (2019). https://our2019.mts.ru/ru Accessed 30 Apr 2021
24. The Sustainable Development Report of Beeline (PJSC VimpelCom). https://rspp.ru/upload/ uf/fc7/otchet_ob_ust_razvitii2019.pdf. Accessed 25 Apr 2021
25. The Report on the Corporate Social Responsibility and Sustainable Development of Tele 2. https://msk.tele2.ru/api/media/content?contentId=m3170010. Accessed 25 Apr 2021

Study of Relationship Between the Corporate Governance Factors and ESG Ratings of ICT Companies from the Developed Markets

Sergei Grishunin[1]([✉]), Svetlana Suloeva[2]([✉]), Tatyana Nekrasova[2]([✉]), and Alexandra Erorova[1]([✉])

[1] National Research University Higher School of Economics, Moscow, Russia
Sgrishunin@hse.ru
[2] Peter the Great St. Petersburg Polytechnic University, St. Petersburg, Russia
suloeva_sb@spbstu.ru, nekrasova_tp@sbpstu.ru

Abstract. Assessment of corporate governance determinants of ESG ratings is a task of high interest for researchers and practitioners in project management in information and communication industry (ICT). This is underpinned by the growing interest to responsible and sustainable investing. We analyzed key drivers of governance pillar of ESG ratings of ICT companies in the developed markets. The relevance of the topic was underpinned by significant share of the governance in overall ESG assessment of ICT projects. The paper filled research gaps because existing studies on the topic did not address the governance practices specifically in ICT companies. Conversely, the conclusions for some governance drivers were controversial or incomplete. Data were collected for 80 telecommunication and IT companies between years 2005–2019. The dependent variable was Refinitiv ESG rating. The set of explanatory variables consisted of corporate governance activities labeled as best practices in the literature. It was found that existence of corporate social responsibility (CSR) committee, CEO duality, presence of non-executive members in the board, policy independence and chairman's past experience and continuity have positive and significant effect on ESG ratings of ICT companies. The presence of non-executive members in the board had marginal effect on ESG ratings. The growing representation of women in boards and management had positive but marginal effect on ESG score. The results can be used in practice for making recommendations for the development of managerial actions aimed at increase in ESG ratings.

Keywords: Information and communication industry · Project controlling · ESG rating · Corporate governance · Responsible investments

1 Introduction

The development of the responsible and sustainable investing approach as well as tightening of regulation in the area has changed the attitude of banks and other investors to the financing of projects in information and communication (ICT) industry. In the

© Springer Nature Switzerland AG 2022
Y. Koucheryavy et al. (Eds.): NEW2AN 2021/ruSMART 2021, LNCS 13158, pp. 158–169, 2022.
https://doi.org/10.1007/978-3-030-97777-1_13

next decade, only these investment projects will receive funding which will be able to demonstrate (1) their financial, technical, service and consumer superiority over rivals; and (2) their ability to follow responsible business practices. Environmental, social and governance (ESG) factors have become a fundamental route in evaluating of the attractiveness of the projects in ICT industry [24, 25, 27]. But as more companies seek to address ESG issues in their operations [29], how can investors and controllers make meaningful assessments about their relative progress? One solution is the application of ESG ratings assigned by the independent rating agencies. However, methodologies of these agencies remain not transparent and incomparable [30]. These features make it difficult to identify drivers that should be addressed to boost the ratings or reconstruct the ratings. There are only few research efforts to uncover these drivers for ICT companies.

The goal of the paper is to identify and analyze key determinants of the governance pillar of ESG ratings assigned to ICT companies in developed markets. The choice of the pillar was underpinned by its significant share in overall ESG assessment of ICT projects [24]. The governance quality remains a crucial foundation for achieving success in other pillars: environmental and social. This paper contributes to the literature in various ways. Firstly, it addresses ESG issues of ICT companies while other studies lose this focus. Secondly, we used ESG drivers which are either non-sufficiently covered by the literature (generational, gender and racial diversity of the board and top management) or those for which controversial results were received concerning their impact on ESG ratings (e.g., CEO duality). Thirdly, the paper used the data from large timespan from 2005 to 2019. The results can be used by the project controllers for making recommendations for the development of managerial actions to positively influence individual corporate governance drivers. The results can also be useful for the researchers who are working in exploring the impact of ESG factors on projects' success.

2 Sustainable Development Issues in Project Management in Info-Communication

Constantly changing environment broken frontiers between telecommunication and information technology industries. They have merged into a single info-communication industry (ICT) [1]. In 2021–2024 ICT companies will continue to develop such groundbreaking technologies as (1) 5G expansion and gradual transition to 6G; (2) artificial intelligence and machine learning; (3) cloud, mobile, social and big data analytics; and (4) expansion of internet of things applications [2]. However, development of these technologies requires significant investments while competition for investors' money is growing. In the following years, only these investment projects will receive funding which are able to demonstrate not only their technical, service and consumer superiority over its rivals but also their ability to follow sustainable investing practices. SRI - socially responsible investment in a broad sense is defined as an investment process that includes the recognition of companies with the efficient corporate social responsibility practices [4]. According to a 2018 US SIF report[1], socially responsible investing in the

---

[1] US SIF and US SIF Foundation. Report on US Sustainable, Responsible and Impact. Investing Trends (2018).

US reached $ 12 trillion, 38% higher than it was in 2016. SRI requires companies to work out and implement managerial methods and tools that allow investment projects to achieve environmental, social, and governance development goals (ESG) [5]. A number of global organizations continues working on ESG reporting standards and facilitating incorporation of these factors into the investment process [4].

To assess the extent to which ESG projects have achieved their goals, investors analyze a large number of non-financial factors reflecting projects' key risks and growth opportunities. These are incorporated in ESG ratings, assigned by specialized reputable agencies such as MSCI, Refinitiv, ISS-Oekom, Sustainalytics or Vigeo-EIRIS. ESG ratings have strong correlation with market value of the companies [28].

According to the conventional wisdom the application CSR practices should have negligible effect on ICT companies. This is not true. Companies in ICT industry can impact global sustainability via complex, indirect effects on energy consumption, data privacy and security as well governance and transparency [25, 27]. ICT companies will emit up to 5%–6% of the world's carbon emission by 2025 due to the exponential rise in connectivity needs and data traffic. New projects shall become more energy efficient for the powering of equipment [24] while enabling other industries to reduce their carbon emission. In the social pillar ICT has above-average exposure to risks related to data security and systems stability [25, 27].

Literature shows [24] that the corporate governance perhaps is the most influential ESG pillar for ICT companies. According to a joint study of Deutsche Asset Management and the University of Hamburg of the impact of ESG-factors on the financial performance of ICT companies [3], the share of corporate performance (G-factors) in the financial stability of those companies reached around 60%. One of the most important but least studied among the G-factors is the diversity of the leadership in ICT companies. Female board representation is associated with greater innovative success and thus enhances firm performance in innovation-intensive industries such as ICT. Yet, there is still limited participation of women in leadership of ICT companies due to harmful stereotypes and a lack of digital confidence on the part of women[2].

To conclude, investors in ICT industry pay special attention of progress in SRI area of industry participants and often apply ESG ratings as one of the key assessment criteria of such progress. The most influential pillar for ICT industry is the governance one. Thus, to increase the chances to attract investments, ICT companies need to understand (1) what corporate governance factors can drive the progress in SRI area; and (2) what steps the company shall take to achieve progress in the area.

3   Governance Factors Affecting ESG Ratings. Literature Review

ESG Factors and Company's Performance

Many research efforts indicates that that socially responsible behavior can have a positive impact on a company's bottom line. Barbero and Marchiano [6] showed that socially

---

[2] Women in the ICT sector. European institute for gender equality, https://eige.europa.eu/publications/work-life-balance/eu-policies-on-work-life-balance/women-in-ict, last accessed 2021/06/20

responsible activities better served the interests of non-owner stakeholders such as employees, customers, suppliers, debtors or regulators. Jones found that following more efficient ESG practices could provide more beneficial contracting conditions [7]. In [8] a positive relationship was found among eco-efficiency indicators, operational factors and market value. In [9] it was reported positive association between ESG disclosure and firm performance in diverse set of companies in Malaysia [9]. Ghoul et al. [10] found that achieving high standards in corporate social responsibility had stronger impact on firms' value and their ability to access funding in the countries with weaker market institutions. However, there were limited number of studies which consider the impact of ESG factors on ICT companies' performance. Given that SRI is the new management practice, the conclusions of several studies are controversial. In [11–14] the negative or insignificant relationship between the effectiveness of ESG and value of companies was identified. Thus, additional research is necessary to enrich the research filed and address the controversial conclusions.

Impact of Corporate Governance on ESG Ratings
Despite the growth in the number of ESG ratings, investors experience difficulties in interpreting them. Rating methodologies are largely undisclosed publicly and have a significant expert component. This determines the practical and scientific interest in the study of the quantitative dependence of these ratings on the ESG factors of companies.

Analysis of the methodologies of ESG rating agencies demonstrated the differences in approaches. For example, MSCI identifies two groups of corporate factors: corporate governance (the board and supervisory board, remuneration and accounting) and business behavior (business ethics and tax transparency) [15]. Sustainalytics assesses companies' governance on honesty and quality of management, composition of directors, remuneration, rights of shareholders and owners of companies, financial reporting and interaction with stakeholders [16]. The governance pillar of Refinitiv rating includes such themes as: (1) SCR strategy and ESG reporting; (2) board and management composition and management compensation; and (3) shareholder rights.

Board composition, diversity and efficiency is a critical governance issue affecting the CSR and ESG scores of the companies in various industries. Firms with boards consisting of independent directors, women directors and directors possessing financial expertise can achieve superior ESG performance [23]. Another study, which considered Fortune 500 companies, indicated that gender and racial diversity of the board had the strong impact on corporate social responsibility (CSR) ratings [27]. However, board independence did not enhance the ratings. Interestingly, CEO duality had negative impact on ESG and CSR ratings which may reflect the disadvantages of separating CEO and chair of the board position. In contrast, the existence of efficient corporate responsibility arms such as CSR committee and policy independence increased the CSR ratings. Lu and Wang demonstrated that the following of the best practices in corporate governance such as separation of board chair and CEO, establishing ESG committees and gender diversity in the board helped the companies to improve environmental performance and to disclose more CSR-related information [17]. Ferrero-Ferrero et al. demonstrated that such board diversity factor as age and age range positively affected CSR performance [19]. Several researches showed that as the number of female directors increased, so did the firm's corporate social responsibility rating [18, 22]. They showed that women brought certain strengths to the board such as increased sensitivity to SRI and participative decision-making styles. In those studies, it was found that CEO duality positively impacted corporate social responsibility ratings because it increased the effectiveness of board monitoring.

Let's conclude. Analysis of studies revealed gaps in the literature. There were no studies of impact of corporate governance practices on ESG ratings specifically for companies from info-communication industry. There was limited number of studies exploring the impact of corporate governance factors on ESG ratings. There were controversial results of impact of some corporate governance factors on ESG scores: e.g., generational diversity or CEO duality.

4 Data and Methods

Research Hypothesis
We tested the following hypothesis:

H1. An effective composition of directors has a positive effect on the company's position in the ESG rating. This hypothesis will check the literature conclusion that an effective composition of directors has a positive effect on disclosure of corporate social responsibility and leads to improved environmental performance [17, 23].

H2. The number of women on the board of directors increases the company's position in the ESG rating. Several studies show that companies with women in management have better ESG scores than firms with no gender difference among senior executives [18, 22, 23, 26].

H3. Diversification of age groups in the composition of directors leads to higher positions in the ESG rating. The studies indicated that the more age groups are included in the management, the better the interaction of employees with each other, as well as the better the relationship with stakeholders [19].

The Model
We applied ordered logistic regression model to prove the above hypothesis [20]. The model has one categorical dependent variable Y, which is the ESG rating of a company, and several explanatory indicators $x_1.....x_n$

$$log\left(\frac{Pr(y \leq m|x)}{Pr(y > m|x)}\right) = \tau_m - \beta x (1 \leq m < M), where: \qquad (1)$$

m is a rating category of y, τ – is a cut point and β is a vector of logit coefficients, which are the same across the logit equations. Coefficients in the model are estimated with maximum likelihood estimation. To express m in numerical form, we have converted rating into the integers, presented in ascending order (Table 1).

The Data
We analyzed 80 info-communication and technology firms from developed markets according to the Bloomberg industry classification. Time horizon for data sampling - 15 years between 2005 and 2019. The list of firms included both the leading companies

Table 1. Numerical scale for dependent variable

Rating letter	A+	A	A-	B+	B	B-	C+	C	C-	D+	D	D-
Rating number	12	11	10	9	8	7	6	5	4	3	2	1

Source: Refinitiv ESG score

in the industry (Apple Inc, Microsoft Corp, Vodafone Group PLC, Deutsche Telekom AG, AT&T Corp, Telefonica SA) as well as medium and small organizations (for example, Open Text Corporation, Obic Company, etc.). The distribution of companies by countries was the following: Japan (30), United States (20); European Union and UK (18); Canada (6) and other developed market (6). In total, companies from 12 countries were considered. The dependent variable (Y) was Refinitiv ESG rating [21], which ranges from the highest "A+" to the lowest "D-" (see Table 1). We chose Refinitiv rating because of its long history of publication.

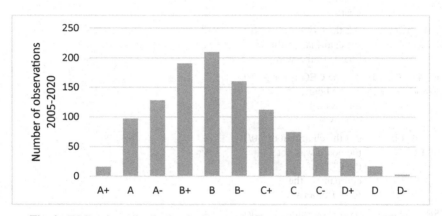

Fig. 1. ESG ratings distribution in the sample **Source:** Thomson Reuters Eikon

As Fig. 1 shows, the majority of ESG ratings in the sample are concentrated in B- - B + range, however the frequency of ratings in lower bands (C, D) is lower than in higher bands. The explanatory variables $(x_1 \ldots x_n)$ are presented in the Table 1. The source of the data was Thomson Reuters Eikon and Bloomberg (for variables to test hypothesis 2).

We checked data for pairwise correlation to avoid multicollinearity. The quality criterion was the correlation between factors below 0.8. We excluded independent members (IM) variable due to its tense correlation with non-executive members' factor (NEM). The choice of NEM over IM was underpinned by that the concept of a non-executive director is more formal than the term of an independent director since it is more difficult to determine whether or not an official is interested in the company's performance. The rest of the factors have a low or medium strength of connection. After data cleaning our sample included 839 observations.

Table 2. Explanatory variables

Variable	Description	Unit	Expected influence on Y	Mean	Standard deviation
Factors for testing H1					
Policy Independence	0 if there is no policy of independence, 1 otherwise	0/1	"+"	–	–
Non-Executive Members	Percentage of non-executive directors on the board	%	"+"	58.7	31.3
Independent Members	Percentage of independent directors on the board	%	"+"	50	32.8
CEO Chairman Duality	0 if the CEO is also the chairman of the board, 1 otherwise	0/1	"+"	–	–
CEO is a Board Member	0 if the CEO is not on the board of directors, 1 otherwise	0/1	"-"	–	–
Chairman is ex-CEO	0 if the chairman of the board was not the CEO of the company in the past, 1 otherwise	0/1	"-"	–	–
CSR Committee	0 - no committee, 1 if there is one	0/1	" +"	–	–
Factors for testing H2					
Women in board	Percentage of women on board	%	"+"	11.5	11.9
Female CEO	0 if the CEO is a man, 1 if a woman	0/1	"+"	–	–
Female Chair	0 if the chairman of the board of directors is a man, 1 if a woman	0/1	"+"	–	–
Factors for testing H3					
Age Range	Age range of board members	year	"-"	21.3	7.6
Average Age	Average age of board members	year	"-"	61.5	3.3

(continued)

Table 2. (*continued*)

Variable	Description	Unit	Expected influence on Y	Mean	Standard deviation
Control variable					
Governance Score	Reflects that board members and managers act in the best interests of shareholders	1–12	"+"	–	–

Source: Thomson Reuters Eikon, Bloomberg

5 Results and Discussion

We estimated the model with STATA. The results of estimation are in Table 2.

Table 3. The results of the model estimation

Variables	Coef.	St. Err.	t-value	p-value	5%–95% Confidence Interval	
Policy Independence**	.403	.179	2.26	.024	.053	.754
Non-Executive Members*	.006	.003	1.96	.05	0	.013
CEO Chairman Duality***	−.527	.202	−2.61	.009	−.923	−.131
CEO is a Board Member	−.375	.234	−1.60	.11	−.834	.084
Chairman is ex-CEO***	.656	.192	3.42	.001	.28	1.033
CSR Committee***	1.747	.172	10.18	0	1.41	2.083
Women in board*	.013	.007	1.78	.075	−.001	.028
Female CEO	−.011	.383	−0.03	.978	−.761	.74
Female Chair	.528	.449	1.17	.24	−.353	1.408
Age Range	.007	.009	0.76	.448	−.01	.024
Average Age	.008	.021	0.38	.707	−.033	.049
Governance Score***	.748	.035	21.13	0	.678	.817
Pseudo r-squared	0.234		Obs		839.000	
Chi-square	851.855		Prob > chi2		0.000	
Akaike crit. (AIC)	2838.707		BIC		2947.548	

*** $p < 0.01$, ** $p < 0.05$, * $p < 0.1$

The obtained regression is adequate, that is, the coefficients are not equal to zero at all levels of significance, since the p-value = 0.000 (Table 3). Also, the control variable, a component of corporate governance, has a positive and significant impact, which means that the model is adequately specified. For correct interpretation of the impact of each factor on ESG rating, the odds ratio must be considered (Table 4).

Table 4. Log odds ratios for explanatory variables

Variables	Logit coefficient	Odds ratio
Policy Independence	0.403**	1.497**
Non-Executive Members	0.00649*	1.007*
CEO Chairman Duality	−0.527***	0.590***
Chairman is ex-CEO	0.656***	1.927***
CSR Committee	1.747***	5.737***
Women in board	0.0132*	1.013*
Governance Score	0.748***	2.112***

The log odds ratios can be interpreted as follows: when the value of policy independence variable is increased by one unit the chances of getting a higher ESG score increase by 1.497 times, provided all other variables are unchanged. The existence of corporate social responsibility committee has the greatest influence on ESG rating. An increase in this variable by one lead to a fivefold increase in the chances of getting higher ESG rating. Conversely, if the position of CEO and chairman is divided the chance of getting a higher rating becomes 0.59 – the rating will decrease. The consolidated research results are presented in Table 5.

Hypothesis 1 is Confirmed. Efficient corporate governance practices such as an existence of CSR committee, presence of non-executive members in the board, policy independence and chairman's past experience and continuity have positive and significant effect on ESG ratings of ICT companies. Presence of the efficient CSR committee has the most significant impact on ESG rating. This is followed by "chairman is ex-CEO" and "policy independence" factors. The impact of presence of non-executive members in the board had marginal effect on ESG ratings. These results coincided with those obtained earlier in the literature that board independence did not enhance ESG scores. However, the impact of segregation of duties between CEO and the chairman of the board had negative and significant impact on ESG ratings of ICT companies. This corresponded with the conclusion given in [18, 22, 27], but did not correspond to that from [17]. It means that for ICT companies strong leadership overweight the agency problem of CEO duality. Due to its controversy, this question needs further research.

Hypothesis 2 is Partly Confirmed. For ICT companies, the growing representation of women in board of directors had positive but marginal effect on ESG score. Such factors as woman CEO or chair of the board had insignificant impact on ratings. Therefore, on one hand, our finding corresponded with those in [17, 22, 23, 27], however the marginality of effect demonstrated that ICT industry is still considered as "men territory".

Table 5. Result of hypothesis testing

Variable	Significant?	Expected sign	Actual sign
Hypothesis 1			
Policy Independence**	Yes	" + "	" + "
Non-Executive Members*	Yes	" + "	" + "
CEO Chairman Duality***	Yes	" + "	" − "
CEO is a Board Member	No	" − "	" − "
Chairman is ex-CEO ***	Yes	" − "	" + "
CSR Committee***	Yes	" + "	" + "
Hypothesis 2			
Percent of Women in board*	Yes	" + "	" + "
Female CEO	No	" + "	" − "
Female Chairperson	No	" + "	" + "
Hypothesis 3			
Age Range	Yes	" − "	" + "
Average Age	Yes	" − "	" + "
Control			
Governance Score***	Yes	" + "	" + "

Hypothesis 3 is Rejected. In ICT industry generational diversity of the board did not have significant impact of ESG ratings. This result could be obtained because our sample included mature telecommunications companies and young IT companies. Additional investigation of this issue is required.

6 Conclusion

ESG ratings are becoming one of the key tools in project selection in project controlling in telecommunication. Yet, the ESG rating methodologies remain not transparent. This makes it difficult for ICT companies' managers to determine individual ESG factors that should be influenced to increase the rating level or reconstruct the ratings. There are few research efforts devoted to determination of ESG rating drivers specifically for ICT industry. We closed the gap in the literature and identified key determinants of G (governance) pillar of ICT companies in advanced markets. This pillar is the most influential part of ESG score in the industry. We showed that the efficient corporate governance practices such as effective CSR committee, presence of non-executive members in the board, policy independence and chairman's past experience as company CEO have positive and significant effect on ESG ratings of ICT companies. The segregation of roles of chairman of board and CEO in ICT companies had negative and significant impact on ESG ratings. Additionally, the growing representation of women in board of directors of ICT companies had positive but marginal effect on ESG ratings. Conversely, in ICT industry generational diversity of the board did not have significant impact of ESG ratings.

This is our first paper in a series of studies of ESG practices in telecommunications. The future research directions will include expanding the research to other pillars of ESG rating: environmental and social. Other direction includes expanding the number of explanatory factors in the governance pillar. We also plan to expand the study to companies from emerging markets. Another extension of area will be the comparison of ESG rating scales of various ratings agencies and developing an ESG rating for companies and projects in ICT industry.

References

1. Glukhov, V., Balashova, E.: Economics and Management in Info-Communication: Tutorial. Piter, Saint Petersburg (2012)
2. Technology, media and telecommunications predictions 2021. Deloitte Insights. https://www2.deloitte.com/content/dam/insights/articles/US93838_TMT_Predictions_2021/DI_2021-TMT-predictions.pdf, Accessed 20 June 2021
3. Rittenhouse, G., Goyal, S., Neilson, D.T., Samuel, S.: Sustainable telecommunications. In: 2011 Technical symposium at ITU telecom world, pp. 19–23. International telecommunication union, Geneva (2011)
4. Renneboog, L., Ter Horst, J., Zhang, C.: Socially responsible investments: institutional aspects, performance, and investor behavior. J. Bank. Finan. **32**(9), 1723–1742 (2008)
5. Governance and Accountability Institute. Flash report: 85% of S&P 500 index® companies publish sustainability reports in 2017. https://www.sustainability-reports.com/85-of-sp-500-index-companies-publish-sustainability-reports-in-2017. Accessed 20 June 2021
6. Barbero, E.R., Marchiano, M.: Stakeholders or shareholders? Board members' personal values and corporate identity. Revista brasileira de gestão de negócios **18**(61), 348–369 (2016)
7. Jones, T.M.: Ethical decision making by individuals in organizations: an issue-contingent model. Acad. Manag. Rev. **16**(2), 366–395 (1991)
8. Guenster, N., Bauer, R., Derwall, J., Koedijk, K.: The economic value of corporate eco-efficiency. Eur. Financ. Manag. **17**(4), 679–704 (2011)
9. Mohmmad, M., Waisuzzaman, S.: Environmental, social and governance (ESG) disclosure, competitive advantage and performance of firms in Malaysia. Clean. Environ. Syst. **2**(100015), 725–731 (2021)
10. Ge, W., Liu, M.: Corporate social responsibility and the cost of corporate bonds. J. Account. Public Policy **34**(6), 597–624 (2015)
11. Brammer, S., Brooks, C., Pavelin, S.: Corporate social performance and stock returns: UK evidence from disaggregate measures. Financ. Manage. **35**(3), 97–116 (2006)
12. McGuire, J.B., Sundgren, A., Schneeweis, T.: Corporate social responsibility and firm financial performance. Acad. Manag. J. **31**(4), 854–872 (1988)
13. Aupperle, K.E., Carroll, A.B., Hatfield, J.D.: An empirical examination of the relationship between corporate social responsibility and profitability. Acad. Manag. J. **28**(2), 446–463 (1985)
14. Horváthová, E.: Does environmental performance affect financial performance? A meta-analysis. Ecol. Econ. **70**(1), 52–59 (2010)

15. MSCI. MSCI ESG Ratings Methodology. https://www.msci.com/documents/1296102/219 01542/MSCI+ESG+Ratings+Methodology+-+Exec+Summary+Nov+2020.pdf, Accessed 20 June 2021

16. The ESG Risk Rating: Frequently Asked Questions for Companies. Sustainalytics. https://www.sustainalytics.com/esg-research/resource/sfs-brochures/the-esg-risk-rating-frequently-asked-questions-for-companies, Accessed 20 June 2021

17. Lu, J., Wang, J.: Corporate governance, law, culture, environmental performance, and CSR disclosure: a global perspective. J. Int. Finan. Mark. Instit. Money **70**, 101624 (2021)

18. Velte, P.: Women on management board and ESG performance. J. Glob. Responsib. **7**(1), 98–109 (2016)

19. Ferrero-Ferrero, I., Ángeles, F.-I., Jesús, M.-T.: Integrating sustainability into corporate governance: an empirical study on board diversity. Corp. Soc. Responsib. Environ. Manag. **22**(4), 193–207 (2013)

20. McCullagh, P.: Regression models for ordinal data. J. Roy. Stat. Soc. B **42**, 109–142 (1980)

21. Refinitiv environmental, social and governance (ESG) scores. https://www.refinitiv.com/content/dam/marketing/en_us/documents/methodology/refinitiv-esg-scores-methodology.pdf, Accessed 20 June 2021

22. Bear, S., Rahman, N., Post, C.: The impact of board diversity and gender composition on corporate social responsibility and firm reputation. J. Bus. Ethics **97**(2), 207–221 (2010)

23. Shaukat, A., Qiu, Y., Trojanowski, G.: Board attributes, corporate social responsibility strategy, and corporate environmental and social performance. J. Bus. Ethics **135**(3), 569–585 (2016)

24. Derue, V.: Putting ESG to work: a case study in the telecoms sector. https://realassets.axa-im.com/content/-/asset_publisher/x7LvZDsY05WX/content/ri-putting-esg-to-work-a-case-study-in-the-telecoms-sector/23818, Accessed 20 June 2021

25. Tataru, I.M., Fleaca, E., Fleacă, B.: Insights on the impact of telecommunication companies on the environment. In: Proceedings of the International Conference on Business Excellence vol. 14(1), pp. 202–213. Society of business excellence, Romania (2020)

26. Kim, O., Kuang, Y.F., Qin, B.: Female representation on boards and CEO performance induced turnover: evidence from Russia. Corp. Govern. Int. Rev. **28**, 235–260 (2020)

27. Moss, M.L., Kaufman, S.M., Townsend, A.M.: The relationship of sustainability to telecommunications. Technol. Soc. **28**(1–2), 235–244 (2006)

28. Kim, S., Li, Z.F.: Understanding the impact of ESG practices in corporate finance. Sustainability **13**, 3746 (2021)

29. Grishunin, S., Suloeva, S., Nekrasova, T.: Development of the mechanism of risk-adjusted scheduling and cost budgeting of R&D projects in telecommunications. In: Galinina, O., Andreev, S., Koucheryavy, Y. (eds.) NEW2AN ruSMART 2018, LNCS, vol. 11118, pp. 456–470. Springer, Heidelberg (2018). https://doi.org/10.1007/978-3-030-01168-0_41

30. Dimson, E., Marsh, P., Staunton, M.: Divergent ESG ratings. J. Portfolio Manag. **47**(1), 75–86 (2020)

Improving Project Management for the Development of New Internet Applications

Tatyana Nekrasova📧 and Natalia Alekseeva(✉)📧

Peter the Great St. Petersburg Polytechnic University (SPbPU), Polytechnicheskaya, 29, 195251 St. Petersburg, Russia
dean@fem.spbstu.ru, alekseeva_ns@spbstu.ru

Abstract. The rise in the use of mobile phones and the ubiquitous availability of wireless networks, easier access to the Internet, and user interest in instantaneous services have led to an increased demand for Internet applications. The purpose of the research is to develop the managerial issues of the projects for the creation and development of Internet applications. The object of the research is a project for the development of a new Internet application. The performed analysis of the mobile applications market indicates an increased competition among the manufacturers of Internet applications, which necessitates improving the quality of project management in the sphere. The authors proposed a conceptual model of project management where the subsystems of project, product, and operational management are identified, and this can be viewed as a special feature of the model. The management within the project faces the uncertainty of both characteristics of the newly created application and some input parameters of the project. Besides, the management of the project has to pay some special attention to the motivation system that is stipulated by special conditions for generating cash-flows, by the project activities of the competitors, and the need for employees of generation Z. Analysis and systematization of all the circumstances of the creation of Internet applications, as well as the features of their management, made it possible to propose an empirically obtained dependence of the effectiveness of the project on the organizational and economic relations within the project.

Keywords: Internet application · Development · Management · Project · Efficiency · Model

1 Introduction

Computational digital technologies are widely used in the industrial and scientific spheres, as well as in the everyday life [1]. Research on the trends in the introduction of digital technologies [2] indicates the full-scale and increasing use around the world. The exponential growth in mobile phone use and availability of wireless networks has changed the Internet usage paradigm. This not only made it easier to access the Internet but also increased the interest of users of instant mobile services. Naturally, interest in using Internet applications has grown significantly.

© Springer Nature Switzerland AG 2022
Y. Koucheryavy et al. (Eds.): NEW2AN 2021/ruSMART 2021, LNCS 13158, pp. 170–178, 2022.
https://doi.org/10.1007/978-3-030-97777-1_14

The growth in the number of Internet applications touches upon the issues of information distribution through various channels and platforms [3], meeting the dynamically growing needs of heterogeneous subscribers. In this regard, many researchers note that today developers of Internet applications are facing the problems of scalability of their software [4], security [5], and data privacy. The possibilities of various networks for organizing Internet architectures are investigated. Some sources highlight the inefficiency of existing Internet structures [6]. Some researchers consider so-called information-oriented networks [7] or content-oriented networks [8] as alternatives.

Other authors say that architectures flexible enough exist anyway, as well as reliable Internet accessories for hosting applications. Some authors believe that it is necessary to investigate the issues of machine learning to improve the quality of Internet applications [9], others are putting stress on the issue of choosing an interface [10]. It is proposed to predict the click-through rate of an ad using machine learning [9]. The adaptability of various networks to the use of machine learning is widely discussed [11], as well as public biases and prejudgments that occur when using web-based machine learning systems.

One can find special studies oriented on creating and managing Internet applications with various functions: for home health care [12], fund-raising [13], creating multimedia content [14], e-learning [15], online games [16, 17], online reviews [18], standardization management [19]. However, these articles do not pay much attention to the issues of project management in the development of new Internet applications [20, 21]. This work summarizes the available research experience and presents a comprehensive vision of the management process of the creation and development of Internet applications. The purpose of the research is to develop the issues of project management of the creation and development of Internet applications. The tasks implied to achieve this goal are:

1. Analysis of the Internet applications market.
2. Development of a conceptual model of project management for the development of a new Internet application.
3. Revealing the dependence of the effectiveness of the project on the organizational and economic relations occurring within the project.

The object of the research is a project on the development of a new Internet application. The subject of the research is organizational and economic relations arising within the project.

2   Materials and Methods

The work uses general scientific methods: methods of observation, polling, analysis, and synthesis. Also, the graphic method was used in the work. The data for the analysis of the Internet applications market was obtained from open sources. The research horizon is limited by the data available for analysis. The study was carried out as of June 2021. The MS Excel software and its functionality for constructing bar charts were used in the research.

   The conceptual model of project management for the development of a new Internet application was obtained empirically, based on the analysis of scientific literature, interviews of top management officials, analysis of internal documentation of enterprises, and personal experience of the authors.

3 Results

3.1 A Subsection Sample

The number of applications available for download on the two most well-known platforms is increasing every year (see Fig. 1), which intensifies competition on the market for developing new applications.

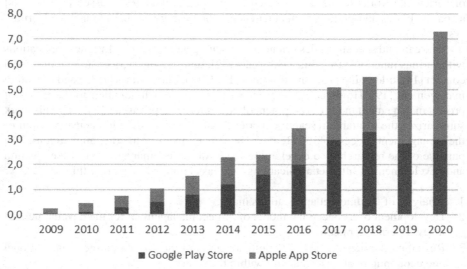

Fig. 1. The number of applications available for download, mln. (compiled by the authors based on the data [22, 23]).

   According to [22], more than 100,000 new applications appear in the Google Play Store every month, and more than 30,000 in the Apple App Store. The presented data indicate a high level of supply in this market. Despite the continued growth in the number of applications available on the market, the number of applications downloaded by users is starting to fall. This trend was first noticed in the United States in the 1st quarter of 2019, then it was noted in other countries as well. According to the report in The State of Mobile 2020 [24], the average number of applications used by a user in a month is 30. Between one-third and one-half of the applications installed on the phone are opened once a month [24]. Studies in many countries have shown that, on average, a user opens no more than 10 mobile applications per day [24]. The presented data indicate a limited demand for applications, as well as a high level of saturation of this demand.

Nevertheless, mobile app market researchers note that expert polls show that users are still ready to install new apps on their smartphones.

The analysis of the mobile applications market also indicates an increase in competition among the developers of Internet applications, which stipulates the need to increase the quality of newly created applications. The higher quality of applications can be achieved by improving the quality of project management while developing new Internet applications. The latter determines the relevance of this work.

The improvements in the quality of project management are proposed to be achieved by developing a project management model for creating Internet applications. The conceptual model allows determining the semantic and meaningful structure of the considered area of project management. The proposed model is one of the first stages of creating an organizational and economic management mechanism that allows making a comprehensive idea of the management system of the subject area under consideration. Further, a graphical view of the conceptual model of project management for the creation and development of a new Internet application is presented (see Fig. 2).

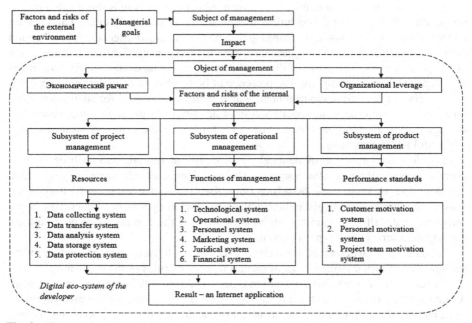

Fig. 2. The conceptual model of project management for the development of a new Internet application.

The main elements of the conceptual model are the subject of management, represented by the top management of the developing company, the object of management is the project for creating an Internet application, and the managerial goal. The latter is formulated by the subject of management based on the analysis of the factors and risks of both the internal and external environment in which the developing company operates, as well as the market for the newly created Internet application. The goal of management may be to create an Internet application in a certain market segment, designed for a certain circle of users. The goal is set within the time constraints and the resources involved. Specific quantitative or qualitative characteristics of the goal are set by the top management based on the company's development strategy. The goal's measurability and its applied nature serve as an important condition for achieving the goal.

The subject of management influences the factors and risks of the internal environment of the company through the systems of organizational and economic leverages. A feature of creating Internet applications is the impact of economic and organizational leverages on two subsystems - the project management subsystem of the company and the product management subsystem. This division becomes useful in case of uncertainty in the characteristics of the developed product. Internet applications are products with a high degree of uncertainty in their characteristics. This circumstance is due to the combination of such factors as high competitiveness and youth of the market, the constantly evolving needs of users, the possibility of inexpensive testing of the product at the intermediate stages, and a quick response to the results of such testing.

In the described situation, the product management subsystem is responsible for the formation and changes of the technical specifications for the newly created application under the influence of constantly changing data on the reaction of users to the beta version of the product. The project management subsystem is responsible for the implementation of the project itself. The goals of these subsystems are antagonists, which determines their separation in the company. The presence of both subsystems in the company leads to conflicts in the internal environment, which increases the need for such managerial functions as organization and coordination of activities. At the same time, successful management of all these subsystems makes the final result the company produces more successful and competitive.

The described subsystems demand an allocation of resources to each of them to operate successfully. Since the resources are limited some coordinating body is needed that alongside other functions should determine the allocation of resources for the project. This circumstance objectively indicates the need for an operational subsystem in the company, that will be constantly functioning even in the conditions of continuously developing a series of all types of products.

Each of the three described subsystems executes a full list of management functions and operates within the framework of certain norms and rules of the company.

The creation of an internet application is performed entirely in a digital environment. A feature of the product itself is its existence only in the digital space, which stipulates some increased requirements for the availability and the quality of support of the systems working with data, highlighted in Fig. 2 as a separate area.

Some special attention should be paid to the systems of motivation, also separately highlighted in Fig. 2. An Internet application has a feature that is the form of payment. Most of the applications are financed by additional features that can be obtained by the user in the applications, as well as by placing advertisements in them. At the same time, about 30% of deletions of applications occur due to intrusive advertising [vc.ru]. Thus, the use of an Internet application is not yet a guarantee of getting an income, and the placement of income-generating content in the application may even induce the user to stop using the application. Therefore, when developing an application, some special efforts should be made to ensure the income-generating potential of the application in the future, so that it won't be used only with the basic functions.

Let's move on to the personnel motivating system of the developing company and the team of the project. Here a well-known task in project management can be distinguished. Namely, the task of attracting personnel to work for a specific project when they are involved in other projects of the company. When the work for different projects is unequally paid, then the staff has a different motivation, which should be taken into account and corrected by the company management. The alignment of the personnel motivation can be performed either by the subsystem of the project management or operational management, depending on the organizational structure of the company. The personnel motivating mechanisms should be developed, clearly described, communicated to the personnel, and systematically applied by all the participants.

A less developed problem in the development of Internet applications is the entry of Generation Z into the labor market. It's of no doubt, that attracting young employees to this industry is necessary. Generation Z is creative, which is in demand in the sector. They also represent a significant share of buyers of Internet applications, so it is critically important for a developing company to recruit people who understand and share the interests of potential consumers. However, the values of the generation sometimes differ significantly from the previous ones, and therefore the system of motivation in the company should be substantially revised and adapted for the people with a different lifestyle in the team.

Thus, the analysis of the proposed conceptual model of project management for the development of a new Internet application made it possible to determine that the effectiveness of such a project will depend on the effective functioning of the subsystems of project management, product management, and operational management (x_1, x_2, x_3 respectively), on the quality of implementation of managerial functions (x_4), on the availability of the necessary resources (x_5), on the availability and implementation of the rules and norms of the project and operational activities (x_6), on the organization of data working systems (x_7), on the full operation of all the systems of the developing company (x_8) and the development and implementation of the motivation system (x_9). The empirically obtained dependence can be represented as follows:

$$y = f\,(x_1, x_2, x_3, x_4, x_5, x_6, x_7, x_8, x_9) \rightarrow \max \qquad (1)$$

where y – the effectiveness of the project.

The resulting dependence can be used to develop expert questionnaires to study the current project activities for the development of applications in the company. This can be useful to identify the growth points. The development of such questionnaires is also useful for the company for setting tactical goals for changing internal policies, redistributing the responsibilities of participants and project supervisors, modifying technological and operational maps of project implementation. All these steps can serve to improve the quality of the created products. The development of expert questionnaires based on the obtained dependence is the field of further research of the authors.

4   Discussion

The development of the digital economy brings about new markets for digital products, one of them is the market of Internet applications. The market data show an active stage of growth of this market, an intensive phase of creating various applications. The market can be also characterized by the unformed needs of the user, and severe competition between developers. It was stated that the number of existing applications is significantly exceeding the needs of users, but the quality of the Internet applications lags behind the existing and future requirements. This circumstance enables launching some new products on the market that may get significant market shares. The presented research discusses the issues of improving project management for the development of new Internet applications that can be relevant in the current market conditions.

The quality of project management for the creation of Internet applications can be improved by applying the developed project management model. The proposed conceptual model is influenced by the following circumstances:

1. Uncertainty of the characteristics of the created product.
2. Existence of Internet application only in the digital environment.
3. Market-driven need to improve the quality of Internet applications.
4. Conflicting goals within the project, aimed, on the one hand, at changing the characteristics of the product during the creation period and, on the other hand, accelerating the launch of the product to the market.
5. Features of getting cash-inflows from Internet applications.
6. Competition of projects within the developing company.
7. Entry of generation Z into the labor market.

The above-mentioned points make it necessary to distinguish the subsystems of project management, product management, and operational management in the model. The implementation of the model determines the nature of organizational and economic relations within the project of developing a new Internet application. Some special role in the model is played by the data working system and the motivating system oriented on the customers, the staff of the developer, and the project team. The quality of operation of the systems can have a decisive impact giving the developer either breakthrough results of the creation of Internet application, or a failure, starting with the loss of all data.

The analysis and systematization of all the circumstances of the creation of Internet applications, as well as the features of their management, made it possible to propose an empirically determined dependence of the effectiveness of the project for the development of a new Internet application on the organizational and economic relations in the project. There were found 9 parameters of the internal environment of the developing company that influences the effectiveness of the project implementation. A more detailed study of the impact of these parameters makes up the basis of further research of the authors.

The impact on the parameters will increase the effectiveness of the project by reducing the risks and more efficient use of resources. The expert estimates are the reduction of the application development time by about 30% and saving of financial resources by at least 20%.

5   Conclusion

The conducted analysis of the mobile applications market shows an increase in competition among the developers of Internet applications, which stipulates higher quality of newly created applications. Improving the quality of applications can be achieved by improving the quality of project management, which determines the relevance of this work.

The authors proposed a conceptual model of project management for the development of a new Internet application. A feature of the model is distinguishing the subsystems of project, product, and operational management, due to the uncertainty of the characteristics of the newly created application. Another feature of the proposed model is special attention paid to the motivation systems. This is important due to the existing conditions for creating cash-flows from the applications, the project activity of the company, and the generation Z employees.

The analysis of the conceptual model developed by the authors made it possible to propose an empirically obtained dependence of the effectiveness of a project for the development of a new Internet application on the organizational and economic relations within the project. The dependence can be used to develop expert questionnaires that can improve the quality of developed products.

References

1. Nekrasova, T., Leventsov, V., Gluhov, V.: Development of infocommunications services in Russia. In: Galinina, O., Andreev, S., Balandin, S., Koucheryavy, Y. (eds.) NEW2AN/ruSMART-2019. LNCS, vol. 11660, pp. 505–514. Springer, Cham (2019). https://doi.org/10.1007/978-3-030-30859-9_43
2. Babkin, A.V., Nekrasova, T.P., Alekseeva, N.S., Babkin, I.A.: Research of tendencies of introduction of digital technologies in telecommunication branch on the basis of the analysis of publication activity. In: Khalid S.S. (eds.) 34th IBIMA Conference, pp. 3176–3185. IBIMA, Madrid (2019)
3. Namiot, D., Sneps-Sneppe, M., Pauliks, R.: On data stream processing in IoT applications. In: Galinina, O., Andreev, S., Balandin, S., Koucheryavy, Y. (eds.) NEW2AN/ruSMART-2018. LNCS, vol. 11118, pp. 41–51. Springer, Cham (2018). https://doi.org/10.1007/978-3-030-01168-0_5
4. Sopin, E., Zolotous, N., Ageev, K., Shorgin, S.: Analysis of the response time characteristics of the fog computing enabled real-time mobile applications. In: Galinina, O., Andreev, S., Balandin, S., Koucheryavy, Y., (eds.) NEW2AN 2020, ruSMART 2020: Internet of Things, Smart Spaces, and Next Generation Networks and Systems, LNCS, vol. 12525, pp. 99–109. Springer, St. Petersburg (2020). https://doi.org/10.1007/978-3-030-65729-1
5. Pavlov, A., Voloshina, N.: Analysis of IDS alert correlation techniques for attacker group recognition in distributed systems. In: Galinina, O., Andreev, S., Balandin, S., Koucheryavy, Y., (eds.) NEW2AN 2020, ruSMART 2020: Internet of Things, Smart Spaces, and Next Generation Networks and Systems, LNCS, vol. 12525, pp. 32–42. Springer, St. Petersburg (2020). https://doi.org/10.1007/978-3-030-65729-1
6. Bilal, M., Kang, S.-G.: Network-Coding Approach for Information-Centric Networking. IEEE Syst. J. **13**(2), 8451876, 1376–1385 (2019)
7. Khelifi, H., Luo, S., Nour, B., Hussain, R., Ksentini, A.: Named data networking in vehicular ad hoc networks: state-of-the-art and challenges. IEEE Commun. Surv. Tutor. **22**(1), 8624354, 320–351 (2020)

8. Christopher Arokiaraj, A.P., Muthumani, N.: A survey and analysis of content centric networking approaches. Int. J. Sci. Technol. Res. **9**(1), 3613–3617 (2020)
9. Jie-Hao, C., Xue-Yi, L., Zi-Qian, Z., Ji-Yun, S., Qiu-Hong, Z.: A CTR prediction method based on feature engineering and online learning. In: ISCIT 2017, pp. 1–6. IEEE, Cairns (2017). https://doi.org/10.1109/ISCIT.2017.8261198
10. Sosunova, I., Zaslavsky, A., Matvienko, A., Sadov, O., Fedchenkov, P., Anagnostopoulos, T.: Context-driven heterogeneous interface selection for smart city applications. In: Galinina, O., Andreev, S., Balandin, S., Koucheryavy, Y. (eds.) NEW2AN/ruSMART -2018. LNCS, vol. 11118, pp. 23–32. Springer, Cham (2018). https://doi.org/10.1007/978-3-030-01168-0_3
11. Li, K.-W., Huang, P.-H., Wen, C.H.-P.: Reducing network cost of minimal-migration based VM management in cloud datacenters. In: NOF 2016, 7810130. IEEE, Buzios (2017). https://doi.org/10.1109/NOF.2016.7810130
12. Korotkov, K.G., Semenov, K.P., Malyugin, V.I., Kiesewetter, D.V.: Developing of emerging internet applications for home healthcare. In: Galinina, O., Andreev, S., Balandin, S., Koucheryavy, Y., (eds.) NEW2AN 2017, ruSMART 2017, NsCC 2017, LNCS, vol. 10531, pp. 3–12. Springer, St. Petersburg (2017). https://doi.org/10.1007/978-3-319-67380-6
13. Liu, Q., Wang, G., Zhao, H., Xu, T., Chen, E.: Enhancing campaign design in crowdfunding: a product supply optimization perspective. In: IJCAI, pp. 695–702 (2017). https://doi.org/10.24963/ijcai.2017/97
14. Rosa, C., Arsenio, A.: Mobile live video on demand for social groups. In: ICCE-Berlin 2015, pp. 335–339. IEEE, Berlin (2016). https://doi.org/10.1109/ICCE-Berlin.2015.7391273
15. Tan, E.L.: Fundamental implicit FDTD schemes for computational electromagnetics and educational mobile apps (invited review). Prog. Electromag. Res. **168**, 39–59 (2020)
16. Posea, V., Balint, M., Dimitriu, A., Iosup, A.: An analysis of the BBO Fans online social gaming community. In: RoEduNet 2010, pp. 218–223. IEEE, Sibiu (2010)
17. Liao, G.-Y., Pham, T.T.L., Huang, T.-L., Cheng, T.C.E., Teng, C.-I.: Impact of workplace frustration on online gamer loyalty. Ind. Manag. Data Syst. **121**(5), 1008–1025 (2021)
18. Zhao, S.: Thumb up or down? a text-mining approach of understanding consumers through. Rev. Dec. Sci. **52**(3), 699–719 (2021)
19. Klochkov, Y., Glushkova, A., Gazizulina, A., Koldov, E.: Standardization of road quality assessment by developing mobile applications. In: Galinina, O., Andreev, S., Balandin, S., Koucheryavy, Y., (eds.) NEW2AN 2020, ruSMART 2020: Internet of Things, Smart Spaces, and Next Generation Networks and Systems, LNCS, 12525, pp. 176–193. Springer, St. Petersburg (2020). https://doi.org/10.1007/978-3-030-65729-1
20. Leventsov, V., Radaev, A., Nikolaevskiy, N.: Design issues of information and communication systems for new generation industrial enterprises. In: Galinina, O., Andreev, S., Balandin, S., Koucheryavy, Y. (eds.) NEW2AN/ruSMART/NsCC -2017. LNCS, vol. 10531, pp. 142–150. Springer, Cham (2017). https://doi.org/10.1007/978-3-319-67380-6_13
21. Shchepinin, V.E., Leventsov, V.A., Zabelin, B.F., Konnikov, E.A., Kasianenko, E.O.: The content aspect of the tendency to reflect the actual result of management. In: Reliability, Infocom Technologies and Optimization (Trends and Future Directions) 6th international Conference ICRITO. Excellent Publishing House, pp. 685–690 (2018). https://doi.org/10.1109/ICRITO.2017.8342509
22. vc.ru Homepage. https://vc.ru/marketing/245003-statistika-mobilnyh-prilozheniy-2021-zagruzki-trendy-i-dohodnost-industrii. Accessed 06 Aug 2021
23. Statista Homepage. https://www.statista.com/statistics/266210/number-of-available-applications-in-the-google-play-store/. Accessed 06 Aug 2021
24. App Annie Homepage. https://www.appannie.com/ru/go/state-of-mobile-2020/. Accessed 06 Aug 2021

Specifics of Forming an Innovation Sector When Developing Industry 4.0 Technology

Valery Leventsov[1]([envelope]), Vladimir Gluhov[1], Anna Kamyshova[2],
and Denis Skripnichenko[2]

[1] Peter the Great St. Petersburg Polytechnic University, Saint-Petersburg, Russia
{vleventsov,vicerector.me}@spbstu.ru
[2] St. Petersburg State University of Economics, Saint Petersburg, Russia

Abstract. The global economy is currently operating under the formation and development of the fourth industrial revolution, within which new technology such as the Internet of Things, intellectual spaces and new generation networks and systems are being generated. In similar transitional periods, the appearance of so much drastically new technology has traditionally been accompanied by radical changes not only to the industrial structure but to the national structure as well, in terms of global changes to the world economy. The emergence of these processes is already exhausting the global hyper-competition, above all, between the two current centers of the world economy with their alternative types of economic systems: the USA with its predominantly market economy and China with its predominantly planned economy. Mainstreaming the problems occurring during the formation and development of the fourth industrial revolution necessitates research of the fundamental bases of the phenomena mentioned above, in particular, the factors of the determining types of alternative economic systems. The goal of this research is to verify the impact the efficiency of the national economy's real sector has on the type of economic system. The methodological basis for the authors' research is the theory of alternative economic systems, which is based on D.Y. Miropolsky's dual-sector model of economics. The theory of alternative economic systems was developed in the context of a neo-Marxist synthesis based on the methods of the dialectal approach. The main theoretical conclusion of the theory of alternative economic systems is the statement that the type of economic system is determined by the ratio between the basic and pioneering sector of the national economy, which, in turn, depends on the system of characterizing the division of labor. At the same time, this theoretical analysis validates the nature of how the ratio between the basic and pioneering sectors are influenced by such characteristics of the division of labor within a system that reflect the efficiency of the real sector of the national economy: specific resource efficiency, specific resource intensity and growth rate of productivity in the pioneering sector. When researching the specifics of forming an innovation sector during the development of Industry 4.0 technology based on a correlation-regression analysis of empirical data on the performance and development of the national economic sectors in Russia for 2005–2019, it was revealed that the biggest influencer on the ratio between the basic and pioneering sectors is the efficiency of the pioneering economic sector. The results of the regression compiled by the authors prove the existence of an inverse connection between the specific resource intensity of the pioneering

© Springer Nature Switzerland AG 2022
Y. Koucheryavy et al. (Eds.): NEW2AN 2021/ruSMART 2021, LNCS 13158, pp. 179–190, 2022.
https://doi.org/10.1007/978-3-030-97777-1_15

sector and a direct link between the growth rate of productivity in the pioneering sector, on the one hand, and with the ratio between the basic and pioneering sectors on the other. In terms of the Russian economy, it was proven that there is a reduced level in the resource surplus of its basic sector and an increased level in the resource deficiency of the pioneering sector, creating objective preconditions for restricting the efficient operation of redistributive mechanisms based on market mechanisms, thus giving reason to strengthen planning economic mechanisms. Promising areas for further research of these issues include verifying the influence of the ratio between the basic and the pioneering sectors of the national economy on the type of economic system, determining the optimality criteria of this proportion and the conditions for its achievement, and identifying the level of influence government and market regulators have on this ratio. The results of such research will allow a set of scientifically based proposals to be developed on the formation of a system of government regulatory tools aimed at sustainably developing the national economy and increasing the level of its global competitiveness.

Keywords: Theory of alternative economic systems · Real economic sector · Innovation · Sector efficiency of the national economy · Redistributive mechanism

1   Introduction

A statistical intersystem theoretical analysis based on the methods of D.Y. Miropolsky's dual-sector model of the national economy [1] is extrapolated to a dynamic analysis of one economic system. In other words, instead of two systems, one system will be examined in different time periods. Next, the logically drawn conclusion from such an analysis will be the existence of (other things being equal):

1. a direct correlation between the level of the specific resource efficiency of the basic sector and the ratio between the basic and pioneering economic sectors [2, p. 203–205].
2. an inverse relationship between the level of the specific resource intensity of the pioneering sector and the ratio between the basic and pioneering economic sectors [2, p. 206–207].
3. a direct correlation between the growth rate of productivity in the pioneering sector and the ratio between the basic and pioneering economic sectors [3, p. 140–141].

Formally, in the most general form, these conclusions can be presented as follows:

$$\left(\frac{BS}{PS}\right)_t = f\left(RE_t^{B^+}, RI_t^{P^-}, RE_t^{P^+}\right), \tag{1}$$

where BS is the scale of the national economy's basic sector.

PS is the scale of the national economy's pioneering sector.

$\left(\frac{BS}{PS}\right)_t$ is the value of the ratio between the basic and pioneering sectors of the national economy for the current period.

RE_t^B is the specific resource efficiency of the national economy's basic sector for the current period.

RI_t^P is the specific resource intensity of the national economy's pioneering sector for the current period.

RE_t^P is the growth rate of productivity in the national economy's pioneering sector for the current period.

In other words, an increased level of the specific resource efficiency of the basic sector and the growth rate of productivity in the pioneering sector over time, as well as the reduced level of the specific resource intensity of the pioneering sector, other things being equal, lead to an increase in the ratio between the basic and pioneering sectors. This, thereby, demonstrates the trend for strengthening market organization of the economy and market mechanisms for developing the national economy. Accordingly, the opposite is also true.

These conclusions are verified based on the statistical data on the operation of the Russian economy for the period 2005–2019.

2   Method of Research

Checking and proving the proposed hypothesis involves several steps of verifying the positions of the authors' theory by conducting an empirical analysis of the statistical data on the Russian economy for 2005–2019:

- determining a set of statistical indicators that measure the variables of the functional dependency;
- dividing the russian economy into basic and pioneering sectors;
- calculating the values of the variables for the functional dependency;
- preparing the obtained time series for using methods of correlation-regression analysis;
- analyzing multicollinearity;
- conducting a correlation-regression analysis.

2.1   Determining a Set of Statistical Indicators that Measure the Variables of the Functional Dependency

The statistical indicators used to measure the annual result of subjects for the Russian economy as a whole and for certain types of economic activity were:

- Organization turnover (without subjects of small businesses, budgetary organizations, banks, insurance and other financial and credit organizations), mln. rubles [4].
- Number of innovation products, jobs, services, mln. rubles [5].
- Percentage of innovation products, jobs and services in the overall total of products shipped, performed jobs and services, % [6].

The statistical indicators used to measure the spending of Russian economic subjects were:

– Costs for producing and selling products (jobs, services) for a full range of organizations, mln. rubles [7].
– Costs for innovation activities in organizations, or costs for technological innovations in organizations, mln. rubles [8].
– Percentage of costs for innovation activities in the overall total of shipped products, performed jobs and services, % [9].

The source for the values of these indicators was the Unified Interdepartmental Statistical Information System (UniSIS). At the same time, the earliest possible time period for analysis was 2005, the first year for which Rosstat provides information about the number of innovation products, jobs and services. The latest possible year for analysis was 2019, the last year for which Rosstat published information for each of the indicators used as of the moment this research was carried out.

2.2 Dividing the Russian Economy into Basic and Pioneering Sectors

It should first be clarified that this paper uses a narrow definition of the dual-sector economic model, according to which the national economy can be divided into two sectors: basic and pioneering [1, p. 160–163]. Using such an approach, a base product is created in the basic economic sector by traditional means and satisfies the vital needs necessary to exist. In the pioneering sector, a new method is used to produce a pioneering product, which satisfies new, non-vital needs [3, p. 93, 133]. Thus, in this research, pioneering products are those that the Rosstat determines to be innovation products, jobs and services [10].

Second, it is worth mentioning the need to select as the scale of the pioneering sector (PS) either the magnitude of its result or the magnitude of its costs.

Third, it is noted that at least two methods can be suggested for directly dividing the national economy into the basic and pioneering sectors [11, p. 9–11]. The first method is based on the percentage of either the innovation products, jobs and services, or the costs for innovation activities in the overall amount of shipped products, performed jobs and services. The second method is based on general absolute values for all the innovation products, jobs and services, or the costs for the innovation activities of organizations.

The main drawback of the first method is the lack of representativeness of its assessments of both the results and of the costs of the pioneering and, thus, the basic economic sectors. The use of this method leads to an artificial contraction or expansion of the pioneering sector scale depending on which statistical indicator is selected as the indicator of results or costs of the pioneering sector. This disadvantage does not make it possible to use the first method for the goals of this paper. However, a notable advantage of this method is the ability to conduct both a statistical and dynamic analysis of the industrial components and structure of the pioneering and basic sectors.

In the second method, the pioneering sector includes all types of economic activity that produces innovation products. In this case, the well-defined indicator for the results of the pioneering sector are the values of all innovation products, jobs and services for the national economy as a whole. For the indicator of costs of the pioneering sector, the costs of innovation activities in organizations or the costs for technological innovations of organizations is used for the national economy as a whole. This option is due to the lack of any other public statistical information that would allow for a more exact, although indirect, evaluation of the full costs of producing and selling specifically innovation products to be conducted. It is also due to the main disadvantage of the first method.

Thus, for the goals of this paper, the second method was selected for dividing the economy into the basic and pioneering sectors. At the same time, the value of the results as an unambiguous and exact statistically measurable value is used as the indicator for the scale of the pioneering sector.

2.3 Calculated Values of the Variables for the Functional Dependency Given in Tables 1, 2, 3

Table 1. Indicators for the operation of the basic and pioneering sectors of the Russian economy

t	Year	TR_t, mln. rubles	PS_t, mln. rubles	BS_t, mln. rubles
1	2	3	4	5
1	2005	28286484.12	545540	27740944.12
2	2006	35602976.25	777458.15	34825518.10
3	2007	44577641.82	958928.74	43618713.08
4	2008	53822945.72	1103365.54	52719580.19
5	2009	52218856.35	934589.04	51284267.30
6	2010	63540 559.00	1243712.48	62296846.53
7	2011	79039 408.00	2106740.73	76932667.22
8	2012	87651 322.00	2872905.12	84778416.98
9	2013	94791100.24	3507866.00	91283234.23
10	2014	102965068.30	3579923.83	99385144.47
11	2015	111801236.27	3843428.70	107957807.60
12	2016	120158889.41	4364321.68	115794567.70
13	2017	130141390.50	4166998.65	125974391.90
14	2018	150802579.80	4516276.36	146286303.40
15	2019	16347230.84	4863381.90	158483848.90

Scale of the pioneering sector of the national economy (column 4):
PS – total innovation products, jobs and services.
Scale of the basic sector of the national economy (column 5):

$$BS = TR - PS = col.3 - col.4, \qquad (2)$$

where TR is the turnover of organizations (column 3).

Ratio between the basic and pioneering sectors of the national economy (column 9):

$$\frac{BS}{PS} = \frac{col.5}{col.4}. \tag{3}$$

Costs of the pioneering sector of the national economy (column 7):

TC^P – costs for the innovation activities of organizations, or costs for the technological innovations of organizations.

Costs of the basic sector of the national economy (column 8):

$$TC^B = TC - TC^P = col.6 - col.7, \tag{4}$$

where TC is the costs for producing and selling products (jobs, services) (column 6).

Table 2. Indicators of the operation of the basic and pioneering sectors of the Russian economy

t	Year	TC_t, mln. rubles	$TC^P{}_t$, mln. rubles	$TC^B{}_t$, mln. rubles
1	2	6	7	8
1	2005	18151498.20	143222.60	18008275.60
2	2006	22006498.20	215650.30	21790847.90
3	2007	27226339.60	241696.20	26984643.40
4	2008	33387196.53	317710.20	33069486.33
5	2009	32584437.47	408689.50	32175747.97
6	2010	38877035.95	411008.80	38466027.15
7	2011	47182868.55	748540.10	46434328.45
8	2012	52559013.59	915366.20	51643647.39
9	2013	57645430.23	1134237.50	56511192.73
10	2014	61912396.04	1231476.90	60680919.14
11	2015	67558508.82	1211294.40	66347214.42
12	2016	73481340.76	1298444.50	72182896.26
13	2017	81783124.03	1416922.80	80366201.23
14	2018	90518804.00	1484901.10	89033902.90
15	2019	98585278.97	1954133.32	96631145.65

Specific resource efficiency of the basic sector of the national economy (column 10):

$$RE^B = \frac{BS}{TC^B} = \frac{col.5}{col.8}. \tag{5}$$

Specific resource intensity of the pioneering sector of the national economy (column 11):

$$RI^P = \frac{TC^P}{PS} = \frac{col.7}{col.4}. \tag{6}$$

Productivity in the pioneering sector of the national economy (column 12):

$$RE^P = \frac{PS}{TC^P} = \frac{CT.4}{CT.7}. \tag{7}$$

Growth rate of productivity in the pioneering sector of the national economy (column 13):

$$\dot{RE}_t^P = \frac{RE_t^P}{RE_{t-1}^P}. \tag{8}$$

Table 3. Indicators of the operation of the basic and pioneering sectors of the Russian economy

t	Year	BS_t/PS_t	RE^B_t	RI^P_t	RE^P_t	$\dot{RE}_t^P$
1	2	9	10	11	12	13
1	2005	50,85	1,54	0,26	3,81	
2	2006	44,79	1,60	0,28	3,61	0,95
3	2007	45,49	1,62	0,25	3,97	1,10
4	2008	47,78	1,59	0,29	3,47	0,88
5	2009	54,87	1,59	0,44	2,29	0,66
6	2010	50,09	1,62	0,33	3,03	1,32
7	2011	36,52	1,66	0,36	2,81	0,93
8	2012	29,51	1,64	0,32	3,14	1,12
9	2013	26,02	1,62	0,32	3,09	0,99
10	2014	27,76	1,64	0,34	2,91	0,94
11	2015	28,09	1,63	0,32	3,17	1,09
12	2016	26,53	1,60	0,30	3,36	1,06
13	2017	30,23	1,57	0,34	2,94	0,87
14	2018	32,39	1,64	0,33	3,04	1,03
15	2019	32,59	1,64	0,40	2,49	0,82

2.4 Preparing the Obtained Time Series for Using Methods of Correlation-Regression Analysis

A modeling of the tendencies in the obtained time series of values for the variables of functional dependency is performed. To do this, analytical functions characterizing the dependencies of time series data levels on time, or trends, are constructed (Table 4). In other words, an analytical alignment of these time series is conducted using the method of least squares (Table 2).

Table 4. Data of regression statistics and analysis of variance results for trend equations of the variables of functional dependency

№ In order	Equations/Coefficients	R	Value of Fisher's F-test		Value of Student's t-test	
			Actual	Table $\alpha = 0.05$; $k_1 = 1, k_2 = 13$	Actual	Table $df = 13$
1	$\left(\frac{BS}{PS}\right)_t = 51,83 - 1,78t + \varepsilon_t$	0.78	20.11	4.67		
	$a = 51,83$				14.34	3.01
	$b = -1,78$				I4.48I	for $\alpha = 0.01$
2	$RE_t^B = 1,57t^{0,015}\theta_t$	0.6	6.99	4.67		
	$a = 1,57$				40.29	3.01
	$b = 0,015$				2.64	2.16 for $\alpha = 0.05$
3	$RI_t^P = 0,26t^{0,109}\rho_t$	0.6	6.53	4.67		
	$a = 0,26$				I15.62I	3.01 for $\alpha = 0.01$
	$b = 0,109$				2.56	2.16 for $\alpha = 0.05$
4	$RE_t^P = 1,21t^{-0,119}\chi_t$	0.64	5.43	5.32		
	$a = 1,21$				2.22	1.86 for $\alpha = 0.1$
	$b = -0,119$				I2.33I	2.31 for $\alpha = 0.05$

The actual values of the correlation coefficients (Table 2), according to Chaddock's scale, reflect the high, strong and close relation for the trend equations between the basic and pioneering sectors of the economy and the noticeable average relation for trend equations of the specific resource efficiency of the basic sector, the specific resource intensity of the pioneering sector and the growth rate of productivity in the pioneering sector. An increase in the actual values of Fisher's F-test above those in the table points to the statistical significance of all the regression equations as a whole. An increase in the actual values of Student's t-tests above those in the table confirms the statistical importance of each individual coefficient of all the equations.

Thus, the Russian economy saw the following stable trends in 2005–2019 (Table 5):

- Reduced values for the ratio between its basic and pioneering sectors, which demonstrates the trend of increased preconditions for strengthening the planned organization of the economy and planning mechanisms for developing the national economy.
- Growth of the specific resource efficiency of the basic sector
- Growth of the specific resource intensity of the pioneering sector
- Reduced growth rates of productivity in the pioneering sector

2.5 Analyzing Multicollinearity (Table 3) Based on Converted Calculated Values of Dependency Variables Smoothed Out According to the Correlating Trend Equations (Table 2)

Table 5. Matrix of pair correlation coefficients

	$\left(\widehat{\frac{BS}{PS}}\right)_t$	$\widehat{RE_t^B}$	$\widehat{RI_t^P}$	$\widehat{RE_t^P}$
$\left(\widehat{\frac{BS}{PS}}\right)_t$	1.0000			
$\widehat{RE_t^B}$	−0.9415	1.0000		
$\widehat{RI_t^P}$	−0.9533	0.9993	1.0000	
$\widehat{RE_t^P}$	0.9385	−0.9730	−0.9703	1.0000

This analysis shows that the factors are multicollinear to each other. For this reason, factors excluded from the model are those whose pair correlation coefficient values with productive attributes are smaller, specifically, the factors $\widehat{RE_t^B}$ and $\widehat{RE_t^P}$.

Furthermore, this analysis confirms the conclusions of the theoretical analysis about the nature of how the ratio between the basic and pioneering economic sectors is dependent, on the one hand, on the level of specific resource intensity and, on the other, on the growth rate of productivity in the pioneering sector. At the same time, the theoretical conclusion about the existence of a direct dependence between the specific resource efficiency level of the basic sector and the ratio between the basic and pioneering sectors was not confirmed.

2.6 Correlation-Regression Analysis

By applying the generic least squares method to the converted data of the traits remaining in the model after analyzing multicollinearity, the following equation is given:

$$\left(\widehat{\frac{BS}{PS}}\right)_t = 218,5 - 547\widehat{RI_t^P} + \varphi_t, \tag{9}$$

where $\left(\widehat{\frac{BS}{PS}}\right)_t$ is the converted calculated values of the ratio between the basic and pioneering economic sectors smoothed out according to the trend equation of this ratio (Eq. 1, Table 2).

$\widehat{RI_t^P}$ is the converted calculated values of the specific resource intensity of the pioneering sector smoothed out according to its trend equation (Eq. 3, Table 2).

The coefficient of determination for this equation is $R^2 = 0,999$, which demonstrates the very high, very strong relationship between these variables. The actual value of the Fisher F-test (1291.04) exceeds its table value (4.75) at the significance level: $\alpha = 0,05$ and at a degrees of freedom number: $k_1 = 1$ and $k_2 = 12$. This reflects the statistical significance of the regression equation as a whole. The actual values of Student's t-test for coefficients a (42.43) and b (|35.93|) exceed its table value (3.05) at the significance level: $\alpha = 0,01$ and at a degrees of freedom number: $df = 12$, which points to the statistical significance of each coefficient individually.

3 Conclusion

The econometric analysis of the empirical data on the operation and development of the real economic sector of Russia for the period 2005–2019 revealed that a noticeable stable growth trend of the specific resource intensity of the pioneering sector of Russia's national economy has created over the past 15 years objective preconditions for the trend of strengthening the planned organization of the economy and planning mechanisms for developing the Russian economy. This conclusion makes it possible to assert the need to change the balance of government and market regulators of the emerging innovation sector towards strengthening the role of government regulators when developing Industry 4.0 technology [12–15].

The logical explanation of the differences in the nature of the relationship between the specific resource efficiency of the basic sector and the ratio between the basic and pioneering sectors, revealed through theoretical (direct relation) and empirical (inverse relation) analysis, is due mainly to the "other things being equal" condition not being fulfilled in practice. In other words, in economic practice, the type of economic system is simultaneously impacted by several characteristics of the national economy's real sector at once, i.e. all characteristics of the division of labor within the system, which influence the ratio between the basic and pioneering sectors.

Furthermore, such a simultaneous change of several factors at once can have the opposite effect on the efficiency traits, whose final total is determined not only by the scale of changes of the factors themselves, but also by the level of influence of each of them on the efficiency trait. As shown in the data from Table 1, the Russian economy in 2005–2019 was characterized by (Table 6):

- more significant relative expansion of the scale of the pioneering sector compared to the relative expansion of the basic sector.
- more significant increase in the specific resource intensity of the pioneering sector compared to the growth of the specific resource efficiency in the basic sector.
- more significant reduction in the productivity growth rates in the pioneering sector compared to the reduced productivity in the basic sector.

Table 6. Basic growth rates for performance indicators of the real economic sector of Russia for 2005–2019.

Indicator	Growth rates of indicator (in %) in the:	
	BASIC sector	PIONEERING sector
Scale	69	163
Costs	58	303
Specific resource efficiency (productivity)	7	− 35
Specific resource intensity	− 6	53
Productivity growth rate	− 4	− 14

Thus, on the one hand, the level of resource surplus in the basic economic sector of Russia shrunk due mainly to the reduced productivity growth rate in the pioneering sector, which slowed down the transfer of pioneering products into the basic category and, among other things, affected the decline in the growth rates of resource efficiency in the basic sector. On the other hand, the increase in the resource intensity of the pioneering sector and in its growth rates led to a higher level of resource deficiency in the pioneering sector of the Russian economy.

As a result, the empirical analysis also showed the objective trend of a growing number of preconditions for strengthening the planned organization of the economy and planning mechanisms for developing the innovation sector of the national economy when developing Industry 4.0 technology, characterized by the stable trend of reduced values for the ratio between the basic and pioneering sectors of the Russian economy against the background of the stable trend of the increasing specific resource efficiency in its basic sector.

References

1. Miropolsky, D.Y.: Economic theory and types of economic systems [Ekonomicheskaya teoriya i tipy khozyaystvennykh sistem]. Econ. Manag. **2**, 22–28 (2007)
2. Eurasian political economics: Textbook. In: Maksimtseva, I.A., Miropolsky, D.Y., Tarasevich, L.S. (Ed.). SPb. UNECON Publishers, p. 767 (2016)
3. Miropolsky, D.Y.: Russian economics in Eurasian integration: macro economical and regional levels [Rossiyskaya economiya v evraziyskoy integratsii: makroekonomicheskiy i regional'nyy urovin]. In: Miropolsky, D.Y., Selischeva, T.A., Dyatlov, S.A., Selischeva, T.A. (ed.) SPb. UNECON Publishers, p. 180 (2018)

4. Organization turnover (without subjects of small businesses, budgetary organizations, banks, insurance and other financial and credit organizations) [Electronic resource]. https://gks.ru/free_doc/new_site/business/prom/oborot.htm. Accessed 4 Mar 2021

5. Innovations. Total innovation products, jobs and services [Electronic resource]. System requirements: Microsoft Office Excel. https://rosstat.gov.ru/folder/14477. Accessed 4 Mar 2021

6. Innovations. Percentage of innovation products, jobs and services in the overall total of shipped products, performed jobs and services [Electronic resource]. System requirements: Microsoft Office Excel. https://rosstat.gov.ru/folder/14477. Accessed 4 Mar 2021

7. Costs for producing and selling products (jobs, services) for a full range of organizations [Electronic resource]. https://gks.ru/free_doc/new_site/business/prom/zatr.htm. Accessed 4 Mar 2021

8. Innovations. Costs for innovation activities in organizations, or costs for technological innovations in organizations [Electronic resource]. System requirements: Microsoft Office Excel. https://rosstat.gov.ru/folder/14477. Accessed 4 Mar 2021

9. Innovations. Percentage of costs for innovation activities in the overall total of shipped products, performed jobs and services [Electronic resource]. System requirements: Microsoft Office Excel. https://rosstat.gov.ru/folder/14477. Accessed 4 Mar 2021

10. Innovations. Innovations, methodology. Innovation statistics (Methodology for "innovations" rubric) [Electronic resource]. System requirements: Microsoft Office Word. https://rosstat.gov.ru/folder/14477. Accessed 4 Mar 2021

11. Miropolsky, D.Y.: Economic Transformation and Structural Constraints: Experience of Russia. UNECON News 4, 5–25 (2002)

12. Miropolsky, D.Y.: Alternative principles of economic politics in [Al'ternativnye printsipy ekonomicheskoy politiki v EAES] EAEU. In: In the collection: Eurasian Economic Perspective. Collection of presentations from the V International Economic Forum, pp. 24–31 (2018)

13. Kamyshova, A., Leventsov, V.: The state and the market in the process of formation and development of the information economy in Russia. In: 36th IBIMA Conference, 4–5 November 2020, Granada, Spain

14. Balance of government and market regulators of socio-economic development in conditions of a digital economy. J. Legal Econ. Stud. 4, 205–211 (2020)

15. Kamyshova, A.B.: Government and market regulators: prospects of interaction in the Eurasian space/Government and market: mechanisms and institutions for Eurasian integration in conditions of strengthening the global hyper-competition [Gosudarstvennye i rynochnye regulyatory: perspektivy vzaimodeystviya v Evraziyskom prostranstve/Gosudarstvo i pynok: mekhanizms i instituty Evraziyskoy integratsii v usloviyakh usilyeniya global'noy giperkonkurentsii]. In: Collective monograph. Dyatlov, S.A., Miropolsky, D.Y., Selischeva, T.A. (ed.) SPb.: UNECON Publishers, pp. 206–217 (2017)

Increasing the Competitiveness of Info-Telecommunications Enterprises Through Building a Mobile Eco-system

Irina Krasyuk[1], Valery Leventsov[1(✉)], Olga Kartavenko[1], Maria Kolgan[2], and Yulia Medvedeva[2]

[1] Peter the Great St. Petersburg Polytechnic University, Saint Petersburg, Russia
{vleventsov,kartav_oa}@spbstu.ru
[2] Don State Technical University, Rostov-on-Don, Russia
{mkolgan,ymedvedeva}@donstu.ru

Abstract. The rapid development and growing competition among mobile companies actualize the need to work out approaches to modern enterprise management in this sector, which must be aimed at increasing the social and emotional value of services for consumers. The ability of an enterprise to make a desired impression on the consumer will determine the company's competitive position and success on the market. Thus, the problem of increasing the competitiveness of services provided by telecommunications companies using digital tools is important. Moreover, since the convergence of information and telecommunications technology is fast, the popular concept of a business eco-system aimed at forming the service value chain has become wide-spread. This paper studies the effects from the integration and interaction of info-telecommunications enterprises. First we reveal the link between the competitiveness of an enterprise and its business model system, then we focus on studying the impact of various types of relations on the values of the customer, competitor and other participants in the eco-system. The results obtained give grounds for understanding a complex interplay between the participants of the created added value in the eco-system of mobile business.

Keywords: Info-telecommunications · Service value · Competitiveness · Eco-system

1 Introduction

Developing modern business in the telecommunications sector is largely dependent on the adaptiveness of enterprises to the modern conditions of the market economy. This process implies increased competitiveness of enterprises and creation of competitive advantages in the periods when the market is volatile. Managing the competitiveness of an enterprise is a totality of measures aimed at consistent improvement of production process, continuous search for new distribution channels, new groups of consumers, enhanced service, advertising [1]. It should be considered as an integral part of the enterprise management system. Every enterprise when it enters the market with a product

© Springer Nature Switzerland AG 2022
Y. Koucheryavy et al. (Eds.): NEW2AN 2021/ruSMART 2021, LNCS 13158, pp. 191–200, 2022.
https://doi.org/10.1007/978-3-030-97777-1_16

or service (or plans to do so), first of all, encounters an obstacle that makes it adapt its activities to certain market parameters. This obstacle is other firms that do business in this market, i.e. competitors. The relationship between them is defined by the term "competition".

Stable operation of telecommunications companies in the conditions of unfavorable external environment directly depends on the success of the enterprise's activities and its competitiveness level. The competitiveness of a telecommunications enterprise represents a totality of interconnected building blocks aimed at ensuring for the company's strong competitive positions, maintaining and developing the existing competitive advantages and creating new ones.

Competitiveness is an economic category whose essence does not have a single and unambiguous interpretation. To understand competition deeper, let us have a look at the definitions given by various authors. Competition is a form of mutual rivalry between market economy players, which is preconditioned by a sovereign right of each of them to implement their economic potential [2].

I.M. Lifshits, the author of "Competitiveness of products and services", point out that there are three approaches to defining the term competitiveness: 1) "Competitiveness is a certain action on the market. The approach is based on understanding competence as rivalry for achieving better results" [3]. 2) Competitiveness is one of the main performance evaluation criteria. The approach is based on understanding competitiveness as an integral property of the market.

Competition in the mobile business is getting fiercer as more and more competitive enterprises enter the market and the info-telecommunications sector is transforming due to the faster convergence of information and communications technology. The ranking of the role that the ICT of our country plays is very significant in the structure of the global competitiveness index among various countries and production drivers (Fig. 1). The situation makes enterprises to reveal its strategic and innovative potential and strive for its most effective use, as well as create new competitive positions. The Russian business stably grows it digital potential, as shown by statistical data for years 2015–2019, and provokes the info-telecommunications sector to carry out technological, organizational and marketing innovations (Fig. 2). Having these positions in this industry is one of the key elements for gaining profit today that allows the enterprises to survive and grow.

Analyzing the publications that discuss the problems of competitive positions, we come to a conclusion that this category is complex and multi-faceted and learn that there is a differentiated system of interpretation of this term.

Some authors highlight the dynamic nature of competitiveness. J. Schumpeter considered competition as a system of dynamic and developing economic relations [4], while M. Porter compares competition to a dynamic and evolving process, a forever changing landscape where new products and new marketing ways appear, as well as new production processes and new market segments [2]. In his early works, Porter suggests that companies achieve their competitive advantage either by providing their customers with bigger value at a price lower than the price of competitors, or by using unique ways in their activities and create bigger value than their competitors do and, thus, charge the premium price (differentiation). However, in his later publications, the scientist justifies

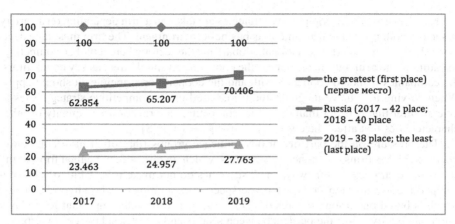

Fig. 1. The world ranking of digital competitiveness

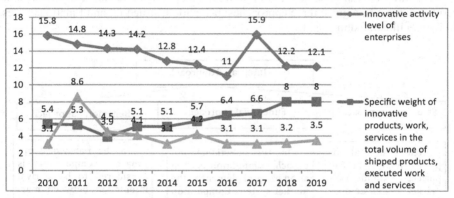

Fig. 2. Major indicators of innovative activities of ICT enterprises in Russia (source: Digital Economics: 2021: brief statistics digest. Moscow: Research university Higher School of Economics, 2021, https://publications.hse.ru/books/420262192)

his new vision of competitiveness, which is based on forming value jointly with the client [6].

A competitive strategy is a specific combination of objectives and measures used by a firm to achieve the goal it sets. Three fundamental areas are in the focus of attention of strategic decision-making in the process of formulating competitive strategies: the sphere of competition, the types of relationships with competitors, the types of competitive advantages [7].

The first of the above areas is the sector of a firm's competitive activities, which is presented by the market where the firm is going to compete offering its products or services. The second area is about the relationships between firms and implies identifying agents that can be seen as competitors or partners. This approach to relationship between firms helps to distinguish the sphere of competition and the sphere of cooperation.

Key decisions about competitive strategies are taken in a firm depending on a variety of factors both inside the firm and in its business environment. The firm must take decisions about the market (local, national, global) and the sector where it will be competing. In addition, the firm must decide about the companies it should treat as key competitors, the companies it should cooperate with and the cooperation principles it should apply. When striving to achieve its goals, the firm, based on its competitive strategy, tries to give an offer that is better than that of its competitor in terms of price, quality or other characteristics that affect the customer's buying decision [8].

The pressure on the part of various influence groups (that often have conflicting interests) makes firms take concrete measures, which, in turn, affect the final form of the competitive strategy. In this way, "net" strategies do not make it possible to achieve a competitive advantage in a longer term perspective. A solution may be a hybrid strategy, which is based on various spheres of choice [9]. It is especially important for today's economic reality, when the borders between sectors and countries, between enterprises and the environment are being erased [10].

Over time we can observe the evolution of standpoints of various economists concerning competition given three approaches: behavioral, structural and functional ones, which are illustrated in Fig. 3.

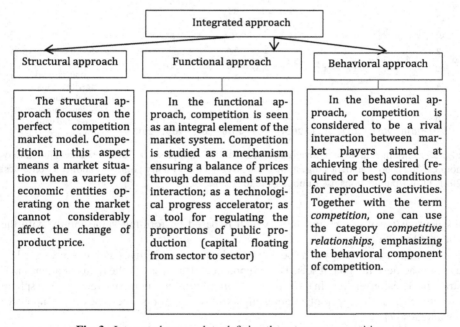

Fig. 3. Integrated approach to defining the category *competition*

Most researchers consider competitive positions from the consumer's perspective, see them as some specifics that brings substantial profits or benefits and are inclined to the idea that these positions must be based on consumer value. However, modern literature lacks a clear definition of this notion. The problems of competitiveness were discussed in the works by various researchers. Michael Porter worked out a theory of competitive positions where competiveness is defined as an ability to compete on the world market having a global strategy. Thus, it can be concluded that competitiveness predetermines the success or failure of a country in specific industries and its place in the system of the world economy, while internal competitiveness depends on the ability of an industry to develop continuously and introduce innovations.

An eco-system can be defined as a totality of relations between various subjects oscillating around a specific problem and cooperating to find comprehensive solutions. In its essence, such an eco-system is created by all organizations which are aimed at developing through innovation. This group of relations is characterized by a symbiosis not only in terms of technical but also a resource component, including knowledge and abilities for development [11].

Thus, the trends for the emergence of business eco-systems determine the importance of interaction in the created value chain. As a result, there is need for response to the demands of companies for synchronized and coordinated activities of their partners who take part in the process of creating, implementing and delivering value to the consumer. This synchronization is possible in case of the information and technical maintenance of the new generation eco-system, which supplements and expands the classical information and technical maintenance with applications and special infrastructure. As a rule, this is done by ICT enterprises.

2 Method of Research

The research methodology is based on general methods of scientific cognition and system approach. The core methods of the research are logical and monographic methods, foresight research, comparison, synthesis and structural analysis.

This paper relies on the information from the following key databases: Scopus, Web of Science, Semantic Scholar, ResearchGate; reports on strategic development of telecommunications companies, statistical data of the Higher School of Economics (Moscow), data from the IMD WORLD COMPETITIVENESS CENTER.

Speaking about the facts affecting the competitiveness of telecommunications enterprises, we cannot but mention the impact of global trends. Changes in the business structure, such as breaking-through technological advances, digitalization and quicker life cycle of products lead to full-scale transformations in the sector we are considering. Distribution channels are changing, profitability zones are shifting, new market players appear on the market. This all profoundly changes the balance of power in the industry and considerably speeds up the introduction of new business models. Comprehensive digitalization leads to the transformations in the activities of the companies operating on this market. Lots of new stakeholders appear on the market and only those enterprises who build their organizational and economic relationships given the requirements of digital trends are becoming the leaders. As a result, the eco-system approach to the organization of interaction is getting more and more widely-spread. It becomes one of the issues that attract the interest of scientific community and is a prospective area for practical application in the activities of various companies. (Ratten, 2020), (Kandiah &

Gossain, 1998; Scaringella & Radziwon, 2018; Sklyar et al., 2019; Stam & van de Ven, 2019; Tsujimoto et al., 2018; Tsvetkova & Gustafsson, 2012; Valkokari, 2015) [12–19].

2.1   Role and Significance of Marketing in Forming the Competitive Advantages of Mobile Business Enterprises

Competitiveness is based on a set of competitive advantages that are sustained for a long period of time. In order to achieve competitiveness, ICT enterprises have to look for possible sources for finding and gaining such advantages. It is thanks to competitiveness that enterprises can grow, introduce innovations in their activities and develop their business. Otherwise, they will lose their market share and go bankrupt [20]. For this reason, mobile business enterprises have to develop the relevant management strategy and tactics and always improve and update them.

In its essence, the quality of provided services is an important component of service marketing, which acts as a main requirement for establishing the quality of servicing in the mind of consumers to satisfy them. In the very dynamic and competitive environment of this business, the quality of servicing is attracting more and more attention [21]. For consumers, services, being intangible, are the material evidence of their interaction with servicing organizations. Among other things, the material/ physical environment is one of the aspects of the service quality, which establish the prospect of enhancing the service quality for consumers [22]. Clear understanding of material evidence helps to reduce the uncertainty of clients, because they cannot evaluate in advance the quality of services they are provided.

In order to understand the quality of a service, we should define its specific features as a product. Investigating their consumers' emotional need, enterprises must create such a service that would fully satisfy the emotional and motivational needs of the consumer. The concept of the experience economy is transforming the approach to the offer of a mobile service into a multi-level interplay system: "mobile service – mobile service value – mobile service experience" (Fig. 4).

It should be noted that service plays a key role in the perception and experience of consumers. Consequently, the significance of staff is growing in communications with the consumer throughout all the links and processes in which the service value is created as well as in the implementation of the strategic development goals of a mobile business enterprise, because the experience of the consumer is formed by aesthetic aspects, which take shape in service processes and behavioral acts performed in the service space of the "contact zone".

The competitiveness of ICT enterprises largely depends on the specifics of their operation. Various types of enterprises in the industry have considerable distinctions in their methods of work.

The specifics of their activities is confirmed by companies' need to adopt individual approaches to the development strategies focused on their own distinctive population of consumers.

In the competitive business environment, an exceptional place is taken by enterprises that offer customers a wide range of services, actively introduce cutting-edge technologies in production and customer service, work out new methods of promotion, all of which require serious investments.

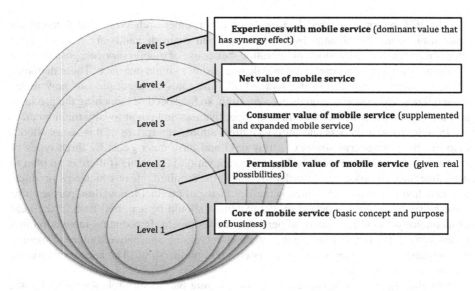

Fig. 4. Diagram of a five-level model in the context of a growing info-telecommunications enterprise

2.2   Eco-system and Successful Development of Telecommunications Business

The development of information technology has resulted in a number of qualitative changes in social relations. It stimulated the growth of non-formal contacts between various business participants in info-telecommunications sphere and considerably transformed the relationships inside enterprises, as well as their corporate environment and culture. Thus, one of the scientific ICT problems arising in the context of digital transformation is the optimization of relationship in the chain of producer-customer interaction. Considerable economic and technical advantages are achieved if many of the various agents of this sector are integrated. For this purpose, we investigate enterprises and partners in a wider context of the distribution channel – digital eco-system, where stimuli and criteria may be selected in a way to bring about close and open communications between participants, leading to the joint gain of competitive advantages.

In order to describe the landscape of the business eco-system on the ICT market, we tried to categorize enterprises and group them by various criteria into certain archetypes. These studies had some constraints because the borders between different types of enterprises can be blurred and each industry can have various distinctions at the same time [11]. Despite this fact, we made an attempt to specify the landscape of the business eco-system on the ICT market, as the transition to the "eco-system" landscape can be carried out by many types of players.

It is common for the business model of an ICT enterprise to have a structural landscape. It can be figuratively called as "focused on consumers" and it allows meeting consumers' demands, offering new products, services and creating alternative business models.

The ICT sector is a typical example of a consumer archetype. The demand for innovation is mostly dictated by consumers. Their main demands are reducing time spent on operations, 24/7 mode of operation, better use of mobile services, possibility of obtaining other services apart from mobile ones using a single interface. These demands are the innovation drivers in the sector [23]. The rates of generation of new ideas, technologies and business models are very high, so the speed of launching the products and their quality are the key factors of competitiveness and client loyalty maintenance.

In order to be a success and introduce innovations, enterprises of this sector should map out their long-term strategy in this field and have clear goals by three types of innovation. No effective work with process innovation is possible if there is no plan to digitalize internal processes. In order to achieve the required rate at which new products are launched to the market, which is the key factor of product innovation, partnerships must be set up while the necessary competences should be acquired both in the field of technology and in the sphere of personnel development. Introducing innovation in a business model, it is essential to concentrate on increasing alternative sources of income and develop the company's own eco-systems and partnerships. The success factors in this process are as follows.

Concluding partnership agreements. Developing partnership relations with banks, financial technology companies, non-banking companies (of course, telecommunications companies and IT companies) is the way to supplement the existing competences with the new ones and obtain competitive advantage. ICT enterprises should carefully monitor the activities of financial technology companies and start-ups on the market, identify the most promising of them and acquire them or create strategic partnerships with them.

Developing the missing competences. Goal-oriented development work requires new skills in digital technology (work with big data and artificial intelligence, optimization of the internal IT infrastructure), in human resource management (search for talented young professionals that are ready to work with innovative technologies – from regular developers to AI specialists), and the ability to deeply understand the needs of clients (design thinking principles, implying that new solution prototypes are created and continuously tested jointly with end users).

Transforming the company's corporate culture. The culture of effective work in eco-systems implies an agile approach to their development, encouragement of cross-functional interaction, provision of employees with the necessary freedom of action as intangible motivation factors are especially important for perspective young professionals.

In consumer archetype industries, patent-capable knowledge is not the key success factor. For example, in smart phone and solar panel production, no dependence is observed between profits or revenues and the quality of knowledge or patents. The ability to gain profits is determined to a larger degree by fast commercialization and scalability of innovations rather than by an invention itself. The biggest share of profits in such industries is made by the companies that are the first to convey new ideas and bring technology to the consumer. Russian producers have a considerable growth potential in the industries of this kind of archetype since the market is big.

3 Conclusion

In the time of rapidly growing competition in mobile business, some important issues arise such as innovative approaches to managing the development of an enterprise in the competitive environment. They should be creatively innovative so as to increase the social and emotional value of mobile services for consumers. The ability of an ICT enterprise to produce the desired impression on the consumer will determine its competitive positions and success on the market. In the course of the research the following main results were obtained:

1. we consider the essential characteristics of competitiveness and the factors that have an impact on telecommunications enterprises, define the marketing aspects that affect the competitiveness of an enterprise. It is revealed that among today's concepts of competitiveness in the info-telecommunications sector of Russia, one can effectively use the concepts that reveal the competitive advantages of the national industry.
2. a five level model is suggested to manage a mobile service in the aspect of development of an info-telecommunications enterprise. The most important requirement for creating product value is the ability to adapt to the changing needs of clients, new technological advances, the capabilities of enterprises and competition on the market.
3. we suggest an interpretation of the landscape of an eco-system, common for the info-telecommunications industry, which can be figuratively called "customer oriented". In order to ensure the required rate at which new products are launched to the market, which is the key factor of product innovation, partnerships must be set up not only with the key stakeholders on the ICT market, but also with the consumers of services, and, thus, on the basis of iterations, the necessary competences can be ensured both in the field of technology and in the field of personnel development.

References

1. Esty, D.C., Porter, M.E.: Industrial ecology and competitiveness: strategic implications for the firm. J. Ind. Ecol. 2(1), 35–43 (1998)
2. Porter, M.E.: Competitive Advantage: Creating and Sustaining Superior Performance. Collier Macmillan, London (1985)
3. Lifshits, A.S., Zherelova, A.A.: Competitiveness of enterprises during crisis: growth evaluation and reserves. In: The bulletin of Higher Educational Institutions. Series: Economics, Finance and Enterprise Management. No. 2 (44) (2020)
4. Taranukha, Y.: Neoshumpeterian's testing of "creative" competition factors: implications for Russia. Moscow Univ. Econ. Bullet. 2018(5), 21–40 (2018). https://doi.org/10.38050/013001 05201852
5. Bashir, M., Verma, R.: Why business model innovation is the new competitive advantage. IUP J. Bus. Strategy 14(1), 7 (2017)
6. Porter, M.E., Kramer, M.R.: Creating shared value: how to reinvent capitalism—and unleash a wave of innovation and growth. In: Lenssen, G.G., Craig Smith, N. (eds.) Managing Sustainable Business: An Executive Education Case and Textbook, pp. 323–346. Springer Netherlands, Dordrecht (2019). https://doi.org/10.1007/978-94-024-1144-7_16

7. Thompson, J., Arthur, A., Strickland, A.J., Gamble, J.: Crafting and Executing Strategy: The Quest for Competitive Advantage: Concepts And Cases. McGraw-Hill, Boston (2008)
8. Mintzberg, H., Ahlstrand, B., Lampel, J.B.: Strategy safari. – Pearson UK (2020)
9. Lambin, J.-J., Chumpitaz, R., Schuiling, I.: Market-driven management. In: Strategic and Operational Marketing: Translated from French. SPb.: Piter, p. 720 (2018)
10. Teodorescu, M., Korchagina, E.: Applying blockchain in the modern supply chain management: its implication on open innovation. J. Open Innovat. Technol. Market, Compl. 7(1), 80 (2021). https://doi.org/10.3390/joitmc7010080C
11. Krasyuk, I., Leventsov, V., Kolgan, M., Medvedeva, Y.: Building a platform-type business model to form an omnichannel integration in the telecommunications industry. In: Galinina, O., Andreev, S., Balandin, S., Koucheryavy, Y. (eds.) Internet of Things, Smart Spaces, and Next Generation Networks and Systems: 20th International Conference, NEW2AN 2020, and 13th Conference, ruSMART 2020, St. Petersburg, Russia, August 26–28, 2020, Proceedings, Part II, pp. 328–337. Springer International Publishing, Cham (2020). https://doi.org/10.1007/978-3-030-65729-1_28
12. Ratten, V.: Entrepreneurial ecosystems. In: Thunderbird International Business Review(2020). https://doi.org/10.1002/tie.22164
13. Kandiah, G., Gossain, S.: Reinventing value: the new business ecosystem. In: Strategy & Leadership(1998). https://doi.org/10.1108/eb054622
14. Scaringella, L., Radziwon, A.: Innovation, entrepreneurial, knowledge, and business ecosystems: Old wine in new bottles? Technol. Forecast. Soc. Chang. 136, 59–87 (2018). https://doi.org/10.1016/j.techfore.2017.09.023
15. Sklyar, A., Kowalkowski, C., Tronvoll, B., Sörhammar, D.: Organizing for digital servitization: a service ecosystem perspective. J. Bus. Res. 104, 450–460 (2019). https://doi.org/10.1016/j.jbusres.2019.02.012
16. Stam, E., van de Ven, A.: Entrepreneurial ecosystem elements. Small Bus. Econ. 56(2), 809–832 (2019). https://doi.org/10.1007/s11187-019-00270-6
17. Tsujimoto, M., Kajikawa, Y., Tomita, J., Matsumoto, Y.: A review of the ecosystem concept — Towards coherent ecosystem design. Technol. Forecast. Soc. Chang. 136, 49–58 (2018). https://doi.org/10.1016/j.techfore.2017.06.032
18. Tsvetkova, A., Gustafsson, M.: Business models for industrial ecosystems: a modular approach. J. Clean. Prod. 29–30, 246–254 (2012). https://doi.org/10.1016/j.jclepro.2012.01.017
19. Valkokari, K.: Business, innovation, and knowledge ecosystems: how they differ and how to survive and thrive within them. Technol. Innov. Manag. Rev. 5(8), 17–24 (2015). https://doi.org/10.22215/timreview919
20. Bondarenko, V., Kostoglodov, D., Nekrasova, T.: Telecommunications techniques in the healthcare development: Foreign experience and Russian realities. Presented at the (2020). https://doi.org/10.1007/978-3-030-65729-1_27
21. Chkalova, O., Bolshakova, I., Kopasovskaya, N., Mukhanova, N., Gluhov, V.: Transformation of online consumer behavior under the influence of the pandemic and the development of telecommunications. In: Galinina, O., Andreev, S., Balandin, S., Koucheryavy, Y., (eds.) Internet of Things, Smart Spaces, and Next Generation Networks and Systems. NEW2AN 2020, ruSMART 2020. LNCS, vol. 12526. Springer, Cham (2020). https://doi.org/10.1007/978-3-030
22. Krymov, S.M., Kolgan, M.V., Suvorova, S.L., Martynenko, O.: Digital technologies and transformation of modern retail. IOP Conf. Ser. Mater. Sci. Eng. 497, 012126 (2019). https://doi.org/10.1088/1757-899X/497/1/012126
23. Nekrasova, T., Leventsov, V., Gluhov, V.: Development of info communications services in Russia. In: Galinina, O., Andreev, S., Balandin, S., Koucheryavy, Y. (eds.) NEW2AN/ruSMART -2019. LNCS, vol. 11660, pp. 505–514. Springer, Cham (2019). https://doi.org/10.1007/978-3-030-30859-9_43

Structural Shifts on Derivatives Markets at the Time of Increasing Digitalization and Post-pandemic Transformation of the Market

Vladimir Gluhov[1], Olga Kartavenko[1(✉)], Anna Kamyshova[2], Ekaterina Popova[2], and Nikita Kapustin[2]

[1] Peter the Great St. Petersburg Polytechnic University, Saint Petersburg, Russia
{vicerector.me,kartav_oa}@spbstu.ru
[2] St. Petersburg State University of Economics, Saint Petersburg, Russia

Abstract. The increasing pressure of exogenous factors on the activities of mega-regulators at the time of the post-pandemic transformation of the market and changing monetary policy leads to lower profitability of deposits at commercial banks and at the same rises the yield curve of weighted average interest rates on interbank loans granted in euros, dollars, pounds and other currencies. The trading processes on the futures market are being intensively digitalized and so the post-pandemic transformation of the market is causing market players seeking to hedge risks to change their behavior. Changes that occurred on the debt capital market during the pandemic have increased investors' interest in international derivatives market instruments and sped up the transformation of regional features of the derivatives market. These changes are mainly caused by the spread of the coronavirus infection and its impact on the global economy, which contributes to the development of digital technologies as instruments of interregional trade. International economic activity has been transformed by the opening and closing cycles of the economies of different countries, which affects the logistics and business processes of economic agents. The transformation of economic activity manifested in structural shifts occurring on the derivatives markets is confirmed by the changes in the dynamics of underlying assets of the derivatives market, such as stock indices, stocks, commodities, currencies, interest rates and ETFs. The analysis of the condition and specifics of the international derivatives market has revealed two problems worthy of independent research: 1) identifying major structural shifts in the international derivatives market that occurred during the pandemic; 2) evaluating the impact of the post-pandemic transformation of the market on the Russian derivatives market. The main parameters of the derivatives market, such as capitalization and trading activity, were determined in order to solve the indicated problems. The study of the dynamics of these indicators in the aggregate system of data of the international derivatives market allowed us to identify the main development trends on this market and assess the degree of influence of the pandemic on its main tools. The analysis of the regional characteristics of the international derivatives market made it possible to find out the main changes that took place on American, European, Asian, Middle Eastern and African exchange markets affected by growing digitalization. The data obtained

© Springer Nature Switzerland AG 2022
Y. Koucheryavy et al. (Eds.): NEW2AN 2021/ruSMART 2021, LNCS 13158, pp. 201–211, 2022.
https://doi.org/10.1007/978-3-030-97777-1_17

made it possible to identify the place of the Russian derivatives market in the system of world economic relations on the derivatives markets during the period of post-pandemic transformation of the market and to compare the changes that took place in the Russian derivatives market with the trends of the international derivatives market.

Keywords: Derivatives market · Futures contracts · Post-pandemic transformation of the market · Structural shifts · Digitalization

1 Introduction

The development of the world economy during post-pandemic transformation is accompanied by a number of changes, which are expressed in the structural shifts occurring on the global and national markets affected by increasing digitalization [1, 2]. The international derivatives market has not been an exception to the aforementioned trends of modern global economic development and transformed too during the pandemic. In order to analyze the changes that occurred in the international derivatives market during the pandemic, two main problems have to be resolved:

- Evaluating trading activity on the derivatives market and identify major trends;
- Determining the level of capitalization of the international derivatives market.

The main parameters have changed (trading activity, expressed through the number of traded contracts, and total market capitalization, represented by the value of traded contracts).

From 2017 to 2020, a steady increase was observed in trading activity on the international derivatives market. Market capitalization increased from 2017 to 2019, but declined during the coronavirus pandemic. Figure 1 shows the dynamics of capitalization and trading activity on the international derivatives market. The increasing trading activity on the international derivatives market is associated with a growing interest in underlying assets such as stock indices, commodities, stocks and ETFs. Table 1 shows the distribution of trading activity by underlying assets. From 2017 to 2020, the players of the international derivatives market had a growing interest in underlying assets such as stock indices, commodities and stocks. It is worth noting that ETF trading increased significantly during the pandemic. In addition, there is a noticeable reduction in trading derivatives, whose underlying assets are interest rates. The trade decreased from 4.52 billion contracts in 2019 to 3.98 billion contracts in 2020.

The changing trading activity on the interest rate market has had a significant impact on the capitalization of the international derivatives market [3].

According to the World Federation of Exchanges, the capitalization of the international derivatives market decreased by 14% in 2020. The value of traded contracts on the international derivatives market went down from $2.8 billion in 2019 to $2.41 billion in 2020 [4]. A significant change in the capitalization of the international derivatives market is associated with a decrease in the capitalization of the interest rate market, which is the largest among all underlying assets, according to the data in Table 2. The capitalization

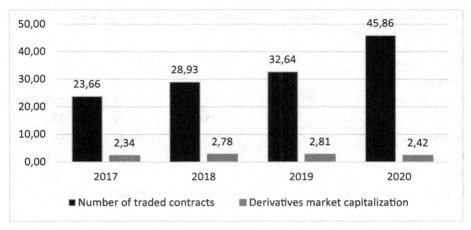

Fig.1. Dynamics of trading activity and capitalization on the international derivatives market, billion US dollars

Table 1. Distribution of trading activity on the international derivatives market by underlying assets, billion contracts

Underlying asset	2017	2018	2019	2020
Stock indices	5.75	7.81	10.30	15.43
Commodities	5.62	5.65	6.85	9.28
Stocks	4.41	5.50	6.08	10.40
Interest rates	3.52	4.37	4.52	3.98
Currency	2.76	3.63	3.12	3.71
ETF	1.60	1.97	1.78	3.07
Cumulative trading activity	23.66	28.93	32.64	45.86

of the interest rate market decreased from $2.3 billion in 2019 to $1.7 billion in 2020, which shows the significant changes in monetary policy of various countries, to which economic agents were forced to respond [5].

From the data on trading activity and capitalization of the interest rate market, we can conclude that the players of the international derivatives market preferred to reduce their positions in interest-rate forward contracts. This is because of increased volatility and decreased liquidity in this market caused by a significant growth of yield curves of weighted average interest rates on interbank loans given in euros, dollars, pounds and other currencies [6].

It should be noted that the capitalization of markets whose underlying assets are stock indices, stocks, commodities, currencies and ETFs increased significantly in 2020. The steady upward trend in the size of these markets continued during the pandemic.

Table 2. Distribution of capitalization on the international derivatives market by underlying assets, million US dollars

Underlying asset	2017	2018	2019	2020
Stock indices	239.25	313.54	308.33	402.51
Commodities	109.52	132.59	137.16	138.95
Stocks	10.28	15.15	14.90	20.29
Interest rates	1 880.87	2 272.39	2 302.44	1 748.14
Currency	92.91	37.96	33.37	36.61
ETF	6.39	7.50	12.82	70.11
Cumulative capitalization	2 339.22	2 779.12	2 809.03	2 416.60

2 Method of Research

Analysis of the state and specifics of the international derivatives market has shown that the following three problems should be considered more thoroughly:

- Identifying trade activity in each region and the reasons for its formation;
- Determining the Level of Capitalization in Each Region and the Reasons for Its Decline During the Pandemic;
- Detecting the development trends on the Russian derivatives market in the system of the international market of futures contracts.

2.1 Regional Features of Trading Activity on the International Derivatives Market

Regional characteristics of trading activity in the international derivatives market are considered given the geographical data distribution. The analysis interprets the data on the following regions: American, Asian and Europe- Middle East-Africa.

Trade activity between 2017 and 2020 was growing steadily in all three regions. The greatest trading activity was concentrated in the U.S. region. It should be noted that Asian derivatives exchanges are actively attracting new market participants, as shown in Table 3. During the pandemic, Asian exchanges made a qualitative leap in trading activity compared with other exchanges, from 13.64 to 19.05 billion traded contracts.

Each region of the international derivatives market is different. As the analysis of trading activity shows, market participants in each region prefer to trade certain underlying assets. These preferences reveal the features of each region of the international derivatives market, see Table 4.

Table 3. Distribution of trading activity on the international derivatives market by region, billion contracts.

Region	2017	2018	2019	2020
American region	10.08	12.17	13.44	19.60
Asian region	8.68	11.05	13.64	19.05
Europe- Middle East- Africa region	4.90	5.71	5.55	7.21
Total number of traded contracts	23.66	28.93	32.64	45.86

Table 4. Distribution of trading activity of regional derivatives markets by underlying assets, %

Region	2017	2018	2019	2020
American region	*100.00*	*100.00*	*100.00*	*100.00*
Stock indices	15.58	18.02	21.63	25.30
Commodities	11.92	9.88	9.13	6.31
Stocks	27.37	27.34	27.42	33.67
Interest rates	24.53	23.69	23.48	13.85
Currency	4.76	4.92	5.10	5.23
ETF	15.83	16.15	13.23	15.64
Asian region	*100.00*	*100.00*	*100.00*	*100.00*
Stock indices	33.58	37.59	44.28	46.98
Commodities	37.59	29.30	30.86	33.03
Stocks	10.10	11.06	9.89	10.12
Interest rates	2.52	2.04	1.83	1.18
Currency	16.17	19.98	13.12	8.68
ETF	0.03	0.03	0.04	0.04
Europe-Africa-Middle East region	*100.00*	*100.00*	*100.00*	*100.00*
Stock indices	25.79	25.57	24.22	21.09
Commodities	23.62	21.18	25.42	24.24
Stocks	15.80	16.60	18.77	26.00
Interest rates	16.82	22.16	19.99	14.42
Currency	17.95	14.48	11.60	14.25
ETF	0.02	0.01	0.00	–

The American region is characterized by the following characteristics of the derivatives market:

- The most traded underlying assets are: stock indices, stocks, ETFs and currencies;

- a steady increase in trading activity is observed in the following underlying assets: stock indices, stocks and currencies.
- a steady decline in trading activity is observed in the commodity segment of the U.S. derivatives market;
- during the pandemic, trading activity reduced on the interest rate market and increased in ETF products.

The Asian region is characterized by the following characteristics of the derivatives market:

- The most traded underlying assets are: stock indices and commodities
- steady growth in trading activity is observed in the following underlying assets: stock indices and commodities;
- a steady decline in trading activity is observed in the interest rates and currencies market;
- during the pandemic, trading activity decreased in the currency segment of the derivatives market

The Europe - Africa - Middle East region is characterized by the following characteristics of the futures market:

- The most traded underlying assets are: stock indices and commodities;
- stable growth of trading activity is observed in the segment of stocks;
- During the pandemic, trading activity declined in interest rates and ETFs

2.2 Determining the Level of Capitalization in Each Region and the Reasons for its Decline During the Pandemic

An analysis of the international market capitalization by region, presented in Table 5, shows that the largest derivatives exchanges are concentrated in the American region, the second largest in terms of capitalization is the Europe-Africa-Middle East region, while the Asian market is inferior to the other regions. However, unlike the American and Europe-Africa-Middle East regions, the Asian derivatives market increased its capitalization during the pandemic.

Table 5. Distribution of international derivatives market capitalization by region, million US dollars

Region	2017	2018	2019	2020
American region	1 621.38	1 837.13	1 962.79	1 593.84
Asian region	155.98	189.08	217.75	258.92
Europe-Africa-Middle East region	561.87	714.80	596.34	563.84
Capitalization of the derivatives market	2 339.22	2 741.01	2 776.88	2 416.60

A structural analysis of the capitalization of the international derivatives market allowed us to identify the underlying assets that make up the total regional capitalization, as well as to find out about the individual characteristics of each region (Table 6).

Table 6. Distribution of capitalization of regional derivatives markets by underlying assets, %.

Region	2017	2018	2019	2020
American region	*100.00*	*100.00*	*100.00*	*100.00*
Stock indices	5.93	5.24	4.90	11.34
Commodities	3.56	3.63	3.19	3.55
Stocks	0.04	0.21	0.24	0.67
Interest rates	84.54	88.67	89.51	78.01
Currency	5.53	1.84	1.51	2.04
ETF	0.39	0.41	0.65	4.40
Asian region	*100.00*	*100.00*	*100.00*	*100.00*
Stock indices	61.76	65.59	58.90	64.76
Commodities	7.74	7.88	14.28	18.61
Stocks	2.84	2.81	2.19	2.52
Interest rates	26.31	22.07	23.34	12.97
Currency	1.33	1.64	1.28	1.13
ETF	0.03	0.02	0.02	0.01
Europe-Africa-Middle East regions	*100.00*	*100.00*	*100.00*	*100.00*
Stock indices	8.32	7.73	8.68	9.60
Commodities	7.08	7.13	7.28	6.06
Stocks	0.92	0.83	0.92	0.56
Interest rates	83.48	84.16	82.96	83.57
Currency	0.20	0.15	0.17	0.22
ETF	0.00	0.00	0.00	0.00

The American region is characterized by the following features of the derivatives market:

- the main capitalization is generated by the interest rate market;
- stable capitalization growth is observed in the markets of currencies, ETFs and stocks;
- there is no steady decline in capitalization in the underlying asset markets;
- during the pandemic, there is a significant increase in the capitalization of the market of stock indices, currencies and ETFs. A decrease in capitalization is observed on the interest rate market.

The Asian region is characterized by the following features of the derivatives market:

- the main capitalization is generated by the market of stock indices;
- stable growth of capitalization is observed in the commodities market;
- a steady decline in capitalization in the currency and ETF markets;
- during the pandemic, there is a significant decline in the capitalization of the interest rate market

The Europe - Africa - Middle East region is characterized by the following features of the derivatives market:

- the main capitalization is generated by the interest rate market;
- steady capitalization growth in the underlying asset markets is not observed;
- there is no steady decline in capitalization in the underlying asset markets;
- during the pandemic, the capitalization of the stock indices, interest rates and currencies market increased. The steady upward trend in the capitalization of the commodity derivatives market ceased during the pandemic.

2.3 Features of Russian Derivatives Market Development Trends in the System of the International Derivatives Market

The Russian derivatives market is quite a young market in the structure of the international derivatives market [7]. Its capitalization in 2020 was $2.11 million (Table 6) with the trading activity being 2.1 billion traded contracts (Table 7).

The structure of capitalization of the Russian market is characterized by the following features:

- the capitalization of the Russian derivatives market is generated by the high capitalization of the currency and commodity markets;
- stock indices and stock markets are emerging markets with a total of $389.96 million;
- the interest rate market is underdeveloped;
- there is no market for ETF products;
- there are no stable upward and downward trends in the capitalization of the derivatives market for underlying assets;
- there is a significant increase in the capitalization of currency and commodity markets during the pandemic

The structure of trading activity on the Russian derivatives market is characterized by the following features of the derivatives market.

- trading activity is most intensive on the currency market with 874.63 billion contracts;
- stock indices and commodities are actively traded markets, with total trading activity of 830.56 billion contracts
- interest rate market has weak trading activity;
- there are no steady upward or downward trends in trading activity for the underlying assets;

Table 7. Distribution of capitalization of the Russian derivatives market by underlying assets, million US dollars

Underlying asset	2017	2018	2019	2020
Stock indices	190.69	170.12	121.37	190.34
Commodities	491.35	483.15	663.69	859.63
Stocks	203.96	237.17	208.29	199.62
Interest rates	1.46	0.29	0.46	0.27
Currency	697.17	607.97	461.24	870.08
ETF	0.00	0.00	0.00	0.00
Cumulative capitalization	1 584.63	1 498.70	1 455.05	2 119.94

- during the pandemic, an increase in trading activity is observed in currency derivatives and futures contracts on stock indices, while a decrease in trading activity is observed in the commodity segment of the derivatives market (Table 8).

Table 8. Distribution of trading activity in the Russian derivatives market by underlying assets, billion contracts

Underlying asset	2017	2018	2019	2020
Stock indices	395.27	378.32	303.02	451.43
Commodities	283.59	336.28	429.90	379.13
Stocks	58.88	71.06	68.02	54.42
Interest rates	0.28	0.18	0.18	0.18
Currency	717.41	622.28	470.40	874.63
ETF	0	0	0	0
Cumulative trading activity	1 455.43	1 408.11	1 271.52	1 759.78

The Russian derivatives market is a developing market in the structure of the international derivatives market. This is due to the low capitalization of the interest rate market, which is the key market in the structure of the international market. General trends of the international derivatives market development emphasize the importance of the interest rate market for strategic development of all derivative trading. This is why the development of this market in the long term will increase the total capitalization of the Russian derivatives market and stabilize its trading activity. There are no options on the Russian interest rate market, which narrows the capabilities of this market.

The Russian derivatives market is mainly used for hedging currency and commodity risks, since the main trading activity is concentrated in the currency and commodity segment [8].

The pandemic period had a positive effect on the Russian derivatives market, which resulted in the qualitative growth of aggregate capitalization and trading activity.

3 Conclusion

In the course of the study, we obtained the following main results, which substantiate the presence of structural shifts on the international and national derivatives markets:

1. The period of post-pandemic market transformation had a negative impact on the capitalization of the international derivatives market. There has been a decline in total capitalization by almost half, from $2.3 billion in 2019 to $1.7 billion in 2020. The main reasons are related to the decline of the interest rate capitalization market in the American region;
2. In the American region, there has been a steady growth in trading activity of futures contracts on the following underlying assets: stock indices, stocks and currencies. In the Asian region, derivatives, the underlying assets of which are stock indices and commodities, became the drivers of trading activity growth. In the Europe-Africa-Middle East region, the growth of trading activity is observed on the market of futures contracts with underlying assets for stocks and stock indices;
3. The trend of increasing digitalization during the pandemic had a positive impact on the development of the Russian derivatives market, which was reflected in the qualitative growth of aggregate capitalization and trading activity. During the spread of the coronavirus infection, players on the Russian derivatives market used its tools to hedge currency and commodity risks, which is confirmed by the growing trading activity and capitalization in these market segments.

Acknowledgments. The reported study was funded by RFBR, project number 20-010-00942 A.

References

1. Kamyshova, A.B.: Interrelation of state and market regulators of social and economic development in the digital economy. J. Legal Econ. Stud. **4**. 205–211 (2020)
2. Kamyshova, A., Leventsov, V.: The state and the market in the process of formation and development of the information economy in Russia. In: 36th IBIMA Conference: 4–5 November 2020, Granada, Spain
3. Crispoldi, C., Wigger, G., Larkin, P.: Interest rate derivatives markets. SABR and SABR LIBOR Market Models Pract. **275**, 5–10 (2015)
4. Derivatives Market Highlights. World-exchanges.org: internet resource. https://statistics.world-exchanges.org/
5. Jeffrey, C., Tyler, P., Dave, S., David, W.: What's the Fed doing in response to the COVID-19 crisis? What more could it do? Brookings.edu: internet resource. https://www.brookings.edu/research/fed-response-to-covid19/
6. Brian, C.: Will 1% Yield force the fed into curve control? 2020. https://www.bloomberg.com/opinion/articles/2020-12-07/will-1-10-year-treasury-yield-force-the-fed-into-curve-control Accessed 7 Dec 2020

7. Radkovskaya, N.P., Klochkova, E.N., Lvova, Y.N., Stepkina, Y.A.: Global risks and the search for a development model in the post-pandemic period. Econ. Entrepren. **12**. 140–144 (2020)
8. Popova, E.M., Lvova, Y.N.: Infrastructural changes in the Russian derivatives market. News of St. Petersburg State Econ. Univ. **3**(105) 29–33 (2017)
9. Nekrasova, T., Leventsov, V., Gluhov, V.: Development of info communications services in Russia. In: Galinina, O., Andreev, S., Balandin, S., Koucheryavy, Y. (eds.) NEW2AN/ruSMART -2019. LNCS, vol. 11660, pp. 505–514. Springer, Cham (2019). https://doi.org/10.1007/978-3-030-30859-9_43
10. Leventsov V.A. Finances and Engineering: theory and practice [Finansy i inzhiniring: teoriya i praktika]. In: Leventsov, V.A., Leventsov, A.N., Kryukov, I. N. SPb.: Polytechnic University, p. 334 (2014)
11. The virus is drowning world markets. Internet resource. https://www.finam.ru/analysis/new sitem/mirovye-rynki-tonut-v-virusnom-fone-20200227-093057/?utm_source=morning_r evi&utm_medium=new&utm_content=27.02.2020&utm_campaign=all_morning. Accessed 27 Dec 2020
12. Oil prices plummet 30%. Internet resource. https://www.rbc.ru/economics/09/03/2020/5e6 56d349a79474203e30da2. Accessed 09 Apr 2020
13. Russia starts a big game with a power move: foreign experts on the effects of Russia leaving OPEC+. Internet resource. http://actualcomment.ru/rossiya-nachinaet-bolshuyu-igru-del aya-silnyy-khod-zarubezhnye-eksperty-o-posledstviyakh-vykhoda-rf--2003091026.html. Accessed 09 Nov 2020
14. WHO announces the coronavirus pandemic in the world. Internet resource. https://www. finam.ru/analysis/newsitem/voz-ob-yavila-pandemiyu-koronavirusa-v-mire-20200311-200 943/?utm_source=morning_revi&utm_medium=new&utm_content=12.03.2020&utm_cam paign=all_morning. Accessed 12 Dec 2020
15. Expert from China names an end date for the coronavirus epidemic. Internet resource. https://sovetov.su/news/109_Ekspert_iz_KNR_nazval_sroki_okonchaniya_epi demii_koronavirusa.html. Accessed 12 Dec 2020
16. Federal Reserve reduces base target rate to zero. Internet resource. https://www.finam.ru/analysis/newsitem/frs-snizila-osnovnuyu-procentnuyu-stavku-do-nulya-20200316-014934/. Accessed 16 Dec 2020
17. Experts predict a further drop in the rouble and oil. Internet resource. https://quote.rbc.ru/news/article/5e660bf09a79476d130d65a7. Accessed 13 Mar 2020
18. How much does oil really cost and what are the prospects of Russia in the oil war. Internet resource. http://krizis-kopilka.ru/archives/73982. Accessed 13 Dec 2020
19. Russian oil has dropped to $19 a barrel. Internet resource. https://www.rbc.ru/economics/19/03/2020/5e7344249a7947add13aeb78. Accessed 19 Dec 2020
20. Buffet: the situation on the market is not comparable to the crisis of 2008. Internet resource. https://investfuture.ru/news/id/baffet-situaciya-na-rynkah-ne-sravnima-s-kri zisom-2008-goda?utm_referrer=https%3A%2F%2Fpulse.mail.ru&utm_source=pulse_ mail_ru. Accessed 13 Dec 2020
21. Bank of America: an economic crisis has begun in the USA. Internet resource. https://sensay. mirtesen.ru/blog/43824663633/Bank-of-America-v-SSHA-nachalsya-ekonomicheskiy-kri zis?utm_referrer=mirtesen.ru&utm_campaign=transit&utm_source=main&utm_medium= page_0&domain=mirtesen.ru&paid=1&pad=1. Accessed 23 Dec 2020

Coarse Estimation of the Distance to the Harmonic Sound Source by DAS for the Determination of Optical Cable Location

Vladimir A. Burdin⬡, Olga Yu. Gubareva⬡, and Vladimir O. Gureev$^{(\boxtimes)}$ ⬡

Povolzhsky State University of Telecommunications and Informatics, Samara, Russia
v.gureev@psuti.ru

Abstract. The methods of coarse estimation of the distance to the harmonic sound source by DAS to determine totally dielectric optical cable location are considered in this paper. Using numerical simulation, we investigated restrictions and errors of distance determination methods under the harmonic acoustic source impact. We got results for such algorithms of DAS data processing as simple triangulation algorithm and triangulation algorithm with source offset. There are determined conditions and demonstrated possibilities of applying these algorithms for optical cable location searching.

Keywords: Optical fiber · Ph-OTDR · Distributed acoustic sensor · Gauge length · Optical cable localization · Array signal processing · Triangulation

1 Introduction

The continuous growth of digital universe is fundamentally changing the life of a person and his environment. The digital vortex covers an increasing number of industries [1–3]. With the introduction of 5G/6G technologies, these trends are expected to intensify significantly. Fiber-optic communication networks serve as the physical foundation for the development of these processes. Only fiber-optic cable lines can provide the bandwidth required for future technologies [4, 5].

One of the most important advantages of optical cables is their electro-magnetic compatibility. The ability to develop fully dielectric optical cables allows us to lay them in areas of hazardous electromagnetic fields (close to high voltage lines and electrified railways). This does not require additional costs for electrical safety measures. In particular, for equipment and maintenance of control and measuring points, grounding, etc. The most significant problem of using optical cable lines without metal elements is the search for cable routing and localization of places of its damage. Route prospecting is an integral part of the vast majority of cable maintenance work. The absence of extended metal elements along the cable line significantly complicates, and in many cases completely excludes the use of traditional methods for these purposes. This requires the development of new or improvement of known methods for determining the location of the optical cable.

© Springer Nature Switzerland AG 2022
Y. Koucheryavy et al. (Eds.): NEW2AN 2021/ruSMART 2021, LNCS 13158, pp. 212–220, 2022.
https://doi.org/10.1007/978-3-030-97777-1_18

One of the most promising ways to search for an optical cable are acousto-optical methods [5–8]. These methods are based on the use of distributed acoustic sensors (DAS). These are acoustic monitoring systems with a phase-sensitive optical reflectometer (Ph-OTDR) operating in the time domain, to which an optical fiber is connected, which serves as a sensor. DAS features high sensitivity and satisfactory resolution. DAS market in on the rise and is expected that by 2025 it will have overshot by 2 billion dollars [9].

When implementing acousto-optical methods for searching for an optical cable, an optical fiber of the cable under test is used as a distributed acoustic sensor. To determine the location of the cable laying on the cable route near the cable, move the source of vibro-acoustic impact, using the DAS measure the distribution along the cable of acoustic signals induced in the optical fiber of the cable, and as a result of their processing determine the location of the cable (Fig. 1).

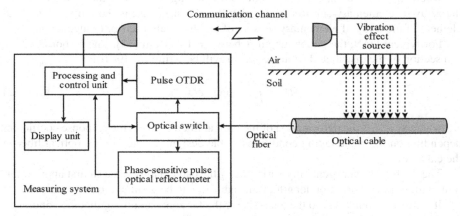

Fig. 1. Scheme for determining the location of the route of laying and localizing the place of damage of the optical cable.

For the convenience of performing route-search work, it is desirable to know the distance from the source of vibro-acoustic impact to the cable. This is necessary, first of all, to determine the direction of movement of the source over the cable. At the same time, high accuracy of measuring this distance is not required. The location of the cable is subsequently specified either by the method of halving, or in another way by the points of location of the source, in which certain distributions of acoustic signals are induced [6, 7]. This makes it possible to use fairly simple approximate data processing algorithms to determine the distance from the cable to the source.

We will use the most widely used DAS data processing method. Namely, analyzes of the phase characteristics induced in the fiber as a result of vibro-acoustic exposure to the signal using the ASP method (The array signal processing) [10, 11]. We will consider the algorithm for processing the results of measurements by the ASP method using the simplest triangulation scheme [12] and the algorithm for processing the data obtained from the results of measurements for two points of the source location when the source is displaced along the normal to the cable axis. In what follows, we will call it the source offset triangulation algorithm (SOTA). In this work, we present the results of numerical modeling, estimate the constraints imposed on the algorithms under consideration and the expected errors in determining the desired distances.

2 Simulation of Signals Induced in DAS by an Acoustic Source

We will consider the impact of one acoustic source. In this case, we will restrict ourselves to the analysis of harmonic impact. Let's imagine an optical fiber as a sequence of elementary sections, the length of which is equal to the gauge length of the DAS. Then, respectively

$$\Delta x = x_{i+1} - x_i \tag{1}$$

where x_i, x_{i+1} are the coordinates of the beginning and end of the i -th element of the array of elementary sensors of the distributed sensor; Δx is the length of the i-th element of the array of elementary sensors of the distributed sensor (gauge length).

For typical DAS, the gauge length is between 1.0–10 m [13]. The response of the i-th section of the distributed acoustic sensor will be written as [9, 10]

$$s_i(t) = \int_{x_{i,0}}^{x_{i,1}} \eta(x) \cdot \varepsilon(x, t) dx \tag{2}$$

where $\varepsilon(x, t)$ is the deformation of the optical fiber; $\eta(x)$ - is the response coefficient depending on the cable laying conditions, cable design, position of the optical fiber in the cable, etc.

The coefficient $\eta(x)$ generally varies along the cable. However, as a first approximation, within the construction length of the cable, it can be assumed to be constant.

If we restrict ourselves to the analysis for the far zone, assuming that the conditions for this assumption are satisfied, then the acoustic field of a point source acting on the optical fiber of the cable is described as [14]

$$P(t, x) = \frac{P_0}{r} \exp[j(\omega t - kr)]$$
$$r = \sqrt{(z - z_0)^2 + (y - y_0)^2 + (x - x_0)^2} \tag{3}$$

where x_0, y_0, z_0 – coordinates of the source of acoustic signals, x, y, z – coordinates of some point of the optical fiber, ω – circular frequency, t – time; k is the wavenumber, P_0 – is the amplitude of the acoustic signal at the source output.

Figure 2 shows the results of calculating the distributions of the amplitude and phase of the ratio $P(t, x)/P_0$ along the fiber provided that the cable is laid in a straight line. It was assumed that the source of the acoustic signal and the optical cable are in the air, $(z - z_0) = 1$ m, $(y - y_0) = 2$ m, the frequency of the acoustic signal is 2 kHz and the speed of sound propagation in the air is 331 m/s.

Taking into account (2) and (3) the recorded DAS signal from an optical fiber on an elementary cable section is described as

$$P_C(t, x_i) = P_0 \cdot \exp(j\omega t) \int_{x_{i,0}}^{x_{i,1}} \frac{\eta(x)}{r} \exp(-jkr) dx \tag{4}$$

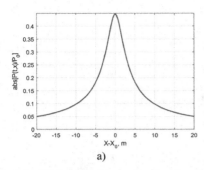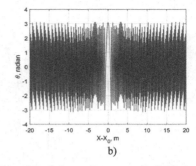

a) b)

Fig. 2. Distributions of the amplitude (a) and phase (b) of the acting acoustic field along the optical fiber.

Figure 2(b) shows the estimates of the distributions of the phase of the ratio $P_C(t, x)/P_0$ depending on the coordinates x and y, calculated by the formula (4) for the conditions considered above at $\Delta x = 1$ m и $\eta = 1$. The integral was calculated numerically by the trapezoidal method.

3 Algorithm of Simple Triangulation

The processing of the results of the distribution along the cable of the phase of the received DAS signal based on the ray method using the Algorithm of simple triangulation (AST) is as follows. Determine the angle of incidence of the beam on the i-th elementary section of the optical fiber sensor by the formula

$$\alpha_i = \arccos\left(\frac{\varphi_{i+1} - \varphi_i}{k \cdot \Delta x}\right) \tag{5}$$

We calculate the estimate of the distance from the cable to the source of the vibro-acoustic signal for the $(i + 1)$-th elementary section of the fiber-optic sensor as

$$y_i = x_{i+1} \cdot tg\alpha_i \tag{6}$$

We calculate the required estimate of the distance as the average

$$y_m = \frac{\sum_{i=2}^{N-1} y_i}{N-1} \tag{7}$$

The relative estimation error in percent was determined by the formula

$$\delta = 100 \cdot \frac{y_z - y_m}{y_z}, \% \tag{8}$$

$$y_z = \sqrt{y^2 + z^2}$$

Here y_z is the distance from the source to the cable, specified in the simulation of the signal induced on the fiber by acoustic exposure; z – cable laying depth (Fig. 3).

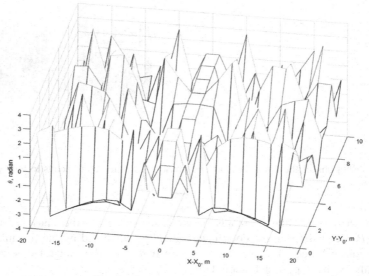

Fig. 3. DAS signal phase distribution.

Let us assume $X_g = \Delta x/\lambda$, $X_y = \Delta x/y$. Here λ – is the acoustic wavelength. Figures 4 and 5 show the dependences of the error estimates on the entered values X_g and X_y. Figure 6 shows the dependences of the errors on X_y and the signal-to-noise ratio (SNR) at $X_y = 0.36$. Additive interference was considered.

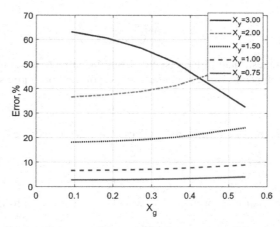

Fig. 4. Dependences of errors on the normalized parameters of the gauge length DAS.

As shown by the simulation results, the region of variation of the parameters X_g and X_y, in which the errors are acceptable are small. So that the errors do not exceed 10%, it is necessary to fulfill the conditions $X_g < 0.3$–0.4 and $X_y < 0.4$–0.5. The limitations on X_g are explained by the fact that the phase incursion at the gauge length did not

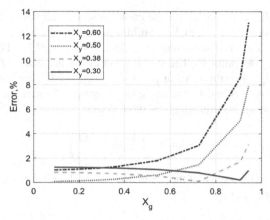

Fig. 5. Dependences of errors on the normalized parameters of the gauge length DAS.

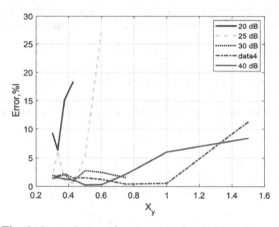

Fig. 6. Dependences of errors on the level of interference.

exceed 2π to make measurements. Such a narrow range of changes in the parameter X_g significantly limits the ability to select the frequency of the acoustic signal, which is undesirable in conditions of interference. This is clearly demonstrated by the graphs in Fig. 6. An increase in errors with an increase in X_y is expected. Since in this case the dependence of the phase incursion on the y coordinate decreases in comparison with the dependence on the gauge length.

4   Source Offset Triangulation Algorithm

When using SOTA, the distribution along the cable of the phase of the signal induced by the acoustic impact in the DAS at some point A is preliminarily measured. This distribution is used to determine the point corresponding to the coordinate of the source on the axis of the cable. The source is displaced from point A and, moving it, point B is found, the coordinate of which on the cable axis coincides with point A. Drawing a straight line through points A and B, build a normal to the cable axis. Displace the source from point A along the normal by a distance $\Delta y < 0.3\lambda$. The location of the source is designated as point C. The distribution along the cable of the phase of the acoustic-induced signal in the DAS at point C is measured. Then, from the results of measurements at points A and C, the angle of deflection of the ray incident on the i-th section from the normal is determined by the formula

$$\gamma_i = \arccos\left(\frac{\varphi_{C,i} - \varphi_{A,i}}{k \cdot \Delta y}\right) \tag{9}$$

Then the angle of incidence of the beam on the i-th elementary section of the optical fiber sensor is determined as

$$\alpha_i = \frac{\pi}{2} - \gamma_i \tag{10}$$

An estimate of the distance from the cable to the source of the vibro-acoustic signal for the i-th elementary section of the fiber-optic sensor is calculated as

$$y_i = y_i \cdot tg\alpha_i \tag{11}$$

Then, using formulas (7), (8), the required distance and the estimation error are calculated.

Figures 7 and 8 show the dependences of the error estimates on the entered quantities X_g and X_y.

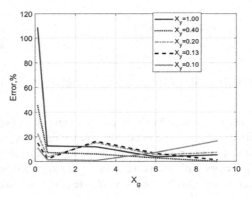

Fig. 7. Dependences of errors on the normalized parameters of the gauge length DAS.

As follows from the graphs, the error does not exceed 15% when X_g changes in the range from 0.5 to 9.0. This allows you to change the frequency of the source of vibro-acoustic exposure in a fairly wide frequency range. The parameter X_y as for AST, should not exceed 0.4–0.5 to obtain a satisfactory error.

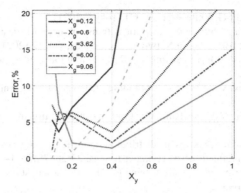

Fig. 8. Dependences of errors on the normalized parameters of the gauge length DAS.

5   Conclusion

As a result of the simulation, it is shown that the considered algorithms make it possible to estimate the distance from the optical cable to the location of the source of harmonic acoustic exposure with an error of up to 10–15% or less. This allows them to be used to find the location of the optical cable and the places of its damage along the route using DAS.

When using AST, the parameter X_g of the normalized gauge length DAS should not exceed 0.3–0.4, which significantly limits the range of permissible frequencies of the vibro-acoustic signal source. When using SOTA, the allowable range of changes for this parameter is significantly greater, from 0.5 to 9.0. Accordingly, the range of permissible frequencies of the source of the vibro-acoustic signal is much larger.

Both of the considered algorithms do not allow obtaining satisfactory errors in the near-field zone. For both AST and SOTA, the parameter X_y should not exceed 0.4–0.5.

It is quite possible that the use of improved algorithms will make it possible to reduce errors depending on the parameter X_g and further expand the range of its permissible changes. However, in our opinion, it is not possible to remove the restrictions on the parameter X_y.

Undoubtedly, the obtained results of modeling require experimental confirmation. At the same time, they inspire confidence, since AST has been known and well tested for a long time period.

References

1. Yokoi T., Shan J., Wade M., Macaulay J.: Digital vortex 2019. Continuous and Connected Change. Global Center for Digital Business Transformation (2019). https://www.imd.org/res earch-knowledge/reports/digitalvortex2019/. Accessed 11 July 2021
2. Udovita, P.V.M.V.D.: Conceptual review on dimensions of digital transformation in modern era. Int. J. Sci. Res. Publ. **10**(2), 520–529 (2020)
3. Digital vortex 2021. Digital Disruption in a COVID World. Global Center for Digital Business Transformation, 2021. https://www.imd.org/research-knowledge/reports/digital-vortex-report-2021/. Accessed 11 July 2021

4. Abe, Y.: Beyond 5G/6G White Paper. NICT, Tokyo (2021)
5. Ranaweera, C., et al.: Rethinking of optical transport network design for 5G/6G mobile communication. In: IEEE Future Networks Tech Focus, vol. 12 (2021)
6. Burdin, V.A.: Method of Route Search and Determining Place of Optical Cable Fault. Patent RU 2656295 (2018)
7. Burdin, V.A., Gureev, V.O.: Method for Finding the Route of Laying an Optical Cable. Patent RU 2748310 (2021)
8. Gureev, V.O., Burdin, V.A., Shaban, O.V.: Optical cable location methods. Proc. SPIE **11793**, 117931A (2021)
9. Muanenda, Y.: Recent advances in distributed acoustic sensing based on phase-sensitive optical time domain reflectometry. Hindawi J. Sens. **23**(3897873), 1–16 (2018)
10. Liang, J., et al.: Distributed acoustic sensing for 2D and 3D acoustic source localization. Opt. Lett. **44**(7), 1690–1693 (2019)
11. Wang, Z., Lu, B., Ye, Q., Cai, H.: Recent progress in distributed fiber acoustic sensing with Φ-OTDR. Sensors **20**(22), 6594 (2020)
12. Hwang, J.-H., Soonwon, S., Park, C.-S.: Position estimation of sound source using three optical Mach-Zehnder acoustic sensor array. Curr. Opt. Photon. **1**(6), 573–578 (2017)
13. Fenta, M.C., Potter, D.K., Szanyi, J.: Fibre optic methods of prospecting: a comprehensive and modern branch of geophysics. Surv. Geophys. **42**, 551–584 (2021)
14. Lependin, L.F.: Acoustics. Higher School, Moscow (1978)

Fiber Optic System for Monitoring Coolant Parameters in Nuclear Power Plants

Roman Davydov[1](✉) ⓘ, Semen Logunov[3] ⓘ, Denis Nikolaev[1] ⓘ,
Vadim Davydov[1,2,3] ⓘ, and Valentin Dudkin[3] ⓘ

[1] Peter the Great Saint Petersburg Polytechnic University, St. Petersburg 195251, Russia
davydovrv@spbstu.ru

[2] Department of Ecology, All-Russian Research Institute of Phytopathology, Moscow Region,
B. Vyazyomy, Odintsovo 143050, Russia

[3] The Bonch-Bruevich Saint - Petersburg State University of Telecommunications, Saint
Petersburg 193232, Russia

Abstract. Problems that are extremely difficult to solve without the development of special systems using optical fibers are identified. In this work, we substantiated the need to measure the parameters of the coolant to control the operation of a nuclear reactor and ensure efficient heat transfer to increase the efficiency of electric power generation. We developed the fiber optic system's design to control the coolant parameters and determined the requirements for the type of fiber. The negative influence of γ - radiation on the optical fiber and the processes of relaxation of E' centers have been investigated. In this work, we proposed methods for measuring the flow rate of the coolant q and the level of oxygen activity and presented the results of experimental studies and measurements.

Keywords: Fiber optic system · Nuclear power plant · Laser radiation · Gamma radiation · Optical signal attenuation

1 Introduction

Currently, in conditions of many various kinds of interference (for example, electromagnetic, vibration), there are problems with transmitting information, especially under challenging conditions [1–5]. These problems are solved in various ways and methods [3, 5–8]. The most promising of them is using a fiber-optic transmission system (FOTS) [6, 9–11]. The use of FOTS makes it possible to transmit information, carry out measurements (fiber-optic sensors) in difficult conditions in the presence of many interferences [11–15]. The use of other measuring devices under these conditions is very hard.

One of these cases occurs at nuclear power plants when it is necessary to measure the parameters of the coolant's current flow inside the reactor's protective zone. The efficiency of electricity production and the safety of a nuclear power plant depend on the optimal choice of these parameters. Molten lithium, lead with nickel, sodium, or water-salt solution at different temperatures are used as a heat carrier [16–19]. High temperature and chemical activity and many interferences create many problems with the use of

© Springer Nature Switzerland AG 2022
Y. Koucheryavy et al. (Eds.): NEW2AN 2021/ruSMART 2021, LNCS 13158, pp. 221–229, 2022.
https://doi.org/10.1007/978-3-030-97777-1_19

various meters, even with the use of fiber-optic communication lines for information transmission—the error in measuring various parameters increases, which complicates the control of the reactor operation. Therefore, the development of new systems for measuring the coolant parameters with an error of 1% is extremely important. One of the possible options for solving this problem is the fiber-optic system developed by us.

2   Fiber Optic System for Monitoring the Parameters of the Coolant

Studies [20–25] have shown that modern designs of optical fibers are resistant to the noted negative factors up to specific values of temperatures (up to 873 K), pressures (up to 25 MPa), vibration (up to 3 kHz), and humidity (up to 100% with special coating). These are incredibly harsh operating conditions. The most harmful effect on optical fiber is produced by γ - radiation (the fiber darkens). Attenuation of the optical signal increases [25–27]. Due to the formation of E' centers in the optical fiber, laser radiation is absorbed. Using this physical phenomenon, we propose using it to control the coolant parameters in nuclear power plants. We have developed the following measuring structure with a fiber-optic system (Fig. 1).

One of the operation features in most nuclear reactors is the presence of oxygen activity $^{16}O(n, p)^{16}N$ in the coolant. Oxygen activity is present only when the reactor is operating at high energy levels of power and decreases almost immediately after the termination of the chain reaction. When a coolant with oxygen activity flows through the pipeline, additional γ-quanta are emitted due to the decay of ^{16}N nuclei. An addition is made to the "natural" background of radioactive radiation present in this zone. This additive to the exposure dose of radiation acting on the optical fiber is of a pulsed nature. It appears in a certain zone of the pipeline due to the uneven distribution of neutrons with an energy of more than 9 meV in the coolant, which, when interacting with the oxygen nuclei that make up the coolant, form ^{16}N nuclei because of the reaction (n, p).

The appearance of this γ-quanta in the area of the optical fiber's coils sharply increases the number of E'-centers [25–27]. Radiation-induced losses α_s increase, which is determined by the following formula:

$$\alpha_s = 10 \lg \frac{P_{out}}{P_{in}} / l \qquad (1)$$

where P_{in} is the power of laser radiation introduced into the optical fiber, P_{out} is the power at the exit from the optical fiber, l is the length of the optical fiber.

1 - a pipeline with a coolant; 2 and 3 - spools with optical fiber (sensors); 4 - protective radiation shields; 5 - multifunctional power supply driver; 6 - transmitting optical module ($\lambda = 1550$ nm); 7 - pulse power driver; 8 - semiconductor laser ($\lambda = 1310$ nm); 9 and 10 - optical dividers with a division ratio of 2; 11, 12, 13 and 14 - multiplexers; 15 and 16 - photo receivers; 17 and 18 - optical power meters; 19 and 20 - comparators; 21 - logical device; 22 - processing and control device; 23 - display device; 24 - central computer.

The P_{out} value recorded on photodetectors 15 and 16 (Fig. 1) decreases. Suppose two coils with optical fiber are located on the pipeline with a distance L between them and the coolant's flow, separated by protective screens. In that case, decreasing the value of Pout in the second coil will begin after some time Δt, which corresponds to the flow

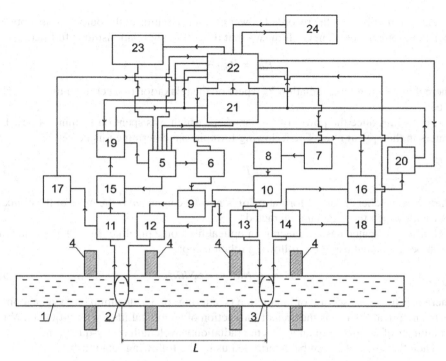

Fig. 1. Structural diagram of the fiber-optic measuring system.

of this segment of the coolant from the first coil to the second through the pipeline. Having established the same cutoff value for P_{out}, provided that two coils receive laser radiation from one source with the same power, it is possible to determine Δt using comparison circuits. Then the value of the flow rate of the coolant q is determined using the following relationship:

$$q = \pi d^2 / 4L\Delta t \qquad (2)$$

where d is the inner diameter of the pipeline.

After measuring Δt, using the previously developed method for controlling the relaxation rate of E' centers in an optical fiber [27, 28], α_s is restored to its initial value (before the appearance of bursts of γ-radiation with a high exposure dose from flowing coolant). And the process of measuring q can be carried out again.

Another critical parameter of the coolant is the level of oxygen activity (the number of emitted γ-quanta per unit time). It also needs to be measured. The previously developed ionization chambers for measuring the flux of γ-quanta in the zone will work with significant failures, and there will be a problem with the transfer of information.

Our studies of the effect of γ-radiation on the formation of E' centers in an optical fiber [27, 28] allowed us to establish that at a certain laser power P_{in}, an equilibrium can be established between two processes (the formation of new and relaxation of existing

E′ centers). In this case, the recorded power of laser radiation at the output of the optical fiber Pout remains unchanged. It means that the following relationship is fulfilled:

$$P_{in} = P_{out} + P_{ec} \tag{3}$$

where the power of laser radiation P_{ec} spent on the relaxation of a certain number of (N) E′ centers.

Let us introduce the power of γ-quanta P_γ, which was spent on forming N new E′ centers in the optical fiber. The following formula can determine this power:

$$P_\gamma = \frac{E}{m} \tag{4}$$

where E is the energy for the formation of N new E′-centers, m is the mass of the optical fiber with which the γ-quanta interacted.

For the presented case of placing an optical fiber on a pipeline (Fig. 1), the value of E can be calculated using the following relationship:

$$E = \sigma SNh\nu = \sigma SNh\lambda/c \tag{5}$$

where σ is the cross-section of interaction (scattering) of a γ-quantum on oxygen atoms O_2 in an optical fiber, S is the area of interaction of an optical fiber with γ-quanta, N is the number of emitted γ-quanta, λ is the radiation wavelength of a γ-quantum.

Then the value of N can be determined using the following relationship:

$$N = cm\frac{Pin - Pout}{\sigma Sh\lambda} \tag{6}$$

In relation (6), the values of the laser radiation power Pin and Pout are measured. The value of σ is established experimentally for each type of fiber since it will depend on the percentage of doping of the core of the optical fiber with germanium oxide GeO_2 and the temperature of the optical fiber T_f. Therefore, when conducting studies of the oxygen activity of the coolant, it is necessary to control two temperatures ($T_{coolant}$ and T_f) and its flow rate q. Time in relation (6) is entered through the units of measurement of the speed of light c.

3   Results and Discussion

In Fig. 2 shows the results of studies of changes in the power of laser radiation P_{out} at the output of optical fiber from time t when exposed to γ-radiation in the form of a pulse with a duration of 2 s (exposure dose of radiation 100 Gy) for various types of the fiber core. In Fig. 3, as an example, the process of controlling the relaxation processes of E′ centers in an optical fiber after the termination of γ-radiation while maintaining the radioactive background is presented.

The obtained results (Fig. 2 and Fig. 3) show that fiber with a pure quartz core is less sensitive to γ-radiation. With an increase in the degree of doping of the optical fiber core, the loss of α_s and the steepness of their rise increase. Therefore, the system developed by us uses fibers with a high degree of doping with germanium oxide.

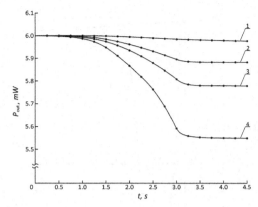

Fig. 2. Dependence of the change in the power of laser radiation P_{out} on the time t at a wavelength of $\lambda = 1550$ nm for a single-mode fiber at T $= 294.2$ K. Graphs 1, 2, 3, and 4 correspond to different types of optical fiber core: pure silica SiO_2; SiO_2 - GeO_2 (alloying 1.5%); SiO_2 - GeO_2 (alloying 4%), SiO_2 - GeO_2 (alloying 15%).

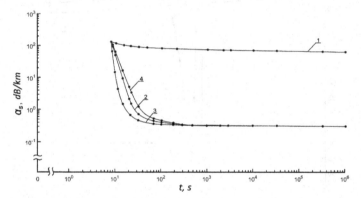

Fig. 3. Dependence of the change in losses α_s on the time t at a wavelength of $\lambda = 1550$ nm for a single-mode fiber core SiO2 - GeO2 (alloying 1.5%) at T $= 294.2$ K. Graphs 1, 2, and 3 correspond to a different power of pulsed laser radiation of rectangular shape with $\lambda = 1310$ nm to mW: 0; 200; 400. Graph 4 - constant level of laser radiation with $\lambda = 1310$ nm with a power of 100 mW.

Figure 4 shows the dependences of the change in voltage U_{ph} at the outputs of two photodetectors 15 and 16 on the time t.

According to the presented changes in voltages on the comparators 15 and 16 using key circuits, the value of the coolant flow rate q is determined. Further, by measuring the values of P_{in} and P_{out} using (6), we determine N. The results obtained are presented in the following form. For example, for a reactor with a water-salt solution of the coolant at T $= 896.5$ K, the value q $= 126$ m^3/s, N ≈ 109 for 1 s. Such data, if necessary, are presented in the form of a table in which the date and time of measurement are entered.

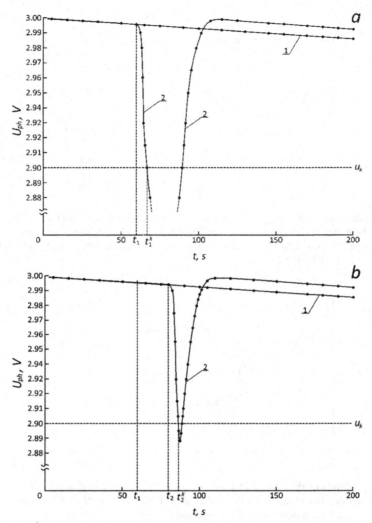

Fig. 4. Dependence of voltage change U_{ph} on the time t on two photodetectors: a) - 15; b) - 16. Graph 1 corresponds to the case when there is no coolant with oxygen activity in the pipeline. Graph 2 - the passage through the pipeline zone, on which the coil with the optical fiber is located, of the coolant with oxygen activity (burst of γ-quanta).

4   Conclusion

The obtained results show that the fiber-optic system developed by us makes it possible to measure the coolant parameters (flow rate q and the level of oxygen activity N). It makes it possible to control the reactor's operation and ensure optimal heat exchange between the coolant and feed water in the second loop.

By adjusting the coolant parameters, it is possible to ensure the best mode of operation of the steam generator at a nuclear power plant. It will reduce losses in electricity generation and increase the service life of the equipment.

References

1. Al-Bahri, M., Kirichek, R., Aleksey, B.: Integrating Internet of Things with the digital object architecture. In: Galinina, O., Andreev, S., Balandin, S., Koucheryavy, Y. (eds.) Internet of Things, Smart Spaces, and Next Generation Networks and Systems. NEW2AN 2019, vol. 11660, pp. 540–547 (2019). https://doi.org/10.1007/978-3-030-30859-9_47
2. Pirmagomedov, R., Kirichek, R., Blinnikov, M., Koucheryavy, A.: UAV-based gateways for wireless nanosensor networks deployed over large areas. Comput. Commun. **146**, 55–62 (2019)
3. Bachevsky, S.V., Fokin, G.A., Simonov, A.N., Sevidov, V.V.: Positioning of radio emission sources with unmanned aerial vehicles using TDOA-AOA measurement processing. In: Journal of Physics: Conference Series, vol. 1368, no. 4, p. 042040 (2019)
4. Podstrigaev, A.S., Smolyakov, A.V., Davydov, V.V., Myazin, N.S., Grebenikova, N.M., Davydov, R.V.: New method for determining the probability of signals overlapping for the estimation of the stability of the radio monitoring systems in a complex signal environment. In: Galinina, O., Andreev, S., Balandin, S., Koucheryavy, Y. (eds.) NEW2AN/ruSMART -2019. LNCS, vol. 11660, pp. 525–533. Springer, Cham (2019). https://doi.org/10.1007/978-3-030-30859-9_45
5. Ateya, A.A., Muthanna, A., Gudkova, I., Abuarqoub, A., Vybornova, A., Koucheryavy, A.: Development of intelligent core network for tactile internet and future smart systems. J. Sens. Actuator Netw. **7**(1), 7 (2018)
6. Kiesewetter, D., Malyugin, V., Makarov, S., Korotkov, K., Ming, D., Wei, X.: Application of the optical fibers in the system of determining the distance of jump at ski springboard. In: Proceedings – 2016 Advances in Wireless and Optical Communications, RTUWO 2016, p. 7821845, pp. 5–8 (2017)
7. Ateya, A.A., Muthanna, A., Vybornova, A., Darya, P., Koucheryavy, A.: Energy - aware offloading algorithm for multi-level cloud based 5G system. In: Galinina, O., Andreev, S., Balandin, S., Koucheryavy, Y. (eds.) NEW2AN/ruSMART -2018. LNCS, vol. 11118, pp. 355–370. Springer, Cham (2018). https://doi.org/10.1007/978-3-030-01168-0_33
8. Dinh, T.D., Pham, V.D., Kirichek, R., Koucheryavy, A.: Flying network for emergencies. Commun. Comput. Inf. Sci. **919**, 58–70 (2018)
9. Moroz, A.V., Davydov, R.V., Davydov, V.V.: A new scheme for transmitting heterodyne signals based on a fiber-optical transmission system for receiving antenna devices of radar stations and communication systems. In: Galinina, O., Andreev, S., Balandin, S., Koucheryavy, Y. (eds.) NEW2AN/ruSMART -2019. LNCS, vol. 11660, pp. 710–718. Springer, Cham (2019). https://doi.org/10.1007/978-3-030-30859-9_62
10. Ermolaev, A.N., Krishpents, G.P., Vysoczkiy, M.G.: Compensation of chromatic and polarization mode dispersion in fiber-optic communication lines in microwave signals transmission. In: Journal of Physics: Conference Series, vol. 741, no. 1, p. 012071 (2016)
11. Kirichek, R., Kulik, V.: Long-range data transmission on Flying Ubiquitous Sensor Networks (FUSN) by using LPWAN protocols. Commun. Comput. Inf. Sci. **678**, 442–453 (2016)
12. Davydov, V.V., Karseev, A.Yu., Nepomnyashchay, E.K., Petrov, A.A., Velichko, E.N.: Fiber – optic super – high – frequency signal transmission system for sea – based radar station. In: Balandin, S., Andreev, S., Koucheryavy, Y. (eds.) Internet of Things, Smart Spaces, and Next Generation Networks and Systems. NEW2AN 2014, vol. 8638, pp. 694–702 (2014). https://doi.org/10.1007/978-3-319-10353-2_65

13. Tarasenko, M.Yu., Sharova, N.V., Lenets, V.A.: Feature of use direct and external modulation in fiber optical simulators of a false target for testing radar station. Lecture Notes in Computer Science, 8638 LNCS, pp. 227–232 (2017)

14. Davydov, R.V., et al.: Fiber-optic transmission system for the testing of active phased antenna arrays in an anechoic chamber. In: Galinina, O., Andreev, S., Balandin, S., Koucheryavy, Y. (eds.) NEW2AN/ruSMART/NsCC -2017. LNCS, vol. 10531, pp. 177–183. Springer, Cham (2017). https://doi.org/10.1007/978-3-319-67380-6_16

15. Koucheryavy, A., Bogdanov, I., Paramonov, A.: The mobile sensor network life-time under different spurious flows intrusion. In: Balandin, S., Andreev, S., Koucheryavy, Y. (eds.) NEW2AN/ruSMART -2013. LNCS, vol. 8121, pp. 312–317. Springer, Heidelberg (2013). https://doi.org/10.1007/978-3-642-40316-3_27

16. Davydov, V.V., Myazin, N.S., Kiryukhin, A.V.: Nuclear-magnetic flowmeter-relaxometers for monitoring coolant and feedwater flow and status in NPP. At Energy 127(5), 274–279 (2020). https://doi.org/10.1007/s10512-020-00623-5

17. Klinov, D.A., Gulevich, A.V., Kagramanyan, V.S.: Challenges and motivation for the development of sodium fast reactors in modern conditions. At Energy 125(3), 131–135 (2020)

18. Vel't, I.D., D'yakonova, E.A., Mikhailova, Y.V., Terekhina, N.V.: Magnetic flowmeter for fast sodium reactors. Atom. Energy 122(4), 243–251 (2017). https://doi.org/10.1007/s10512-017-0262-8

19. Davydov, V.V., Dudkin, V.I., Karseev, A.: Fiber – optic communication line for the NMR signals transmission in the control systems of the ships atomic power plants work. Opt. Memory Neural Netw. (Inf. Opt.) 23(4), 259–264 (2014)

20. Myazin, N.S., et al.: Fiber – optical system for governance and control of work for nuclear power stations of low power. In: Galinina, O., Andreev, S., Balandin, S., Koucheryavy, Y. (eds.) NEW2AN/ruSMART -2019. LNCS, vol. 11660, pp. 744–756. Springer, Cham (2019). https://doi.org/10.1007/978-3-030-30859-9_66

21. Moroz, A.V.: Fiber-optical system for transmitting heterodyne signals in active phased antenna arrays of radar stations. In: Journal of Physics: Conference Series, vol. 1368, no. 2, pp. 022024 (2019)

22. Moroz, A.V.: Features of transmission bearing and heterodyne receivers for signals in fiber-optic communication line in active phased array antenna. In: Journal of Physics: Conference Series, vol. 1410, no. 1, p. 012212 (2019)

23. Myazin, N., Neronov, Y., Dudkin, V., Petrov, A.: On the need for express control of the quality of consumer goods within the concept 'Internet of Things'. In: IOP Conference Series: Materials Science and Engineering, vol. 497, no. 1, p. 012111 (2019)

24. Pham, V.D., Grishin, I., Okuneva, D., Kirichek, R. Method of constructing node Map in wireless mesh sensor network. In: Galinina, O., Andreev, S., Balandin, S., Koucheryavy, Y. (eds.) Internet of Things, Smart Spaces, and Next Generation Networks and Systems. NEW2AN 2020, ruSMART, vol. 12526, pp. 16–27 (2020). https://doi.org/10.1007/978-3-030-65729-1_2

25. Tomashuk, A.L., Filippov, A.V., Kashaykin, P.F., Guryanov, A.N., Semjonov, S.L.: 1.55-μm-light absorption induced by pulsed-X-ray radiation in pure-silica-core fiber: effects of light power and temperature. J. Non-Cryst. Solids 521, 119504 (2019)

26. Tomashuk, A.L., Filippov, A.V., Kashaykin, P.F., Byshkova, E.A., Guryanov, A.N., Dianov, E.M.: Role of inherent radiation-induced self-trapped holes in pulsed-radiation effect on pure-silica-core optical fibers. J. Lightwave Technol. 37(3), 956–962 (2019)

27. Dmitrieva, D.S., Pilipova, V.M., Rud, V.Y.: Fiber-optical communication line with a system for compensation of radiation-induced losses during the transmission of information. In: Galinina, O., Andreev, S., Balandin, S., Koucheryavy, Y. (eds.) Internet of Things, Smart Spaces, and Next Generation Networks and Systems. NEW2AN 2020, vol. 12526, pp. 348–356 (2020). https://doi.org/10.1007/978-3-030-65729-1_30
28. Dmitrieva, D.S., Pilipova, V.M., Davydov, V.V., Valiullin, L.R.: About compensation of radiation - induced losses in optical fibers. In: Journal of Physics: Conference Series, vol. 1695, no. 1, p. 012130 (2020)

Fiber-Optic Sensor for Monitoring Radiation Level

Diana S. Dmitrieva[1]($\boxtimes$) (iD), Valeria M. Pilipova[1] (iD), Valentin I. Dudkin[1] (iD),
Roman V. Davydov[2] (iD), and Vadim V. Davydov[2,3] (iD)

[1] The Bonch-Bruevich Saint - Petersburg State University of Telecommunications, Saint Petersburg 193232, Russia
dmitrievadiana1405@gmail.com

[2] Peter the Great Saint Petersburg Polytechnic University, St. Petersburg 195251, Russia

[3] All-Russian Research Institute of Phytopathology, Moscow Region, B. Vyazyomy, Odintsovo 143050, Russia

Abstract. The necessity of improving the functional capabilities of the fiber-optic sensor for monitoring radioactive radiation is substantiated. The new method of constructing a communication lane with the fiber-optic sensor for controlling exposure dose of radiation in a range of its variations in several orders of magnitude in remote mode is proposed. The sensor design for long distance measurements (more than 10 km from laser transmitting module and photodetector) is developed. Particular attention to the implementation of long-term radiation situation control at high exposure doses of radiation is paid. Functional capabilities of the fiber-optic sensor are identified. The experimental results are presented.

Keywords: Fiber-optic sensor · Radioactive radiation · Radiation-induced losses · Transparency · Laser radiation · Power

1 Introduction

In modern world are constantly being posed the new tasks, for the solution of which is required the use of radioactive materials [1–5]. Every year the number of their use increases, especially in nuclear energy and in scientific researches [3, 6–8]. It inevitably leads to the increase in the number of radiation leakage both into soil and into the atmosphere, which must be controlled [8–11]. It should be noted that radioactive pollution has negative influence on the quality of information transmission in various communication systems [12–17].

Main difficulties appear with the control of powerful radioactive radiation, for example, in the areas of nuclear reactor and heat exchange systems of nuclear electric setups, where present a radioactive coolant, in exclusion zones, and also at special test sites [6–8, 10, 11, 18, 19]. In these cases, control the radiation situation must be carried out continuously in automatic mode. In some cases, control should be realized at the distance more than 10000 m from the location of the center of laser transmitting module and photodetector. It should be noted that the exposure dose D_R in control zone can change

© Springer Nature Switzerland AG 2022
Y. Koucheryavy et al. (Eds.): NEW2AN 2021/ruSMART 2021, LNCS 13158, pp. 230–239, 2022.
https://doi.org/10.1007/978-3-030-97777-1_20

by several orders in a short period of time. In such operation conditions, it is extremely difficult to use most of dosimetry devices. Devices often go off (without the possibility of further entering to measurement mode). Electronics for transmission information is out of order. Moreover, radiation, which poses a great danger to humans for a long time, accumulates on the device case and its functional units.

One of the perspective directions for the implementation of remote control of radiation level is the use of fiber-optic sensors [20–23]. The fiber-optic sensors developed nowadays, which operation principle is based on the measurements of change in radiation-induced losses or laser radiation polarization under the γ-radiation influence (the latter allows to register small D_R changes, which cause a decrease in the laser radiation power by 0.05 dB), have several disadvantages. At high D_R values laser radiation in them is completely damped and sensor stopped its work for a long time. The relaxation process without interventions takes 10^5 s and more [1, 2, 20–22], because for measurements are used small powers (no more than 5 mW). The use of more powerful radiation does not allow to conduct measurements with small D_R values and can damage photosensitive layer in photodetector module. Therefore, the purpose of our work is to develop a new design of a fiber-optic sensor based on the research carried out, which will make it possible to carry out the measurements D_R of long-term to time and record small changes a this parameter in the presence of constant background γ-radiation. The use of this design of the optical sensor will allow solving a number of additional tasks. For example, the long-term investigations to the operation of nuclear facilities protective structures or the changes dynamics a value D_R after depressurization of containers with radioactive elements. In addition, the use of the developed optical sensors significantly expands the possibilities of continuous environmental monitoring of different territories in remote regime.

2 Fiber-Optic Sensor with Controlled Relaxation Velocity of E′ Centers

The E′ - centers appear in an optical fiber after γ-radiation influence [2, 21–26]. The E′ - centers are appeared as the changes result in the structure of the optical fiber. The amount of these defects directly depends on the two effects in the optical fiber, which are appeared after irradiation. There are displacement and ionization effects. The displacement is the atoms shift under the γ-radiation influence. It can lead to the destruction of the optical fiber structure. This effect can become irreversible at high exposure doses of radiation. The optical fiber will be destructed at the area of the γ-radiation influence.

Analysis of the experimental results obtained earlier [21–28] showed, that it is necessary to provide additional researches of γ-radiation influence on the optical fiber for develop a new design of the fiber-optic sensor. To carry out the necessary research, an experimental setup was developed and assembled. Its block diagram is presented at the Fig. 1.

In contrast to earlier researches provided by other scientists [1, 2, 20–28], the use of the developed experimental setup makes it possible to measure losses both at the moment of the γ-radiation influence on fiber, and immediately after its ending. There is no large time interval between the time of the γ-radiation influence and the beginning of

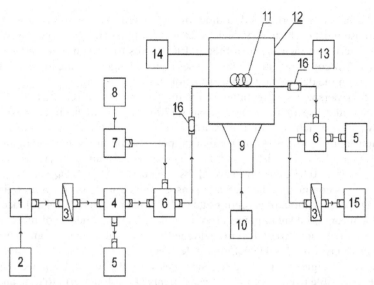

Fig. 1. The block diagram of the experimental setup: 1 - laser transmitting module; 2 - power driver; 3 - polarizer; 4 - optical divider; 5 - optical power meter; 6 - мультиплексор; 7 - pulsed semiconductor laser; 8 - pulse power driver; 9 - source of γ - radiation; 10 - control unit of the source of γ - radiation; 11 - optical fiber; 12 - closed volume of a polymeric material; 13 - a device for changing the temperature; 14 - a device for controlling the dose of radiation; 15 - receiving optical module; 16 - optical adapter.

measurements. It allows to establish a number of new features for optical fibers, which relate to the color centers relaxation.

For providing researchers in the experimental setup is used modified transmitting module DMPO131-23M (company Dilaz). A wavelength is $\lambda = 1550$ nm, variation of radiation power is from 0.1 to 5.4 mW. Radiation-induced losses α_s are determined with using following formula [1, 2, 20]:

$$\alpha_s = 10 \lg(P_{out}/P_{in})/L \tag{1}$$

where P_{in} – the power, input into the optical fiber, P_{out} – the power output from the optical fiber, L – the length of the optical fiber.

For using formula (1) were calculated losses, which appear on the connecting elements and different converters in the experimental setup were calculated (Fig. 1). To implement different connections, were used detachable connections, which have typical losses $\alpha_{pc} = 0.2$ dB. There are 11 such connections. The losses in the optical adder are 0.46 dB. There are 2 such adders. The losses on the optical polarizer are 0.32 dB. Total losses are 3.44 dB.

For registration in the experimental setup was used the receiving optical module DFDSH40-16M (company Dilaz), which has highly sensitive in the wavelength range of 980–1650 nm. The use a set of two devices from one company in the FOCL systems allows to obtain a higher signal-to-noise ratio of the registered optical signal at a low power of laser radiation [29, 30].

At the Fig. 2 as an example are presented the dependences of the α_s losses in single-mode fibers with the exposure dose of γ-radiation.

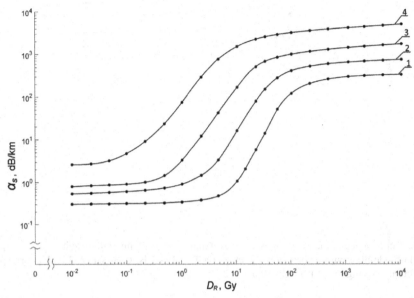

Fig. 2. Dependence of the α_s changes at a wavelength $\lambda = 1550$ nm with irradiation dose D_R for a single-mode fiber with a core $SiO_2 - GeO_2$ at a T $= 294.2$ K. Charts 1, 2, 3 and 4 correspond to different alloying in %: 1.5; 4.0; 10.0 and 20.0.

Obtained results show, that an increase in alloying percentage increases formation velocity of E' centers in optical fiber under the γ-radiation influence. The sensitivity of optical fiber increases to the changes of exposure dose D_R. It allows to register the changes in small D_R values, which lead to the decrease of the laser radiation power at the output of FOCL by 0.2 dB.

At the Fig. 3 as an example are presented the research results of velocity of the optical properties recovery after γ-radiation influence with a dose 100 G.

Analysis of the obtained results shows that the optical properties recovery becomes faster with an increase of alloying percentage of its core (relaxation velocity of E' centers higher).

Therefore, in the work, it was proposed the following design of fiber-optic sensor. An optical fiber with pure quartz core is proposed to connect through optical connectors 16 (Fig. 1) to an optical fiber 200 m long with a core $SiO_2 - GeO_2$ and alloying percentage of 20%. The alloying degree (percentage) can be changed depending on the solving tasks. To recover the optical fiber properties in work uses a method developed earlier by us for trunk FOCL with using an additional laser radiation with $\lambda = 1310$ nm [21, 22, 25]. At the Fig. 4 and Fig. 5 are presented the research results of velocity of the optical properties recovery after γ-radiation influence with a dose 100 G for pulsed

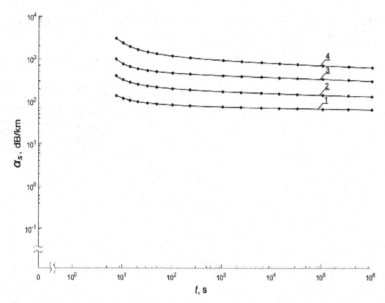

Fig. 3. Dependence of the α_s changes at a wavelength $\lambda = 1550$ nm with irradiation dose D_R for a single-mode fiber with a core $SiO_2 - GeO_2$ at a T = 294.2 K. Charts 1, 2, 3 and 4 correspond to different alloying in %: 1.5; 4.0; 10.0 and 20.0.

and continuous laser radiation of various power. In the research was used pulsed laser radiation with a duration 0.1 with various powers during 10 s.

Analysis of the obtained results shows that the use of additional laser radiation allows to increase relaxation velocity of E' centers and recover the optical properties of an optical fiber in less 10 s. Moreover, it was established, that the use of additional laser radiation for optical fiber recovery is more effective than continuous. It should be noted, it is easier to realize higher power in pulsed mode then in continuous.

In addition, to determinate the optimal operation mode for recover the optical properties of an optical fiber, the dependence of the changes in α_s losses with time t (after ending γ-radiation influence on an optical fiber) was researched for various pulse durations τ of an additional laser radiation. For conducting researches was used a single-mode fiber with a core $SiO_2 - GeO_2$ (alloying 1.5%). Exposure dose was $D_R = 100$ G. Additional laser radiation with a wavelength $\lambda = 1310$ nm and power $P_{ex} = 0.2$ W was input into the optical fiber. At the Fig. 6 as an example is presented one of such dependences.

Obtained results show, that the pulse duration of laser radiation with using meander does not influence a lot on the the changes in the relaxation velocity of E' centers. Main influence is exerted by the laser radiation power, which cannot be increase to infinity, because an additional laser radiation with $\lambda = 1310$ nm begins to influence on radiation with $\lambda = 1550$ nm. It increases the measurements error when control small D_R changes.

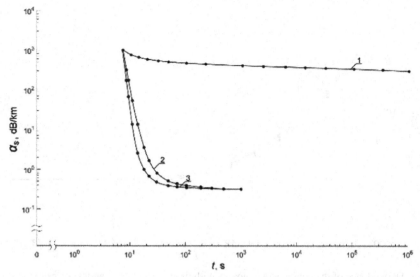

Fig. 4. Dependence of the changes in α_s losses with time t at a wavelength $\lambda = 1550$ nm for a single-mode fiber with a core $SiO_2 - GeO_2$ (alloying 10.0%) and polymer cladding at T = 294.3 K. Charts 1, 2 and 3 correspond to different laser radiation powers in mW: 0; 40; 80.

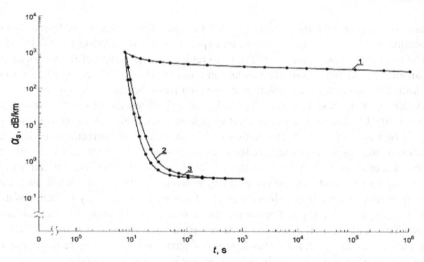

Fig. 5. Dependence of the changes in α_s losses with time t at a wavelength $\lambda = 1550$ nm for a single-mode fiber with a core $SiO_2 - GeO_2$ (alloying 10.0%) and polymer cladding at T = 294.3 K. Charts 1, 2 and 3 correspond to different laser radiation powers in mW: 0; 20; 40.

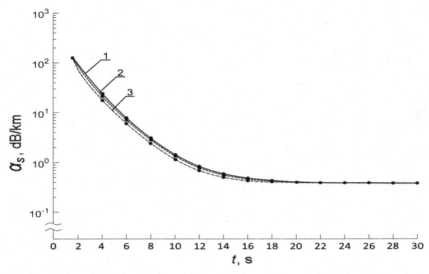

Fig. 6. Dependence of the changes in α_S losses with time t. Charts 1, 2 and 3 correspond to pulse durations τ in s: 0.1; 0.2; 0.8.

3 Conclusion

Obtained experimental results show, that the fiber-optic sensor developed by us can work in continuous mode for remote control an exposure dose of radiation from 0.1 to 1000 G. The use of this design allows not only to register the presence of the γ-radiation in certain area, but also to obtain data about radiation via FOCL. It is not necessary to use an additional communication line to transmit data from the measurement area.

Analysis of the results at the Fig. 2, 3, 4 and 5 allows to set the following. At a certain value D_R and power of an additional laser radiation, a static equilibrium can occur between two processes (formation of E' centers and its relaxation). In this case, the value α_S increases insignificantly for a certain period under the γ-radiation influence on fiber, for example, for 10^5 s (less than 1% from its initial state). The influence of the radioactive background γ-radiation γ-radiation which is always present in such cases a during measurements in developed design of sensor a successfully is compensating. Therefore, the new developed fiber-optic sensor will be in stable mode of a radioactive release. This will make it possible in the future, after additional research, to develop a remote system for large areas state control of territories with an increased danger of pollution. Such a task is extremely difficult to implement at the moment.

Another promising direction for further research may be the development of a fiber-optic sensor for continuous control to changes dynamic of the value D_R value in the central protective zone of reactor. This will provide new data about the reactor operation and the flowing nature of chain reactions. To implement this project, new designs of optical fibers are needed, since the radiation level in this zone of the reactor is very high. These fibers are currently being developed according to our guidelines.

References

1. Kashaykin, P.F., Tomashuk, A.L., Vasiliev, S.A., Chikhray, Y.V., Semjonov, S.L.: Radiation resistance of single-mode optical fibres with view to in-reactor applications. Nucl. Mater. Energy **27**, 100981 (2021)
2. Tomashuk, A.L., et al.: Light absorption induced in undoped-silica-core panda-type birefringent optical fiber by pulsed action of ionizing radiation. Bull. Lebedev. Phys. Inst. **45**(12), 385–388 (2018). https://doi.org/10.3103/S1068335618120047
3. Myazin, N.S., Yushkova, V.V., Taranda, N.I., Rud, V.Yu.: On the need to control the state of the flowing media by the values of relaxation constants. In: Journal of Physics: Conference Series, vol. 1410, no. 1, p. 012130 (2019)
4. Davydov, R., Antonov, V., Makeev, S., Dudkin, V., Myazin, N.: New high-speed system for controlling the parameters of a nuclear reactor in a nuclear power plant. In: E3S Web of Conferences, vol. 140, p. 02001 (2019)
5. Myazin, N.S., Rud, V.Yu., Yushkova, V.V., Dudkin, V.I.: New method for determining the composition of liquid media during the express control of their state using the nuclear magnetic resonance phenomena. In: Journal of Physics: Conference Series, vol. 1400, no. 6, p. 066008 (2019)
6. Gryznova, E., Batov, Y., Myazin, N., Rud, V.: Methodology for assessing the environmental characteristics of various methods of generating electricity. In: E3S Web of Conferences, vol. 140, p. 09001 (2019)
7. Davydov, V.V., Myazin, N.S., Kiryukhin, A.V.: Nuclear-magnetic flowmeter-relaxometers for monitoring coolant and feedwater flow and status in NPP. At Energy **127**(5), 274–279 (2020). https://doi.org/10.1007/s10512-020-00623-5
8. Gryznova, E., Grebenikova, N., Ivanov, D., Bykov, V.: The study of the environmental efficiency of energy production from various sources of raw materials. In: IOP Conference Series: Earth and Environmental Science, vol. 390, no. 1, p. 012044 (2019)
9. Nikitina, M., Grebenikova, N., Dudkin, V., Batov, Y.: Methodology for assessing the adverse effects of the use of nuclear energy on agricultural land. In: IOP Conference Series: Earth and Environmental Science, vol. 390, no. 1, p. 012024 (2019)
10. Fadeenko, V., Fadeenko, I., Dudkin, V., Nikolaev, D.: Remote environmental monitoring in the area of a nuclear power plant. In: IOP Conference Series: Earth and Environmental Science, vol. 390, no. 1, p. 012022 (2019)
11. Fadeenko, V.B., Fadeenko, I.V., Vasiliev, D.A., Rud, V.Yu.: Investigation of radiation formation (plasmoid) in the air environment by radar method. In: Journal of Physics: Conference Series, vol. 1697, no. 1, p. 012057 (2020)
12. Al-Bahri, M., Ruslan, K., Aleksey, B.: Integrating Internet of Things with the digital object architecture. In: Galinina, O., Andreev, S., Balandin, S., Koucheryavy, Y. (eds.) NEW2AN/ruSMART -2019. LNCS, vol. 11660, pp. 540–547. Springer, Cham (2019). https://doi.org/10.1007/978-3-030-30859-9_47
13. Pirmagomedov, R., Kirichek, R., Blinnikov, M., Koucheryavy, A.: UAV-based gateways for wireless nanosensor networks deployed over large areas. Comput. Commun. **146**, 55–62 (2019)
14. Moroz, A., Davydov, R., Davydov, V.: A new scheme for transmitting heterodyne signals based on a fiber-optical transmission system for receiving antenna devices of radar stations and communication systems. In: Galinina, O., Andreev, S., Balandin, S., Koucheryavy, Y. (eds.) NEW2AN/ruSMART -2019. LNCS, vol. 11660, pp. 710–718. Springer, Cham (2019). https://doi.org/10.1007/978-3-030-30859-9_62

15. Makolkina, M., Pham, V., Kirichek, R., Gogol, A., Koucheryavy, A.: Interaction of AR and IoT applications on the basis of hierarchical cloud services. In: Galinina, O., Andreev, S., Balandin, S., Koucheryavy, Y. (eds.) NEW2AN/ruSMART -2018. LNCS, vol. 11118, pp. 547–559. Springer, Cham (2018). https://doi.org/10.1007/978-3-030-01168-0_49

16. Ateya, A.A., Muthanna, A., Gudkova, I., Abuarqoub, A., Vybornova, A., Koucheryavy, A.: Development of intelligent core network for tactile internet and future smart systems. J. Sens. Actuator Netw. 7(1), 7 (2018)

17. Ateya, A., Muthanna, A., Vybornova, A., Darya, P., Koucheryavy, A.: Energy - aware offloading algorithm for multi-level cloud based 5G system. In: Galinina, O., Andreev, S., Balandin, S., Koucheryavy, Y. (eds.) NEW2AN/ruSMART -2018. LNCS, vol. 11118, pp. 355–370. Springer, Cham (2018). https://doi.org/10.1007/978-3-030-01168-0_33

18. Elokhin, A.P., Zhilina, M.V.: Determination of gas-aerosol radioactive impurity characteristics from arms γ-ray detector indications. Atom. Energy 112(4), 269–280 (2012)

19. Fadeenko, V.B., Fadeenko, I.V., Vasiliev, D.A., Yu Rud, V.: Multifunctional radar system for remote control of environment and the Earth's surface. In: Journal of Physics: Conference Series, vol. 1745, no. 1, p. 012023 (2021)

20. Tomashuk, A.L., Kashaykin, P.F., Semjonov, S.L., Kolosovskii, A.O., Chamorovskiy, Y.: Pulsed-X-ray-irradiation of radiation-resistant PANDA fibers: dependence on dose, probe light power, and temperature. Opt. Mater. 109, 110384 (2020)

21. Dmitrieva, D.S., Pilipova, V.M., Rud, V.Y.: Fiber-optical communication line with a system for compensation of radiation-induced losses during the transmission of information. In: Galinina, O., Andreev, S., Balandin, S., Koucheryavy, Y. (eds.) Internet of Things, Smart Spaces, and Next Generation Networks and Systems. NEW2AN 2020, ruSMART 2020, vol. 12526, pp. 348–356 (2020)

22. Dmitrieva, D.S., Pilipova, V.M., Davydov, V.V., Valiullin, L.R.: About compensation of radiation - induced losses in optical fibers. In: Journal of Physics: Conference Series, vol. 1695, no. 1, p. 012130 (2020)

23. Kashaykin, P.F., Tomashuk, A.L., Khopin, V.F., Semjonov, S.L., Dianov, E.M.: New radiation colour centre in germanosilicate glass fibres. Quantum Electron. 48(12), 1143–1146 (2018)

24. Dmitrieva, D.S., Pilipova, V.M., Dudkin, V.I., Davydov, V.V., Rud, V.Yu.: The possibility of controlling the relaxation rate of color centers in the optical fibers. In: Journal of Physics: Conference Series, vol. 1697, no. 1, p. 012145 (2020)

25. Dmitrieva, D., Pilipova, V., Andreeva, E., Dudkin, V., Davydov, V.: Method for determination of negative influence to γ - radiation on fiber optic information transmission systems. In: Proceedings of ITNT 2020 - 6th IEEE International Conference on Information Technology and Nanotechnology, Samara, Russia, vol. 9253348. IEEE (2020)

26. Tomashuk, A.L., Filippov, A.V., Kashaykin, P.F., Guryanov, A.N., Semjonov, S.L.: 1.55-μm-light absorption induced by pulsed-X-ray radiation in pure-silica-core fiber: effects of light power and temperature. In: J. Non-Crystal. Solids 521, 119504 (2019)

27. Kashaikin, P.F., Tomashuk, A.L., Salganskii, M.Y., Gur'yanov, A.N., Dianov, E.M.: Prediction of radiation-induced light absorption in optical fibers with an undoped silica core for space applications. Tech. Phys. 64(5), 701–707 (2019). https://doi.org/10.1134/S10637842 19050098

28. Davydov, R.V., Dmitrieva, D.S., Pilipova, V.M., Dudkin, V.I., Andreeva, E.I.: The research of radioactive exposure compensation on optical material for optical fibers by powerful laser radiation. In: Proceedings - International Conference Laser Optics 2020, ICLO 2020, Saint-Petersburg, Russia, vol. 9285820. IEEE (2020)

29. Tarasenko, M.Yu., Sharova, N.V., Lenets, V.A.: Feature of use direct and external modulation in fiber optical simulators of a false target for testing radar station. In: Galinina, O., Andreev, S., Balandin, S., Koucheryavy, Y. (eds.) Internet of Things, Smart Spaces, and Next Generation Networks and Systems. ruSMART 2017, NsCC 2017, NEW2AN 2017, vol. 8638, pp. 227–232 (2017). https://doi.org/10.1007/978-3-319-67380-6_21

30. Davydov, R.V., et al.: Fiber-optic transmission system for the testing of active phased antenna arrays in an anechoic chamber. In: Galinina, O., Andreev, S., Balandin, S., Koucheryavy, Y. (eds.) NEW2AN/ruSMART/NsCC -2017. LNCS, vol. 10531, pp. 177–183. Springer, Cham (2017). https://doi.org/10.1007/978-3-319-67380-6_16

Experimental Study of Temperature Impact on Fiber Optic Current Sensor Elements

Valentina Temkina[1]($\boxtimes$) (iD), Andrei Medvedev[1] (iD), Alexey Mayzel[2] (iD),
Eduard Sivolenko[3] (iD), Ekaterina Poletaeva[1], and Iuliia Dudnik[1]

[1] Peter the Great St. Petersburg Polytechnic University, St. Petersburg, Russia
temkina.vs@edu.spbstu.ru, andrey.medvedev@inbox.ru,
katuwka11_12@mail.ru, malykhina.yuliya@bk.ru
[2] Software-Defined Systems LLC, St. Petersburg, Russia
amayzel@gmail.com
[3] Radiophysics and Electronics, Yerevan State University, Yerevan, Armenia
eduard.sivolenko@gmail.com

Abstract. Fiber optic current sensors must meet 0.2S accuracy class in various environmental conditions in order to achieve a competitive position in the digital measuring device market. However, a number of external factors still limit their use. One of these factors is temperature. In this paper, we studied the temperature impact on the operation of optical elements that make up a fiber optic current sensor. Each element responds differently to changes in ambient temperature. Therefore, we considered each element of the optical scheme separately and experimentally investigated the evolution of the polarization state of light during heating and cooling of these elements. The study showed that the circulator is not affected by temperature, the modulator operates like a phase plate, and a parasitic polarization mode is excited in the delay line. The most affected by temperature are the quarter-wave plate and the sensitive spun fiber. It will lead to significant errors in the fiber optic current sensor measurements. Therefore, to ensure the high-precision operation of the device, it is necessary to develop algorithms for compensating the temperature dependences.

Keywords: Fiber optic current sensor · Temperature impact · Polarization state · Poincare sphere

1 Introduction

The development of Smart Grid networks and the integration of digital substations entail the inevitability of replacing instrument current transformers with digital measuring devices. For this reason, recently, fiber optic current sensors (FOCS) have been rapidly developed [1–5]. It is designed to measure with high accuracy the amplitude and spectral composition of the industrial frequency current and convert the measured values into a digital data stream in accordance with the IEC 61850-9-2 (2011) standard for use by digital substation devices. Resistance to electromagnetic interference, small dimensions and weight, good electrical insulation characterize the FOCS. The entire measuring

© Springer Nature Switzerland AG 2022
Y. Koucheryavy et al. (Eds.): NEW2AN 2021/ruSMART 2021, LNCS 13158, pp. 240–253, 2022.
https://doi.org/10.1007/978-3-030-97777-1_21

(optical) part of the current sensor located in the high voltage region is made of dielectric materials. It ensures the minimum probability of electrical breakdown.

To achieve a competitive position in the energetics' market of measuring instruments, FOCSs must provide measurement error of no more than ±0.2% in the entire range of environmental conditions during the service life. However, research has shown that ensuring this accuracy is challenging. Mechanical disturbances, temperature changes of optical elements, polarization mismatches, the residual linear birefringence inside the sensing coil, etc. worsen the FOCS measurement error [6–10]. Therefore, it is necessary to revise the existing design solutions and signal processing algorithms used in the FOCS.

2 Challenge

The FOCS operation principle is based on the effect of light modulation (Faraday Effect) in a special optical fiber (spun fiber) when it is exposed to an external magnetic field. A current flowing through the conductor creates this magnetic field. As a result, the FOCS output signal is proportional to the measured current.

We have built the FOCS laboratory prototype according to the optical scheme shown in Fig. 1. The used signal processing algorithm is based on the synchronous detection of the first, second and fourth harmonics of the modulation frequency and analysis of their ratio. The optical scheme and signal processing algorithm are de-scribed in detail in article [11]. In this scheme, the circulator also performs the functions of a polarizer, since the connector key are aligned to the slow axis and fast axis is blocked. The FOCS error is measured by a comparison device, which traditionally used for verification of measuring instruments in energetics.

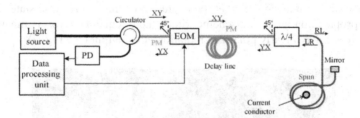

Fig. 1. FOCS optical scheme.

During experiments it was found that mechanical disturbances of a fiber and temperature changing of various optical elements lead to significant increase in the FOCS measurement error. It is unacceptable for such devices. At the same time, it is not difficult to isolate the circuit from mechanical influences, but it is almost impossible to maintain the temperature of all optical elements constant. Firstly, the fiber quarter-wave plate and sensitive spun fiber are spaced from the rest of the circuit and located directly next to a current conductor in a high-voltage region. Therefore, these elements are most affected by the ambient temperature and the dielectric structure of the FOCS measuring part must not be disturbed. Secondly, the thermal stabilization system of optical elements leads to an increase in the finished device cost. Thus, thermal exposure is the most important parasitic factor that should be studied and taken into account.

The research is complicated by the fact that the FOCS error, determined using a comparison device, does not give us an unambiguous answer what physical processes occur in the scheme when the optical elements' temperature changes. The error on the comparison device shows only the total contribution of all circuit imperfections and external parasitic factors. Since the FOCS is built according to the self-consistent interferometer scheme, the influence of parasitic factors should be mutually compensated for the forward and backward light passage through the optical elements. However, it is not seen in a real sensor. In order to investigate the reasons for this behavior and understand how to deal with the FOCS temperature dependence, we decided to analyze each element of the FOCS optical scheme separately.

3   Experimental Research of Temperature Impact on FOCS Optical Elements

The research method consisted in sequential heating and cooling of FOCS optical elements and simultaneous measurement of the polarization state of light propagating through these elements. We used the polarimeter PAX1000IR2/M (Thorlabs) to measure the polarization state. Since the polarimeter operates with coherent narrow-band input optical radiation, the laser DFB-1550-PM-20 (Optilab) with a wavelength $\lambda = 1550$ nm was chosen as a light source.

3.1   Circulator

The FOCS is built according to the polarization interferometer scheme. Therefore, it is very important to understand what the evolution of the polarization state of light is during its propagation along the scheme. Since the circulator performs functions of a polarizer, we receive linearly polarized radiation at its output (see Fig. 2).

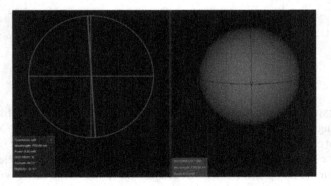

Fig. 2. Polarization state of light at the circulator output.

We isolated the circulator in a small chamber, heated by a Peltier element in the range from 22 °C to 50 °C and then cooled it down. For this reason, a triangular signal was applied to the control input of the used thermostat. One complete cycle (heating and cooling) took about 40 min. The temperature of the heated element was measured using a thermocouple. The experiment showed that the point characterizing the polarization state remained almost stationary at the Poincare sphere equator. The point deviations from the equator are so small that they are visible only on the dependences of the polarization state ellipticity on the circulator temperature (see Fig. 3).

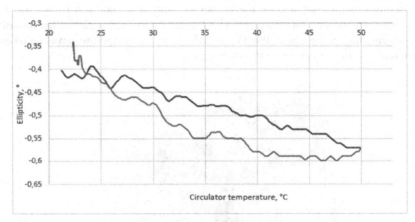

Fig. 3. Ellipticity of the polarization state of light at the circulator output vs. Circulator temperature. Blue line corresponds to heating, red line – cooling. (Color figure online)

It can be assumed that the polarization state remains linear over the entire temperature range of the circulator. Thus, the circulator does not introduce an error in the FOCS readings, but reduces the optical radiation power in the FOCS scheme.

3.2 Electro-Optical Modulator

An electro-optical modulator (EOM) in the FOCS scheme follows the circulator (see Fig. 1). Two light waves with orthogonal linear polarizations are excited at the modulator input. Consequently, the phase shift between these modes should lead to a change in the total polarization state of light at the modulator output.

To conduct an experimental study of temperature impact on EOM, an optical circuit was assembled, shown in Fig. 4. The circuit included an electro-optical phase modulator manufactured at the Ioffe Institute based on a lithium niobate crystal, in which an optical waveguide is created. The Eigen polarization axes of the fiber leading to the modulator are oriented at an angle of 45° to the Eigen polarization axes of the lithium niobate crystal. It leads to the excitation of two orthogonal linearly polarized modes of equal intensity in the modulator. Depending on the phase shift be-tween two polarization modes, either a linear, elliptical, or circular polarization state is formed at the modulator output.

Like the circulator, we slowly heated and cooled the modulator in the range of 23 °C to 47 °C. One complete cycle (heating and cooling) took about 70 min. EOM was in the case, so it was impossible to measure the crystal temperature. In experiment, two

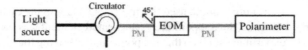

Fig. 4. Optical circuit for experimental study of temperature impact on the EOM.

thermocouples were used to measure the temperature (see Fig. 5). The first was fixed on a duralumin plate mounted on the Peltier element. The modulator case was fixed on this plate. The second thermocouple was located on the upper part of the modulator case. Subsequently, we assumed that the modulator crystal temperature was equal to the average temperature of these two thermocouples.

Fig. 5. The location of the thermocouples for measuring the EOM temperature.

When the modulator temperature changes, it was expected that the point character-izing the polarization state at the EOM output would move on the Poincare sphere in a circle (along the meridian). In this case, the point must pass through the poles R and L, corresponding to the right and left circular polarizations, respectively. The number of circles during heating and cooling should be the same, but in a different direction. However, the trajectory of the point along the Poincare sphere had the following form in the experiment (see Fig. 6).

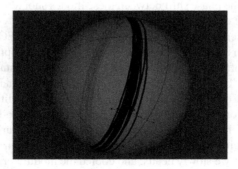

Fig. 6. Evolution of the polarization state during heating and cooling of the modulator.

It can be seen that a point on the Poincare sphere really moved in a circle, but this circle had an inclination and the point did not pass exactly through the poles R and L of the sphere. This may mean that the rotation angle of the Eigen polarization axes at the modulator input does not correspond exactly to 45° and the excited orthogonal linearly polarized modes have unequal intensity. It was recorded that the polarization state of light passes one complete circle along the Poincare sphere with an increase in temperature by 3 °C.

Figure 7 shows the dependence of the polarization state ellipticity at the modulator output on the average temperature of two thermocouples.

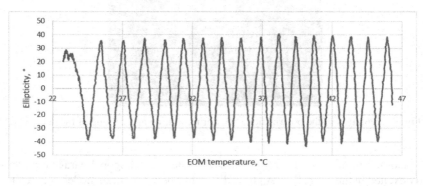

Fig. 7. Ellipticity of the polarization state of light at the modulator output vs. EOM temperature (heating).

It can be seen here that the linear orthogonal modes excited at the modulator input had unequal intensity, since the ellipticity value did not reach ±45°. This means that the polarization at the modulator output does not become either right or left circular.

3.3 Fiber Delay Line

The delay line in our FOCS prototype is a coil of birefringent Bow-Tie type fiber HB1250 (Fibercore). The length of this fiber is 200 m. To study the temperature impact on the delay line, an optical circuit was assembled, shown in Fig. 8.

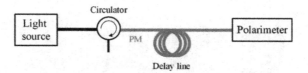

Fig. 8. Optical circuit for experimental study of temperature impact on the delay line.

We placed the entire coil of the delay line in an insulating box, slowly heated by a lamp in the range from 24 °C to 50 °C and then cooled by turning off the lamp. One complete cycle (heating and cooling) took about 50 min.

Since we supplied linearly polarized radiation to the delay line input, it was expected that the point characterizing the polarization state would not move along the Poincare sphere and would remain at the equator. This would mean maintaining the linear polarization of light. However, as can be seen from Fig. 9, the assumption was not confirmed.

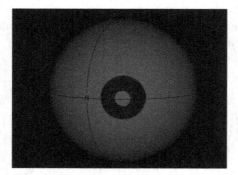

Fig. 9. Evolution of the polarization state during heating and cooling of the delay line.

In addition to the main linearly polarized mode, an orthogonal parasitic mode was clearly excited in the delay line. A phase difference between these modes occured under the action of temperature. As a result, a point on the Poincare sphere moved along a small circle centered on the equator.

The parasitic mode can be excited in the optical connector between the circulator output and the delay line input. Either it may mean that there are inhomogeneities in the delay line fiber or parasitic internal stresses arising from poor-quality winding of the fiber onto a coil. As a consequence, optical power is transferred from one mode to another.

Figure 10 shows the dependence of the ellipticity on the delay line temperature. It can be noted that the average radius of the circle on the Poincare sphere corresponds to an ellipticity equal to 3.3°.

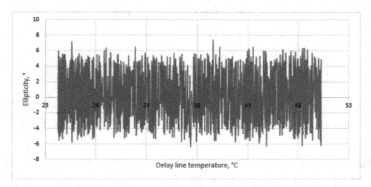

Fig. 10. Ellipticity of the polarization state of light at the delay line output vs. Delay line temperature (heating).

We assumed that the parasitic mode intensity (and hence the circle radius on the Poincare sphere) can be reduced by introducing a small polarization mismatch at the delay line input. With this polarization mismatch, we suppose to compensate for mismatches arising in the optical connector. We carried out a series of experiments and obtained the dependence shown in Fig. 11.

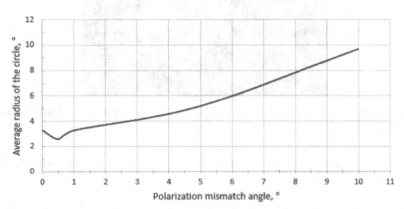

Fig. 11. Average radius of the circle on the Poincare sphere when the delay line is heated vs. Polarization mismatch at the delay line input.

Hence, it can be seen that an increase in the polarization mismatch angle at the delay line input leaded to an increase in the circle radius of polarization state evolution on the Poincare sphere. However, the minimum radius (and hence the minimum possible amplitude of the parasitic mode) was obtained at an angle of polarization mismatches not 0°, but 0.5°. In this way, we can try to improve the FOCS scheme.

In the FOCS scheme, EOM is located in front of the delay line. Therefore, we also investigated the circuit shown in Fig. 12. In this case, two orthogonal linearly polarized modes propagated in the delay line. Accordingly, we saw the total polarization state of these two modes on the polarimeter.

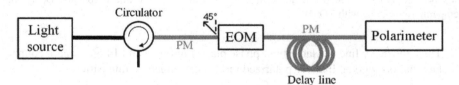

Fig. 12. Optical circuit for experimental study of temperature impact on the delay line (with EOM).

We heated the delay line from 24 °C to 50 °C and then cooled. The evolution of the polarization state of light at the delay line output is shown in Fig. 13.

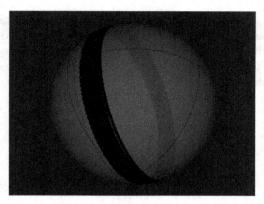

Fig. 13. Evolution of the polarization state during heating and cooling of the delay line (scheme with EOM).

Figure 14 shows the dependence of the polarization state ellipticity on the delay line temperature.

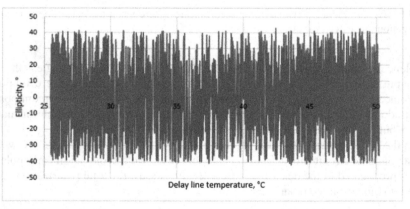

Fig. 14. Ellipticity of the polarization state of light at the delay line output vs. Delay line temperature (scheme with EOM).

Thus, the delay line is a large fiber phase plate. Figure 13 and 14 once again confirm the fact that orthogonal linearly polarized modes have unequal intensities.

3.4   Fiber Quarter-Wave Plate

Fiber quarter-wave plate (QWP) is the most important FOCS element. It must convert linearly polarized radiation into circularly polarized one, which is stored in the sensitive spun fiber. We made a phase plate of Bow-Tie birefringent fiber HB1250 (Fibercore) with a beat length of 3.28 mm. The length of this plate is 0.82 mm, which almost corresponds to the first order QWP.

To study the temperature impact on the phase plate, an optical scheme was assembled, shown in Fig. 15. Using a Peltier element, we subjected the manufactured phase plate to slow heating in the range from 20 °C to 64 °C and subsequent cooling. It took about 40 min to complete this cycle. The evolution of the polarization state of light at the phase plate output is presented on the Poincare sphere (see Fig. 16). The dependence of the polarization state ellipticity on the phase plate temperature is shown in Fig. 17.

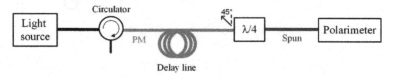

Fig. 15. Optical circuit for experimental study of temperature impact on fiber phase plate.

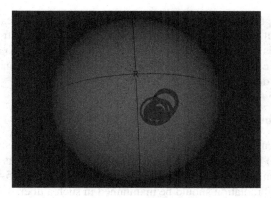

Fig. 16. Evolution of the polarization state during heating and cooling of the fiber phase plate.

It was observed that with an increase in the phase plate temperature, the point on the Poincare sphere moved away from the pole R, and the temperature dependence of ellipticity had a monotonic decreasing trend. It should be noted that the longer the phase plate is, the more pronounced this effect. Therefore, it can be assumed that the polarization state as close as possible to circular can be obtained by continuing of the phase plate cooling. However, the QWP is located in the high voltage region in a real FOCS, directly next to the wire. Therefore, it is not possible to keep the plate temperature constant. In this case, a change in the plate temperature will lead to FOCS errors. Thus, it is necessary to apply algorithms to compensate for this error in the FOCS signal processing. Active research is being carried out in this direction. For example, there are compensation methods through optimizing initial phase delay in QWP [12, 13]. In contrast, we have developed the algorithm to compensate for the error caused by a QWP temperature change without implementing direct temperature measurements, complicating the QWP manufacturing method and increasing the cost of the FOCS design. This algorithm is described in paper [14].

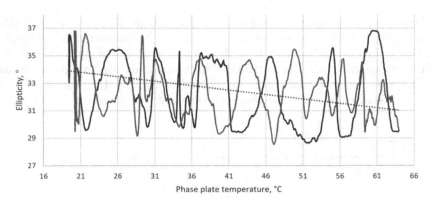

Fig. 17. Ellipticity of the polarization state of light at the fiber phase plate output vs. Phase plate temperature. Blue line corresponds to heating, red line – cooling. (Color figure online)

In addition, experiments have shown that the phase plate provides not ideal circular polarization of light at its output, but elliptical. When light reflected from the mirror, the polarization state is not converted to orthogonal, but is converted to another elliptical. Consequently, the contrast of the interference signal of the sensor and its sensitivity to the magnetic field decrease.

3.5 Sensitive Spun Fiber

The sensing element of our FOCS is a spun fiber coil. This coil has 159 turns of fiber SHB1500(8.9/125) (Fibercore) with a radius of 8 cm. Spun fiber is manufactured by spinning a preform with a strong built-in linear birefringence [15–17]. As a result, circularly polarized radiation should be maintained in such a fiber.

To study the temperature impact on the spun fiber, an optical scheme was assembled, shown in Fig. 18.

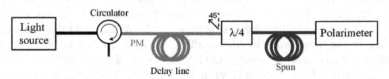

Fig. 18. Optical circuit for experimental study of temperature impact on sensitive spun fiber.

We placed the entire coil of spun fiber in an insulating box, slowly heated by a lamp in the range from 20 °C to 57 °C and then cooled by turning off the lamp. One complete cycle (heating and cooling) took about 1 h. The evolution of the polarization state of light at the spun fiber output is presented on the Poincare sphere (see Fig. 19). The dependence of the polarization state ellipticity on the spun fiber temperature is shown in Fig. 20.

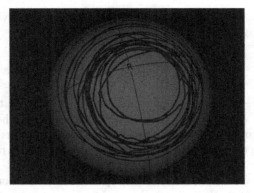

Fig. 19. Evolution of the polarization state during heating of the spun fiber coil.

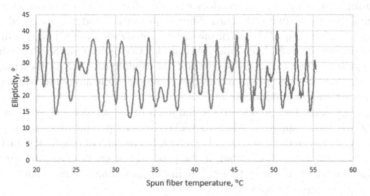

Fig. 20. Ellipticity of the polarization state of light at the spun fiber output vs. Spun fiber temperature (heating).

As can be seen from Fig. 19, we did not excite a circularly polarized mode in the spun fiber, but an elliptical one. This is because a parasitic orthogonal mode of low intensity was already present at the delay line output (see Fig. 9), which leaded to the formation of elliptically polarized light at the QWP output. In addition, the QWP temperature affects its output light polarization.

When the spun fiber was heated, we observed that a point along the Poincare sphere moved in a circle around the pole R. If the spun fiber were ideal and not subjected to any external influences, the point on the Poincare sphere would move along the same circle, symmetric with respect to the pole R. It would mean maintaining of the right elliptical polarization of light. However, the spun fiber in the FOCS prototype was wound on a coil. Therefore, additional induced anisotropy of fiber appeared due to fiber bends, internal stresses, and mechanical deformation during winding, etc. This leaded to a displacement and tilt of the circle on the Poincare sphere and, as a consequence, a change in the ellipticity of the polarized radiation. As in the case of the QWP, this effect will entail an increase the FOCS error and a decrease the sensitivity to the magnetic field.

4 Conclusion

In this paper, we presented the experimental study results of the temperature impact on FOCS elements. We considered each element of the optical scheme separately and investigated the evolution of the polarization state of light during heating and cooling of these elements. As a result of the work, following conclusions can be drawn:

1. The circulator used in the FOCS prototype performs the functions of a polarizer. In this case, a part of the optical radiation power is lost, however we have one ideal linearly polarized light mode at the circulator output. The circulator is stable in the operating temperature range and does not affect the FOCS measurement error.
2. At the EOM input, two orthogonal linearly polarized modes are excited, but their intensities are not equal. It can be caused by polarization mismatches at the optical connectors or the modulator input. When the EOM is heated, the phase difference between these modes changes. As a result, the modulator operates like a phase plate. The polarization state of light passes one complete circle along the Poincare sphere with an increase in temperature by 3 °C.
3. In the fiber delay line, in addition to the main linearly polarized mode, a parasitic orthogonal mode appears. When the delay line temperature increases, the phase difference between them changes. Therefore, not linear, but elliptical polarization of light can come at the QWP input. In the paper we proposed a method for reducing the parasitic mode intensity by introducing an additional polarization mismatch at the delay line input, equal to 0.5°.
4. The QWP temperature affects the ellipticity of the polarization state at its output, and, consequently, the FOCS measurement error. The greater the QWP order, the stronger this impact is. It is possible to make the polarization state as close to circular as possible by changing the QWP temperature. However, in a real device, it is advisable to compensate for the QWP temperature dependence when processing the sensor signal.
5. When the spun fiber coil is heated, the point on the Poincare sphere, which characterizes the polarization state at the spun fiber output, moves in a circle around the sphere pole. Fiber bends, internal stresses, mechanical deformations lead to the induction of additional anisotropy in the fiber. As a consequence, this circle on the Poincare sphere is not symmetrical about the pole, is inclined and constantly displaced. It leads to an increase in the FOCS measurement error and a decrease in the sensitivity to the magnetic field.

Acknowledgments. This research was supported by the Peter the Great Saint Petersburg Polytechnic University in the framework of the Russian state assignment for basic research (project N FSEG-2020-0024).

References

1. Silva, R.M., et al.: Optical current sensors for high power systems: a review. Appl. Sci. **2**, 602–628 (2012)
2. Lenner, M., Frank, A., Yang, L., Roininen, T., Bohnert, K.: Long-term reliability of fiber-optic current sensors. IEEE Sens. J. **20**(2), 823–832 (2019)
3. Boev, A., et al.: Fibre-optic current sensor. Patent RU 2437106 C2, G01R 15/24, G01R 19/2. Date of publication: 20.12.2011 Bull. 35
4. Bohnert, K., Frank, A., Yang, L., Gu, X., Muller, G.M.: Polarimetric fiber-optic current sensor with integrated-optic polarization splitter. J. Lightw. Technol. **37**(14), 3672–3678 (2019)
5. Li, Y.S., Zhang, W.W., Liu, X.Y., Liu, J.: Characteristic analysis and experiment of adaptive fiber optic current sensor technology. Appl. Sci. **9**(2), 333 (2019)
6. Wang, W., Wang, X., Xia, J.: The nonreciprocal errors in fiber optic current sensors. Opt. Laser Technol. **43**(8), 1470–1474 (2011)
7. Bohnert, K., Gabus, P., Nehring, J., Brandle, H.: Temperature and vibration insensitive fiber-optic current sensor. J. Lightwave Technol. **20**(2), 267–276 (2002)
8. Bohnert, K., Hsu, C., Yang, L., Frank, A., Müller, G.M., Gabus, P.: Fiber-optic current sensor tolerant to imperfections of polarization-maintaining fiber connectors. J. Lightwave Technol. **36**(11), 2161–2165 (2002)
9. Huang, Y., Xia, L., Pang, F., Yuan, Y., Ji, J.: Self-compensative fiber optic current sensor. J. Lightwave Technol. **39**(7), 2187–2193 (2021)
10. Gao, H., Wang, G., Gao, W., Li, S.: A chiral photonic crystal fiber sensing coil for decreasing the polarization error in a fiber optic current sensor. Opt. Commun. **469**, 125755 (2020)
11. Temkina, V., Medvedev, A., Mayzel, A.: Research on the methods and algorithms improving the measurements precision and market competitive advantages of fiber optic current sensors. Sensors **20**(21), Article № 5995, 1–22 (2020)
12. Hu, H., Huang, J., Xia, L., Yan, Z., Peng, S.: The compensation of long-term temperature induced error in the all fiber current transformer through optimizing initial phase delay in λ/4 wave plate. Microw. Opt. Technol. Lett. **61**(7), 1769–1773 (2019)
13. Muller, G.M., Frank, A., Yang, L., Gu, X., Bohnert, K.: Temperature compensation of interferometric and polarimetric fiber-optic current sensors with spun highly birefringent fiber. J. Lightw. Technol. **37**(18), 4507–4513 (2019)
14. Temkina, V., Medvedev, A., Mayzel, A., Mokeev, A.: Compensation of fiber quarter-wave plate temperature deviation in fiber optic current sensor. In: 2019 IEEE International Conference on Electrical Engineering and Photonics (EExPolytech), St. Petersburg, pp. 339–341. IEEE (2019)
15. Polynkin, P., Blake, J.: Polarization evolution in bent spun fiber. J. Lightwave Technol. **23**, 3815–3820 (2005)
16. Gubin, V.P., et al.: Use of Spun optical fibres in current sensors. Quantum Electron. **36**(3), 287–291 (2006)
17. Hu, H., Huang, J., Huang, Y., Xia, L., Yu, J.: Modeling of the birefringence in spun fiber. Opt. Commun. **473**, Article No. 125919 (2020)

Fiber-Optic Recirculating Memory Loop for Wideband Microwave Signal

Sergei I. Ivanov$^{(\boxtimes)}$, Alexander P. Lavrov , Dmitrii V. Kondakov ,
and Yurij A. Matveev

Peter the Great Saint-Petersburg Polytechnic University, St. Petersburg, Russian Federation
ivanov_si@spbstu.ru

Abstract. A fiber-optic recirculating delay line for wideband microwave signals
is described. The core of delay line is an analogue wideband fiber-optic link,
with two radio frequency switches at input and output of fiber-optic link. The
link itself is intensity modulated direct detection type one with an integrated-
optical Mach-Zehnder modulator. The delay medium is single mode fiber; its
length determines the minimum delay time – time discrete. Switches control allows
to realize recirculation throw an analogue wideband fiber-optic link. So, the total
time delay is controlled in steps: multiples of the time discrete. In recirculation
loop a back arm is radio frequency path, so in this arm we use additional radio
frequency amplifier to adjust recirculation loop gain close to 1. We pay attention
to adjusting recirculation loop gain – theoretically and in experiments in lab setup.
We exam coupling between maximum number of recirculation and recirculation
loop gain, and also influence of gain unflatness across frequency bandwidth. Lab
setup has instantaneous bandwidth 0.5...14 GHz, limited by used radio frequency
switches. Two fibers with length approx. 25 m and 100 m were used in lab setup.
Time control for switches was from FPGA based time control unit with time
discrete 2 ns. The number of recirculation in the memory loop varied from 1 to
30.

Keywords: Wideband analogue fiber-optic line · Recirculating memory loop ·
Microwave signal · Switchable time delay

1 Introduction

Delay lines (DL) are important in the construction of many electronic systems. Delay
lines are used to test the operation of receivers in radars [1, 2], in instantaneous frequency meters [2–4], in microwave signal processing (including microwave filters) [2,
5–7], signal generation [5, 7], in radio countermeasures [3, 4, 10], in phased arrays
antenna beamforming according to true-time-delay (TTD) principle [1, 2, 6, 11, 12, 16],
in constructing photonic ADCs [2, 13] and etc. DLs are implemented on a different element base: coaxial cables and waveguides, surface acoustic waves (SAW), magnetostatic
waves, optics – bulk optics, fiber and integrated optics, etc. [14, 15]. The current trend
in the construction of electronic systems is the use of ultra-wideband signals [1, 17, 18],

© Springer Nature Switzerland AG 2022
Y. Koucheryavy et al. (Eds.): NEW2AN 2021/ruSMART 2021, LNCS 13158, pp. 254–267, 2022.
https://doi.org/10.1007/978-3-030-97777-1_22

and in this case, optical technologies and optical components sage become fundamental (principal) solutions [2, 18–20]. Other advantages of using optical technologies in radio electronic systems: low signal attenuation during its transmission over long distances – specific attenuation 0.2 dB/km for SMF-28 fiber in optical telecom C-band, insensitivity to electromagnetic interference, small dimensions of the DL with long delay time, very large time-bandwidth (TBW) product values for DL: frequency bandwidth – tens of gigahertz, delay times – tens of microseconds without regeneration [2, 18–20].

Speaking about optical DL of microwave signals, it should be noted that the signals themselves belong to the radio (RF) or microwave (MW) range, and the signal propagation medium is optical, therefore, 2 transformations are performed in the optical DL of microwave signals: at the input of the DL – the conversion "radio->optics" (this conversion is the modulation of the optical carrier), and at the output of the DL – the inverse conversion "optics->radio" (this conversion is the demodulation of the optical carrier) [2].

For the implementation of the actual optical DLs, multiple and very different designs have been proposed. Possible classification for optical DLs can be found in [13–15]:

- by the physical effect used – dispersive DL: the dispersion $D(\lambda)$ of the single-mode fiber itself or dispersion in fiber Bragg grating (FBG) - both discrete and chirped ones (in such systems, the wavelength of the used optical radiation must change - switch (for example, when using a dense wavelength division multiplexing (DWDM) approach) or smoothly tune (tunable laser source - TLS)) [21];
- by the structure of the delay medium (with switching of wave paths with different path lengths): cascade, parallel on a single-mode fiber, or (as an alternative) based on multicore fiber [22, 23], while the optical switches can be different type: integrated-optical e.g., high-speed switches on LiNbO3 [24], or low-millisecond-speed micro-electro-mechanical systems (MEMS) switches [25];
- by the value of delay time regulation range: small changes in the delay time - with the use of stretchers [26–29], or large changes in delay time - with the use of switches: and here the direction "recirculating DL" stands out [30–37]. In recirculating DLs, the output signal is again fed to the LD input. The signal delay time in these type DLs can vary within wide range by controlling the number of recirculations.

In recirculating DLs, an obligatory components are switches at the input and output of recirculation loop. The recirculation loop can be completely optical, and then optical switches can be used in the DL, for example, [24]. An alternative construction of a recirculation loop is using microwave switches at the input and output of the recirculation loop. In this case, two optics-radio conversions are performed in each recirculation cycle. Philosophically (physically) it is clear that any additional signal transformations can lead to a decrease in the quality characteristics of the implemented radio-electronic system. In addition, it is also clear that optical processes are much faster than electronic processes in "purely" electronic - semiconductor components (transistors) (their time constants are compared), and, thus, the use of microwave switches leads to a limitation of the operating frequency band in recirculating DL. However, the use of microwave switches gives a gain in the size and cost of the DLs. We consider this circumstance as essential in the construction of electronic systems, placed, for example, on mobile platforms.

Fiber optic recirculating DLs with microwave switches have been studied for a long time and widely [32–37]. However, interest in them is not waning at the present time. These type DLs are characterized by an increase in noise level at the DL output with a large number of regeneration cycles. The desire to make the signal recirculation with a small signal change during the total delay time leads to self-excitation of the DL – it turns into an auto-generator. We have previously obtained experimentally these type preliminary results on the recirculation DL models [30, 31]. In this paper, we investigate the relationship between the frequency unevenness of the transfer coefficient in the recirculation loop with the maximum number of recirculation cycles. A related problem was considered earlier in [34].

2 Fiber-Optic Recirculating Memory Loop for Wideband Microwave Signal

The block diagram of the fiber-optic recirculating memory loop is presented in Fig. 1. In practice it is an analogue fiber-optic switchable recirculating delay line. The base of DL is a wideband analogue fiber-optic link. In the laboratory set-up we used Optiva OTS-2 (Emcore) link. This link is intensity modulation direct detection type (IM-DD) one [38, 39].

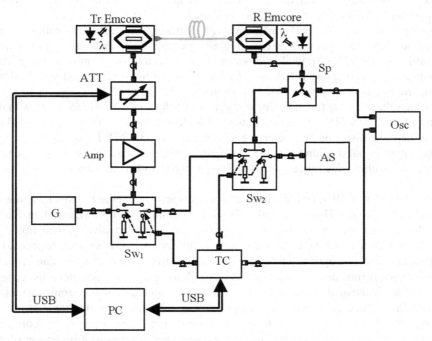

Fig. 1. The block diagram of the fiber-optic recirculating memory loop.

An input RF signal comes through switch Sw1, amplifier Amp, and attenuator ATT to input of RF-optic converter Tr Emcore. This link transmitter module realizes intensity modulation (IM) of DFB laser radiation (telecom C-band, ITU grid) by MZM modulator driven by input RF signal with frequencies in 0.05...18 GHz range. We can comment: analogue optical transmitters with external intensity modulation by MZM modulators have significantly wider RF bandwidth than optical transmitters with direct intensity modulation by laser injection current modulation [2, 39]. Intensity modulated optical signal is delayed in the fiber optic coil, and then the delayed signal is converted back to RF frequency domain by this link receiver module R Emcore (direct detection). In our lab experimental setup of DL the receiver output RF signal comes through splitter Sp in two ways. The one way – back to link input (to switch Sw1), so forming loop for recirculating functioning, the second way – for RF signal registration on oscilloscope OCS. At the output of recirculating DL there is the switch for snatch (pull out) delayed RF signal. In our lab setup it is switch Sw2 installed after the splitter. The snatched RF signal we can exam by spectrum analyzer SA. The switches Sw1 and Sw2 work under control from time control (TC) unit.

The switching time of an RF switches may be in nanosecond range: 10 ns as in [40]. TC unit also gives synchro pulse to 'trigger' input of OSC. Some details concerning our exam of the Optiva OTS-2 18 GHz link: link gain, 1 dB compression point, output noise level, own intrinsic time delay in the 'transmitter + receiver' modules pair one can find in [41].

The time delays T_Σ implemented in our DL depend on the fiber segment length L_F as well as the number n of recirculation assigned to the DL from TC unit: $T_\Sigma = T(n + 1)$. The minimum delay time (when $n = 0$) is $T = (L_F n_0)/c$, where n_0 is the effective refractive index of fiber mode (single mode fiber SMF-28 type), c is the light velocity in free space. In the DL lab setup we use 37 m and 112 m fiber segment (fiber spoon), so T_1 equals 180 ns for 37 m length and 552 ns for 112 m length. The length L_F of fiber segment determines time discrete (resolution = step) when one switches total time delay in DL. This time discrete depends on the DL application (Radar, Radio communication intelligence, Radio countermeasure).

We can measure time delay in analogue fiber-optic links with high precision using vector network analyzer (VNA) [27]. A VNA measures the S-parameters (S_{11}, S_{12}, S_{21}, and S_{22}) of microwave two-port networks. To measure network time delay the parameter S_{21} is important: $|S_{21}(f)|$ is the amplitude response of a two-port device, and $\arg[S_{21}(f)]$ is its phase response, $\varphi(f)$. From the measured phase response $\varphi(f)$ in an analogue FO link specified frequency band Δf, the group delay time T_{del} is determined: $T_{del} = \Delta\varphi(f)/(\Delta f \cdot 360)$, where $\Delta\varphi(f)$– phase change, in degrees.

For phase unwrapping in $\Delta\varphi(f)$ a VNA has to measure $S_{21}(f)$ with large amounts of points in measurement trace. We use the VNA S5085 (Planar) with number of points in $S(f)$ traces up to 200001 [42].

We add also that the VNA S5085 software allows selecting superimposed RF signals (case of multipath RF signal propagation through a two-port networks under test), and this possibilities was used in our research of delay line based on LiNbO$_3$ crystal [43].

Fig. 2. General view of the experimental setup.

The general view (a photo) of the lab experimental setup is shown in Fig. 2. Some additional details concerning performances of components used in the recirculation delay line lab setup one can find in [31].

3 Mathematical Model of Recirculating Analogue Fiber-Optic Delay Line. Main Parameters of the Delay Line Calculation

The main parameters of a recirculating fiber-optic delay line (FODL) with an switchable delay time are: the range of time delays changes and the discrete in delay change, the device operating frequency range (bandwidth), the accuracy and stability of the delay time, insertion loss and dynamic range (including the noise figure).

The time discrete T and the maximum delay time T_{DLmax} of the recirculating FODL are determined, respectively, by the length L_F of the fiber-optic line itself and the maximum number of signal recirculations in the line. To calculate the number n_{max}, let us consider a mathematical model of the recirculating FODL shown in Fig. 3. The radio frequency switch Sw, in a time interval not exceeding the discrete T, connects the radio frequency signal $s(t)$ to the line input (see Fig. 3).

Due to the linearity of the device under consideration, the resulting random signal $n(t)$ from all noise sources in device can be recalculated to the line input as shown in Fig. 3.

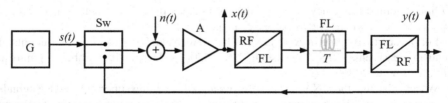

Fig. 3. Functional diagram of analogue Fiber-Optic recirculating delay line, which is an explication for constructing a mathematical model of the device.

Element A in Fig. 3 is a variable gain amplifier and we consider it determines the sum effect of all frequency dependent elements of the line (the remaining elements are thus frequency independent with a gain equal to unity). The inertial properties of element A are characterized by its pulse (Dirac) response h(t) [44].

The input amplified RF signal is denoted by $x(t)$, the output RF signal arriving at the input during recirculation is denoted by $y(t)$ (see Fig. 3). The proposed functional diagram adequately describes the processes of signal recirculation in the line, but significantly simplifies the mathematical model in comparison with the functional diagram considered earlier.

For a mathematical description of the signal transformation in the line, we use the method of sequential integration [45], with the help of which the solution continues forward, that is, in the direction of increasing time t from one subinterval to next one. The entire observation time t is divided into sub intervals of duration T (discrete)

$$t \in (-\infty, nT] = (-\infty, 0] \cup (0, T] \cup (T, 2T] \cup \cdots ((n-1)T, nT]. \tag{1}$$

In the first-time interval, when the device is in initial state (inoperative), zero initial conditions are assumed to be satisfied

$$t \in (-\infty, 0]; \; s(t) \equiv 0; \; n(t) \equiv 0; \; x_{-1}(t) \equiv 0; \; y_{-1}(t) \equiv 0. \tag{2}$$

In the second time interval, the RF signal $s(t)$ in sum with the noise $n(t)$ is fed to the device input. In this case, the output signal $y(t)$ is absent (equal to zero)

$$t \in (0, T]; \; s(t) \equiv s(t); \; n(t) \equiv n(t); \; y_0(t) \equiv 0; \tag{3}$$

$$x_0(t) = \int_{-\infty}^{t} \left[s(t_0) + n(t_0) + y_0(t_0) \right] h(t - t_0) dt_0 = \int_{0+0}^{t} [s(t_0) + n(t_0)] h(t - t_0) dt_0. \tag{4}$$

At the next and subsequent intervals, the signal $s(t)$ is absent, the noise $n(t)$ is fed to the device input together with the output signal $y(t)$ delayed by the time T

$$t \in (T, 2T]; \; s(t) \equiv 0; \; n(t) \equiv n(t); \; y_1(t) = x_0(t - T); \tag{5}$$

$$x_1(t) = \int_{T+0}^{t} \left[n(t_1) + y_1(t_1) \right] h(t - t_1) dt_1$$
$$= \int_{T+0}^{t} \left\{ n(t_1) + \int_{0+0}^{t_1-T} [s(t_0) + n(t_0)] h(t_1 - T - t_0) dt_0 \right\} h(t - t_1) dt_1. \tag{6}$$

On the last n-th interval, we have

$$t \in ((n-1)T, nT]; \; s(t) \equiv 0; \; n(t) \equiv n(t); \; y_{n-1}(t) = x_{n-2}(t - T); \tag{7}$$

$$x_{n-1}(t) = \int_{(n-1)T}^{t} \left[n(t_{n-1}) + y_{n-1}(t_{n-1}) \right] h(t - t_{n-1}) dt_{n-1}. \tag{8}$$

Let us introduce the following notations: for the power gain $K(f)$ as square of the Fourier transform modulus of $h(t)$

$$K(f) = |\Im\{h(t)|t: t \in (0, T]\}|^2, \tag{9}$$

and for the power spectral density (PSD) of noise

$$N(f) = \frac{1}{T}\langle|\Im\{n(t)|t: t \in ((i-1)T, iT]\}|^2\rangle, \quad i = 1, 2, \dots n \tag{10}$$

and for RF input signal spectrum

$$S(f) = \frac{1}{T}\langle|\Im\{s(t)|t: t \in (0, T]\}|^2\rangle, \tag{11}$$

where (see (10) and (11)) the angle brackets denote the statistical averaging of the corresponding quantity. Taking into account the statistical independence of the noise at different time intervals T (uncorrelated Gaussian quantities), from relations (3)–(8) we obtain the following expressions for the output radio frequency signal PSD at the n recirculation interval

$$S_n(f) = S(f)K^n(f), \tag{12}$$

and for the output noise PSD

$$N_n(f) = \frac{1 - K^n(f)}{1 - K(f)}N(f)K(f). \tag{13}$$

Let us consider the factors influencing the number of maximum recirculations nmax, and, consequently, the maximum duration of the signal time delay $s(t)$. One of these factors is the nonlinearity of the operating mode of the device when the signal power exceeds $P_{s\,0}$. In this case, the n_{max} value is determined from (12) by the relation

$$n_{max} - 1 \le \frac{10 \log L}{10 \log K_0}, \quad L = \frac{P_{s\,max}}{P_{s0}}. \tag{14}$$

The dependence of n_{max} as a function of K_0 for different values of parameter L is shown in Fig. 4, a). Obviously, the n_{max} increases when K_0 come closer to 1 and the parameter L increases. It is important to note that in order to achieve the maximum time delay, it is necessary to adjust the gain K_0 equal to 1 with a closed back loop of the delay line. However, in practice, such a condition will always be met up with error - with minimum allowed step of changing gain K_0. Therefore, we can always assume that

$$K_0 = 1 + \Delta K, \tag{15}$$

where the minimum value of ΔK is determined by the technical capabilities of components used in delay line construction.

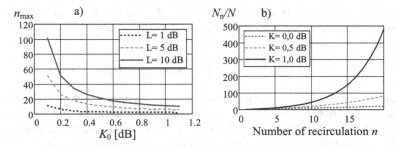

Fig. 4. a) n_{max} vs K_0 for different values of the parameter L; b) The Normalized noise spectral density N_n/N vs n for different values of the parameter K_0.

Another factor limiting the n_{max} value is an increase in the noise level with an increase in the number of recirculations n in accordance with expression (13). When calculating the noise level, it is necessary to consider two possible types of the form of the amplitude-frequency characteristic (AFC) of the device, shown in Fig. 5. The first AFC form in Fig. 5, a) is characterized by homogeneous ripples near the mean value of K_0. The second AFC form in Fig. 5, b) is characterized by one large inhomogeneity ΔK_0 at a fixed frequency f_0.

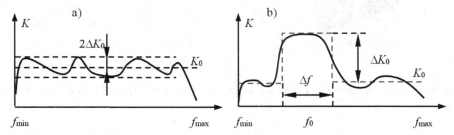

Fig. 5. Frequency response of the device: a) – homogeneous ripples, b) – large inhomogeneity at frequency f_0.

The graph of the dependence of the noise PSD normalized value N_n/N as a function of the recirculation number n for different value K_0 for the first type of the AFC form is shown in Fig. 4, b). For the second type of frequency response form (see Fig. 5, b), the increase in the noise level with the recirculation number n is determined by the ratio

$$\frac{[P_{noise}(f)]_{out}}{[P_{noise}(f)]_{in}} = \frac{1 - K_0^n}{1 - K_0}K_0(1 - M) + \frac{1 - K^n(f_0)}{1 - K(f_0)}K(f_0)M, \quad M = \frac{\Delta f}{f_{max} - f_{min}}. \quad (16)$$

The increase in the noise level in accordance with (16) can be significant and in case when the second term in (16) is much larger than the first one, the random output signal is quasi-harmonic with a frequency f_0.

With increasing recirculation number n the noise level with respect to the signal component increases, so the signal-to-noise ratio (SNR) decreases, and therefore the noise figure F_n increases. If for technical reasons the value of F_n is specified, then the maximum number of recirculations can be found from the ratio

$$\frac{\text{SNR}_{\text{in}}}{\text{SNR}_{\text{out}}} = F_n = \frac{1 - K_0^n(f)}{[1 - K_0(f)]K_0^{n-1}(f)}. \tag{17}$$

Figure 6 a) shows 3-D plot of the noise figure F_n dependence of the noise figure F_n on n and K_0. Figure 6, b) shows cross-sections of 3-D plot at various values of the noise F_n. A smaller value of the noise figure F_n requires more stringent restrictions on the maximum allowable number of cycles n for a given gain control step ΔK.

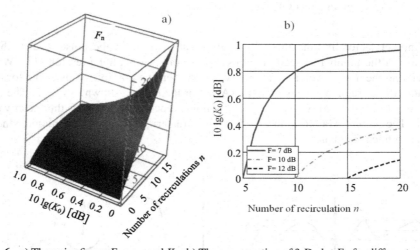

Fig. 6. a) The noise figure F_n vs n and K_0; b) The cross section of 3-D plot F_n for different values F_n.

4   Results of Experimental Studies of Recirculating Fiber-Optic Delay Line Model and Discussions

To test the developed mathematical model describing the recirculating FODL and the proposed method for calculating delay line parameters, experimental studies were carried out on the delay line laboratory model, a description of which is given in Sect. 2. Figure 7 shows a graph of the frequency response (parameter S_{21} of the S-parameter matrix) of the developed model with open feedback loop. The feedback loop is realized by a short dispersionless RF coaxial cable with negligible losses.

The operating frequency range is 150…300 MHz and the frequency response of the entire device is determined by the frequency response of an amplifier with adjustable gain. This amplifier was used because of restricted bandwidth of available oscilloscope. It can be seen from the graph that the frequency response of the investigated recirculation radio-photonic line has a pronounced maximum at a frequency of 175 MHz. According to

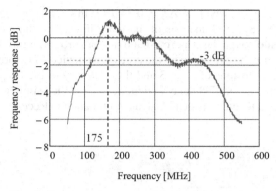

Fig. 7. Frequency response of the investigated device.

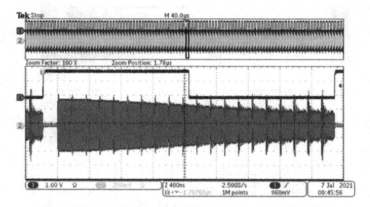

Fig. 8. Waveform of the signal recirculating in the delay line.

the Sect. 3 results, with a large number of recirculations n_{max}, the output noise spectrum will be narrowband with a center frequency of about 175 MHz.

Figure 8 shows waveform of the signal $x(t)$ (see Fig. 3) recirculating in the FODL during the total time delay interval nT. The total length of the fiber-optic line itself was approx. 40 m, which determines the minimum time discrete T, equal to 180 ns. The duration of the RF input signal (like impulse) with a frequency of 250 MHz did not exceed T. The minimum gain control step was $\Delta K = 0.5$ dB.

Adjusting the gain in closed feedback loop made it possible to set the K_0 value approximately equal to 1, when the attenuation (amplification) of the RF signal is minimal during the total delay time (see Fig. 8). Experimental studies have shown that the maximum recirculations number n_{max} under these conditions is 20..22 cycles, while the maximum time delay is about 4 ms, which is in agreement with the calculated value according to the formula (14). Figure 9 shows a waveform of increase in noise level for the same parameters of the delay time and the gain K_0, as for Fig. 8. Figure 10 shows a comparison of the measurement data and calculations according to the method described in Sect. 3. The calculation by formula (13) of the normalized noise level as a function of the recirculation cycle at $\Delta K = 0.35$ dB is in satisfactory agreement with the experimental results. Spectral analysis of the noise in each of the recirculation cycles showed that the random signal is a narrow-band random process with a central frequency of 180 MHz. This result is explained by the type of the device AFC form shown in Fig. 7 and confirms the conclusions of Sect. 3 and the adequacy of the proposed mathematical model. On our laboratory FO delay line model we fulfilled similar experiments with another fiber segment length between FO Transmitter and FO Receiver – approx. 112 m.

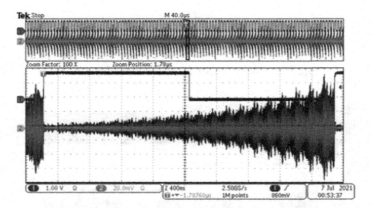

Fig. 9. Waveform of the noise recirculating in the delay line.

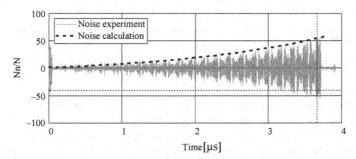

Fig. 10. Comparison of the experimental and theoretical growth of the noise recirculating in the delay line.

The obtained estimates of the delay line operating parameters based on the measurement results, based on discussed approach, are also in satisfactory agreement with the calculations according to the proposed method.

5 Conclusion

The rigorous mathematical and physically consistent model of informative (useful) signal and noise transformation in recirculating analogue fiber-optic delay line is proposed. This model takes into account the flatness of the loop gain $K(f)$, the resolution of the gain control $\Delta K(f)$, the permissible value of the noise figure Fn and the margin in maximum permissible signal power level P_{max}. A method is proposed for calculating the maximum number of recirculation cycles n_{max} and, accordingly, the maximum time delay $n_{max}T$. Experimental studies carried out using a model of a recirculating radio-photon delay line with a fiber-optic line length of 40 and 112 m are in satisfactory agreement with the calculations according to the proposed method. The experimental estimate of the n_{max} value in the range 22...25 coincides with the calculated estimate for a given amplitude-frequency characteristic $K(f)$. The performed measurements of the time dynamics of the noise level during the recirculation process are in satisfactory agreement with the corresponding theoretical calculations. We believe that a delay line of this type could be of interest not only in radar and countermeasures, but also in other applications, for example in meteorological radars and lidar systems to imitate return pulses in them and also in another type optical delay line investigation [46, 47].

Acknowledgments. This research was funded by RFBR, project number 20-07-00928.

References

1. Skolnik, M.: Radar Handbook, 3rd edn. McGraw-Hill Companies, New York (2008)
2. Urick, V.J., McKinney, J.D., Williams, K.J.: Fundamentals of Microwave Photonics. Wiley, Hoboken (2015)
3. Tsui, J.B.: Microwave Receivers with Electronic Warfare Applications. SciTech Publishing, Raleigh (2005)
4. Poisel, R.A.: Electronic Warfare Receivers and Receiver Systems, 3rd edn. Artech House, Boston (2014)
5. Yao, J.: Microwave photonics. IEEE J. Lightwave Technol. **27**(3), 314–335 (2009)
6. Berceli, T., Herczfeld, P.R.: Microwave photonics – a historical perspective. IEEE Trans. Microw. Theory Tech. **65**(5), 1891–1903 (2017)
7. Minasian, R.A., Chan, E.H.W., Yi, X.: Microwave photonic signal processing. Opt. Express **21**(19), 22918–22936 (2013)
8. Diehl, J.F., Singley, J.M., Sunderman, C.E., Urick, V.J.: Microwave photonic delay line signal processing. Appl. Opt. **54**(31), F35–F41 (2015)
9. Capmany, J., Mora, J., Gasulla, I., Sancho, J., Lloret, J., Sales, S.: Microwave photonic signal processing. J. Lightwave Technol. **31**, 571–586 (2013)
10. Belkin, M.E., Fofanov, D., Sigov, A.: Microwave photonics approach as a novel smart fabrication technique of a radio communication jammers. Procedia Comput. Sci. **180**, 950–957 (2021)
11. Volkov, V.A., Gordeev, D.A., Ivanov, S.I., Lavrov, A.P., Saenko, I.I.: Photonic beamformer model based on analog fiber-optic links' components. J. Phys. Conf. Ser. **737**, 012002 (2016). https://doi.org/10.1088/1742-6596/737/1/012002
12. Ivanov, S.I., Lavrov, A.P., Saenko, I.I., Filatov, D.L.: Chirped fiber grating beamformer for linear phased array antenna. In: Galinina, O., Andreev, S., Balandin, S., Koucheryavy, Y. (eds.) NEW2AN/ruSMART -2018. LNCS, vol. 11118, pp. 594–604. Springer, Cham (2018). https://doi.org/10.1007/978-3-030-01168-0_53
13. Zmuda, H., Fanto, M., McEwen, T., Pawloski, J., Norelli, K.: A photonic recirculating delay line for analog-to-digital conversion and other applications. Proc. SPIE **6975**, 69750F (2008). https://doi.org/10.1117/12.783962

14. Shahoei, H., Yao, J.: Delay lines. In: Webster, J. (ed.) Wiley Encyclopedia of Electrical and Electronics Engineering, pp. 1–15. Wiley, Hoboken (2014). https://doi.org/10.1002/047134 608X.W8234
15. Belkin, M.E.: Ultra-wideband long-term RF-signal delay devices: optimal decisions analysis. Infocommun. Radio Technol. 1(1) 103–120 (2018). https://doi.org/10.15826/icrt.2018.01. 1.08. (in Russian)
16. Riza, N.A.: Selected Papers on Photonic Control Systems for Phased Array Antennas. SPIE Press, vol. MS136 (1997)
17. Ghavami, M., Michael, L.B., Kohno, R.: Ultra Wideband Signals and Systems in Communication Engineering. Wiley, Chichester (2004)
18. Immoreev, I., Tao, T.: UWB radar for patient monitoring. IEEE Aerosp. Electron. Syst. Mag. 23(11), 11–18 (2008). https://doi.org/10.1109/MAES.2008.4693985
19. Iezekiel, S.: Microwave Photonics: Devices and Applications. Wiley, Chichester (2009)
20. Ghelfi, P., et al.: A fully photonics-based coherent radar system. Nature 57, 341–345 (2014). https://doi.org/10.1038/nature13078
21. Kashyap, R.: Fiber Bragg Gratings, 2nd edn. Elsevier, Amsterdam (2009)
22. Egorova, O.N., Astapovich, M.S., Belkin, M.E., Semjonov, S.L.: Multicore optical fibre and fibre-optic delay line based on it. Quantum Electron. 46(12), 1134–1138 (2016). https://doi. org/10.1070/QEL16224
23. Gasulla, I., Capmany, J.: Microwave photonics applications of multicore fibers. IEEE Photonics J. 4(3), 877–888 (2012). https://doi.org/10.1109/JPHOT.2012.2199101
24. https://agiltron.com/category/fiber-optic-switches/nanospeed-fiber-optical-switches. Accessed 08 July 2021
25. https://www.sercalo.com/products/mems-switches-products. Accessed 08 July 2021
26. https://lunainc.com/sites/default/files/assets/files/data-sheets/FST-001%20Data%20Sheet. pdf. Accessed 08 July 2021
27. Lavrov, A., Ivanov, S., Saenko, I.: Measurements and stabilization of the radio signals time delay when their transmitting over long wideband analog fiber optics links. In: 2019 IEEE International Conference on Electrical Engineering and Photonics (EExPolytech), pp. 50–53 (2019). https://doi.org/10.1109/EExPolytech.2019.8906807
28. Vekshin, Yu.V., Tsaruk, A.A., Vytnov, A.V., Zotov, M.B., Karpichev, A.S., Khvostov, Y.Y.: Fiber optic transmission lines for the radio astronomy receivers. Trans. IAA RAS (50), 16–22 (2019). https://doi.org/10.32876/ApplAstron.50.16-22
29. Shillue, B., et al.: The ALMA photonic local oscillator system. Proc. SPIE 8452, 845216 (2012)
30. Podstrigaev, A.S., Lukiyanov, A.S., Galichina, A.A., Lavrov, A.P., Parfenov, M.V.: Wideband tunable delay line for microwave signals based on RF photonic components. In: Galinina, O., Andreev, S., Balandin, S., Koucheryavy, Y. (eds.) Internet of Things, Smart Spaces, and Next Generation Networks and Systems, pp. 424–431. Springer, Cham (2020). https://doi.org/10. 1007/978-3-030-65726-0_38
31. Kondakov, D.V., Ivanov, S.I., Lavrov, A.P.: A broadband analog fiber-optic line with recirculating memory loop for variable microwave signal delay. J. Phys. Conf. Ser. (2021)
32. Newberg, I.L., Gee, C.M., Thurmond, G.D., Yen, H.W.: Long microwave delay fiberoptic link for radar testing. IEEE Trans. Microw. Theory Tech. 38(5), 664–666 (1990)
33. Wurtz, L.T., Wheless, W.P.: Design of a programmable 2–18 GHz microwave fiber-optic delay line. In: IEEE Southeastcon 1997 Conference, pp. 11–19 (1997). https://doi.org/10. 1109/SECON.1997.598600
34. Koffman, I., Herczfeld, P.R., Daryoush, A.S., Even-Or, B., Markowitz, R.: A fiber optic recirculating memory loop for radar applications. Microw. Opt. Technol. Lett. 1(7), 232–235 (1988)

35. Singley, J., Diehl, J., McDermitt, C., Sunderman, C., Urick, V.: Design and performance of a 560-microsecond Ku-band binary fiber-optic delay line. NRL Memorandum Report, NRL/MR/5650-14-9545 (2014)
36. Nguyen, T.A., Chan, E.H.W., Minasian, R.A.: Photonic multiple frequency measurement using a frequency shifting recirculating delay line structure. J. Lightwave Technol. **32**(20), 3831–3838 (2014)
37. Vizoso, B., Vfizquez, C., Civera, R., Lopez-Amo, M., Muriel, M.A.: Amplified fiber-optic recirculating delay lines. J. Lightwave Technol. **12**(2), 294–305 (1994)
38. Optiva OTS-2 18 GHz Unamplified Microwave Band Fiber Optic Links. https://emcore. com/wp-content/uploads/2016/03/Optiva-OTS-2-18GHz-Unamplified.pdf. Accessed 10 July 2021
39. Ivanov, S.I., Lavrov, A.P., Saenko, I.I.: Main characteristics study of analog fiber-optic links with direct and external modulation in transmitter modules. In: 2018 IEEE International Conference on Electrical Engineering and Photonics (EExPolytech), pp. 264–267 (2018). https://doi.org/10.1109/EExPolytech.2018.8564391
40. Switch HMC347ALP3E datasheet. https://www.analog.com/en/products/hmc347alp3e.html. Accessed 10 July 2021
41. Ivanov, S.I., Lavrov, A.P., Saenko, I.I.: Investigation of key components of photonic beam-forming system for receiving antenna array. In: Balandin, S., Andreev, S., Koucheryavy, Y. (eds.) ruSMART 2015. LNCS, vol. 9247, pp. 679–688. Springer, Cham (2015). https://doi. org/10.1007/978-3-319-23126-6_61
42. S5085 2-Port 8.5 GHz Analyzer. Extended Specification Sheets. https://coppermountaintech. com, https://online.fliphtml5.com/pbaab/jjxa/#p=1. Accessed 10 Apr 2021
43. Varlamov, A.V., Ivanov, S.I., Lavrov, A.P., Shamray, A.V.: Time-frequency analysis of acoustic waves in an integrated acousto-optical modulator based on LiNbO3 crystal. J. Phys. Conf. Ser. **1697**, 012174 (2020). https://doi.org/10.1088/1742-6596/1697/1/01217
44. Siebert, W.McC.: Circuits, Signals, and Systems, vol. 2. The MIT Press, Cambridge; London (1988)
45. Bellman, R., Cooke, K.L.: Differential-Difference Equations. Academic Press, New York; London (1963)
46. Privalov, V.E., Shemanin, V.G.: Lidar system for monitoring radioactive contamination of atmospheric air. J. Opt. Technol. **84**(5), 289–293 (2017). https://doi.org/10.1364/JOT.84. 000289
47. Markvart, A.A., Liokumovich, L.B., Ushakov, N.A.: Tunable optical delay lines based on a system of coupled whispering gallery mode resonators. J. Phys. Conf. Ser. **1326**, 012017 (2019)

Simulation and Experimental Study of Multi-source Application Layer ARQ for FANET

Irina Kaisina$^{(\boxtimes)}$ ⓘ, Albert Abilov ⓘ, Danil Vasiliev ⓘ, Mohammed Amin Lamri ⓘ, and Anatoli Nistyuk ⓘ

Department of Communication Networks and Systems, Kalashnikov Izhevsk State Technical University, ul. Studencheskaya, 7, 426069 Izhevsk, Russia
{irina.kaysina,albert.abilov,danil.s.vasilyev,lamri.amin,
kafsts}@istu.ru
http://www.istu.ru/

Abstract. This paper discusses a FANET consisting of several source nodes and one destination node in the form of a ground station. As data for transmission, a video stream was considered, which was broadcasted in real time simultaneously by several source nodes. Simulation of the multi-stream data transmission process was carried out in NS-3 environment. Several variations of multi-stream transmission modeling were considered, in the first of which the Application class was used to create several source nodes, in the second the Poisson Pareto Burst Process (PPBP) traffic generator was used. Based on the simulation results, it was concluded that an increase in the number of flying source nodes negatively affects QoS: the requirement for Goodput increases, the destination node buffer is overloaded and video data packets are dropped, and PDR decreases. To solve the above problem, the Multi-Source Application Layer ARQ (MS-AL-ARQ) method is proposed, the main principle of which is to repeat the lost data chunks at the application level. This paper describes the principle of operation of MS-AL-ARQ for working with separate input buffers and a common input buffer at the destination node. Both variations of the MS-AL-ARQ operation are implemented in software, the effectiveness of their application was experimentally proven.

Keywords: FANET · Multi-source · MS-AL-ARQ · Buffer · PDR · Goodput · PPBP

1 Introduction

Unmanned aerial vehicles are more and more actively developed and disseminated, they find their application in performing tasks of monitoring terrains and pipelines; and are used in emergency zones and etc. [1–5]. From a practical point of view, UAVs are most often used for direct data transfer from a source node (a camera on a UAV board, a thermal imager, or other payload) to a ground control station. In this case, for the transmission of video data, communication channels are used that are specially

© Springer Nature Switzerland AG 2022
Y. Koucheryavy et al. (Eds.): NEW2AN 2021/ruSMART 2021, LNCS 13158, pp. 268–283, 2022.
https://doi.org/10.1007/978-3-030-97777-1_23

developed for UAVs, which allow data transmission over long distances. A separate group of UAV applications, including a large number of them, can be attributed to the drone show, which has been especially popular for the last few years, where each small UAV does not transmit data to a ground station, but only receives data about the position change at a certain interval. From the point of view of scientific research, the use of ad-hoc mode in UAV networks and the deployment of entire flying ad-hoc networks (FANETs) have been considered for several years now [6–11]. In addition, many scenarios have already been investigated to date, which describe the process of data transmission in such networks: "source node - destination node"; "source node - relay node - destination node"; "source node - swarm of relay nodes - destination node" [12]. In the presence of several relay nodes, routing protocols are used, some of which have been investigated and improved through measuring metrics, using an inter-layer approach, applying the geographical location of nodes and using artificial intelligence systems [13–15]. All these improve the quality of data transmission in the FANET with a single source node.

Increasing the number of source nodes in the FANET can reduce the mission fulfillment time. This scenario can be considered in different variations: "source nodes - destination node"; "source nodes - relay node - destination node"; "source nodes - swarm of relay nodes - destination node". The use of several source nodes is promising and can be used in emergency situations when it is important to explore a large area, for example, a forest, as soon as possible. However, an increase in the number of source nodes can adversely affect QoS due to an overflow in the input buffer at the destination node and relay nodes. The primary task is to study in detail the simplest scenario "source nodes - destination node" and develop new methods and algorithms for improving QoS.

2   Simulation of the Process of Data Transmission from Several Source Nodes to a Ground Station in NS-3

The Network Simulator 3 (NS-3) was chosen as the environment for simulation. NS-3 is a discrete event network simulator designed primarily for research activities. The simulator is open source for researchers to contribute and share their program assets. The code is written in the C++ programming language, which is used to implement the simulation script. The section considers several scenarios: data transmission from several UAVs to a ground station using the Application class, it also presents the results of the previously published paper describing the effect of the number of flying source nodes on Goodput using a PPBP traffic generator [16]. At the same time, in both programs being developed, the Free-Space Mode model was used as a signal propagation medium, which is based on Harold Friis formula:

$$R_x = T_x + 10log_{10}\left(\frac{\lambda^2}{(4\pi d)^2 L}\right) \tag{1}$$

where Tx - is the power at the transmitter, dBm; d - distance between transmitter and receiver, m; L - system losses. To achieve results that are closest to reality, the transmitter power did not exceed 25 dBm, which corresponds to the parameters of Raspberry Pi 3 Model B microcomputer. 802.11n was chosen as the communication standard, supported

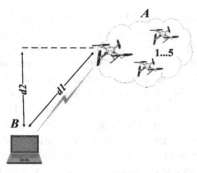

Fig. 1. Illustration of a scenario for simulating multi-stream transmission of video data using PPBP

in reality by microcomputers. In both simulation scenarios, the source nodes were put at distance d1 from the destination node, as shown in Fig. 1.

When generating video traffic using PPBP, video data was transmitted through an intermediate gateway node as shown in Fig. 1. In both simulation scenarios, the number of flying source nodes increased from 1 to 5 with a step of one node.

2.1 Assessing the Effect of the Number of Flying Source Nodes on PDR When Using the Application Class

Using the Application class, the transmission of video data from one or several source nodes in the form of a UAV to a ground station was implemented. The stream was transmitted using UDP at the transport layer. During the simulation, the MCS values varied from 0 to 7, the interval between the transmission of each packet was varied too. The channel width chosen was 20 or 40 MHz, respectively and distance *d1* between the source nodes and the destination node increased. Moreover, the frequency remained unchanged and equaled 5 GHz, the channel number and other settings were taken from the recommendations to work with the *wifi-phy-configuration* link layer [17]. Dependencies of the influence of the number of flying source nodes on the Packet Delivery Rate – PDR were obtained, which was defined as the ratio of the number of received packets to the number of sent packets. Figures 2, 3, 4, 5 and 6 show the simulation results for 20 MHz channel width.

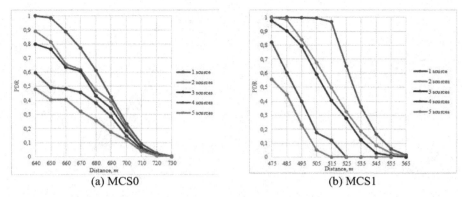

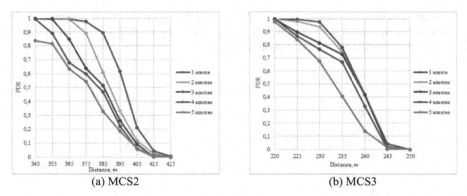

Fig. 2. Dependence of PDR on the distance between the destination node and the source nodes with values of MCS0 (a), MCS1 (b) and 20 MHz channel width

Fig. 3. Dependence of PDR on the distance between the destination node and the source nodes with values of 2 MCS (a), MCS3 (b) and 20 MHz channel width

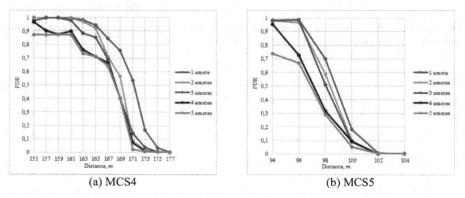

Fig. 4. Dependence of PDR on the distance between the destination node and the source nodes with values of MCS4 (a), MCS5 (b) and 20 MHz channel width

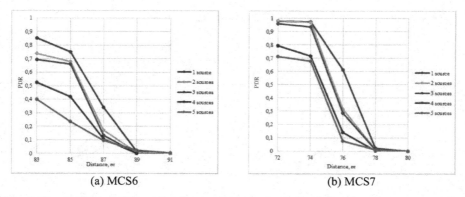

(a) MCS6   (b) MCS7

Fig. 5. Dependence of PDR on the distance between the destination node and the source nodes with values of MCS6 (a), MCS7 (b) and 20 MHz channel width

From the graphs presented in Figs. 2, 3, 4 and 5 it follows that an increase in the number of flying source nodes negatively affects PDR. Figures 6, 7, 8, 9, 10 and 11 show the simulation results for 40 MHz channel width.

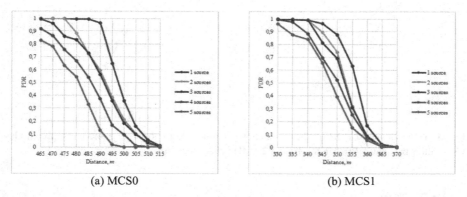

(a) MCS0   (b) MCS1

Fig. 6. Dependence of PDR on the distance between the destination node and the source nodes with values of MCS0 (a), MCS1 (b) and 40 MHz channel width

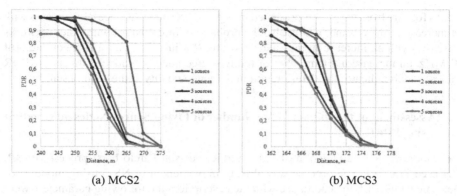

(a) MCS2   (b) MCS3

Fig. 7. Dependence of PDR on the distance between the destination node and the source nodes with values of MCS2 (a), MCS3 (b) and 40 MHz channel width

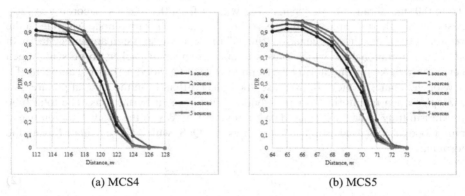

(a) MCS4   (b) MCS5

Fig. 8. Dependence of PDR on the distance between the destination node and the source nodes with values of MCS4 (a), MCS5 (b) and 40 MHz channel width

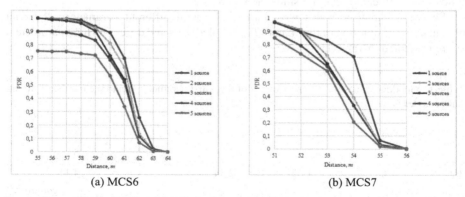

(a) MCS6   (b) MCS7

Fig. 9. Dependence of PDR on the distance between the destination node and the source nodes with values of MCS6 (a), MCS7 (b) and 40 MHz channel width

As follows from the graphs presented in Figs. 6, 7, 8 and 9, distance d1 decreases with an increase in the channel width, also the probability of collisions with other networks increases with an increase in the channel width. But just like with a channel width of 20 MHz, an increase in the number of flying source nodes negatively affects the PDR values, which indicates the deterioration in the video quality at the ground station.

2.2 Assessment of the Impact of the Number of Flying Source Nodes on Goodput Using PPBP

For a more realistic simulation of video traffic, Poisson Pareto burst process (PPBP) was used [18, 19]. The process was already implemented in NS-3 using modules of the same name [20]. In accordance with the description, the following parameters were changed in the model during the simulation: the number of active source nodes n, the Hurst parameter H and the duration of the data burst T_{on}. Restrictions were set for each of the aforementioned parameters as follows: the Hurst parameter H took values from 0.6 to 0.9; the duration of the "burst" T_{on} was set from 0.1 to 0.5 s, according to [20]. Also, such a short duration of the "burst" of data at each source node was due to the peculiarities of the chosen scenario. "Bursts" in video transmission are associated with an abrupt frame change, which causes a larger number of packets to be sent. When performing tasks for monitoring a certain terrestrial territory, a "burst" can occur if a new object comes in view. In this case, the object differs from the general picture. For example, when monitoring a field, a building gets caught by the lens. The total time for transmitting streaming video data from several UAVs to the ground station was 5 min. Goodput was used as a metric for assessing QoS, which was calculated using the formula:

$$Goodput = \frac{buffer*1370*8}{time} \qquad (2)$$

Where $buffer$ - the number of packets in the buffer at the destination node at the end of the simulation; 1370 - the packet size; 8 - the number of bits in a byte; $time$ - the running time of the application that transmits the video data.

Several simulation cycles were carried out with different parameters, the data obtained for the duration of the "burst" T_{on} equaled 0.1 s and different Hurst parameters H are presented in Table 1:

Table 1. Goodput values for different values of the Hurst parameter H and the number of flying source nodes is n

H	n				
	1	2	3	4	5
0,6	0,85	1,65	2,44	3,29	4,11

(*continued*)

Table 1. (*continued*)

H	n				
	1	2	3	4	5
0,7	0,96	1,88	2,78	3,71	4,54
0,8	1,14	2,27	3,23	4,36	5,01
0,9	1,5	2,9	4,05	5,03	5,34

It was determined that the increase in the number of source nodes increases the requirements for Goodput. So, with an increase in the number of source nodes from one to five, the Goodput increases from 0.8–1.5 Mbit/s up to 4.1–5.3 Mbit/s for different values of the Hurst parameter H in the considered scenario.

Based on the results of modeling the process of transmitting video data from several flying source nodes to a ground station, we can conclude that an increase in sources causes an increase in Goodput requirements and a decrease in PDR, while overloads appear on the input buffer of the destination node, which leads to degradation of the video quality. The solution to the problem can be the development of a retransmission request algorithm for a UAV network with several source nodes at the application level.

3 Multi-source Application Layer ARQ (MS-AL-ARQ)

The MS-AL-ARQ method and algorithm are based on the principles of the AL-ARQ algorithm [21]. One of the basic principles of the algorithm is to determine the lost chunk from one of the source nodes based on the sequence number with the identifier of the IP address. After identifying the lost piece of data, NACK is sent into the buffer to the source node. In this case, a retransmission timeout (RTO) is set, after which NACK is sent again. This action will be repeated until: a chunk of data is received, until the waiting timeout for a chunk of data (RTO) expires. Several options of MS-AL-ARQ operation were implemented: for separate input buffers at the destination node and for the common input buffer at the destination node. At the same time, at the start of the broadcast each data stream was broadcasted to a separate application, i.e. a separate port must be allocated for each source node. RTO was calculated based on the approximation of statistics on the round trip time of the two-way transmission RTT (Round Trip Time), the value of the current smoothed cycle time SRTT (Smoothed Round Trip Time) was also set. These values were taken from the TCP protocol [22]. TCP uses a sender-initiated retransmission scheme that uses RTO retransmission timeouts and duplicate acknowledgment (ACK) times.

3.1 Description of the MS-AL-ARQ Method

The process of transmission from n source nodes shown in Fig. 10 will be studied. The squares in the figure illustrate data chunks that contain the source IP address, port number (in the figure, the first digit before the dot), and the sequence number of the data chunk.

All chunks are sequentially transmitted from n source nodes to one destination node. The destination node can have one common or separate buffers that store the received chunks of data. In this case, the buffers are updated with the arrival of each chunk and are limited in size. Once the buffer is full, chunks of data are sent to a streaming video application such as VLC (VideoLAN Client). Each application runs on a specific socket, i.e. each source node has a separate application, which is associated with different IP addresses and ports.

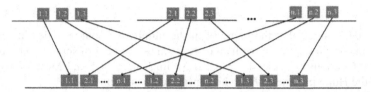

Fig. 10. The process of transmitting data chunks from n source nodes

When implementing retransmission with multiple source nodes, it is necessary to send NACK, which will contain information about the source node (source IP address, port number) and the sequence number of the lost data chunk. Based on this information, NACK will be delivered to the specific source node, and the lost chunk will be resent, as shown in Fig. 11.

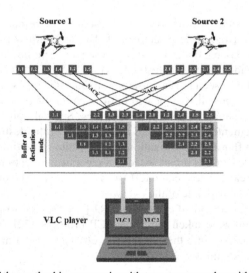

Fig. 11. Operation of the method in a scenario with two source nodes with separate input buffers

In Fig. 11, two source nodes send chunks of data to a destination node. When transmitting data through a communication channel, the first node loses the second piece of data, and the second node loses the first piece. NACK for the first node comes in the form of a response to the third piece of data. At this time, the fourth chunk is being transmitted, and after that the second chunk is resent from the first source node. NACK comes to the second source node after the second piece of data. At this time the third piece is sent and after that, the first piece of data is resent from the second source node. All chunks are sent to the buffer, after which, in accordance with the port number and IP address, they are broadcasted to the VLC application.

In addition to the formation of separate input buffers at the destination node, an algorithm with a common input buffer at the destination node can be implemented. The software implementation of the retransmission method with a common input buffer in the future can serve as a basis for the development of new methods and algorithms prioritized by the source node with the highest value of loss of application-level data chunks.

3.2 Experimental Evaluation of MS-AL-ARQ Performance with Separate Input Buffers

Several experiments were performed to evaluate the effectiveness of MS-AL-ARQ with separate input buffers and with a common input buffer. In the first experiment, Raspberry Pi 3 Model B microcomputers were chosen as the source nodes. The choice is related to the fact that these microcomputers are used in UAVs (for example, Coex Clover). The built-in antenna M620720 was used for data transmissions. It supported 2.4 GHz frequency bands and had 1.7 dBi. A specialized version of Ubuntu MATE 18.04 for the Raspberry Pi was chosen as the system on microcomputers. The destination node was a laptop. The laptop specifications: Pentium B940 processor, 4 GB DDR3 RAM, 802.11 b/g/n network card up to 300 Mb/s. The built-in VLC media player was used for streaming video. The data was captured using the tcpdump program. The data were analyzed in Wireshark software through the "counter" function prescribed in the software implementation.

As a transmitted video, a video clip of 1920 × 1080 Full HD resolution was chosen, and H.264 codec. The variable bit rate with an average of 3501 Kbps was selected. The video was 5 min long with the frame rate of 23.976 per second, which is 7192 full frames. The audio was cut from the video and the video was processed using the meGUI software. The communication between all devices was carried out using the 802.11 standard. For the convenience of research, 1 channel with the central frequency of 2.412 GHz was selected; the Wi-Fi analyzer utility was used to select the channel. To reproduce several streams and correct the operation of the MS-AL-ARQ algorithm in conditions of multi-stream data transmission, the work with separate ports was implemented, i.e. each source node transmitted data to its dedicated port.

PDR was calculated for a different number of source nodes for UDP at the transport layer in conjunction with the MS-AL-ARQ application layer, for only UDP at the transport layer and for TCP at the transport layer. The reference values were chosen for the sent number of packets. The results of the experimental study are shown in Fig. 12.

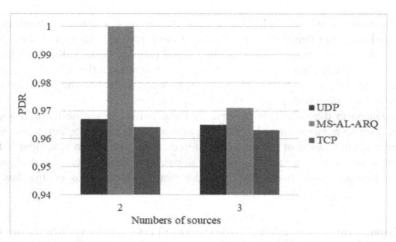

Fig. 12. Dependence of PDR on 2 and 3 source nodes when MS-AL-ARQ operates with separate input buffers

As follows from the graphs presented in Fig. 12, the proposed MS-AL-ARQ algorithm completely restored the lost chunks of application-level data from two source nodes. So, PDR for two source nodes for UDP was 0.967, when the MS-AL-ARQ algorithm is running PDR metric was 1, for the TCP transport layer protocol the PDR value was 0.964. With the increase in the number of source nodes to three, the PDR value began to deteriorate in all cases. So, with 3 source nodes, when the MS-AL-ARQ algorithm was running, PDR was 0.971. When only the UDP transport layer was operating, PDR was 0.965. For the TCP transport layer PDR was 0.963. The losses among the source nodes may point at the operation of the RTS/CST mechanism, which is responsible for preventing collisions in the standards of the 802.11 family.

3.3 Experimental Evaluation of MS-AL-ARQ Effectiveness with a Common Input Buffer

In the experimental study of the MS-AL-ARQ algorithm efficiency with a common input buffer, Clover small educational UAVs acted as source nodes while a laptop acted as a destination node. The source nodes broadcasted the streaming video to the destination node at each control point; the 1st control point was located at the distance of 5 m, the 12th control point was located at the distance of 60 m from the destination node, i.e. the source nodes were removed from the destination node at the distance of 60 m with the step of 5 m as shown in Fig. 13.

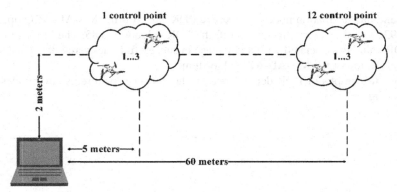

Fig. 13. Scenario of conducting experimental studies of the MS-AL-ARQ algorithm efficiency with the common input buffer

At each checkpoint, the video data was broadcasted with the MS-AL-ARQ algorithm enabled with the UDP protocol at the transport layer and without the MS-AL-ARQ algorithm also using the UDP protocol at the transport layer.

The data obtained were analyzed in the same way as described in the previous section, and the PDR was calculated. Figure 14 shows the results of the experimental study of the MS-AL-ARQ algorithm efficiency with the common input buffer in the form of the graph of PDR versus the distance between two flying source nodes and the destination node.

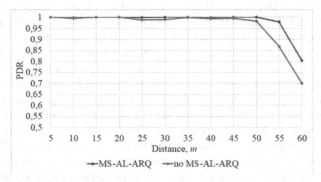

Fig. 14. Dependence of PDR on the distance between two flying source nodes in the form of a UAV and a ground station

As follows from the graphs presented in Fig. 14, the use of the MS-AL-ARQ algorithm improves the PDR value: at the distance of 50 m the PDR value without the MS-AL-ARQ algorithm was 0.98, when using the MS-AL-ARQ algorithm PDR was 0.99; when the distance was increased to 55 m, PDR without the use of the algorithm was 0.86, with the use of the algorithm was 0.97; at the distance of 60 m PDR without the use of the algorithm was 0.7, while with the use of the algorithm it was 0.8. Thus, when the transmission deteriorates at the distance of 50 to 60 m between the source nodes and the destination node, the average PDR value during MS-AL-ARQ operation was 0.93, with the algorithms turned off, the PDR value was 0.85. The improvement in the PDR value is associated with an increase in successfully delivered data packets due to the operation of the MS-AL-ARQ algorithm.

Also, the graphs of PDR dependence on the distance for three source nodes were plotted (Fig. 15).

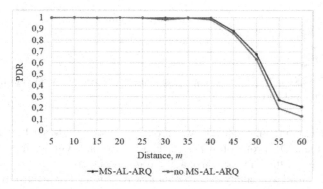

Fig. 15. Dependence of PDR on the distance between three flying source nodes in the form of a UAV and a ground station

As follows from the graphs presented in Fig. 15, the use of the MS-AL-ARQ algorithm improves the PDR value. At the distance of 35 m, the PDR value without the MS-AL-ARQ algorithm was 0.99, when using the MS-AL-ARQ algorithm PDR was 1; when the distance was increased to 40 m, PDR without the use of the algorithm was 0.98 while with the use of the algorithm it was 0.99; at the distance of 45 m PDR without the use of the algorithm was 0.86, with the use of the algorithm it was 0.88; at the distance of 50 m, the PDR value without the MS-AL-ARQ algorithm was 0.63 while with the MS-AL-ARQ algorithm PDR was 0.67; when the distance increased to 55 m, PDR was 0.2 without the use of the algorithm, and 0.27 with the use of the algorithm; at the distance of 60 m the PDR without the use of the algorithm was 0.12, and when using the algorithm it was 0.21. Thus, when the communication deteriorates at the distance of 35 to 60 m between the source nodes and the destination node, the average PDR value during MS-AL-ARQ operation was 0.67, with the algorithms turned off the PDR value was 0.61. As in the previous case, an improvement in the PDR value is associated with an increase in successfully delivered data packets due to the operation of the MS-AL-ARQ algorithm.

In addition to the dependence of PDR on the distance between two and three flying source nodes and a destination node, the value of the gain from the application of the MS-AL-ARQ algorithm was calculated and presented in Fig. 16. The gain was calculated as the ratio of PDR using the algorithm to PDR without the use of the MS-AL-ARQ algorithm.

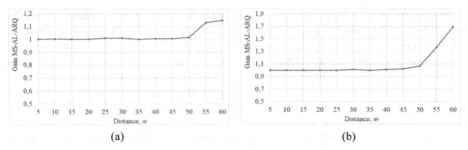

(a)   (b)

Fig. 16. Gain from the MS-AL-ARQ algorithm a) for two source nodes b) for three source nodes

From the results of the experimental study of the MS-AL-ARQ algorithm efficiency for separate input buffers and a common input buffer, it follows that the use of the MS-AL-ARQ algorithm gives an advantage. For example, the use of the algorithm provides an increase in PDR in up to 1.13 –1.15 times with two source nodes and up to 1.2–1.7 times with three source nodes, as presented in Fig. 16.

4 Conclusion

In this paper the results of simulation of the process of data transmission from several flying source nodes to a ground station were presented. It was determined that an increase in the number of source nodes increases the requirements for Goodput. So, with an increase in the number of source nodes from one to five, Goodput increased from 0.8–1.5 Mbit/s to 4.1–5.3 Mbit/s with different values of the Hurst parameter Hin in the considered scenario. At the same time, the overloads can occur on the input buffer of the destination node, which will lead to the loss of data chunks of application layer; a decrease in PDR and deterioration in video quality.

The paper proposes the MS-AL-ARQ method and algorithm the main idea of which is a request for retransmission of lost chunks of application-level data from flying source nodes. The software was developed to implement the MS-AL-ARQ algorithm for working with separate input buffers and a common input buffer at the destination node. The developed software for recovering lost chunks of application-level data based on retransmission from several flying source nodes made it possible, through experimental studies, to evaluate the efficiency of MS-AL-ARQ when transmitting multi-stream video data in real conditions.

Several experiments were carried out to evaluate the MS-AL-ARQ algorithm efficiency when using separate input buffers and a common input buffer at the destination node. Based on the results of the first experiment using separate input buffers at the destination node, it was determined that the MS-AL-ARQ algorithm completely recovered all lost packets at two source nodes. In the second experiment, the Clever small educational UAVs acted as the source nodes, which broadcasted data to the ground station. In the course of the experiment, the MS-AL-ARQ algorithm efficiency with a common input buffer was evaluated. With two flying source nodes, the application of the MS-AL-ARQ algorithm provided an improvement in PDR with an increase in the distance from 50 to

60 m by an average of 10%. With an increase in the number of source nodes to three, the use of the MS-AL-ARQ algorithm provided an improvement in PDR with an increase in the distance from 35 to 60 m by an average of 22%. The value of the gain from the application of the MS-AL-ARQ algorithm was calculated, so, the use of the algorithm provided an increase in PDR in up to 1.13–1.15 times with two source nodes and up to 1.2–1.7 times with three source nodes. The improvement in the PDR value is associated with an increase in the proportion of successfully delivered packets due to the operation of the MS-AL-ARQ algorithm.

In future, a promising direction is the development of prioritization algorithms for the source node with the highest value of packet loss rate measured on the application layer.

Acknowledgments. The reported study was funded by RFBR according to the research project No. 19-29-06076.

References

1. Bujari, A., Palazzi, C.E., Ronzani, D.: FANET application scenarios and mobility models. In: Proceedings of the 3rd Workshop on Micro Aerial Vehicle Networks, Systems, and Applications, pp. 43–46 (2017)
2. Gapeyenko, M., Petrov, V., Moltchanov, D., Andreev, S., Himayat, N., Koucheryavy, Y.: Flexible and reliable UAV-assisted backhaul operation in 5G mmWave cellular networks. IEEE J. Sel. Areas Commun. **36**, 2486–2496 (2018)
3. Pirmagomedov, R., Kirichek, R., Blinnikov, M., Koucheryavy, A.: UAV-based gateways for wireless nanosensor networks deployed over large areas. Comput. Commun. **146**, 55–62 (2019)
4. Nex, F., Remondino, F.: UAV for 3D mapping applications: a review. Appl. Geomat. **6**(1), 1–15 (2013). https://doi.org/10.1007/s12518-013-0120-x
5. Menouar, H., Guvenc, I., Akkaya, K., Uluagac, A.S., Kadri, A., Tuncer, A.: UAV-enabled intelligent transportation systems for the smart city: applications and challenges. IEEE Commun. Mag. **55**, 22–28 (2017)
6. Dinh, T.D., Vishnevsky, V., Le, D.T., Kirichek, R., Koucheryavy, A.: Determination of subscribers coordinates using flying network for emergencies. In: 2021 23rd International Conference on Advanced Communication Technology (ICACT), pp. 1–10. IEEE, February 2021
7. Bekmezci, I., Sen, I., Erkalkan, E.: Flying ad hoc networks (FANET) test bed implementation. In: Proceedings of7th International Conference on Recent Advances in Space Technologies (RAST), pp. 665–668. IEEE (2015)
8. Srivastava, A., Prakash, J.: Future FANET with application and enabling techniques: anatomization and sustainability issues. Comput. Sci. Rev. **39**, 100359 (2021)
9. De Rango, F., Potrino, G., Tropea, M., Santamaria, A.F., Fazio, P.: Scalable and ligthway bio-inspired coordination protocol for FANET in precision agriculture applications. Comput. Electr. Eng. **74**, 305–318 (2019)
10. Chriki, A., Touati, H., Snoussi, H., Kamoun, F.: FANET: Communication, mobility models and security issues. Comput. Netw. **163**, 106877 (2019)
11. Bekmezci, I., Sahingoz, O.K., Temel, Ş: Flying ad-hoc networks (FANETs): a survey. Ad Hoc Netw. **11**, 1254–1270 (2013)

12. Vasiliev, D.S., Meitis, D.S., Abilov, A.: Simulation-based comparison of AODV, OLSR and HWMP protocols for flying ad hoc networks. In: Balandin, S., Andreev, S., Koucheryavy, Y. (eds.) NEW2AN 2014. LNCS, vol. 8638, pp. 245–252. Springer, Cham (2014). https://doi.org/10.1007/978-3-319-10353-2_21
13. Khan, M.F., Yau, K.L.A., Noor, R.M., Imran, M.A.: Routing schemes in FANETs: a survey. Sensors **20**(1), 38 (2020)
14. Zhao, L., Saif, M.B., Hawbani, A., Min, G., Peng, S., Lin, N.: A novel improved artificial bee colony and blockchain-based secure clustering routing scheme for FANET. China Commun. **18**(7), 103–116 (2021)
15. Khan, I.U., et al.: Smart IoT control-based nature inspired energy efficient routing protocol for flying ad hoc network (FANET). IEEE Access **8**, 56371–56378 (2020)
16. Kaisina, I.A., et al.: NS-3 simulation of Poisson-Pareto burst process in multi-source FANET scenario with network coding. In: Moscow Workshop on Electronic and Networking Technologies (MWENT), Moscow, pp. 1–5. IEEE (2020)
17. Tom Henderson: NS-3. wifi-phy-configuration.cc (2021). https://www.nsnam.org/doxygen/wifi-phy-configuration_8cc_source.html. Accessed 10 June 2021
18. Addie, R.G., Neame, T.D., Zukerman, M.: Performance evaluation of a queue fed by a Poisson Pareto burst process. Comput. Netw. **40**(3), 377–397 (2002)
19. Zukerman, M., Neame, T.D., Addie, R.G.: Internet traffic modeling and future technology implications. In: IEEE INFOCOM 2003. Twenty-second Annual Joint Conference of the IEEE Computer and Communications Societies (IEEE Cat. No. 03CH37428), vol. 1, pp. 587–596. IEEE, March 2003
20. Ammar, D., Begin, T., Guerin-Lassous, I.: A new tool for generating realistic internet traffic in ns-3. In: Proceedings of the 4th International ICST Conference on Simulation Tools and Techniques – ICST, Barcelona, Spain, 22–24 March 2011, pp. 81–83 (2011)
21. Vasiliev, D., et al.: Application layer ARQ and network coding for QoS improving in UAV-assisted networks. In: Proceedings of 25th Conference of Open Innovations Association (FRUCT), pp. 353–360. IEEE (2019)
22. Jacobson, V.: Congestion avoidance and control. ACM SIGCOMM Comput. Commun. Rev. **18**(4), 314–329 (1988)

Deep Learning Approach for Predicting Energy Consumption of Drones Based on MEC

Ali R. Abdellah[1,2][✉], Abbas Alzaghir[2], and Andrey Koucheryavy[2]

[1] Electronics and Communications Engineering, Electrical Engineering Department,
Al-Azhar University, Qena 83513, Egypt
alirefaee@azhar.edu.eg
[2] The Bonch-Bruevich Saint-Petersburg State University of Telecommunications,
St. Petersburg 193232, Russia
abbasaltamimi89@gmail.com, akouch@mail.ru

Abstract. Drones or UAVs are one of the major emerging use cases of 5G networks, which is promised to have numerous applications in many fields. The integration of unmanned aerial vehicles (UAV) and artificial intelligence (AI) is beginning to attract the attention of researchers. AI technology is an important solution to the challenges of drones, improving capabilities and opening the door to various sectors. Recently, AI has emerged as a key component needed to process a large amount of collected data. In recent years, Deep Learning (DL) is a state-of-the-art method to solve various problems in wireless networks such as network management and optimization, predictive analytics, lifetime value prediction, etc. In this paper, we have proposed the approach Deep Learning with a LSTM network to predict the energy consumption of drones based on MEC. The prediction accuracy has been evaluated using the RMSE and MAPE.LSTM Deep Learning.

Keywords: Traffic prediction · UAV · Drone · Deep Learning · AI · LSTM

1 Introduction

Unmanned Aerial Vehicles (UAVs) are becoming an integral part of 5G and are expected to play an essential role in the continued functionality of 5G networks and have many applications, including military, medical care, surveillance and monitoring, telecommunications. In particular, UAV networks can support existing cellular communications to quickly restore service and provide the offloading of traffic from highly congested areas in a cost-effective manner. In addition, UAVs can be used as a cellular network to enable various applications such as packet transmissions and lifetime data flows. Moreover, UAVs use to gather information from IoT tools on the ground [1].

The original version of this chapter was revised: an orthographic error in an author's name was corrected. The correction to this chapter is available at
https://doi.org/10.1007/978-3-030-97777-1_42

© Springer Nature Switzerland AG 2022, corrected publication 2022
Y. Koucheryavy et al. (Eds.): NEW2AN 2021/ruSMART 2021, LNCS 13158, pp. 284–296, 2022.
https://doi.org/10.1007/978-3-030-97777-1_24

For solving the challenges of devices with limited resources to achieve low latency and low energy consumption, the Mobile Edge Computing (MEC) platform, which evolved from 5G and significantly incorporates radio access networks(RAN) with Internet service provider (ISP), was used. It able to enhance and store the transmission capacity resources and decrease the computation capability of wireless end user. The MEC provides computing power, storage, and processing on the wireless network side. The main goal of MEC is to provide the end-users with intelligent facilities and processing capabilities. MEC will be near wireless access networks for creating a carrier-level service environment with low latency, great efficiency, and great transmission capacity. Also, it speeds up the quick download for different content. content, applications, and services on the network to maintain the network with high-quality network experience [5].

In wireless networks, which is based on the unmanned aerial vehicles to provide low-latency and ultra-reliable services to meet the needs of end-users [2]. I.e., UAVs need the use of 5G ultra-reliable communication channels, in order to allow for real-time control of such an apparatus with a low-latency mode [3]. In this case, more attention is being paid to the deep learning methods, which are based on the data, in order to optimize the performance of your network, using a vast amount of data generated, and thus, to meet the QoS conditions of wireless networks [4].

Drones or UAVs are unmanned flying devices that are used for many purposes. In their early days, these devices were manually controlled and remotely monitored. Today, however, drones are often equipped with artificial intelligence and the automation of either some or all processes. AI-integration allows the operator of an unmanned aircraft to exploit information from sensors connected to the drone for collection and implementation of the visible and environmental information. This information enables unmanned or supported flight and makes operations more manageable and accessible. Therefore, drones well-suited to intelligent mobility contributions that nowadays commercially accessible to businesses and users [18].

Artificial intelligence (AI) can add a predictive measure to unmanned aerial systems by coupling failure prediction with an image processing system that could detect objects on the ground to avoid in the event of an emergency landing due to system or flight failure. The AI system makes predictions based on variables such as the aircraft's current position, power state, altitude, and wind speed and then invokes an algorithm to steer the aircraft to a safe landing site. The AI could even predict failures before they occur so that maintenance can be performed to avoid the potential loss and subsequent crash [19].

This work implements a time series prediction of energy consumption for drone-based MEC using a deep learning approach based on an LSTM network. The accuracy was measured in four cases according to the learning rate used in training. We evaluated the prediction accuracy in terms of RMSE and MAPE as a measure of prediction accuracy to investigate the best prediction accuracy and the maximum average improvement in prediction accuracy. Table 1 describes the list of used abbreviations in the paper.

The paper is organized as follows: Sect. 2 introduces the related works; Sect. 3 presents deep learning with LSTM network; Sect. 4 introduces the multi- drone network simulation; Sect. 5 introduces simulation results; Sect. 6 conclusion.

Table 1. List of abbreviation

Abbreviation	Meaning
RMSE	Root Mean Square Error
MSE	Mean Square Error
SSE	Sum of squared errors
MAE	Mean Absolute Error
MAPE	Mean absolute percentage error
DNN	Deep neural network
UAV	Unmanned aerial vehicle
MEC	Mobile Edge Computing
RAN	Radio access network
ANN	Artificial Neural Network
AI	The artificial intelligent
ML	Machine Learning
RNN	Recurrent neural network
NARX	A non-linear auto-associative with external input
MSP	Multi-step prediction
GRU	Gated Recurrent Units
CNN	Convolution neural network
IoT	The Internet of Things
QoS	Quality of Service
LSTM	Long Short-Term Memory
VANET	Vehicular Ad hoc Network
MLNN	Multitask Learning Neural Network

2 Related Work

In recent years, several researchers have focused on time series prediction of wireless network traffic using ML methods and in 5G technology. Our goal in this paper is to predict the energy consumption of UAV enabled MEC using Deep Learning with LSTM network. Therefore, in this section, we present the outstanding works that are relevant to our field in this work.

The author [6] presented IoT traffic time series prediction based on the ML approach. He used MSP with Time Series NARX Recurrent Neural Networks. The prediction accuracy was measured using the loss functions MSE, SSE and MAE, and MAPE. Also, IoT delay prediction was implemented using DNN: a multi-parameters method, DNN [7].

Ali R. Abdellah et al. [8] examined the prediction of IoT traffic-based deep learning with LSTM networks. In [9], the VANET traffic throughput was predicted using deep learning based on long short-term memory. Furthermore, predictive analytics have been implemented to predict packet transmission delay in ad hoc networks using a regression graph [10]. G. White et al. [11] studied the prediction of quality of service in IoT environments, including service response time and throughput.

Abdellah et al. [12] investigated long-short term prediction and implemented IoT traffic prediction in time series using Deep Learning with an LSTM network. Traffic speed prediction was implemented using a deep learning approach in [13]. Moreover, Karthika et al. [14] used the deep learning method to predict the extensive mobility data in urban traffic. The progress of the graph DL structure for predicting traffic flow in large networks with high accuracy and efficiency was investigated in [15].

Tao et al. [16] used multiple tasks learning neural network (MLNN) to solve the speed prediction task for three short time intervals by integrating the Convolutional Neural Network (CNN) and Gated Recurrent Units (GRU) networks. The author [17] has provided a review of NN techniques for short-term traffic forecasting and also suggests research directions for further applications of NN models.

3   Deep Learning with LSTM Network

To overcome the problems of 5G networks, technologies that improve the predictive accuracy of network traffic are needed to avoid degradation of system QoS and Improving Energy Efficiency. Visual technologies need to be predictive to avoid weakly interacting solutions; therefore, a traffic forecasting variant is necessary. Several ML methods have been used to optimize traffic forecasting performance. Among the most important methods is DNN which is relied on the ANN techniques.

DL relies on multilayer neural networks and related algorithms that often process large data sets. Some methods are superior to traditional NNs to process the data of the previous case. RNN is one of the techniques that consist of several network loops, and these networks allow the continuation of the information. Each network in the loop takes the input and data from the preceding network, performs the respective operation, generates an output, and passes the information to the following network. Some applications only need new data, while others may need more of the previous data.

Ordinary RNNs are very poor at dealing with situations where something has to be "memorized" over a long period of time. The learning delay becomes very large when there is no connection between the information that was needed in the past and the principle that is needed. The effect of a hidden state or input with step t on subsequent states of the feedback network drops exponentially. The solutions currently offered in Deep Learning consist mainly of changing and complicating the architecture of a "building block" of the recurrent network. It turns out that instead of a single number affected by all subsequent states, we can construct a certain type of cell in which we explicitly simulate in one form or another a "long memory", the processes of writing and reading from this "memory cell" and so on. Of course, such a cell will not have just one set of weights, like a typical neuron, but several, and learning will be more difficult, but in practice it often proves rewarding.

One of the most well-known and commonly used structures from each of these cells is an LSTM (Long Short-Term Memory); DL with LSTM model, are the special kind of RNNs that can learn like predictions. These networks are accurately created to open the case of long memory of feedback networks. LSTMs are great at retaining datum over a long period of time. As more prior information can influence the model's performance, LSTMs are a real option for employment. The advantages are that LSTMs can be active to support autonomous connections without having to be mined. The network also needs to be trained to decide what information is on the bus, the study, the network, and a clear idea of what needs to be stored. There is no fear of entering new data and destroying important information.

When training deep networks, LSTM is used repeatedly. A typical LSTM cell architecture is shown in Fig. 1. In LSTM, there are three main types of nodes called gates: Input gates, Forget gates, and Output gates, as well as the actual recurrent cell with a hidden state. Gates in LSTM are the sigmoid transfer functions Eq. (1), that is, their output a value equal to 0 or 1 and usually it is either 0 or 1.

$$\text{sig(t)} = \frac{1}{1 + e^{-t}} \tag{1}$$

Additional connections that increase the model's connectivity (we will talk about this below). If we denote by x_t the input vector at the time t, h_t is the hidden state vector at time t, Wi (with different second powers) are the weight matrices applicable to the input, W_h is the weight matrices in feedback connections, and b are vectors of accessible terms, we obtain the next formal definition of how the LSTM works: Given the next input x_t with a hidden state from the previous step h_{t-1} and the current state of the cell c_{t-1}, we sequentially compute *the equations for input gates, forget gates, and output gates in LSTM are:*

$$i_t = \sigma(W_{xi}x_t + W_{hi}h_{t-1} + b_i) \tag{2}$$

$$f_t = \sigma\left(W_{xf}x_t + W_{hf}h_{t-1} + b_f\right) \tag{3}$$

$$o_t = \sigma(W_{xo}x_t + W_{ho}h_{t-1} + b_o) \tag{4}$$

The equation for *candidate cell state, cell state, and block output (the final output) are:*

$$c'_t = tanh(W_{xc}x_t + W_{hc}h_{t-1} + b_{c'}) \tag{5}$$

$$c_t = f_t \times c_{t-1} + i_t \times c'_t \tag{6}$$

$$h_t = o_t \times tanh\left(c'_t\right) \tag{7}$$

It does not look obvious for a single link in the network. We illustrated the LSTM cell in Fig. 1, shows the actual structure of the LSTM; the dashed lines are for convenience only and establish relationships related to the hidden state of h_t (not c_t). But even the picture looks very complicated. So, let us understand what these formulas mean step by step.

Two vectors are fed to the LSTM input, as in the "normal" RNN: a new vector from the input data x_t and a hidden state vector h_{t-1}, which was obtained from the hidden state of this cell at the previous step. In addition, inside, everyone LSTM block is a "cell" - a vector that performs the function of memory. The cell vector at step t was designated above by c_t, and c'_t obtained in the first equation, is a vector obtained from the input and the previous hidden state, which becomes a candidate for a new memory value. It turns out from x_t and h_{t-1}, by a very usual transformation for neural networks: first a linear function, then a hyperbolic tangent, everything is like in ordinary neural networks but c'_t is only a candidate for a new meaning memory. Before it is written, instead of c_{t-1}, the candidate value, and the old value pass through two more gates: the input gate i_t and the forgetting gate f_t.

Consider the formula in Eq. (7) where the new value is obtained as a linear combination of the old one with the coefficients of the forgetting gate f_t and the new candidate c'_t with the coefficients of the input gate it. If the values of the forgetting gate vector f_t are close to zero, the old value of c_{t-1} is "forgotten", and if the values of it are large, the new input vector is added to what was in memory [8, 9, 12].

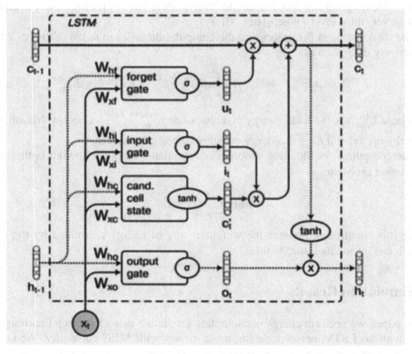

Fig. 1. LSTM cell structure

4 Multi-drone Network Simulation

The model comprises of a multi-drone network connected to a base station via a wireless channel, and the base station is equipped with an edge computing server, as shown in Fig. 1. drone-m has a set of M independent computational tasks, indicated by M = {1; 2...; M}, which must be processed locally in drone-m (drone1; drone2 ....; drone-m)or will be offloaded and executed either in one of the neighboring drones or remotely in the edge computing server. The scenario considers that drone-m stay unchanged during a period when computations are offloaded, while it can be moved to another location during other periods.

The communication model proposed in this work has a multi-drone network connected to a single base station through a wireless channel, where the base station is prepared with edge computing resources. The multi-drone network consists of a number of drones wirelessly connected to each other, one of which is considered as drone-m, which has M independent computational tasks to perform. The considered scenario is a multi-stage computation offloading mode, so we considered two decision offloading variables denoted as βi, and αi is a binary computation offloading decision, where {βi = 1} indicates, that computational task i is assigned by drone-m to be (at first level, {βi = 0} indicates that computational task i is offloaded from drone-m and processed either at one of the neighboring drones (second level), where {$\alpha i = 1$}, or remotely at an edge cloud server (third level), where{$\alpha i = 0$}.}

The total overhead for processing the computation task i in terms of energy can be respectively expressed as:

$$E_i^{total} = \beta_i E_{i,m}^{local} + (1 - \beta_i)\left[\alpha_i E_{i,m}^{nearby\_UAV} + (1 - \alpha_i)E_{i,m}^{edge}\right] \tag{8}$$

Where $E_{i,m}^{local}$ is the local energy consumption; $E_{i,m}^{nearby\_UAV}$ is energy consumption of nearby drone; and $E_{i,m}^{edge}$ is energy consumption at edge server.

The computation offloading problem is formulated as the following optimization formulation problem:

$$\min \sum_{i=1}^{N} E_i^{total} \tag{9}$$

Where this equation minimizes the weighted sum of energy consumed by the drone through task offloading distributions.

5 Simulation Results

In this paper, we perform energy consumption prediction using the Deep Learning approach with an LSTM network for multiple drones with MEC capability. We studied the performance in four cases with respect to the learning rate used in training. The prediction accuracy was measured using the RMSE and MAPE.

The datasets are from a drone enabled MEC network. The model was simulated using MATLAB after the dataset was collected and processed. This was split into 70%,

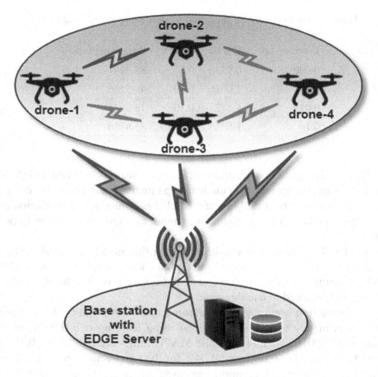

Fig. 2. Multi-drone network model

30% for training and 30% for testing. The RMSE and MAPE were used to measure the prediction accuracy as shown in Eqs. (11), (12).

$$RMSE = \sqrt{\frac{1}{N} \sum_{t=1}^{n} (x_t - \hat{x}_t)^2} \tag{10}$$

$$MAPE = \frac{1}{N} \sum_{t=1}^{n} \left| \frac{x_t - \hat{x}_t}{x_t} \right| \tag{11}$$

Where N is the total number of observations, x_t is the actual value, while $\hat{x}_t$ is the predicated value.

Table 2 shows the prediction accuracy for the VANET throughput using RMSE and MAPE.

Table 2. The accuracy for predicted models using RMSE and MAPE.

Learning rate	RMSE	MAPE	Processing time
0.0001	0.9530	0.06	55.3281
0.001	1.0016	0.09	49.5156
0.01	1.1123	0.10	38.2031
0.1	1.5325	0.60	35.8750

Table 2 shows the prediction accuracy for energy consumption in multi-UAV offloading traffic in four cases depending on the learning rate used in training. We evaluated the prediction accuracy in terms of RMSE and MAPE as a measure of prediction accuracy to study the best prediction accuracy and maximum average improvement in prediction accuracy.

From the tabulated results, it can be seen that the model predicted in the case of learning rate of 0.0001 has the best prediction accuracy in terms of both RMSE and MAPE. The maximum average improvement in this case is 0.54%; however, the longest training time was required to use this case.

Also, the prediction accuracy using learning rates 0.001 and 0.01 has a prediction accuracy approximately equal to the case of using learning rate 0.0001, in terms of RMSE values of 1.0016 and 1.1123, while MAPE values are 0.09% and 0.1%, respectively. MAPE decreased to 0.03% and 0.04% for the two learning rates 0.001 and 0.01. Therefore, the maximum average improvement in this case is 0.51% and 0.50% for the two learning rates 0.001 and 0.01. From the tabulated results, it can be seen that the network trained with learning rates 0.001 and 0.01 has the faster training times than learning rate 0.0001.

On the other hand, the prediction accuracy in the case of using learning rate 0.1 has the lowest prediction accuracy in both RMSE and MAPE values compared to its peers; however, this case has the fastest training speed.

Figures 3, 4, 5 and 6 show the predicted models in four cases with respect to the learning rate used in training. Each figure has three curves for actual, predicted and losses with time series. Figure 3 shows the responses in the case of using 0.0001, if we look at the first curve, the actual energy increases randomly with time, but the predicted energy in the second curve decreases gradually with time up to time 6 and then increases gradually up to time 17, which gives the best prediction accuracy in this case. From the loss curve, we can also see that the loss randomly with time and the highest loss occurs at time 13.

Figure 4 shows the resulting responses in the case of using the learning rate 0.001. In the first curve for the actual energy as a function of time, one can see that the energy also increases randomly with time. On the other hand, in the second curve, the predicted model gradually decreases from time 1 to time 11 and then slightly increases with time until time 17, which gives the best prediction accuracy in this case. From the loss curve, we can also see that the loss increases randomly with time and the highest loss occurs at time 13.

From Figs. 5 and 6, in the cases of using learning rates 0.01, 0.1, it can be seen that the predicted models are random with time and semi-equal to the actual model in these cases. It can also be seen from the loss curves that the loss increases randomly with time and the highest loss occurs at time points 5 and 12, respectively.

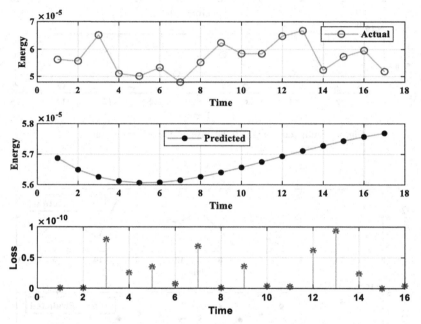

Fig. 3. Predicted models in the case of using learning rate 0.0001

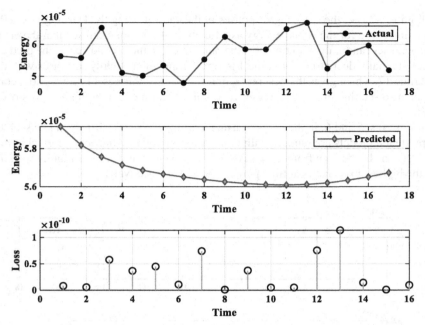

Fig. 4. Predicted models in the case of using learning rate 0.001

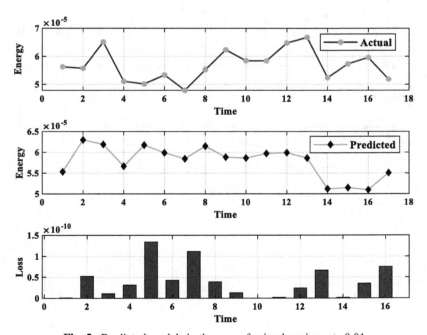

Fig. 5. Predicted models in the case of using learning rate 0.01

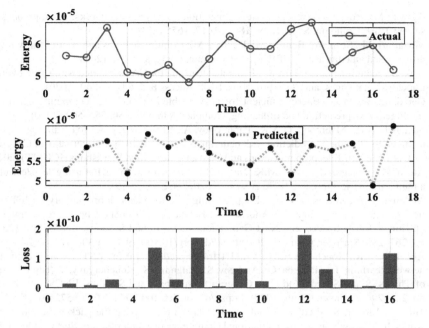

Fig. 6. Predicted models in the case of using learning rate 0.1

6   Conclusion

In this paper, the approach to predict the energy consumption of drones based on MEC using Deep Learning with a LSTM network has been investigated. Deep Learning is becoming popular due to its superiority in accuracy when trained on large datasets. LSTMs are very strong in predicting time series because they can remember the historical information over a long period of time. LSTM is good for predicting time series when the lags are of unknown duration. The prediction accuracy of the model DL was measured using the RMSE and MAPE. The simulation results show that the model with learning rate 0.0001 outperforms its competitors and has the best prediction accuracy, but it has required the longest training time. On the other hand, the prediction accuracy in the case of using learning rate 0.1 has the lowest prediction accuracy compared to the others; however, it required the fastest training speed.

Acknowledgments. This research is based on the Applied Scientific Research under the SPbSUT state assignment 2021.

The researcher [Ali R. Abdellah] is funded by a scholarship [Ph.D.] under the Joint (Executive Program between the Arab Republic of Egypt and the Russian Federation).

References

1. Liu, X., et al.: Trajectory design and power control for multi-UAV assisted wireless networks: a machine learning approach. IEEE Trans. Veh. Technol. **68**(8), 7957–7969 (2019)

2. Agiwal, M., Roy, A., Saxena, N.: Next generation 5G wireless networks: a comprehensive survey. IEEE Commun. Surv. Tutor. **18**(3), 1617–1655 (2016)
3. Mozaffari, M., Saad, W., Bennis, M., Debbah, M.: Communications and control for wireless drone-based antenna array. IEEE Trans. Commun. **67**(1), 820–834 (2019)
4. Brik, B., Ksentini, A., Bouaziz, M.: Federated learning for UAVs-enabled wireless networks: use cases, challenges, and open problems. IEEE Access **8**, 53841–53849 (2020)
5. Gaoxiang, W., et al.: Energy efficient for UAV-enabled mobile edge computing networks: Intelligent task prediction and offloading. Comput. Commun. **150**, 556–562 (2020)
6. Abdellah, A.R., Mahmood, O.A.K., Paramonov, A., Koucheryavy, A.: IoT traffic prediction using multi-step ahead prediction with neural network. In: IEEE 11th International Congress on Ultra-Modern Telecommunications and Control Systems and Workshops (ICUMT) (2019)
7. Ateeq, M., Ishmanov, F., Afzal, M.K., Naeem, M.: Predicting delay in IoT using deep learning: a multiparametric approach. IEEE Access **7**, 62022–62031 (2019)
8. Abdellah, A.R., Koucheryavy, A.: Deep learning with long short-term memory for IoT traffic prediction. In: Galinina, O., Andreev, S., Balandin, S., Koucheryavy, Y. (eds.) Internet of Things, Smart Spaces, and Next Generation Networks and Systems. LNCS, vol. 12525, pp. 267–280. Springer, Cham (2020). https://doi.org/10.1007/978-3-030-65726-0_24
9. Abdellah, A.R., Koucheryavy, A.: VANET traffic prediction using LSTM with deep neural network learning. In: Galinina, O., Andreev, S., Balandin, S., Koucheryavy, Y. (eds.) Internet of Things, Smart Spaces, and Next Generation Networks and Systems. LNCS, vol. 12525, pp. 281–294. Springer, Cham (2020). https://doi.org/10.1007/978-3-030-65726-0_25
10. Tuli, H., Kumar, S.: Prediction analysis of delay in transferring the packets in adhoc networks. In: Proceedings of 3rd International Conference on Computing for Sustainable Global Development (INDIACom), pp. 660–662, March 2016
11. White, G., Palade, A., Cabrera, C., Clarke, S.: IoTPredict: collaborative QoS prediction in IoT. In: IEEE PerCom, pp. 1–10, March 2018
12. Abdellah, A.R., Artem, V., Muthanna, A., Gallyamov, D., Koucheryavy, A.: Deep learning for IoT traffic prediction based on edge computing. In: Vishnevskiy, V.M., Samouylov, K.E., Kozyrev, D.V. (eds.) DCCN 2020. CCIS, vol. 1337, pp. 18–29. Springer, Cham (2020). https://doi.org/10.1007/978-3-030-66242-4_2
13. Jia, Y., Wu, J., Du, Y.: Traffic speed prediction using deep learning method. In: IEEE 19th International Conference on Intelligent Transportation Systems (ITSC), pp. 1–5, November 2016. https://doi.org/10.1109/ITSC.2016.7795712
14. Karthika, B., UmaMaheswari, N., Venkatesh, R.: A Research of traffic prediction using deep learning techniques. Int. J. Innov. Technol. Explor. Eng. (IJITEE) **8**, 725–728 (2019)
15. Zhang, Y., Cheng, T., Ren, Y.: A graph deep learning method for short-term traffic forecasting on large road networks. Comput.-Aided Civil Infrastruct. Eng. **34**(10), 877–896 (2019)
16. Tao, Y., Wang, X., Zhang, Y.: A multitask learning neural network for short-term traffic speed prediction and confidence estimation. In: Tetko, I.V., Kůrková, V., Karpov, P., Theis, F. (eds.) ICANN 2019. LNCS, vol. 11728, pp. 434–449. Springer, Cham (2019). https://doi.org/10.1007/978-3-030-30484-3_36
17. Do, L.N.N., Taherifar, N., Vu, H.L.: Survey of neural network-based models for short-term traffic state prediction. WIREs Data Mining Knowl. Discov. **9**, 1–24 (2018). https://doi.org/10.1002/widm.1285
18. Lahmeri, M.-A., Kishk, M.A., Alouini, M.-S.: Artificial intelligence for UAV-enabled wireless networks: a survey. IEEE Open J. Commun. Soc. **2**, 1015–1040 (2020)
19. Khan, A.I., Al-Mulla, Y.: Unmanned aerial vehicle in the machine learning environment. Procedia Comput. Sci. **160**, 46–53 (2019). https://doi.org/10.1016/j.procs.2019.09.442

Predicting Energy Consumption for UAV-Enabled MEC Using Machine Learning Algorithm

Abbas Alzaghir[2], Ali R. Abdellah[1,2(✉)], and Andrey Koucheryavy[2]

[1] Electronics and Communications Engineering, Electrical Engineering Department, Al-Azhar University, Qena 83513, Egypt
alirefaee@azhar.edu.eg
[2] The Bonch-Bruevich Saint-Petersburg State University of Telecommunications, St. Petersburg 193232, Russia

Abstract. Unmanned aerial vehicles (UAVs) are a promising technology for 5G networks and beyond. Artificial Intelligence (AI) is on the rise and proving to be very successful, mainly because it can process large amounts of data. Recently, many researchers have started integrating intelligence into UAV networks by using AI algorithms in solving various UAV-related problems. Several types of research have been conducted to improve the predictive accuracy of wireless network traffic applications. Traffic prediction systems have the potential to improve network traffic and reduce travel delays by enabling better utilization of available capabilities and monitoring, managing, and controlling the transportation system. In this paper, time series prediction of energy consumption in UAV-based MEC is performed using recurrent NARX neural networks. The prediction accuracy was calculated using the RMSE and MAPE.

Keywords: 5G · UAV · Machine learning · AI · Traffic prediction

1 Introduction

5G technology is designed to be adaptable to a wide range of requirements. In other words, 5G is massive connectivity that will be able to connect a massive number of things through the ability to scale data rates, power, and mobility to provide extremely cost-effective solutions. Another feature of the 5G network is Ultra-Reliable Low Latency Communication (URLLC), enabling highly reliable low latency connections. 5G will also enable new mission-critical services, such as remote control of critical infrastructure, Industrial IoT (IIoT), vehicles, and medical procedures. These developments in communication technology will lead to an increase in end-user devices and, therefore, a massive amount of data that needs to be processed. Mobile Edge Computing (MEC) is one of the solutions found to address the problem of limited resources of end devices in 5G technology such as UAVs, where the MEC provides the computational and storage capacity; also, MEC servers will be located near the end devices to achieve low latency and low energy consumption [1, 2].

The original version of this chapter was revised: an orthographic error in an author's name was corrected. The correction to this chapter is available at https://doi.org/10.1007/978-3-030-97777-1_42

© Springer Nature Switzerland AG 2022, corrected publication 2022
Y. Koucheryavy et al. (Eds.): NEW2AN 2021/ruSMART 2021, LNCS 13158, pp. 297–309, 2022.
https://doi.org/10.1007/978-3-030-97777-1_25

Unmanned aerial vehicles (UAVs) are end devices with limited resources considered the main component of the 5G network and will play an essential role in communication networks. Due to their unique characteristics such as flexibility, mobility, and adaptive altitude, they can be used as mobile base stations in various applications such as cellular systems, smart cities, etc. Moreover, UAVs can collect data from autonomous sensor devices, especially in agriculture [3]. UAVs and MEC servers' integration will help overcome all the challenges faced by UAVs, where the MEC server provides computational and storage data, resulting in reduced delay and energy consumption.

It is expected that the context of machine learning (ML) will address various problems already identified in the use of UAVs for communication purposes and help achieve energy efficiency [4].

ML algorithms are widely used in 5G networks, where the use of ML can lead to far-reaching developments in the applications or infrastructure, moreover, ML can be used to improve network management, avoid congestion, and optimize resource allocation, as well as analyze data and make decisions in real time or offloading. There are many ML algorithms that can improve the energy efficiency of 5G networks, such as neural network-based techniques that can help in the efficient processing of Big Data [5]. Moreover, integrating artificial intelligence (AI) and machine learning (ML) technologies into wireless networks can leverage intelligence to solve various problems. Thus, the combination of AI/ML and drones seems to be tightly integrated into multiple disciplines, applications, and in all layers of the network, promising unprecedented performance improvements and reduced complexity [4].

One of the ML algorithms used to improve the energy efficiency of the 5G network is supervised learning, where a model trains the set of labeled data to predict the optimal solutions. Massive MIMO is considered an example of an application of supervised learning for energy efficiency. A supposed problem is channel estimation and detection due to the high number of antennas. Unsupervised learning is another method that is different from supervised learning. It works with unlabeled inputs and is suitable for dimensionality reduction and clustering. Unsupervised learning can be used to cluster base stations with similar behavior for energy-efficient operation under different load conditions [6].

Network traffic prediction is one of the most hopeful research areas in artificial intelligence (AI) for data communication networks. Prediction can be an effective approach for network management and operational tasks. It aims to predict subsequent network traffic based on previous network traffic data. It has applications in large areas and has attracted many studies recently. Many researchers focused on analyzing various challenges in current computer network applications. Network traffic prediction is an efficient method to ensure security, accuracy, and secure network communication. Various methods are used and tested for network traffic prediction, including ML methods and data mining techniques. Several notable groups of network prediction methods are applied to achieve efficient and effective performance [5, 10, 11, 14–16].

In this paper, we implement time series prediction of energy consumption in a MEC with multiple UAVs using recurrent NARX neural networks. We studied the performance in four cases as a function of k-step ahead predictions using the different number of hidden neurons. The prediction accuracy was calculated using the RMSE and MAPE.

The paper is structured as follows: Sect. 2 discusses the literature review; Sect. 3 presents the modeling of multi-UAV offloading; Sect. 4 presents the neural networks of NARX; Sect. 5 gives our experimental results; Sect. 6 Conclusion (Table 1).

Table 1. List of abbreviation

Abbreviation	Meaning
UAV	Unmanned aerial vehicle
MEC	Mobile Edge Computing
ML	Machine Learning
AI	The artificial intelligent
ANN	Artificial Neural Network
RNN	Recurrent neural network
MAPE	Mean absolute percentage error
RMSE	Root Mean Square Error
SSE	Sum of squared errors
MSE	Mean Square Error
MAE	Mean Absolute Error
NARX	A non-linear auto-associative with external input
MSP	Multi-step prediction
IoT	The Internet of Things
Trainlm	Levenberg-Marquardt backpropagation
Trainrp	The resilient backpropagation algorithm (RPROP)
Traincgf	Conjugate gradient backpropagation with Fletcher-Reeves updates
SDN	Software-defined networking
URLLC	Ultra-Reliable Low Latency Communication

2 Literature Review

Recently, there are many works and studies that focus on network traffic prediction using ML techniques and in the area of 5G networks. Our focus in this paper is on predicting the energy consumption of UAV-based MEC using recurrent NARX neural networks, especially k-step-ahead prediction, hence the rest of this section highlights the previous studies on our focus in this paper.

The authors in [7] gave a general overview of supervised and unsupervised ML techniques applied in UAV networks. They also briefly presented the reinforcement learning technique implemented for UAV networks. For each of the three methods considered, they made several concluding remarks discussing current limitations and challenges, as well as several interesting open problems.

Moreover, in [4], the authors presented a detailed study of all related research where ML techniques are applied to UAV-based communication to improve the various design and functional aspects such as positioning, resource management, channel modeling, and security.

The paper [5] proposed a single-stage and multi-stage prediction process for predicting delay in IoT based on NARX recurrent neural network. The prediction was estimated using three neural network training algorithms: Trainlm, Traincgf, Trainrp, with MSE as a performance function in terms of using Root Mean Square Error (RMSE) and Mean Absolute Percentage Error (MAPE) as a measure of prediction accuracy.

In addition, the research [8] highlighted the role of the federated deep learning concept to overcome some challenges of UAV-enabled wireless networks. The authors presented a general introduction to federated learning and its fundamentals. They also highlighted many use cases of federated learning in UAV-enabled networks ranging from 5G networks and beyond, IoT, edge computing, and caching to Flying Ad-Hoc Networks.

Moreover, a novel approach for predictive deployment of UAV base stations to provide on-demand wireless service to mobile users was proposed [9]. The authors formulated a power minimization problem to optimize the service area sharing of each UAV while minimizing the UAV power required for downlink communication and mobility. They developed a novel ML context based on the Gaussian mixture model (GMM) and a weighted expectation-maximization algorithm (WEM) to predict the potential network congestion.

Ali R. Abdellah et al. [10] presented a time series prediction approach for IoT traffic with MSP using recurrent NARX neural networks, and the prediction accuracy was evaluated using the cost functions MSE, SSE and MAE, besides mean absolute percentage error (MAPE) as a measure of prediction accuracy.

In [11], IoT traffic prediction was performed with neural networks based on SDN infrastructure using recurrent NARX neural networks. The ANN was trained using three neural network training algorithms: Trainlm, Traincgf, Traincgp, and the prediction accuracy was measured using MAPE. In addition, to improve the latency performance for H2M traffic over access networks, machine learning based bandwidth prediction for low latency H2M applications was performed [12].White et al. [13] investigated QoS prediction in IoT environments; they predicted service latency and throughput.

3   Multi-UAV Network Model

The model comprises of a multi-UAV network connected to a base station via a wireless channel, and the base station is equipped with an edge computing server, as shown in Fig. 1. UAV-m has a set of M independent computational tasks, indicated by M = {1; 2...; M}, which must be processed locally in UAV-m or will be offloaded and executed either in one of the neighboring UAVs or remotely in the edge computing server. The scenario considers that UAV-m stay unchanged during a period when computations are offloaded, while it can be moved to another location during other periods.

The communication model proposed in this work has a multi-UAV network connected to a single base station through a wireless channel, where the base station is prepared with edge computing resources. The multi-UAV network consists of a number of UAVs wirelessly connected to each other, one of which is considered as UAV-m, which has M independent computational tasks to perform. The considered scenario is a multi-stage computation offloading mode, so we considered two decision offloading variables denoted as βi, and αi is a binary computation offloading decision, where {βi = 1} indicates, that computational task i is assigned by UAV-m to be (at first level, {βi = 0} indicates that computational task i is offloaded from UAV-m and processed either at one of the neighboring UAVs (second level), where {αi = 1}, or remotely at an edge cloud server (third level), where {αi = 0}.)

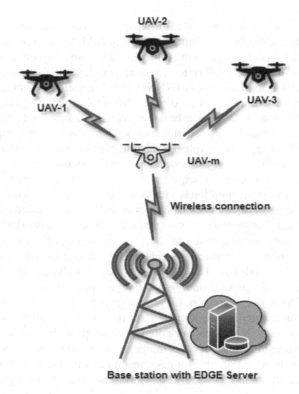

Fig. 1. Multi-UAV network model.

The total overhead for processing the computation task *i* in terms of energy can be respectively expressed as:

$$E_i^{total} = \beta_i E_{i,m}^{local} + (1 - \beta_i)\left[\alpha_i E_{i,m}^{nearby\_UAV} + (1 - \alpha_i)E_{i,m}^{edge}\right] \tag{1}$$

Where $E_{i,m}^{local}$ is the local energy consumption; $E_{i,m}^{nearby\_UAV}$ is energy consumption of nearby UAV; and $E_{i,m}^{edge}$ is energy consumption at edge server.

The computation offloading problem is formulated as the following optimization formulation problem:

$$\min \sum_{i=1}^{N} E_i^{total} \tag{2}$$

Where this equation minimizes the weighted sum of energy consumed by the UAV through task offloading distributions.

4 NARX Neural Networks

The architectural approach proposed in this paper to solve the prediction of energy consumption in the offloading of multi-UAVs using NARX recurrent neural networks or so-called NARX models "Nonlinear Autoregressive with exogenous inputs." NARX is a powerful class of models well suited for nonlinear modeling systems [5, 10, 11].

Using Artificial Neural Networks (ANNs) to solve various problems in different applications, including time series prediction. ANNs are methods that rely on math modeling to the neuron of the human brain and can train, save, and retrieve historical data. ANNs can approximate any function and perform a nonlinear mapping of aggregated inputs to output capacities while the relationships between inputs and outputs are unfamiliar. They have been designed on the basis of modeling by mathematics. ANN model selection, based on previous experience of the system developed.

Assume that energy consumption is a historical series. The neural network NARX is an efficient time series predictor used in this paper. NARX is a nonlinear autoregressive network with external inputs and is a dynamic recurrent neural network (RNN) that uses feedback around many of the network layers. It relies on the ARX time series model to simulate various nonlinear dynamical systems and their use cases in several applications, including time series modeling. The NARX is a feedback dynamical neural network. It has recurrent connections surrounding many layers of the network. To use the total capacity of the NARX neural network for predicting the nonlinear historical series. It is necessary to exploit its memory capacity by using the historical values of the expected or real historical series. The NARX network predictor uses preceding values of the current time series and preceding values of other inputs to predict the value of the target series. Thus, NARX is a robust tool suitable for nonlinear modeling systems. Moreover, NARX learns more efficiently than other neural network time series using a gradient descent learning algorithm.

Figure 2 shows a generalized recurrent network architecture based on a multilayer perceptron with a hidden layer du = dy = 2. u (k) is the model's input, and the corresponding output is y (k + 1). It indicates that the output of the model predicts its input by one step of the time. The signal vector fed to the information of the perceptron contains the following elements:

- Current and previous input values: u (k), u (k − 1),...,u (k − du), representing external information for networks.
- Values of the output y (k), y (k − 1)..., y (k − d y) in the previous time points the variables on which the output of the model y (k + 1) depends.

Thus, the dynamics of the described NARX simulation model is expressed by the next nonlinear equation:

$$y(k + 1) = \varphi\{u(k), u(k - 1), \ldots, u(k - du), y(k), y(k - 1), \ldots, y(k - dy)\} \quad (3)$$

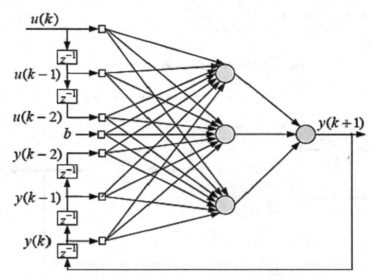

Fig. 2. A generalized recurrent network architecture

Neural networks of NARX can be trained in two different methods: open-loop training architecture and closed-loop architecture.

In the open-loop architecture, the training of the dynamical feedback NARX network is done as in a conventional stable network. The recurrent link is resolved, and each time delay is processed as a single input. The recurrent inputs are provided with the actual outputs rather than data obtained from the network's response. Upon completion of training, the trained network is adapted to the performance of a NARX network. Accordingly, multi-step-ahead prediction, which is often desired for predictive control, may have numerous prediction errors. Since the network uses actual information for training rather than predictive information, the prediction error is more significant when the recurrent path is closed.

The closed-loop architecture uses dynamic learning algorithms (i.e., backpropagation algorithms) for training. These algorithms are more computationally intensive than traditional stable network algorithms. Training in the closed-loop form is also much more prone to early convergence to the min-loss function, and the training results are incredibly dependent on the past information Figs. 3 and 4 show the open-loop and closed-loop architectures.

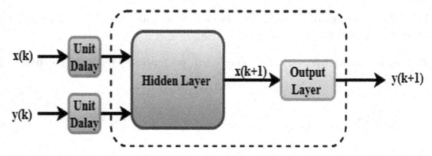

Fig. 3. NARX neural network - open-loop form

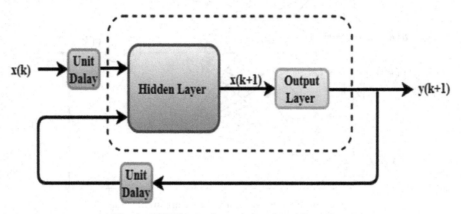

Fig. 4. NARX neural network - closed-loop form

5 Simulation Results

In this work, we performed time series prediction using MATLAB environment to implement and simulate the energy consumption of UAV-based MEC using NARX recurrent neural networks. We investigated the performance in four cases as a function of the k-step predictions using the different number of hidden neurons. The datasets were generated from the MEC with multi-UAV model, and we also simulated the model using the MATLAB simulator. After collecting and preparing the dataset, we divided it into 70%, 30% for training and 30% for testing. To evaluate the prediction accuracy for the traffic data, we used the RMSE and MAPE as shown in Eqs. (4) and (5). Table 2 shows the prediction accuracy for IoT throughput using RMSE and MAPE.

$$RMSE = \sqrt{\frac{1}{N} \sum_{t=1}^{n} (y_t - \hat{y}_t)^2} \tag{4}$$

$$MAPE = \frac{1}{N} \sum_{t=1}^{n} \left| \frac{y_t - \hat{y}_t}{y_t} \right| \tag{5}$$

Where N is the total number of observations, y_t is the actual value, whereas $\hat{y}_t$ is the predicated value.

Table 2. Prediction accuracy for the predicted models using RMSE and MAPE.

Hidden layer size	10		15		17		20	
K-step prediction	RMSE	MAPE	RMSE	MAPE	RMSE	MAPE	RMSE	MAPE
1-step	0.2574	12.3273	0.2100	11.4484	0.1187	10.0160	0.1071	8.0379
10-steps	0.5770	10.1151	0.4970	8.5736	0.3295	4.3579	0.2807	3.2652
15-steps	0.5316	11.1624	0.4982	8.5779	0.4619	6.7046	0.3733	2.5661
20-steps	0.5491	4.6681	0.5249	3.0331	0.4976	1.4025	0.4600	1.0032

Table 2 illustrates the prediction accuracy for energy consumption in multi-UAV loading traffic in four cases depending on the k-step predictions and using the different number of neurons used in training based on the recurrent neural network NARX predictor. We evaluated the prediction accuracy using RMSE and MAPE to measure the prediction accuracy to investigate the best prediction accuracy and the maximum average improvement in prediction accuracy considering MSE as a loss function.

The tabulated results show that the model has the best prediction accuracy in the 1-step case with 20 hidden neurons for RMSE and MAPE. The maximum average improvement, in this case, is 4.3%. Also, the model predicted with 17 hidden neurons has a prediction accuracy approximately equal to that of the model with 20 hidden neurons; moreover, the maximum average improvement is 2.3%. On the other hand, the models predicted with 15 and 10 hidden neurons have the lowest prediction accuracies compared to the others.

As shown in the table in the 10-step case, the model predicted with 20 hidden neurons outperforms its competitors, and the maximum average improvement, in this case, is 6.85%. On the other hand, the model predicted with 17 hidden neurons has a prediction accuracy approximately equal to that of the model with 20 hidden neurons; moreover, the maximum average improvement is 5.76%.

In the 15-step case, the prediction model with 20 hidden neurons has better accuracy than the others, and the maximum average improvement is 8.6%. Also, the prediction models with 17 and 15 hidden neurons have approximately equal prediction accuracy, and the maximum average improvement is 4.46% and 2.6%, respectively. On the other hand, the prediction model with 10 hidden neurons has lower prediction accuracy than the others.

In the 20-step, the prediction models with 20 and 17 hidden neurons have semi-equal and better accuracy than the others; the maximum average improvements are 3.66% and 3.3%, respectively. Also, the model predicted with 15 steps has lower performance than the models with 20 and 17 hidden neurons, and the maximum average improvement is 1.635%. On the other hand, the model predicted with 10 hidden neurons has the lowest prediction accuracies compared to the others.

Figures 5, 6, 7 and 8 show the predicted models for energy in four cases according to the number of hidden neurons used in each case, and the corresponding k-steps ahead prediction in each case. From the figures, it can be seen that the predicted energy models change randomly with time in all cases.

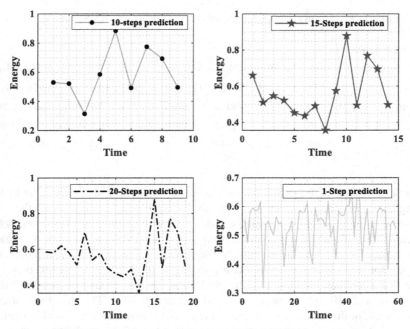

Fig. 5. Predicted models in the case of using 20 hidden neurons.

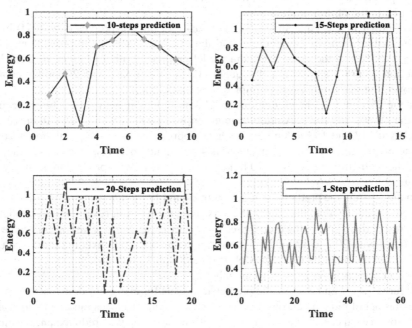

Fig. 6. Predicted models in the case of using 17 hidden neurons.

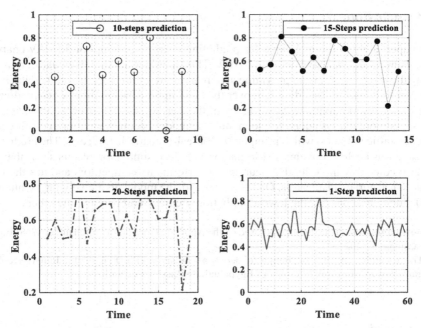

Fig. 7. Predicted models in the case of using 15 hidden neurons.

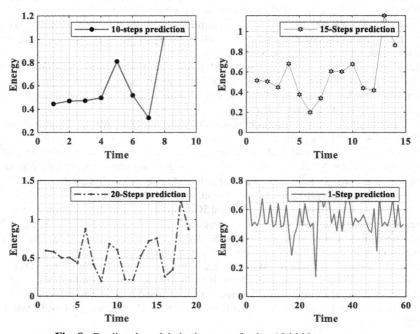

Fig. 8. Predicted models in the case of using 10 hidden neurons.

6 Conclusion

This paper is about the technique for predicting energy consumption in UAV-enabled MEC using recurrent neural network NARX. This technique has the advantage of remembering the historical data and providing a more accurate estimate of the future data in the time series. It also has an advantage over the other approaches to time series prediction in that it serves to maximize the accuracy of the learning method over the training iterations. As more data is added to the model, the model becomes smarter and can better evaluate traffic volumes, which is important for real-time traffic forecasts. The prediction accuracy was evaluated using RMSE and MAPE. The simulation results show that the model predicted with 20 hidden neurons outperforms its competitors and has the best prediction accuracy in all cases. On the other hand, the model predicted with the number of 10 hidden neurons has the lowest prediction accuracy compared to the others.

Acknowledgments. This research is based on the Applied Scientific Research under the SPbSUT state assignment 2021.

The researcher [Ali R. Abdellah] is funded by a scholarship [Ph.D.] under the Joint (Executive Program between the Arab Republic of Egypt and the Russian Federation).

References

1. Trung, Q., Duong, Chu, X., Suraweera, H.A.: Ultra-Dense Networks for 5G and Beyond: Modelling, Analysis, and Applications. Wiley, New York (2019)
2. Abdellah, A., Koucheryavy, A.: Survey on artificial intelligence techniques in 5G networks. J. Inf. Technol. Telecommun. **8**(1), 1–10 (2020). SPbSUT, Russia. http://www.sut.ru/doci/nauka/1AEA/ITT/2020_1/1-10.pdf
3. Kovalenko, V., Alzaghir, A., Volkov, A., Muthanna, A., Koucheryavy, A.: Clustering algorithms for UAV placement in 5G and beyond networks. In: 2020 12th International Congress on Ultra Modern Telecommunications and Control Systems and Workshops (ICUMT), pp. 301–307. IEEE, October 2020
4. Bithas, P.S., et al.: A survey on machine-learning techniques for UAV-based communications. Sensors **19**(23), 5170 (2019)
5. Abdellah, A.R., Mahmood, O.A., Koucheryavy, A.: Delay prediction in IoT using machine learning approach. In: 2020 12th International Congress on Ultra Modern Telecommunications and Control Systems and Workshops (ICUMT) Brno, Czech Republic, pp. 275–279 (2020). https://doi.org/10.1109/ICUMT51630.2020.9222245
6. Mughees, A., et al.: Towards energy efficient 5G networks using machine learning: taxonomy, research challenges, and future research directions. IEEE Access **8**, 187498–187522 (2020)
7. Lahmeri, M.-A., Kishk, M.A., Alouini, M.-S.: Artificial Intelligence for UAV-enabled wireless networks: a survey. IEEE Open J. Commun. Soc. **2**, 1015–1040 (2021)
8. Brik, B., Ksentini, A., Bouaziz, M.: Federated learning for UAVs-enabled wireless networks: use cases, challenges, and open problems. IEEE Access **8**, 53841–55384 (2020)
9. Zhang, Q., et al.: Machine learning for predictive on-demand deployment of UAVs for wireless communications. In: 2018 IEEE Global Communications Conference (GLOBECOM). IEEE (2018)

10. Abdellah, A., Mahmood, O.A.K., Paramonov, A., Koucheryavy, A.: IoT traffic prediction using multi-step ahead prediction with neural network. In: 2019 11th International Congress on Ultra Modern Telecommunications and Control Systems and Workshops (ICUMT), Dublin, Ireland, pp. 1–4 (2019). https://doi.org/10.1109/ICUMT48472.2019.8970675

11. Volkov, A., Abdellah, A.R., Muthanna, A., Makolkina, M., Paramonov, A., Koucheryavy, A.: IoT traffic prediction with neural networks learning based on SDN infrastructure. In: Vishnevskiy, V.M., Samouylov, K.E., Kozyrev, D.V. (eds.) DCCN 2020. LNCS, vol. 12563, pp. 64–76. Springer, Cham (2020). https://doi.org/10.1007/978-3-030-66471-8_6

12. Ruan, L., Dias, M.P.I., Wong, E.: Machine learning-based bandwidth prediction for low-latency H2M applications. IEEE Internet Things J. **6**(2), 3743–3752 (2019). https://doi.org/10.1109/JIOT.2018.2890563

13. White, G., Palade, A., Cabrera, C., Clarke, S.: IoTPredict: collaborative QoS prediction in IoT. In: IEEE PerCom, pp. 1–10, March 2018

14. Abdellah, A.R., Artem, V., Muthanna, A., Gallyamov, D., Koucheryavy, A.: Deep learning for IoT traffic prediction based on edge computing. In: Vishnevskiy, V.M., Samouylov, K.E., Kozyrev, D.V. (eds.) DCCN 2020. CCIS, vol. 1337, pp. 18–29. Springer, Cham (2020). https://doi.org/10.1007/978-3-030-66242-4_2

15. Abdellah, A.R., Koucheryavy, A.: Deep learning with long short-term memory for IoT traffic prediction. In: Galinina, O., Andreev, S., Balandin, S., Koucheryavy, Y. (eds.) Internet of Things, Smart Spaces, and Next Generation Networks and Systems, NEW2AN 2020, ruSMART 2020. LNCS, vol. 12525, pp. 267–280. Springer, Cham (2020). https://doi.org/10.1007/978-3-030-65726-0_24

16. Abdellah, A.R., Koucheryavy, A.: VANET traffic prediction using LSTM with deep neural network learning. In: Galinina, O., Andreev, S., Balandin, S., Koucheryavy, Y. (eds.) Internet of Things, Smart Spaces, and Next Generation Networks and Systems. NEW2AN 2020, ruSMART 2020. LNCS, vol. 12525, pp. 281–294. Springer, Cham (2020). https://doi.org/10.1007/978-3-030-65726-0_25

Investigation Methods of Dehydrated Protein Films for Biomolecular Electronics

Maksim Baranov$^{(\boxtimes)}$ ⓘ and Elena Velichko ⓘ

Peter the Great St. Petersburg Polytechnic University (SPbPU), St. Petersburg 195251, Russia
baranovma1993@gmail.com

Abstract. This work is devoted to the study of biomolecular films for the development of biomolecular electronics functional devices. It is shown that the properties of biomolecular films indicate the formation of spatial structures in dry films. Experimental studies of the formation of structures in dehydrated films have been carried out at various concentrations of protein and salt in the initial solutions. To quantitatively estimate the energies of protein nanosystems, computational experiments were carried out using the method of molecular modeling. A description of the obtained experimental results is given, further fields of research are discussed.

Keywords: Self-assembly · Biomolecular electronics · Thin films · Nanoelectronics

1 Introduction

Currently, scientific and technical problems require not only theoretical and practical research, but also the construction of computational models and they perform an appropriate experiment. In addition, most modern developments are at the junction of several sciences at once, for example, physics, biology, and chemistry [1–7]. One of such applied scientific problems is the development of a new type of electronics, which is based on the use of not only standard silicon technology, but also organic molecules, such as proteins, amino acids, and nucleic acids [8–11]. They have unique properties, including the ability to assemble into organized molecular layers. Therefore, thin films created from biological molecules can form the basis of biomolecular electronics [10, 12–15].

Self-organized biomolecular films are ordered molecular structures [6]. They are created by drying an initial liquid solution of biomolecules on a solid support. It has already been shown earlier that it is possible to obtain various structure types, which depends on the amount of salts in the initial protein solution [3, 16, 17]. Typically, structures are classified into 2 types: cracks and dendrites. Cracks are mainly formed from water solutions of the original proteins, and they are linear, radial, spiral. The dendrites are usually formed as salt crystals found in the initial protein solution and can be in various sizes and shapes. In [16] experimental results are presented on the study of the geometric parameters of dendritic structures, depending on various parameters of the experiment.

© Springer Nature Switzerland AG 2022
Y. Koucheryavy et al. (Eds.): NEW2AN 2021/ruSMART 2021, LNCS 13158, pp. 310–320, 2022.
https://doi.org/10.1007/978-3-030-97777-1_26

The structures formed in the films because molecule self-organization is evidence of self-organization processes in the macrolevel. By monitoring the dehydration of solutions and the subsequent growth of biomolecular films, it is possible to obtain various ordered molecular groups by changing the properties of these films [3, 18, 19]. In addition, the presence, shape, and form of structures can provide information about the stability of films which is an important parameter of maintaining their structure under insignificant mechanical impacts [20].

Some protein films properties and their applications are described in [3, 16, 21–23]. It has been shown that such materials can be used in various applications, for example, drug delivery, antimicrobial coatings, electronics, optics, and probing [24]. The creation of protein films for various packaging is being studied. Polyethylene glycol or glycerin is used as a plasticizer. It has been shown that by changing the concentration of the plasticizer it is possible to regulate the solubility of the films in water, as well as to change their mechanical properties [25, 26]. Creation of biological sensors based on protein films and wires is promising research. It has been shown that a sensor based on a protein nanowire responds to a wide range of concentrations of various gases, for example, ammonia [27, 28]. Protein-based gas sensors of this type can be used in environmental monitoring, industry and agriculture.

The study of film's "behavior" under the influence of various external factors is promise field of research. In particular, we are not interested in the physical behavior of the film, although its formation under the influence of a field is described [3], but in its behavior: change conformation, dipole moment, ability to accumulate charge, etc.

Thus, the aim of this work is to study the properties of biomolecular films formed from albumin protein solution. In this work, a study of the dependence of the formation of dissipative structures on the temperature of dehydration of biomolecular films is carried out. Experimental results of molecular dynamics modeling are also presented. The energy of molecular clusters is calculated depending on the modeling temperature and the magnitude of the applied electric fields.

2 Experimental Part

There are several methods for creating biomolecular films on a solid substrate. Various drying methods prevail, including spraying, sublimation and supercritical fluid drying. However, these methods are quite expensive and require special expensive equipment.

The method of isothermal dehydration was chosen as a promising method for obtaining biomolecular films. Removal of water (dehydration) is regulated by fundamental physical principles: the loss of neutral particles (water molecules) from the surface can be derived from the Clausius-Clapeyron equation:

$$n_a = bT^{\frac{1}{2}} \exp\left(-\frac{l_a}{kT}\right), \tag{1}$$

where n_a – number of molecules evaporating from unit surface in unit time; l_a, J, – latent heat of vaporization per molecule; T, K, – temperature; k, $\frac{J}{K}$, – Boltzmann constant; b, $K^{-\frac{1}{2}}$, – evaporation constant.

In practice, mass transfer at the surface of liquid water depends not only on the temperature and composition of the gas phase; it depends on osmotic pressure, presence of surfactants, bulk rheological properties, kinetics of heat transfer at the surface, and on the geometry of the dried volume. As has been shown, because of drying, structures of various types are formed in the film. To analyze them in this work, we used the method of optical microscopy. Optical microscope Olympus CX 43 and Altami USB camera (model UCMOS10000 KPA) were used to obtain protein film images. These images have following properties: an area about 0.1 cm^2, a resolution of 1280×960 pixels, a depth of 24 bits. Optical analysis provides information only on macrostructures. To understand the internal processes, it is necessary to supplement this method with modeling of intramolecular processes.

One of these characteristics is the free energy of thin films. It is responsible for the formation of certain structures or patterns within the film, as well as for the organization of stable molecular structures.

The total energy of the films is of interest; therefore, it makes sense to pay attention to the Hamiltonian [2, 29, 30]. In the classical representation, it is defined as the sum of the kinetic and potential energies of the system

$$H(p, r) = K(p) + V(r). \tag{2}$$

The kinetic energy in this case does not depend on the position of the particles, if configuration restrictions are not applied and is defined as:

$$K(p) = \sum_{i=1}^{N} \frac{p_i^2}{2m_i}. \tag{3}$$

Potential energy is the sum of various potential energies that describe bound and unbound interactions between particles, as well as special, "non-physical" interactions:

$$V(r) = U^{phys}(r) + U^{special}(r) = U^{bon}(r) + U^{nonb}(r) + U^{special}(r). \tag{4}$$

It makes sense to consider each of the components separately when studying the configuration of molecular clusters and the conformation of molecules.

The molecular dynamics (MD) method was used to study the free energy. Molecular system models were modeled using Visual Molecular Dynamics (VMD). Each of them was a system of two albumin protein molecules. The minimum distance between individual regions of these molecules was about 3 Å. The studies were carried out in a cubic water volume with the addition of Na$^+$ and Cl$^-$ ions. The studies were carried out at NPT configuration (constant value of the number of particles, pressure, and temperature). All simulations were carried out with a CHARMM27 force field using the NAMD package under periodic boundary conditions and a cutoff radius for unrelated interactions with a switching function, starting from 12 Å and reaching zero at 14 Å.

Simulation took place in several stages: minimization energy, heating, equilibration, and dynamics. The simulation time was at most 5 ns.

3 Results

This section presents the experimental results obtained using isothermal dehydration methods and molecular dynamics modeling. The images obtained during the research and the graphs of the dependence of the energies of molecular clusters on time for various variations of the experimental conditions are described.

3.1 Dehydration Temperature

For these experiments, albumin protein solutions were prepared with a concentration of 5% since this is the optimal concentration to obtain standard spiral structures [3]. Then the usual drying of experimental samples was carried out at various dehydration temperatures: 293, 298, 303, 308 and 313 K. The results of these studies are presented in Fig. 1.

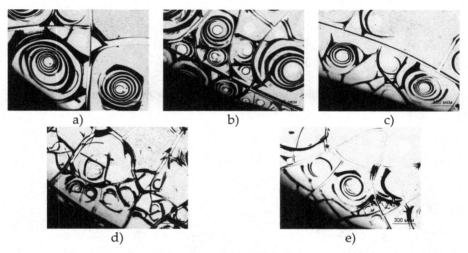

Fig. 1. Images of protein films, formed with 293 K, 298 K, 303 K, 308 K, and 313 K temperature presented five micro photos from a) to e) points, respectively

As can be seen from the images, the number of spiral structures decreases with increasing temperature. Also, the films become less stable, and the nuclei of future spirals begin to form without the formation of spiral cracks.

A graph was plotted as the number of spiral structures versus temperature. This dependence are shown in Fig. 2.

Studies of the processes of self-organization were carried out using the method of molecular simulation. Calculations were carried out at the same temperatures. Graphs of the dependences of the energy of molecular clusters from time to time are presented in Fig. 3.

Analyzing Fig. 3 it can be noted that with an increase in modeling temperature, the total energy of molecular clusters increases. As you can see, in all experiments this value has a negative sign. Relying on the results of previous studies, it can be said that with such an energy sign, the peptide film has a positive adhesion to the surface. With a change of adhesion sign disappears. Comparing the results in Fig. 3 and Figs. 1 and 2, it could be noted that with an increase in the dehydration temperature, the number of helical

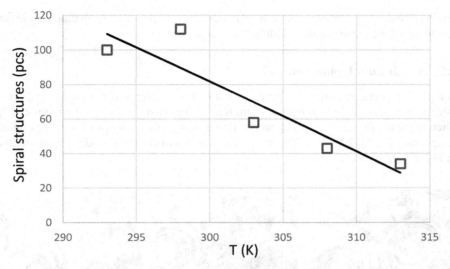

Fig. 2. Numbers of spiral structures as a function of dehydration temperature

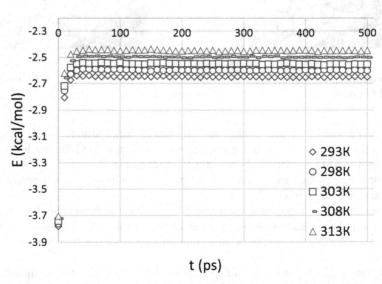

Fig. 3. Energies of molecular cluster with 293 K, 298 K, 303 K, 308 K, and 313 K temperature shown as a function of time by five lines from top to bottom, respectively

structures in the films decreases, and the energy of the biomolecular cluster increases, tending to the positive range of values. As stated in the article [31], the free energy of the peptide film is related to its stability: high energy results less stability. Thus, it can be concluded that the studied biomolecular films lose stability with increasing temperature.

3.2 External Electric Field

Current research is aimed at studying the properties of thin films. Since in the future these films may become a material for creating elements of devices for biomolecular electronics, the properties and stability of these films under the influence of direct electric fields of various magnitudes are currently being studied. An aqueous solution of albumin protein was used with different values of the volumetric concentration of protein in the solution: 5% and 2%. External electric field was applied to the samples with 0.25, 0.5, 1, 1.5, 2, 3, 4 и 5 V/cm intensity. The area of the film surface was the same for all experiments and was equal to 0.1 cm^2. Various images were obtained containing quasiperiodic structures consisting of certain cells about 200 nm in size each (Figs. 4 and 5).

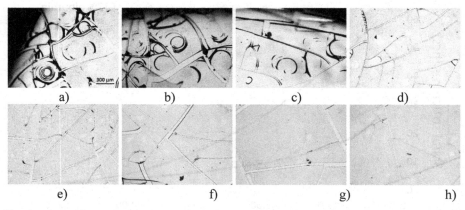

Fig. 4. Albumin protein solutions films 2%, formed under the influence of an external electric field: a – 0.25 V/cm; b – 0.5 V/cm; c – 1 V/cm; d – 1.5 V/cm; e – 2 V/cm; f – 3 V/cm; g – 4 V/cm; h – 5 V/cm

Figures 4 and 5 shows photos of sections of films in which spiral structures are formed.

Figure 6 shows a graph of the dependence of the number of spiral structures on the value of the applied electrical field. The structures were counted on the entire surface of the films.

Analyzing this dependence, it can be concluded, that the external electric field affects the cracking of protein films. In addition, considering the resulting images it is worth noting that the films formed under the influence of the electric field are unstable and have a weak adhesion to the substrate.

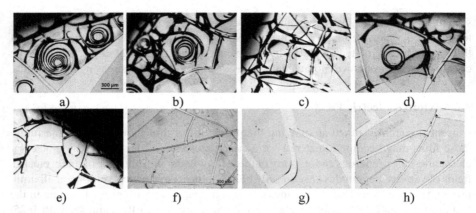

Fig. 5. Albumin protein solution films 5% concentration, formed under the influence of an external electric field: a – 0.25 V/cm; b – 0.5 V/cm; c – 1 V/cm; d – 1.5 V/cm; e – 2 V/cm; f – 3 V/cm; g – 4 V/cm; h – 5 V/cm

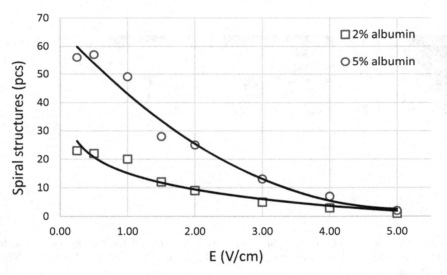

Fig. 6. Number of spiral structures in dehydrated protein films with 2 and 5% albumin volume fractions are shown as a function of external electric field volume by two lines from bottom to top, respectively

The MD method showed, that with small changes of the external electrical field, the order of the V/cm units, the total energy of the molecular cluster remains almost unchanged. This is presented in Fig. 4. However, with an increase in fields per unit kcal/(mol $\times$ Å $\times$ e), the energy of clusters begins to change significantly (Figs. 7 and 8).

In Fig. 8, we can see that the energies of molecular clusters are increased by 2 tenths of a power, in comparison with Fig. 7. For 5 ns, the energy indicators do not have time

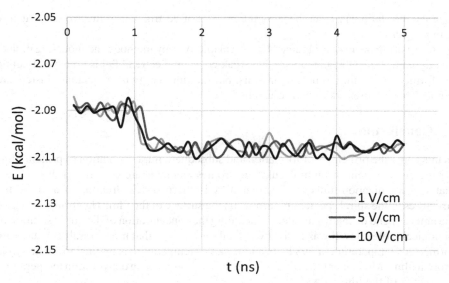

Fig. 7. Energies of molecular cluster with intensity of external electric field of 1, 5, and 10 V/cm shown as a function of time by four lines from top to bottom, respectively

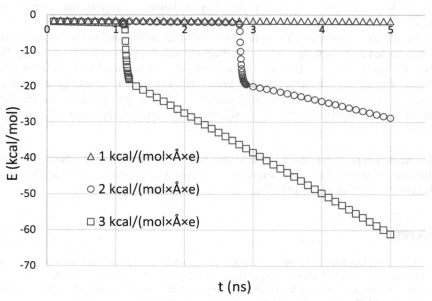

Fig. 8. Energies of molecular cluster with intensity of external electric field of 4.3×10^6, 8.7×10^6 and 13×10^6 V/cm which corresponds 1, 2 and 3 kcal/(mol $\times$ Å $\times$ e) shown as a function of time by four lines from top to bottom, respectively

to reach the stationary level, because the process of destruction of the protein structure is in progress.

Comparing the results obtained by optical microscopy methods and modeling molecular dynamics it can be concluded that weak constant electrical fields do have effect on the formation of thin biomolecular films, but the full energy of molecular clusters are stable. This requires additional research.

4 Conclusion

In this paper the principles of formation and subsequent implementation of protein films for the development of biomolecular electronics elements are considered. It is shown that self-organization films can be created by isothermal dehydration. As a result, the structures of the spiral species are formed on the surface of the film. The form and size of the latter depend on many parameters including the concentration of the initial solution of biological molecules. It was found by optical microscopy that more spiral structures are formed at a temperature of 298 K. In addition, this temperature is optimal to create stable protein films. Molecular modeling showed that with increasing dehydration temperature, the energy of the film grows.

The energy values of the molecular cluster were obtained by computer simulation of protein molecules in the water. Based on the analysis of the obtained data, it can be assumed that the mesh spiral-elliptic, resulting from the dehydration of the aqueous solutions of the protein, has an electric nature. It can be assumed that the distribution of both the electric potential and the fields in the volume charge of the domain has a solenoidal structure in the form of cylindrical harmonics.

The effect of an external electric field on the formation of protein films is investigated. It was revealed that when the fields are applied, the order of units in V/cm has weak effect on the formation of films. In addition, the films created in the electric field lose their stability. The method of molecular simulation shows that the total energy of molecular clusters is poorly changed when small electric fields are applied. However, the fields with the value of kcal/(mol $\times$ Å $\times$ e) are capable of significantly change the energy of protein molecules in water.

Acknowledgments. This research was funded by RSF, grant number №21-72-20029. The results of the work were obtained using computational resources of Peter the Great Saint-Petersburg Polytechnic University Supercomputing Center (www.spbstu.ru).

References

1. Chiralt, A., González-Martínez, C., Vargas, M., Atarés, L.: Edible films and coatings from proteins. Elsevier Ltd. (2018). https://doi.org/10.1016/B978-0-08-100722-8.00019-X
2. Alessandrini, A., Gerunda, M., Facci, P.: Tuning molecular orientation in protein films. Surface Sci. **542**, 64–71 (2003). https://doi.org/10.1016/S0039-6028(03)00922-1
3. Velichko, E., Zezina, T., Baranov, M., Nepomnyashchaya, E., Tsybin, O.: Dynamics of polypeptide cluster dipole moment for nano communication applications. In: Galinina, O., Andreev, S., Balandin, S., Koucheryavy, Y. (eds.) NEW2AN/ruSMART -2018. LNCS, vol. 11118, pp. 675–682. Springer, Cham (2018). https://doi.org/10.1007/978-3-030-01168-0_62

4. Bibi, F., Villain, M., Guillaume, C., Sorli, B., Gontard, N.: A review: origins of the dielectric properties of proteins and potential development as bio-sensors. Sensors **16**, 1232 (2016). mdpi.com, https://doi.org/10.3390/s16081232

5. Allouche, A.: Software news and updates Gabedit — a graphical user interface for computational chemistry softwares. J. Comput. Chem. **32**, 174–182 (2012). https://doi.org/10.1002/jcc

6. Velichko, E., Tsybin, O.: Biomolecular Electronics. Introduction (2011)

7. Baev, A., Prasad, P.N., Ågren, H., Samoć, M., Wegener, M.: Metaphotonics: an emerging field with opportunities and challenges. Phys. Rep. **594**, 1–60 (2015). https://doi.org/10.1016/j.physrep.2015.07.002

8. Wang, N., Yang, A., Fu, Y., Li, Y., Yan, F.: Functionalized organic thin film transistors for biosensing. Acc. Chem. Res. **52**(2), 277–287 (2019). https://doi.org/10.1021/acs.accounts.8b00448

9. Siqueira, J.R., Caseli, L., Crespilho, F.N., Zucolotto, V., Oliveira, O.N.: Immobilization of biomolecules on nanostructured films for biosensing. Biosens. Bioelectron. **25**, 1254–1263 (2010). https://doi.org/10.1016/j.bios.2009.09.043

10. Torculas, M., Medina, J., Xue, W., Hu, X.: Protein-based bioelectronics. ACS Biomater. Sci. Eng. **2**, 1211–1223 (2016). https://doi.org/10.1021/acsbiomaterials.6b00119

11. Amdursky, N., Głowacki, E.D., Meredith, P., Amdursky, N., Głowacki, E.D., Meredith, P.: Macroscale biomolecular electronics and ionics. Wiley Online Libr. **31**, 1802221 (2018). https://doi.org/10.1002/adma.201802221

12. Withayachumnankul, W., O'Hara, J.F., Cao, W., Al-Naib, I., Zhang, W.: Limitation in thin-film sensing with transmission-mode terahertz time-domain spectroscopy. Opt. Express **22**, 972 (2014). https://doi.org/10.1364/oe.22.000972

13. Mohan, A., Rajendran, S.R.C.K., He, Q.S., Bazinet, L., Udenigwe, C.C.: Encapsulation of food protein hydrolysates and peptides: a review. RSC Adv. **5**, 79270–79278 (2015). https://doi.org/10.1039/c5ra13419f

14. Xin, S., Li, X., Wang, Q., Al., E.: Novel layer by layer structured nanofibrous mats coated by protein films for dermal regeneration. J. Biomed. Nanotechnol. **10**, 803–810 (2014)

15. Guvendiren, M., Yang, S., Burdick, J.A.: Swelling-induced surface patterns in hydrogels with gradient crosslinking density. Wiley Online Libr. **19**, 3038–3045 (2009). https://doi.org/10.1002/adfm.200900622

16. Baranov, M., Velichko, E., Greshnevikov, K.: Analysis of fractal structures in dehydrated films of protein solutions. Symmetry **13**, 123 (2021). mdpi.com, https://doi.org/10.3390/sym13010123

17. Velichko, E., Nepomnyashchaya, E., Baranov, M.: Study of self-assembled molecular films as a method of search for promising materials in nanoelectronics and nanocommunications. In: Galinina, O., Andreev, S., Balandin, S., Koucheryavy, Y. (eds.) NEW2AN/ruSMART -2018. LNCS, vol. 11118, pp. 691–701. Springer, Cham (2018). https://doi.org/10.1007/978-3-030-01168-0_64

18. Baranov, M., Velichko, E., Shariaty, F.: Determination of geometrical parameters in blood serum films using an image segmentation algorithm. Opt. Mem. Neural Netw. (Inf. Opt.) **29**, 330–335 (2020). https://doi.org/10.3103/S1060992X20040037

19. Baranov, M.A., Rozov, S.V.: Study of the dielectric parameters of biological liquids. J. Phys. Conf. Ser. **1326**, 012006 (2019). https://doi.org/10.1088/1742-6596/1326/1/012006

20. Baranov, M.A., Klimchitskaya, G.L., Mostepanenko, V.M., Velichko, E.N.: Fluctuation-induced free energy of thin peptide films. Phys. Rev. E. **99**, 022410 (2019). https://doi.org/10.1103/PhysRevE.99.022410

21. Baranov, M., Velichko, E., Rozov, S.: Dehydrated films of protein solutions: structural properties. St. Petersburg Polytech. State Univ. J. Phys. Math. **12**, 25–37 (2019). https://doi.org/10.18721/JPM.12403

22. Baranov, M., Tsybin, O., Velichko, E.: Structured biomolecular films for microelectronics. St. Petersburg Polytech. State Univ. J. Phys. Math. **14**, 85–99 (2021). https://doi.org/10.18721/JPM.14106
23. Baranov, M.A., Dudina, A.I., Nepomnyaschaya, E.K.: Optical analysis of protein-metal interactions. J. Phys. Conf. Ser. **1226**, 012005 (2019). https://doi.org/10.1088/1742-6596/1226/1/012005
24. Taylor, P.A., Jayaraman, A.: Molecular modeling and simulations of peptide-polymer conjugates. Annu. Rev. Chem. Biomol. Eng. **11**, 257–276 (2020)
25. Proaño, J., Salgado, P.: Physical, structural and antioxidant properties of brewer's spent grain protein films. Wiley Online Libr. **100**, 5458–5465 (2020). https://doi.org/10.1002/jsfa.10597
26. Sarıcaoglu, F.: Physicochemical, antioxidant and antimicrobial properties of mechanically deboned chicken meat protein films enriched with various essential oils. Food Packag. Shelf Life **25**, 100527 (2020). Elsevier
27. Smith, A.F., et al.: Bioelectronic protein nanowire sensors for ammonia detection. Nano Res. **13**(5), 1479–1484 (2020). https://doi.org/10.1007/s12274-020-2825-6
28. Liu, X., Fu, T., Ward, J., Gao, H.: Multifunctional protein nanowire humidity sensors for green wearable electronics. Wiley Online Libr. **6**, 2000721 (2020). https://doi.org/10.1002/aelm.202000721
29. Phillips, J.C., et al.: Scalable molecular dynamics with NAMD. J. Comput. Chem. **26**, 1781–1802 (2005). https://doi.org/10.1002/jcc.20289
30. Wang, Y., Harrison, C.B., Schulten, K., McCammon, J.A.: Implementation of accelerated molecular dynamics in NAMD. Comput. Sci. Discov. **4**, 015002 (2011). https://doi.org/10.1088/1749-4699/4/1/015002
31. Velichko, E.N., Baranov, M.A., Mostepanenko, V.M.: Change of sign in the Casimir interaction of peptide films deposited on a dielectric substrate. Mod. Phys. Lett. A. **35**, 1–6 (2020). https://doi.org/10.1142/S0217732320400209

Applying Deep Learning Techniques to Extract Diagnostic Information from ECG Images

Georgy M. Kostin[1]([⊠]) [iD], Vitalii A. Pavlov[1]([⊠]) [iD], Sergey V. Zavjalov[1]([⊠]) [iD],
and Tatiana M. Pervunina[2]([⊠]) [iD]

[1] Institute of Physics, Nanotechnology and Telecommunications, Peter the Great St. Petersburg,
Polytechnic University, 195251 St. Petersburg, Russia
gekkonist@gmail.com, {pavlov_va,zavyalov_sv}@spbstu.ru
[2] Almazov National Medical Research Centre, 197341 St. Petersburg, Russia
ptm.pervunina@yandex.ru

Abstract. This work is devoted to the implementation of an algorithm for extracting diagnostic information from ECG images using deep learning methods. The U-Net neural network architecture was chosen to search and segment the ECG signal area in the image. The training was conducted based on the developed data set. The values of the DICE coefficient were obtained to assess the reliability of the neural network architecture, which indicates the high accuracy of the proposed method for solving the problem.

Keywords: Computer vision · Electrocardiogram · Convolutional neural networks · Segmentation · Deep learning · U-Net

1 Introduction

Electrocardiography (ECG) is a common instrumental method for the diagnosis of cardiovascular diseases. The essence of the method is very simple: registration of the potential difference from the surface of the patient's body. The electrical activity of the heart is reflected by the change in the potential difference during diagnosis. These are the processes of propagation of the wave of contraction through the heart, polarization and depolarization of pacemakers and pathways.

Today, there is an extensive class of devices that allow you to get an electrocardiogram, but most models of heart disease are based on outdated data sets and step-by-step algorithms for interpreting ECG results. From this, we can conclude that the subjective assessment of the operator, in our case, a medical professional, is the main disadvantage, since due to insufficient experience and related circumstances, such as distracting events and fatigue, the probability of an error in the diagnosis increases, which, sometimes, can lead to tragic consequences for the patient under study.

The transition of ECG charts from a paper form to electronic ECG signals allows the use of additional software for automatic analysis, followed by the identification of signs that the operator should pay attention to. Now, the digitized signals allow us to objectively evaluate parameters such as PR-, QRS-, QT-intervals, variance, and height

© Springer Nature Switzerland AG 2022
Y. Koucheryavy et al. (Eds.): NEW2AN 2021/ruSMART 2021, LNCS 13158, pp. 321–328, 2022.
https://doi.org/10.1007/978-3-030-97777-1_27

of ST, as well as previously missed readings, such as the morphology of the T-wave or the spatial angle of QRS-T. An example of such a system is bedside monitors, which automatically signal heart rhythm disorders.

According to statistics provided by the World Health Organization, the first place in all deaths is occupied by diseases related to the heart and blood vessels. Thus, in 2016, 17.9 million people died from cardiovascular diseases (CVD), 85% of whose deaths are associated with strokes and heart attacks [1]. It is also an interesting fact that middle-and low-income countries are more susceptible to CVD than others. Most low-cost medical facilities do not have the ability to instantly update existing devices to obtain electrocardiograms, which makes it impossible to use the additional software for automatic ECG analysis.

It is worth noting that advances in machine learning have had a significant impact in areas related to signal processing. It is safe to say that collecting big data from ECG signal sets makes them suitable for machine learning approaches. Thus, the first stage is the reliable extraction of diagnostic information from ECG images, followed by the reproduction of the digitized waveform.

In 2007, an algorithm for digitizing the conversion of ECG and other paper medical records into digital analogues was introduced [2]. The essence of this algorithm is to digitize the original image, correct a possible skew, and convert binary data into vectors. The advantages of this method include the classical architecture, which does not require large computing capabilities of the device, but behind it lies the main drawback, namely the direct presence of an operator to mark the original ECG image for further separation.

The paper [3] presents an algorithm for automatic selection of a digital ECG signal and recognition of the QRS interval. This algorithm is based on the division of a 3-channel image into separate scenes, followed by processing to extract the shape of the ECG signal and then digitize it. The QRS interval is classified by hardware, showing acceptable results. The disadvantages of this development include the inability to work with two or more ECG signals simultaneously, which requires an operator for manual segmentation, as well as with complex cases of the studied forms of ECG, which are due to the specifics of the disease.

In [4], an algorithm for identifying a person using an ECG is presented. The digital signal is converted to an image and classified using CNN. This implementation shows high performance but has high computational complexity.

Another interesting project is the processing of electrocardiogram images and the extraction of numerical information [5], published in 2016. This algorithm allows you to digitize ECG signals with R-peak classification with high accuracy. But, unfortunately, it requires an operator that will mark the beginning and end of the studied ECG signal on the X-axis, as well as the maximum and minimum values on the Y-axis on the original ECG image.

In [6], an algorithm for classifying the ECG signal using deep learning methods is presented. This development is interesting for its ability to work in real time, namely sending data to the cloud and automatic processing. In the future, the user can view their results at any time convenient for them. The disadvantages of this work include the need to work with images rather than numerical data, as well as the unsuitability for a complex form of the ECG signal.

During the review of the existing methods of ECG signal classification [2–7], several shortcomings were identified, including the need for manual input of input parameters by the user, as well as the inability to work with complex cases of signals.

The aim of this work is to implement and apply an algorithm for extracting diagnostic information from ECG images based on convolutional neural networks to provide a reliable and reproducible digitized ECG signal form from ECG images. The results of the work can be used:

- to digitize ECG signals received from obsolete measuring instruments;
- reduce the transmission time of diagnostic information in low bandwidth networks;
- classify diagnostic information that signals atrial contractions.

2   Description of the Proposed Algorithm

The first stage of the algorithm development is the use of the U-Net neural network architecture [8] to obtain segmented zones of electrocardiogram signals. For her training, 100 images of electrocardiograms were used, which were in the public domain. The original image was marked with areas with a previously known label of the "signal" or "background" class. An example of training images and masks created for them is shown in Table 1. The training took place on an NVIDIA GeForce GTX 1650 video card with 4 GB of video memory. The results of the U-Net architecture trained on the developed dataset are shown in Fig. 1.

Table 1. Dice coefficient results

№ image	d, %	№ image	d, %	№ image	d, %
1	88.08	28	87.52	53	89.64
7	87.77	31	91.20	61	87.60
14	90.23	36	88.21	70	90.23
18	89.60	42	88.02	76	89.91
24	89.90	44	87.50	84	90.26

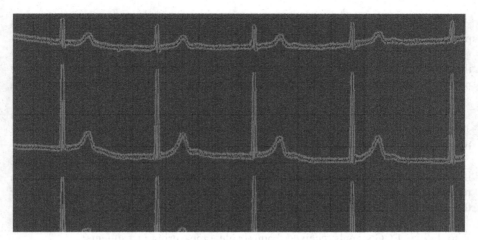

Fig. 1. The result of segmenting the ECG image using U-Net

To check the validity of the segmentation of ECG images, we use the Dice coefficient according to the formula 1:

$$d = (2 \times (A \cap B))/(|A| + |B|), \tag{1}$$

where A is the reference mask, and B is the mask obtained because of segmentation of the semi-convolutional neural network U-Net. Since the denominator is the sum of all the elements of the two masks under consideration without subtracting their connection, it is necessary to multiply the number by 2. The case when the masks completely intersect means that $|A| = |B| = |A \cap B|$ and the coefficient of the cubes will be equal to 1. Table 1 shows an excerpt from the results of calculating the Dice coefficient for images from the training database. The obtained results are justified by the fact that during segmentation, "broken pixels" are formed inside the mask, which must be removed in the course of further work of the algorithm.

The next stage of the developed algorithm is the search and digitization of millimeter lines that correspond to 0.5 mV vertically and 1 cm horizontally per cell, respectively, for further normalization of the digitized ECG signal.

This is followed by the "improvement" of the mask, namely, the closure of the "empty" areas inside the contour obtained during the operation of the fully convolutional U-Net neural network. To do this, it was decided to use the classic morphological image processing functions, namely "imclose", "imerode" and "imdilate". When recalculating the dice coefficient according to formula 1, it can be argued that the above manipulations had a beneficial effect and increased the average value by 5%.

Since the U-Net neural network architecture performs semantic segmentation of objects, namely, many objects of the same class are defined as a single mask, it is necessary to perform a separation into layers. To do this, we will use the classical algorithm for segmentation of morphological watersheds [9]. This method allows you to separate objects in the image by assigning unique values to closed contours.

The last and final stage is the digitization of the ECG signals that were segmented and layered in the previous stages, as well as the classification of the R-peak. Initially, the mask is multiplied by the original ECG image, which allows you to get rid of unnecessary information and avoid digitizing the unexplored ECG signal. Next, you need to go through all the columns of the source image to find an element corresponding to the color of the ECG signal, the value of the row of which will be written to the created variable, the data is normalized with respect to the "central" row and adjusted for the values of the original cells of the millimeter that were found earlier.

To classify the R-peak, it is necessary to take the first derivative of the received ECG signal. After performing this iteration, the result of which is shown in Fig. 2, sharp rises and falls between the Q-, R- and S-peaks are clearly recorded and allow us to determine the location of the R-peak with a greater probability than from the original signal.

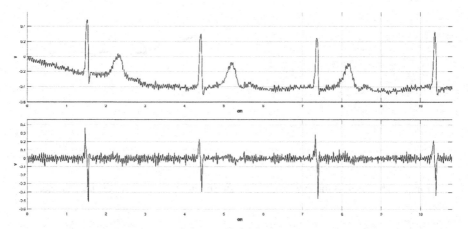

Fig. 2. The original ECG signal (top) and its first derivative (bottom)

Initially, we are looking for S-peaks that have maximum negative values. To do this, using the built-in *min* function, the minimum value of the entire first derivative of the ECG signal is found, and the elements whose values are greater than or equal to "0.25" of the calculated maximum negative value are assigned the value "0". This boundary value is chosen for reasons of filtering out minor bursts that are present on the first derivative. Then a loop is started that search for the minimum value and having found it, writes the values of the X and Y axes, while deleting the interval of 5 conventional units along the X axis before and after the found value. This iteration is necessary to prevent overwriting previously found values. Now when the minimum value is "0", the algorithm stops working.

The search for R-peaks is performed in 25 conventional units strictly to the left of the found values of S-peaks. Since there is an increase between the Q- and R-peaks in the initial ECG signal, it will be significantly amplified on the graphs of the first derivative, which allows searching using the built-in *max* function. The structure of the algorithm completely repeats the search for S-peaks.

The Q-peaks on the graphs of the first derivative are the inflection points after the R-peaks, which makes them easier to find. The algorithm calculates the coordinates and adds them to the final table containing the values of the Q-, R -, and S-peaks.

3   Results

As a result of the work, a database was obtained indicating the location of R-peaks on the initial ECG signal, as well as the QRS interval, which display information about atrial contractions and ventricular excitation processes. The results of digitized ECG signals with a demonstration of the R-peak classifier are shown in Figs. 3 and 4.

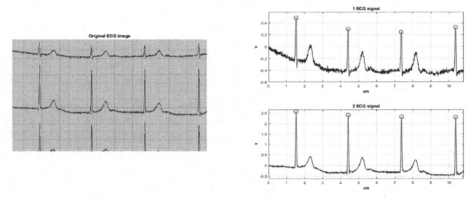

Fig. 3. The result is the extraction of diagnostic information from the ECG image

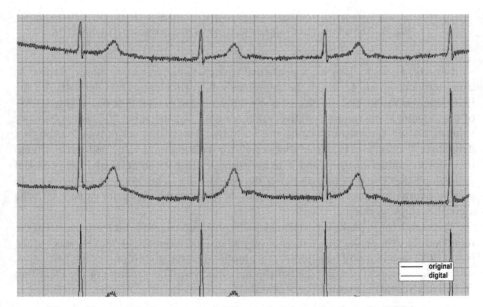

Fig. 4. The result is the extraction of diagnostic information from the ECG image

Table 2 shows an excerpt from the results of testing the R-peak classifier on test images. As you can see, the algorithm copes with the task in 97% of cases. Further modification may improve the results.

Table 2. Results of automatic extraction of diagnostic information

№ image	Real number of R-peaks	The number of R-peaks found	№ image	Real number of R-peaks	The number of R-peaks found
103	12	12	135	11	11
108	12	12	139	12	12
114	9	8	148	12	11
120	14	13	154	15	14
122	10	10	163	6	6

4 Conclusion

The proposed algorithm allows you to digitize ECG images obtained from outdated measuring devices, thereby reducing the amount of stored and sent information. The developed classifier captures R-peaks with a small margin of error, indicating to medical personnel atrial contractions.

Using the algorithm in practice will allow you to extend the service of outdated measuring devices, without losing the effectiveness of modern diagnostics.

References

1. Cardiovascular diseases (CVDs). World Health Organization official site (2017). https://www.who.int/en/news-room/fact-sheets/detail/cardiovascular-diseases-(cvds). Accessed 21 Apr 2021
2. Silva, A., de Oliveira, H.M., Lins, R.D.: Converting ECG and other paper legated biomedical maps into digital signals. In: Liu, W., Lladós, J., Ogier, J.-M. (eds.) GREC 2007. LNCS, vol. 5046, pp. 21–28. Springer, Heidelberg (2008). https://doi.org/10.1007/978-3-540-88188-9_3
3. Shuang, W., Shugang, Z., Zhen, L., Lei, H., Zhiqiang, W.: Automatic digital ECG signal extraction and normal QRS recognition from real scene ECG images. Comput. Methods Programs Biomed. **187**, 1–34 (2020)
4. Bote, J.M., Recas, J., Rincon, F., Atienza, D., Hermida, R.: A modular low-complexity ECG delineation algorithm for real-time embedded systems. IEEE J. Biomed. Health Inform. **22**(2), 429–441 (2018)
5. Gurve, D., Srivastava, A.K., Mukhopadhyay, K., Prasad, N.E., Shukla, S., Muthurajan, H.: Electrocardiogram (ECG) image processing and extraction of numerical information. Int. J. Eng. Technol. Sci. Res. (IJETSR) **3**, 2394–3386 (2016)
6. Yeh, L.-R., Chen, W.-C., Chan, H.-Y., et al.: Integrating ECG monitoring and classification via IoT and deep neural networks. Biosensors **11**, 1–12 (2021)

7. Rahman, T., et al.: COV-ECGNET: COVID-19 detection using ECG trace images with deep convolutional neural network, arXiv.org, pp. 1–24 (2021). https://arxiv.org/abs/2106.00436
8. Ronneberger, O., Fischer, P., Brox, T.: U-net: convolutional networks for biomedical image segmentation. In: Navab, N., Hornegger, J., Wells, W.M., Frangi, A.F. (eds.) MICCAI 2015. LNCS, vol. 9351, pp. 234–241. Springer, Cham (2015). https://doi.org/10.1007/978-3-319-24574-4_28
9. Kornilov, A.S., Safonov, I.V.: An overview of watershed algorithm implementations in open source libraries. J. Imaging **4**, 1–15 (2018)

Application of Wavelet Transform for ECG Processing

Veronika Malysheva[1]([⊠]) [ID], Diana Zaynullina[1] [ID], Alena Stosh[1] [ID],
and Gregory Cherepennikov[2] [ID]

[1] Peter the Great St. Petersburg Polytechnic University, Saint-Petersburg, Russia
{malysheva.vn,zajnullina.dm,stosh.ao}@edu.spbstu.ru
[2] Saint-Petersburg State University of Aerospace Instrumentation,
Saint-Petersburg, Russia

Abstract. The paper describes an algorithm for processing a cardiac signal, which can be applied to a wireless electrocardiogram (ECG) monitoring device with the ability to collect and analyze the data. The processing consists of automated noise removal, smoothing and extraction of the PQRST complex in the ECG signal using wavelet transform. The cardiac signal, due to the wavelet transform, is decomposed into approximating and detailing coefficients, which are responsible for the low-frequency and high-frequency components of the signal respectively. The cleaned signal is the reconstruction of the signal by approximating and modified detailing coefficients. PQRST waves are extracted by approximation coefficients with further search of peaks amplitudes in the purified signal.

Keywords: ECG · Wavelet transform · Filtering · PQRST-complex extraction

1 Introduction

Myocardial infarction (MI) is a clinical syndrome resulting from damage to the heart muscle when there is a discrepancy between the need for the myocardial oxygen and the possibility of its delivery [1]. In other words, MI results from necrosis caused by prolonged myocardial ischemia. Atherosclerosis is one of the most common causes of myocardial infarction. With this disease, fat deposits or plaques occur on the walls of the arteries. They can thicken, thereby reducing blood flow through the artery. If atherosclerosis affects coronary arteries, coronary heart disease occurs. With a pronounced lack of blood supply to the heart tissue, necrosis of the muscle cells of the heart can develop, leading to myocardial infarction.

In order to save the patient's life, it is necessary to recognize this state of health in time. The first signs of approaching MI for men appear in 3–7 days, while for women they can be detected a few weeks before the attack. Thus, determining the condition of the patient's body is a very important task. Timely signs

© Springer Nature Switzerland AG 2022
Y. Koucheryavy et al. (Eds.): NEW2AN 2021/ruSMART 2021, LNCS 13158, pp. 329–338, 2022.
https://doi.org/10.1007/978-3-030-97777-1_28

of MI prevent the development of coronary heart disease. Each individual symptom is not specific to a heart attack, as it can develop against the background of other diseases, but in total they can indicate a heart attack. The clinical picture of MI usually is the sudden onset of intense pain in the chest localization. Pain is usually compressive and pressing. Pain syndrome is accompanied by agitation of the patient, at the same time paleness of the skin, increased sweating, tachycardia, arrhythmia, normal or reduced blood pressure are noted [2].

Currently, myocardial infarction is considered one of the main causes of death in the population. The World Health Organization (WHO) estimates that 17.9 million people died from cardiovascular disease (CVDs) in 2016, accounting for 31% of all global deaths, of which 85% were due to coronary heart disease and stroke [3].

One of the modern methods of diagnosing CVDs is obtain an electrocardiogram, which allows you to determine heart rate indicators. This examination is the most accessible and informative, it has high diagnostic value in various pathologies.

Currently, many researchers are working on a portable device, which is capable of removing ECGs over a long period of time. An example of such a development is Savvy ECG [4,5]. This device is able of long-term monitoring of cardiac activity. Two disposable electrodes are used to remove the ECG. It is also worth mentioning a wearable wireless ECG monitoring system with dynamic transmission power control. This development also allows you to capture data for a long period of time. The device uses 3 electrodes and is capable of detecting, amplify, filter and transmit the ECG signals [6].

However, the received signal will not carry any value without its subsequent filtering and analysis. One of the simplest ways to clean the heart signal from high-frequency components (noise) is to use a frequency filter. Nevertheless, since the frequency range of the useful signal intersects with the interference frequencies, it is difficult to establish a cutoff frequency that would completely separate the ECG signal from the noise. Using a low cutoff frequency will lead to a filter that will not be able to completely eliminate the noise of the isoline (baseline), while using a high cutoff frequency will lead to distortion of the ST segment [7]. To avoid this problem and get a high-quality signal, it is necessary to create an adaptive filter that can separate interference without changing the shape of the useful signal. However, this is a very time-consuming task.

It is worth mentioning the Savitsky-Goley filter (SG) - a smoothing least squares filter [8]. It can be used to remove the effect of breathing from the isoline [9]. Savitsky-Goley filters are more effective at preserving the high-frequency components of the signal, but less effective at suppressing noise.

Another way to clear the ECG from interference is to use a wavelet transform. The wavelet analysis effectively solves the problem of getting rid of the signal from the noise components. The purpose of this work is to develop an algorithm for automated noise removal, smoothing and isolation of PQRST features in an ECG signal using a wavelet transform. One of the most convenient mathematical packages that support wavelet analysis is the Matlab development environment.

2   Method

2.1   Theory

The wavelet analysis effectively solves the problem of removing the noise components from the captured signal. In the simplest model, a noisy signal consists of a useful part of the signal and a component that represents a combination of the noise level and Gaussian white noise (a stationary random sequence that has a constant spectrum at all frequencies). The purpose of the analysis is to get rid of the noise part and restore the useful part of the signal.

The wavelet transform is based on two functions: scaling and wavelet. A filter is built for each of these functions. The signal is passed through each filter, followed by the extraction of only even elements. As a result, the signal is converted into two sequences: a sequence of approximating coefficients that represent the low-frequency elements of the signal, and a sequence of detailing coefficients. The latter describe the high-frequency part of the signal (noise).

Repeating the same operation on the approximation coefficients gives two more sets of coefficients: the approximation coefficients and the depth detail 2. The transformation can be repeated as long as the sequence of approximation coefficients has sufficient length. As a result of N-procedures, we get a wavelet transform of depth N, the output of which is N sets of detail coefficients and one set of approximation coefficients.

This transformation is reversible and linear. That allows to perform an inverse wavelet transform, as a result of which the reconstructed signal will be.

Therefore, to clear the signal, it is necessary to modify the detailing coefficients. It is also possible to consider the noise component as a signal less absolute value than valuable. The simplest way to remove noise is to equate to zero values of coefficients, which are less than a certain threshold value (cutoff frequency).

Thus, the removal of high-frequency signal components using wavelet transform consists of several actions:

1. Wavelet decomposition of the cardiac signal to a level that preserves the shape and location of the PQRST waves of the cardiac signal in the approximation coefficients;
2. Setting the type and threshold values of signal cleaning by the nature of noise in the original signal [10];
3. Influence on the detailed coefficients of the wavelet transform according to the signal cleaning conditions;
4. Signal recovery by approximation and modification coefficients over detailing coefficients.

It is important to choose the right threshold value, since the quality of signal cleaning depends on it. Setting a small threshold value leads to insignificant noise reduction, and a large value can lead to the loss of an important part of the information about the cardiac signal.

The Stein's unbiased risk estimate allows us to determine the optimal threshold value corresponding to the level of signal decomposition at which this function takes minimum values [11].

The quality of the noise reduction of the signal also depends on the method of applying thresholding. There are the following methods of threshold processing:

1. General thresholding, the threshold in this case is fixed at all levels of decomposition;
2. Multi-level thresholding, in which the threshold changes during the transition between the decomposition levels;
3. Local thresholding, using a variable threshold, which is different when moving from level to level, as well as depending on the detail coefficients at this level.

2.2   Comparison with Other Methods

In addition to cleaning the signal from noise using wavelet tools, there are other methods: Fourier transform [12], moving average method, smoothing by 3, 7 points, etc.

Wavelet transformations have almost all the advantages of Fourier transforms, and are also more informative. The disadvantage of Fourier analysis is that it does not have time resolution, that is, it is impossible to determine when different frequencies appear in the signal. And also the basis functions of the Fourier method are only the set of sines and cosines of various frequencies other than zero on the entire numerical line. Because of this, the method can only be applied to a narrow class of tasks.

The moving average method is also not the best way to remove the high-frequency component, since it does not remove the noise component, only unevenly weakens it. The same situation with smoothing on the 3rd, 7th points. In addition, these methods do not store the locations of PQRST waves in the signal, which leads to the need for additional operations.

In contrast to the above methods, the wavelet transform has the following positive qualities:

1. The wavelet transform has quite a lot of basic functions, the properties of which are different and have extensive applications;
2. The basic functions of the wavelet transform are localized in frequency and time;
3. The wavelet transform effectively gets rid of the high-frequency part of the signal, and also preserves the shape and heights of the PQRST peaks.

The disadvantage of the wavelet transform is its difficulty, but this problem is solved using programming packages.

Thus, the wavelet converter is one of the most effective methods of processing a cardiac signal, having the highest performance and capabilities compared to other methods.

2.3   Signal Filtering

One method for removing noise and smoothing the cardiac signal is to use built-in functions in the MATLAB environment [13]. For example, the function *wdencmp*, based on the decomposition using the Wavlet Dobeshi 4. The recommended threshold for signal cleaning can be obtained using the *ddencmp* function. However, using this method, the removal of high-frequency signal elements is incorrect. The shape of the isoline changes, although the correct arrangement of the PQRST complex waves for the purified signal is preserved (Fig. 1). The solution to this problem lies in changing the thresholds at different levels of decomposition or creating an adaptive wavelet [14].

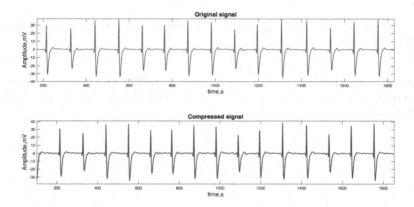

Fig. 1. Using the wdencmp function to compare the original and cleaned signal.

Another method of processing is the direct decomposition of the cardiosignal using a mother wavelet, which has a the same splash as PQRST complex. And also removing the detailing coefficients, which is responsible for the high-frequency part of the signal. After the decomposition done, a direct reconstruction is performed using the approximation coefficients to represent the purified signal.

The Daubechy Wavelet 4 is used as a basic wavelet in the work. It is possible to create an adapted wavelet by taking a QRS complex as a sample. Decomposition to the first level is considered, because the approximating coefficients for higher levels of decomposition contain insufficient information of the initial cardiac signal (Fig. 2).

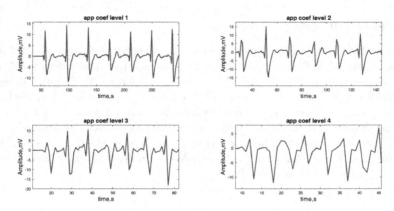

Fig. 2. Graphs of approximating coefficients in the decomposition using the Daubechy Wavelet 4.

Recovery by the first level of approximation (Fig. 3 and 4) clears the signal from noise well. At the same time, the shape and location of the peaks of the PQRST complex are preserved.

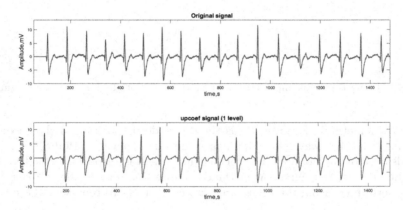

Fig. 3. Comparison of the graphs of the original signal and the restored one by the 1st level of approximation.

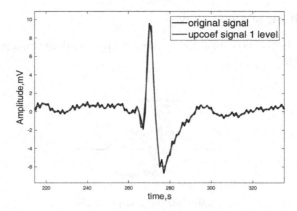

Fig. 4. Superposition of the original signal and the reconstructed one according to the 1st approximation level.

For clarity, we will output the error between the original and the restored signal at the 1st level of approximation (Fig. 5). As you can see from the graph, the error does not exceed 1.4%. This means that the shape of the PQRST complex and the height R of the peak, in particular, are preserved. This confirms the rationality of using approximating coefficients of the 1st level for signal reconstruction.

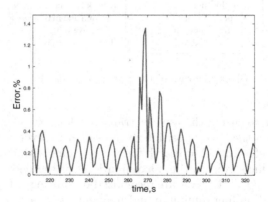

Fig. 5. The value of the error between the original and restored signal according to the 1st level of approximation.

2.4   Recognition of ECG Waves

The next task is to recognize the waves of the cardiogram, i.e. the PQRST complex (Fig. 6).

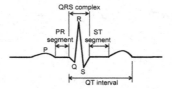

Fig. 6. PQRST-complex [15].

The main problem in identifying PQRST features is finding the exact location of the waves. The solution of this problem greatly simplifies the determination of the amplitudes and forms of the PQRST complex. To find the location of the waves, first of all, it is necessary to determine the QRS complex, which has large amplitudes. Then T and P waves are recognized, since they are the smallest of the waves of the PQRST complex (Fig. 7).

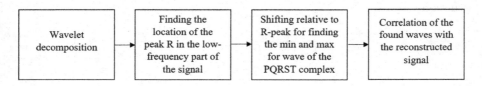

Fig. 7. Block diagram of the pqrst wave search algorithm

The algorithm for using the wavelet transform for recognizing ECG waves is performed through the decomposition of the signal to level 1, the allocation of approximation coefficients. The search for waves begins with finding the location of the peak R, which exceeds the maximum level of the decomposed signal by more than 50%. P, Q, S, T waves are recognized by shifting left and right relative to the R-peak and finding minimum and maximum for each wave, respectively. Then the found waves are correlated with the reconstructed signal (Fig. 8).

Thus, the algorithm performs automated recognition of the position of P, Q, R, S, T peaks in the ECG signal using MATLAB environment.

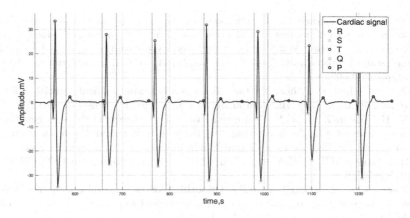

Fig. 8. Isolation of the QRS complex and peaks in the reconstructed signal.

3   Conclusions

In this paper, one of the methods of ECG processing was considered. It is based on the use of the classical theory of the wavelet transform, modernized for efficiency and ease of use. In practice, this method can be used as software for various types of wearable wireless ECG monitoring. The wavelet analysis has shown its effectiveness in filtering the cardiac signal. In the future, it is planned to take an adaptive wavelet for the characteristic surge of the PQRST complex as the base wavelet and find the optimal way to find the threshold value for removing the high-frequency components of the signal.

References

1. Liu, P., Wang, Y., Jin, Z.: Myocardial infarction. In: Jin, Z., Lu, B., Wang, Y. (eds.) Cardiac CT, pp. 9–14. Springer, Singapore (2020). https://doi.org/10.1007/978-981-15-5305-9_2
2. Roth, E.J.: Myocardial infarction. In: Kreutzer, J., DeLuca, J., Caplan, B. (eds.) Encyclopedia of Clinical Neuropsychology, p. 66. Springer, Cham (2018). https://doi.org/10.1007/978-3-319-56782-2_2192-2
3. Cardiovascular diseases (CVDs). https://www.who.int/news-room/fact-sheets/detail/cardiovascular-diseases-(cvds). Accessed 4 June 2021
4. Trobec, R., Tomašić, I., Rashkovska, A., Depolli, M., Avbelj, V.: Body Sensors and Electrocardiography. SAST, Springer, Cham (2018). https://doi.org/10.1007/978-3-319-59340-1
5. Rashkovska, A., Depolli, M., Tomašić, I., Avbelj, V., Trobec, R.: Medical-grade ECG sensor for long-term monitoring. Sensors **20**(1695), 1–17 (2020). https://doi.org/10.3390/s20061695
6. Wang, Y., Doleschel, S., Wunderlich, R., Heinen, S.: A wearable wireless ECG monitoring system with dynamic transmission power control for long-term homecare. J. Med. Syst. **39**(3), 1–10 (2015). https://doi.org/10.1007/s10916-015-0223-5

7. Lundstrom, L., Karlsson, P., Ohlsson, T.: Method and Device for Filtering out Baseline Fluctuations from an Electrocardiogram. US Patent No. 5469856 (1995)
8. Savitzky, A., Golay, M.J.E.: Smoothing and differentiation of data by simplified least squares procedures. Anal. Chem. 1627–1639 (1964). https://doi.org/10.1016/j.sigpro.2005.02.002
9. Zheng, L., Lall, C., Chen, Y.: Low-distortion baseline removal algorithm for electrocardiogram signals. In: Computing in Cardiology, pp. 769–772 (2012)
10. He, H., Wang, Z., Tan, Y.: Noise reduction of ECG signals through genetic optimized wavelet threshold filtering. In: IEEE International Conference on Computational Intelligence and Virtual Environments for Measurement Systems and Applications (CIVEMSA), pp. 1–6 (2015). https://doi.org/10.1109/CIVEMSA.2015.7158597
11. Belov, A.A., Proskurjakov, A.J.: Smoothing of time numbers on the basis of wavelet-transformation in the automate ecological monitoring systems. Methods Devices Transm. Process. Inf. 1, 21–24 (2010)
12. Touseef, Y., Saira, A., Sajid, A., Mohamed-Slim, A., Osama, A.: Fractional fourier transform based QRS complex detection. In: ECG Signal, ICASSP 2020 Virtual Conference, Slide Count: 0:14:39 (2020)
13. Official website of MathWorks. https://www.mathworks.com/. Accessed 20 May 2021
14. Analyze and synthesize signals and images using Wavelet Toolbox. https://www.mathworks.com/products/wavelet.html. Accessed 28 May 2021
15. Son, J., Park, J., Oh, H., Bhuiyan, M.Z.A., Hur, J., Kang, K.: Privacy-preserving electrocardiogram monitoring for intelligent arrhythmia detection. Sensors 17(6), 1–21 (2017). 1360

Analysis of Nonlinear Distortions of FTN Signals Transmitted Through TWT Amplifier

Ekaterina Smirnova$^{(\boxtimes)}$ and Sergey Makarov$^{(\boxtimes)}$

Peter the Great St. Petersburg Polytechnic University, St. Petersburg, Russian Federation
smirnova.en@edu.spbstu.ru, makarov@cee.spbstu.ru

Abstract. Nonlinear distortions of FTN signals conditioned by using TWT amplifier are investigated. Influence of TWT with AM-AM and AM-PM conversions on of the energy spectrum distortions and an increase in the level of energy losses is analyzed. Signal waveforms, spectrums and BER performance are obtained at the input and output TWT amplifier.

Keywords: FTN signals · Nonlinear distortion · TWT

1 Introduction

An increase in the transmission rate in a continuous channel with limited bandwidth is achieved by using FTN (Faster-Than-Nyquist Signaling) signals [1–5]. As a rule, the basic ideas of FTN signal formation are based on the use of the filter method. It is based on the formation of RRC (Root-Raised-Cosine) pulses. Temporal and spectral characteristics of such pulses depend on the amplitude-frequency characteristic shape of the RRC-filter with rounding $1 > \alpha > 0$.

The reception power efficiency is determined by the correlation properties of the transmitted random sequence of FTN signals based on RRC pulses. When the signal duration Ts is long, random intersignal interference occurs in the signal sequence and leads to energy losses [5]. In this case Ts significantly exceeds the transmission time interval of bit T of the original channel message. The random signal sequence based on the RRC pulse has a high PAPR of the radiated oscillations. PAPR is determined by the duration of the signals or the level of random intersignal interference. It also depend on the shape of the pulse and the transmission rate of the channel alphabet symbols.

Recently, the options for using FTN signals in satellite application systems are being actively considered [6]. This is especially true for structures of the second generation of modulation systems for digital broadcasting. In particular, there are many cases in satellite broadcasting systems, such as DVB S2/S2X [6–8]. These cases are related to the problem of increasing the spectral efficiency. It can be done by FTN signals. However

© Springer Nature Switzerland AG 2022
Y. Koucheryavy et al. (Eds.): NEW2AN 2021/ruSMART 2021, LNCS 13158, pp. 339–351, 2022.
https://doi.org/10.1007/978-3-030-97777-1_29

the transmission of such signals from a satellite repeater occurs with the amplifiers based on traveling wave tubes (TWT – Traveling - Wave Tube) [9, 10]. These power amplifiers introduce harmonic distortion in the transmitted signals. This is especially true for signals with a high value of PAPR. In this case, there is not only a limitation on the amplitude (AM-AM), but also on the phase of the oscillation (AM-PM). The presence of such restrictions leads to significant distortions of the energy spectrum and an increase in energy losses.

Signal distortions associated with TWT for classical types of modulation are well studied [11–14]. To study nonlinear distortions, it is proposed to use nonlinear models of amplifiers based on TWT based on a two-parameter formula for AM-AM and AM-PM [15]. At the same time it remains open to study the effect of limitation the amplitude of a random sequence of signals on the spectral and energy characteristics of signals with phase modulation and quadrature phase modulation, which have a compact frequency spectrum and intersignal interference associated with the formation conditions of such signals.

The purpose of this work is to analyze the influence of TWT with limitation in amplitude (AM-AM) and in phase (AM-PM) on of the energy spectrum distortions of a random sequence of FTN signals and an increase in the level of energy losses.

2 TWT Amplifier Nonlinear Model

Nonlinear distortion occurs when the FTN signal passes through the TWT amplifier. It leads to distortion in the signal amplitude (AM-AM) and in the phase (AM-PM). The presence of such distortions leads to the energy spectrum changes of a signal random sequence and increase in energy losses. In general terms, a relatively narrowband signal at the input of the TWT can be written in the following form:

$$y(t) = r(t) \cos(2\pi f_0 t + \psi(t)), \tag{1}$$

where $r(t)$ is envelope and $\Psi(t)$ – phase of input signal.

Then, in the nonlinear amplitude-phase model, the output signal of TWT amplifier can be represented as follows:

$$z(t) = A[r(t)] \cos\{2\pi f_0 t + \psi(t) + \Phi[r(t)]\}, \tag{2}$$

where $A[r(t)]$ – even function from $r(t)$, representing AM-AM conversion, $\Phi[r(t)]$ – even function from $r(t)$, representing AM-PM conversion.

The characteristics of a TWT amplifier are [15]:

$$A[r(t)] = A_{sat}^2 \frac{r(t)}{r^2(t) + A_{sat}^2},$$ (3)

$$\Phi[r(t)] = \frac{\pi}{3} \frac{r^2(t)}{r^2(t) + A_{sat}^2}$$ (4)

In (3, 4) the value A_{sat} is the saturation voltage at the amplifier input. Figure 1 shows the normalized TWT characteristics at $A_{sat} = 1$.

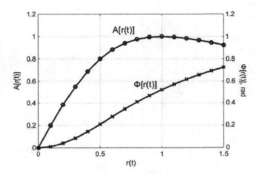

Fig. 1. Normalized TWT characteristics

It is obvious that the presence of phase distortions of the input signal should lead to distortions of the energy spectrum and correlation properties of the transmitted quadrature signals.

Let's analyze the signal distortion due to nonlinear transformation in accordance with expressions (3) and (4). The shape of the real envelope $a(t)$ of single FTN signal based on RRC can be represented as:

$$a(t) = \frac{\sin(\pi t/T)}{\pi t} \frac{\cos(\pi t\beta/T)}{1 - 4\beta^2 t^2/(T)^2}, \quad \beta = 0.3.$$ (5)

FTN signal with duration Ts = 8 T and phase modulation with angle $[+\pi/2; -\pi/2]$ and real envelope (5) passed through TWT for different values of input signal amplitude $A_{r(t)}$ with $A_{sat} = 1$ (Fig. 2):

Figure 2 shows the FTN signal shapes for the amplitude value of RRC symbol $A_{r(t)} = 1$ (Fig. 2 a, b); 0.5 (Fig. 2 c, d) and 0.25 (Fig. 2 e, f). As can be seen from the comparison of these figures, significant distortion of the FTN signal shape is observed for $A_{r(t)} = 1$ (Fig. 2 a, b). The shape of the RRC pulse changes both near the main lobe and the side lobes. This leads to a change in the correlation properties of the transmitted signals.

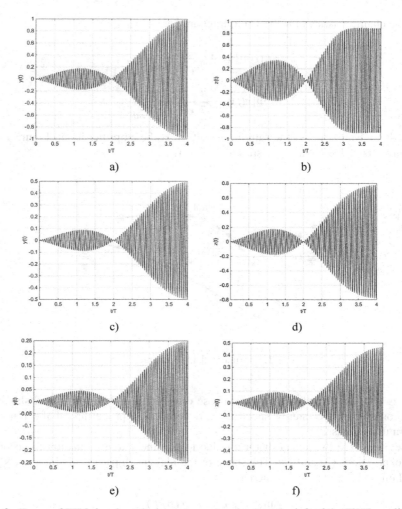

Fig. 2. Forms of FTN signals at the input (a, c, e) and output (b, d, f) of the TWT amplifier

The spectral characteristics of FTN signals at the input and output of the TWT amplifier are shown in Fig. 3. Figure 3, a shows the normalized energy spectrum of the signals at the input of the TWT amplifier, Fig. 3b and c - at the output of the TWT amplifier for $A_{r(t)} = 1$ and $A_{r(t)} = 0.25$, respectively.

As we see from Fig. 3, shape of the spectrum in the frequency band is distorted and the level of out-of-band emissions increases with $A_{r(t)} = 1$. For example, when offset is 6/T, the level of out-of-band emissions increases by 15 dB. With a small amplitude $A_{r(t)} = 0.25$ (Fig. 3, c), the shape of the energy spectrum in the frequency band practically does not change, but the level of out-of-band emissions increases by 10 dB.

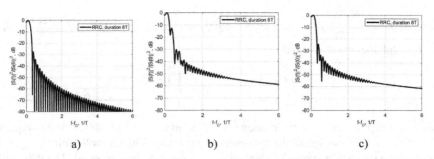

Fig. 3. Energy spectrum of FTN signals at the input (a) and output of the TWT amplifier (b, c)

Figure 4 shows the shapes of the FTN signal phase change for different values $A_{r(t)}$ = 1 (Fig. 4, a) and $A_{r(t)}$ = 0.25 (Fig. 4, b). As can be seen from these figures, a total signal delay of about 0.15 T is observed and it does not depend on the amplitude value. At a high value $A_{r(t)}$ = 1, additional phase modulation appears due to the non-linear character of the signal amplification.

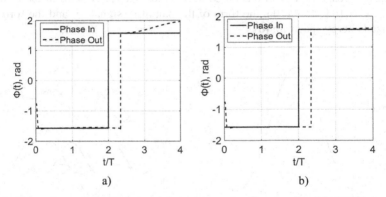

Fig. 4. Phase shape of the FTN signal at the input (a) and output (b) of the TWT amplifier

The effects of complex waveform distortion considered on single FTN signals. Consider these distortions on a sequence of FTN signals with offset quadrature phase shift keying (OQPSK).

3 Quadrature FTN Signals

It is convenient to represent a sequence of N such signals with amplitude and envelope $a(t)$ in the following form:

$$y(t) = y_1(t) - y_2(t), \tag{6}$$

$$y_1(t) = (A_0/\sqrt{2})u_1(t)\cos(\omega_0 t + \varphi_0), \quad y_2(t) = (A_0/\sqrt{2})u_2(t)\sin(\omega_0 t + \varphi_0),$$

where $u_1(t) = \sum_{k=0}^{(N-1)/2} a(t - 2kT)d_r^{(2k)}$, $u_2(t) = \sum_{k=0}^{(N-1)/2} a(t - 2kT - T)d_r^{(2k+1)}$, $d_r^{(k)}$-

channel alphabet symbol equal to

$$d_r^{(k)} = \begin{cases} 1, r = 1 \\ -1, r = 2 \end{cases}, \quad \psi_T(t) = \begin{cases} 1 - 0 < t < T \\ 0 - T < t, t < 0 \end{cases}$$

and the initial phase of the high-frequency oscillation is $\varphi_0 = \pi/4$. Note that the sequence (6) is divided into two quadrature streams of even and odd symbols, following at the transmission rate. Each symbol is transmitted at a doubled time interval. The RRC pulse $a(t)$ can be written as:

$$a(t) = \frac{\sin(\pi t/2T)}{\pi t} \frac{\cos(\pi t \beta/2T)}{1 - 4\beta^2 t^2/(2T)^2}, \quad \beta = 0.3. \tag{7}$$

The function exists on the time interval $-LT/2 < t < LT/2$ ($L = 2.4,...$) and is equal to zero on all other time intervals. Figure 5 shows the waveforms of $a(t)$, the waveforms of RRC pulses in each quadrature channel of an FTN signal with OQPSK modulation (b), which correspond to the transmitted binary message for $N = 10$ of the form: $(-1; 1; 1; -1; -1; 1; 1; 1; -1; 1)$, the form of the bandpass signal (c) and the form of the normalized energy spectrum (d).

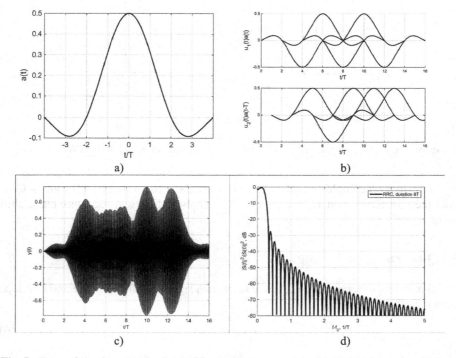

Fig. 5. Form of envelope (a), the form of the quadrature components (b), bandpass signal (c) and the form of the energy spectrum (d) for the duration Ts = 8 T

Consider the parameters of the PAPR and the frequency band occupied by FTN signals with OQPSK modulation for different signal durations. Let us determine the PAPR of sequence (6), averaged over all possible j-th realizations with average power $P_{average}$ and peak power P_{max}, as follows:

$$\max\{PAPR\} = \max\{P_{max}/P_{average}\}$$

$$= \max\left\{\max_{j}\left\{\left|y^{(j)}(t)\right|^2\right\}\middle/\frac{1}{2^N}\sum_{j=1}^{2^N}\int_{0}^{(N-1)T+LT}\left|y^{(j)}(t)\right|^2 dt\right\} \quad (8)$$

Figure 6 illustrates PAPR dependence of signal duration Ts with N = 1000.

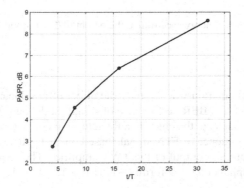

Fig. 6. PAPR of the signal duration dependence

It can be seen from Fig. 6 PAPR increases with an increase in the duration of FTN signals with OQPSK modulation. So, for at Ts = 4 T, the PAPR is 2.7 dB, and at Ts = 32 T, it is 8.6 dB.

The presence of nonlinear distortions leads to the energy spectrum changes of a signal and increase in energy losses. Figure 7 shows the shapes of the energy spectrum (out-of-band emission decay curves plotted from the maximum values $|S(f)|^2/|S(0)|^2$).

It can be seen that the appearance of AM-AM and AM-PM distortions leads to an increase in the level of out-of-band emission. This growth is observed in the range of values $|S(f)|^2/|S(0)|^2$ below -20 dB. However, with increasing signal duration, the influence of the effect of nonlinear signal distortion on the form of the energy spectrum decreases.

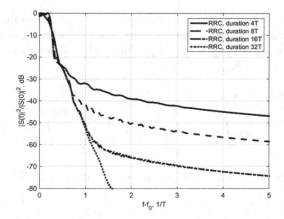

Fig. 7. Energy spectrum at the output of TWT amplifier

4 Simulation

The purpose of the simulation was to study the effect of nonlinearity on the temporal, spectral characteristics and BER perfomance of signals at the output of the TWT amplifier. First of all, let us analyze the change in the temporal characteristics at the output of the TWT amplifier. Sequence of FTN signals based on RRC pulses. Figure 8 shows the waveforms at the input and output of the TWT amplifier. The sequence of symbols of the channel binary alphabet has the form: $(-1; 1; 1; -1; -1; 1; 1; 1; -1; 1)$ at $A_{sat} = 1$.

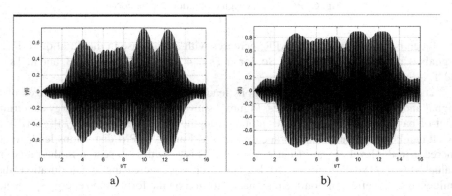

a)   b)

Fig. 8. Signal waveforms at the input (a) and output (b) of the TWT amplifier for $T_S = 8\,T$

As can be seen from Fig. 8, at the output of the TWT amplifier there is a near-constant level of the amplitude of the radiated oscillation. Figure 9 shows the shapes of the real and imaginary parts (Fig. 9, a and b) of the complex envelope of the transmitted signal at the output of the TWT amplifier and the phase change of the oscillation (Fig. 9, c). In these figures, the solid lines represent the waveforms at the input and the dashed lines at the output of the TWT amplifier.

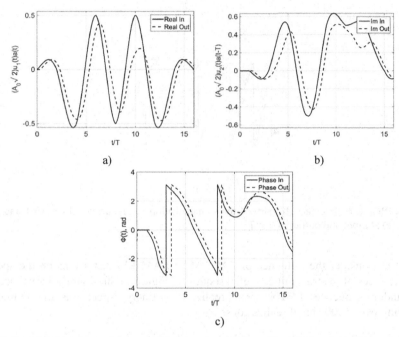

Fig. 9. Real (a), imaginary (b) parts of the signal envelope at Ts = 8 T and the phase change (c) at input and output of TWT

Figure 10 shows the shapes of the real (Fig. 10, a) and imaginary (Fig. 10, b) parts and phase change (Fig. 10, c) of signal obtained as a result of simulation. Transmitted signal has duration Ts = 16 T and an envelope of the form (7). In this case, the sequence of symbols of the channel binary alphabet has the form corresponded to the previous example.

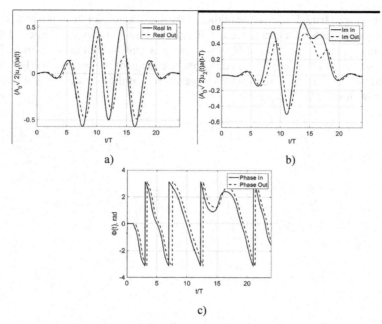

Fig. 10. Real (a), imaginary (b) parts of the signal envelope with duration Ts = 16 T and phase change (c) at input and output of TWT

Let us consider the influence of AM-AM and AM-PM distortions on the spectral characteristics of the transmitted signal sequence. Figure 11 shows the energy spectrum of a random sequence of FTN signals realizations. Energy spectrums are obtained by averaging over 1000 signal realizations.

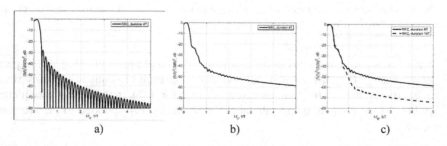

Fig. 11. Energy spectrum of the signal at the input (a) and at output of TWT amplifier (b, c)

Figure 11, a shows the shape of the energy spectrum of a sequence of quadrature signals with an envelope of the form (7) with duration Ts = 8 T at the input of TWT. Figure 11, b shows the shape of the energy spectrum of these signals at the output of TWT. For comparison, Fig. 11, c shows the shapes of the energy spectrum of signals with a duration of Ts = 8 T and Ts = 16 T. Due to the nonlinear nature of the amplitude and phase characteristics of the TWT amplifier, the levels of out-of-band emissions significantly increase. Moreover, this growth is most significant in the region of the occupied frequency band (near the frequency offset by 1/T). As expected, an increase in the signal duration from Ts = 8 T to Ts = 16 T leads to a slight decrease in the level of out-of-band emissions within 1–2%.

Consider the BER performance of OQPSK-FTN signals with AWGN channel. As a transmission channel, a channel with additive Gaussian noise (AWGN) with an average power spectral density $N_0/2$ is used. The demodulator implements the optimal algorithm of element-wise coherent reception. The calculation of the probability of erroneous reception occurs in a synchronous mode. For this, at least 10,000 implementations are used. Figure 12 shows the BER performance. Figure 12, a curves are shown for the case of the absence of a nonlinear amplifier, and in Fig. 12, b - with AM-AM and AM-PM distortions at the output of the TWT amplifier for a $A_{sat} = 1$. Demodulation algorithm is algorithm of coherent element-wise reception of signals with an analysis interval equal to Ts.

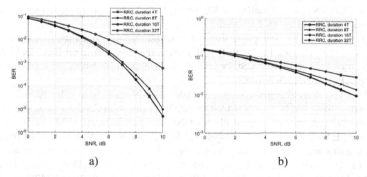

a)   b)

Fig. 12. BER perfomance for FTN signals with OQPSK modulation based on RRC pulses

Comparing the dependences of the error probability in Fig. 12, a and b, we can conclude that the presence of nonlinear effects with amplitude limitation of oscillations leads to BER performance degradation. The magnitude of these energy losses reaches 6–7 dB with the error probability equal to 10^{-2}.

5 Conclusion

The influence of a TWT amplifier with AM-AM and AM-PM distortions on the energy spectrum changes and an increase in the level of energy losses of FTN signals based on RRC pulses are analyzed.

It is shown that parasitic amplitude and phase modulation occurs at the output of the TWT amplifier. The spectral characteristics of random signal sequences degrade by these effects. With signal amplitude value equal 1 the spectrum shape is distorted and the level of out-of-band emissions increases for binary phase modulation. The level of out-of-band emissions increases by 15 dB at offset by 6/T. With a small signal amplitude value equal 0.25 the shape of the energy spectrum in the frequency band practically does not change, but the level of out-of-band emissions increases by 10 dB.

Due to the nonlinear amplitude and phase characteristics of the TWT amplifier, OOBE level increase by more than 20 dB at 6/T offset for OQPSK modulation.

The presence of TWT amplifier distortions of the phase and amplitude of a random sequence of signals leads to an increase in energy losses. The magnitude of these energy losses reaches 6–7 dB with the error probability equal to 10^{-2}.

The results of the work were obtained with the support of the grant of Russian Science Foundation № 21-71-10,007.

References

1. Makarov, S.B., et al.: Optimizing the shape of Faster-Than-Nyquist (FTN) signals with the constraint on energy concentration in the occupied frequency bandwidth. IEEE Access **8**, 130082–130093 (2020). https://doi.org/10.1109/ACCESS.2020.3009213
2. Li, Q., Gong, F.-K., Song, P.-Y., Li, G., Zhai, S.-H.: Joint channel estimation and precoding for faster-than-Nyquist signaling. IEEE Trans. Veh. Technol. **69**(11), 13139–13147 (2020). https://doi.org/10.1109/TVT.2020.3021065
3. Gelgor, A., Gelgor, T.: New pulse shapes for partial response signaling to outperform faster-than-Nyquist signalling. In: 2019 IEEE International Conference on Electrical Engineering and Photonics (EExPolytech), St. Petersburg, Russia, pp. 144–148 (2019). https://doi.org/10.1109/EExPolytech.2019.8906884
4. Kang, W., Wu, Z.: Probabilistic shaping in faster-than-Nyquist system. In: 2020 IEEE Wireless Communications and Networking Conference Workshops (WCNCW), Seoul, Korea (South), pp. 1–6 (2020). https://doi.org/10.1109/WCNCW48565.2020.9124739
5. Smirnova, E.N., Makarov, S.B., Zavjalov, S.V., Polozhintsev, B.: Influence of the amplitude limitation of signals with the sin(x)/x envelope on the spectral and energy characteristics. In: 2020 IEEE International Conference on Electrical Engineering and Photonics (EExPolytech), pp. 164–167 (2020). https://doi.org/10.1109/EExPolytech50912.2020.9243855
6. Puzko, D., Batov, Y., Gelgor, A., Tkachenko, D., Angueira, P., Montalban, J.: Evaluation of finite discrete RRC-pulse parameters to simulate DVB-S2 with LDM. In: 2019 IEEE International Conference on Electrical Engineering and Photonics (EExPolytech), St. Petersburg, Russia, pp. 140–143 (2019). https://doi.org/10.1109/EExPolytech.2019.8906847
7. ETSI EN 302 307-1: Digital Video Broadcasting (DVB); Second generation framing structure, channel coding and modulation systems for Broadcasting, Interactive Services, News Gathering and other broadband satellite applications; Part 1: DVB-S2
8. ETSI EN 302 307-2: Digital Video Broadcasting (DVB); Second generation framing structure, channel coding and modulation systems for Broadcasting, Interactive Services, News Gathering and other broadband satellite applications; Part 2: DVB-S2 Extensions (DVBS2X)
9. Ghosh, S.K.: Travelling-wave tubes for space application: present and future. In: 2020 URSI Regional Conference on Radio Science (URSI-RCRS), Varanasi, India, pp. 1–3 (2020). https://doi.org/10.23919/URSIRCRS49211.2020.9113591
10. Nguyen, K.T., et al.: Oscillation characteristics in waveguide-based TWT amplifiers. In: 2015 IEEE International Vacuum Electronics Conference (IVEC), Beijing, pp. 1–2 (2015). https://doi.org/10.1109/IVEC.2015.7223810
11. Santella, G., Mazzenga, F.: A hybrid analytical-simulation procedure for performance evaluation in M-QAM-OFDM schemes in presence of nonlinear distortions. IEEE Trans. Veh. Technol. **47**(1), 142–151 (1998). https://doi.org/10.1109/25.661041

12. Chini, A., Wu, Y., El-Tanany, M., Mahmoud, S.: Hardware nonlinearities in digital TV broadcasting using OFDM modulation. IEEE Trans. Broadcasting **44**(1), 12–21 (1998). https://doi.org/10.1109/11.713052
13. Dardari, D., Tralli, V., Vaccari, A.: A theoretical characterization of nonlinear distortion effects in OFDM systems. IEEE Trans. Commun. **48**(10), 1755–1764 (2000). https://doi.org/10.1109/26.871400
14. Zou, L., Jiang, M., Zhao, C., He, Y., Zhu, D., Huang, Q.: BLDnet: robust learning-based detection for high-order QAM with nonlinear distortion. In: 2020 IEEE/CIC International Conference on Communications in China (ICCC), pp. 262–266 (2020). https://doi.org/10.1109/ICCC49849.2020.9238959
15. Saleh, A.A.M.: Frequency-independent and frequency-dependent nonlinear models of TWT amplifiers. IEEE Trans. Commun. **29**(11), 1715–1720 (1981). https://doi.org/10.1109/TCOM.1981.1094911

Selecting a Receiver for Wideband Spectrum Sensing in Cognitive Radio Systems Based on an Assessment of the Signal Environment Complexity

Alexey S. Podstrigaev[1]([✉]) [iD], Andrey V. Smolyakov[1] [iD], Vladimir P. Likhachev[2], Sergei E. Efimov[3] [iD], and Vadim V. Davydov[4,5]

[1] Saint Petersburg Electrotechnical University "LETI", St. Petersburg, Russia
ap0d@ya.ru
[2] Zhukovsky-Gagarin Air Force Academy, Voronezh, Russia
[3] Saint Petersburg State University of Aerospace Instrumentation, Saint Petersburg, Russia
[4] Peter the Great Saint Petersburg Polytechnic University, St. Petersburg 195251, Russia
[5] The Bonch-Bruevich Saint - Petersburg State University
of Telecommunications, Saint Petersburg 193232, Russia

Abstract. A matrix receiver and a sub-Nyquist receiver are shown to provide the processing of the largest number of time-superimposed pulses. In practice, still, the number of pulses' overlaps depends on the signal environment complexity. Besides, from the point of view of the wideband analyzer, random factors determine this environment. Therefore, to select the receiver type suitable for the developed wideband analyzer (WBA), a quantitative indicator of the signal environment complexity is required. In this paper, the probability of overlap not less than M pulses is proposed as such an indicator. The expressions obtained for calculating this probability allowed to plot the probability of overlapping in time of M and more pulses against the number of radio emission sources at different duty-off factors of the pulse sequences emitted the sources. To ease the attribution of obtained probabilities to actual operating conditions of the WBA, the paper provides the numbers of radars of various purposes which can form a signal environment with given complexity. The paper also gives recommendations on selecting an optimal receiver for the developed wideband analyzer considering implementation complexity and the desired ratio overlapped pulses processing efficiency. The latter is understood to be a ration of successfully processed overlapped pulses under predicted analyzer's operational conditions characterized by types and numbers of radio emission sources. To summarize, the presented results make it possible to select a receiver for the wideband spectrum sensing depending on the potential complexity of the signal environment.

Keywords: Cognitive radio system · Wideband spectrum sensing · Sub-Nyquist receiver · Undersampling receiver · Matrix receiver · Multichannel receiver · Complex signal environment · Complex electronic environment · Wideband analyzer · Broadband receiver · Software-defined radio

© Springer Nature Switzerland AG 2022
Y. Koucheryavy et al. (Eds.): NEW2AN 2021/ruSMART 2021, LNCS 13158, pp. 352–364, 2022.
https://doi.org/10.1007/978-3-030-97777-1_30

1 Introduction

Cognitive radio (CR) technology improves radio spectrum utilization by providing users with dynamic access to its unused parts [1–5]. As a result, the tasks of organizing intelligent networks, public safety, broadband cellular communications, medicine, and radar are more effectively solved [6–16]. And the efficiency of spectrum utilization is crucial in complex signal environments with the overloaded ether [17–20]. For searching of a "spectrum hole", defined as a frequency band not being used at time and place of CR system operation, spectral analysis is performed using wideband analyzers (WBA) [3].

Six main types of receivers are used for wideband spectrum sensing (WSS). Table 1 presents a qualitative assessment of the characteristics of these receivers. In the table P_0 is the sensitivity, Δf_{inst} is the instantaneous processing bandwidth, and DSP is digital signal processing. A more detailed description of the receivers can be found in, e.g. [21–25], and [26–33] provide an overview of narrowband and broadband processing technologies used in CR systems with different receivers.

Table 1 Characteristics of receivers used for WBA

Receiver type	P_0	Δf_{inst}	Overlapped pulses processing	DSP complexity	Weight and dimensions	Cost
Scanning	High	Low	Narrow bandwidth	Avg	Medium	Avg
Multichannel	High	High	Possible	Very high	Very high	High
Matrix	Avg	High	Difficult	Avg	High	High
IFM receiver	Below avg	High	Missing	Low	High	Avg
Single-bit ADC	Below avg	High	Missing	Avg	Low	Low
Sub-Nyquist	Avg	High	Possible	High	Medium	Avg

Given the rapid development of CR, the number of users will increase in the future, which means that the WBAs will need to expand their frequency range. However, scanning a wide frequency band will cause a delay in finding a spectrum hole. Therefore, promising WBA should have a wide instantaneous processing bandwidth (multiband sensing mode), which is also noted, for example, in [29–35]. But, with the expansion of the analysis band, the number of possible overlaps of the emitted pulses increases [36–38].

According to the data presented in Table 1, receivers of only three types allow processing of overlapped pulses, namely multichannel, matrix (multi-stage multichannel), and a sub-Nyquist receiver. Therefore, it is advisable to use the remaining receivers to detect and then process powerful signals against the background of weak interference, overlapped short-pulse signals with a large duty-off factor, or in the absence of interfering signals. However, these three receiver types also have their features when processing overlapped pulses. So, in the matrix receiver, processing such pulses is possible only in implementation with high design complexity [39, 40]. For a sub-Nyquist receiver increasing the number of overlaps leads to an increase in processing errors [41–43]. A multichannel receiver has difficulties transmitting and processing significant traffic of pulse descriptor words (PDW) from all channels. Additionally, the processing of signal fragments received by different channels is particularly complicated in such a receiver. Furthermore, the processing complexity dramatically increases if many such signals are being received simultaneously.

Thus, many receivers and processing technologies are known to be suitable for CR systems. At the same time, the signal environment complexity from the point of view of the WBA's operation effectiveness has not yet been evaluated. Therefore, this paper aims to substantiate the criteria for selecting the receiver for a WSS of the CR system under development based on an assessment of the potential signal environment complexity.

2 Receiver Channel Capacity

Receivers with a wide instantaneous analysis bandwidth are often yield frequency measurement ambiguity that occurs when pulses overlap in a broadband radio frontend. It is this ambiguity that limits the throughput of receivers in terms of the number of simultaneously processed pulses.

Matrix receiver, supplemented by the broadband fiber-optic delay line at its input [44] or other means of reducing the frequency measurement ambiguity [39, 40, 45], allows to handle up to 2...3 overlapped pulses. However, this makes the receiver more complex and expensive.

For a sub-Nyquist receiver, the maximum number of simultaneously transmitted PDWs $L_{\text{ptx } max}$ can be defined as

$$L_{\text{ptx } max} = v_b T_{\text{p min}}/N_y, \tag{1}$$

where v_b is the effective data transfer rate (without the communication channel overhead), N_y – size of the one PDW, $T_{\text{p min}}$ is the minimum pulse repetition interval $\lfloor \ \rfloor$ – operation of rounding downward.

For $N_y = 100$ bits, $T_{\text{p min}} = 1$ us, and $v_b = 800$ Mbit/s (for a Gigabit Ethernet interface (1000BASE-X) with an overhead of 20%), according to (1), L_{ptxmax} equals 8.

However, in practice, the sub-Nyquist receiver throughput can be limited both by the throughput of the FPGA transceivers and by the number of pulses overlaps, at which the processing errors rate exceeds the acceptable threshold. The throughput of modern systems FPGA's high-speed serial transceivers [46] allows the processing of up to 3...5 overlapped pulses with the error rate remaining sufficiently low.

As for the multichannel receiver, in theory, it can process an arbitrarily large number of overlapped pulses. In practice, though, there is a limit primarily defined by the number of receiving channels, so a tradeoff between this number and the implementation complexity is to be found. Thus, on the one hand, the increase in the number of channels increases both the design complexity (and, as a result, cost, mass, and dimensions) and the pulse deinterleaving algorithm's complexity. On the other hand, such an increase narrows each channel's frequency band, which, with all other things being equal, improves the frequency resolution (when using spectral analysis) and reduces the probability of pulses overlap in each channel.

If we assume that the CR system's bandwidth is approximately 1 GHz [2, 47], and the bandwidth of each channel is 100 MHz, then the number of processed overlapped pulses will be at least 10 (equals to the number of channels). However, due to the above-described limitations of Gigabit Ethernet, the throughput will be limited to 8 pulses.

Thus, we further assume that the throughput of the matrix receiver is up to 2…3, the sub-Nyquist receiver is up to 3…5, and the multichannel receiver is up to 8 superimposed pulses. However, it is unknown at what complexity of the signal environment and what probability this or that number of overlaps occurs.

3 Determining the Probability of Pulse Overlap

Let assume that one source generates only one pulse sequence. Then the probability of time-overlap of pulses from the different sequences emitted by N sources is a function of the parameters of the corresponding pulse sequences (Fig. 1):

$$P = f\left(\tau_1, \ldots \tau_N, T_1 \ldots, T_N, \tau_1', \ldots \tau_N', T_1' \ldots, T_N', t_{01}, \ldots t_{0N}\right), \qquad (2)$$

where τ_n – nth source's pulse width $\left(n = \overline{1, N}\right)$, T_n is the nth source's pulse repetition interval, τ_n' – duration of the nth source's pulse burst emitted in the direction of the WBA, T_n' – repetition interval of the nth source's burst emitted in the direction of the WBA, t_{0n} – the moment of the of nth source's radiation start.

The sources signal parameter vectors $\left(\tau_n, T_n, \tau_n', T_n', t_{0n}\right)$ are independent, but the joint probability density functions of vectors' elements are unknown. The nature of the functional dependence itself, which relates probability (2) to the specified parameters of the source signals, is also unknown. This makes it impossible to determine the statistical characteristics of probability (2).

When predicting a potential signal environment, the detailed description of the source signal structure in a particular mode of operation is usually unknown. Therefore, to make it possible to determine the probability P, it is advisable to characterize the sources signal by its duty-on factor

$$\overline{R}_n = \frac{\overline{\tau_n'}}{\overline{T_n'}} \cdot \frac{\overline{\tau_n}}{\overline{T_n}}. \qquad (3)$$

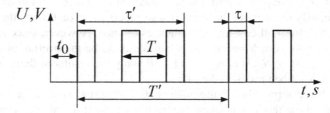

Fig. 1. Structure of the pulse sequence of a single source

This value is inversely proportional to the duty-off factor of the source signal $\overline{S_n} = 1/\overline{R_n}$.

If the pulses are emitted in bursts and a space scan is performed, the average duty-on factor of the sequence τ_n'/T_n' depends on the space scanning algorithm.

Thus, the probability function of combining sources pulses in time (2) can be represented as

$$P = f(R_1, \ldots, R_N, t_{01}, \ldots, t_{0N}). \tag{4}$$

Nevertheless, even with all the assumptions made, it is still difficult to determine an explicit analytical relation for the probability P since the probability density functions of the emission start moments and the nature of the function f are unknown.

Thus, an analytical description of the probability P as a function of random variables is not possible. Therefore, there is a need to solve this problem in other ways.

4 Methods

The first and obvious way to determine the probability of pulse overlap is to repeatedly simulate the simultaneous operation of several sources with different vectors $\overrightarrow{t_0}$ and average the obtained results. The time required to complete such a simulation can be approximated as

$$T_{\text{sim}} \approx T_{\text{sim0}} q^{-(N-1)}, \tag{5}$$

where q is the number of variations in the emission start moments, N is the number of considered sources, T_{sim0} is the time of one simulation with a fixed combination of the emission start moments.

To correctly determine the desired probability, T_{sim0} must significantly exceed the maximum period of the simulated sequences, defined as $(1/\max\{R_n\})\tau_x$, where τ_x is an arbitrary single radiation period assumed to be the same for all sources. It can be seen from (5) that the simulation algorithm has complexity $O(q^N)$. That is the time required for simulation increases rapidly both with the increasing complexity of the signal environment under consideration and with increasing requirements for the accuracy of the analysis. This makes it difficult to apply simulation in analyzing a complex signal environment (CSE), for which signal overlaps are usual [36–38].

The second way to solve the problem is to consider the desired probability as the probability of some random event. Most papers use this method [48–51] consider the problem of pulse overlap concerning signal interception. Since all conditions must be met simultaneously to intercept the signal, these papers focus on finding the probability of pulses overlap from all considered sequences at once. However, since in this paper the event of overlap from N sequences is considered to be the overlap of any number of pulses M ($2 \leq M \leq N$), it is not possible to apply the results of these works to the solution of the described problem directly.

However, basic approaches to the mathematical description of pulse sequences are universal. Thus, the authors of the classic paper in the field of signal interception analysis [48] interpret the average duty-on factor R_n as the probability of detecting a pulse from the nth source at any point in its duration at a random moment. If we accept this interpretation, the problem of determining the probability of pulses from several sequences time-overlap can be formulated as the problem of determining the probability of a random event consisting in the simultaneous occurrence of two or more events out of N possible ones with probabilities R_n, $n = \overline{1, N}$. If a set of similar sources forms the signal environment under consideration, we can assume that all average duty-on factors R_n are approximately the same and equal to R. In this case, the overlap probability of M or more pulses from N identical sources can be determined using the Bernoulli formula:

$$P_M = 1 - \sum_{m=0}^{M-1} P'_m = 1 - \sum_{m=0}^{M-1} C_N^m R^m (1 - R)^{N-m}, \qquad (6)$$

where P'_m are the overlap probabilities of exactly m pulses from N, and C_N^m are the binomial coefficients.

Since digital processing of received signals is performed over several samples, rather than one at a time, short-term pulse overlaps may not pose a threat to the correctness of its results. In this case, when calculating the probability (6), it is possible to introduce a limit on the minimum allowable overlap duration τ_o by modifying the probabilities R_n

$$R'_n = \frac{\tau'_n}{T'_n} \frac{(\tau_n - \tau_o)}{\overline{T_n}}. \qquad (7)$$

The complexity of calculating the required probability (6) is $O(N^2)$.

Because the required expression is obtained now, instead of the average duty-on factors R_n we will use more familiar duty-off factors $\overline{S_n} = 1/R_n$.

5   Signal Environment Modelling

A review of reference materials about radars of the International Telecommunication Union (ITU) was performed to determine the typical sources' signals' duty-off factors. The materials contain characteristics of typical radars operating in the frequency range from 30 MHz to 36 GHz. Radars are used widely nowadays, and they are a powerful source of interference, so we use them as an example in this paper. A summary of the review results is presented in Table 2.

Table 2. Signals duty-off factors of radars of various purposes

Purpose of the radar station	Duty-off factor S
Target tracking	$10^1 \ldots 10^2$
Surveillance and search	$10^2 \ldots 10^4$
Navigation	$10^3 \ldots 10^5$

Following (6), the probability P_M of overlap in time M and more pulses ($M = 3 \ldots 5$) was plotted against the number N of radio emission sources. The graphs were obtained for different duty-off factors S (Fig. 2). The graphs show curves corresponding to the radar stations of various purposes (Table 2).

6 Criteria for the Signal Environment Complexity

If the acceptable number of pulse overlaps is exceeded, errors and ambiguities arise in determining the time-frequency parameters and the type of intra-pulse modulation. Moreover, errors can occur for multiple signals at once. Practice shows that errors significant for secondary processing occur at approximately $P_M \geq 10\%$ (in Fig. 2, this boundary is marked by a dashed-dotted line with two dots). Such an overlap probability and a short observation time result in noticeable errors in the definition and classification of the signal preventing their automatic recognition.

Dependencies presented in Fig. 2 assume that all considered signals have the same duty-off factor, each source emits only one pulse sequence, and the emission starts moments are distributed uniformly.

Accordingly, from the point of view of wideband signal analysis, the following criteria for the signal environment complexity can be formulated:

for $P_M < 10\%$ at $M \geq 2$ the complexity is low, so almost any of the known receiver's schemes can be used, including those with a narrow instantaneous analysis bandwidth [21–24];

for $P_M \geq 10\%$ if $2 \leq M \leq 3$ and $P_M < 10\%$ when $M > 3$ the complexity is medium; the use of a matrix receiver is advised [25, 39, 40, 52–54];

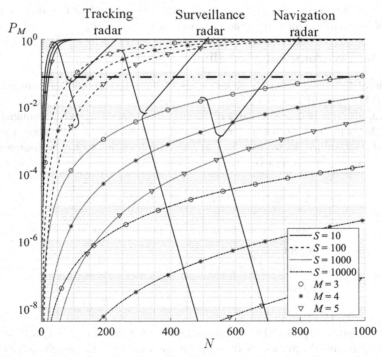

Fig. 2. The probability of overlapping in time M or more pulses depending on the number of sources N for a different duty-off factors S of pulse sequences

for $P_M \geq 10\%$ when $4 \leq M \leq 5$ and $P_M < 10\%$ when $M > 5$ the complexity is high; the use of the sub-Nyquist receiver is advised [35, 41, 43, 55];

For $P_M \geq 10\%$ and $M \geq 6$ complexity is very high; either the multichannel receiver has to be used [21, 22, 40], or a further increase of the efficiency of other receivers is needed.

7 Criteria for Selecting a Receiver for WSS

Based on the above-described criteria and the modelling results (Fig. 2), the numbers of radars of various purposes which can form a signal environment with given complexity are calculated and presented in Table 3. In practice, these data can be used to assess the complexity of the signal environment and select the optimal receiver for the developed WBA. The receiver in this case will be optimal in terms of processing efficiency (Fig. 2) and implementation complexity (Table 1).

Table 3. Relationship between the signal environment complexity, its composition, and the optimal receiver for the WSS

The signal environment complexity	Complexity criteria	Radar forming the environment			Optimal receiver
		Purpose	S	Quantity	
Low	$P_M < 10\%$ at $M \geq 2$	Tracking	10^1	Less than 6	Any
			10^2	Less than 54	
		Surveillance	10^3	Less than 533	
			10^4	Much more than 4000	
		Navigation			
Avg	$P_M \geq 10\%$ at $2 \leq M \leq 3$ and $P_M < 10\%$ at $M > 3$	Tracking	10^1	6 … 18	Matrix
			10^2	54…175	
		Surveillance	10^3	533…1745	
High	$P_M \geq 10\%$ at $4 \leq M \leq 5$ and $P_M < 10\%$ at $M > 5$	Tracking	10^1	19 … 32	Sub-Nyquist
			10^2	176…316	
		Surveillance	10^3	1746…3152	
Very high	$P_M \geq 10\%$ at $M \geq 6$	Tracking	10^1	More than 32	Multi-channel

(*continued*)

Table 3. (*continued*)

The signal environment complexity	Complexity criteria	Radar forming the environment			Optimal receiver
		Purpose	S	Quantity	
			10^2	More than 316	
		Surveillance	10^3	More than 3152	

As can be seen from Table 3, any of the typical schemes can be used in CR system's WBA if the signal environment complexity is low. With higher complexity, it is advisable to use a matrix receiver, a sub-Nyquist receiver, or a multichannel receiver depending on the expected number of overlapped pulses. It is worth noting that in all three receivers operating frequency range can be set programmatically, which is cohesive with the CR concept.

Figure 2 and Table 3 also show that if the CSE is formed to a greater extent by signals from navigation radars, then there is no threat to the stability of the WBA operation: even with 100 navigation radars located in the operation area, the probability of their pulses overlap does not exceed 0.01%. If the CSE is formed by tracking radars, the situation worsens significantly: even with 10...20 functioning radars, the pulses overlap probability may exceed 10%.

It can be concluded from the given environment's examples that existing receivers allow WBA to work reliably even in a very saturated signal environment. Nevertheless, it is still reasonable to further develop the reception methods to increase their throughput, defined as the number of overlapped pulses being processed.

8   Conclusion

All receivers have physical limitations on the number of simultaneously processed time-overlapped pulses. At the same time, a matrix receiver, a sub-Nyquist receiver, and a multichannel receiver provide the largest number among other receivers types of overlaps that can be processed.

In practice, the number of overlaps depends on the signal environment complexity. An indicator and criteria for assessing this complexity are proposed. Since from the point of view of the wideband analyzer, random factors determine this environment, the probability of overlap not less than M pulses is advised to be used as such an indicator. The expressions obtained for calculating this probability allowed to plot the probability of overlapping in time of M and more pulses against the number of radio emission sources at different duty-off factors of the pulse sequences emitted the sources.

Based on the modelling results, variants of the composition and purpose of the sources are proposed using the example of radars, which can create a certain level of complexity of the signal environment. Receivers optimal for use in WBA in terms of processing efficiency and implementation complexity are proposed, considering the composition, quantity, and purpose of the sources forming a potential signal environment.

Thus, it is shown that the described receivers allow performing instantaneous spectrum analysis in a wide frequency band. This increases the efficiency of spectrum utilization, speed of providing a user with access to the radio channel, and, consequently, the system's overall throughput.

References

1. Mitola, J., Maguire, G.Q.: Cognitive radio: making software radios more personal. IEEE Pers. Commun. **6**(4), 13–18 (1999). https://doi.org/10.1109/98.788210
2. Nguyen, V.T., Villain, F., Le Guillou, Y.: Cognitive radio RF: overview and challenges. VLSI Des. (2012). https://doi.org/10.1155/2012/716476
3. Zeng, Y., Liang, Y.-C., Hoang, A.T., Zhang, R.: A review on spectrum sensing for cognitive radio: challenges and solutions. EURASIP J. Adv. Signal Process. (2010). https://doi.org/10.1155/2010/381465
4. Zhang, L., Wang, Y., Tao, W., Jia, Z., Song, T., Pan, C.: Intelligent reflecting surface aided MIMO cognitive radio systems. IEEE Trans. Veh. Technol. **69**(10), 11445–11457 (2020). https://doi.org/10.1109/TVT.2020.3011308
5. Onumanyi, A.J., Abu-Mahfouz, A.M., Hancke, G.P.: Low power wide area network, cognitive radio and the internet of things: potentials for integration. Sensors **20**, 6837 (2020)
6. Wang, J., Ghosh, M., Challapali, K.: Emerging cognitive radio applications: a survey. IEEE Commun. Mag. **49**(3), 74–81 (2011). https://doi.org/10.1109/MCOM.2011.5723803
7. Kaur, M.J., Uddin, M., Verma, H.K., Ambedkar, B.R.: Role of cognitive radio on 4G communications a review. J. Emerg. Trends Comput. Inf. Sci. **3**(2), 272–276 (2012)
8. Al-Bahri, M., Ruslan, K., Aleksey, B.: Integrating internet of things with the digital object architecture. In: Galinina, O., Andreev, S., Balandin, S., Koucheryavy, Y. (eds.) NEW2AN/ruSMART -2019. LNCS, vol. 11660, pp. 540–547. Springer, Cham (2019). https://doi.org/10.1007/978-3-030-30859-9_47
9. Pirmagomedov, R., Kirichek, R., Blinnikov, M., Koucheryavy, A.: UAV-based gateways for wireless nanosensor networks deployed over large areas. Comput. Commun. **146**, 55–62 (2019)
10. Simonov, A., Fokin, G., Sevidov, V., Sivers, M., Dvornikov, S.: Polarization direction finding method of interfering radio emission sources. In: Galinina, O., Andreev, S., Balandin, S., Koucheryavy, Y. (eds.) NEW2AN/ruSMART -2019. LNCS, vol. 11660, pp. 208–219. Springer, Cham (2019). https://doi.org/10.1007/978-3-030-30859-9_18
11. Moroz, A.V., Davydov, R.V., Davydov, V.V.: A new scheme for transmitting heterodyne signals based on a fiber-optical transmission system for receiving antenna devices of radar stations and communication systems. In: Galinina, O., Andreev, S., Balandin, S., Koucheryavy, Y. (eds.) NEW2AN/ruSMART -2019. LNCS, vol. 11660, pp. 710–718. Springer, Cham (2019). https://doi.org/10.1007/978-3-030-30859-9_62
12. Liu, F., Masouros, C., Petropulu, A.P., Griffiths, H., Hanzo, L.: Joint radar and communication design: applications, state-of-the-art, and the road ahead. IEEE Trans. Commun. **68**(6), 3834–3862 (2020). https://doi.org/10.1109/TCOMM.2020.2973976
13. Filin, S., Harada, H., Murakami, H., Ishizu, K.: International standardization of cognitive radio systems. IEEE Commun. Mag. **49**(3), 82–89 (2011). https://doi.org/10.1109/MCOM.2011.5723804
14. Onumanyi, A.J., Abu-Mahfouz, A.M., Hancke, G.P.: Adaptive threshold techniques for cognitive radio-based low power wide area network. Trans. Emerg. Telecommun. Technol. **31**, e3908 (2020)

15. Xu, D., Yu, X., Sun, Y., Ng, D.W.K., Schober, R.: Resource allocation for IRS-assisted full-duplex cognitive radio systems. IEEE Trans. Commun. **68**(12), 7376–7394 (2020). https://doi.org/10.1109/TCOMM.2020.3020838

16. Thanuja, T.C., Daman, K.A., Patil, A.S.: Optimized spectrum sensing techniques for enhanced throughput in cognitive radio network. In: 2020 International Conference on Emerging Smart Computing and Informatics (ESCI), pp. 137–141 (2020). https://doi.org/10.1109/ESCI48226.2020.9167576

17. Makolkina, M., Pham, V.D., Kirichek, R., Gogol, A., Koucheryavy, A.: Interaction of AR and IoT applications on the basis of hierarchical cloud services. In: Galinina, O., Andreev, S., Balandin, S., Koucheryavy, Y. (eds.) NEW2AN/ruSMART -2018. LNCS, vol. 11118, pp. 547–559. Springer, Cham (2018). https://doi.org/10.1007/978-3-030-01168-0_49

18. Ateya, A.A., Muthanna, A., Gudkova, I., Abuarqoub, A., Vybornova, A., Koucheryavy, A.: Development of intelligent core network for tactile internet and future smart systems. J. Sens. Actuator Netw. **7**(1), 7 (2018)

19. Ateya, A.A., Muthanna, A., Vybornova, A., Darya, P., Koucheryavy, A.: Energy - aware offloading algorithm for multi-level cloud based 5G system. In: Galinina, O., Andreev, S., Balandin, S., Koucheryavy, Y. (eds.) NEW2AN/ruSMART -2018. LNCS, vol. 11118, pp. 355–370. Springer, Cham (2018). https://doi.org/10.1007/978-3-030-01168-0_33

20. Yazdani, H., Vosoughi, A., Gong, X.: Achievable rates of opportunistic cognitive radio systems using reconfigurable antennas with imperfect sensing and channel estimation. IEEE Trans. Cogn. Commun. Netw. (2021). https://doi.org/10.1109/TCCN.2021.3056691

21. Tsui, J.: Microwave receivers with electronic warfare applications (2005)

22. Tsui, J.: Special Design Topics in Digital Wideband Receivers (2010)

23. Poisel, R.: Electronic Warfare Receivers and Receiver Systems-Artech (2014)

24. Tsui, J.: Digital Techniques for Wideband Receivers (2004)

25. Anderson, G.W., Webb, D.C., Spezio, A.E., Lee, J.N.: Advanced channelization for RF, microwave, and millimeter wave applications. Proc. IEEE **79**(3), 355–388 (1991)

26. Javed, J.N., Khalil, M., Shabbir, A.: A survey on cognitive radio spectrum sensing: classifications and performance comparison. In: 2019 International Conference on Innovative Computing (ICIC), pp. 1–8. IEEE (2019)

27. Yucek, T., Arslan, H.: A survey of spectrum sensing algorithms for cognitive radio applications. IEEE Commun. Surv. Tutorials **11**(1), 116–130 (2009)

28. Haykin, S., Thomson, D.J., Reed, J.H.: Spectrum sensing for cognitive radio. Proc. IEEE **97**(5), 849–877 (2009). https://doi.org/10.1109/jproc.2009.2015711

29. Axell, E., Leus, G., Larsson, E., Poor, H.: Spectrum sensing for cognitive radio: state-of-the-art and recent advances. IEEE Signal Process. Mag. **29**(3), 101–116 (2012). https://doi.org/10.1109/msp.2012.2183771

30. Martian, A., Al Sammarraie, M.J.A., Vlădeanu, C., Popescu, D.C.: Three-event energy detection with adaptive threshold for spectrum sensing in cognitive radio systems. Sensors **20**, 3614 (2020)

31. Aswini, V., Vamshidhar Reddy, A., Narendar, Ch., Renuka, N.: Probability of detection and probability of false alarm in cooperative spectrum sensing for cognitive radio systems using hard fusion rules. In: AIP Conference Proceedings, vol. 2358, p. 080020 (2021). https://doi.org/10.1063/5.0058411

32. Liu, X., Zheng, K., Chi, K., Zhu, Y.H.: Cooperative spectrum sensing optimization in energy-harvesting cognitive radio networks. IEEE Trans. Wireless Commun. **19**(11), 7663–7676 (2020). https://doi.org/10.1109/TWC.2020.3015260

33. Salama, G.M., Taha, S.A.: Cooperative spectrum sensing and hard decision rules for cognitive radio network. In: 2020 3rd International Conference on Computer Applications & Information Security (ICCAIS), pp. 1–6 (2020). https://doi.org/10.1109/ICCAIS48893.2020.9096740

34. Quan, Z., Cui, S., Sayed, A.H., Poor, H.V.: Optimal multiband joint detection for spectrum sensing in cognitive radio networks. IEEE Trans. Signal Process. **57**(3), 1128–1140 (2008)
35. Aswathy, G.P., Gopakumar, K.: Sub-Nyquist wideband spectrum sensing techniques for cognitive radio: a review and proposed techniques. AEU-Int. J. Electron. Commun. **104**, 44–57 (2019)
36. Podstrigaev, A.S., Smolyakov, A.V., Maslov, I.V.: Probability of pulse overlap as a quantitative indicator of signal environment complexity. J. Russ. Univ. Radioelectronics **23**(5), 37–45 (2020). https://doi.org/10.32603/1993-8985-2020-23-5-37-45
37. Podstrigaev, A.S., Smolyakov, A.V., Davydov, V.V., Myazin, N.S., Grebenikova, N.M., Davydov, R.V.: New method for determining the probability of signals overlapping for the estimation of the stability of the radio monitoring systems in a complex signal environment. In: Galinina, O., Andreev, S., Balandin, S., Koucheryavy, Y. (eds.) NEW2AN/ruSMART -2019. LNCS, vol. 11660, pp. 525–533. Springer, Cham (2019). https://doi.org/10.1007/978-3-030-30859-9_45
38. Podstrigaev, A.S., Smolyakov, A.V., Davydov, V.V., Myazin, N.S., Slobodyan, M.G.: Features of the development of transceivers for information and communication systems considering the distribution of radar operating frequencies in the frequency range. In: Galinina, O., Andreev, S., Balandin, S., Koucheryavy, Y. (eds.) NEW2AN/ruSMART -2018. LNCS, vol. 11118, pp. 509–515. Springer, Cham (2018). https://doi.org/10.1007/978-3-030-01168-0_45
39. Patent RU2587645 (2016)
40. Kim, J., Utomo, D.R., Dissanayake, A., Han, S.K., Lee, S.G.: The evolution of channelization receiver architecture: principles and design challenges. IEEE Access **5**, 25385–25395 (2017)
41. Huang, S., Zhang, H., Sun, H., Yu, L., Chen, L.: Frequency estimation of multiple sinusoids with three sub-Nyquist channels. Signal Process. **139**, 96–101 (2017)
42. Yen, C.-P., Tsai, Y., Wang, X.: Wideband spectrum sensing based on sub-Nyquist sampling. IEEE Trans. Signal Process. **61**(12), 3028–3040 (2013). https://doi.org/10.1109/tsp.2013.225 1342
43. Patent US5293114 (1994)
44. Podstrigaev, A.S., Lukiyanov, A.S., Galichina, A.A., Lavrov, A.P., Parfenov, M.V.: Wideband tunable delay line for microwave signals based on RF photonic components. In: Galinina, O., Andreev, S., Balandin, S., Koucheryavy, Y. (eds.) Internet of Things, Smart Spaces, and Next Generation Networks and Systems, pp. 424–431. Springer, Cham (2020). https://doi.org/10.1007/978-3-030-65726-0_38
45. Patent RU2422845 (2011)
46. Jiao, B.: Leveraging UltraScale Architecture Transceivers for High-Speed Serial I/O Connectivity, p. 24 (2015). https://www.xilinx.com/support/documentation/white_papers/wp458-ult rascale-xcvrs-serialio.pdf
47. Akyildiz, I.F., Lee, W.Y., Vuran, M.C., Mohanty, S.: A survey on spectrum management in cognitive radio networks. IEEE Commun. Mag. **46**(4), 40–48 (2008)
48. Self, A.G., Smith, B.G.: Intercept time and its prediction. IEE Proc. F Commun. Radar Signal Process. **132**(4), 215–220 (1985). https://doi.org/10.1049/ip-f-1.1985.0052
49. Kelly, S.W., Noone, G.P., Perkins, J.E.: Synchronization effects on probability of pulse train interception. IEEE Trans. Aerosp. Electron. Syst. **32**(1), 213–220 (1996). https://doi.org/10.1109/7.481263
50. Apfeld, S., Charlish, A., Koch W.: An adaptive receiver search strategy for electronic support. In: Sensor Signal Processing for Defence, Edinburgh, pp. 1–5 (2016). https://doi.org/10.1109/SSPD.2016.7590587
51. Vaughan, I., Clarkson, L.: Optimisation of Periodic Search Strategies for Electronic Support. IEEE Trans. Aerosp. Electron. Syst. **47**(3), 1770–1784 (2011). https://doi.org/10.1109/TAES.2011.5937264

52. Anderson, G.W., Webb, D.C., Spezio, A.E., Lee, J.N.: Advanced channelization for RF, microwave, and millimeterwave applications. Proc. IEEE **79**(3), 355–388 (1991). https://doi. org/10.1109/5.75091
53. Grover, R.: Kent: disrupting the net: ECM against advanced radars. Signal **32**(6), 10–13 (1978)
54. Likhachev, V.P., Podstrigaev, A.S., Nhan, N.T., Davydov, V.V., Myazin, N.S.: Study of the accuracy of determining the location of radio emission sources with complex signals when using autocorrelation and matrix receivers in broadband tools for analyzing the electronic environment. In: Galinina, O., Andreev, S., Balandin, S., Koucheryavy, Y. (eds.) Internet of Things, Smart Spaces, and Next Generation Networks and Systems, pp. 326–333. Springer, Cham (2020). https://doi.org/10.1007/978-3-030-65726-0_29
55. Kondakov, D., Kosmynin, A., Lavrov, A.: A method of simultaneous signals spectrum analysis for instantaneous frequency measurement receiver. In: Galinina, O., Andreev, S., Balandin, S., Koucheryavy, Y. (eds.) Internet of Things, Smart Spaces, and Next Generation Networks and Systems, pp. 200–209. Springer, Cham (2018). https://doi.org/10.1007/978-3-030-01168-0_19

Instantaneous Interference Evaluation Model for Smart Antennas in 5G Ultra-Dense Networks

Vadim Davydov[1], Grigoriy Fokin[2(✉)] (ID), Angelina Moroz[1] (ID), and Vitaly Lazarev[2] (ID)

[1] Peter the Great Saint Petersburg Polytechnic University, Saint-Petersburg, Russia
[2] The Bonch-Bruevich SPbSUT, Saint-Petersburg, Russia
grihafokin@gmail.com

Abstract. The rapidly increasing number of simultaneously transmitting devices in the upcoming 5G Ultra-Dense Networks (UDN) leads to the relevant problem of unacceptable interference level in densified multi-user radio access network. Transition to millimeter-wave frequencies and evolving massive MIMO systems on the physical layer is essential for minimizing the interference level of devices, using the same frequency resource, by means of angular and spatial multi-user separation with smart antennas. Its adaptive 3D-beamforming capability is expected to alleviate the 5G UDN interference problem by means of steering the transmitted signal of interest (SOI) toward the desired direction and simultaneously, avoiding signal of no interest (SNOI) transmission or reception from the unwanted direction. This well-known problem was already well treated in the past decade for stationary devices. However, the case of user mobility had not yet been thoroughly investigated. The challenge here consists in the instantaneous dependency of signal to interference ratio (SIR) on devices angular and spatial separation, which changes during their motion. Current work presents an instantaneous SIR evaluation model for the special case of two mobile devices and two stationary base stations, equipped with smart antennas, which perform location-aware beamforming (LAB) during mobile devices motion, accounting for their SOI and SNOI roles. Simulation results demonstrate considerable SIR fluctuation that needs to be accounted for when assessing device angular and spatial separation.

Keywords: 5G · Ultra-dense networks · Instantaneous interference · Location-aware beamforming · Antenna radiation pattern · Spatial and angular separation

1 Introduction

The upcoming decade is expected to demonstrate 5G networks worldwide commercial emergence with its intrinsic technical challenges [1–5]. From the radio access network operation and maintenance point of view, one of the most important problems is 5G network densification, which leads to considerable device angular and spatial concentration, and subsequently, interference level growth [6]. The use in some cases of fiber-optic systems for the backhaul areas does not solve this problem [7–10].

© Springer Nature Switzerland AG 2022
Y. Koucheryavy et al. (Eds.): NEW2AN 2021/ruSMART 2021, LNCS 13158, pp. 365–376, 2022.
https://doi.org/10.1007/978-3-030-97777-1_31

Traditional for 2G-4G radio access network approach with interference maintenance and control by spatial separation of base stations, utilizing the same frequency resource, is modeled by frequency reuse cluster [11]. This approach, however, is inadequate for 5G Ultra-Dense Networks (UDN) with up to million devices per one square kilometer [12]. Transition to millimeter-wave [13] promises to alleviate device spatial densification by means of evolving and miniaturization of massive MIMO systems [14] on the device physical layer. Space division multiple access (SDMA) seems to be a promising solution for 5G UDN [15], which is realized through multiuser transmit beamforming [16] and can help interference avoidance [17]. 5G UDN interference analysis [18] should consider, in general, the following challenge. In close device angular and spatial separation scenarios, when the user equipment (UE), which is the receiver of the signal-of-interest (SOI), is in the maximum of base station (BS) antenna radiation pattern (ARP) lobe, but at the same time, there is interference from neighboring BSs, directed to their own UEs, which are signal-not-of-interest (SNOI), and incurs interference increase for the target UE. Works [19–21] investigate three-dimensional (3D) beamforming as intrinsic massive MIMO capability from the single and multi-user cases and prove its potential for interference avoidance. This problem, due to the increasing number of simultaneously transmitting devices, was usually treated in the past decade for stationary cases, however, the case of device mobility had not yet been thoroughly investigated. One of the promising approaches and solution for this problem is so-called location-aware beamforming (LAB) [22]–[24], which was investigated by authors in [25–30] for the stationary case. The aim of the current work is to develop the model for the instantaneous signal to interference ratio (SIR) evaluation, depending on stationary and mobile devices angular and spatial separation using the LAB approach.

An interesting approach for interference evaluation in 5G is presented in [31–36], however, for stationary cases. In this paper we develop a simulation model to investigate the interference of BSs and UEs ARP influence in UDN scenarios with different spatial separation distances of neighboring UE and BSs, using SOI/SNOI evaluation accounting for their azimuth and elevation angle separation. The resulting spatial distance and angular separation metric could serve as a measure for interference control in 5G ultra-dense networks with beamforming. The material in the paper organized in the following order. System-level instantaneous interference evaluation model for smart antennas [37–40] in 5G UDN is formalized in the second part. Corresponding simulation SIR model, implemented with MATLAB toolboxes [41, 42], are presented in the third part. Finally, we draw the conclusions in the fourth part.

2   Interference Evaluation Model Description

System level interference evaluation model contains base scenario for dense-urban-like environment model [30] and specialcollision and non-collision cases for two BSs with LAB, placed on the top of traffic or street lamp, and two moving UEs.

2.1 Base Scenario Layout Description

An illustration of the base scenario with two BS and two UE is in Fig. 1. The distance between BSs and UEs is parametrized and can be adjusted. The minimal distance between any BS and UE is about 7 m (different roadsides).

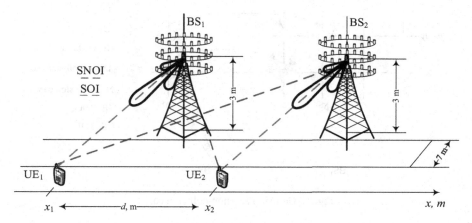

Fig. 1. The dense urban base scenario layout example

In all scenarios UE can be stationary or move in different directions, being beam tracked by the corresponding BS (LAB). We assume that corresponding BS to UE SOI direction should be the major lobe or ARP maximum, which can be obtained via array factor (AF) by electrical steering vector adjustment on BS [38]:

$$AF = \mathbf{w}^T \mathbf{v}(k), \tag{1}$$

where $\mathbf{w}^T$ is the transposed vector of antenna array element weights, $\mathbf{v}(k) - N \times 1$ complex vector of steering weights, representing antenna element phase shifts. The direction from BS to another UE is the minor SNOI lobe direction. Beam tracking of the UE leads to instantaneous interference, resulting in change of SOI/SNOI ratio and can be denoted as SIR metric, which can be found for the case of two links using equation:

$$SIR = \frac{SOI}{SNOI} = \frac{AF_0 P_0 / L_0}{AF_i P_i / L_i}, \tag{2}$$

where P_0 or P_i is BS transmitted power and L_0 or L_i is a free space loss for a given wavelength and distance between corresponding BS and UE in SOI or SNOI direction respectively. For simulation model we consider only the downlink (DL) transmission link and assume that BS antennas are directional and UE antennas are omnidirectional. According to scenario in Fig. 1, we propose several cases for simulation investigation: a) two UEs are moving towards each other along the same line trajectory with a chance of actual collision in the middle of trajectory (the collision case); b) two UEs are moving towards each other with some shifts between their line trajectories (the non-collision case); c) combination of collision and non-collision cases, where the trajectory shift is a variable value, for which we can compute SIR grid.

2.2 Collision and Non-collision Cases Description

The main area of interest in both collision and non-collision cases is SNOI direction that depends on UE_2 position and affects SIR level. Both cases are depicted in Fig. 2.

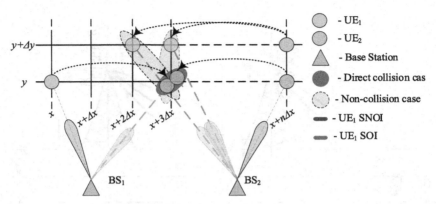

Fig. 2. Collision and non-collision cases

In both cases UE_1 moves along a fixed line (y is constant) from left to right.

In the first case UE_2 moves from right to left along the same line as UE_1 (direct collision), and in some point in the middle of trajectory both BS beams appear to be directed to the same point.

In the second case UE_2 moves from right to left on the line, which is shifted from UE_1 line by Δy, and in some point UE_1 appear to be placed on the boresight of the BS_2.

For every UE_1 and UE_2 trajectory coordinates (x, y), azimuth φ and elevation θ angles are calculated. Using this information, BS_1 and BS_2 ARP with AF (1) can be adjusted, and using (2) simulation model computes instantaneous SIR.

2.3 Instantaneous SIR Grid Description

Expanding the collision and non-collision cases, different trajectory shifts Δy produce a coordinate grid and instantaneous SIR for every point can be found using (2) and UE_1 and UE_2 coordinates; for every grid point azimuth and elevation angles are calculated. Using this information, BS_1 and BS_2 ARP can be adjusted with the proper steering vector coefficients (1). At this point, two main simulation approaches can be used: when UE_1 is stationary and UE_2 is moving along all line trajectories with different Δy shifts, and when both of the UEs are moving, but UE_1 is staying on the same y shift, whereas UE_2 Δy shift can be changed. Both approach layouts are representing close to real world dense-urban and are depicted in the Fig. 3 and Fig. 4, respectively.

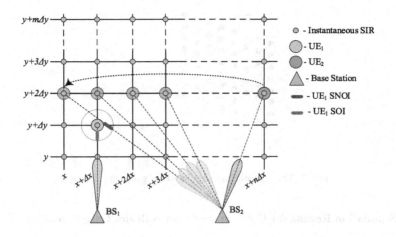

Fig. 3. Stationary case for instantaneous SIR grid calculation

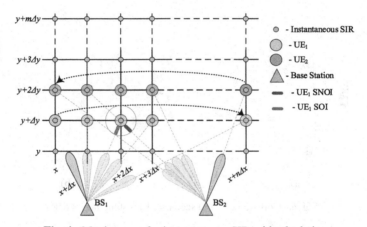

Fig. 4. Moving case for instantaneous SIR grid calculation

Instantaneous SIR results for both cases are provided further in chapter 3.

3   Interference Evaluation Model Simulation Results

3.1   Simulation Parameters

Simulation model uses two BSs, mounted on traffic light objects with uniform rectangular antenna arrays (URA), developed with MATLAB toolboxes [41, 42]. The array direction (boresight) is LAB controlled by a digital steering vector (1). Simulation model uses 3 GHz carrier, which fits the FR1 5G, and 64 (8 × 8) element URA (Fig. 5).

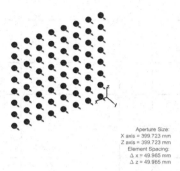

Aperture Size:
X axis = 399.723 mm
Z axis = 399.723 mm
Element Spacing:
Δ x = 49.965 mm
Δ z = 49.965 mm

Fig. 5 The uniform rectangular array geometry example

3.2   Simulation Results for Collision and Non-collision Case Scenarios

Scenario and SIR for collision and non-collision cases are shown in Fig. 6 and Fig. 7.

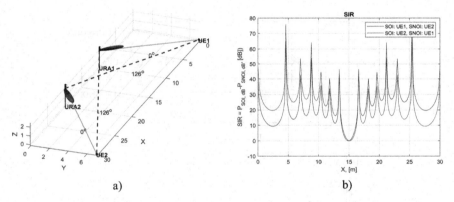

a)   b)

Fig. 6. Collision case: a) scenario; b) instantaneous SIR

Figure 6b and 7b with instantaneous SIR show, that besides predictable low SOI to SNOI level at the half of the UEs trajectory (due to symmetry), where ARP major lobes overlap, UEs experience severe interference fluctuation in many other areas during their movement. Also, comparing two scenarios in Fig. 6a and 7a, despite two UEs do not intersect in the non-collision case where Δy is nonzero, there is still severe interference fluctuation area, where SIR tends to zero. For further investigation we need to get instantaneous SIR dependency, where Δy shift between UEs trajectories is a variable.

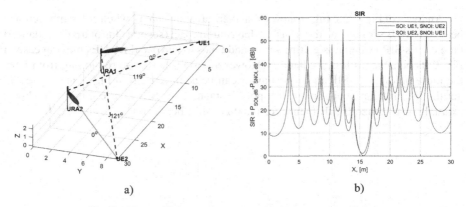

a)   b)

Fig. 7. Non-collision case: a) scenario; b) instantaneous SIR

3.3 Instantaneous SIR Grid Simulation

For instantaneous SIR simulation with variable Δy shift between two UEs we consider two cases. Figure 8 illustrates SIR grid for the case, when UE_1 is stationary and placed in the point with coordinates (15, 7) and UE_2 moves along line with coordinates (0, 7) and (30, 7). Figure 9 illustrates SIR grid for the case when two UEs move simultaneously towards each other along line with coordinates (0, 7) and (30, 7). Both cases (due to symmetry) assume UE_1 as SOI and UE_2 as SNOI.

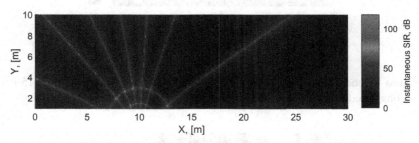

Fig. 8. Instantaneous SIR with variable shift for one UE stationary case

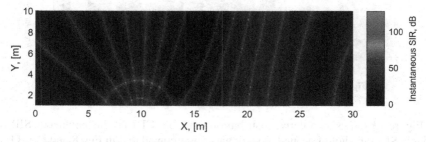

Fig. 9. Instantaneous SIR with variable shift for two moving UEs case

Analysis of Fig. 8 and Fig. 9 shows, that there are many areas, when cross-interference between two BSs antenna arrays has a deleterious impact (several tens of dB degradation) on the UEs SIR (when it is getting lower and tends to zero) and for UEs moving case in Fig. 9 its behavior is less predictable. However, the farther UEs are moving from BSs, the more predictable SIR metric behavior can be achieved. From Fig. 8 and 9 we can get the information about areas with poor instantaneous SIR metric. Figure 10 shows example instantaneous SIR metric for fixed Δy shift between UEs, as in Fig. 7b.

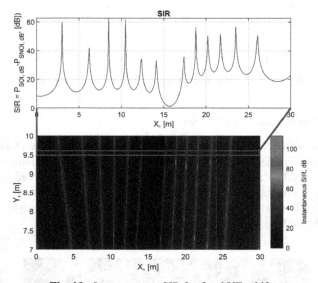

Fig. 10. Instantaneous SIR for fixed UEs shift

Figure 11 and Fig. 12 demonstrates areas with SIR above threshold of 15 dB for cases, considered in Fig. 8 and Fig. 9 respectively.

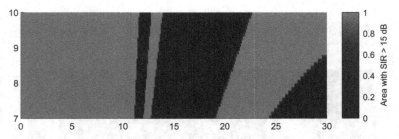

Fig. 11. Areas with SIR above 15 dB for one UE stationary case

Figure 13 shows cumulative distribution function (CDF) of instantaneous SIR with variable SIR threshold for one UE stationary case, considered in Fig. 8 and Fig. 11, and two moving UEs case, considered in Fig. 9 and Fig. 12.

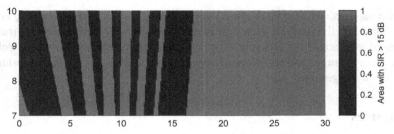

Fig. 12. Areas with SIR above 15 dB for two moving UEs case

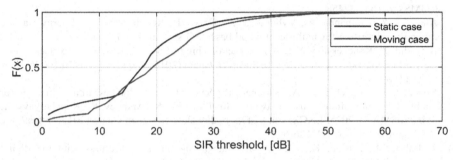

Fig. 13. SIR CDF

Analysis of SIR CDF in Fig. 13 shows, that probability of instantaneous SIR, being less than SIR threshold, depends on UEs mobility, specifically, in the working area from 1 to 30 dB static case with one UE stationary case has less areas with low instantaneous SIR than in the moving case with two moving UEs case. Based on this information, different MIMO system parameters, such as antenna element number, antenna array patterns and beamforming algorithms should be adjusted for achieving higher instantaneous SIR and resulting UDN performance.

4 Conclusion

Presented instantaneous interference evaluation model for the special case of two mobile devices and two stationary base stations, equipped with smart antennas, helps to investigate instantaneous signal to interference ratio evaluation for location-aware beamforming during mobile devices motion, accounting for their SOI and SNOI roles. Revealed problem consists in the instantaneous signal to interference ratio dependency on devices angular and spatial separation, which changes during their motion and can lead to deleterious impact with SIR degradation by several tens of dB. Simulation results demonstrate considerable SIR fluctuation, especially in the case of mobile devices, that needs to be accounted for, when assessing device angular and spatial separation. This fluctuation can be a significant limitation for communication sessions between separated devices in the case dense-urban-like environment scenarios. For mitigating the neighboring base stations deleterious interference impact in worst cases, when SOI and SNOI antenna radiation patterns are directed to closely located devices, SIR margin needs to be taken into account. Preliminary location information about mobile devices and their angular and spatial separation with different smart antennas parameters, such as antenna element number, array patterns and beamforming algorithms should be selected and substantiated in further investigations.

References

1. Agiwal, M., Roy, A., Saxena, N.: Next generation 5G wireless networks: a comprehensive survey. IEEE Commun. Surv. Tutorials **18**(3), 1617–1655 (2016). https://doi.org/10.1109/COMST.2016.2532458
2. Ateya, A.A., Muthanna, A., Vybornova, A., Darya, P., Koucheryavy, A.: Energy - aware offloading algorithm for multi-level cloud based 5G system. In: Galinina, O., Andreev, S., Balandin, S., Koucheryavy, Y. (eds.) Internet of Things, Smart Spaces, and Next Generation Networks and Systems, pp. 355–370. Springer, Cham (2018). https://doi.org/10.1007/978-3-030-01168-0_33
3. Koucheryavy, A., Vladyko, A., Kirichek, R.: State of the art and research challenges for public flying ubiquitous sensor networks. In: Balandin, S., Andreev, S., Koucheryavy, Y. (eds.) ruSMART 2015. LNCS, vol. 9247, pp. 299–308. Springer, Cham (2015). https://doi.org/10.1007/978-3-319-23126-6_27
4. Al-Bahri, M., Ruslan, K., Aleksey, B.: Integrating internet of things with the digital object architecture. In: Galinina, O., Andreev, S., Balandin, S., Koucheryavy, Y. (eds.) NEW2AN/ruSMART -2019. LNCS, vol. 11660, pp. 540–547. Springer, Cham (2019). https://doi.org/10.1007/978-3-030-30859-9_47
5. Pirmagomedov, R., Blinnikov, M., Kirichek, R., Koucheryavy, A.: Wireless nanosensor network with flying gateway. In: Chowdhury, K.R., Di Felice, M., Matta, I., Sheng, Bo. (eds.) WWIC 2018. LNCS, vol. 10866, pp. 258–268. Springer, Cham (2018). https://doi.org/10.1007/978-3-030-02931-9_21
6. Kamel, M., Hamouda, W., Youssef, A.: Ultra-dense networks: a survey. IEEE Commun. Surv. Tutorials **18**(4), 2522–2545 (2016). https://doi.org/10.1109/COMST.2016.2571730
7. Kiesewetter, D., Malyugin, V., Makarov, S., Korotkov, K., Ming, D., Wei, X.: Application of the optical fibers in the system of determining the distance of jump at ski springboard. In: 2016 Advances in Wireless and Optical Communications (RTUWO), pp. 5–8 (2016). https://doi.org/10.1109/RTUWO.2016.7821845
8. Tarasenko, M.Y., Davydov, V.V., Lenets, V.A., Akulich, N.V., Yalunina, T.R.: Features of use direct and external modulation in fiber optical simulators of a false target for testing radar station. In: Galinina, O., Andreev, S., Balandin, S., Koucheryavy, Y. (eds.) NEW2AN/ruSMART/NsCC -2017. LNCS, vol. 10531, pp. 227–232. Springer, Cham (2017). https://doi.org/10.1007/978-3-319-67380-6_21
9. Dmitrieva, D.S., Pilipova, V.M., Davydov, R.V., Davydov, V.V., Rud, V.Y.: Fiber-optical communication line with a system for compensation of radiation-induced losses during the transmission of information. In: Internet of Things, Smart Spaces, and Next Generation Networks and Systems, vol. 12526. LNCS, pp. 348–356. Springer, Cham (2020). https://doi.org/10.1007/978-3-030-65729-1_30
10. Myazin, N.S., Dudkin, V.I., Grebenikova, N.M., Davydov, R.V., Davydov, V.V., Rud', V.Y., Podstrigaev, A.S.: Fiber – optical system for governance and control of work for nuclear power stations of low power. In: Galinina, O., Andreev, S., Balandin, S., Koucheryavy, Y. (eds.) NEW2AN/ruSMART -2019. LNCS, vol. 11660, pp. 744–756. Springer, Cham (2019). https://doi.org/10.1007/978-3-030-30859-9_66

11. Harada, H., Prasad, R.: Simulation and Software Radio for Mobile Communications. Artech House (2002)
12. Baldemair, R., et al.: Ultra-dense networks in millimeter-wave frequencies. IEEE Commun. Mag. **53**(1), 202–208 (2015). https://doi.org/10.1109/MCOM.2015.7010535
13. Uwaechia, A.N., Mahyuddin, N.M.: A comprehensive survey on millimeter wave communications for fifth-generation wireless networks: feasibility and challenges. IEEE Access **8**, 62367–62414 (2020). https://doi.org/10.1109/ACCESS.2020.2984204
14. Larsson, E.G., Edfors, O., Tufvesson, F., Marzetta, T.L.: Massive MIMO for next generation wireless systems. IEEE Commun. Mag. **52**(2), 186–195 (2014). https://doi.org/10.1109/MCOM.2014.6736761
15. Bai, L., Li, T., Xiao Z., Choi, J.: Performance analysis for SDMA mmWave systems: using an approximate closed-form solution of downlink sum-rate. IEEE Access **5**, 15641–15649 (2017). https://doi.org/10.1109/ACCESS.2017.2734739
16. Björnson, E., Bengtsson, M., Ottersten, B.: Optimal multiuser transmit beamforming: a difficult problem with a simple solution structure [Lecture Notes]. IEEE Sig. Process. Mag. **31**(4), 142–148 (2014). https://doi.org/10.1109/MSP.2014.2312183
17. Halbauer, H., Saur, S., Koppenborg, J., Hoek, C.: Interference avoidance with dynamic vertical beamsteering in real deployments. In: 2012 IEEE Wireless Communications and Networking Conference Workshops (WCNCW), pp. 294–299 (2012). https://doi.org/10.1109/WCNCW.2012.6215509
18. Rachad, J., Nasri, R., Decreusefond, L.: Interference analysis in dynamic TDD system combined or not with cell clustering scheme. In: 2018 IEEE 87th Vehicular Technology Conference (VTC Spring), pp. 1–5 (2018). https://doi.org/10.1109/VTCSpring.2018.8417679
19. Koppenborg, J., Halbauer, H., Saur, S., Hoek, C.: 3D beamforming trials with an active antenna array. In: 2012 International ITG Workshop on Smart Antennas (WSA), pp. 110–114 (2012). https://doi.org/10.1109/WSA.2012.6181190
20. Rachad, J., Nasri, R., Decreusefond, L.: A 3D beamforming scheme based on the spatial distribution of user locations. In: 2019 IEEE 30th Annual International Symposium on Personal, Indoor and Mobile Radio Communications (PIMRC), pp. 1–7 (2019). https://doi.org/10.1109/PIMRC.2019.8904392
21. Razavizadeh, S.M., Ahn, M., Lee, I.: Three-dimensional beamforming: a new enabling technology for 5G wireless networks. IEEE Sig. Process. Mag. **31**(6), 94–101 (2014). https://doi.org/10.1109/MSP.2014.2335236
22. Taranto, R.D., Muppirisetty, S., Raulefs, R., Slock, D., Svensson, T., Wymeersch, H.: Location-aware communications for 5G networks: how location information can improve scalability, latency, and robustness of 5G. IEEE Sig. Process. Mag. **31**(6), 102–112 (2014). https://doi.org/10.1109/MSP.2014.2332611
23. Zhou, B., Liu, A., Lau, V.: Successive localization and beamforming in 5G mmWave MIMO communication systems. IEEE Trans. Sig. Process. **67**(6), 1620–1635 (2019). https://doi.org/10.1109/TSP.2019.2894789
24. Kela, P., et al.: Location based beamforming in 5G ultra-dense networks. In: IEEE 84th Vehicular Technology Conference, pp. 1–7 (2016). https://doi.org/10.1109/VTCFall.2016.7881072
25. Fokin, G., Lazarev, V.: Location accuracy of radio emission sources for beamforming in ultra-dense radio networks. In: 2019 IEEE Microwave Theory and Techniques in Wireless Communications (MTTW), pp. 9–12 (2019). https://doi.org/10.1109/MTTW.2019.8897228
26. Fokin, G., Lazarev, V.: 3D location accuracy estimation of radio emission sources for beamforming in ultra-dense radio networks. In: 2019 11th International Congress on Ultra-Modern Telecommunications and Control Systems and Workshops (ICUMT), pp. 1–6 (2019). https://doi.org/10.1109/ICUMT48472.2019.8970939

27. Lazarev, V., Fokin, G., Stepanets, I.: Positioning for location-aware beamforming in 5G ultra-dense networks. In: 2019 IEEE International Conference on Electrical Engineering and Photonics (EExPolytech), pp. 136–139 (2019). https://doi.org/10.1109/EExPolytech.2019.890 6825
28. Fokin, G.: Interference suppression using location aware beamforming in 5G ultra-dense networks. In: 2020 IEEE Microwave Theory and Techniques in Wireless Communications (MTTW), pp. 13–17 (2020). https://doi.org/10.1109/MTTW51045.2020.9245050
29. Fokin, G., Bachevsky, S., Sevidov, V.: System level performance evaluation of location aware beamforming in 5G ultra-dense networks. In: 2020 IEEE International Conference on Electrical Engineering and Photonics (EExPolytech), pp. 94–97 (2020). https://doi.org/10.1109/EExPolytech50912.2020.9243970
30. Lazarev, V.O., Fokin, G.A.: Positioning performance requirements evaluation for grid model in ultra-dense network scenario. In: 2020 Systems of Signals Generating and Processing in the Field of on-Board Communications, pp. 1–6 (2020). https://doi.org/10.1109/IEEECONF4 8371.2020.9078650
31. Bechta, K., Kelner, J.M., Ziółkowski, C., Nowosielski, L.: Inter-beam co-channel downlink and uplink interference for 5G new radio in mm-Wave bands. Sensors **21**, 793 (2021). https://doi.org/10.3390/s21030793
32. Bechta, K., Ziółkowski, C., Kelner, J.M., Nowosielski, L.: Modeling of downlink interference in massive MIMO 5G macro-cell. Sensors **21**, 597 (2021). https://doi.org/10.3390/s21020597
33. Ziółkowski, C., Kelner, J.M.: Antenna pattern in three-dimensional modelling of the arrival angle in simulation studies of wireless channels. IET Microwaves Antennas Propag. **11**, 898–906 (2017). https://doi.org/10.1049/IET-MAP.2016.0591
34. Kelner, J.M., Ziółkowski, C.: Interference in multi-beam antenna system of 5G network. Int. J. Electron. Telecommun. **66**(1), 17–23 (2020). https://doi.org/10.24425/ijet.2019.130260
35. Ziółkowski, C., Kelner, J.M.: Statistical evaluation of the azimuth and elevation angles seen at the output of the receiving antenna. IEEE Trans. Antennas Propag. **66**(4), 2165–2169 (2018). https://doi.org/10.1109/TAP.2018.2796719.
36. Xue, Q., Li, B., Zuo, X., Yan, Z., Yang, M.: Cell capacity for 5G cellular network with inter-beam interference. In: 2016 IEEE International Conference on Signal Processing, Communications and Computing (ICSPCC), pp. 1–5 (2016). https://doi.org/10.1109/ICSPCC.2016.7753608
37. Litva, J.: Digital Beamforming in Wireless Communications. Artech House (1996)
38. Balanis, C.: Antenna Theory: Analysis and Design, 4th edn. Wiley (2016)
39. Mailloux, R.J.: Phased Array Antenna Handbook, 3rd edn. Artech House (2017)
40. Gross, F.: Smart Antennas with MATLAB, 2nd edn. McGraw-Hill (2015)
41. Antenna Toolbox™ User's Guide, The MathWorks (2019). https://www.mathworks.com/help/releases/R2019b/pdf_doc/antenna/antenna_ug.pdf
42. Phased Array System Toolbox™ User's Guide, The MathWorks (2019). https://www.mathworks.com/help/pdf_doc/phased/phased_ug.pdf

The Effect of Error Burst When Using a Decision Feedback Algorithm for Receiving Non-orthogonal Multi-frequency Signals

Sergey B. Makarov[1] , Dac Cu Nguyen[1](✉) , Sergey V. Zavjalov[1] ,
Anna S. Ovsyannikova[1] , and Canh Minh Nguyen[2]

[1] Peter the Great St. Petersburg Polytechnic University, St. Petersburg, Russia
makarov@cee.spbstu.ru, daccu91.spb@gmail.com,
zavyalov_sv@spbstu.ru
[2] University of Transport and Communications, Hanoi, Vietnam
ncminh@utc.edu.vn

Abstract. An algorithm for coherent element-by-element detection with decision feedback is proposed for signals with non-orthogonal subcarrier frequency spacing. The simulation results in the Matlab environment show that the proposed algorithm is quite effective. The admissible boundary values of the signal-to-noise ratio are determined, at which the effect of the error burst is manifested. The error burst of decision feedback affects the reduction of the performance of detection, starting from the values of the bit error rate BER = 0.1–0.3 at the normalized frequency spacing α = 0.3–0.4. In addition, it is determined that the decision feedback depth is effective in value of not more than 4.

Keywords: Coherent detection · Non-orthogonal · BER · Iterative algorithm · Decision feedback · Error burst

1 Introduction

An increase in the spectral efficiency of multi-frequency signals of duration T is possible by reducing the spacing Δf between subcarriers while maintaining their total number [1–5]. Since the signals transmitted on the subcarriers are not orthogonal, inter-channel interference (ICI) occurs due to the influence of the signals transmitted on adjacent subcarriers on each other. This influence introduces additional interference during the demodulation of the signals transmitted on each subcarrier frequency [6–9].

Algorithms for processing multi-frequency signals in the presence of ICI for channels with additive white Gaussian noise (AWGN) with an average power spectral density of $N_0/2$, as a rule, are based on the methods of element-by-element detection at each subcarrier frequency, or maximum-likelihood sequence estimation (MLSE) of a sequence of N transmitted signals on the duration T. When using algorithms of coherent detection MLSE of message packets under ICI conditions, it is possible to obtain high energy efficiency [10–12]. However, their implementation turns out to be very difficult. Computational complexity, which is understood as the amount of computational resources

© Springer Nature Switzerland AG 2022
Y. Koucheryavy et al. (Eds.): NEW2AN 2021/ruSMART 2021, LNCS 13158, pp. 377–389, 2022.
https://doi.org/10.1007/978-3-030-97777-1_32

(speed, computational time and memory) required to implement the algorithm, grows in power-law dependence on the length of received message packet.

It is simpler to apply algorithms of element-by-element coherent detection in conditions when inter-channel interference is noise [13–15]. This method is the simplest to implement, but the use of such reception algorithms does not allow obtaining high performance of detection. The development of the element-by-element detection is the use of an iterative algorithm of element-by-element processing with decision feedback at each subcarrier frequency [11]. This algorithm is a compromise between the element-by-element coherent detection algorithm, but under conditions where ICI is partially compensated for, and the detection algorithm MLSE, when decisions about the received signal depend on decisions about the received signals transmitted on adjacent subcarriers.

ICI cancellation at the n-th subcarrier frequency caused by received signals at adjacent subcarriers at non-orthogonal spacing is possible only if all channel alphabet symbols transmitted at subcarriers preceding (subcarrier numbers 0, 1, 2, ..., $(n - 1)$) n-th subcarrier frequency are received correctly. With erroneously received signals, ICI increases, which leads to a decrease in performance of detection. These erroneous decisions can obviously cause a series of errors when receiving signals on the n-th subcarrier frequency. It is obvious that the error burst is strongly manifested at low signal-to-noise ratios (SNR), which are typical for many radio communication channels. With an increase in the level of ICI at each subcarrier frequency the error burst will lead to a decrease in the performance of detection not only in the region of low SNR, but also in the range of values these ratios providing the error probabilities $p = 10^{-2} - 10^{-3}$.

The aim of this work is to evaluate the performance of the detection of non-orthogonal multi-frequency signals at small values of the spacing between subcarriers when using the algorithm of coherent element-by-element detection with decision feedback and to determine the permissible boundary values of the SNR, at which the effect of error burst is manifested.

2 Representation of Multi-frequency Non-orthogonal Signals

A random sequence $y(t)$ of multi-frequency non-orthogonal signals in the general case of infinite length, with the number N of used subcarriers ω_p and complex channel alphabet symbols $C_{pk}^{(r)}$ on the p-th subcarrier and on the k-th time interval, the index r of which determines the value of this symbol, can be represented as:

$$y(t) = \sum_{k=-\infty}^{\infty} \sum_{p=0}^{N-1} a(t - kT) C_{pk}^{(r)} e^{j\omega_p t}, t \in (-\infty; \infty) \tag{1}$$

where the amplitude pulse $a(t)$ can have an arbitrary shape and duration, which are determined by the requirements for the degree of compactness of the spectrum. In the simplest case, $a(t)$ is rectangular and can be represented by the following formula:

$$a(t) = \begin{cases} 1, & t \in [0, T] \\ 0, & \text{otherwise} \end{cases} \tag{2}$$

Over a time interval $t \in [0; T]$, the signal $s(t)$ can be written in the following form:

$$s(t) = \sum_{p=0}^{N-1} a(t) C_p^{(r)} e^{j\omega_p t} \tag{3}$$

For classical OFDM (orthogonal frequency-division multiplexing) signals, the normalized frequency spacing $\alpha = \Delta f \cdot T$ of adjacent subcarriers is 1. For multi-frequency non-orthogonal signals, the value $\alpha < 1$, and the parameter α plays the role of the frequency division multiplexing factor. With decreasing α, the spectrum width decreases by $(1 - \alpha) \cdot 100\%$ in comparison with OFDM signals.

Expression (1) for a random sequence $y(t)$ of non-orthogonal multi-frequency signals can be written in a convenient form by dividing into a useful signal transmitted at the n-th subcarrier frequency and ICI caused by the influence of signals transmitted on adjacent subcarriers. Then the signals $s(t)$ at each subcarrier frequency in the time interval can be represented as:

$$s(t) = s_n^{(r)}(t) + s_-^{(i)}(t) + s_+^{(q)}(t) \tag{4}$$

Here, $s_n^{(r)}(t)$ is a useful signal transmitted at the n-th subcarrier frequency with an amplitude pulse $a(t)$ and a channel alphabet symbol (see (3)). With a value of $\alpha < 1$, signals transmitted at adjacent subcarriers will fall into the analysis interval. The minus (−) index defines the signals transmitted at frequencies preceding the n-th subcarrier frequency, and the plus (+) index defines the signals transmitted at frequencies following it. Index $i = M^n$, where M^n determines the number of possible combinations of symbols of the channel alphabet with volume M, following before the analyzed one. Index $q = M^{N-n-1}$, where M^{N-n-1} is the number of possible combinations of characters following the analyzed one. Then:

$$s_-^{(i)}(t) = \sum_{p=0}^{n-1} a(t) C_p^{(r)} e^{j\omega_p t} \tag{5}$$

$$s_+^{(q)}(t) = \sum_{p=n+1}^{N-1} a(t) C_p^{(r)} e^{j\omega_p t} \tag{6}$$

As seen from expressions (5) and (6), the ICI depends on the value of subcarrier difference $|\omega_p - \omega_{p-1}|$ (the frequency spacing $\alpha = \Delta f \cdot T$) and the type of the amplitude pulse $a(t)$.

3 Algorithm of Element-by-Element Detection with Decision Feedback

We will assume that signals are received separately at each transmission subcarrier. When analyzing coherent signal processing, as in the case of receiving classical OFDM signals, the measurement of the initial phase of the bandpass signal is determined using a phase-locked loop. For this, additional subcarriers are used, which are added to the bandpass signal at the stage of its formation. Clock synchronization is also determined from a periodic sequence of symbols transmitted on additional subcarriers. Under these conditions, in the general case, the analyzed process at the input of the receiving device, taking into account (1), has the form:

$$r(t) = \mu y(t) + n(t)$$

Here $n(t)$ is additive white Gaussian noise (AWGN) with an average power spectral density of $N_0/2$, μ is the transmission coefficient over the communication channel, which is determined by the level of fading.

The element-by-element coherent detection at each subcarrier frequency in the $t \in [0; T]$ time interval can be considered as detection against the background of ICI $s_-^{(i)}(t)$ and $s_+^{(q)}(t)$. The optimal algorithm for element-by-element detection of signals at the n-th subcarrier assumes averaging over all $i = M^n$ and $q = M^{N-n-1}$ possible combinations of channel alphabet symbols. This algorithm essentially does not provide for any measures to combat ICI.

Assuming that the signals $s_+^{(q)}(t)$ following the analyzed one at the current symbol interval are additional interference and a priori information about the form of implementation of this interference is not taken into account in processing, the following algorithm can be obtained:

the l-th symbols is registered if the inequality holds:

$$\int_0^T r(t)\left(s_n^{(l)}(t) - s_n^{(r)}(t)\right)dt > \frac{1}{2}\mu\left(\int_0^T \left(s_n^{(l)}(t) + s_-^{(i)}(t)\right)^2 dt - \int_0^T \left(s_n^{(r)}(t) + s_-^{(i)}(t)\right)^2 dt\right) \quad (7)$$

Consider the implementation of the feedback algorithm based on the solution (7) for signals with $a(t)$ rectangular shape (2) and with binary ($M = 2$) symbols of the channel alphabet. In this case, for $r = 1$ symbol $C_n^{(1)} = 1$, and for $r = 2$ symbol $C_n^{(2)} = -1$. Then we have $s_n^{(1)}(t) = -s_n^{(2)}(t)$, and simplifying (7), we obtain the following rule for making a decision:

$$\int_0^T r(t)s_n^{(l)}(t)dt \underset{<}{\overset{>}{=}} \mu\int_0^T s_n^{(l)}(t)s_-^{(i)}(t)dt \quad (8)$$

As can be seen from this expression, the values of the correlation integral are compared with a threshold value that depends on the amount of ICI. The same algorithm can be rewritten in a different way:

$$\int_0^T (r(t) - \mu s_-^{(i)}(t))s_n^{(l)}(t)dt \underset{<}{\overset{>}{=}} 0 \quad (9)$$

In algorithm (9), in the integrand expression, ICI caused by signals transmitted at frequencies preceding the n-th subcarrier frequency is subtracted from the received analyzed process. Compensation of the ICI indicated in (10) is possible only if all the channel alphabet symbols transmitted on the subcarriers preceding the n-th subcarrier frequency are received correctly. With erroneously received symbols, ICI increases, which leads to a decrease in performance of detection.

The implementation of algorithms (8) and (9) assumes that signals are received at frequencies preceding the n-th subcarrier frequency and there are estimates of the channel alphabet symbols. Of course, it is not possible to obtain such estimates at once (at time $t = T$ on the interval). Therefore, it is necessary to provide an iterative procedure for the appearance of a solution when receiving multi-frequency signals.

For the convenience of presenting the iterative procedure, first of all, we rewrite algorithm (8) taking into account (5) in the following form:

$$C_n^{(l)} \int_0^T r(t) e^{j\omega_n t} dt \underset{<}{\overset{>}{\gtrless}} \mu C_n^{(l)} \int_0^T e^{j\omega_n t} \left(\sum_{p=0}^{n-1} \overline{C}_p^{(r)} e^{j\omega_p t} \right) dt . \tag{10}$$

On the right side of inequality (10) (threshold $\Lambda_n = \mu C_n^{(l)} \int_0^T e^{j\omega_n t} \left(\sum_{p=0}^{n-1} \overline{C}_p^{(r)} e^{j\omega_p t} \right) dt$),

$\overline{C}_p^{(r)}$ are estimates of the received symbols transmitted by signals at frequencies preceding the n-th subcarrier frequency.

In this regard, the following iterative procedure is expedient. At the first step, a signal is received at the extreme subcarrier frequency ω_0 without using feedback (algorithm (10) with a threshold value equal to zero). At the next step, signals are received at subcarrier frequency ω_1. At this frequency, when forming the decision threshold, the estimate of the symbol received at the previous step is taken into account. At the third step, the estimates of the symbols adopted at the first and second steps will be taken into account. This procedure continues until the N-th step, when a decision is made on the symbols received on subcarrier ω_{N-1}.

However, with a large number N of subcarriers (more than 128), the introduction of decision feedback on a time interval over the entire signal sequence turns out to be very difficult. In addition, even for small α ($\alpha < 0.5$), the number of neighboring subcarriers, on which signals that interfere with the reception of the given one are transmitted, turn out to be no more than 4–5. Therefore, we will restrict ourselves to considering an example of constructing a receiving device with a decision feedback, taking into account no more than 3 signals transmitted at 3 subcarriers preceding the n-th subcarrier frequency at the same time interval T (Fig. 1).

Figure 1 shows a block diagram of a multi-frequency correlation receiver with decision feedback. The analyzed process is fed to the input of a low-noise amplifier (LNA) and through a band-pass filter (BPF) to N correlators. The bandwidth of this filter is selected based on the occupied bandwidth of the received multi-frequency signals. Oscillators in correlators have frequencies corresponding to the frequencies of the subcarriers of the channels of the multi-frequency signals. The block diagram of Fig. 1 does not show the devices for carrier phase recovery and clock frequency recovery, since they do not differ from the known ones [16]. The outputs of the integrators are connected to the Rangekeeper (RK) through the switches $K_i (i = 0, 1, 2, \ldots N - 1)$. The operation of the switch is controlled by a synchronization system that generates pulse sequences with a pulse repetition period equal to $T_{sync} = T$. Starting with the correlator tuned to the frequency, the outputs of the integrators are connected to the RK through time delay elements $k \Delta t (k = 1, 2, \ldots N - 1)$. It is advisable to choose the time interval based

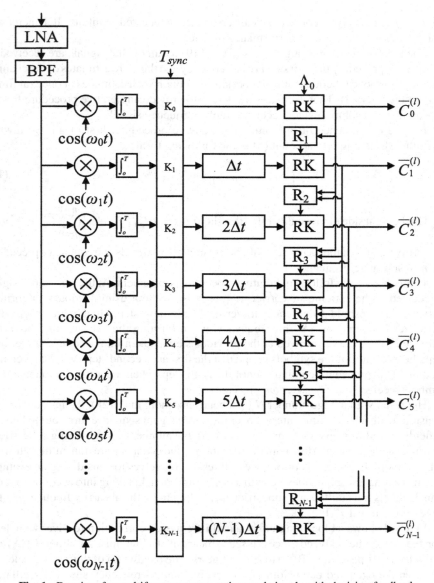

Fig. 1. Receiver for multifrequency non-orthogonal signals with decision feedback

on the performance capabilities of the signal demodulator, the transmission rate of the channel alphabet symbols, and the methods of digital implementation of the algorithm (10). In its simplest case, the value $\Delta t = T/N$.

The elements of the operational memory $R_p (p = 1, 2, \ldots N - 1)$ contain sets of values of the correlation coefficients of signals transmitted at subcarriers in accordance with the right side of expression (10). The sizes of the sets of these values of the correlation coefficients turn out to be different depending on the value of the index p in R_p.

The value of the threshold at the inputs of the RK depends on the symbol decisions transmitted at frequencies preceding the n-th subcarrier frequency. As can be seen from Fig. 1, when receiving a signal at the subcarrier frequency ω_n, the estimates of decisions about the symbols transmitted at the 3 previous subcarriers at the time interval $t \in [0; T]$ are taken into account by the threshold value. Thus, at the outputs of the receiving device with feedback according to the decision on the time interval $t \in [T; 2T]$, estimates $\overline{C}_p^{(r)}$ of the received symbols will be formed.

4 Simulation Results

The purpose of the simulation was to evaluate the performance of detection of multi-frequency signals with non-orthogonal frequency spacing using algorithm (10) with decision feedback and to determine the error burst parameters at low SNR values and small subcarrier spacing. The simulation model is built in the Matlab environment. The simulation parameters are chosen as follows:

- type of modulation on each subcarrier frequency: BPSK
- number of used subcarriers: $N = 32$–128
- normalized frequency spacing of adjacent subcarriers $\alpha = 0.7; 0.4; 0.3$;
- the total number of transmitted symbols: 10,000.

Figure 2 shows the dependences of BER on E_b/N_0, where $E_b = \int_0^T [s_n^{(r)}(t)]^2 dt$ is the energy of the useful signal at the n-th subcarrier frequency, at various values, taken into account when forming the threshold, the number of decisions on the received signals transmitted at frequencies preceding the n-th subcarrier frequency. In this case, the value of the normalized frequency spacing is $\alpha = 0.7$. The number of subcarriers is $N = 32$.

Figure 2, a–c) show the dependences of BER on the signal-to-noise ratio E_b/N_0 when using the detection algorithm with decision feedback (dashed line) and when using the classical algorithm of element-by-element detection (solid line) without feedback (threshold in (10) is equal to zero). Figure 2, a) shows the case of feedback using one previous subcarrier frequency; in Fig. 2, b) - two previous subcarriers; and in Fig. 2, c) - two previous subcarriers with an extended interval of E_b/N_0 values. From the analysis of these dependencies, the following conclusions can be drawn. First, it can be seen from the graphs in Fig. 2, a) that there is a point of intersection of the error probability curves (in the region of -3.5 dB of E_b/N_0 ratios) after which the algorithm with decision feedback turns out to be more effective than the classical detection algorithm. In the region $E_b/N_0 < -3.5$ dB, the effects of burst error begin to affect and the performance of the algorithm with decision feedback decreases and becomes lower than that of the classical detection algorithm. Secondly, with the value of the normalized frequency spacing $\alpha = 0.7$, the ICI from signals transmitted at adjacent subcarriers turns out to be insignificant. Therefore, the efficiency of using the results of detection at the two previous subcarriers in the feedback loop is insignificant (the error probabilities BER $= 0.1$ are achieved at E_b/N_0

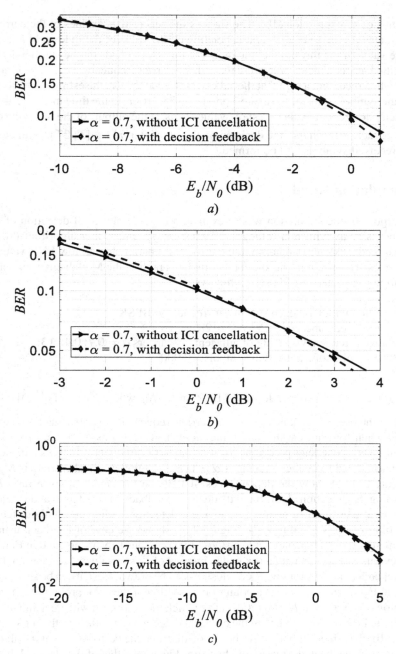

Fig. 2. Dependence of BER on E_b/N_0 for $\alpha = 0.7$

= 0 dB in Fig. 2, *b*)), although the threshold value of the start of error burst is shifted to the region of $E_b/N_0 < 1.5$ dB. Third, the energy gain when using the algorithm with decision feedback at BER = 0.03 is less than 1 dB (Fig. 2, *c*).

Let us consider the dependences of BER performance on E_b/N_0 on the normalized frequency spacing of adjacent subcarriers $\alpha = 0.4$ (Fig. 3 for $N = 32$).

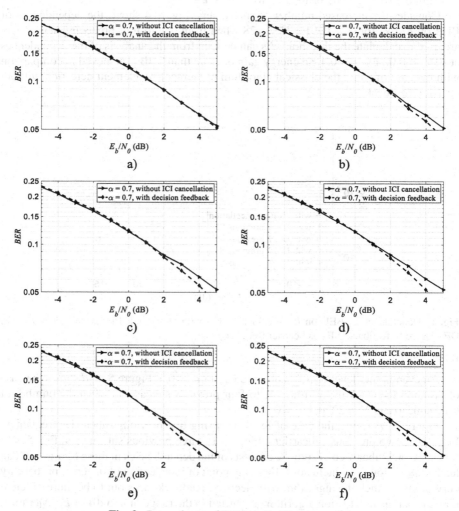

Fig. 3. Dependence of BER on E_b/N_0 for $\alpha = 0.4$

Figure 3, *a–f* illustrates the case of feedback using from one to six previous subcarriers, respectively. From the analysis of the dependencies in these figures, the following conclusions can be drawn. First, the point of intersection of the error probability curves after which the decision feedback algorithm turns out to be more efficient than the classical detection algorithm is in the range of 0.5–1.5 dB of the E_b/N_0 ratio. This occurs when the depth of the feedback increases, which is caused by the increase in the number of subcarriers taken into account while processing this signal. Secondly, with the value of the normalized frequency spacing $\alpha = 0.4$, ICI from signals transmitted at adjacent subcarriers turns out to be significant. Therefore, it is necessary to use at least 4 subcarriers for the feedback loop (Fig. 3, a–d). Third, the energy gain when using the feedback algorithm at BER $= 0.05$ is about 1 dB (Fig. 3, e).

Consider the increased number of subcarriers. Figure 4 shows the dependences of BER on E_b/N_0 for $\alpha = 0.4$ for $N = 128$ when from one to four preceding subcarriers are used to calculate the threshold. As can be seen from the analysis of the dependences at BER $= 0.02$ for $\alpha = 0.4$, an energy gain of more than 7 dB is achieved in comparison with the case of using the classical algorithm of element-by-element detection without decision feedback.

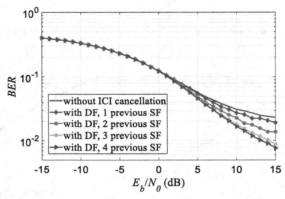

Fig. 4. Dependence of BER on E_b/N_0 for $\alpha = 0.4$ with an extended range of values E_b/N_0. DF – decision feedback, SF – subcarrier frequency.

An even higher level of ICI is observed at for $\alpha = 0.3$. Figure 5, a–d shows the case of decision feedback using from one to four previous subcarriers when the number of used subcarriers $N = 32$ and $\alpha = 0.3$.

Figure 5, a) shows the case of feedback using one previous subcarrier frequency; Fig. 5, b) - two previous subcarriers; Fig. 5, c) - three previous subcarriers; Fig. 5, d) - four previous subcarriers. From the analysis of the dependencies in these figures, we can lead to the following conclusions. First, the point of intersection of the error probability curves, after which the algorithm with decision feedback turns out to be more efficient than the classical detection algorithm, is shifted to the range of 4–5 dB of E_b/N_0 ratios, which significantly exceeds the boundary signal-to-noise values at $\alpha = 0.4$ and 0.7. At the same time, the BER values are in the range of BER $= 0.1$–0.15. This is not surprising, because the spectrum of multi-frequency signals was compressed by more than 3 times and the correlation of signals transmitted at subcarriers increased significantly. Second, the energy gains increased significantly when using the feedback algorithm. So, with BER $= 0.13$, this gain is more than 4–5 dB (Fig. 5, c–d). Third, the error burst at E_b/N_0

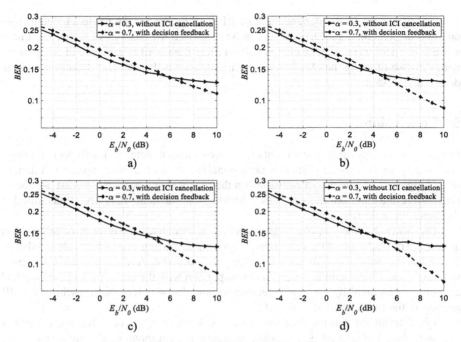

Fig. 5. Dependence of BER on E_b/N_0 for $\alpha = 0.3$

< 4–5 dB looks more significant (the loss is about 2 dB at BER $= 0.2$), which must be taken into account when using detection algorithms with decision feedback.

Consider the increased number of subcarriers. Figure 6 shows the dependence of BER on E_b/N_0 ratio for $\alpha = 0.3$ for $N = 128$.

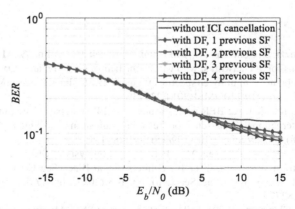

Fig. 6. Dependence of BER on E_b/N_0 for $\alpha = 0.3$ with an extended range of values E_b/N_0. DF – decision feedback, SF – subcarrier frequency

This figure shows the dependences of BER on E_b/N_0 for the feedback depth from one to four preceding subcarriers. As can be seen from the analysis of the dependences at BER < 0.15 for $\alpha = 0.3$, an energy gain of more than 9 dB is achieved in comparison with the case of using the classical algorithm of element-by-element detection without decision feedback.

5 Conclusions

In this work, an algorithm of coherent element-by-element detection with decision feedback is proposed for signals with non-orthogonal subcarrier frequency spacing. A feature of this algorithm is the use of decisions on the received symbols transmitted at subcarriers before the analyzed moment when deciding on the value of symbol transmitted at the n-th subcarrier frequency.

It is shown that the proposed algorithm is quite effective. The error burst of decision affects the degradation of the detection performance, starting from the values of BER = 0.1–0.3 at the normalized frequency spacing $\alpha = 0.3$–0.4. At the same time, for these spacing, a significant gain is observed in comparison with the case of using the classical algorithm of element-by-element detection without decision feedback, reaching 7–9 dB already in the range of BER = 0.1–0.2.

It is determined that the decision feedback depth is effective if feedback depth is not more than 4. This makes it possible to reduce the computational complexity of the algorithm of element-by-element detection with decision feedback.

Acknowledgments. The results of the work were obtained with the support of the scholarship of the President of the Russian Federation to young scientists and graduate students carrying out promising research and development in priority areas of modernization of the Russian economy for 2021–2023 (СП-1671.2021.3).

References

1. Banelli, P., Buzzi, S., Colavolpe, G., Modenini, A., Rusek, F., Ugolini, A.: Modulation formats and waveforms for 5G networks: who will be the heir of OFDM?: an overview of alternative modulation schemes for improved spectral efficiency. IEEE Signal Process. Mag. **31**(6), 80–93 2014. https://doi.org/10.1109/MSP.2014.2337391
2. Gorbunov, S., Rashich, A.: BER performance of SEFDM signals in lte fading channels. In: 2018 41st International Conference on Telecommunications and Signal Processing (TSP), pp. 1–4 (2018). https://doi.org/10.1109/TSP.2018.8441462
3. Gelgor, A., Gorlov, A., Nguyen, V.P.: Performance analysis of SEFDM with optimal subcarriers spectrum shapes. In: 2017 IEEE International Black Sea Conference on Communications and Networking (BlackSeaCom), pp. 1–5 (2017). https://doi.org/10.1109/BlackS eaCom.2017.8277680
4. Darwazeh, I., Ghannam, H., Xu, T.: The first 15 years of SEFDM: a brief survey. In: 2018 11th International Symposium on Communication Systems, Networks & Digital Signal Processing (CSNDSP). IEEE, pp. 1–7 (2018). https://doi.org/10.1109/CSNDSP.2018.8471886

5. Kanaras, I., Chorti, A., Rodrigues, M., Darwazeh, I.: Spectrally efficient FDM signals: bandwidth gain at the expense of receiver complexity. In: Proceedings of the IEEE International Conference on Communications, ICC 2009, June 2009

6. Yin, Z., Jia, M., Lyu, F., Wang, W., Guo, Q., Shen, X.: Spectral efficiency analysis of SEFDM systems with ICI mitigation. In: 2019 IEEE 90th Vehicular Technology Conference (VTC2019-Fall), pp. 1–5 (2019). https://doi.org/10.1109/VTCFall.2019.8891303

7. Ghannam, H., Darwazeh, I.: SEFDM: spectral efficiency upper bound and interference distribution. In: 2018 11th International Symposium on Communication Systems, Networks & Digital Signal Processing (CSNDSP), pp. 1–6 (2018). https://doi.org/10.1109/CSNDSP.2018.8471782

8. Isam, S., Darwazeh, I.: Characterizing the intercarrier interference of non-orthogonal spectrally efficient FDM system. In: 2012 8th International Symposium on Communication Systems, Networks & Digital Signal Processing (CSNDSP), pp. 1–5 (2012). https://doi.org/10.1109/CSNDSP.2012.6292762

9. Kanaras, I., Chorti, A., Rodrigues, M., Darwazeh, I.: Spectrally efficient FDM signals: bandwidth gain at the expense of receiver complexity. In: IEEE International Conference on Communications, pp. 1–6 (2009)

10. Guo, M.: Simplified maximum likelihood detection for FTN non-orthogonal FDM system. IEEE Photon. Technol. Lett. **29**(19), 1687–1690 (2017). https://doi.org/10.1109/LPT.2017.2743244

11. Lee, W., Hill, F.: A maximum-likelihood sequence estimator with decision-feedback equalization. IEEE Trans. Commun. **25**(9), 971–979 (1977). https://doi.org/10.1109/TCOM.1977.1093930

12. Kanaras, I., Chorti, A., Rodrigues, M., Darwazeh, I.: A combined MMSE-ML detection for spectrally efficient non orthogonal FDM signal. In: Proceedings of IEEE Broadnet Conference, September 2008

13. Kanaras, I., Chorti, A., Rodrigues, M., Darwazeh, I.: A new quasi-optimal detection algorithm for a non orthogonal spectrally efficient FDM. In: International Symposium on Communication and Information Technologies, pp. 460–465, September 2009

14. Rashich, A., Kislitsyn, A., Fadeev, D., Nguyen, T.N.: FFT-based trellis receiver for SEFDM signals. In: 2016 IEEE Global Communications Conference (GLOBECOM), pp. 1–6. IEEE (2016)

15. Zavjalov, S.V., Makarov, S.B., Volvenko, S.V.: Nonlinear coherent detection algorithms of nonorthogonal multifrequency signals. In: Balandin, S., Andreev, S., Koucheryavy, Y. (eds.) NEW2AN 2014. LNCS, vol. 8638, pp. 703–713. Springer, Cham (2014). https://doi.org/10.1007/978-3-319-10353-2_66

16. Haeb, R., Meyr, H.: A systematic approach to carrier recovery and detection of digitally phase modulated signals of fading channels. IEEE Trans. Commun. **37**(7), 748–754 (1989). https://doi.org/10.1109/26.31167

Software Implementation of the Algorithm for Optimal Joint Estimation and Detection of an Arbitrary Waveform

Nikita Ilchenko$^{(\boxtimes)}$ and Eugenii Popov

Peter the Great Saint Petersburg Polytechnic University, Saint-Petersburg 195251, Russia
nikita.ilchenko1998@gmail.com

Abstract. In this paper, we investigate the problem of joint detection and estimation of the duration of an arbitrary waveform. The main problem is the nondifferentiability of the logarithm of the likelihood ratio functional and, consequently, the need to use the mathematical apparatus of Markov processes to find the characteristics of noise immunity. A solution to the Fokker – Planck – Kolmogorov equation with time-dependent coefficients is proposed. After that, simulation of the algorithm was carried out. Based on the simulation results, a comparison was made between the theoretically obtained dependences and those obtained during the experiment, as well as with the dependence for a completely known signal. The case of signal detection in the absence of information about the signal shape is also considered, while assuming that the signal has a rectangular shape. At the end, numerical results are presented, and the further direction of research is determined.

Keywords: Optimal detecting · ML-estimation · FPK-equation

1 Introduction

At the current stage of human development, radar methods have found wide application. Their use is due to the security issues of both individuals and organizations, and entire states. By means of radio location, it is possible to ensure control of the situation in the air, space, ground, and surface spaces.

Each radar station (radar) has its own characteristics, which are associated with its specific purpose. But of all the stations, it is worth highlighting the radar detection system, because on Earth, in space, in the air, and at sea, the radar detection method is the main one.

However, when detecting, sometimes it turns out to be very difficult, and sometimes even impossible, to determine a priori information about the signal. So, we cannot know the probability of the appearance of a signal or the amplitude of the signal, which took place during the transmission of information, in addition, the duration of the pulse may also be unknown, as well as the shape of the signal, if we just want to understand whether the signal was transmitted. Considering all the above, it is necessary to use detection

© Springer Nature Switzerland AG 2022
Y. Koucheryavy et al. (Eds.): NEW2AN 2021/ruSMART 2021, LNCS 13158, pp. 390–404, 2022.
https://doi.org/10.1007/978-3-030-97777-1_33

methods and algorithms that allow, together with the decision on the presence of a signal, to produce and estimate unknown parameters.

To date, a fairly large number of works are known related to the joint detection-evaluation of signals [1–3]. In particular, in [2], this problem of unknown duration was investigated in detail for a rectangular signal.

To summarize the results, in this paper, a joint estimation-detection algorithm for arbitrary waveforms is considered. Dependencies for the probability of false alarm and correct detection are also obtained.

2 Optimal Joint Detection–Estimation Algorithm

2.1 Statement of the Problem

First, you need to formulate the task that will be considered. Thus, the problem of signal detection on the observation interval $[0; T]$, the shape of which is different from rectangular and is described by the function $g(t)$. It is also known that the signal amplitude is equal to A_0, which considers the channel multiplier μ, the signal duration τ is unknown, but the values are taken from the a priori interval $[T_1; T_2]$. The detected signal then has the form:

$$s(t) = \begin{cases} A_0 g(t), \ 0 \le t \le \tau; \\ 0, \ t < 0, t > \tau; \end{cases}, \ 0 \le T_1 \le \tau \le T_2 \le T \tag{1}$$

The very task of detection is to compare some statistics with a threshold value. The role of this statistic is played by the likelihood ratio functional or its logarithm, and the threshold value depends on the criterion used. Here, the threshold value is selected from the Neumann – Pearson criterion. In detection tasks, this criterion is used since it fixes the probability of a false alarm and maximizes the probability of correct detection. Also, unlike the same criterion of average risk or the criterion of the maximum posterior probability, the Neumann – Pearson criterion does not imply knowledge of a priori information, price matrix and the probability of a signal. In addition, it is important for the user to obtain the minimum false alarm probability and the maximum correct detection probability, but this is impossible, and among all strategies with the same false alarm probability, the criterion used has the highest probability of correct detection.

2.2 Joint Detection–Estimation Algorithm

To form the algorithm, it is necessary to find the logarithm of the likelihood ratio functional (LRF), which is written in general form:

$$\ln \Lambda[z(t)] = \frac{2}{N_0} \int_0^T z(t)s(t)dt - \frac{1}{N_0} \int_0^T s^2(t)dt, \tag{2}$$

where $z(t)$ – received oscillation equal to $z(t) = s(t) + n(t)$;
$n(t)$ – additive white Gaussian process with zero mean and variance $N_0/2$.

Considering in (1) that the signal lasts less than the observation time, the LRF logarithm takes the form:

$$\ln \Lambda[z(t), \tau] = \frac{2A_0}{N_0} \int\limits_0^\tau z(t)g(t)dt - \frac{A_0^2}{N_0} \int\limits_0^\tau g^2(t)dt. \tag{3}$$

The presence of the parameter τ in square brackets emphasizes the dependence of the LRF also on the unknown duration. As an estimate of the unknown parameter, the maximum likelihood estimate (ML–estimate) is used. This is due, firstly, to the fact that its finding is easier from the point of view of calculations and technically, and, secondly, this estimate is effective or asymptotically effective.

In estimation theory, in order to determine the ML–estimate, it is necessary to find the derivative of expression (3) with respect to the parameter τ and equate it to zero. However, this is not feasible, since the functional is a function nondifferentiable with respect to the duration parameter. For such cases, the value [2]:

$$\tau^* = \underset{\tau \in [T_1; T_2]}{\arg\max} (\ln \Lambda[z(t), \tau]). \tag{4}$$

Then, taking into account (4), the final algorithm can be written:

$$\Lambda^* = \frac{2A_0}{N_0} \int\limits_0^{\tau^*} z(t)g(t)dt - \frac{A_0^2}{N_0} \int\limits_0^{\tau^*} g^2(t)dt > \ln \Lambda_{NP}. \tag{5}$$

The threshold value $\ln \Lambda_{NP}$ in (5) is calculated from the integral relation:

$$\int\limits_{\Lambda_{NP}}^{+\infty} w_\zeta (z/H_2)dz = P_{FA}, \tag{6}$$

where $w_\zeta (z/H_2)$ – distribution density of the analyzed oscillation at the receiver input in the absence of a useful signal;

P_{FA} – the probability of a false alarm or, in other words, the probability of a type I error.

According to the final expression (5) and considering (4), we can conclude about the structural diagram of the detector. So, it will be a multichannel receiver [4], on each channel of which the value of the LRF logarithm will be generated, then the maximum of all channels is selected and compared with the threshold, after these procedures a decision is made on the presence or absence of a signal. The structure of the detector is shown schematically in Fig. 1.

2.3 Noise Immunity Characteristics

The Probability of a False Alarm

In this clause, the parameters of noise immunity will be determined, that is, the dependence of the probability of a false alarm on the threshold value and the dependence of the

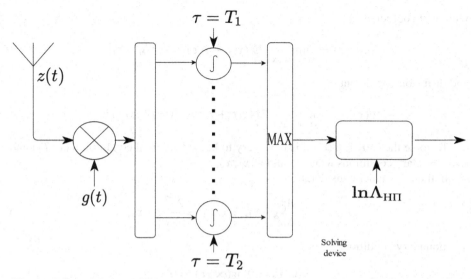

Fig. 1. Schematic of a multichannel receiver for an arbitrary waveform and unknown duration.

probability of correct detection on the signal-to-noise ratio. First, we find the probability of a false alarm.

Let us assume that $z(t) = n(t)$ – there is no useful signal, that is:

$$\mu(\tau) \equiv \ln \Lambda[z(t), \tau/z(t) = n(t)] = \frac{2A_0}{N_0} \int_0^\tau n(t)g(t)dt - h^2(\tau),$$

where $h(\tau) = \sqrt{A_0^2 \int_0^\tau g^2(t)dt/N_0}$ – signal-to-noise ratio. Then the probability of a false alarm is defined as:

$$\alpha \equiv P_{FA} = P\left(\max_{T_1 \leq \tau \leq T_2} \mu(\tau) > \ln \Lambda_{NP}\right)$$

or equivalently

$$\alpha = 1 - P(\mu(\tau)) \leq \ln \Lambda_{NP}) = 1 - P(\ln \Lambda_{NP} - \mu(\tau)) \geq 0).$$

It is worth noting that the process

$$x(\tau) = \ln \Lambda_{NP} - \mu(\tau) = \ln \Lambda_{NP} - \frac{2A_0}{N_0} \int_0^\tau n(t)g(t)dt + h^2(\tau) \qquad (7)$$

is Wiener (as an integral of a Gaussian process); therefore, its probability density $w(x, \tau)$ obeys the Fokker – Planck – Kolmogorov (FPK) equation:

$$\frac{\partial w(x, \tau)}{\partial \tau} = -\frac{\partial}{\partial x}[a(x, \tau)w(x, \tau)] + \frac{1}{2}\frac{\partial^2}{\partial x^2}[b(x, \tau)w(x, \tau)], \qquad (8)$$

with drift coefficient

$$a(x, \tau) = \lim_{\Delta\tau \to 0} \frac{1}{\Delta\tau} \mathbf{E}[(x(\tau + \Delta\tau) - x(\tau))/x(\tau)]$$

and diffusion coefficient

$$b(x, \tau) = \lim_{\Delta\tau \to 0} \frac{1}{\Delta\tau} \mathbf{E}\left[(x(\tau + \Delta\tau) - x(\tau))^2/x(\tau)\right].$$

To solve the FPK Eq. (8), it is necessary to know the initial condition $w(x, T_1)$ and two boundary conditions $w(x_1, \tau)$ and $w(x_2, \tau)$.

In the case under consideration

$$a(x, \tau) = \frac{A_0^2}{N_0} g^2(\tau), \ b(x, \tau) = \frac{2A_0^2}{N_0} g^2(\tau), \tag{9}$$

and boundary conditions

$$w(0, \tau) = 0, \ w(\infty, \tau) = 0.$$

Since the process $x(\tau)$ is Gaussian, the initial condition is the Gaussian distribution at $\tau = T_1$ with the expectation

$$\mathbf{E}[x(T_1)] = \ln \Lambda_{NP} + h^2(T_1)$$

and variance

$$\mathbf{D}[x(T_1)] = \mathbf{E}\left[\left(\left(\frac{2A_0}{N_0}\int_0^{T_1} n(t)g(t)dt\right)\right)^2\right] = \mathbf{E}\left[\left(\frac{2A_0}{N_0}\right)^2 \int_0^{T_1}\int_0^{T_1} n(t_1)n(t_2)g(t_1)g(t_2)dt_1 dt_2\right]$$

$$= \frac{2A_0^2 \int_0^{T_1} g^2(t)dt}{N_0} = 2h^2(T_1).$$

To solve Eq. (8), we make a change of variables similar to the one used in article [5]:

$$U(x, \tau) = w(x, \tau)\exp\left(-\frac{\text{sgn}[a(x,\tau)]x}{2} + \frac{h^2(\tau)}{4}\right);$$
$$w(x, \tau) = U(x, \tau)\exp\left(\frac{\text{sgn}[a(x,\tau)]x}{2} - \frac{h^2(\tau)}{4}\right). \tag{10}$$

This replacement reduces the original equation to the equation for $U(x, \tau)$:

$$\frac{\partial U(x, \tau)}{\partial \tau} - \frac{b(\tau)}{2}\frac{\partial^2 U(x, \tau)}{\partial x^2} = 0 \tag{11}$$

with boundary conditions

$$U(0, \tau) = 0, \ U(\infty, \tau) = 0.$$

and the initial condition

$$U(x, T_1) = w(x, T_1) \exp\left(-\frac{x}{2} + \frac{h^2(T_1)}{4}\right)$$

$$= \frac{1}{\sqrt{2\pi \cdot 2h^2(T_1)}} \exp\left[-\frac{\left(x - \ln \Lambda_{\mathrm{NP}} - h^2(T_1)\right)^2}{2 \cdot 2h^2(T_1)}\right] \exp\left(-\frac{x}{2} + \frac{h^2(T_1)}{4}\right).$$

The solution to Eq. (11) with the indicated initial and boundary conditions is the function

$$U(x, \tau) = \frac{1}{\sqrt{4\pi\left(h^2(\tau) - h^2(T_1)\right)}} \int_0^\infty U(s, T_1)\left\{\exp\left[-\frac{(x - s)^2}{4\left(h^2(\tau) - h^2(T_1)\right)}\right]\right.$$

$$\left. - \exp\left[-\frac{(x + s)^2}{4\left(h^2(\tau) - h^2(T_1)\right)}\right]\right\} ds. \tag{12}$$

Substituting the initial condition, we obtain

$$U(x, \tau) = \frac{1}{\sqrt{4\pi\left(h^2(\tau) - h^2(T_1)\right)}} \int_0^\infty \frac{1}{\sqrt{4\pi h^2(T_1)}} \exp\left[-\frac{\left(s - \ln \Lambda_{\mathrm{NP}} - h^2(T_1)\right)^2}{4h^2(T_1)}\right]$$

$$\times \exp\left(-\frac{s}{2} + \frac{h^2(T_1)}{4}\right)\left\{\exp\left[-\frac{(x - s)^2}{4\left(h^2(\tau) - h^2(T_1)\right)}\right] - \exp\left[-\frac{(x + s)^2}{4\left(h^2(\tau) - h^2(T_1)\right)}\right]\right\} ds$$

and

$$w(x, \tau) = \frac{1}{4\pi\sqrt{(h^2(\tau) - h^2(T_1))h^2(T_1)}} \exp\left(\frac{x}{2} - \frac{h^2(\tau)}{4}\right) \exp\left(\frac{h^2(T_1)}{4}\right)$$

$$\times \int_0^\infty \exp\left[-\frac{\left(s - \ln \Lambda_{\mathrm{NP}} - h^2(T_1)\right)^2}{4h^2(T_1)}\right] \exp\left(-\frac{s}{2}\right)$$

$$\times \left\{\exp\left[-\frac{(x - s)^2}{4\left(h^2(\tau) - h^2(T_1)\right)}\right] - \exp\left[-\frac{(x + s)^2}{4\left(h^2(\tau) - h^2(T_1)\right)}\right]\right\} ds, \ x \geq 0, \ \tau \geq 0. \tag{13}$$

Now, when the density $w(x, \tau)$ is found as a solution to the FPK equation, the false alarm probability is [3]

$$\alpha = 1 - P(x(T_2) \geq 0) = 1 - \int_0^\infty w(x, T_2)dx = 1 - \int_0^\infty \int_0^\infty \frac{1}{4\pi\sqrt{(h^2(T_2) - h^2(T_1))h^2(T_1)}}$$

$$\times \exp\left(-\frac{h^2(T_2)}{4}\right) \exp\left(\frac{h^2(T_1)}{4}\right) \exp\left[-\frac{\left(s - \ln \Lambda_{\mathrm{NP}} - h^2(T_1)\right)^2}{4h^2(T_1)}\right] \exp\left(-\frac{s}{2}\right)$$

$$\times \exp\left(\frac{x}{2}\right)\left\{\exp\left[-\frac{(x - s)^2}{4\left(h^2(T_2) - h^2(T_1)\right)}\right] - \exp\left[-\frac{(x + s)^2}{4\left(h^2(T_2) - h^2(T_1)\right)}\right]\right\} dsdx.$$

We change the order of integration in such a way that the inner integral over the variable x

$$I = \int\limits_0^\infty \exp\left(\frac{x}{2}\right)\left\{\exp\left[-\frac{(x-s)^2}{4\left(h^2(T_2)-h^2(T_1)\right)}\right] - \exp\left[-\frac{(x+s)^2}{4\left(h^2(T_2)-h^2(T_1)\right)}\right]\right\}dx,$$

express through the tabulated function

$$\mathrm{erfc}(x) = \frac{2}{\sqrt{\pi}}\int\limits_x^\infty \exp\left(-y^2\right)dy,$$

implemented in MATLAB. We have:

$$I = \sqrt{\frac{2\pi\left(h^2(T_2)-h^2(T_1)\right)}{2}}\,\exp\left(\frac{h^2(T_2)-h^2(T_1)}{4}\right)$$

$$\left[\exp\left(\frac{s}{2}\right)\mathrm{erfc}\left(-\frac{h^2(T_2)-h^2(T_1)+s}{\sqrt{4\left(h^2(T_2)-h^2(T_1)\right)}}\right)\right.$$

$$\left.-\exp\left(-\frac{s}{2}\right)\mathrm{erfc}\left(-\frac{h^2(T_2)-h^2(T_1)-s}{\sqrt{4\left(h^2(T_2)-h^2(T_1)\right)}}\right)\right],$$

Then

$$\alpha = 1 - P(x(T_2)\geq 0) = 1 - \frac{1}{2\sqrt{4\pi h^2(T_1)}}\int\limits_0^\infty \exp\left[-\frac{\left(s-\ln\Lambda_{\mathrm{NP}}-h^2(T_1)\right)^2}{4h^2(T_1)}\right]$$

$$\times\left[\mathrm{erfc}\left(-\frac{h^2(T_2)-h^2(T_1)+s}{\sqrt{4\left(h^2(T_2)-h^2(T_1)\right)}}\right) - \exp(-s)\mathrm{erfc}\left(-\frac{h^2(T_2)-h^2(T_1)-s}{\sqrt{4\left(h^2(T_2)-h^2(T_1)\right)}}\right)\right]ds. \qquad (14)$$

Taking into account the values of the FPK coefficients, it is possible to give a physical meaning to the parameters appearing in (14):

$h^2(T_1) = h_1^2$ – signal-to-noise ratio for the studied signal with duration T_1;
$h^2(T_2) = h_2^2$ – signal-to-noise ratio for the studied signal with duration T_2;
$h^2(T_2) - h^2(T_1) = h_\Delta^2$ – signal-to-noise ratio for the studied signal with duration Δ.
Then

$$\alpha = P_{\mathrm{FA}} = 1 - \frac{1}{4h_1\sqrt{\pi}}\int\limits_0^\infty \exp\left[-\frac{\left(s-\ln\Lambda_{\mathrm{NP}}-h_1^2\right)^2}{4h_1^2}\right]$$

$$\times\left[\mathrm{erfc}\left(-\frac{h_\Delta^2+s}{2h_\Delta}\right) - \exp(-s)\mathrm{erfc}\left(-\frac{h_\Delta^2-s}{2h_\Delta}\right)\right]ds. \qquad (15)$$

If we assume that $T_1 \rightarrow T_2$, then.

$$h_1 \rightarrow h_2 \equiv h, h_\Delta \rightarrow 0, \mathrm{erfc}\left(-\frac{h_\Delta^2 + s}{2h_\Delta}\right) \rightarrow 2, \mathrm{erfc}\left(-\frac{h_\Delta^2 - s}{2h_\Delta}\right) \rightarrow 0$$

and the probability of a false alarm then

$$\alpha \rightarrow 1 - \frac{1}{2h\sqrt{\pi}} \int_0^\infty \exp\left[-\frac{(s - \ln \Lambda_{\mathrm{NP}} - h^2)^2}{4h^2}\right] ds = 1 - F_0\left(\frac{\ln \Lambda_{\mathrm{NP}} + h^2}{h\sqrt{2}}\right)$$

$$= \frac{1}{2}\left[1 - \mathrm{erf}\left(\frac{\ln \Lambda_{\mathrm{NP}}}{2h} + \frac{h}{2}\right)\right]$$

coincides with the expression that is obtained in the case of detection of a completely known signal [6s].

To express explicitly the dependence of the threshold value $\ln \Lambda_{\mathrm{NP}}$ on the probability of false alarm P_{FA} is a very time-consuming task, therefore, in what follows, we will use only dependence (5).

The Probability of Correct Detection

After the expression for P_{FA} has been found, we determine the probability of correct detection of P_{CD}, that is, when the signal $s(t)$ is present at the input of the receiver:

$$P_{\mathrm{CD}} = 1 - \beta = P\left(\max_{T_1 \leq \tau \leq T_2} \mu(\tau) > \ln \Lambda_{\mathrm{NP}}/z(t) = s(t) + n(t)\right),$$

where β – probability of missing a target:

$$\beta = P(\mu(\tau) \leq \ln \Lambda_{\mathrm{NP}}/z(t) = s(t) + n(t)) = P(x(\tau) \geq 0/z(t) = s(t) + n(t))$$

$$= \int_0^\infty w(x, T_2/z(t) = s(t) + n(t)) dx. \tag{16}$$

A feature of this situation is that LRF depends on the ratio τ and τ_0 (true duration): if $T_1 \leq \tau < \tau_0$, then

$$\ln \Lambda[z(t), \tau/z(t) = s(t) + n(t)] = \frac{2A_0}{N_0} \int_0^\tau n(t)g(t)dt + \frac{A_0^2}{N_0} \int_0^\tau g^2(t)dt;$$

if $\tau_0 \leq \tau < T_2$, then

$$\ln \Lambda[z(t), \tau/z(t) = s(t) + n(t)] = \frac{2A_0}{N_0} \int_0^\tau n(t)g(t)dt - \frac{A_0^2}{N_0} \int_0^\tau g^2(t)dt + \frac{2A_0^2}{N_0} \int_0^{\tau_0} g^2(t)dt$$

or, combining,

$$\ln \Lambda[z(t), \tau/z(t) = s(t) + n(t)] = \frac{2A_0}{N_0} \int_0^\tau n(t)g(t)dt$$

$$+ \frac{2A_0^2}{N_0} \int\limits_0^{\min(\tau,\tau_0)} g^2(t)dt - \frac{A_0^2}{N_0} \int\limits_0^{\tau} g^2(t)dt. \tag{17}$$

This leads to the fact that the drift coefficient in the FPK equation has different values depending on the indicated ratios:

$$a(x,\tau) = \begin{cases} -a_1 = -\frac{A_0^2}{N_0} g^2(\tau), \ T_1 \leq \tau < \tau_0; \\ a_1 = \frac{A_0^2}{N_0} g^2(\tau), \ \tau_0 \leq \tau \leq T_2, \end{cases} \quad a_1 > 0, \tag{18}$$

the diffusion coefficient is still equal to

$$b(x,\tau) = \frac{2A_0^2}{N_0} g^2(\tau). \tag{19}$$

Thus, it is necessary to find a solution to Eq. (8) with the initial condition.

$$w_1(s_1, T_1) = \frac{1}{\sqrt{4\pi h^2(T_1)}} \exp\left[-\frac{(s_1 - \ln \Lambda_{NP} + h^2(T_1))^2}{4h^2(T_1)} \right],$$

boundary conditions

$$w(0,\tau) = 0, \ w(\infty, \tau) = 0.$$

and coefficients (18) and (19).

Since the drift coefficient changes abruptly at $\tau = \tau_0$, the solution to Eq. (8) must be sought separately for the intervals $[T_1; \tau_0)$ and $[\tau_0; T_2]$. Note that to find the probability (16), it is necessary to know the density $w(x, \tau)$ only on the second interval (specifically at the point T_2), however, to find $w(x, \tau)$ on the second interval $[\tau_0; T_2]$ it is necessary to know the expression for $w(x, \tau)$ on the first interval $[T_1; \tau_0)$. In this case, the value $w(x, \tau)$ found on the interval $[T_1; \tau_0)$, at $\tau = \tau_0$ will be the initial condition for finding $w(x, \tau)$ on the interval $[\tau_0; T_2]$.

Let $T_1 \leq \tau < \tau_0$. The solution to Eq. (8) is determined by expression (13) and at $\tau = \tau_0$ considering the values of the coefficients a and b

$$w(x,\tau_0) = \frac{1}{\sqrt{4\pi (h^2(\tau_0) - h^2(T_1))}} \exp\left(-\frac{x}{2} - \frac{h^2(\tau_0)}{4}\right) \exp\left(\frac{h^2(T_1)}{4}\right) \int\limits_0^{\infty} \exp\left(\frac{s_1}{2}\right)$$

$$\times w_1(s_1, T_1) \left\{ \exp\left[-\frac{(x-s_1)^2}{4(h^2(\tau_0) - h^2(T_1))} \right] - \exp\left[-\frac{(x+s_1)^2}{4(h^2(\tau_0) - h^2(T_1))} \right] \right\} ds_1. \tag{20}$$

Expression (20) is the initial condition for solving Eq. (8) on the second interval $[\tau_0; T_2]$.

To simplify writing, we introduce the function

$$f(y_1, y_2, y_3) = \exp\left[-\frac{(y_1 - y_2)^2}{4y_3}\right] - \exp\left[-\frac{(y_1 + y_2)^2}{4y_3}\right]. \tag{21}$$

Considering (21), then we can write:

$$w(x, \tau_0) \equiv w_2(x, \tau_0) = \frac{1}{\sqrt{4\pi\left(h^2(\tau_0) - h^2(T_1)\right)}} \exp\left[-\frac{h^2(\tau_0) - h^2(T_1)}{4}\right]$$

$$\times \int_0^\infty w_1(s_1, T_1) \exp\left[\frac{s_1 - x}{2}\right] f\left(x, s_1, h^2(\tau_0) - h^2(T_1)\right) ds_1. \tag{22}$$

Next, we look for a solution to Eq. (8) for $\tau_0 \le \tau < T_2$ with boundary conditions.

$$w(0, \tau) = 0, w(\infty, \tau) = 0.$$

and the initial condition $w_2(x, \tau_0)$ defined by (22). We then have:

$$w(x, \tau) = \frac{1}{\sqrt{4\pi\left(h^2(\tau) - h^2(\tau_0)\right)}} \exp\left(\frac{x}{2} - \frac{h^2(\tau)}{4}\right) \exp\left(\frac{h^2(\tau_0)}{4}\right)$$

$$\times \int_0^\infty w_2(s_2, \tau_0) \exp\left(-\frac{s_2}{2}\right) f\left(x, s_2, h^2(\tau) - h^2(\tau_0)\right) ds_2$$

$$= \frac{1}{4\pi\sqrt{\left(h^2(\tau) - h^2(\tau_0)\right)\left(h^2(\tau_0) - h^2(T_1)\right)}} \exp\left(\frac{x}{2} - \frac{h^2(\tau)}{4}\right) \exp\left(\frac{h^2(\tau_0)}{4}\right)$$

$$\times \exp\left[-\frac{h^2(\tau_0) - h^2(T_1)}{4}\right] \int_0^\infty \int_0^\infty w_1(s_1, T_1) \exp\left[\frac{s_1 - s_2}{2}\right] \exp\left(-\frac{s_2}{2}\right)$$

$$\times f\left(s_2, s_1, h^2(\tau_0) - h^2(T_1)\right) f\left(x, s_2, h^2(\tau) - h^2(\tau_0)\right) ds_1 ds_2. \tag{23}$$

After substituting (23) at the point $\tau = T_2$ into formula (16), the final distribution takes the form:

$$P_{CD} = 1 - \frac{1}{4\pi\sqrt{\left(h^2(T_2) - h^2(\tau_0)\right)\left(h^2(\tau_0) - h^2(T_1)\right)}} \int_0^\infty \exp\left(\frac{x}{2} - \frac{h^2(T_2)}{4}\right) \exp\left(\frac{h^2(\tau_0)}{4}\right)$$

$$\times \exp\left[\frac{h^2(T_1) - h^2(\tau_0)}{4}\right] \int_0^\infty \int_0^\infty w_1(s_1, T_1) \exp\left[\frac{s_1 - s_2}{2}\right] \exp\left(-\frac{s_2}{2}\right)$$

$$\times g\left(s_2, s_1, h^2(\tau_0) - h^2(T_1)\right) g\left(x, s_2, h^2(T_2) - h^2(\tau_0)\right) ds_1 ds_2 dx. \tag{24}$$

Applying the same method as for the dependence of the probability of a false alarm, and applying the same notation, we can simplify expression (24) as follows:

$$
P_{CD} = 1 - \frac{1}{4\sqrt{\pi\left(h_0^2 - h_1^2\right)}} \exp\left[\frac{h_1^2 - h_0^2}{4}\right] \times \int_0^\infty \int_0^\infty w_1(s_1, T_1) \exp\left[\frac{s_1 - s_2}{2}\right]
$$

$$
\times \left[erfc\left(-\frac{\left(h_2^2 - h_0^2\right) + s_2}{\sqrt{4\left(h_2^2 - h_0^2\right)}}\right) - \exp(-s_2)erfc\left(-\frac{\left(h_2^2 - h_0^2\right) - s_2}{\sqrt{4\left(h_2^2 - h_0^2\right)}}\right) \right]
$$

$$
\times g\left(s_2, s_1, h_0^2 - h_1^2\right) ds_1 ds_2, \tag{25}
$$

where $h^2(T_0) = h_0^2$ – signal-to-noise ratio for the studied signal of duration T_0 (true signal-to-noise ratio).

Thus, in this clause, the noise immunity characteristics of the algorithm for detecting an arbitrary waveform with an unknown duration were obtained.

3   Modeling

To simulate the operation of the algorithm, we will form the logarithm of the likelihood ratio functional in discrete form. To do this, we assume that there are M samples of the received oscillation, and the samples of the noise process correspond to the following form:

$$
n_k = \frac{1}{\Delta t} \int_{t_k}^{t_k + \Delta t} n(t)dt,
$$

where $\Delta t = \frac{T}{M-1}$; $t_k = k\Delta t$, $k = \overline{0, M-1}$.

These samples of the Gaussian process have zero mean and variance equal to:

$$
\mathbf{D}[n_k] \equiv \sigma^2 = \frac{1}{\Delta t^2}\mathbf{E}\left[\int_{t_k}^{t_k + \Delta t}\int_{t_k}^{t_k + \Delta t} n(t_1)n(t_2)dt_1 dt_2\right]
$$

$$
= \frac{1}{\Delta t^2}\frac{N_0}{2}\mathbf{E}\left[\int_{t_k}^{t_k + \Delta t}\int_{t_k}^{t_k + \Delta t} \delta(t_1 - t_2)dt_1 dt_2\right] = \frac{N_0}{2\Delta t}.
$$

The information signal has the form:

$$
s_k = \begin{cases} A_0 g_k, & k \in [0, k_\tau - 1]; \\ 0, & k \in [k_\tau - 1, M - 1], \end{cases}
$$

where k_τ – the index corresponding to the duration so that $k_\tau \Delta t = \tau$.

The received waveform is a sample of M samples, each of which is described as follows:

$$z_k = s_k + n_k, \ k = \overline{0, M - 1}.$$

The LRF logarithm will be represented by the following expression:

$$\ln \Lambda[\mathbf{z}, k_\tau] = \frac{A_0}{\sigma^2} \sum_{k=0}^{k_\tau - 1} z_k - \frac{A_0^2}{2\sigma^2} \sum_{k=0}^{k_\tau - 1} g_k^2, \tag{26}$$

The ML-estimate is the value that maximizes the LRF (26), that is:

$$\Lambda^* = \ln \Lambda[\mathbf{z}, k^*] > \ln \Lambda_{\text{NP}}.$$

Further, according to the algorithm given below, simulation modeling was carried out, during which the dependence of the false alarm probability P_{FA} on the threshold value $\ln \Lambda_{\text{NP}}$ was obtained as the following condition

$$P_{\text{FA}} = P\{\Lambda^* > \ln \Lambda_{\text{NP}}/z_k = n_k\},$$

and the dependence of the probability of correct detection P_{CD} on the true signal-to-noise ratio h_0, determined by the formula:

$$P_{\text{CD}} = P\{\Lambda^* > \ln \Lambda_{\text{NP}}/z_k = s_k + n_k\}.$$

Simulation is carried out for the Nyquist signal given by the formula:

$$s_k = \begin{cases} A_0 \operatorname{sinc}(k/M) \cdot \frac{\cos(\pi \cdot \beta \cdot k/M)}{1 - 4 \cdot \beta^2 \cdot k^2/M^2}, & k = 0, \ldots, k_\tau - 1; \\ 0, & k = k_\tau, \ldots, M - 1, \end{cases}$$

where β – impulse shape smoothing factor; $\operatorname{sinc}(x) = \sin(x)/\pi x$.

Observation interval $[0; T]$, where $T = 1$ s, prior interval $[T_1; T_2]$, where $T_1 = 0.4$ s and $T_1 = 0.6$ s, the true duration is 0.5 s, counts in the signal $M = 256$. The very procedure for conducting modeling has the following structure:

1. The received oscillation is formed by adding the useful signal with Gaussian noise with zero mean and known intensity.
2. Using formula (26), a set of values of the LRF logarithm is formed for each possible duration, as described in Fig. 1. The maximum value is selected, which corresponds to the estimate of the duration, and it is additionally assumed that there is no useful signal.
3. Several values of the threshold value $\ln \Lambda_{\text{NP}}$ is set and by means of multiple repetitions of the algorithm for each value from a given series, as a result, the dependence of the logarithm of the threshold value on the probability of a false alarm is constructed.
4. The value of the probability P_{FA} is set, and the corresponding dependence is constructed according to the formula (15). This dependence is then used to find the value of $\ln \Lambda_{\text{NP}}$ corresponding to the given value of the probability.

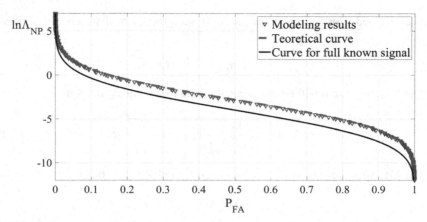

Fig. 2. Dependence of the false alarm probability on the threshold value at SNR h = 2

5. By using several specified SNR of the signal, multiple tests of the algorithm are carried out for the case of the presence of a useful signal at the receiver input with the threshold value from the previous paragraph, based on the results of which the dependence of the probability of correct detection on the signal-to-noise ratio is constructed at a fixed value of the probability of false alarms.

Below in Figs. 2, 3 the obtained dependences are shown, as well as the theoretical curves and dependences corresponding to the case of a completely known signal.

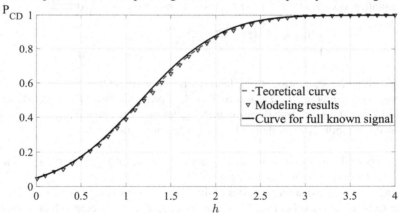

Fig. 3. Dependence of the probability of correct detection on SNR at the probability of a false alarm $P_{FA} = 0.05$

It is also interesting if we do not know the waveform and assume that the signal is rectangular. In this case, the signal energies are considered equal. Figure 4 shows the simulation results.

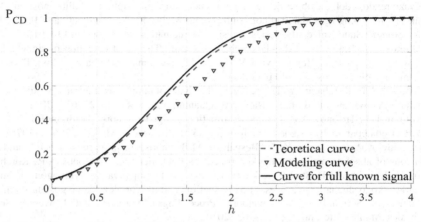

Fig. 4. Dependence of the probability of correct detection on SNR at the probability of a false alarm $P_{FA} = 0.05$ and the assumption upon reception that the signal is rectangular

4 Conclusion

Thus, in the course of the work, a solution was found, and a method was proposed for solving the Fokker–Planck–Kolmogorov (FPK) equation with time-dependent coefficients. Since all the calculations in this paper are carried out in a general form, now you can use finite expressions to find a solution to the FPK–equation for other signal forms. To do this, you only need to check the coefficients of the FPK–equation.

Modeling was also carried out, according to the results of which it can be concluded that ignorance of the signal duration leads to a slight deterioration in the noise immunity parameters, for example, when the probability of correct detection of $P_{CD} = 0.8$, the difference in the SNR is 0.2 dB. At the same time, if we additionally consider the signal form unknown and take it rectangular, then the noise immunity losses are 1.5 dB in the SNR.

This detector can be used in systems that would detect signals from devices whose access is prohibited in this territory. That is, in systems for monitoring unauthorized entry.

The next stage of research is to consider another form of signal, as well as the additional lack of information about the signal amplitude and the determination of the optimal algorithm for joint detection–estimating the duration and amplitude of the signal.

References

1. Trifonov, A.P., Korchagin, Yu.E., Linvinov, E.V.: Quasi likelihood detection of the signal with unknown amplitude and duration. [Trifonov A.P., Korchagin Yu.E., Linvinov E.V. Kvazipravdopodobnoe obnarujenie signalov s neizvestnymi amplitudoi i dlitel'nost'yu]. Vestnik Voronezhskogo gosudarstvennogo universiteta. Seriya: Fizika. Matematika — Proceedings of Voronezh State University. Series: Physics. Mathematics, no. 1, pp. 41–49 (2016)
2. Akimov, I.S., Bakut, P.A., Bogdanovich, V.A., et al.: Theory of detection of signals. [Akimov I.S., Bakut P.A., Bogdanovich V.A. i dr. Teoriya obnaruzheniya signalov]. Radio and communications, Moscow, 440 p. (1984)
3. Trifonov, A.P., Korchagin, Yu.E.: Receiving the signal of unknown duration. Izvestiya vysshix uchebnyx zavedenij. Radiofizika Radiophy. Quantum Electr. **45**(5), 625–637 (2002)
4. Kulikov, E.I., Trifonov, A.P.: Parametr estimation of signals in noise. [Kulikov E.I., Trifonov A.P. Ocenka parametrov signalov na fone pomekh]. Sov. Radio, Moscow, 296 p. (1978)
5. Trifonov, A.P., Korchagin, Yu.E., Bespalova, M.B.: Statistical properties of height and provisions of absolute maximum markov processes Bachelier type. [Trifonov A.P., Korchagin Yu.E., Bespalova M.B. Statisticheskie svoistva vysoty i polojeniya absolyutnogo maksimuma markovskogo sluchainogo processa tipa Bashel'e]. Vestnik Voronezhskogo gosudarstvennogo universiteta. Seriya: Fizika. Matematika — Proceedings of Voronezh State University. Series: Physics. Mathematics, no. 4, pp. 54–65 (2014)
6. Gelgor, A.L., Gorlov, A.I., Popov, E.A.: General theory of communication. Hypothesis testing. Parameter estimation. Optimal signal reception. [Gel'gor A. L., Gorlov A. I., Popov E. A. Obshchaya teoriya svyazi. Proverka statisticheskih gipotez. Ocenivanie parametrov. Optimal'nyj priyom signalov]. Saint Peterburg State Polytechnic University, St. Peterburg, 227 p. (2013)

Application of Neural Network to Demodulate SEFDM Signals

Anastasiia I. Semenova$^{(\boxtimes)}$ (ID) and Sergey V. Zavjalov$^{(\boxtimes)}$ (ID)

Peter the Great St. Petersburg Polytechnic University, St. Petersburg, Russia
semenova.aigor@gmail.com, zavyalov_sv@spbstu.ru

Abstract. The paper presents a research of the effectiveness of using neural networks to demodulate SEFDM signals when passing through a channel with AWGN. Investigation of the questions of numbers of subcarriers for structure for analogue full search, realization the architecture, of analogue full search for processing SEFDM signals with different bandwidth compression factor between subcarriers are considered. Simulation modeling and comparison with element-by-element signal demodulation algorithms are carried out. Also, considered comparison with analogue full search, which realized in another work.

Keywords: SEFDM · Neural networks · Demodulation · Full search

1 Introduction

The 5-6G standards focus on spectral efficiency, which is calculated as the ratio of the data transfer rate to the bandwidth width [1–4]. Therefore, a non-orthogonal SEFDM (Spectrally Efficient Frequency Division Multiplexing) waveform is being developed, which shows improved spectral efficiency due to a more compact and dense arrangement of the subsystems in the frequency domain. The advantage of the SEFDM signal is the saving of bandwidth [5–8].

In SEFDM, the signals on neighboring carrier frequencies overlap each other and this creates interference that affects the stability of the reception. To solve this problem, it is necessary to use full search algorithms [9], Viterbi algorithms [10], and algorithms with compensation [11], but these algorithms are difficult to implement, and this in turn reduces the battery life.

In real systems, it is necessary to use complex algorithms, which leads to an increase in complexity and high-power consumption [12]. Recently, machine learning has been used in telecommunications systems due to its ability to work with complex systems for which it is impossible to perform mathematical modeling.

Currently, deep learning methods are used in communication systems to solve complex mathematical problems. These algorithms were proposed to be used for physical layer applications. Deep learning uses many hidden layers to extract more features and build an efficient neural network [13].

Most signal processing algorithms are usually linear and stationary. However, in practice, the information transmission systems are affected by numerous factors. These

© Springer Nature Switzerland AG 2022
Y. Koucheryavy et al. (Eds.): NEW2AN 2021/ruSMART 2021, LNCS 13158, pp. 405–412, 2022.
https://doi.org/10.1007/978-3-030-97777-1_34

factors are difficult to consider when constructing reception algorithms, but they can lead to degradation of BER (bit error rate) performance of reception and the speed of information transmission. In this case, it is more convenient to use deep learning in the processing block since it will be better optimized for a specific hardware platform and channel [14].

To determine the types of suitable neural network architectures for demodulating SEFDM signals, a literature review was made [12–16]. It was decided to use a fully connected neural network architecture. This architecture has the property of accounting for interference between subcarriers, since all the neurons of this network are connected to each other (information comes from each neuron to each neuron of the subsequent layer).

The aim of the work is to evaluate effectiveness of using of neural networks for demodulating SEFDM signals. The feature of the algorithm is that it can be used for any number of subcarriers divided into subgroups of four. This algorithm does not overload the work of the computing device and can be implemented in field-programmable gate array (FPGA).

In this paper, we consider the neural network (NN) structure designed for BPSK (Binary Phase Shift Keying) demodulation. The motivation of using BPSK is due to obtaining the lower border of the reception BER performance.

2   The Structure of Neural Network

In this paper, we implemented the structure of a fully connected neural network for full search. Figure 1 shows the structure of the analogue of full search for the case of 4 subcarriers.

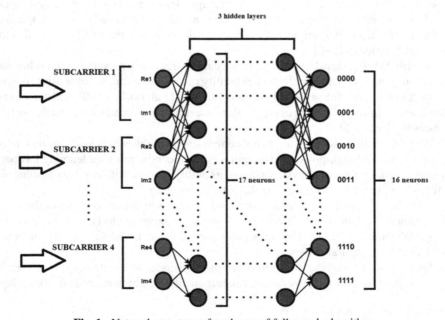

Fig. 1. Network structure of analogue of full search algorithm.

The idea is as follows: implementing a neural network structure to demodulate SEFDM signals for more subcarriers is difficult due to the high computational complexity than for 4 subcarriers. Therefore, the idea was proposed to divide the subcarriers into subgroups (each subgroup has 4 subcarriers). The input of the network is fed sequentially samples of signals from subcarrier frequencies. The number of subcarriers arriving at the input of the neural network can be any, the computational complexity increases slightly, thereby allowing you to use any number of subcarriers at the input without complicating the learning process. Each output neuron encodes a bit sequence that is transmitted to the subcarriers. For example, if four information symbols «0» are transmitted on four subcarriers, then the response should be on the first neuron, which is equivalent to the four symbols «0». The work of the direct pass will be presented below using the example of the work of a single neuron (Fig. 2).

The input is supplied with complex samples of the signal, divided into real and imaginary components. These groups are multiplied by the corresponding weight coefficients, and then added together. Then, the calculation is performed using the activation function, which calculates the output value of the neuron and feeds it to the output of the neural network in this example. The activation function calculates the output value and feeds it to the network output in this example (Fig. 2). Note that an example is given without hidden layers, for the convenience of understanding how a direct pass occurs. In this paper, the hyperbolic tangent activation function was selected. The selection was made considering the range of input data values in the range from -1 to $+1$.

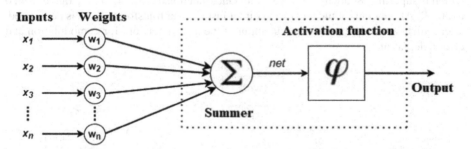

Fig. 2. A model of an artificial neuron. Direct passage.

To train the neural network, the built-in toolbox Neural Network MATLAB library was used. The training process is performed until the minimum error is reached (Fig. 3). The minimum error criterion is set before the start of training and is the value of the error function $\leq 10^{-5}$. The error at the network output is calculated using the root-mean-square error (MSE). The formula is presented below.

$$\frac{1}{N} \sum_{i=1}^{N} (a_i - y_i)^2,$$

where N – is the number of subcarriers, i – is the ordinal number of subcarriers, a –the received value at the network output, y – the initial value that should be obtained at the network output.

The procedure for teaching this architecture is described in detail in the following literature [17].

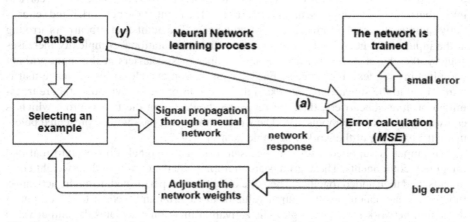

Fig. 3. The process of training a neural network. The example in the figure indicates a complex count.

When analyzing the BER performance, the SEFDM signal is formed at the first stage, which is superimposed with additive white Gaussian noise (AWGN) in the range from 0 to 20 dB. At the input of the receiver, a direct fast Fourier transform (FFT) is performed, after which the samples are fed to the input of the neural network for demodulation and error calculation.

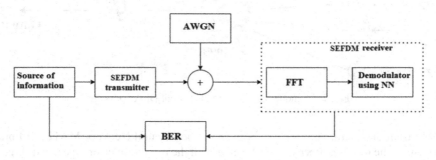

Fig. 4. Block diagram of the simulation model.

In the third chapter, we will present the results of comparing the BER performance curves of SEFDM, considering the neural network in the channel with the AWGN with the element-by-element reception. The result of comparison with the algorithm of reception based on full search, implemented in [18], will also be presented. To simulate multi-frequency signals, the following parameters were selected: number of subcarriers 32, compaction coefficients (0.8, 0.9, 1), BPSK modulation. At least 10^6 information bits were transmitted to each point according to the error probability.

3 Results

Figure 5 shows the results of the BER performance of SEFDM signals for different values of the compaction coefficient for the AWGN channel. The network structure of this reception is shown in Fig. 1. Based on the result in Fig. 5, we note that the energy gain at alpha 0.8 and 0.9 was 3 dB in terms of the probability of error 10^{-3} relative to the element-by-element reception. The energy loss is equal to 1 dB in terms of the probability of error 10^{-3} relative to the potential BER performance of receiving BPSK signals.

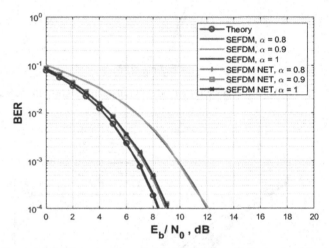

Fig. 5. Reception BER performance for the algorithm of full search of 4 subcarriers.

Figure 6 shows the result for 8 subcarriers (analogous of full search, we divided 8 subcarriers into two subgroups of 4 subcarriers each). In this result, there is an energy gain of about 3 dB for the case of alpha 0.9 and an energy gain of about 6 dB for the case of alpha 0.8. In comparison with Fig. 5, there is a doubling of the energy gain for the case of alpha 0.8.

Figure 7 shows the result of the BER performance of SEFDM signals with 32 subcarriers divided into subgroups. In the case of alpha 0.8, there is an energy gain of about 2 dB compared to Fig. 6. In the case of 0.9, there is an energy gain of 4 dB of the BER performance curve, considering the neural network.

Figs. 5, 6, 7 show a comparison with the element-by-element method. Let us consider a comparison with the algorithm for accepting a full search, implemented in [18] (Fig. 8).

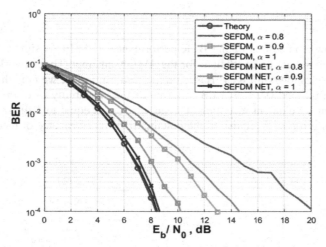

Fig. 6. Reception BER performance for a modified full-search algorithm for 8 subcarriers.

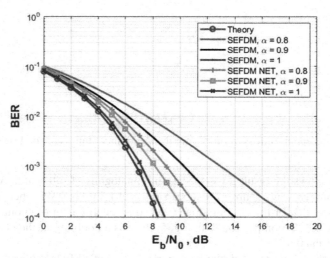

Fig. 7. Reception BER performance for a modified analogue full search algorithm for 32 subcarriers.

Let us compare the results of the BER performance of receiving SEFDM signals in a channel with AWGN between the algorithm of full search of NN (divided into subgroups), the algorithm with feedback of NN, and the algorithm of reception based on full search [18]. The number of subcarriers is 32, BPSK modulation. The energy gain is present in the reception algorithm based on a full search with a compaction coefficient equal to 0.5 [18].

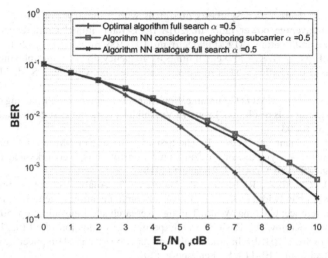

Fig. 8. Comparison of algorithms considering the NN and the reception algorithm based on a full search [18].

4 Conclusions

As a result of experiments, it was found that for a complete search, the architecture for 4 subcarriers is optimal according to the criteria of computational complexity and the signal-to-noise ratio.

The BER performance of reception taking into account the neural network has an energy gain compared to the element-by-element reception when using any number of subcarriers, but loses in energy terms compared to the full search algorithm.

Acknowledgements. The results of the work were obtained with the support of the scholarship of the President of the Russian Federation to young scientists and graduate students carrying out promising research and development in priority areas of modernization of the Russian economy for 2021–2023 (СП-1671.2021.3) and used computational re-sources of Peter the Great Saint-Petersburg Polytechnic University Supercomputing Center (http://www.scc.spbstu.ru).

References

1. Makarov, S.B., et al.: Optimizing the shape of Faster-Than-Nyquist (FTN) signals with the constraint on energy concentration in the occupied frequency bandwidth. IEEE Access **8**, 130082–130093 (2020)
2. Makarov, S.B., Markov, A.M.: Incoherent reception "in a whole" of spectrally effective signals formed on the basis of phase pulses of the shape $\sin^p x$. Radioeng. **84**(12) (24), 43–51 (2020)
3. Irfan, M., Aïssa, S.: Generalization of index-modulation: breaking the conventional limits on spectral and energy efficiencies. In: IEEE Transactions on Wireless Communications, pp.1–1 (2021)

4. Sadovaya, Y., Gelgor, A.: Synthesis of signals with a low-level of out-of-band emission and peak-to-average power ratio. In: 2018 IEEE International Conference on Electrical Engineering and Photonics (EExPolytech), pp. 103–106, St. Petersburg (2018)

5. Slyusar, V.I., Vasil'ev, K.A.: Potential limits of frequency division multiplexing of N-OFDM signals based on Hartley's basis functions. Radioelectron. Commun. Syst. **51**(3), 129–133 (2008)

6. Slyusar, V.I., Smolyar, V.G.: Communication channels frequency multiplexing on the basis of superrayleigh signals resolution. Izvestiya Vysshikh Uchebnykh Zavedenij. Radioelektronika **46**(7), 30–39 (2003)

7. Darwazeh, I., Ghannam, H., Xu, T.: The first 15 years of SEFDM: a brief survey. In: 2018 11th International Symposium on Communication Systems, Networks and Digital Signal Processing (CSNDSP), pp. 1–7, Budapest (2018)

8. Kanaras, I., Chorti, A., Rodrigues, M., Darwazeh, I.: Analysis of sub-optimum detection techniques for bandwidth efficient multi-carrier communication system. In: Cranfield Multi-Strand Conference: Creating Wealth Through Research and Innovation, pp. 505–510 (2008)

9. Kislitsyn, A., Krylov, A., Rashich, A.: Experimental evaluation of SEFDM trellis based demodulator. In: 2020 IEEE International Conference on Electrical Engineering and Photonics (EExPolytech), pp. 110–113, St. Petersburg, (2020)

10. Gelgor, A., Gorlov, A., Nguyen, V.P.: Performance analysis of SEFDM with optimal subcarriers spectrum shapes. In: 2017 IEEE International Black Sea Conference on Communications and Networking (BlackSeaCom), Istanbul, pp. 1–5 (2017)

11. Xu, T., Darwazeh, I.: Design and prototyping of neural network compression for non-orthogonal IoT signals. In: 2019 IEEE Wireless Communications and Networking Conference (WCNC), Marrakesh, pp. 1–6 (2019)

12. Xu, T., Xu, T., Darwazeh, I.: Deep learning for interference cancellation in non-orthogonal signal based optical communication systems. In: 2018 Progress in Electromagnetics Research Symposium (PIERS-Toyama), pp. 241–248, Toyama (2018)

13. Haykin, S.: Neural networks and learning machines. Pearson; 3rd edition, p. 936 (2008)

14. Jia, M., Yin, Z., Guo, Q., Liu, G., Gu, X.: Downlink design for spectrum efficient IoT network. IEEE Internet of Things J. **5**(5), 3397–3404 (2018)

15. Sun, Y., Wang, C., Cai, H., Zhao, C., Wu, Y., Chen, Y.: Deep learning based equalizer for MIMO-OFDM systems with insufficient cyclic prefix. In: 2020 IEEE 92nd Vehicular Technology Conference (VTC2020-Fall), pp. 1–5 (2020)

16. O'Shea, T., Hoydis, J.: An introduction to deep learning for the physical layer. In: IEEE Transactions on Cognitive Communications and Networking, pp. 563–575 (2017)

17. Xu, T., Darwazeh I.: Deep learning for over-the-air non-orthogonal signal classification. In: 2020 IEEE 91st Vehicular Technology Conference (VTC2020-Spring), pp. 1–5 (2020)

18. Kislitsyn, A.B.: Algorithms for receiving spectral-effective multi-frequency signals with non-orthogonal frequency compaction: dissertation of the Candidate of Technical Sciences, St. Petersburg, p. 143 (2016)

Electromagnetic Waves Propagation in Low-Profile SIW Structures

Ekaterina Kiseleva$^{(\boxtimes)}$ [ID], Artem Galushko [ID], and Alexander Sochava [ID]

Peter the Great St.Petersburg Polytechnic University (SPbPU), Polytechnicheskaya, 29, St. Petersburg 195251, Russia
kate.danilchenko96@gmail.com

Abstract. In this work the investigation of the substrate integrated waveguides (SIW) characteristics is presented. The losses in the SIW structure with different parameters were calculated. The analytical calculation is based on the theory of the Kontorovich's averaged boundary conditions. The numerical calculation was carried out using the Ansys HFSS software package. The distribution of the electromagnetic field along one low-profile SIW structure and several adjacent structures was obtained numerically. Another interesting result is the obtained field distribution for a long SIW structure. The results of this study can be useful for the development of devices based on SIW structures transmitting electromagnetic waves.

Keywords: SIW structure · S-parameters · Averaged boundary conditions · Ansys HFSS

1 Introduction

SIW structures have been actively studied and applied for the past 20 years [1]. Various devices can be manufactured based on these structures. For example, antennas, couplers, millimeter-wave chips, etc. [2, 3].

SIW waveguides make it possible to significantly reduce the dimensions of the transmitting part, in comparison with classical rectangular waveguides. This feature makes the waveguides of this structure in demand in microwave systems due to continuing miniaturization of such systems.

In this article, the SIW structure losses are analytically calculated by the Kontorovich method [4] and compared with the analytical calculations given by Bozza and etc. [5, 6]. In the Kontorovich method, the SIW vias rows of waveguide are represented as the surface of parallel conductors. An electromagnetic wave illuminates this surface at the angle of $\varphi = 90^0$ (Fig. 1). This approach can also be found in the works of Yatsenko and etc. [7].

No less interesting is the numerical calculation of electromagnetic field inside the SIW waveguide structure. Such a distribution can be obtained using the finite element method in the Ansys HFSS program both for one structure and for several adjacent structures. Also in this software package there is a possibility of numerical calculation of losses, which will allow comparing the results of numerical and analytical calculations.

© Springer Nature Switzerland AG 2022
Y. Koucheryavy et al. (Eds.): NEW2AN 2021/ruSMART 2021, LNCS 13158, pp. 413–426, 2022.
https://doi.org/10.1007/978-3-030-97777-1_35

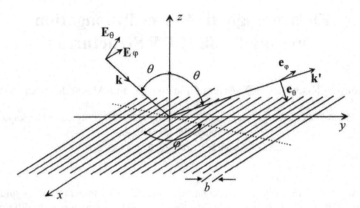

Fig. 1. The model for a vias row used in the framework of the Kontorovich method.

The adjacent SIW structures considered in this work could be used to construct slotted antenna arrays, for example, for satellite communication antennas (television antennas), security systems, flying objects, etc. [8]. This type of implementation of slotted antennas is easy, technologically advanced and cost effective.

2 Analytical Calculation of Losses in the SIW Structure

2.1 The Kontorovich's Averaged Boundary Conditions Method

As it was said to calculate the loss factor, we represent the vias boundaries of waveguide in the form of a parallel conductors system. To find the fields created by all currents and charges in the plane of the grid, we use the formula (1) from sources [4, 7]: Eq. (11)

$$\vec{E} = -i\frac{\omega}{c}\vec{A}_m - grad\ \varphi_m \tag{1}$$

The average vector and scalar potentials can be expressed as follows:

$$\vec{A}_m = \frac{\mu}{c}\int_S \vec{j_m}\,\Psi\,dS;\ \varphi_m = \frac{1}{\varepsilon}\int_S \sigma_m\Psi\,dS \tag{2}$$

Constraints imposed by the averaged Kontorovich boundary conditions (b - distance between conductors; r_0 - radius of conductors):

$$b \ll \lambda;\ 2r_0 \ll b \tag{3}$$

Considering that the current flows only along one axis, we will neglect the currents j_y. Then the electric field vector potential of the parallel conductors grid:

$$A_x = \frac{\mu}{c}\int_F \vec{j_x}\,(x, y)\Psi(R)dF + \frac{\mu}{c}2\vec{j_x}\,b\,ln\left(\frac{b}{2\pi r_0}\right) \tag{4}$$

There are no vertical and horizontal conductors in the model under consideration. Hence we got an electric field:

$$E_x = -E_x^s + \frac{2i\omega\,\mu b}{c^2} \ln\frac{b}{2\pi r_0}\left[(1 + F_0)j_0 + \frac{1}{k^2}\frac{\partial^2 j_x}{\partial x^2}\right] \qquad (5)$$

$$F_0 = -\frac{\mu_i f(s)}{4\,\mu\,\ln\frac{b}{2\pi r_0}}; f(s) = \begin{cases} 1 - \frac{1}{s^2}, & \text{if "}s\text{" is small} \\ 1 - \frac{i}{s}, & \text{if "}s\text{" is large} \\ 0, & \text{if } \sigma = \infty \end{cases} \qquad (6)$$

$$s = -\frac{r_0\sqrt{\pi\,\mu_i\sigma\omega}}{\sqrt{2}c} \qquad (7)$$

The E-field reflection coefficient from the surface can be obtained through the relation:

$$R_{\parallel}^e = \frac{\left(\overrightarrow{E^{ref}}\,\vec{e}_\theta\right)}{E_0^e} \qquad (8)$$

We substitute the previously obtained electric field into Eq. (8) and have a formula for calculating the reflection coefficient.

$$R_{\parallel}^e = \frac{\cos^2\theta}{1 - \sin^2\theta}\left[1 + i\frac{2b}{\lambda}\ln\frac{b}{2\pi r_0}\cos\theta\left(1 + \frac{F_0}{1 - 1 - \sin^2\theta}\right)\right]^{-1} \qquad (9)$$

The angle θ depends on the free space wavenumber (n - mode number):

$$\theta = arccos\left(\frac{n\lambda}{2b}\right) \qquad (10)$$

Then the Maclaurin's series expansion approximation can be applied. Therefore, consider the incident field in Fig. 1 as a plane wave:

$$\overrightarrow{E^{inc}} = \vec{E}e^{-i\vec{k}\vec{r}} \qquad (11)$$

Each numbered wire will create an electric field:

$$E_{xn}^W = -\frac{\eta}{4k}\left(k^2 - k_x^2\right)I_n H_0^{(2)}\left(\sqrt{k^2 - k_x^2}r_n\right) \qquad (12)$$

$\eta = \sqrt{\frac{\mu_a}{\varepsilon_a}}$ – wave impedance of the environment; $r_n = \sqrt{(y - y_n)^2 - z^2}$; $H_0^{(2)}$ – the second kind Hankel function.

The current on the n conductor will be:

$$I_n = Ie^{-ik_x x}e^{-ik_y y} \qquad (13)$$

$$k_x = k\,\sin\theta; k_y = k\,\sin\theta; k_z = k\,\cos\theta$$

The local field from the n-conductor will be equal to:

$$E_x^{loc} = E_x e^{-jk_x} - \frac{\eta}{2k}\left(k^2 - k_x^2\right)Ie^{-jk_x}\sum_{n=1}^{\infty}\cos(k_y bn)H_0^{(2)}\left(\sqrt{k^2 - k_x^2}bn\right) \quad (14)$$

The boundary condition for the first conductor with index 0 can be written as follows:

$$E_x^{loc} + E_{x0}^W = ZIe^{-jk_x} \quad (15)$$

This model corresponds to the condition of the small conductor radius ($kr_0 \ll 1$). For this condition the Hankel function can be simplified (C - Euler's constant).

$$H_0^{(2)}\left(\sqrt{k^2 - k_x^2}r_0\right) \approx 1 - j\frac{2}{\pi}\left(log\frac{\sqrt{k^2 - k_x^2}r_0}{2} + C\right) \quad (16)$$

Then the first conductor field can be represented as follows:

$$E_x - \frac{\eta}{2k^2 b}\left(k^2 - k_x^2\right)I(1 + j\alpha) = ZI \quad (17)$$

α – mesh density parameter:

$$\alpha = \frac{kb}{\pi}\left[ln\frac{b}{2\pi r_0} + \frac{1}{2}\sum_{n=-\infty}^{\infty}\left(\frac{2\pi}{\sqrt{(2\pi b + k_y b)^2 - (k^2 - k_x^2)b^2}} - \frac{1}{|n|}\right)\right] \quad (18)$$

Next, we can introduce the surface current density:

$$J = \frac{I}{b} = \frac{2}{\eta}\frac{E_x\cos\theta}{(1 + j\alpha\cos\theta) + \left(\frac{2}{\eta}\right)Zb\cos\theta} \quad (19)$$

For the far zone, the field incident on the grating is defined as a plane wave:

$$E_\theta^{ref} = \vec{e_\theta}\overrightarrow{E^{ref}} = -\frac{\eta}{2}J \quad (20)$$

Then we can get the reflectance of the incident wave:

$$R_{TE} = \frac{E_\theta^{ref}}{E_\theta} = -\frac{1}{(1 + j\alpha\cos\theta) + (2/\eta)Zb\cos\theta} \quad (21)$$

2.2   Alternative Method for Calculating the Loss Factor in a SIW Structure

Substrate integrated waveguide is a rectangular waveguide bounded above and below by flat metal plates. The side walls are presented in the form of metal vias. The vias have a radius r_0 and are located at a distance p from each other. The height of the waveguide is h, the distance between the rows of vias is W.

To avoid high losses of the radiated field outside the waveguide part, the article [9] gives the conditions for the optimal distance between the landing of the vias and their diameter d (Fig. 2):

$$d < \frac{\lambda_g}{5} \tag{22}$$

$$p < 2d \tag{23}$$

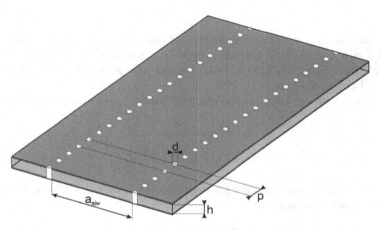

Fig. 2. Calculated model geometry

For such waveguide, we accepted the width of an equivalent rectangular waveguide. In [10], an analysis of the SIW structure calculated for the frequency range of 10–15 GHz was presented. The electric field distributions were obtained for the SIW structure and for an equivalent waveguide with uniform dielectric filling $\varepsilon = 2.2$ and the same height $b = 0.8$ mm in the single mode. The width of an equivalent rectangular waveguide was calculated based on the formula (1) [10]:

$$a_e = a_{siw} - \frac{4r^2}{0,95c_1} \tag{24}$$

a_e – equivalent waveguide width (10.73 mm), a_{siw} – SIW structure width (11 mm), r - radius of vias, c_1 – distance between the vias centers.

The critical frequency of the TE_{10} and SIW structure is given in [9] and is equal to:

$$f_c(TE_{10}) = \frac{c}{2\sqrt{\varepsilon}} * \left(a_{siw} - \frac{4r^2}{0,95c_1} \right)^{-1} \tag{25}$$

$$f_c(TE_{20}) = \frac{c}{\sqrt{\varepsilon}} * \left(a_{siw} - \frac{4r^2}{1.1c_1} - \frac{8r^3}{6.6c_1^2}\right)^{-1} \tag{26}$$

According to [10], the critical frequency TE_{m0} of the mode can be calculated using the following formula:

$$f_c(TE_{m0}) = \frac{m}{2a_{\vartheta}\sqrt{\varepsilon\mu}} \tag{27}$$

However, it is necessary to take into account the nonlinear dependence of the equivalent width a_e depending on the mode. With a rare succession of vias, the field begins to penetrate behind the vias at a lower frequency.

While for a classical rectangular waveguide, the critical frequency can be calculated as follows, taking into account the critical wavelength:

$$f_c = \frac{c}{2} * \sqrt{\left(\frac{m}{a}\right)^2 + \left(\frac{n}{b}\right)^2} \tag{28}$$

Consider the SIW structure with a radius of pins of 0.5 mm and a distance between them of 5 mm at the critical frequency of 5 GHz. Based on the formula for the SIW structure critical frequency (25) and the classical waveguide (28), their width will be similar: 3.1 cm versus 3 cm.

The wavelength can be calculated using the formula for a classical waveguide:

$$\lambda_g = \frac{\lambda_0}{\sqrt{\varepsilon_r\left(1 - \left(\frac{f_c}{f}\right)^2\right)}} \tag{29}$$

Losses in such waveguides have several components: dielectric losses, ohmic losses, and leakage radiation losses:

$$\alpha = \alpha_d + \alpha_c + \alpha_r \tag{30}$$

α_d - dielectric losses (β - propagation phase constant):

$$\alpha_d = \frac{k^2 \tan\delta}{2\beta} \tag{31}$$

The study of electromagnetic fields for various dielectrics is given in the article [11].

α_c - ohmic losses:

$$\alpha_c = \frac{R_s}{a^3 b\beta k\eta}\left(2b\pi^2 + a^3 k^2\right) \tag{32}$$

α_r leakage radiation loss:

$$\alpha_r = \frac{\frac{1}{a_{siw}}\left(\frac{d}{a_{siw}}\right)^{2.84}\left(\frac{p}{d} - 1\right)^{6.28}}{4.85\sqrt{\left(\frac{2a_{siw}}{\lambda_g}\right)^2 - 1}} \tag{33}$$

3 Computer Simulation of Losses in a SIW Structure

3.1 Field Distribution in a SIW Structure and Loss Calculation

The geometry, sources and boundary conditions are specified for the model. The electromagnetic field is calculated by the finite element method based on Maxwell's transformations.

The first step in the model numerical calculation is the construction of its geometry. The distance between the rows of vias is taken as 6 cm. The initial waveguide height h is 2 mm. The distance between the vias is 8 mm, and the radius of the vias r is taken equal to 0.4 mm.

The SIW structure model consists of two metal slabs 0.2 mm thick, located at a distance taken as the waveguide height h. Each metal vias is a separate element, connecting the metal slabs. The space between the metal slabs and the vias is filled with a dielectric. Dielectric constant of the material used is 2.2.

The boundaries of dielectric between the rows of vias are represented as the input and output ports. In Fig. 3 they are marked in red and yellow, respectively. The other boundaries of the dielectric are open boundaries from which energy can be radiated. The waveguide length Y_L equals to 60 cm. The width of the model X_L equals to 18 cm.

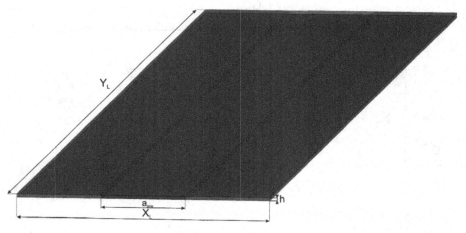

Fig. 3. Constructed model

The losses inside such a waveguide are calculated as:

$$\alpha = \frac{1}{L} \cdot 20 \cdot log \frac{E_0}{E_{np}} \qquad (34)$$

The reflection coefficient is taken as the reflection coefficient of the TE wave (21). Then we finally get the losses inside the waveguide (in dB/m):

$$\alpha = \frac{1}{L} \cdot 20 \cdot log \frac{1}{R_{TE}^n} \qquad (35)$$

Further, the radiation losses were calculated analytically and in HFSS without taking into account ohmic losses and losses in the dielectric. A similar calculation was carried out using the Bozzi formula [6]. Figures 4, 5 and 6 show the dependences of losses on frequency, the radius of the vias and the distance between them.

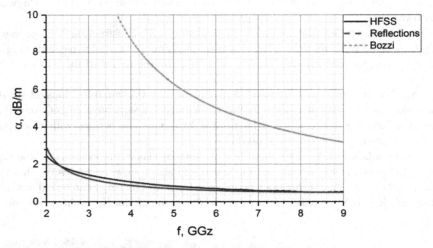

Fig. 4. Frequency dependence of radiation losses

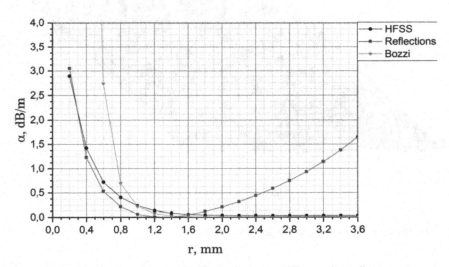

Fig. 5. Dependence of radiation losses on different vias radius

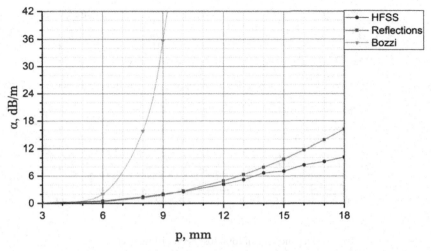

Fig. 6. Dependence of radiation losses on different distances between vias

The results obtained by formula (35) are designated "Theory" and are compared with the results obtained by numerical simulation. In Fig. 7 shows the frequency dependence of the total losses for the SIW structure.

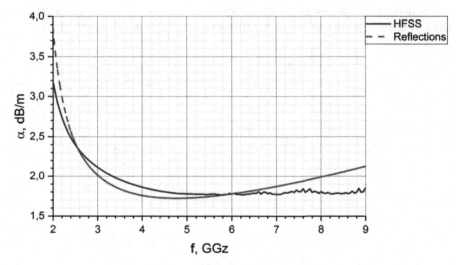

Fig. 7. Frequency dependence of total losses

The dependences of losses on the radii of vias, calculated at a frequency of 2 GHz, are shown in Fig. 8:

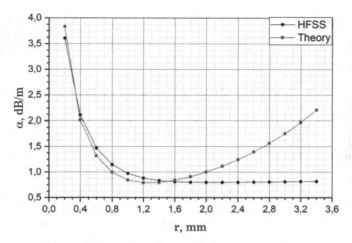

Fig. 8. Dependence of total losses on different vias radius

Despite the closeness of the analytically calculated and modeled losses with an increase in the radius of the vias, the dependences have an excellent character. It is necessary to take into account that the analytical calculation will converge provided that the grid parameter α (18) should be less than 0.3. When the grid parameter exceeds 0.3 ($r > 1.5$) the accuracy of the calculation decreases.

The dependence of losses on the distance between vias was also calculated. The graphs of the dependence of losses at a frequency of 2 GHz are shown in Fig. 9:

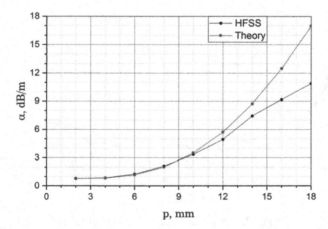

Fig. 9. Dependence of total losses on different distances between vias

In the Ansys HFSS package, we can plot the distribution of an electromagnetic wave inside the volume of a dielectric. This feature allows us to additionally check how much the field inside the waveguide flows out of its aisles. As seen in Fig. 10 and Fig. 11, where the waveguide models have 0.4 mm and 1 mm vias' radius, respectively, the field leakage significantly depends on the waveguide parameters, which accordingly affects the field intensity inside the waveguide.

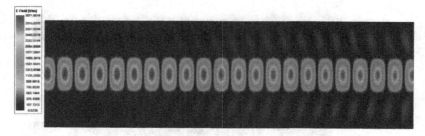

Fig. 10. Field distribution inside the dielectric for r = 0.4 mm

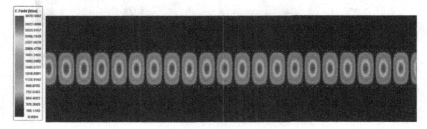

Fig. 11. Field distribution inside the dielectric for r = 1 mm

The obtained results confirm that it is possible to change the amount of losses due to the SIW structure by changing the lattice parameter.

3.2 Field Distribution in Adjacent SIW Structures

Within the framework of this research, it is planned to use such SIW structures for antenna arrays. So, the grating is made of several coupled waveguides, the calculation of the field inside two (Fig. 12) and three (Fig. 13) coupled SIW structures 60 cm long was performed. The radius of the vias in the model is 0.4 mm, the distance between them is 8 mm. A similar study was previously carried out for structures with other parameters [12].

As shown in references [10], the adjacent waveguide model behaves like a directional coupler. However, the amount of branching energy can be controlled by changing the density and radius of the SIW structure vias.

3.3 Field Distribution in Adjacent Long SIW Structures

In the final part of this work, an investigation of three adjacent SIW structures with a length of one and two meters was carried out (Fig. 14, 15). Such a calculation is interesting for predicting the field distribution in antenna arrays based on SIW waveguides [13].

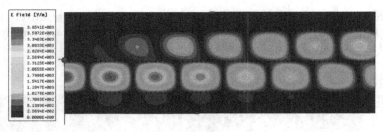

Fig. 12. Field distribution inside the dielectric in two coupled SIW structures

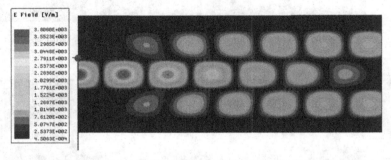

Fig. 13. Field distribution inside the dielectric in three coupled SIW structures

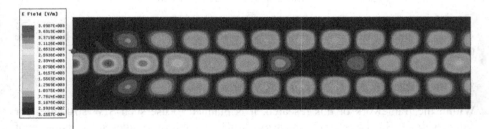

Fig. 14. Field distribution in three coupled SIW structures (length – 1 m)

Fig. 15. Field distribution in three coupled SIW structures (length – 2 m)

As a result, a parasitic effect was revealed. Due to the insufficient density of the SIW grating, energy flows into adjacent waveguides. There are maxima and minima of the field inside the waveguide, which may not allow the required phase shift for the antenna array.

4 Conclusion

The analytical calculation of the loss parameters in a low-profile SIW structure can be considered as the main result of this work. The characteristics obtained by such calculation and calculation using numerical methods turned out to be similar. The distribution of the field inside the waveguide structure with different lattice parameters and for several adjacent structures of different lengths was also obtained numerically. The obtained results prove the fact of a decrease in losses in the structure with a decrease in the distance between the lattice vias or an increase in their radius.

It is important to note that numerical calculation helps to predict various effects without resorting to laborious analytical calculations. This parasitic effect has been found for long coupled structures. With increasing length, energy peaks and drops appear in the waveguide part. Further research and development using SIW structures for antenna arrays will be carried out taking into account the obtained effect.

References

1. Bozzi, M., Perregrini, L., Wu, K., Arcioni, P.: Current and future research trends in substrate integrated waveguide technology. Radioengineering 18(2), 201–209 (2009)
2. Doghri, A., Djerafi, T., Ghiotto, A., Wu, K.: Substrate integrated waveguide directional couplers for compact three-dimensional integrated circuits. IEEE Trans. Microw. Theory Tech. 63(1), 209–219 (2015)
3. Liu, J., Tang, X., Li, Y., Long, Y.: Substrate integrated waveguide leaky-wave antenna with H-shaped slots. IEEE Trans. Antennas Propag. 60(8), 3962–3967 (2012)
4. Kontorovich, M.I., Astrakhan, M.I., Akimov, V.P., Fersman, G.A.: Electrodynamics of Network Structures. Radio i Svyaz', Moscow (1987). (in Russian)
5. Bozzi, M., Pasian, M., Perregrini, L., Wu, K.: On the losses in substrate-integrated waveguides and cavities. Int. J. Microw. Wirel. Technol. 1(5), 395–401 (2009)
6. Bozzi M., Pasian M., Perregrini L.: Modeling of losses in substrate integrated waveguide components. In: International Conference on Numerical Electromagnetic Modeling and Optimization for RF, Microwave, and Terahertz Applications (NEMO) (2014)
7. Yatsenko V.V., Tretyakov S.A., Maslovski S.I., Sochava A.A.: Higher-order impedance boundary conditions for sparse wire grids. IEEE Trans. Antennas Propag. 48(5), 720–727 (2000)
8. Daniil, V., Ekaterina, K., Alexander, S., Sergei, B.: Experimental investigation of radiation characteristics of the controlled slot antenna array. In: Velichko, E., Vinnichenko, M., Kapralova, V., Koucheryavy, Y. (eds.) International Youth Conference on Electronics, Telecommunications and Information Technologies. SPPHY, vol. 255, pp. 747–754. Springer, Cham (2021). https://doi.org/10.1007/978-3-030-58868-7_81
9. Djerafi, T., Doghri, A., Wu, K.: Substrate integrated waveguide antennas. In: Chen, Z., Liu, D., Nakano, H., Qing, X., Zwick, T. (eds.) Handbook of Antenna Technologies. Springer, Singapore. (2016). https://doi.org/10.1007/978-981-4560-44-3_57

10. Rahali, B., Feham, M.: Substrate integrated waveguide power divider, circulator and coupler in [10–15] GHz band. Int. J. Inf. Sci. Tech. **4**(1/2), 10 (2014)
11. Haider, F., Dade, M.: A brief study and analysis to investigate the effect of various dielectric materials on substrate-integrated waveguide. In: Rawat, B.S., Trivedi, A., Manhas, S., Karwal, V. (eds.) Advances in Signal Processing and Communication. LNEE, vol. 526, pp. 337–344. Springer, Singapore (2019). https://doi.org/10.1007/978-981-13-2553-3_32
12. Danilchenko, E.V.: Slit antenna based on several coupled dielectric filled waveguides: bachelor's work: 03.16.01. Peter the Great St. Petersburg Polytechnic University, Institute of Physics of Nanotechnology and Telecommunications; Scientific Hands. A. A. Sochava., St. Petersburg (2017). (in Russian)
13. Kiseleva, E., Sochava, A., Cherepanov, A.: Telecommunication slot antenna based on a low-profile SIW structure. In: 2018 IEEE International Conference on Electrical Engineering and Photonics, EExPolytech 2018, Peter the Great St. Petersburg Polytechnic University (SPbPU), pp. 48–51, St. Petersburg, Russian Federation (2018)

Observation Interval Analysis
for Faster-Than-Nyquist Signals Coherent
Detection with Decision Feedback

Ilya Lavrenyuk[1]([⊠]) [iD], Sergey Makarov[1] [iD], and Wei Xue[2] [iD]

[1] Peter the Great St. Petersburg Polytechnic University, St. Petersburg, Russia
knaiser@mail.ru
[2] College of Information and Communication Engineering, Harbin Engineering University,
Harbin, China

Abstract. The method of transmitting signals above the Nyquist limit seems to be promising in terms of increasing bandwidth efficiency, but its practical application is limited by the complexity of the implementation of receiver devices, which should apply complex detection algorithms to eliminate the negative effect of inter-symbol interference in the signal. In this paper, we consider a simple algorithm of elementwise detection with decision feedback and its modification, which makes it possible to increase the detection BER performance without increasing the computational complexity. The modification involves the optimization on obser-vation interval to minimize the interference of subsequent signals during detection procedures.

Keywords: Faster-than-Nyquist · Detection algorithm · Decision feedback · Intersymbol interference

1 Introduction

Random sequences of binary Faster-than-Nyquist (FTN) signal $s(t)$ can provide a data transmission rate R above the Nyquist limit [1]. The duration of such signals exceeds the time T_b of transmission for one information symbol. High spectral efficiency is achieved with application of signals with energy E_s and duration $T_s = LT$ ($L = 2, 3, \ldots$), which are formed, particularly, using a filter with an extremely narrow passband, or as a solution of the optimization problem [2, 3].

The transmission occurs in the condition of intersymbol interference (ISI), which significantly affects on the BER performance at high symbol rates of data transmission. The properties of these FTN signals are considered and estimation of the bandwidth and energy efficiency in AWGN channels are given in [4, 5].

Usually, coherent detection algorithms applied for Faster-than-Nyquist signal trans-mission. These algorithms include maximum-likelihood-sequence-estimation (MLSE) approach, providing a weighted enumeration of all possible combinations of received signals under ISI conditions. However, the hardware implementation complexity (the number of required computational operations) of such algorithms limits their application.

© Springer Nature Switzerland AG 2022
Y. Koucheryavy et al. (Eds.): NEW2AN 2021/ruSMART 2021, LNCS 13158, pp. 427–437, 2022.
https://doi.org/10.1007/978-3-030-97777-1_36

Reducing the complexity of such processing algorithms achieved by using implementations based on the Viterbi algorithm [4, 6, 7]. However, even so it is not possible to achieve significant gains in reducing the number of computational.

There are some elementwise coherent detection algorithms, that make it possible to obtain the maximum speed of the signal demodulator. However, such algorithms demonstrate energy losses, especially for high symbol rates over the Nyquist limit. These algorithms include algorithms with averaging over all possible waveforms falling within the analysis interval; algorithms that are optimal in the sense of the maximum likelihood criterion and others, described in [8–10].

Effective detection algorithms for FTN signals include algorithms for detection with decision feedback, which occupy an intermediate position between easily implemented elementwise processing and algorithms for detection signals taking into account ISI.

The application of nonlinear iterative algorithms for coherent detection with decision feedback makes it possible to obtain a sufficiently high detection energy efficiency. At the same time, it does not require significant increase in the number of computational operations even at high transmission rates over Nyquist barrier (values of $R > 2 / T$). The main idea of these algorithms is in utilization of decisions obtained on previous iterations to eliminate interference on current iteration. When the observation interval is equal to the pulse duration T_s, all symbols following the analyzed one form intersymbol interference. A feature of the applied pulse shapes in FTN signaling is that the time characteristic of the pulse has a clearly defined central section and a rather extended section with low energy for the rest of the signal duration. This makes it possible to reduce the influence of intersymbol interference from signals following the analyzed one by choosing an analysis interval less than T_s.

The main goal of this work is to estimate the BER performance of binary FTN signals coherent detection with decision feedback processing and optimal analysis interval.

2 Definition of FTN Signals

Let an FTN signal $s_r(t)$ with an arbitrary amplitude pulse shape $a(t)$, having a maximum value A_0, a carrier frequency f_c and a duration $T_s = LT$ ($L > 1$). Then we represent $s_r(t)$ in the following form:

$$s_r(t) = A_0 a(t) d_r^{(0)} cos(2\pi f_0 t) \tag{1}$$

where $d_r^{(0)}$ is the value of the modulation symbol in the time interval from 0 to T of transmission of one message bit. For BPSK, $d_r^{(0)} = \pm 1$ and r = 1, 2.

A random sequence of N signals (1), for an arbitrary message transmission rate written as:

$$y(t) = A_0 \sum_{n=-N/2}^{N/2} a(t - \xi nT) d_r^{(n)} cos(2\pi f_0 t) \tag{2}$$

Sequence (2) provides binary data transmission at a rate R = 1 / ξT ($0 < \xi \leq 1$) above the Nyquist limit. Random sequences of FTN signals (2) can be based on square root raised cosine (RRC) pulses. The formation of such FTN signals occurs using a low-pass filter with an frequency response of the root raised cosine type with a coefficient β of the frequency response rounding equal to $1 > \beta > 0$. Note that for the value of the parameter $\beta = 0$, the form of the amplitude pulse $a(t)$ coincides with the form of the function $sin(x)/x$. This amplitude pulse has the maximum amplitude side lobes and, accordingly, creates the highest level of intersymbol ISI interference in sequence (2). Intersymbol interference affects both the parameters of the peak to average power ratio (PAPR) and the BER performance of signal detection. For example, Fig. 1, a) shows the forms of the binary FTN signals built on the basis of RRC pulses, for the duration $T_s = 16\,T$, corresponding to the transmitted sequence of the following information symbols: $\{0, 1, 0, 0, 1, 1, 1, 0, 0, 1\}$. Figure 1, b) shows the form of the passband signal.

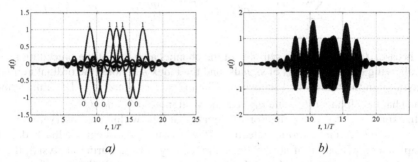

Fig. 1. Forms of the RRC pulse sequence: a) the form of individual pulses $a(t)$, and b) the form of the passband signal.

As can be seen from the Fig. 1, in the implementation of coherent elementwise detection of such FTN signals the observation interval equals 16 T. In this case, in the observation interval fall eight previous and eight subsequent pulses, and they form intersymbol interference. If we assume that with ideal feedback decisions it is possible to use the on the previous received symbols as known, we can eliminate negative influence on current analysis interval. The interference from the subsequent pulses can minimized by decreasing the observation interval. In general, in a random sequence of signals based on RRC pulses, the level of intersymbol interference will enlarge with an increase in the transmission rate R over Nyquist limit.

3   Decision Feedback Detection of FTN Signals

The analyzed process at the input of the receiving device has the form:

$$r(t) = \mu s_r(t) + \mu y_-(t, i) + \mu y_+(t, q) + n(t). \tag{3}$$

Here, $n(t)$ it is additive white Gaussian noise (AWGN) with an average power spectral density of $N_0/2$, and μ is the transmission coefficient over the communication channel, which is determined by the level of fading. On the observation interval T_s, when a certain k-th signal is received, the form of two sequences of preceding $y_-(t, i)$ and subsequent

$y_+(t, q)$ signals depend on the transmission rate $R = 1 / \xi T$. The indices i and q denote the numbers of specific combinations of I preceding and Q subsequent signals, so that, for example, when using the binary alphabet for $R = 1 / T$ we have $i = 1, 2, ..., 2^I$; $q = 1, 2, ..., 2^Q$. By setting the value $T = 1$ we can choose in integer form the number of preceding $I = LR_{obs} - 1$ and subsequent $Q = LR_{obs} - 1$ signals falling into the observation interval T_s. Then for $k = 0$ we write the expressions for the sequences of preceding $y_-(t, i)$ and subsequent $y_+(t, q)$ signals in the form:

$$y_-(t, i) = \sum_{p=-1}^{-(LR_{obs}-1)} s_{ri}^{(p)}(t - p\xi T) = \sum_{p=-1}^{-(LR_{obs}-1)} d_{ri}^{(p)} a(t - p\xi T) \cos(2\pi f_0 t); \quad (4)$$

$$y_+(t, q) = \sum_{p=1}^{LR_{obs}-1} s_{rq}^{(p)}(t - p\xi T) = \sum_{p=1}^{LR_{obs}-1} d_{rq}^{(p)} a(t - p\xi T) \cos(2\pi f_0 t). \quad (5)$$

In this case, $d_{ri}^{(p)}$ and $d_{rq}^{(p)}$ are symbols of the channel alphabet of the preceding i and of the following q combinations of signals, and the index p denotes the ordinal number of the symbol in the transmitted sequence. When $Q = I = 1$ and $R = 1 / T$, the symbols of the channel alphabet $d_{ri}^{(p)}$ and $d_{rq}^{(p)}$ can be written as: $d_i^{(p)}$ and $d_q^{(p)}$.

In expression (5), a combination of signals that falls within the observation interval T_{obs} is an interference during detection. If we assume the ideal feedback decisions (complete compensation of all the signals preceding current during analysis), then the value of $T_{obs} < T_s$ can be reduced, keeping the beginning of the interval T_{obs} equal to zero. Thus, it becomes possible to reduce the negative influence of signal in (5) on the signal detection in the presence of ISI.

Let us obtain an algorithm of elementwise detection with decision feedback, assuming that all signals following the analyzed one on the current symbol interval are additional interference. A priori information about the form of this interference is not taken into account during processing. We choose the analysis interval equal to $T_{obs} < T_s$. Then we get:

$$\exp\left(\frac{1}{N_0}\left(2\mu\int_0^{T_{obs}} r(t)(s_l(t) + y_-(t, i))dt - \mu^2\int_0^{T_{obs}} (s_l(t) + y_-(t, i))^2 dt\right)\right)$$
$$> \exp\left(\frac{1}{N_0}\left(2\mu\int_0^{T_{obs}} r(t)(s_r(t) + y_-(t, i))dt - \mu^2\int_0^{T_{obs}} (s_r(t) + y_-(t, i))^2 dt\right)\right).$$
$$(6)$$

Then, expanding (6) in a power series and limiting it only to the first terms of the expansion, and taking into account that $s_1(t) = -s_2(t)$, we obtain the following rule for making a decision: the l-th symbol is registered if the inequality (7) holds.

$$\int_0^{T_{obs}} r(t)s_l(t)dt \gtrless \mu \int_0^{T_{obs}} s_l(t)y_-(t, i)dt. \quad (7)$$

As can be seen from (7), the values of the correlation integral compared with the threshold value, which depends on the value of intersymbol interference. The same algorithm can be rewritten in a different way:

$$\int_0^{T_{obs}} (r(t) - \mu y_-(t, i))s_l(t)dt \gtrless 0 \qquad (8)$$

In the integrand expression (8) intersymbol interference caused by signals preceding current one is subtracted from the received analyzed process. Note that if this interference is not taken into account, then the algorithm (8) is transformed into the well-known algorithm of elementwise coherent detection. Compensation of the intersymbol interference indicated in (8) is possible only if all the symbols transmitted by the previous signals received correctly. With incorrectly received symbols, intersymbol interference will increase, which will lead to BER performance degradation. However, at large signal-to-noise ratios, at which the transition from (6) to (7) is valid, the indicated detection algorithm with decision feedback provide high reliability of signal detection.

Consider representation of (7) through baseband quadrature components. Let's express $r(t)$ and $s_l(t)$ in the form:

$$r(t) = A_{rc}(t) \cos(2\pi f_0 t) - A_{rs}(t)sin(2\pi f_0 t) \qquad (9)$$

$$s_l(t) = A_{lc}(t) \cos(2\pi f_0 t) - A_{ls}(t)sin(2\pi f_0 t)$$

Taking into account (2) and (10), we rewrite (7) in the following form:

$$d_l^{(0)} \int_0^{T_{obs}} A_{rc}(t)a(t)dt \gtrless \mu d_l^{(0)} \int_0^{T_{obs}} a(t) \sum_{p=-1}^{-(LR_{obs}-1)} d_{ri}^{(p)} a(t - p\xi T)dt. \qquad (10)$$

As can be seen from (10), the algorithm for coherent detection with decision feedback involves comparing the result of correlation processing of a signal in the interval of analysis and comparing this result with a threshold, the value of which is determined by the magnitude of the interference of the previous signal combinations. In addition, the level of the threshold depends on the transmission ratio μ of the communication channel, which is determined by the level of fading. Algorithm (10) provides feedback to the depth $(LR - 1)$ of symbols. Of course, the depth of feedback can also vary depending on the requirements for the hardware and software implementation of (10). Algorithms (7) and (10) can be performed on the basis of correlators or matched filters.

Let us consider a block diagram of the implementation of algorithm (10) using digital signal processing methods. Figure 2 shows a general block diagram of a digital receiver (Fig. 2, a) and a microprocessor program (Fig. 2, b). The input of the digital receiver receives a sum of the useful signal and additive noise, which, after amplification and band-pass filtering, is converted by means of an analog-to-digital converter (ADC) into a sequence of digital samples. From the ADC output, a sequence of digital samples is fed to the microprocessor. The microprocessor carries out signal processing during the observation interval in accordance with the algorithm (10). As the input parameters of the microprocessor operation, the values of the observation interval duration T_{obs},

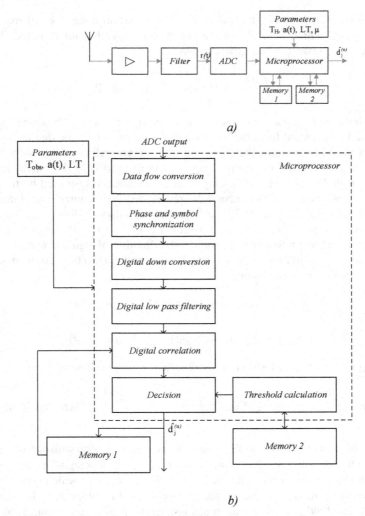

Fig. 2. a) Block diagram of a digital receiver; b) schematic flow chart of the implementation of the detection algorithm on a microprocessor device

the type of the amplitude pulse $a(t)$, the duration of the useful signal $T_s = LT$ and the transmission coefficient over the communication channel μ are entered.

A sequence of digital samples from the input signal (Fig. 2, b) is fed through the data flow converter to the "Phase and symbol synchronization" block. These blocks are executed programmatically. The measurement of the initial phase of the high-frequency oscillation is determined by the phase-locked loop algorithm according to the preamble before the sequence (2). Symbol synchronization is carried out with help of periodic sequence of symbols using in synchronization system. Under these conditions, from the analyzed process $r(t)$ at the input of the detection device with the help of phase and symbol synchronization, a reference oscillation extracted from the message preamble. After transferring the analyzed process $r(t)$ to zero frequency and low-pass filtering from the components at the doubled carrier frequency, digital correlation processing takes place in accordance with (10).

The microprocessor (Fig. 2, a) is supported by two memory blocks: memory 1 and memory 2. Memory 1 block stores operational values about the estimates of all previous received symbols $\hat{d}_{ri}^{(p)}$ included in (10). These estimates are read into the microprocessor with a clock interval delay. For example, at a transmission rate of $R = 1/T$, the delays Z^{-k} ($k = 1, 2...L-1$) in transmitting the symbol estimates will be a multiple of T. As R increases, the number of memory elements in this block increases accordingly. Memory 2 block stores the values of the cross-correlation coefficients of the transmitted signals included in the right-hand side of inequality (10). These coefficients $R_{(i)}$ ($i = 1, 2, ...$ $L - 1$), for example, for $R = 1/T$ are equal:

$$R_{(1)} = \int_0^{LT} a(t)a(t-T)dtL; R_{(2)} = \int_0^{LT} a(t)a(t-2T)dt; .....R_{(L-1)}$$
$$= \int_0^{LT} a(t)a(t-(L-1)T)dt$$

After digital correlation processing, which is carried out on the observation interval T_{obs}, its result is sent to the deciding device. The operation algorithm of this device corresponds to the algorithm (10). At the output of the decision block, estimates $\hat{d}_j^{(n)}$ of the received symbols appear. These estimates are taken into account when choosing the threshold value, and real-time values about the evaluations of all previous received symbols $\hat{d}_{ri}^{(p)}$ are stored in memory 1. The coefficients $R_{(i)}$ taking into account μ are added to the value of the threshold value for decision block.

Of course, parts of the signals following the analyzed signal will also fall into the integration interval. They will be an interference. It is possible to reduce the influence of these signals by choosing the observation interval.

4   Simulation Results

Let us consider the results of simulation of a nonlinear algorithm with decision feedback when receiving FTN signals formed on the basis of RRC pulses of different duration. The purpose of the simulation is to estimate the BER performance of coherent detection of FTN signals in the presence of additive white Gaussian noise (AWGN) in the transmission channel with an average power spectral density $N_0/2$ at various transmission rates and with optimized observation interval. Binary phase modulation was used in the simulation. Number of signals in sequence (2) N $= 10^6$. Feedback depth equals $T_s/2$.

Simulation was performed in the following sequence. In the first part, we will consider the sensitivity of the error probability from the choice of the observation interval for various parameters of the transmitted signals. In the second part, choosing the optimal values of the observation interval, we obtain the dependences of the error probability on the signal-to-noise ratio in the transmission channel.

Let's look at the first part of the simulation. Figure 3 shows the dependences of the error probability (BER) on the value of the observation interval T_{obs} for a given E_b/N_0 = 8 dB. Here E_b is the signal $s_r(t)$ energy in (1). As a modulation RRC pulse, we took a pulse with a duration of $T_s = 4T$ and roll-off of the frequency characteristic $|H(f)|^2$ of the filter $\beta = 0$ (equivalent of a pulse with the form $sin(x)/x$); $\beta = 0.3$ and $\beta = 0.5$. The normalized transmission rate is $R = 1 / \xi T = 1 / 0.8T = 1.25 / T$. As can be seen from this figure, the optimal value of the observation interval is equal to $T_{opt} = 2.3T$. This value is practically independent of the roll-off factor of the frequency characteristic $|H(f)|^2$ of the filter that forms the RRC pulse.

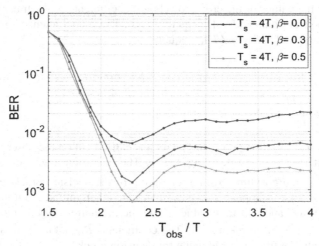

Fig. 3. Dependences of the probability of bit errors on the size of the observation interval for RRC pulses with duration $T_s = 4sT$ and different roll-off factors β

Let us estimate the value of the observation interval for various parameters of the transmission rate and roll-off factor of the $|H(f)|^2$ of the shaping filter. Figure 4 shows the dependences of BER on T_{obs}/T for FTN signals based on RRC pulses with a duration of $T_s = 8T$ at a given $E_b/N_0 = 8$ dB. Figure 4 a) shows the dependences for the roll-off factor of $|H(f)|^2$ $\beta = 0.3$ at various values of the message transmission rate equal to $R = 1.25 / T$; $1.42 / T$ and $1.66 / T$. Figure 4 b) shows the dependences for the transmission rate parameter R = 1.25 / T for different roll-off factors of $|H(f)|^2$ $\beta = 0.0$, 0.3 and 0.5. From the analysis of the curves in these figures it can be seen that the optimal value of the observation interval is equal to $T_{opt} = (4.2–4.3)T$. It does not depend on the message rate and the parameters of the roll-off factor of the shaping filter.

Figure 5 shows the dependences of BER on T_{obs}/T for FTN signals based on RRC pulses with duration $T_s = 16T$ for a given $E_b/N_0 = 8$ dB for a transmission rate = 1.25 / T, roll-off factor of $|H(f)|^2$ $\beta = 0.0$, 0.3 and 0.5. It can be seen from this figure that the optimal value of the observation interval is $T_{opt} = (8.2–8.3)T$.

Let's move on to the second part of the simulation. Figure 6 shows the dependences of BER on the E_b/N_0 when choosing the optimal values of the observation interval T_{obs}

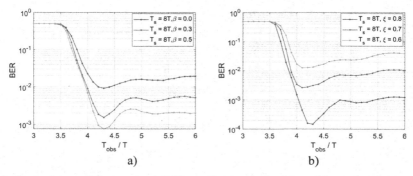

Fig. 4. Dependences of the error probability on the observation interval for various parameters β and ξ

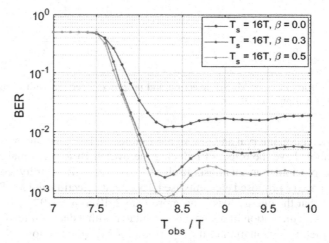

Fig. 5 Dependences of the error probability on the observation interval for an FTN signal with a duration of $T_s = 16\,T$

$/\,T$ for FTN signals based on RRC pulses with a parameter $\beta = 0.3$ and duration $T_s = 8T$ at a transmission rate of $R = 1.25\,/\,T$.

For comparison, Fig. 6 shows the BER performance for different detection algorithms for FTN signal: optimal MLSE detection and proposed detection algorithm with decision feedback with and without changing the observation interval. From the analysis of the given dependences in Fig. 6, the following conclusions can be drawn. Firstly, the application of the algorithm with decision feedback with optimal observation interval makes it possible to increase the BER performance in comparison with the same algorithm but with fixed duration of the analysis interval. The energy gain at the data transmission rate $R = 1.25\,/\,T$ is more than 2 dB for $T_s = 8T$ and the value of observation interval $T_{opt} = (4.2–4.3)\,T$ in the range of bit error probabilities $p = 10^{-4}$–10^{-5}. Secondly, there is a threshold phenomenon associated with the grouping of errors when using decision feedback. Moreover, this phenomenon is more pronounced when using

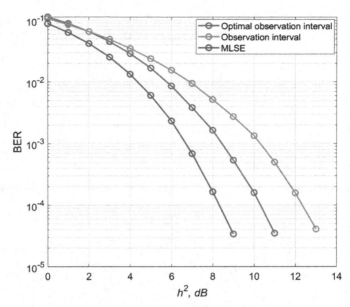

Fig. 6. BER performance for MLSE detection and proposed detection with decision feedback and optimal observation interval

a reduced observation interval and low signal-to-noise ratios, when incorrectly received previous symbols have the effect of reducing the overall BER performance. In Fig. 6, this threshold phenomenon manifests itself at $E_b/N_0 = 2$ dB. Thirdly, comparing the BER performance of proposed elementwise FTN signal detection and MLSE detection, it can be seen that the energy loss is no more than 2 dB at $p = 10^{-4}$–10^{-5}. However, the practical implementation of a signal demodulator with a decision feedback is much simpler than the implementation of the algorithm for MLSE detection.

5   Conclusions

As a result of this work, the following is shown:

1. The application of the detection algorithm with decision feedback and optimal observation interval makes it possible to increase the BER performance in comparison with the use of the same algorithm but with fixed observation interval at data transmission rates higher than the Nyquist barrier by (20–40) %. The energy gain is more than 2 dB in the range of error probabilities $p = 10^{-4}$–10^{-5}.
2. The sensitivity of the algorithm with decision feedback and the optimal observation interval to the accuracy of the choice of the value of this interval turns out to be rather small. In particular, the choice of the observation interval is practically independent of the message transmission rate, the parameters of the roll-off factor of frequency characteristic of the shaping filter and is determined only by the pulse duration.

3. The BER performance of proposed approach is slightly inferior to the MLSE. Energy losses are no more than 2 dB at $p = 10^{-4}$–10^{-5}. However, the practical implementation of a signal demodulator with a decision feedback is much simpler than the implementation of the MLSE detection algorithm.
4. There is a threshold phenomenon associated with the grouping of errors when using decision feedback for low E_b/N_0 values.

Acknowledgements. The reported study was funded by RFBR according to the research project № 20-37-90007\20

References

1. Mazo, J.: Faster-than-Nyquist signaling. Bell Syst. Tech. J. **54**(8), 1451–1462 (1975)
2. Lavrenyuk, I., Ovsyannikova, A., Zavjalov, S., Volvenko, S., Makarov, S.: Improving energy efficiency of finite time FTN pulses detection by choosing optimal envelope shape. In: 26th International Conference on Telecommunications 2019, pp. 289–294. IEEE (2019)
3. Ovsyannikova, A., Zavjalov, S., Volvenko, S.: Influence of correlation coefficient on spectral and energy efficiency of optimal signals. In: 10th International Congress on Ultra-Modern Telecommunications and Control Systems and Workshops 2018, pp.1–4. IEEE (2018)
4. Anderson, J., Rusek, F., Öwall, V.: Faster-than-Nyquist signaling. Proc. IEEE **101**(8), 1817–1830 (2013)
5. Liveris, A., Georghiades, C.: Exploiting Faster-than-Nyquist signaling. IEEE Trans. Commun. **51**(9), 1502–1511 (2003)
6. Anderson, J., Rusek, F., Prlja, A.: Receivers for Faster-than-Nyquist signaling with and without turbo equalization. In: IEEE International Symposium on Information Theory 2008, pp. 464–468. IEEE (2008)
7. Makarov, S., Lavrenyuk, I., Ovsyannikova, A., Zavjalov, S.: BER performance of finite in time optimal FTN signals for the Viterbi algorithm. J. Electron. Sci. Technol. **18**(1), (2020)
8. Bedeer, E., Ahmed, M., Yanikomeroglu, H.: A very low complexity successive symbolby-symbol sequence estimator for Faster-than-Nyquist signaling. IEEE Access **5**, 7414–7422 (2017)
9. Bedeer, E., Ahmed, M., Yanikomeroglu, H.: Reduced complexity optimal detection of binary Faster-than-Nyquist signaling. In: International Conference on Communications 2017, pp. 1–6, France (2017)
10. Ishihara, T., Sugiura, S., Hanzo, L.: The Evolution of Faster-than-Nyquist signaling. IEEE Access **9**, 86535–86564 (2021)

Heuristic Design Algorithm for Scheduling of URLLC and eMBB Traffics in 5G Cellular Networks

Jerzy Martyna[✉][iD]

Institute of Computer Science, Faculty of Mathematics and Computer Science,
Jagiellonian University, ul. Prof. S. Lojasiewicza 6, 30-348 Cracow, Poland
jerzy.martyna@uj.edu.pl

Abstract. In this paper, the radio resource allocation problem of two
5G traffics: Ultra-Reliable Low Latency Communications (URLLC) and
enhanced Mobile BroadBand (eMBB) is studied. While eMBB traffic
demands high data rates, URLLC traffic requires low latency and high
reliability. To solve the formulated problem, an algorithm based on a
heuristic approach is proposed. This enables the maximisation of the
number of eMBB traffics admitted to the system with guaranteed data
rates, while ensuring the allocation of power and bandwidth for all
URLCC traffics with guaranteed latency and reliability requirements.
The results of the simulation tests confirm that the proposed approach
meets the URLLC reliability requirements while maintaining the eMBB
data rates.

Keywords: 5G systems · eMBB · URLLC · Radio resource
management · Scheduling

1 Introduction

Due to the rapid development in technology, 5G wireless mobile networks [1]
have been invented to replace LTE networks and contribute to making our lives
daily lives easier. 5G networks enable, a.o. delivery high data rates up to 10
Gbps with end-to-end latency of 2 to 5 milliseconds [2], allow building wireless
communication systems such as: wireless sensors and actuators, smart grids,
video streaming servers, etc. Implementation of the Internet of Things (IoT) [3]
The implementation of IoT networks based on 5G networks is a natural extension
of data processing capabilities in wireless networks.

In the 5G mobile networks are three types of service traffic, namely: ultra-
reliable low latency communications (URLLC) and enhanced mobile broadband
(eMBB), and massive Machine-Type Communication (mMTC) [4]. The URLLC
services the challenging scheduling tasks, which demand extremely, reliable and
low latency radio transmissions, i.e. one-way radio latency of 1 ms [5]. It supports
applications such as autonomous vehicles, industrial automation and vehicular
communication. The eMBB traffic supports the stable connection for cell-edge

© Springer Nature Switzerland AG 2022
Y. Koucheryavy et al. (Eds.): NEW2AN 2021/ruSMART 2021, LNCS 13158, pp. 438–448, 2022.
https://doi.org/10.1007/978-3-030-97777-1_37

users. This service traffic requires higher data rates than URLLC to further improve the current mobile services such as high definition (HD) video and virtual reality (VR). A third class of service, eMTC, makes possible massive connected solutions for various IoT applications. It covers services that connect a massive number of devices where small data packets are transmitted occasionally. The first two services are mainly supported in the release of 5G wireless networks [4], hence they are the subject of the paper below.

In practice, two approaches are used in the analysis of URLLC and eMBB traffics in 5G wireless mobile networks. In the first approach, the different slices are allocated to each traffic in such a way that they meet all their requirements. Allocated resources (slices) are orthogonal in the frequency time. Additionally, this approach means that there is no interference between these services. This approach entails the inefficient use of resources. The downside to this approach is that resources reserved for URLLC will be wasted in the case where there is no URLLC transmission. This approach was used among others by Zhang et al. [6], Pedersen et al. [7], etc.

In the second approach, resources (slices) are not orthogonal. This means that there is interference between the different traffics. This approach is efficient in terms of reducing of the URLLC latency. However, it may affect the reliability of the eMBB transmission. This approach was applied among others in the papers by Anand et al. [8], Pedersen et al. [9], etc.

In this paper a non-orthogonal scheduling approach is applied. Under this scenario, URLLC traffic is overlapped on eMBB traffic at every mini-slot. Thus, the allocation problem should not just aim at maximising the data rate, but also reduce the URLLC packets' latency. This approach solved a number of problems. Among others, in the paper by Li et al. [10], a dynamic multiplexing of the traffics in both the time and frequency domains has been presented. It has made partitioning bandwidth between eMBB and URLL more efficient. In the paper by Bairagi et al. [11], a mechanism based on a matching game for solving the problem of coexistence of URLLC and eMBB services on the same radio resources was given. Compared to other methods, this solution provided the expected better data rates and fairness to eMBB users.

The main goal of this article is to provide a new algorithm for eMBB and URLLC flows in 5G wireless networks. This algorithm is based on a heuristics that takes into account both URLLC service packet requirements and the minimisation of variance of eMBB user data rate. Moreover, this algorithm provides good parameters for the combined flow of URLLC and eMBB traffics, regardless of network load.

The paper is organised as follows. The next section presents the system model. In Sect. 3, the scheduling problem is formulated as an optimisation problem. Section 4 provides a heuristic algorithm for solving the scheduling problem. In Sect. 5, we present the numerical results illustrating the tradeoff between the services for both URLLC and eMBB. The conclusions are given in Sect. 6.

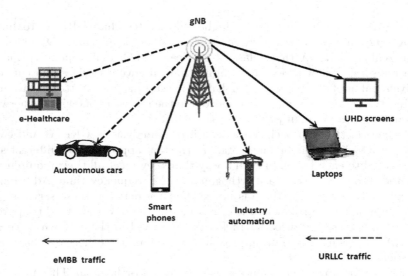

Fig. 1. System model.

2   System Model

It is assumed that the 5G wireless network is one next-generation base station (gNB) with two types of user equipment (UEs) within the range. The first type of UE includes N user equipment demanding URLLC service (see Fig. 1). The data transmission of these UEs is sporadic and limited to short packets with a latency of 0.5 ms. The second type of data transmission provided by licensed network users is a set $\mathcal{M}$ of eMBB users, and it may cover the range of all frequency channels. The traffic generated by these UE users is high and can span the entire width of the frequency spectrum.

Here it is assumed that resource scheduling in downlink mode is done by non-orthogonal slicing, in which each time slot is split into mini-slots of 0.125 ms [12]. Each time slot is divided into the mentioned mini-slots (see Fig. 2) where URLLC packets can be sent. These packets cannot be preempted, unlike eMBB packets, which can still be preempted by gNB. Let B be the total number of resource blocks (RBs), where a RB $b \in \mathcal{B} = \{1, 2, \ldots, B\}$ occupies 12 sub-carrier in frequency.

Let URLLC traffic packets be placed in every slot containing S mini-slots. Then, the data rate of eMBB m user is given by

$$r_{eMBB,b}^m = f_b(1 - \frac{z_{m,b}(t)}{S}) \sum_{i \in \mathcal{N}} \log_2(1 + SINR_{i,b}) \tag{1}$$

where f_b is the bandwidth of the RB b, $z_{m,b}(t)$ is the number of mini-slots from RB of eMBB user m at time slot t, $SINR_{i,m}$ is the *signal-to-noise plus noise ratio* of the i-th URLLC user. Thus, the data rate of the eMBB user m over all allocated RBs is defined as follows:

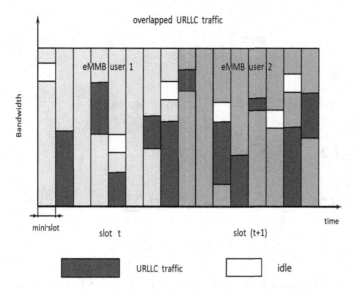

Fig. 2. An example of multiplexing between eMBB and URLLC traffic.

$$r^m_{eMBB} = \sum_{b \in B} c_{m,b}(t) r^m_{eMBB,b}(t) \tag{2}$$

where $c_{m,b}(t)$ is the eMBB user scheduling indicator at time slot t given by:

$$c_{m,b}(t) = \begin{cases} 1, \text{ if the RB } b \text{ is allocated to user } m \text{ at time } t, \quad m \in \mathcal{M} \\ 0, \text{ otherwise} \end{cases} \tag{3}$$

Similarly, the data of the i-th URLLC user on subcarrier b is given by:

$$r^i_{URRLC,b} = \log_2(1 + p_{i,b}\beta_{i,b}) \tag{4}$$

where $p_{i,b}$ is the transmission power to the i-th URLLC user on the subcarrier b, $\beta_{i,b} = h_{i,b}/(N_0 W + I_{i,b})$ is the SINR, $h_{i,b}$ is the channel gain on subcarrier b and the i-th URLLC, N_0 is the noise power, W is the system bandwidth, and $I_{i,b}$ is the interference introduced to the i-URLLC user on the subcarrier b.

3   Heuristic Algorithm for eMBB and URLLC Traffics Scheduling in 5G Systems

In this section the mathematical formulation of resource allocation of URLLC and eMBB traffics in 5G wireless cellular network is formulated.

The achievable eMBB data rate is given by

$$\max \sum_{i \in \mathcal{N}} \sum_{m \in \mathcal{M}} \sum_{b \in \mathcal{B}} w_{i,m} r^m_{eMBB,b} \qquad (5)$$

subject to:

$$C1: \quad r^m_{eMBB,b} \geq r^{req}_{eMBB}, \quad m \in \mathcal{M}, \quad b \in \mathcal{B} \qquad (6)$$

$$C2: \quad \sum_{m \in \mathcal{M}} \sum_{b=1}^{B} r^m_{eMBB,b} \leq P^{max}_{gNB} \qquad (7)$$

$$C3: \quad \sum_{b \in \mathcal{B}} \left(\sum_{m \in \mathcal{M}} r^m_{eMMB,b} x_{m,b} + \sum_{i \in \mathcal{N}} r^i_{URLLC,b} x_{i,b} \right) \leq r,$$

$$x_{m,b} \in \{0,1\}, \ x_{i,b} \in \{0,1\}. \ b \in \mathcal{B} \qquad (8)$$

$$C4: \quad x_{m,b} + x_{i,b} \leq 1, \quad x_{m,b} \in \{0,1\}, \quad x_{i,b} \in \{0,1\},$$

$$m \in \mathcal{M}, \ 1 \in \mathcal{N}, \ b \in \mathcal{B} \qquad (9)$$

$$C5: \quad r^i_{URLLC,b} \leq r^{res}_{URLLC}, \quad i \in \mathcal{N}, b \in \mathcal{B} \qquad (10)$$

$$C6: \quad z_{m,b}(t) \in \{0,1,\ldots,S\}, \quad \forall m \in \mathcal{M}, \ b \in \mathcal{B} \qquad (11)$$

where the $C1$ condition represents a limitation of required data rate for each m-th eMMB traffic user; the $C2$ condition gives a limitation of the gNB, namely P_{max} is the maximum transmission power of the gNB; the $C3$ condition is a limitation of the system data rate for all $\mathcal{M}$ eMMB traffic users and $\mathcal{N}$ URLLC users. Equation $C4$ ensures that the b-th subcarrier will be utilised. The $C5$ condition represents the data rate restriction that can be used by i-th URLLC traffic user. w_{im} is the weight for m-th eMMB user and i-th URLLC traffic user. $x_{m,b}$ denotes the traffic indicator, i.e. $x_{m,b} = 1$ only if the m-th eMMB traffic is allocated to the b-th subcarrier and $x_{m,0} = 0$, otherwise. Condition $C6$ ensures that the number of mini-slots form a RB b can take any integer number less than S.

The optimisation problem in Eq. (5) is nonlinear, non-convex and includes four variables, namely binary $x_{m,b}$, $x_{i,b}$, $w_{i,m}$ and $z_{m,b}(t)$. So, the problem giving in Eq. (5) is a subclass of MINLP (Mixed Integer Nonlinear Programming) problem [13]. The heuristic algorithm for scheduling traffics is presented here as an approximate solution to the above problem.

4   A Heuristic Algorithm for Scheduling URLLC and eMBB Traffics

The heuristic algorithm presented in this section is based on the sliding windows method [14]. This method allows you to make calculations while scanning the data stream. The following data for each packet is necessary for the calculation: arrival time, deadline, distance of the gNB from the packet destination, priority, and packet usability. All packets of both types, eMBB and URLLC, are placed in boxes, the sizes corresponding to the size of the slot t. The t-th slot consists of a set of packets $\{\mathcal{P}\}_t = \{packet_{t,1}, \ldots, packet_{t,l}, \ldots, packet_{t,L}\}$, where L is the number of packets in a single mini-slot.

On the basis of known values, individual parameters for the l packet belonging to $\{\mathcal{P}\}$ are calculated as follows. The standardised time arrival is given by

$$A_l = \frac{AR_l}{US_l} \tag{12}$$

where AR_i and US_l are the standardised time arrival of packet l and standardised usability of packet l, respectively. The priority of packet I is computed by the formula, namely

$$D_l = \frac{DP_l}{US_l} \tag{13}$$

where DP_l is the standardised end-to-end delay of packet l. The communication cost of packet l is given by

$$C_l = \frac{W_l \times D}{US_l} \tag{14}$$

where W_l is the bandwidth for transmission of packet l and D is the distance from gNB and the destination node. The usability of packet l is defined by

$$U_l = \frac{US_l}{TT_l} \tag{15}$$

where TT_l is type of traffic to which the l-th packet belongs. It is assumed here that the parameters $TT = 1$ and $TT = 2$ are equal for the URLLC and eMBB, respectively.

All the parameters listed above have been standardised according to the formula below, namely

$$f(y_k) = \frac{y_k - \min_{packet \in \{\mathcal{P}\}_t}(y_k) + 1}{\max_{packet \in \{\mathcal{P}\}_t}(y_k) - \min_{packet \in \{\mathcal{P}\}_t}(y_k) + 1} \tag{16}$$

In addition, to avoid conflicts between packets resulting from lack of adequate space to fill the mini-slot, the conflict index γ is calculated for each packet l. It is defined as the number of packets conflicting with packet l. Then the degree of conflict DC_l is given as follows:

Algorithm 1. Heuristic algorithm for scheduling of eMBB and URLLC traffics

---

1: **procedure** DYNAMIC SLIDING WINDOW
2: **Require:** $AR_l, US_l, DP_l, W_l, D, TT_l, t$;
3: **Initialisation:**
4:     Let $t \leftarrow 1$;
5:     $\{buffer\} \leftarrow \varnothing\}$;
6:     $\{P\} \leftarrow \varnothing$;
7:     **for** $t \leftarrow 1, T$ **do**
8:         **for** $l \leftarrow 1, L$ **do**
9:             **if** $\{buffer\}_t \neq \varnothing$ **then**
10:                 Copy $\{buffer\}_t \leftarrow \varnothing$;
11:             **else**
12:                 $Put\_packet\_to\{buffer\}_t$;
13:                 $Calculate \ A_l, D_l, C_l, U_l, DC_l, \gamma_l$;
14:                 $Standardisation \ according \ to \ the \ Eq. \ (16)$;
15:                 $Sort\_packets\_in\_\{buffer\}_t$;
16:             **end if**
17:             **while** ($W_l \leq W_{con}$ **and** $r_{eMBB}^m \geq r_{eMBB}^{con}$) **do**
18:                 $Find\_all\_holes\_in\_minislot_t$;
19:                 $Remove\_all\_packets\_with\_highest\_DC_l$;
20:                 $Select\_the\_packets\_to\_\{buffer\}_t$;
21:                 $Put\_\{buffer\}_t\_to\_mini - slot_t$;
22:             **end while**
23:         **end for**
24:         $Copy\_mini - slot_t\_to\{P\}_\sqcup$;
25:     **end for**
26: **end procedure**

Fig. 3. Pseudo-code of scheduling algorithm for eMBB and URLLC traffics.

$$DC_l = \frac{Q_l}{(1 + \gamma_l)^2} \tag{17}$$

where Q_l is the number of packets that are observed by the packet l and are in potential conflict with packet l. If the DC_l value is greater than the set value, the packet l is suspended and placed at the beginning of a new slot.

Figure 3 shows the pseudo-code of the packet scheduling algorithm for eMBB and URLLC traffics for 5G cellular networks. The operation of this algorithm is as follows. After the algorithm is initialised, two loops are performed. In the outer loop, the next mini-slots are placed in the slot. In the inner loop, however, packets are prepared to be placed in the next mini-slots. It first checks if there are any packets in the buffer. If so, they are immediately copied from the buffer to the next mini-slot. The *buffer* is emptied. Then the packets are placed in the buffer. Later, all parameters of these packets ($A_l, D_l, C_l, DC_l, \gamma_l$) are calculated, standardised and sorted. Finally, as long as the bandwidth W and traffic rate conditions for individual eMBB user r_{eMBB}^m are met, packets are placed in the next mini-slot. Next, free holes are found for each mini-slot and non-conflicting

Table 1. Simulation parameters.

Parameter	Value
OFDM symbol number	2
Carrier frequency [MHz]	2000
Modulation method	QPSK
CRC Length [bits]	16
Propagation conditions	Log-Normal shadowing with 5 dB standard deviation; $128.1 + 37.6 \log(D[km])$
Maximum transmit power P_{max}	30 dBm
System bandwidth, W	20 MHz
Signal-to-Noise Ratio (SNR)	5 dB
Total bandwidth of the system, W	20 MHz

packets are placed in it. The packets with the greatest degree of conflict are placed in the *buffer* so that it can end up in the next mini-slot.

5   Simulation Results

In this section, the simulation results of the algorithm presented are provided. To evaluate the performance of the heuristic algorithm implemented in Matlab for the downlink of a single cell, a MISO system was made. It is assumed that the 5G gNB base station is equipped with four transmit antennas. It was assumed that up to 30 URLLC users and a changing number of eMBB users can be found in a single cell within the range of this base station. Both types of eMBB and URLLC users are distributed uniformly around the gNB within a distance of 100 m.

The duration of a time slot was set to 1 ms and each time slot was divided into 8 equally spaced mini-slots. It was assumed that each resource block (RB) is composed of 12 sub-carriers with 14 OFDM symbols. Additionally, it was assumed that the bandwidth of each RB is 180 kHz and each mini-slot consists of 2 OFDM symbols. The total bandwidth of system was set to a value of 20 MHz. The size of each packet is set at a value of 32 bytes. The list of the main simulation parameters is presented in Table 1.

For the comparison of the results obtained, the proportional-fair sharing algorithm was taken into account [15,16]. Two simulation scenarios have been realised. In the first one, it was assumed that the average sum-rate of eMBB users for the changing average load of URLLC traffic is tested. The results obtained are presented in Fig. 4. The values obtained indicate that an increase in the average flow load of URLLC causes a decrease in the average rate of eMBB traffic.

For this simulation scenario, the utilisation of RBs as a function of the eMBB rate r_{eMBB} for both algorithms, namely heuristic and proportional fair sharing, has been used.

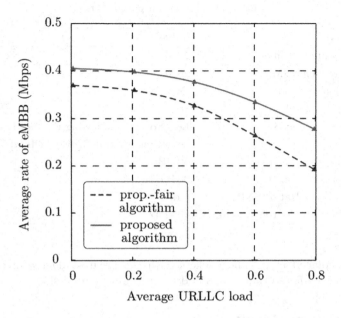

Fig. 4. Average rate of eMBB users as a function of average URLLC load.

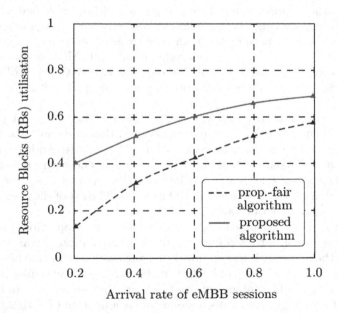

Fig. 5. The resource blocks utilisation as a function of session arrival rate of eMBB users.

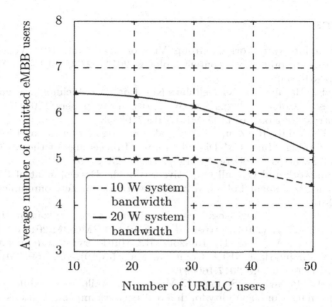

Fig. 6. Average number of admitted eMBB users as a function of URLLC users.

Figure 5 shows the RBs utilisation in dependence of session arrival rate of eMBB users. As can be seen from the graph in Fig. 5, for high values of session arrival rate of eMBB, both algorithms give comparable RB utilisation.

The second simulation scenario was aimed at examining how the average number of URLLC users influences the average number of admitted eMBB users with the adopted bandwidth of the system. Figure 6 shows, for the adopted values of the 10 and 20 MHz bandwidth, the allowed average number of admitted eMBB users depending on the increasing number of URLLC users. It can be seen from the graph that doubling the bandwidth of the system increases the average number of admitted eMBB users allowed by approximately 30 percent for the same number of URLLC users.

6   Conclusion

In this article, the coexistence problem of eMBB and URLLC services in 5G cellular networks is studied. In particular, a heuristic algorithm for scheduling of eMBB and URLLC traffics is presented. The effects of this algorithm are comparable to those described in the literature. It can be successfully used for fulfilling the stringent requirements of URLLC while protecting the eMBB bandwidth requirements.

In further research, an analysis of energy consumption by the base station will be carried out with the algorithm presented here. Energy minimisation while delivering data to users will be crucial in the further development of 5G networks.

References

1. 5G PPP Architecture Working Group, View on 5G Architecture, Version 1.0, July 2016. https://5g-ppp.eu/wp-content/uploads/2014/02/5G-PPP-5G-Architecture-WP-July-2016.pdf
2. Hossain, E., Hasan, M.: 5G Cellular: Key Enabling Technologies and Research Challenges, CoRR. https://arxiv.org/ftp/arxiv/papers/1503/1503.00674.pdf (2015). https://doi.org/10.1109/MIM.2015.7108393
3. Bonomi, F., Milito, R., Zhu, J., Addepalli, S.: Fog computing and its role in the internet of things. In: ACM Digital Library, Proceedings of the MCC 2012, pp. 13–16 (2012). https://doi.org/10.1145/2342509.2342513
4. ITU, Framework and Overall Objectiveness of the Development of IMT for 2020 and Beyond, Document ITU-R M.2083.0 International Telecommunication Union (ITU) (2015)
5. Dahlman, E., et al.: 5G wireless access: requirements and realization. IEEE Comm. Mag. **52**(12), 42–47 (2014). https://doi.org/10.1109/MCOM.2014.6979985
6. Zhang, L., Ijaz, A., Xiao, P., Tafazolli, R.: Multi-service system: an enabler of flexible 5G air interface. IEEE Commun. Mag. **55**(10), 152–159 (2017). https://doi.org/10.1109/MCOM.2017.1600916
7. Pedersen, K., Pocovi, G., Steiner, J., Maeder, A.: Agile 5G scheduler for improved E2E performance and flexibility for different network implementations. IEEE Commun. Mag. **56**(3), 210–217 (2018). https://doi.org/10.1109/MCOM.2017.1700517
8. Anand, A., de Veciana, G., Shakkottai, S.: Joint Scheduling of URLLC and eMBB Traffic in 5G Wireless Networks, pp. 112 (2017). http://arxiv.org/abs/1712.05344
9. Pedersen, K.I., Pocovi, G., Steiner, J., Khosravirad, S.R.: Punctured scheduling for critical low latency data on a shared channel with mobile broadband. In: IEEE Vehicular Technology Conference, vol. 2, pp. 16, (2018) https://doi.org/10.1109/VTCFall.2017.8287951
10. Li, C., Jiang, J., Chen, W., Ji, T., Smee, J.: 5G ultra-reliable and low-latency systems design. In: 2017 Proceedings of the of 2017 European Conference on Networks and Communications (EuCNC), Oulu, pp. 1–5 (2017). https://doi.org/10.1109/EuCNC.2017.7980747
11. Bairagi, A.K., Munir, M.S., Alsenwi, M., Tran, N.H.: A matching based coexistence mechanism between eMBB and uRLLC in 5G wireless networks. In: SAC 2019: Proceedings of the 34th ACM/SIGAPP Symposium on Applied Computing, April 2019, pp. 2377–2384 (2019). https://doi.org/10.1145/3297280.3297513
12. 3GPP TSG RAN WG, Technical report (2020). https://www.3gpp.org/specifications-groups/ran-plenary
13. Luenberger, D.G., Ye, Y.: Primal–dual methods. In: Linear and Nonlinear Programming. ISORMS, vol. 228, pp. 525–558. Springer, Cham (2021). https://doi.org/10.1007/978-3-030-85450-8_15
14. Datar, M., Gionis, A., Indyk, P., Motwani, R.: Maintaining stream statistics over sliding windows. SIAM J. Comput. **31**(6), 1794–1813 (2002). https://doi.org/10.1137/S0097539701398363
15. Kushner, H.J., Whiting, P.A.: Convergence of proportional-fair sharing algorithms under general conditions. IEEE Trans. Wirel. Commun. **3**(4), 1250–1259 (2004). https://doi.org/10.1109/TWC.2004.830826
16. Bu, T., Li, L., Ramjee, R.: Generalized proportional fair scheduling in third generation wireless data networks. In: Proceedings of the IEEE INFOCOM 2006. 25TH IEEE International Conference on Computer Communications, pp. 1–12 (2006). https://doi.org/10.1109/INFOCOM.2006.145

Geometrical Approach to the Plane Tessellation in the IEEE 802.11 Networks Channel Planning

Anton Vikulov[1]([✉]), Alexander Paramonov[1], and Tatiana Tatarnikova[2]

[1] The Bonch-Bruevich State University of Telecommunications,
22 Pr. Bolshevikov, St. Petersburg, Russian Federation
asv012016@gmail.com
[2] Russian State Hydrometeorological University,
79 Voronezhskaya ulitsa, St. Petersburg, Russian Federation

Abstract. The problem of channel planning is typical during the design of the wireless access networks. It can have a geometric interpretation from the point of view of the plane tessellation problem. Since the wireless coverage of the target area by access points coverage zones is very similar to the plane tessellation and is studied in detail in crystallography, we may use appropriate methods of description and research. It makes possible to assess the mutual influence between access points in a distributed network and, thus, to make a conclusion about the applicability of the selected channel plan. Since the number of channels in each specific design task may differ depending on the form and structure of lattice unit cells, the structure of the plane tessellation will be different.

In this paper, channel planning in IEEE 802.11 networks is considered from the plane tessellation problem point of view, taking into account the specifics of spectrum use in these networks. Also we will consider typical structures of a plane tessellation and lattices that correspond to the translational symmetry of such structures, and a method is proposed that considers negative influence between access points of the entire plane.

Keywords: Wireless access network · IEEE 802.11 · Channel planning · Plane tessellation · Lattice · Unit cell

1 Introduction and Related Works

The Nelson-Erdös-Hadwiger problem or the plane chromatic number problem is one of the most famous in combinatorial geometry [1, 2]. It asks for the minimum number of colors needed to color the plane so that there are no two points of the same color at a distance 1 from each other. The problem was formulated in the 1940-s and gained popularity in the scientific world after the publications of H. Hadwiger [3, 4].

Having a simple formulation, this problem remains unsolved by 2021. From the very beginning it was known that the chromatic number n for the plane is $3 < n \leq 7$ [1]. However, by constructing a counterexample in 2018, it was proved that $n > 4$ [5]. There are many works on related topics concerning both the chromatic number for various

© Springer Nature Switzerland AG 2022
Y. Koucheryavy et al. (Eds.): NEW2AN 2021/ruSMART 2021, LNCS 13158, pp. 449–469, 2022.
https://doi.org/10.1007/978-3-030-97777-1_38

dimensions and a large number of related problems, for example Borsuk's conjecture, the problem of plane illumination, etc. A review of these works is given in [1, 6]. Many of these tasks have practical applications in various fields of knowledge.

A special class of problems relate to the coloring of a planar graph, i.e. graph without edges intersection. Here it is necessary to note the "four color theorem" that was proved by the proof of the absence of a counterexample.

The lattices are studied since fundamental works of A. Bravais, C. Hermann, C.V. Mauguin and others. Different tessellations problems were studied by M.C. Escher, H.S.M. Coxeter, M. Gardner and others.

The works [16, 17] are devoted to the problems of building distributed WLANs of the IEEE 802.11 standard. Separate solutions to the problem of estimating the transmission speed for radio-resource management were made in various works, for example [18].

Plane tessellation (parquet construction) problems have been considered in numerous works, in particular [15]. The problem of non-periodic plane tiling by figures of the same shape was considered in [14].

However, considering the chromatic number problems, in the IEEE 802.11 [7] networks channel planning practice, the inverse task is more relevant. We have the given number of colors (channels) and we must find the scheme of the graph coloring that meets certain conditions and thus uses the colors (channels) in the most effective way while taking into account the specifics of IEEE 802.11 wireless data transmission. The example of such problem can be coloring with forbidden distances.

The channel planning problem for various distributed radio networks, for example, in cellular communications, is well known and is typically solved by iterative methods. However, when solving a specific design problem for an IEEE 802.11 WLAN, it is often necessary to estimate the capabilities of various channel plans in terms of the achievable data rates. This is useful both when estimating the applicability of a particular channel plan for specific design conditions, or during existing WLAN audit.

In this paper, we will consider the channel planning problem in IEEE 802.11 networks from the perspective of solving the coloring problem using combinatorial geometry and sphere packing approach, while also taking into account the specifics of spectrum use in these networks. We shall consider these effects in Russian regulatory domain of the IEEE 802.11 networks.

2 IEEE 802.11 Channel Planning Specifics

Under channel planning we understand the choice of channel numbers (central frequencies) and types (widths) in order to provide radio coverage with the characteristics specified in the design task.

The main idea of channel planning is to obtain a continuous coverage of the target area by the coverage areas of the network access points so that the access points (APs) operating on the same channel be located as far from each other as possible. Thus the cellular principle of radio coverage, is applied.

However, in practice we often have additional conditions. For example, existing specialized predictive modelling software does not take into consideration the adjacent-channel interference from formally (according to the signal spectrum mask) non-overlapping channels and thus does not consider its negative impact on the signal-to-noise ratio when calculating heat maps of radio coverage. However, interference from other access points cannot be excluded from consideration without assessing their impact on the design result. In addition, in practice, it makes sense to additionally consider the possible influence of channels located at adjacent central frequencies [8].

The frequency bands 2.4 GHz (ISM) and 5 GHz (UNII) fundamentally differ by the available bandwidth of the electromagnetic spectrum, which greatly affects the channel planning of the network. However, since in the long term we do not expect abandoning the 2.4 GHz band usage, in most cases dual-band radio coverage is required.

In terms of spectral resource, the total available bandwidth of the available spectrum creates the upper bound on the aggregate bandwidth.

In the 2.4 GHz band, there are only 3 non-overlapping 20 MHz channels available in most regulatory domains: these are channels 1, 6, and 11. In addition, in the 2.4 GHz band with minimal spectrum mask overlap, a 4-channel scheme can be used [13].

The 5 GHz UNII sub-bands available in the Russia contain 16 channels HT20/VHT20. They include 8 channels of the UNII-1 and UNII-2 sub-bands (channels: 36, 40, 44, 48, 52, 56, 60 and 64), as well as 8 more channels in the UNII-2ext sub-band and UNII-3 sub-band (channels: 132, 136, 140, 144, 149, 153, 157 and 161) [7]. We should note that channel 165 has very limited support by the client devices and thus we will not consider its usage. Thus, unlike the 2.4 GHz band, the 5 GHz band provides much more spectrum space available for IEEE 802.11 networks. This facilitates the greatest possible spacing of the access points (APs) operating on the same channel and allows to provide higher coverage characteristics.

We also may be limited to use the first 8 channels of the 5 GHz range (UNII-1 and UNII-2) only. The possible reason for this may be the need to provide versatile support for client devices manufactured in other regulatory conditions (for example, when designing a hotel WLAN) [9].

In general, the use of the 5 GHz band has been steadily increasing in recent years and most devices currently support operation at these frequencies [10].

Thus, we can determine the task of channel planning in terms of the available number of specific channels of various types, which practically take place in IEEE 802.11 networks.

3   Plane Coloring Problem Definition from Channel Planning Point of View

Let's assume the following:

1. We generally can use all channels available in the Russian regulatory domain.
2. The radio coverage area of each AP on the plane represents a circle.
3. M is the available number of channels (colors).
4. Only one channel type is used at a time (HT20, VHT20, VHT40, HE20 etc.)
5. R is the radius of the coverage area of all APs. They are equal to each other, regardless of the frequency and channel width used.
6. We understand that the coverage areas of the adjacent APs must have, in practice, overlapping zones. However, we will not take it into account, since it does not impact

on the solution of the problem. Thus, for convenience of geometrical construction, we will consider that adjacent APs coverage areas only touch each other.

7. The area of total space that needs to be covered is much larger than the area covered by a single AP. Since our interest is targeted to the state of the coverage zones inside the covered space, and not at its edges, we will consider the total covered space to be infinite.

8. There are no signal reflections in the medium – we will consider only the direct signal propagation.

For the ISM band, two cases are relevant - with three (M = 3) channels (1, 6 and 11) and four (M = 4) channels (1, 5, 9 and 13) 20 MHz wide (HT20/HE20).

UNII band provides more options. First of all, this is a scenario with the maximum use of all 20 MHz wide channels available in the spectrum. Such a task can occur in the case of deploying a network with a high density of user devices. In this case, the number of channels available in the Russian Federation today is sixteen: 36, 40, 44, 48, 52, 56, 60, 64, 132, 136, 140, 144, 149, 153, 157, 161.

Note also that 16 channels (20 MHz wide) available in the Russian Federation in the 5 GHz spectrum are placed in two non-adjacent groups of 8 channels each (M = 8 + 8). Respectively, for the case of aggregated 40 MHz wide channels, their total number is 8, and taking into account their spectrum location, they are represented by two equal blocks of 4 channels (M = 4 + 4).

The table below shows the main available channels for different possible channel plans (Table 1).

Table 1 Available channels

M	Channel list	Channel width, MHz	Band
3	1, 6, 11	20	ISM
4	1, 5, 9, 13	20	ISM/UNII
8 (4 + 4)	36 + 40, 44 + 48, 52 + 56, 60 + 64, 132 + 136, 140 + 144, 149 + 153, 157 + 161	40	UNII
8	36, 40, 44, 48, 52, 56, 60, 64	20	UNII
15 (5 + 5 + 5)	36, 40, 44, 48, 52, 56, 60, 64, 132, 136, 140, 144, 149, 153, 157	20	UNII
16 (8 + 8)	36, 40, 44, 48, 52, 56, 60, 64, 132, 136, 140, 144, 149, 153, 157, 161	20	UNII

Thus, the following cases will be useful in practice:

– M = 3, corresponding to a 3-channel plan in the ISM band;
– M = 4, corresponding to a 4-channel plan in the ISM band, as well as a four-channel plan with 40 MHz wide channels in the UNII-1 and UNII-2 sub-bands;

- M = 4 + 4 for the case of an 8-channel plan with 40 MHz wide channels using the entire spectrum available in 5 GHz, consisting of two non-contiguous sections.
- M = 8 for 8-channel plan with 20 MHz wide channels in UNII-1 and UNII-2 sub-bands.
- M = 8 + 8 for a 16-channel plan with 20 MHz wide channels using the entire spectrum available in 5 GHz, consisting of two non-contiguous sections.
- M = 5 + 5 + 5 for the case of using 15 20 MHz wide channels using the spectrum available in 5 GHz, except channels 161 and 165;
- in addition, it will also be useful to consider auxiliary case for M = 5.

Note that we will not consider the case for M = 16 because UNII range consists of two non-contiguous channel blocks.

Note that we will not consider channels more than 40 MHz wide due to the fact that, on the one hand, their scope of application is extremely narrow, and on the other hand, this case will be equal to the minimum number of available channels M = 3 and M = 4.

Thus the problem can be formulated as follows.

It is necessary to build a channel plan that will provide:

1. Maximum packing density of the plane by the APs coverage areas.
2. The maximum possible distance between APs of one channel from each other (minimum co-channel interference).
3. If the point 2 is met, provide the maximum possible distance between APs of adjacent channels from each other.
4. Using, whenever possible, all available channels given.

Since it is necessary to ensure the densest filling of the target plane with the AP coverage areas having the shape of a circle, it is convenient to use the apparatus of sphere packs to solve this problem. Therefore, it is necessary to consider a number of questions related to the densest sphere packings [11].

4 Sphere Packing Approach for the Plane Tessellation

Since we will not consider the entire plane tessellation, but only its repeating element, it is convenient to use a unit cell concept which is typically used in crystallography.

A unit cell of structure is a group of elements (in our case, radio coverage zones of APs) associated with each of the lattice points [11].

To describe the paving of a plane, it is also convenient to use the concept of a lattice - an infinite array of points generated by a set of discrete translation operations (vectors). A lattice has translational symmetry if the properties remain constant when translation symmetry operation is applied. Thus, in order to describe the entire covered plane, it is sufficient to specify a unit cell structure and a lattice geometry determined by translation vectors.

The concepts of lattice and structure are connected through the unit cell. The lattice consists of points with translational symmetry between them, and the structure consists of the corresponding unit cells located at the points of the lattice [11].

Therefore, we shall consider unit cells, which, when mapped along translation vectors, will give a plane tessellation (flat structure).

We should also note a concept of the coordination number N - the number of elements located at a minimum distance from the element given. When a structure is represented by graphs, a close term is the order of a vertex - the number of edges incident to a given vertex.

Consider the flat case. The densest hexagonal flat layer is shown in Fig. 1.

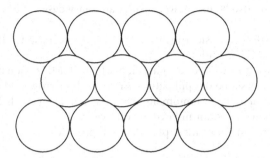

Fig. 1. The densest hexagonal flat layer.

We may note that the number of "holes" between the spheres is twice the number of spheres. Now we will place one more sphere of two different types in each "hole", corresponding to the projections of two additional layers in the three-dimensional structure. The resulting flat structure is a horizontal projection of a three-layer face-centered cubic (FCC) sphere packing. Therefore, the projection of the corresponding layers of the three-dimensional structure on the plane, we will call the "layer" (in quotation marks). Thus, we get a proportionally (by a ratio of 3) scaled layer with spheres of three "layers". In this case, the spheres of one "layer" are at the maximum distance from each other.

The densest three-dimensional sphere packings are of two main types - face-centered cubic – (FCC) and hexagonal closest packing (HCP) [11]. In both cases, we have a maximum plane coordination number of 6 ($N = 6$).

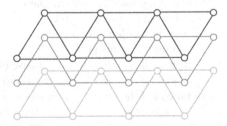

Fig. 2. Horizontal projection of FCC sphere packing with three "layers".

It is convenient to proceed to describe these structures by graphs. APs will be represented as vertices, and edges are drawn between the vertices through the touching points of their coverage areas. Thus we obtain a horizontal projection of the FCC spherical packing. It is shown in Fig. 2.

Note that the HCP packing is the densest for the three-dimensional case with packing density of 74% [15], but the corresponding horizontal projection for the plane case does not meet the conditions of the problem - it has a low density.

Indeed, if we fill only half of the "holes" between the spheres of the first "layer" with the second "layer" spheres, we obtain groups of spheres (marked with ovals) of one "layer" located in proximity to each other, which does not meet the initial requirement (Fig. 3).

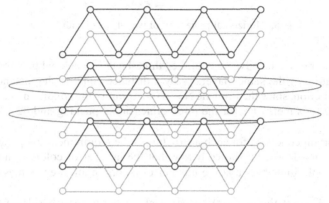

Fig. 3. Horizontal projection of HCP sphere packing with two "layers".

If we keep the equal distances between the "layers" of the same type required by the condition, then the condition of the maximum packing density will not be met - the "holes" are shown with larger circles – see Fig. 4.

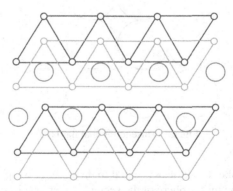

Fig. 4. "Holes" in the horizontal projection of HCP sphere packing with two "layers".

All other variants have a lower coordination number and thus a low plane packing density. For example, the case for a N = 2 is shown in Fig. 5.

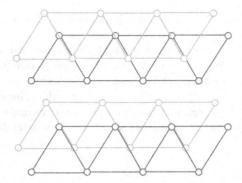

Fig. 5. Horizontal projection of two "layers" with N = 2.

Thus, in our case, the advantage of the "three-layer" hexagonal packing is the maximum separation of the same "layers" - by a distance equal to the distance inside the "layer". In addition, since the in-plane N = 6 (maximum), the condition of the maximum packing density is met: 74% for the three-dimensional packing and 82.7% for the flat packing.

An important condition for such a structure is the requirement to operate with three groups of colors. It will be shown below that the number of colors in a group is not critical. It is only important that the number of colors in all three groups ("layers") is the same.

Another (but not the densest) sphere packing option is a two-layer cubic body-centered packing (BCC) with an in-plane coordination number of 4 (N = 4). The dense tetragonal plane layer corresponding to the BCC packing is shown in Fig. 6.

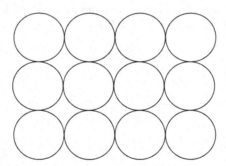

Fig. 6. Dense tetragonal flat layer.

Note that the number of «holes» is equal to the number of spheres. Considering the plane projection, if one more sphere of the second "layer" is placed in each "hole", then we will get a proportionally (twice) scaled up structure with spheres of two "layers". In this case, the spheres of one "layer" will be at the maximum distance from each other as well.

In this case, in a similar way, we get a structure with two "layers". The advantage of the "two-layer" cubic packing is the convenience of construction, since the division of the original group of channels (colors) into two non-adjacent blocks is convenient and logically follows the actual IEEE 802.11 channels placement in the spectrum, as it has been stated above.

The disadvantage of this solution is the lower in-plane coordination number ($N = 4$). As a result, this planar structure is not the densest - three-dimensional density packing is 68%, and two-dimensional - 78.5% [11]. Thus the in-plane packing density is 4.2% lower than for the hexagonal case (Fig. 7).

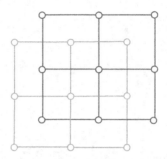

Fig. 7. Horizontal projection of BCC sphere packing.

Thus, the in-plane solutions of the problem corresponding to the maximum plane tessellation can be of two types:

– Cubic solutions (BCC) with two "layers" ($N = 4$)
– Hexagonal solutions (FCC) with three "layers" ($N = 6$)

5   Plane Tessellation Problem Definition

Now we can formulate the requirements for the possible tessellation problem solutions. The problem solution must contain the following elements:

1. Lattice type and its basis
2. The coordination number of the structure, N.
3. The number of "layers" in the structure.
4. The unit cell for the "layer", represented in the form of a graph. Wherein:
- the vertices of the graph are the access points that form the corresponding coverage areas;
- the number of graph vertices corresponds to the number of channels available in the channel plan considered;
- the edges of the graph correspond to geometrically adjacent areas of the AP coverage;
- the graph should take into account translational symmetry on the plane and thus show the mutual influence with similar APs of neighboring unit cells.
5. The criterion that determines the degree of negative impact between APs of a distributed network.

6 Plane Tessellation Model

When considering the plane tessellation, it is convenient to use the concept of translational symmetry, which is widely used in crystallography.

Let's define the following basis. Let a and b be translation vectors (elementary translations) [11] in a flat lattice, and α be the angle between them. Then we can define a flat lattice on an infinite plane, where vectors a and b define transitions between possible neighboring points A. The lattice is shown in Fig. 8.

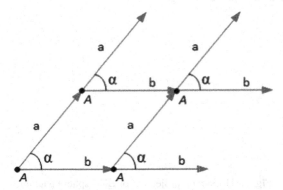

Fig. 8. Translation vectors in flat lattice.

This basis also defines an oblique coordinate system, which is convenient to describe the structure constructed.

As seen in Fig. 8, A point can be symmetrically translated along any sum of vectors a and b and match with itself. Let us now associate a certain group of access points, representing a unit cell, with A point.

A unit cell of structure is a group of elements (in our case, radio coverage zones of access points) associated with each lattice point.

Now, by translating the unit cell along the translation vectors of the lattice, we obtain a plane tessellation by a group of access points, i.e. tessellation structure. We will further consider the construction of various unit cells which correspond to the various channel plans.

We will further represent a unit cell by a planar graph, where the loops and multiple edges are allowed, thereby showing the relationship in the lattice that takes into consideration translation symmetry.

7 Channel Interference Model

Any lattice point, is equivalent to itself after being moved along lattice translation vectors. In this case, the entire set of possible translations can be described by a vector $i\vec{a} + j\vec{b}$, where i and j are integers.

Let the vector r_n - specify the translation between the lattice A point of the considered unit cell and the location of the n-th vertex (AP) of the same unit cell of the structure in order to consider its influence on the target vertex (AP). Obviously, if a considered vertex is located exactly at A point of the lattice, then $r_n = 0$. Thus the entire set of distances to all cells causing interference can be represented as the length of the vector:

$$\vec{d}_{ij} = \vec{r}_n + i\vec{a} + j\vec{b} \quad \text{(m)} \tag{1}$$

$L(f, d)$ is function that determines the signal attenuation (dB) depending on the distance from source d (m), and signal frequency f.

$S_{iw}(f, L(f, d))$ is function that defines the signal spectrum (W) depending on the frequency and the received power level, determined by the signal attenuation during its propagation along vector d.

The spectrum of all adjacent-channel interference from APs of the same WLAN can be described as follows:

$$W = \sum_{i}^{\infty} \sum_{j}^{\infty} S_{iw}\left(f, L\left(f, d_{ij}\right)\right) \quad \text{(W)} \tag{2}$$

Thus, for a given basis and known coordinates of all vertices of the unit cell, i.e. with a predetermined tessellation pattern, the total spectrum of all adjacent-channel interference will depend only on the characteristics of the emitted signal (i.e., its frequency, radiation power, antenna characteristics, etc.). In this case, to solve the problem, it is necessary to determine the geometry of unit cells for the considered channel plans.

8 Cell Units' Geometry

Consider a planar planar graph of equal distances. The order (coordination number N) of each vertex is 6 for the hexagonal "layer" and 4 for the tetragonal "layer".

It is obvious that the degenerate case for M = 1 does not make special sense - the entire plane is covered by access points operating on the same channel, and the unit cell consists of a single vertex. However, M = 1 has application in the rather exotic case of single-channel channel planning implemented by several equipment manufacturers [12]. Despite the obvious disadvantages, such an approach in some cases, may have some benefits. However, we will not consider it here.

For M = 2, the best solution is a "checkerboard" with N = 4. However, the number of channels equal to 2 does not occur in practice, therefore we will not consider this option in detail.

For the rest of the considered cases, we represent the radio coverage area as a graph, the vertices of which correspond to the access points, and the edges correspond to the boundaries of the coverage areas formed by these access points.

Let's now consider M = 3 case. Figure 9 shows the plane tessellation structure with unit cells for 3 available channels with N = 6. Lattice translation vectors for such tessellation are shown by bold lines. Note that the lengths of the lattice translation vectors are equal to each other.

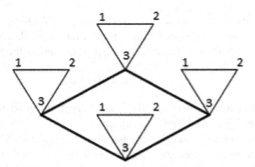

Fig. 9. Plane tessellation for M = 3, N = 6.

Now we will construct a graph corresponding to the unit cell for this structure. When constructing a graph in order to take into account translational symmetry, i.e. the relationship with the unit cells in the tessellated plane, we will show the junctions of the vertices of the graph with similar vertices of neighboring unit cells by additional edges of the graph. Additional edges corresponding to multiplicity more than one will be shown by arcs for clarity. Such a graph for M = 3 is shown in Fig. 10.

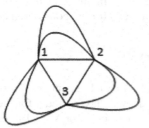

Fig. 10. Graph of the unit cell for M = 3, N = 6.

In this case, we can see that each vertex is connected by a triple edge to each of the other two vertices. The edges are triple due to their own unit cell and also due to two vertices of the same number in the neighboring unit cells. We will use the similar approach in all further constructions of unit cells. Thus, the graph of the unit cell has three triple edges, and all of its edges have the same multiplicity. Note that the graph presented above, taking into account possible permutations, is the only solution for M = 3. Thus, we have constructed a unit cell for the plane tessellation for the case of three channels. We will further consider the cases for the remaining M values in a similar way. Figure 11 shows the plane tessellation for the number of available channels M = 4 with the coordination number N = 6. Lattice translation vectors are shown in bold lines.

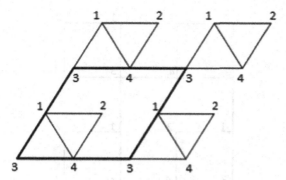

Fig. 11. Plane tessellation for M = 4, N = 6

The graph corresponding to a unit cell for a given structure is shown in Fig. 12.

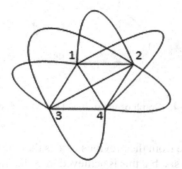

Fig. 12. Graph of the unit cell for M = 4, N = 6

The presented tessellation is the only solution that does not contain edges with multiplicity greater than 2. Note that the graph of the unit cell in this case has six edges with the same multiplicity equal to 2. For a given unit cell, it is possible to propose other variants of translational symmetry on the plane, which, however, will be described by identical graphs.

For M = 4, it is necessary to consider the tessellation case with N = 4. Figures 13 and 14 show the plane tessellation with lattice translation vectors and graph of the unit cell respectively.

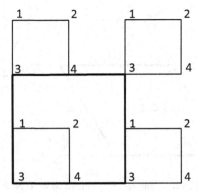

Fig. 13. Plane tessellation for M = 4, N = 4

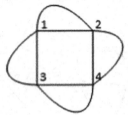

Fig. 14. Graph of the unit cell for M = 4, N = 4

A significant difference from the previous case is that the number of double edges in the graph is four instead of six, but this is achieved by reducing the coordination number, and, consequently, the reducing the packing density of the plane.

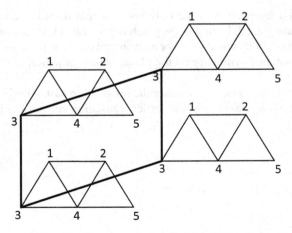

Fig. 15. Plane tessellation for M = 5, N = 6.

Now consider M = 5 case. Figure 15 shows the plane tessellation for 5 available channels with the coordination number of each vertex equal to six. In this case, the lengths of the vectors of elementary translations are not equal to each other.

However, it can be seen from it that the distance between vertices with the same numbers is less than 4R (as for the M = 4 cases) and equal to $2R\sqrt{3}$ (as for the M = 3 case). The graph corresponding to the unit cell for this structure is shown in Fig. 16 and geometrically represents an isosceles trapezoid.

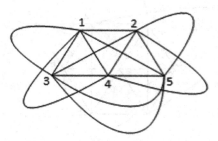

Fig. 16. Graph of the unit cell for M = 5, N = 6.

The presented tessellation considering possible permutations, is the only solution that meets the conditions of the problem statement. Note that this graph has 5 double and 5 single edges. Therefore, in contrast to the previously considered cases, the edges in this graph have different multiplicity.

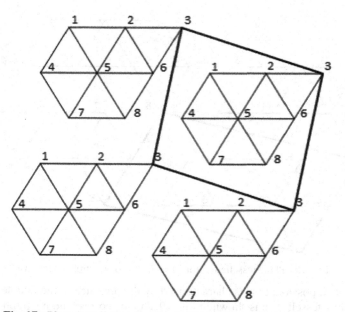

Fig. 17. Plane tessellation for M = 8, N = 6. No multiple edges case.

In the case M = 8, for the coordination number equal to 6 considering possible permutations, two main cases take place. The first case is characterized by the absence of multiple edges in the unit cell graph. The corresponding tessellation is shown in Fig. 17.

The graph corresponding to the unit cell for this structure is shown in Fig. 18.

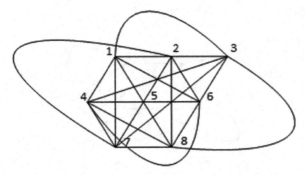

Fig. 18. Graph of the unit cell for M = 8, N = 6. No multiple edges case.

The graph has 24 single edges. The absence of multiple edges in the graph this tessellation means that for each vertex of the target unit cell, the following condition is met: the neighboring unit cells have no adjacent vertices identical to those in the target unit cell.

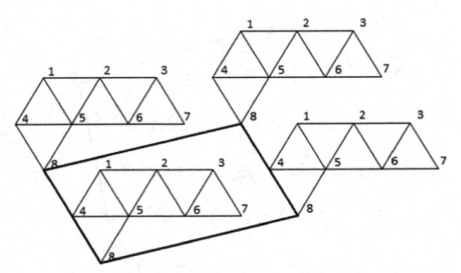

Fig. 19. Plane tessellation for M = 8, N = 6. Multiple edges case.

The second possible case is characterized by the presence of the double edges. The corresponding tessellation is shown in Fig. 19, and the corresponding graph is shown in Fig. 20.

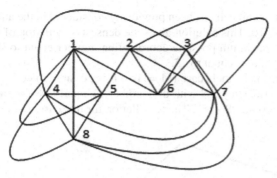

Fig. 20. Graph of the unit cell for M = 8, N = 6. Multiple edges case.

Note that there are several options for constructing a unit cell, but their adjacency matrices are identical. As for the case without multiple edges, it probably makes sense to be considered separately, since here we avoid the usage of multiple edges at the cost of increasing the total number of edges in the graph. This difference will be significant in the further consideration in the interference model.

Now consider the case with 15 channels (M = 15, N = 6). As it has been shown earlier, we have three "layers", while keeping the maximum possible coordination number equal to 6. In this case we have the maximum spatial separation relative to each other. It is possible to construct a solution for 15 channels using three "layers" with the M = 5 for each of them. Let's designate such a case as "5 + 5 + 5". The tessellation for this case is shown in Fig. 21.

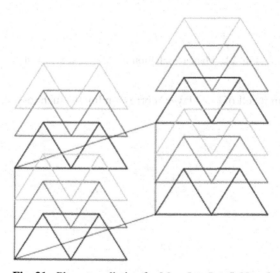

Fig. 21. Plane tessellation for M = 5 + 5 + 5, N = 6

The graph of the unit cell has been previously considered in the auxiliary case for M = 5, shown in Fig. 16. This solution gives the densest tessellation of the plane in three "layers" with the maximum possible coordination number equal to six and the largest number of used channels equal to 15.

Now consider 16 channels case (M = 16). It is possible to construct a solution for 16 channels using two "layers" with the number M equal to 8 for each of them. Let's designate such a case as "8 + 8". The tessellation for this case is shown in Fig. 22.

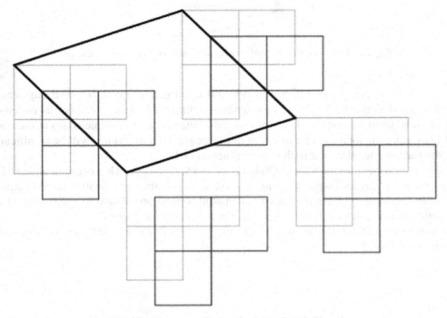

Fig. 22. Plane tessellation for M = 8 + 8. N = 4

Graph of the unit cell of one "layer" corresponding to such tessellation is shown on Fig. 23.

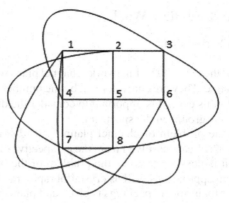

Fig. 23. Graph of the unit cell, M = 8, N = 4

Note that there are no multiple edges in the graph. We should also note that the presented solutions for two "layers" are unique up to the adjacency matrices of the corresponding graphs.

We will summarize the results obtained in Table 2. The table shows the considered cases for the M, and N values, the number of "layers", the lengths of the translation vectors (lattice basis), as well as the number of edges of various multiplicity in the graphs describing the structures of unit cells.

Table 2 Unit cells parameters

M	N	Number of "layers"	$|a|$	$|b|$	α (deg.)	Edges number
3	6	1	$2R\sqrt{3}$	$2R\sqrt{3}$	60	3 triple edges
4	6	1	$4R$	$4R$	60	6 double edges
4	4	1	$4R$	$4R$	90	4 double edges
5	6	1	$2R\sqrt{3}$	$2R\sqrt{7}$	≈80,17	5 double edges, 5 single edges
8	6	1	$2R\sqrt{7}$	$2R\sqrt{7}$	60	24 single edges
8	6	1	$4R$	$2R\sqrt{13}$	≈98,21	4 double edges 16 single edges
5 + 5 + 5	6	3	$2R\sqrt{3}$	$2R\sqrt{7}$	≈80,17	5 double edges 5 single edges
8 + 8	4	2	$4R\sqrt{2}$	$2R\sqrt{10}$	≈98,21	3 triple edges

9   Conclusions and Further Work

In conclusion we should note that:

1. We have analyzed the IEEE 802.11 networks channel plans which are typically used in the design practice. They are characterized by the number of channels equal to 3, 4, 8, 15 and 16. In this case, it is important to consider the division of the channels into non-contiguous groups in the spectrum.
2. It is shown that the problem of channel planning of distributed wireless access networks IEEE 802.11 can be solved from the perspective of the plane tessellation.
3. It is shown that it is possible to solve the problem of the plane tessellation using the sphere packing approach as well as crystallography methods.
4. An analysis of the main sphere packings is given and plane solutions are shown for the plane tessellation for the cases of the coordination number in the plane equal to 4 and 6.
5. The performed analysis showed that it is necessary to take into account the quantity of plane projections of the layers of a three-dimensional structure ("layers"), as well as the number of colors (channels) in their coloring.
6. The problem of constructing the unit cells for the plane tessellations is formulated.
7. A model is proposed in order to estimate the negative influence of APs on each other regarding spectrum resources re-use. It considers the translational symmetry of the plane tessellation, which will be studied by the authors in future works.
8. It is shown that for some values of channel number M used in practice (for example, 8, 15, and 16), in specific conditions, it is necessary to consider the tessellation in several "layers". In particular, possible solutions are, respectively, solutions in "two layers": $4 + 4\ 8 + 8$, as well as in three "layers": $5 + 5 + 5$.
9. For the channel plans most often used in the design practice of IEEE 802.11 networks, unit cell has been constructed that correspond to the statement of the channel planning problem. For some values of M (for example, $M = 4$ and $M = 8$), the existence of different tessellations is noted - cell graphs of the unit cells for them have different edges quantity and multiplicity. This should be taken into account in the further calculations accordingly.
10. The description of unit cells as structural elements of flat lattices is proposed. For some values of M (for example, $M = 5$ and $M = 8$), the existence of different possible tessellations was noted, including both geometrically different unit cells and different lattice basis.
11. The numerical estimations of interference impact between access points are subject to further research.

Acknowledgments. This research is based on the Applied Scientific Research under the SPbSUT state assignment 2021.

References

1. Raigorodskii, A.M.: On the chromatic number of the space. Russian Math. Surv. **55**(2), 351–352 (2000)

2. Jensen, T.R., Toft, B.: Graph coloring problems. In: Wiley-Interscience Series in Discrete Mathematics and Optimization. pp. 150–152 (1995)
3. Hadwiger, H.: Überdeckung des euklidischen Raumes durch kongruente Mengen. Portugal. Math. **4**, 238–242 (1945)
4. Hadwiger, H.: Ungelöste Probleme No. 40. Elem. Math. **16**, 103–104 (1961)
5. De Grey, Aubrey D.N.J.: The chromatic number of the plane is at least 5. Geombinatorics **28**, 5–18 (2018). arXiv:1804.02385
6. Raigorodskii, A.M.: On a bound in Borsuk's problem. Russian Math. Surv. **54**(2), 453–454 (1999). https://doi.org/10.1070/RM1999v054n02ABEH000146
7. IEEE Std 802.11 – 2016. IEEE Standard for Information technology — Telecommunications and information exchange between systems. Local and metropolitan area networks — Specific requirements. Part 11: Wireless LAN Medium Access Control (MAC) and Physical Layer (PHY) Specifications (2016)
8. Aruba High Density Wireless networks for Auditoriums. VRD/Aruba Networks, p. 122 (2010)
9. Aerohive Networks. High Density Wi-Fi Design Principles. Aero hive Networks White Paper. p. 23 (2012)
10. Vikulov, A., Paramonov, A.: Practical retrospective of 5-year evolution of the IEEE 802.11 client device capabilities. In: 2020 12th International Congress on Ultra Modern Telecommunications and Control Systems and Workshops (ICUMT), pp. 296–300 (2020)
11. Nesse, D.W.: Introduction to Mineralogy / Oxford University Press. p. 442 (2000). ISBN 0-19-510691-1
12. WLAN RF architecture primer: single-channel and adaptive multi-channel models. In: Aruba White Paper. Aruba Networks, p. 29 (2013)
13. Balej, J., Zach, P., Pokorný, M.: Four Channel Assignment Schemes for WiFi in 2.4 GHz Band. Acta Universitatis Agriculturae et Silviculturae Mendelianae Brunensis **64**(1), 205–211 (2016). https://doi.org/10.11118/actaun201664010205
14. Socolar, J.E.S., Taylor, J.M.: An aperiodic hexagonal tile. J. Combin. Theory, Seri. A **118**(8), 2207–2231 (2011). https://doi.org/10.1016/j.jcta.2011.05.001
15. Friedenberg, J.: The perceived beauty of regular polygon tessellations. Symmetry **11**(8), 984 (2019). https://doi.org/10.3390/sym11080984
16. Cisco Systems: Cisco Wireless LAN Controller Configuration Best Practices. Cisco Press (2015)
17. Ruckus Wireless. Deploying Very High Density Wi-Fi. Best Practice Design Guide (2012)
18. Gerasimenko, M., et al.: Cooperative radio resource management in heterogeneous cloud radio access networks. IEEE Access **3**, 397–406 (2015). https://doi.org/10.1109/ACCESS.2015.2422266

Advancement of Fingerprint Polarimetric Scheme for Purposes of Authentication

Trubin Pavel(✉) ⒾⒹ, Murashov Aleksandr, Suntsov Dmitriy, and Velichko Elena ⒾⒹ

Higher School of Applied Physics and Space Technologies, Peter the Great St. Petersburg Polytechnic University (SPbPU), Polytechnicheskaya Street. 29, 195251 Saint-Petersburg, Russia

trubin.pk@edu.spbstu.ru

Abstract. Development of laboratory setup for the analysis of polarization features of biological tissues in order to increase the security of fingerprint systems is considered in this work. Calculation method based on Mueller-Stokes measurement of scattered light. Lu-Chipman algorithm of Mueller matrix polar decomposition was used for obtaining polarimetric parameters. During the work automated electromechanical elements were added to the setup. Program for controlling these elements was developed using LABVIEW. Experiments comparing polarimetric parameters of different people were carried out. Images of polarimetric parameters distribution on the surface of the finger were obtained. It is shown that the proposed scheme and data processing algorithm are promising for solving the problem of increasing the reliability of fingerprint sensors.

Keywords: Polarimetry · Mueller matrix · Biotissue · Dactyloscopy · Infosec

1 Introduction

The task of protecting the personal identification process is relevant in the modern world where more and more functions and applications are implemented using mobile devices the security of which is still far from ideal and even necessary. The report by Grand View Research forecasts the growth of the global market for fingerprint access control systems to $ 4.4 billion by 2022 [1, 2]. The growth of e-commerce is considered to be the engine that moves market. The development of this market requires the implementation of secure online payments using new identification methods. The integration of fingerprint access control technology into a smartphone is designed to provide strong authentication when working with mobile applications [3, 4].

Modern methods of protecting fingerprint scanners have significant drawbacks, in particular, the possibility of falsification [4].

Materials popular for the manufacture of counterfeits (gelatin, glue, silicone) have a significantly smaller range of refractive index values, differ in scattering and absorbing characteristics, and are generally more homogeneous in composition and structure than skin [5–7]. Therefore, the optical parameters measurement can be helpful in solving the

© Springer Nature Switzerland AG 2022
Y. Koucheryavy et al. (Eds.): NEW2AN 2021/ruSMART 2021, LNCS 13158, pp. 470–480, 2022.
https://doi.org/10.1007/978-3-030-97777-1_39

problem of identifying a counterfeit. This paper discusses the possibility of applying polarimetry to solving the problem of security of fingerprint scanners.

The aim of this work is to improve the optical scheme [8] and measurement technique of assessing polarimetric tissue inhomogeneities in order to increase the security of optoelectronic fingerprint identification systems.

The tasks of the work include:

- Development of theoretical aspects of the interaction of electromagnetic optical waves with the scattering tissue of human fingers and development of new methods for analyzing experimental data;
- Improvement of the experimental setup, including the addition of automated motorized elements;
- Development of software for controlling the motorized elements;
- Conducting experiments on an improved setup, including experiments comparing the polarimetric parameters of fingerprints of different people.
- Presentation of results, comparison and discussion of the obtained data.

2 Theory

In this work the development of a suitable theoretical basis for the light scattering on the biological tissue of the finger is started [9, 10].

Consider the scattering of light by a point object located at the origin and irradiated by a plane wave at the location of the object ($x = y = z = 0$):

$$E^0 = E_x^0 x_0 + E_y^0 \cos \alpha y_0 + E_y^0 \sin \alpha z_0 \tag{1}$$

At the receiving point x, y, z = h, the field Ex, Ey:

$$E_x = \beta_{11} \frac{e^{-ikr}}{r} E_x^0 + \beta_{12} \frac{e^{-ikr}}{r} E_y^0 \tag{2}$$

$$E_y = \beta_{21} \frac{e^{-ikr}}{r} E_x^0 + \beta_{22} \frac{e^{-ikr}}{r} E_y^0, \tag{3}$$

$$r = \sqrt{x^2 + y^2 + z^2}. \tag{4}$$

The coefficients β_{ij} depend both on the coordinates of the observation point and on the characteristics of the object.

It is assumed that the signal is received by a photodetector which records the intensity of the incoming signals (power). We also assume that a lens focused on an object receives scattered reradiation directed parallel to its optical axis.

In other words, the waves arriving at the photodetector can be considered uncorrelated. Therefore, we are looking for the sum of the power fluxes falling on the light-sensitive elements of the detector. If the photodetector has an area S then it receives a signal

$$P_x = \int_S \frac{1}{r^2} \frac{h}{r} \left| \beta_{11} E_x^0 + \beta_{12} E_y^0 \right|^2 dS \tag{5}$$

$$P_y = \int_S \frac{1}{r^2} \frac{h}{r} \left| \beta_{11} E_x^0 + \beta_{12} E_y^0 \right|^2 dS \tag{6}$$

This is one of the simplest wave propagation options. In general, E_x^0, E_y^0, β_{ij} quantities are complex. Another option for representing an object is small point objects, each gives an uncorrelated field, in this case the power fluxes can be added.

As a result:

$$E_x = \alpha_{11} E_x^0 + \alpha_{12} E_y^0 \tag{7}$$

$$E_y = \alpha_{21} E_x^0 + \alpha_{22} E_y^0 \tag{8}$$

All these quantities are complex. If we have a small point object near which the field E_0 acts then in the direction $r = xx_0 + yy_0 + zz_0$ the field is equal to:

$$E = \frac{\sigma e^{-ikr}}{r} \left\{ E_0 - \frac{r(rE_0)}{r^2} \right\} \tag{9}$$

Let's refer to the Mueller matrix. We register:

$$E_x, E_y, E_x + E_y, E_x + iE_y \tag{10}$$

$$\left| E_x + E_y \right|^2 = |E_x|^2 + \left| E_y \right|^2 + 2|E_x| \left| E_y \right| \cos \delta \tag{11}$$

$$\left| E_x + iE_y \right|^2 = |E_x|^2 + \left| E_y \right|^2 + 2|E_x| \left| E_y \right| \sin \delta \tag{12}$$

Stokes components are defined as:

$$I = |E_x|^2 + \left| E_y \right|^2 \tag{13}$$

$$Q = |E_x|^2 - \left| E_y \right|^2 \tag{14}$$

$$U = \left| E_x + E_y \right|^2 - |E_x|^2 - \left| E_y \right|^2 \tag{15}$$

$$V = \left| E_x + iE_y \right|^2 - |E_x|^2 - \left| E_y \right|^2 \tag{16}$$

We can use four field options as input signals:

$$1) E_X^0 = 1; \ E_y^0 = 0 \tag{17}$$

$$2) E_X^0 = 0; \ E_y^0 = 1 \tag{18}$$

$$3) E_X^0 = 1; \ E_y^0 = 1 \tag{19}$$

$$4) E_X^0 = 1; E_y^0 = i \tag{20}$$

We consider each of these options. For each, we define the Muller matrix:

$$S_{out} = \begin{pmatrix} I_{out} \\ Q_{out} \\ U_{out} \\ V_{out} \end{pmatrix} = \begin{pmatrix} M_{11} & M_{12} & M_{13} & M_{14} \\ M_{21} & M_{22} & M_{23} & M_{24} \\ M_{31} & M_{32} & M_{33} & M_{34} \\ M_{41} & M_{42} & M_{43} & M_{44} \end{pmatrix} \begin{pmatrix} I_{in} \\ Q_{in} \\ U_{in} \\ V_{in} \end{pmatrix} =$$

$$\begin{pmatrix} M_{11}I_{in} + M_{12}Q_{in} + M_{13}U_{in} + M_{14}V_{in} \\ M_{21}I_{in} + M_{22}Q_{in} + M_{23}U_{in} + M_{24}V_{in} \\ M_{31}I_{in} + M_{32}Q_{in} + M_{33}U_{in} + M_{34}V_{in} \\ M_{41}I_{in} + M_{42}Q_{in} + M_{43}U_{in} + M_{44}V_{in} \end{pmatrix} \tag{21}$$

We get the relation between the real coefficients α_{ij} and the coefficients of the matrix.

$$M_{11} = \frac{1}{2}\left(\alpha_{11}^2 + \alpha_{21}^2 + \alpha_{12}^2 + \alpha_{22}^2 \right) \tag{22}$$

$$M_{12} = \frac{1}{2}\left(\alpha_{11}^2 + \alpha_{21}^2 - \alpha_{12}^2 - \alpha_{22}^2 \right) \tag{23}$$

$$M_{21} = \frac{1}{2}\left(\alpha_{11}^2 - \alpha_{21}^2 + \alpha_{12}^2 - \alpha_{22}^2 \right) \tag{24}$$

$$M_{22} = \frac{1}{2}\left(\alpha_{11}^2 - \alpha_{21}^2 - \alpha_{12}^2 + \alpha_{22}^2 \right) \tag{25}$$

$$M_{31} = \alpha_{11}\alpha_{21} + \alpha_{12}dS \tag{26}$$

$$M_{32} = \alpha_{11}\alpha_{21} - \alpha_{12}\alpha_{22} \tag{27}$$

$$M_{13} = \alpha_{11}\alpha_{12} + \alpha_{21}\alpha_{22} \tag{28}$$

$$M_{23} = \alpha_{11}\alpha_{12} - \alpha_{21}\alpha_{22} \tag{29}$$

$$M_{33} = \alpha_{12}\alpha_{21} + \alpha_{11}\alpha_{21} \tag{30}$$

$$M_{44} = \alpha_{12}\alpha_{21} - \alpha_{11}\alpha_{22} \tag{31}$$

$$M_{14} = M_{41} = M_{42} = M_{24} = M_{43} = M_{34} = 0 \tag{32}$$

Biotissue polarimetry is associated with problems arising from multiple scattering, which complicates the existing computational methods developed for transparent media [11]. Various effects due to different constituent parts of a heterogeneous biological tissue are superimposed on each other, which complicates quantitative analysis [12]. Various methods of decomposition of Mueller matrices are used for quantitative analysis [13]. We use the Lu-Chipman algorithm which is based on the factorization of the Mueller matrix into three matrices, each of which describes certain properties of the object (depolarizing, linear birefringence and optical activity, linear and circular dichroism) [14].

In this work, the manual rotary devices of the plates and polarizers were replaced by electromechanical ones, in order to increase the accuracy of the setup and measurements, as well as to reduce the measurement cycle time. Also, a new lens for multiple zooming and more detailed analysis of skin scattering, for example, at the depression and crest of the papillary pattern, was added to the setup.

Example of images obtained with He–Ne laser is shown in Fig. 1.

Fig. 1. Fingerprint image using He–Ne laser.

A He–Ne laser was used in the setup, so there is visible speckle pattern in the image. To preserve high-resolution images and a sufficient number of frames per second, it was decided to use an incoherent light source in the setup. The block diagram of the setup is shown in Fig. 2.

The principle of operation of the scheme: the sample is illuminated by the light of the source (1) passing through the 632 nm filter and optics defining the input polarization (3–6), scattered by the sample, and collected by the optics of the output analyzing elements (7, 8) to the detector (9). One of the 6 states of polarization at the input corresponds to 6 polarization states at the output. 36 measurements are carried out, each of which corresponds to an image that carries information about the effect of the sample on the light of a certain polarization.

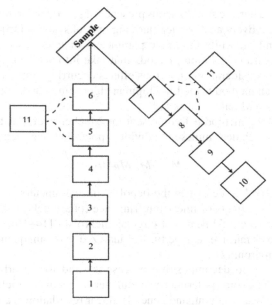

Fig. 2. The block diagram of the laboratory setup. 1 – light source, 2 – red filter, 3 – lense, 4 – linear polarizer, 5 – half-wave plate, 6, 7 – quarter-wave plates, 8 – analyzer, 9 – CCD camera, 10 – PC, 11 – power supply.

After installing the source of incoherent light, the images got rid of the speckle field (Fig. 3).

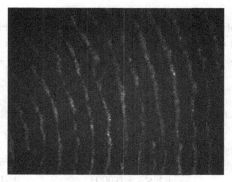

Fig. 3. Fingerprint image obtained using an incoherent light source.

Subtracting and adding these images we can obtain a matrix of images corresponding to the Mueller matrix. The resulting images are converted into numerical arrays, according to the specified scheme, then the Muller matrix is calculated with averaging.

As mentioned earlier, the simultaneous presence of several polarization effects makes it difficult to quantitatively analyze depolarizing optical systems [15]. Matrix elements become interdependent, while biometric parameters of interest to the researcher are masked. In this regard calculation methods that take into account multiple scattering and allow separate consideration of various effects occurring simultaneously are being developed. One such method is the Lu-Chipman algorithm, which determines the polar decomposition of the Mueller matrix [14].

The essence of the method is to represent the Mueller matrix as a product of three matrices, each of which determines an individual polarimetric effect:

$$M = M_\Delta M_R M_D \tag{33}$$

where the matrix M_Δ describes the depolarizing parameters of the medium, M_R is responsible for the effects of linear birefringence (phase delay) and optical activity, M_D includes the effects of linear and circular dichroism [14–16]. After calculation, these composite basis matrices can be further analyzed to obtain quantitative individual properties of the environment.

The above-described decomposition process is valid for an arbitrary matrix and allows one to calculate some polarimetric parameters of media, namely, diattenuation d, depolarization Δ (linear, circular, and general), linear retardation δ, and optical rotation ψ [15].

To control the electromechanical swivel holders, a program was written in the LAB-VIEW environment. The program allows to set the position of the rotational elements of polarizers and plates, to carry out automatic sequential measurements according to a given algorithm and to save images.

3   Experiment

Comparison studies of polarimetric parameters of fingers of different people using He–Ne laser were carried out (see Table 1). The index finger of the left hand was used as the object under study. The random error was calculated based on 20 measurements for each finger.

Table 1. Polarimetric parameters of two different biological samples obtained using a coherent light source.

Parameter	Subject 1	Subject 2
Depolarization (Δ)	0.8944 ± 0.0003	0.918 ± 0.005
Diattenuation (d)	0.053 ± 0.011	0.07 ± 0.03
Linear retardance (δ)	1.11 ± 0.04	1.30 ± 0.06

Table 1 shows that the difference between the depolarization and the diattenuation value lies in the range from 0.01 to 0.03, and the difference between the linear retardance values is in the range from 0.1 to 0.2.

Thus, based on the results of the experiments, it can be seen that with such a number of measurements, it is possible to correctly compare two samples by the value of the linear delay.

Table 2 shows the results of experiments carried out using an incoherent light source.

Table 2. Polarimetric parameters of two different biological samples obtained using an incoherent light source.

Parameter	Subject 3	Subject 2
Depolarization (Δ)	0.889 ± 0.007	0.914 ± 0.004
Diattenuation (d)	0.0542 ± 0.0011	0.0490 ± 0.0022
Linear retardance (δ)	2.779 ± 0.027	2.45 ± 0.03

Table 2 shows that the difference in the depolarization is 0.025 units, the diattenuation value is 0.005, and for the linear retardance difference is 0.32. It can be concluded that the most preferable characteristic for comparison is the value of the linear retardance, since its values differ the most.

Glue models simulating a human finger were also used for the experiments. The manufactured dummies are of poor quality, but even they were able to overcome the protection of smartphones.

Images of the distributions of polarimetric parameters were obtained for an incoherent light source (Fig. 4). The lighter points in the image, the greater the value of the investigated parameter and vice versa. So, from Fig. 4 it can be seen that the magnitude of diattenuation and linear retardance is more influenced by the thickness of the convex portions of the finger (ridges). The depolarization over the image depends on the number of valleys, since the minimum values of this parameter are observed on the ridges. It is rather difficult to judge the structure of the object under study by the magnitude of the circular retardance since the image for this characteristic is noisy.

Table 3 shows the polarimetric parameters obtained by averaging the values in the images from Fig. 4. Biological tissue of the finger depolarizes radiation much more strongly than the material of the fake finger, and also has a greater dependence of the absorption index on the polarization of the incident light (diattenuation parameter).

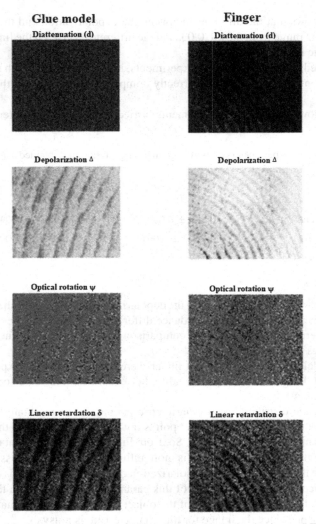

Fig. 4. Polarimetric characteristics of a sample obtained using an LED.

Table 3. Obtained polarimetric parameters.

Parameter	Glue film	Finger
Depolarization (Δ)	0.645 ± 0.002	0.968 ± 0.004
Diattenuation (d)	0.239 ± 0.002	0.030 ± 0.004
Linear retardance (δ)	0.744 ± 0.016	1.17 ± 0.05

4 Conclusion

The security of identification devices is still far from ideal and even necessary, therefore, the task of protecting the process of personal identification remains relevant in the modern world.

The theoretical analysis carried out in the course of the work and the obtained experimental data allow us to indicate the following results:

- The theoretical basis of the interaction of electromagnetic optical waves with scattering biological tissue are determined, the conclusion is drawn that it is necessary to consider the processes of multiple scattering;
- Significant changes were made to the design of the installation, which made it possible to reduce the time of one measurement cycle by more than 5 times ($\approx$5 min/$\approx$30 s), as well as to carry out measurements more accurately;
- A software in the LABVIEW environment was developed to control the measurement process, and the program in the MATLAB package was additionally improved for calculating and displaying images of polarimetric parameters of biological tissue;
- Studies on biological tissue and objects imitating a real finger have been carried out. The difference in polarimetric indicators for different people is shown, which can serve as a basis for personality identification processes;

The results obtained indicate the efficiency of the developed technique, its diagnostic significance and applicability in the field of increasing the protection of information of access systems. The prospects for further research aimed at miniaturizing the installation, simplifying measurements, searching and testing other algorithms for matrix decomposition and calculating biometric parameters, organizing a database of biometric parameters.

Acknowledgements. The reported study was funded by RFBR, project number 20-32-90121.

References

1. Gorshkov, A., Antonov, D.: Biometricheskaya identifikaciya dlya bezopasnosti granic. Tekhnologiya zashchity (2020). http://www.techportal.ru/290053
2. Innovation Spotlight: University of Southampton: Biometrics and Human Identification. (2020). https://www.bccresearch.com/whitepapers/future-of-biometrics-and-human-identification.html
3. Habib, A., Selwal, A.: Robust anti-spoofing techniques for fingerprint liveness detection: a Survey. IOP Conf. Ser. Mater. Sci. Eng. **1033**, 012026 (2021)
4. Husseis, A., Liu-Jimenez, J., Sanchez-Reillo, R.: Fingerprint presentation attack detection utilizing spatio-temporal features. Sensors **21**, 2059 (2021). https://doi.org/10.3390/s21062059
5. Priesnitz, J., Rathgeb, C., Buchmann, N., et al.: An overview of touchless 2D fingerprint recognition. J. Image Video Proc. **2021**, 8 (2021). https://doi.org/10.1186/s13640-021-00548-4

6. Gogoi, A., Konwer, S., Zhuo, G.-Y.: Polarimetric measurements of surface chirality based on linear and nonlinear light scattering. Front. Chem. **8**, 611833 (2021). https://doi.org/10.3389/fchem.2020.611833

7. Calixto, S., et al.: Gelatin as a photosensitive material. Molecules J. Synth. Chem. Nat. Product Chem., p. 22 (2018)

8. Trubin, P., Murashov, A., Suntsov, D., Velichko, E.: Improvement of a dactyloscopic authentication security using polarimetric technique. In: Galinina, O., Andreev, S., Balandin, S., Koucheryavy, Y. (eds.) Internet of Things, Smart Spaces, and Next Generation Networks and Systems. LNCS, vol. 12526. Springer, Cham (2020). https://doi.org/10.1007/978-3-030-657 29-1_6

9. Yu, J., Cheng, X., Li, M.: error analysis and calibration improvement of the imaging section in a mueller matrix microscope. Appl. Sci. **10**(13), 4422 (2020). https://doi.org/10.3390/app 10134422

10. Tuchin, V.V, Tissue optics: light scattering methods and instruments for medical diagnosis. 2nd ed. Bellingham: SPIE Press, vol. 13, p.825 (2007)

11. Baba, J.: The use of polarized light for biomedical applications/PHD dissertation, Texas A&M University, College Station, p. 167 (2003)

12. Layden, D., Ghosh, N., Vitkin, A.: Quantitative polarimetry for tissue characterization and diagnosis. Adv. Biophoton. Tissue Optical Sectioning **5**, 73–108 (2013)

13. Esau, K.L.: Proposed methods for measuring and interpreting mueller matrices in in vivo retinal polarimetry. (2020) UWSpace. http://hdl.handle.net/10012/16601

14. Lu, S., Chipman, R.: Interpretation of Mueller matrices based on polar decomposition. J. Opt. Soc. Am. A **13**, 1106–1113 (1996)

15. Ghosh, N., Wood, M.F.G., Vitkin, A.: Mueller matrix decomposition for extraction of individual polarization parameters from complex turbid media exhibiting multiple scattering, optical activity and linear birefringence. J. Biomed. Optics **13**(4), 1–14 (2008)

16. Sheng, W., Li, W., Qi, J., Liu, T., He, H., Dong, Y., Liu, S., Wu, J., Elson, D.S., Ma, H.: Quantitative analysis of 4 × 4 mueller matrix transformation parameters for biomedical imaging. Photonics. **6**(1), 34 (2019). https://doi.org/10.3390/photonics6010034

Network Slice Degradation Probability as a Metric for Defining Slice Performance Isolation

Nikita Polyakov[1]([✉])[iD], Natalia Yarkina[2][iD], Konstantin Samouylov[1,3][iD], and Yevgeni Koucheryavy[2][iD]

[1] RUDN University, Miklukho-Maklaya Street 6, Moscow 117198, Russia
[2] Unit of Electrical Engineering, Tampere University, 33720 Tampere, Finland
[3] Federal Research Center "Computer Science and Control"
of the Russian Academy of Sciences, 44-2 Vavilov Street, Moscow 119333, Russia

Abstract. Slice isolation is a key feature of the network slicing technique and refers to protecting slices from negative impact of fault, attack or workload increase in other slices. Dynamic resource slicing policies, although provide efficient multiplexing and resource utilization, may lead to situation when a traffic surge in one slice hinders performance of other slices. The level of performance isolation cannot be specified and evaluated without defining an adequate metric. This paper addresses network slice degradation probability as a metric for defining performance isolation of slice. We use teletraffic theory to derive an analytical expression for the degradation probability in a single slice.

Keywords: Network slicing · Slice isolation · Slice degradation

1 Introduction

By logically decoupling the network, the infrastructure owner has the ability to dynamically reallocate virtualized network resources among slice tenants, which permits increasing both the performance and the commercial efficiency of the equipment. However, when applying the network slicing technique in the context of logical segmenting for virtual operators (slice tenants), the requirements for the isolation level and availability of network services must be satisfied [8]. According to the definition of virtual resources' isolation given in [4], a network slice has access to specific range of resources that do not overlap with other network slices.

The aim of this work is to define a metric for slice availability and isolation level while taking into account the dynamic and adaptive character of resource slicing. Reference [7] defines availability of an item as being in a state to perform a required function at a given instant of time or at any instant of time within a

Supported by the RUDN University Strategic Academic Leadership Program. The reported study was funded by RFBR, project number 19-07-00933, 20-07-01064.

© Springer Nature Switzerland AG 2022
Y. Koucheryavy et al. (Eds.): NEW2AN 2021/ruSMART 2021, LNCS 13158, pp. 481–492, 2022.
https://doi.org/10.1007/978-3-030-97777-1_40

given time interval. Availability is usually expressed as a percentage of uptime in a day, month or year. According to [4], communication service availability is a percentage value of the amount of time the end-to-end communication service is delivered according to an agreed QoS, divided by the amount of time the system is expected to deliver the end-to-end service. We propose to define slice availability via service level degradation probability metric. Slice service/SLA degradation was mentioned in [2,11], but not as a key concept.

The concept of service degradation reflects the specifics of packet-switched networks and describes a situation when, if a shortage of resources occurs, an incoming service request is not dropped or queued, but is satisfied, which leads to a temporary decrease in the amount of resources allocated to this and other ongoing sessions below the accepted value. The concept of degradation can be applied to both streaming and elastic traffic. In the first case, it will correspond, for example, to a temporary deterioration in the quality (resolution) of video during a video conference, while in the second case it will describe a breach of the transmission delay requirement.

This work proposes a probabilistic model of a slice which provides a communication service involving elastic (non-GBR) traffic transmission, such as software updates or buffered video streaming. We analyze the availability of the slice in terms of compliance with the SLA between the infrastructure owner and the tenant while maximizing economic benefits. We specifically focus on analytical modeling of slices with non-GBR services, while many authors, e.g. [8], derive formulas for GBR services or analyze system on equipment level [1,5]. In this work, we consider the availability of slices only in terms of the compliance with QoS requirements, without taking into account equipment breakdowns and other external factors.

The paper is structured as follows. Section 2 introduces the basic model assumptions. Section 3 describes a probabilistic model in terms of queuing theory, for which formulas for performance indicators are further derived. Section 5 offers numerical results. Section 6 concludes the paper.

2   Basic Assumptions

For the system model, we overall follow [9] and [6]. We assume the total maximum transmission resource capacity of a 5G base station (BS), $C_{[Gbps]}$, constant and use it as the total amount of resources to be sliced. Let S slices be instantiated at the BS. For each slice s the following parameters are specified in the SLA:

- R_s^{min}—minimum data rate,
- R_s^{max}—maximum data rate,
- N_s^{cont}—contractual maximum number of users for which QoS will be guaranteed,
- R_s^{deg}—data rate threshold under which the slice is considered degraded.

The current state of slice s is assumed to be characterized by the number of active users, N_s, and the current capacity, C_s. The data rate for each slice user is then obtained as $R_s = C_s/N_s$.

By signing a service level agreement, the infrastructure owner commits to provide the tenant with a capacity (bandwidth) $C_s = N_s R_s^{\min}$ as long as $N_s \leq N_s^{\text{cont}}$, where $R_s^{\min}$ and N_s^{cont} are specified in the agreement. If $N_s > N_s^{\text{cont}}$ then only capacity $C_s^{\text{cont}} = N_s^{\text{cont}} R_s^{\min}$ is guaranteed. This bandwidth can be expressed as a share of the total resource capacity $\gamma_s = C_s^{\text{cont}}/C$. In other words, according to the SLA, slice users are guaranteed the data rate $R_s^{\min}$ as long as their number does not exceed N_s^{cont}, while any capacity above that can be provided only if available and without exceeding $R_s^{\max}$ per user.

When the slice bandwidth C_s is not enough to provide end users with the guaranteed minimum data rate $R_s^{\min}$, we talk about degradation of the service level in the slice. Degradation may occur due to an excessive workload increase in the slice itself (the tenant's responsibility) or due to insufficient resource allocation (the infrastructure owner's responsibility). Only in the latter case we refer to the slice isolation breach, i.e. whenever

$$C_s < R_s^{\min} \min\{N_s, N_s^{\text{cont}}\} \stackrel{\text{not}}{=} C_s^{\text{guar}}. \tag{1}$$

Thus, whenever the above condition is true, the availability of the slice is compromised. Moreover, the slice may lose availability due to some other reasons such as equipment failure. We assume that the required availability ratio Av is specified for each slice in the SLA. Reference [3] describes how to apply the reliability theory to the design of wireless networks and defines the steady-state availability as follows:

$$Av = \lim_{T \to \infty} Av(T), \tag{2}$$

where $Av(T) = \mathbb{P}\{\text{"equipment is up at time } T\text{"}\}$. Let us rewrite this as

$$Av = \lim_{T \to \infty} \frac{t^{\,\text{up}}(T)}{T} = 1 - \lim_{T \to \infty} \frac{t^{\,\text{fail}}(T) + t^{\,\text{cap}}(T)}{T}, \tag{3}$$

where T is the total measurement time, $t^{\,\text{up}}(T)$ is the total time of service up, $t^{\,\text{fail}}(T)$ is the total time of service failure and recovery and $t^{\,\text{cap}}(T)$ is the total time when the condition (1) holds.

In this work we do not take into account technical breakdowns, therefore we assume that $t^{\,\text{fail}}(T) = 0$.

Figure 1 illustrates the periods $\Delta_{s,i}^{\text{cap}}$ when the slice capacity falls below the threshold. For simplicity, in the figure it is assumed that $N_s = N_s^{\text{cont}}$ at all times. Here

$$t_s^{\text{cap}}(T) = \sum_{i=1}^{Y_s(T)} \Delta_{s,i}^{\text{cap}}, \quad s = 1, \dots S, \tag{4}$$

where $Y_s(t)$ is the counter of the periods when (1) holds.

3 Stochastic Model of a Single Slice

Queuing theory can provide a convenient analytical framework to model the system described in the previous section. Each slice is modeled as a separate

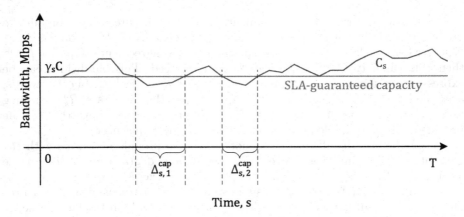

Fig. 1. Periods of slice s isolation breaches assuming that $N_s = N_s^{\text{cont}}$ for all T.

queuing system (QS), which type can be chosen so that it adequately reflects the nature of the service provided in the slice. Jobs in the QS correspond to user sessions. Since in the system model the slices are part of a single network with a total capacity of C, S queuing systems must share a common resource (capacity) C, and its part available to the QS s is denoted by C_s, $s = 1, ..., S$.

Here we consider only one slice type – the one providing best effort (BE) services with a data rate bounded above. Let us denote this type of slices by $BE^{\max}$. It is represented by a QS with egalitarian processor sharing (EPS) discipline with a total resource capacity of C (instead of 1). As in EPS [10], the service rate depends of the resource share per job, R_s, which is determined by their number. However, the resource share per job cannot exceed $R_s^{\max}$, which yields

$$R_s = \min\left\{ \frac{C}{N_s}, R^{\max} \right\}. \tag{5}$$

Such a QS well reflects the provision of services related to the transfer of files or buffered streaming video.

Dynamic resource slicing in this context corresponds to the repeated redistribution of the capacity C among independent QSes according to some slicing policy and following the workloads.

The model under consideration is shown in Fig. 2, where $A_s(x)$ is the distribution law of intervals between session requests, and $B_s(x)$ is the distribution law of the job (file) sizes (corresponding to the service time on a resource unit) for $s = 1, ..., S$. It should be noted that admission control and resource allocation within a slice are individual characteristics for each slice type. For $BE^{\max}$, it is assumed that resources are shared equally among all users (jobs) and the number of jobs in service is unlimited. Since there is no admission control or queue in this slice type, there is a possibility that at a high arrival rate, the number of sessions will be so large that the user data rate will become unacceptable. Therefore, it makes sense to introduce a service speed degradation threshold,

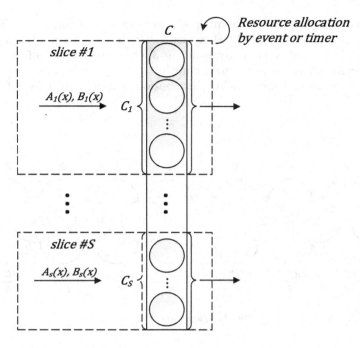

Fig. 2. System of S slices

R_s^{deg}, $0 < R_s^{\text{deg}} \leqslant C$. The threshold will act as an indicator that the service is poorly provided. A decrease in the quality of service in a slice (degradation of a slice) can occur as a result of the arrival of the next request and/or re-slicing of the capacity.

In what follows, for convenience, the term "slice" will be used in the context of a probabilistic model and correspond to the term "QS".

Now let us consider the operation of a single $BE^{\max}$ slice in the system in Fig. 2. In this work we assume that slicing is called only upon model initialization and the slice's capacity, C_s is constant. For convenience, since we are considering one QS, until the end of this section we will omit the index s. Also, by the system we mean this QS.

Let the distribution laws $A(x) = Exp(\lambda)$ and $B(x) = Exp(\theta^{-1})$. Thus, the parameter λ is the mean number of session requests offered per time unit (the arrival rate), and θ is the average size of a job, since elastic traffic is considered. The maximum service speed, which corresponds to the amount of resources allocated per job, is bounded above by $R^{\max}$. The state space of such a QS can be divided into two parts: the states when jobs are served with the maximum speed $R^{\max}$, and when jobs receive less resources. Let M be the maximum number of jobs in the system that can obtain the resource amount of $R^{\max}$,

$$M = \left\lfloor \frac{C}{R^{\max}} \right\rfloor . \tag{6}$$

Let us denote by $N(t)$ the number of jobs in the QS at time $t \geq 0$. The state space of the continuous-time Markov chain $N(t)$ has the form $\{0, 1, 2, ...\}$. The transition diagram of $N(t)$ is shown in Fig. 3. Once the number of jobs exceeds M, the service rate reaches its maximum $\frac{C}{\theta}$.

The stationary state probability distribution $\{p_n,\ n \geq 0\}$ exists if and only if

$$\lambda < \frac{C}{\theta}. \tag{7}$$

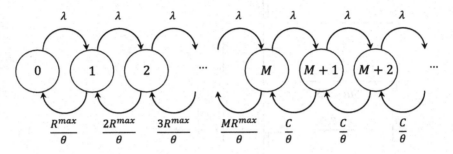

Fig. 3. Transition diagram

Let

$$\rho = \frac{\lambda}{\theta - 1} \tag{8}$$

Then the stationary state probabilities are given by

$$p_n = \begin{cases} \dfrac{1}{n!} \left(\dfrac{\rho}{R^{\max}} \right)^n p_0, & \text{if } 1 \leq n \leq M, \\[2ex] \dfrac{1}{M!} \dfrac{\rho^n}{C^{n-M}(R^{\max})^M} p_0, & \text{if } n \geq M. \end{cases} \tag{9}$$

or, in a more compact form,

$$p_n = \frac{1}{\min\{n, M\}!} \frac{\rho^n}{C^{\max\{0, n-M\}}(R^{\max})^{\min\{n, M\}}} p_0, \quad n \geq 1. \tag{10}$$

Let us find p_0 from the normalization condition:

$$\sum_{n=0}^{\infty} p_n = 1 \implies p_0 = \left(1 + \sum_{n=1}^{M-1} \frac{1}{n!} \left(\frac{\rho}{R^{\max}} \right)^n \right.$$

$$\left. + \frac{1}{M!} \left(\frac{\rho}{R^{\max}} \right)^M \sum_{n=M}^{\infty} \left(\frac{\rho}{C} \right)^{n-M} \right)^{-1}$$

$$= \left(1 + \sum_{n=1}^{M-1} \frac{1}{n!} \left(\frac{\rho}{R^{\max}} \right)^n + \frac{1}{M!} \left(\frac{\rho}{R^{\max}} \right)^M \frac{C}{C-\rho} \right)^{-1}. \tag{11}$$

provided that $\left| \frac{\lambda \theta}{C} \right| < 1$.

4   Slice Performance Measures

The stationary state probabilities obtained in the previous section permit deriving several important performance measures of a $BE^{\max}$ slice. Thus, the slice degradation probability, $P^{\deg}$, can be expressed as the probability that the number of jobs in the system exceeds $\lfloor C/R^{\deg} \rfloor$:

$$P^{\deg} = 1 - \sum_{n=0}^{\lfloor C/R^{\deg} \rfloor} p_n. \tag{12}$$

The required availability ratio Av, as we defined, is equipment uptime, therefore (excluding other factors):

$$Av = 1 - \mathbb{P}\left\{ \frac{C}{R^{\min}} < \min\{N, N^{\text{cont}}\} \right\}. \tag{13}$$

Let UTIL denote the average system utilization. If $0 \le n \le M$, then the system resource C is not fully used, but only its part equal to $nR^{\max}$ is allocated. In other cases, when $n > M$, the entire resource is utilized. Therefore,

$$\text{UTIL} = \frac{\sum_{n=0}^{M} nR^{\max}p_n + \sum_{n=M+1}^{\infty} Cp_n}{C}$$

$$= \frac{R^{\max}}{C} \sum_{n=0}^{M} np_n + \frac{p_0}{M!} \left(\frac{\rho}{R^{\max}} \right)^M \frac{\rho}{C - \rho}. \tag{14}$$

or, by replacing $\sum_{n=M+1}^{\infty} p_n$ with $1 - \sum_{n=0}^{M} p_n$,

$$\text{UTIL} = 1 - \sum_{n=0}^{M} (1 - \frac{nR^{\max}}{C})p_n. \tag{15}$$

The average number of jobs in service, N^{avg}, can be found as

$$N^{\text{avg}} = \sum_{n=1}^{\infty} np_n$$

$$= \sum_{n=1}^{M-1} np_n + Cp_M \left(\frac{M}{C - \rho} + \frac{\rho}{(C - \rho)^2} \right). \tag{16}$$

The average service speed, or the amount or resources per user, is given by

$$R^{\text{avg}} = R^{\max} \sum_{n=1}^{M} p_n + \sum_{n=M+1}^{\infty} \frac{C}{n}p_n = R^{\max} \sum_{n=1}^{M} p_n$$

$$- Cp_M \left(\frac{C}{\rho} \right)^M \left(\ln(1 - \frac{\rho}{C}) + \sum_{n=1}^{M} \frac{1}{n} \left(\frac{\rho}{C} \right)^n \right). \tag{17}$$

Finally, the average service time is determined according to Little's law:

$$T^{\text{avg}} = \frac{N^{\text{avg}}}{\lambda}. \tag{18}$$

Table 1. Parameter values

Slice #	1	2	3	4	5
Traffic type	Buffered video streaming				Files download
Description of traffic	SD	HD	UHD (4K)	VR (8K)	Software update
$R_s^{\min}$, Mbps	2	5	25	50	30
$R_s^{\max}$, Mbps	2.2	8	30	75	C
Average file size θ, GB	0.3	1.2	2.5	5	1

5   Numerical Results

As an example, let us consider five slices with the parameters given in Table 1. We suppose that the five slices are allocated $C = 4$ Gbps and this capacity is shared among them equally. Traffic in the slices has a different degree of elasticity, increasing from slice 1 to 5. The aim of the numerical experiment here is to compare the behavior of the performance measures of slices that have different traffic characteristics. In Fig. 4 and 5 selected performance measures are plotted vs. the offered load ρ_s, while in Fig. 6 and 7 we additionally take into account the difference of the minimum user data rate $R_s^{\min}$.

Figure 4b shows that the capacity utilization grows to its maximum value of 1 when the offered traffic ρ reaches a value close to 0.8 for all slices. In this case, the average number of jobs N_s^{avg} in a slice grows hyperbolically (Fig. 4a). The more elastic the traffic in the slice, the steeper is the growth pattern.

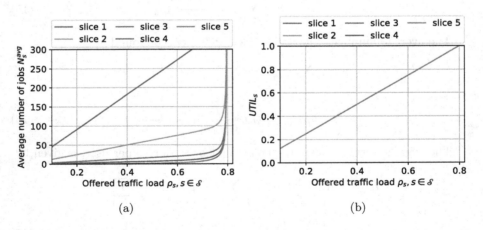

(a)   (b)

Fig. 4. The average number of jobs N_s (a) and the capacity utilization (b) vs. the offered traffic $\rho_s = \rho$.

Figure 5a shows the conditional average user data rate given that the slice is not empty:

$$R_s^{\text{avg}*} = \frac{R_s^{\text{avg}}}{1 - p_0}.$$ (19)

This indicator also depends on the nature of the traffic.

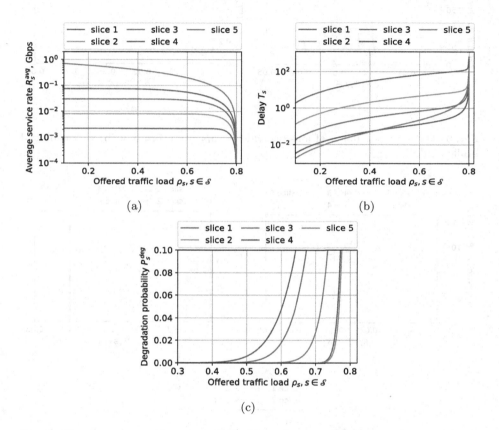

(a)

(b)

(c)

Fig. 5. The average user data rate $R_s^{\text{avg}*}$ (a), the average job service time T_s (b) and the degradation probability P_s^{deg} (c) vs. the offered traffic $\rho_s = \rho$.

The average job service time T_s shown in Fig. 5b demonstrates a different dependency: for higher values of ρ, sessions in slice 5 are longer than in slice 4, which has a higher data rate minimum R_s^{min}, whereas when ρ is low, on the contrary, slice 5 having no constraint on the maximum data rate R_s^{max} shows the best result.

Now consider the degradation probability P_s^{deg} in slices in the range from 0 to 10%. The behavior of this metric in this case is difficult to relate to other indicators, so let us add a dependency on the minimum data rate R_s^{min} to the plots in Fig. 6 and 7.

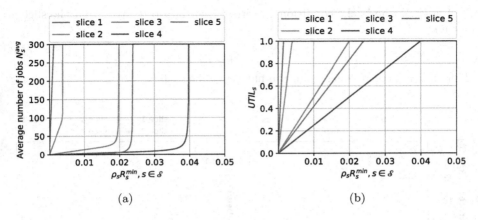

Fig. 6. The average number of jobs (a) and the capacity utilization (b) vs. the offered traffic $\rho_s R_s^{\min}$.

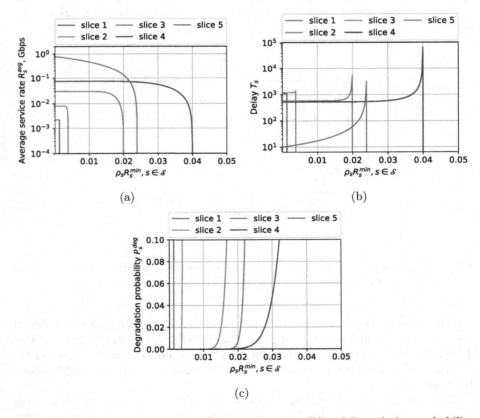

Fig. 7. The average user data rate (a), session duration (b) and degradation probability (c) vs. $\rho_s R_s^{\min}$.

It can be observed in the figures that With a uniform increase in the value of $\rho_s R_s^{\min}$:

- the average number of jobs in a slice still grows hyperbolically (Fig. 6a), but slice 5 overflows faster;
- the capacity utilization in Fig. 6b now behaves differently confirming that slice 5 is overflowing faster;
- the average user data rate (Fig. 7a) and job service time (Fig. 7b) additionally reflect the influence of the threshold of the maximum user data rate $R_s^{\max}$.

The degradation probability $P_s^{\deg}$ as a function of $\rho_s R_s^{\min}$ shows the cumulative effect of slice characteristics:

- Slices 1 and 2 with the least elastic traffic and the smallest job sizes go into degradation much faster. Such traffic is more sensitive to increased load on the system.
- Slice 5 with the most elastic traffic degrades faster than slices 3, 4. This suggests that in general the ratio of the offered traffic load ρ to the threshold of the minimum user data rate $R_s^{\min}$ is of greater importance for the quality of service provided under a static resource slicing, than the threshold of the maximum user data rate $R_s^{\max}$.

6 Conclusion

In this paper we take a closer look at the important metrics for the application of 5G network slicing policies – slice availability and slice degradation probability. We provide an analytical model for a single best-effort slice with a bounded above user data rate. For this model, analytical formulas are derived to calculate the probability of slice degradation and other performance measures.

References

1. Ateya, A.A., Muthanna, A., Gudkova, I., Vybornova, A., Koucheryavy, A.: Intelligent core network for tactile internet system. In: Proceedings of the International Conference on Future Networks and Distributed Systems. ICFNDS 2017, Association for Computing Machinery, New York (2017). https://doi.org/10.1145/3102304.3102326
2. Brik, B., Ksentini, A.: On predicting service-oriented network slices performances in 5G: a federated learning approach. In: 2020 IEEE 45th Conference on Local Computer Networks (LCN), pp. 164–171 (2020). https://doi.org/10.1109/LCN48667.2020.9314849
3. Hößler, T., Scheuvens, L., Franchi, N., Simsek, M., Fettweis, G.P.: Applying reliability theory for future wireless communication networks. In: 2017 IEEE 28th Annual International Symposium on Personal, Indoor, and Mobile Radio Communications (PIMRC), pp. 1–7 (2017). https://doi.org/10.1109/PIMRC.2017.8292773
4. NG, G.: 116-generic network slice template-version 5.0. Tech. rep., Technical report, June 2021

5. Ometov, A., Kozyrev, D., Rykov, V., Andreev, S., Gaidamaka, Y., Koucheryavy, Y.: Reliability-centric analysis of offloaded computation in cooperative wearable applications. Wirel. Commun. Mob. Comput. **2017** (2017)
6. Polyakov, N.A., Yarkina, N.V., Samouylov, K.E.: A simulator for analyzing a network slicing policy with SLA-based performance isolation of slices. Discrete Continuous Models Appl. Comput. Sci. **29**(1), 36–52 (2021). https://doi.org/10.22363/2658-4670-2021-29-1-36-52
7. Recommendation, I.: E. 800: Terms and definitions related to quality of service and network performance including dependability, August 1994 [cited 2013–11-20], pp. 800–200809. http://www.itu.int/rec/T-REC-E
8. Vilà, I., Pérez-Romero, J., Sallent, O., Umbert, A.: Characterization of radio access network slicing scenarios with 5G QoS provisioning. IEEE Access **8**, 51414–51430 (2020). https://doi.org/10.1109/ACCESS.2020.2980685
9. Yarkina, N., Gaidamaka, Y., Correia, L., Samouylov, K.: An analytical model for 5G network resource sharing with flexible SLA-oriented slice isolation. Mathematics **8**, 1177 (2020). https://doi.org/10.3390/math8071177
10. Yashkov, S., Yashkova, A.: Processor sharing: a survey of the mathematical theory. Autom. Remote Control **68**(9), 1662–1731 (2007). https://doi.org/10.1134/S0005117907090202
11. Zanzi, L., Sciancalepore, V.: On guaranteeing end-to-end network slice latency constraints in 5G networks. In: 2018 15th International Symposium on Wireless Communication Systems (ISWCS), pp. 1–6 (2018). https://doi.org/10.1109/ISWCS.2018.8491249

Using a Machine Learning Model for Malicious URL Type Detection

Suet Ping Tung[1,2], Ka Yan Wong[2], Ievgeniia Kuzminykh[3,4](✉) ⓘ, Taimur Bakhshi[5] ⓘ, and Bogdan Ghita[1] ⓘ

[1] University of Plymouth, Drake Circus, Plymouth PL4 8AA, UK
bogdan.ghita@plymouth.ac.uk
[2] HKU School of Professional and Continuing Education, Kowloon Bay, Kowloon, Hong Kong
ivy.wong@teacher.hkuspace.hku.hk
[3] King's College London, Strand, London WC2R 2LS, UK
ievgeniia.kuzminykh@kcl.ac.uk
[4] Kharkiv National University of Radio Electronics, 14 Nauki avenue, Kharkiv, Ukraine
[5] FAST National University of Computer and Emerging Sciences, Lahore, Pakistan
taimur.bakhshi@nu.edu.pk

Abstract. The world wide web, beyond its benefits, has also become a major platform for online criminal activities. Traditional protection methods against malicious URLs, such as blacklisting, remain a valid alternative, but cannot detect unknown sites, hence new methods are being developed for automatic detection, using machine learning approaches. This paper strengthens the existing state of the art by proposing an alternative machine learning approach, that uses a set of 14 lexical and host-based features but focuses on the typical mechanisms employed by malicious URLs. The proposed method employs random forest and decision tree as core mechanisms and is evaluated on a combined benign and malicious URL dataset, which indicates an accuracy of over 97%.

Keywords: Malicious URL · Web Security · Machine Learning · Phishing · Spamming · Malware · Lexical Feature · Traffic

1 Introduction

There are currently over 4.66 billion active Internet users in the world, who rely on it to obtain information, communicate, or to support their work or daily activities [1]. According to the same report, the average user spends almost 7 h on Internet every day for a range of activities, from online shopping and searching for information to social networking and work. While, through the media reports and user education across most organisations, people are aware of various aspects of cybersecurity, the level of knowledge and proficiency in defending against possible attacks is relatively low for a typical user. One of the most common attack vectors are malicious URLs, due to their convenience and ability to disguise or integrate within typical browsing. This trend was confirmed by Google transparency report, which identified over 2 million phishing websites in 2020 [2]. The risks posed by accessing such sites vary from private information

© Springer Nature Switzerland AG 2022
Y. Koucheryavy et al. (Eds.): NEW2AN 2021/ruSMART 2021, LNCS 13158, pp. 493–505, 2022.
https://doi.org/10.1007/978-3-030-97777-1_41

disclosure to installation of malicious software on the computer used by the victim. The underlying attacks also vary, including techniques such as phishing, spamming, or drive-by-download

The initial approach from the research community was to propose a series of counter-measures revolving around blacklisting of malicious URL or identifying malicious hosts. The lists are very dynamic, actively maintained by several organizations and communities, aiming to keep an accurate record of the current threats. While this line of protection is effective, the concept is a reactive one, as blacklists do not identify unknown malicious URLs. Therefore, a more recent alternative approach has been to apply machine learning algorithms that use specific features as inputs in order to detect malicious URLs. Due to their predictive nature, such approaches are far better in dealing with unknown malicious URLs and report a prediction accuracy rate up to 90%. This paper aims to strengthen the machine learning efforts to detect malicious URLs by proposing a hybrid solution that consists of a machine learning model used for detection and support it by manual input in order to evaluate its effectiveness.

The remainder of the paper is organized as follows. Section 2 presents the related work, then Sect. 3 provides an outline of the approach. The model architecture, programming components, data collection and pre-processing, and model prediction measurements are in Sect. 4. The model detection result and comparisons are then discussed in Sect. 5. Section 6 concludes the paper with a summary of its achievements and limitations, as well as with possible avenues for future work.

2 Related Works

Due to its associated potential threat level, malicious URL detection received in recent years a significant amount of attention from the research community. The researchers have used various discriminants to identify the malicious URLs, including lexical features (string properties of the URL, the number of special characters, length of URL, etc.), host-based features (domain name and hostname, IP address, location, etc.), content features (derived from HTML and JavaScript), or link popularity features (ranking, popularity score, reputation).

Based on the type of detection employed, the core mechanisms can be categorized into two areas: non-machine learning approaches and machine learning approaches. Using this criterion, blacklisting is categorized as a non-machine learning method to identify malicious URLs. In this category the research studies proposed implementation of blacklisting based on different techniques such as reputation-based [3] real-time blackhole lists [4], or tracking the top-level domain names [5]. This approach, while effective for known threats, is inherently likely to generate false negatives because of new malicious sites appearing. In addition, to avoid domain name blacklisting, attackers may employ a domain generation algorithm (DGA) to evade blacklists by generating new malicious URLs. The only option to keep ahead of the curve is to design adaptive, intelligent detection techniques, which apply machine learning (ML) algorithms to identify both URLs from the blacklists and the unknown malicious URLs. A summary of studies is presented in Table 1 and identifies what URL features and classifier have been used for detecting the non-benign web pages.

The authors of [6] conducted a comprehensive and systematic survey on malicious URL detection using machine learning techniques. The survey pointed out that support vector machine (SVM) and lexical features are the most widely used machine learning algorithm and type of features respectively. Many studies, such as [7–10], focus on detecting only phishing malicious web pages since vast majority of the malicious links in internet created for phishing purposes [11]. In this context, [7] and [8] used lexical-based URL features only to identify malicious links, while [12] extended the feature extraction with JavaScript client code analysis to achieve a better detection rate.

Considering the type of attack rather than the method of detection, [13] provides an overview of recent phishing URL detection studies. The authors reviewed 13 studies between 2014 and 2019 in terms of algorithms used, performance metrics and proc and cons in the study. Same authors made another survey [9] on the datasets used by researchers about malicious input for feature extraction and training of models [9]. The analysis showed that most studies use imbalanced datasets as the number of phishing sites cannot be compared with that of legitimate URLs.

Other studies aimed to refine the machine learning classification results by combining additional techniques; along this line of research, [14] reduced the false negative rate by using classification based on association (CBA) algorithm. The authors proposed a mix of lexical and comprehensive content-based features, which led to a false negative rate of 1.35%, a significant improvement from the 7.57% in the study that used only lexical features [8]. The authors did not evaluate the complexity of the proposed model, but other works showed that the extraction of content-based features requires more time and creates more delays when analysing a web page when compared to lexical features since reading of source code of the page, search for suspicious functions, iframes, parsing of DOM model are time demanding.

The authors in [15] applied range of ML algorithms such as Logistic Regression, Stochastic Gradient Descent (SGD), Random Forest (RF), Support-Vector Machines (SVM), Naive Bayes, k-Nearest Neighbors (kNN), and Decision Tree (DT) to the dataset with malicious URLs to investigate the prediction accuracy. They extracted the features such as, domain and sub-domain names and suffix to distinguish malicious web site from benign. Their dataset included collection of URLs from different sources and consisted of malware, hidden fraudulent and block listed URLs. All models showed high prediction accuracy, however, random forest algorithm attained the highest F1 score and accuracy. Following up on comparative studies, [16] focused on the host-based features such as domain details, IP addresses and port number to detect malicious web pages. In their experiments, the authors evaluated the effectiveness of different classification algorithms; the tree-based algorithm called Gradient-boosted tree showed the best results with an overall accuracy of 96.9%. The authors in [17] also run a comparative analysis, where they evaluated 7 detection models based on various ML algorithms picked up from their literature review study. Amongst the tested algorithms, the CMU [18] and Endgame [19] models based on bidirectional gated recurrent unit (BGRU) and long short-term memory (LSTM) yielded the highest accuracy.

As part of the machine learning domain, deep learning algorithms are one of the promising areas, due to their ability to replicate more complex behaviour. However, while they are all very effective at learning the patterns exhibited by the targeted phenomena, the inherent issue of deep learning algorithms is their high computational demand, particularly when employing a higher number of variable with wider value ranges [20]. The extent of the computational complexity increase was investigated in [21], where different algorithms were tested in terms of CPU, GPU, and TPU architectures. The deep learning algorithms showed higher accuracy than some of their ML counterparts, but the time required for training and for making decision was 2–4 times higher. In terms of accuracy, the best results showed RF algorithms with 98.68%.

The authors in [22] focused on improving classifiers by applying linear and non-linear transformation. This allowed them to improve the performance of certain ML algorithms, such as k-NN, SVM and Multi-layer Perceptron (MLP). The classifiers were also evaluated in terms of time efficiency on the testing and training subsets. It should be noted that authors used a large set of features (64 inputs in total) that caused the long computational time for the algorithms. Another study [23] used an open-source dataset of malicious URLs [24] (also used by [15] to evaluate the performance of classifiers). The authors established that the Naive Bayes algorithm performed better than logistic regression and convolutional neural network (CNN), with an accuracy 86.25%.

Table 1. Summary of machine learning approach in the literature

Year	Ref.	Features	ML algorithm	Description
2021	[14]	Lexical, Content-based	CBA	Benign page VS Malicious page
2021	[17]	Lexical, Host-based	BGRU, CNN, LSTM	Detect malicious URLs, file paths and registry keys Social media text classification
2021	[15]	Lexical, Host-based	Logistic Regression, SGD, RF, SVM, Naive Bayes, kNN, and Decision Tree	Normal page VS Malicious page
2020	[22]	Lexical, Host-based, Reputation based	kNN, L-SVM, Linear Discriminant Analysis (LDA), Logistic Regression	Normal page VS Malicious page
2020	[23]	Lexical, Host-based,	CNN, Logistic Regression, Naïve Bayes	Normal page VS Malicious page

(*continued*)

Table 1. (*continued*)

Year	Ref.	Features	ML algorithm	Description
2020	[21]	Lexical	RF, Decision Tree, kNN, SVM, Logistic Regression) LDA, AdaBoost, Naive Bayes, Fast.ai and Keras-TensorFlow	Normal page VS Malicious page
2018	[16]	Host-based	Decision Tree, Gradient-boosted tree (GBT), L-SVM, Naive Bayes, Random Forests	Benign page VS Malicious page
2016	[26]	Lexical, Host-based	C4.5, Decision Tree	Benign VS Malicious
2013	[27]	Lexical, Link popularity	Random Forest, Naive Bayes, Logistic Regression, J48, SVM	Normal page VS Malicious page
2013	[28]	Lexical, Host-based	SVM	Benign VS Phishing
2011	[25]	Lexical, Link popularity, Host-based	SVM, RAkEL, kNN	Classify attack types by URL
2011	[29]	Lexical, Webpage Content and Host-Based	Random Forest, Naive Bayes, Logistic regression, J48	Normal page VS Malicious page

The authors in [25] advised that understanding the attack type of malicious URL is useful for the user to respond properly. However, recent research papers seem to focus exclusively on benign and malicious, or benign and phishing. this indicates a lack of research papers addressing multiclass classification to detect the attack type of malicious URLs.

Drawing on the limitations of the existing research, this study aims to investigate the ability of machine learning algorithms to classify different types of malicious URLs using a reduced and robust set of parameters.

3 Methodology

As highlighted by the previous section, machine learning techniques represent an effective approach to identify malicious URLs due to their capacity to formally parse the content of the URL and compare it against recognizable malicious patterns. Following on their success, we propose a model that uses Decision Tree and Random Forest classification algorithms for detecting malicious URLs. This is in line with the conclusions from the authors of [15, 21, 27] who pointed out that Decision Tree and Random Forest are indeed the most likely to improve the detection accuracy, as they are effective classifiers, dynamically learning and adapting to variable domains [30].

The architecture of the proposed model for malicious URLs detection is presented in Fig. 1 and includes the process of extracting features, training phase to the classifiers, as well as the core decision tree and random forest techniques for predicting whether the URL is malicious or benign, as well as the type of attack that may be included in the URL.

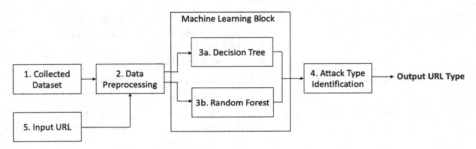

Fig. 1. The architecture of the model

3.1 Datasets

As mentioned before, the aim of the proposed framework is to detect various types of URL attacks. In order to provide a robust knowledge base for training the model, we combined several existing datasets that included URLs of four types: benign, spam, phishing and malware. This led to four single-class datasets, resulting from the mixing of benign and malicious URLs matching a specific type of attack, and one multi-class dataset, including all four categories listed above. The final distribution of URLs in our dataset is presented in Fig. 2.

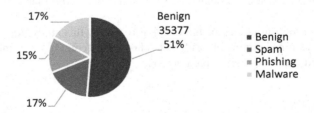

Fig. 2. Types of URLs in the dataset

The dataset with benign URLs was taken from a study undertaken at University of New Brunswick [31]. It contains the URLs that have been collected from different Internet open source repositories, ordered by alexa.com [32]. From a half of million original URLs, the researchers extracted 35,300 that were labeled as benign after removing duplicates and virus checks.

For spam attacks, we used WEBSPAM-UK2007, a publicly available dataset collected by C. Castillo, supported by a team of volunteers [33]. The collection originally crawled 114,529 hosts of the.uk domain, and extracted 12,000 URLs that were labelled as spam web pages.

OpenPhish is one of the service providers that provides a blacklist of phishing URLs [34]. It contains millions of unfiltered URLs from a variety of sources and filter the web pages to detect phishing ones. We selected a subset of 10,000 URLs from this dataset.

DNS-BH is a project of RiskAnalytics that maintains list of domains that possible to spread malware and spyware [35]. A subset of 12,000 URLs, all related to malware websites, were obtained from this source.

In addition, in order to check the presence of a brand name in the domain name and path of each URL, we collected a subset of 50 sites from Alexa separately and added them to the benign dataset.

3.2 Dataset Processing and Features Extraction

The effectiveness of a machine learning algorithm, beyond its ability to identify specific types of patterns, depends on the set of features used as input. The core idea behind our proposed approach is that malicious URLs tend to work either by redirecting the browser to a malicious page through obfuscation or path traversal or by loading an executable. We aim to identify these through an abnormal combination of non-alphanumeric characters such as slashes, equal signs, dashes, underscores, or dots, as well as extensions of executables, such as exe, bin, or configbin. As a result, we selected 14 features related to URL syntax, domain and path that belong to the lexical and host-based categories. Table 2 provides a summary of the features used in our model.

Table 2. Selected URL features for the model

Category	Name	Description
Lexical	url_length	The length of the URL
	sp_char_count	Total specific characters in URL
	slash_count	Number of slashes (/) in URL
	token_count	Number of tokens in URL
	equality_count	Number of equality (=) in URL
	dash_count	Number of dash (–) in URL
	underscore_count	Number of underscore (_) in URL
	dot_count	Number of dots (.) in URL
	exe_count	Number of.exe in URL
	bin_count	Number of.bin URL
	configbin_count	Number of.configbin in URL

(*continued*)

Table 2. (*continued*)

Category	Name	Description
Host-based	is_IP	Presence of IP address in domain name
	brandInSLD	Presence of brand name in domain name
	brandExist	Presence of brand name in path

The novelty and benefits of this approach are two-fold: conceptual and efficiency. From a concept perspective, rather than the lexical or content-based approaches used by prior research, we focus on the typical mechanisms that URLs use for attack. From an efficiency perspective, the models we propose are rather lightweight, using 14 parameters as input rather than 50 + inputs, often including lexical parameters requiring a dictionary comparison.

The datasets listed in the previous section were pre-processed to ensure data consistency (URL format). The features were extracted using a parser and merged with the URL type in order to create the dataset.

3.3   Model Classification and Cross-Validation

Classification of data was done through two machine learning algorithms: Decision Tree [30] and Random Forest [36]. We used the cross-validation technique [37] to train the data. While this technique is typically used for small datasets, we preferred it because it allows to preserve a quality and sample size during splitting the dataset into training and testing sets. The basic approach in cross-validation is showed in Fig. 3 and performed as the data is split into k-folds: the training set is split into k smaller subsets, to average the computed score.

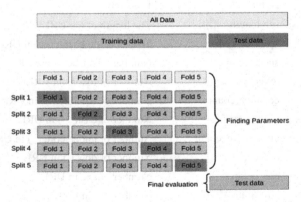

Fig. 3. Visual explanation of data splitting in k-fold cross-valuation [37]

The following procedure is applied to each of the k-folds: the model is trained using k-1 of the folds as training data and then the resulting model is validated on the remaining part of the data (i.e., it is used as a test set to compute a performance measure such as accuracy). The average of the values after each split is the final model performance.

The accuracy of the model was determined by calculating the ratios between the variables describing the outcome of the classification: true positive (TP), false positive (FP), true negative (TN), and false negative (FN). We used three common metrics to evaluate the accuracy of the classifiers: precision, recall and F1-score.

Precision is a true positive predictive value of class, representing the ratio between the number of true positives (TP) and the total number of predicted positive class. Recall, same as sensitivity, is a metric for evaluating the correctness of the class and it is defined as the ratio between the number of true positives and the total number of predictions of the respective class. The F1-score is the harmonic mean of recall and precision. The distinctive feature of F1- score is defined both on the positive and negative classes and F1-score is average these two values. Table 3 below summarises the three indicators.

Table 3. Model accuracy metrics.

Metric	Definition
Precision	TP/(TP + FP)
Recall (sensitivity)	TP/(TP + FN)
F1-Score	2 × (Precision × Recall/Precision + Recall)

4 Results

We applied the k-fold cross-validation technique to the dataset and generated used a 30/70 ratio for the testing/training subsets. As shown in the breakdown from Table 4, out of the total 68,951 URLs, the training subset included 48,265 samples while the testing subset had 20,686 samples. The ratio of benign and malicious samples was approximately 50–50 across the two subsets due to the random nature of selection, which also minimised a possible imbalance between training and testing.

Following the split, the dataset was fit to the two designed models - Decision Tree and Random Forest - and the resulting performance was evaluated using precision, recall and F1-score.

Table 4. Training and testing dataset samples.

Type	Training data	Testing data	Total
Benign	24814	10612	35426
Phishing	6962	2999	9961
Spam	8284	3715	11999
Malware	8205	3360	11565
Total, URLs	48265	20686	68951
Total, %	70	30	100

4.1 Decision Tree

The result of the decision tree model is summarized in Table 5. The final accuracy of Decision Tree model is 96.33% and the F1- score is over 90% of each attack type. The mean of the k-fold cross-validation score is 95.42%, which close to the final testing dataset accuracy.

Table 5. Decision Tree prediction result

Type	Precision	Recall	F1-score
Benign	0.987	0.988	0.987
Phishing	0.913	0.889	0.901
Spam	0.964	0.960	0.962
Malware	0.932	0.956	0.944
Accuracy: 96.33%			

4.2 Random Forest

The results of the Random Forest model are presented in Table 6. The final accuracy of Decision Tree model is 97.49% and F1-score is over 93% of each attack type. The mean of k-fold cross-validation score is 96.67%, which is very close to the final accuracy.

Table 6. Random Forest prediction result

Type	Precision	Recall	F1-score
Benign	0.988	0.995	0.991
Phishing	0.943	0.925	0.934
Spam	0.943	0.925	0.934
Malware	0.943	0.925	0.934
Accuracy: 97.49%			

4.3 Discussion

The performance results of the Decision Tree and Random Forest models showed that Random Forest model is more effective on detection of all the types of malicious URL, given that precision, recall and F1-score of each attack type are higher than Decision Tree, there are over 95% of all the types except phishing.

Our research result is very close to that of the work done by Choi et al. [25]. Although a major part of our experiment datasets (benign, phishing, malware, a portion of spam) are identical, we have extended our dataset with Defacement dataset. Regarding lexical classification outcomes of Choi et al. (Spam 73%Phishing 91.6% and Malware 70.3%), authors did not mention precisely whether their result stems from applying multi-class or single-class classifier. Note that using multi-class classification with additional dataset must degrade the overall performance and accuracy. However, our Random Forest classifier outperforms their lexical feature results in either case of individual and aggregated (multi-class) classifiers yielding around 99% and 97% accuracy respectively even with an addition of Defacement URL dataset.

5 Conclusions

This study proposed a novel parameter set for detection of malicious URL, focused on discriminating various types of behaviour, using two machine learning algorithms, Decision Tree and Random Forest. The dataset for training was consolidated by using several existing datasets with benign and malicious URLs, then fed to both algorithms to predict the attack type of the URL. Selected feature sets applied on supervised classification on a ground truth dataset yields a classification accuracy of 97% with a low false positive rate. Our prediction interval filtering experiment can also be helpful to improve classifier accuracy. In addition, it can be extended to calculate the risk rating of a malicious URL after parameter adjustment and learning with huge training data. The random forest classification accuracy marginally outperformed decision tree, as it was able to identify approximately 97% of the malicious or benign URL.

For future work we are aiming to extend the work to a wider range of variable values, to reflect further, more complex malicious URL behaviour and ensure that the proposed methods remain up to date and continue to detect behaviour in the underlying web technology.

References

1. We Are Social, Hoootsuite: Digital 2021 Global Overview Report. Datareportal.com. 299 (2021)
2. Google: Google: Transparency Report. Google Transpar. Rep. (2010)
3. Prakash, P., Kumar, M., Rao Kompella, R., Gupta, M.: PhishNet: predictive blacklisting to detect phishing attacks. Proc. IEEE INFOCOM. (2010). https://doi.org/10.1109/INFCOM. 2010.5462216
4. Felegyhazi, M., Kreibich, C., Paxson, V.: On the potential of proactive domain blacklisting. LEET 2010 - 3rd USENIX Work. Large-Scale Exploit. Emergent Threat. Botnets, Spyware, Worms, More. (2010)
5. Sinha, S., Bailey, M., Jahanian, F.: Shades of Grey: on the effectiveness of reputation-based blacklists. In: 3rd International Conference Malicious Unwanted Software, MALWARE 2008. 57–64 (2008). https://doi.org/10.1109/MALWARE.2008.4690858
6. Sahoo, D., Liu, C., Hoi, S.C.H.: Malicious URL detection using machine learning: a survey. (2017)
7. Abdelhamid, N., Ayesh, A., Thabtah, F.: Phishing detection based Associative Classification data mining. Expert Syst. Appl. **41**, 5948–5959 (2014). https://doi.org/10.1016/j.eswa.2014. 03.019
8. Jeeva, S.C., Rajsingh, E.B.: Intelligent phishing url detection using association rule mining. Human-centric Comp. Inf. Sci. **6**, (2016). https://doi.org/10.1186/s13673-016-0064-3
9. Aung, E.S., Yamana, H.: URL-based phishing detection using the entropy of non- A lphanumeric characters. ACM Int. Conf. Proceeding Ser. (2019). https://doi.org/10.1145/3366030. 3366064
10. Ravi, R., Shillare, A.A., Bhoir, P.P., Charumathi, K.S.: URL based email phishing detection application. Int. Res. J. Eng. Technol. **8**, 335–360 (2021)
11. Verizon: Data Breach Investigations Report (DBIR). Comput. Fraud Secur. **12**, 8 (2019)
12. Hadi, W., Aburub, F., Alhawari, S.: A new fast associative classification algorithm for detecting phishing websites. Appl. Soft Comput. J. **48**, 729–734 (2016). https://doi.org/10.1016/j.asoc. 2016.08.005
13. Aung, E.S., Zan, T., Yamana, H.: A survey of URL-based phishing detection. pp. 1–8 (2019)
14. Kumi, S., Lim, C., Lee, S.G.: Malicious url detection based on associative classification. Entropy **23**, 1–12 (2021). https://doi.org/10.3390/e23020182
15. Shantanu, D., Janet, B., Kumar, R.J.A.: Malicious URL detection: a comparative study. In: Proceedings of International Conference Artificial Intelligence Smart System ICAIS 2021, pp. 1147–1151 (2021). https://doi.org/10.1109/ICAIS50930.2021.9396014
16. Tan, G., Zhang, P., Liu, Q., Liu, X., Zhu, C., Dou, F.: Adaptive malicious url detection: learning in the presence of concept drifts. In: Proceedings of 17th IEEE International Conference (TrustCom/BigDataSE), pp. 737–743 (2018). https://doi.org/10.1109/TrustCom/BigDataSE. 2018.00107
17. Srinivasan, S., Vinayakumar, R., Arunachalam, A., Alazab, M., Soman, K.: DURLD: malicious URL detection using deep learning-based character level representations. In: Stamp, M., Alazab, M., Shalaginov, A. (eds.) Malware Analysis Using Artificial Intelligence and Deep Learning. Springer, Cham. https://doi.org/10.1007/978-3-030-62582-5_21
18. Dhingra, B., Zhou, Z., Fitzpatrick, D., Muehl, M., Cohen, W.W.: Tweet2Vec: character-based distributed representations for social media. In: 54th Annual Meeting Association Computer Linguistics ACL 2016, pp. 269–274 (2016). https://doi.org/10.18653/v1/p16-2044
19. Anderson, H.S., Woodbridge, J., Filar, B.: DeepDGA: adversarially-tuned domain generation and detection. In: AISec 2016 – Proceedings of 2016 ACM Work. Artificial Intelligence Security co-located with CCS 2016, pp. 13–21 (2016). https://doi.org/10.1145/2996758.299 6767

20. Kuzminykh, I., Shevchuk, D., Shiaeles, S., Ghita, B.: Audio interval retrieval using convolutional neural networks. In: Galinina, O., Andreev, S., Balandin, S., Koucheryavy, Y. (eds.) Internet of Things, Smart Spaces, and Next Generation Networks and Systems. LNCS, vol. 12525. Springer, Cham (2020). https://doi.org/10.1007/978-3-030-65726-0_21

21. Johnson, C., Khadka, B., Basnet, R.B., Doleck, T.: Towards detecting and classifying malicious urls using deep learning. J. Wirel. Mob. Netw. Ubiquitous Comput. Dependable Appl. **11**, 31–48 (2020). https://doi.org/10.22667/JOWUA.2020.12.31.031

22. Li, T., Kou, G., Peng, Y.: Improving malicious URLs detection via feature engineering: linear and nonlinear space transformation methods. Inf. Syst. **91**, (2020). https://doi.org/10.1016/j.is.2020.101494

23. Vundavalli, V., Barsha, F., Masum, M., Shahriar, H., Haddad, H.: Malicious URL detection using supervised machine learning techniques. ACM Int. Conf. Proceeding Ser. (2020). https://doi.org/10.1145/3433174.3433592

24. Urcuqui, C.: Malicious and Benign Websites dataset. https://www.kaggle.com/xwolf12/malicious-and-benign-websites. Accessed 12 Jul 2021

25. Choi, H., Zhu, B.B., Lee, H.: Detecting malicious web links and identifying their attack types. WebApps. **11** (2011)

26. Mašetic, Z., Subasi, A., Azemovic, J.: Malicious web sites detection using C4.5 decision tree. Southeast Eur. J. Soft Comput. **5** (2016). https://doi.org/10.21533/scjournal.v5i1.109

27. Eshete, B., Villafiorita, A., Weldemariam, K., Zulkernine, M.: EINSPECT: evolution-guided analysis and detection of malicious web pages. In: Proceedings of International Computing Software Applied Conference, pp. 375–380 (2013). https://doi.org/10.1109/COMPSAC.2013.63

28. Chu, W., Zhu, B.B., Xue, F., Guan, X., Cai, Z.: Protect sensitive sites from phishing attacks using features extractable from inaccessible phishing URLs. IEEE Int. Conf. Commun. 1990–1994 (2013). https://doi.org/10.1109/ICC.2013.6654816

29. Canali, D., Cova, M., Vigna, G., Kruegel, C.: Prophiler: A fast filter for the large-scale detection of malicious web pages. In: Proceedings of 20th International Conference World Wide Web, WWW 2011. pp. 197–206 (2011). https://doi.org/10.1145/1963405.1963436

30. Murthy, S. K.: Automatic construction of decision trees from data: a multidisciplinary survey. Data Min. Knowl. Discov. **2**(4), 345-89 (1998)

31. Canadian Institute for Cybersecurity: URL dataset (ISCX-URL-2016)

32. Amazon: Alexa Internet, www.alexa.com

33. Castillio, C.: Web Spam Collections. http://chato.cl/webspam/datasets/uk2007/. Accessed 12 Jul 2021

34. OpenPhish: Phishing Intelligence. (2020)

35. Risk Analytics: DNS-BH - Malware Domain Blocklist. (2021)

36. Breiman, L.: Random Forests. Mach. Learn. 5–32 (2001). https://doi.org/10.1023/A:1010933404324

37. Stone, M.: Cross-validatory choice and assessment of statistical predictions. J. R. Stat. Soc. Ser. B. **36**, 111–147 (1974)

Correction to: Internet of Things, Smart Spaces, and Next Generation Networks and Systems

Yevgeni Koucheryavy ⓘ, Sergey Balandin ⓘ, and Sergey Andreev ⓘ

Correction to:
Y. Koucheryavy et al. (Eds.): *Internet of Things, Smart Spaces,*
and Next Generation Networks and Systems, **LNCS 13158,**
https://doi.org/10.1007/978-3-030-97777-1

In an older version of chapters 4, 24, and 25, there was an orthographical error in the name of one of the co-authors. This has been corrected.

The updated version of these chapters can be found at
https://doi.org/10.1007/978-3-030-97777-1_4
https://doi.org/10.1007/978-3-030-97777-1_24
https://doi.org/10.1007/978-3-030-97777-1_25

© Springer Nature Switzerland AG 2022
Y. Koucheryavy et al. (Eds.): NEW2AN 2021/ruSMART 2021, LNCS 13158, p. C1, 2022.
https://doi.org/10.1007/978-3-030-97777-1_42

Author Index

Abdellah, Ali R.   284, 297
Abilov, Albert   268
Abushova, Ekaterina   81
Aleksandr, Murashov   470
Alekseeva, Natalia   170
Alexey, Efimov   108
Alzaghir, Abbas   35, 284, 297
Anufrienko, Alexander   3

Bakhshi, Taimur   493
Baranov, Maksim   310
Bolshakova, Inna   122
Bondarenko, Viktoria   59, 71
Burdin, Vladimir A.   212

Cherepennikov, Gregory   329
Chkalova, Olga   81, 122

Davydov, Roman   221
Davydov, Roman V.   230
Davydov, Vadim   221, 365
Davydov, Vadim V.   230, 352
Dmitrieva, Diana S.   230
Dmitriy, Suntsov   470
Dudkin, Valentin   221
Dudkin, Valentin I.   230
Dudnik, Iuliia   240

Efimov, Sergei E.   352
Efremova, Marina   108
Elena, Velichko   470
Erorova, Alexandra   158
Evseeva, Oksana   108, 147

Fokin, Grigoriy   365

Galushko, Artem   413
Ghita, Bogdan   46, 493
Gluhov, Vladimir   59, 179, 201
Grishunin, Sergei   158
Gubareva, Olga Yu.   212
Gureev, Vladimir O.   212
Guzenko, Natalia   59, 71

Ilchenko, Nikita   390
Ivanov, Sergei I.   254

Kaisina, Irina   268
Kamyshova, Anna   179, 201
Kapustin, Nikita   201
Kartavenko, Olga   191, 201
Kasianenko, Elena   81
Keller, Barbara   22
Kiseleva, Ekaterina   413
Kolgan, Maria   147, 191
Kondakov, Dmitrii V.   254
Kopasovskaya, Natalia   122
Kostin, Georgy M.   321
Koucheryavy, Andrey   35, 284, 297
Koucheryavy, Yevgeni   481
Krasyuk, Irina   147, 191
Kugblenu, Carl   22
Kuzminykh, Ievgeniia   46, 493

Lacis, Gunars   9
Lamri, Mohammed Amin   268
Lavrenyuk, Ilya   427
Lavrov, Alexander P.   254
Lazarev, Vitaly   365
Leventsov, Valery   59, 179, 191
Likhachev, Vladimir P.   352
Logunov, Semen   221

Makarov, Sergey B.   377
Makarov, Sergey   339, 427
Makarov, Vladimir   95
Malysheva, Veronika   329
Martyna, Jerzy   438
Matveev, Yurij A.   254
Mayzel, Alexey   240
Medvedev, Andrei   240
Medvedeva, Yulia   147, 191
Moroz, Angelina   365
Mukhanova, Natalya   71

Nekrasova, Tatyana   122, 158, 170
Nguyen, Canh Minh   377

Nguyen, Dac Cu   377
Nikolaev, Denis   221
Nistyuk, Anatoli   268

Ovsyannikova, Anna S.   377

Paramonov, Alexander   35, 449
Pavel, Trubin   470
Pavlov, Vitalii A.   321
Pervunina, Tatiana M.   321
Pilipova, Valeria M.   230
Plossky, Arseny   95
Podstrigaev, Alexey S.   352
Poletaeva, Ekaterina   240
Polyakov, Nikita   481
Popov, Eugenii   390
Popova, Ekaterina   201

Romanishina, Tatiana   59, 71

Salkutsan, Sergey   71, 122
Samouylov, Konstantin   481
Schneps-Schneppe, Manfred   9
Semenova, Anastasiia I.   405
Shalabaev, Pavel   81
Shimin, Nikolay   108
Sivolenko, Eduard   240
Skripnichenko, Denis   179
Smirnova, Ekaterina   339

Smolyakov, Andrey V.   352
Sochava, Alexander   413
Stosh, Alena   329
Such, Jose M.   46
Suloeva, Svetlana   158

Tatarnikova, Tatiana   449
Tcvetkov, Maxim   108
Temkina, Valentina   240
Tikhvinskiy, Valery   95
Trifonov, Yury   81
Tung, Suet Ping   493

Umanskiy, Roman   95

Vasiliev, Danil   268
Velichko, Elena   310
Vikulov, Anton   449
Vuorimaa, Petri   22

Wong, Ka Yan   493

Xue, Wei   427

Yarkina, Natalia   481

Zavjalov, Sergey V.   321, 377, 405
Zaynullina, Diana   329

Printed in the United States
by Baker & Taylor Publisher Services